Praise for GARRETT M. GRAFF's

THE THREAT MATRIX

"An action-filled, richly detailed portrait of the Federal Bureau of Investigation in its new guise—charged not just with solving crimes already committed, but now with preventing at least some of them.... There's solid storytelling at work here—and quite a story to tell, too."

— *Kirkus Reviews,* starred review

"Graff's two-year-long investigation into the FBI's counterterrorism fight offers insight into the once-classified intelligence the federal government had on bin Laden and other terrorists...leaving readers on the edge of their seats.... Graff's book is a well-written account of the FBI's decades-long fight against terrorism."

—Emily Cahn, TheHill.com

"An invaluable and comprehensive history of the FBI's role in defending our nation (and also in helping our allies) against the terrorist threat in all its forms.... One of the book's greatest strengths is Mr. Graff's discussions of the FBI's involvement in uncovering and thwarting terrorist plots."

—Joshua Sinai, *Washington Times*

"Graff examines the role of the FBI in the United States' war on terror over the past decade— a struggle fraught with myriad unknowns, enemies both domestic and overseas, and longstanding tensions between the agency and the CIA."

—Christopher Schoppa, *Washington Post*'s
Political Bookworm blog

THE
THREAT
MATRIX

ALSO BY GARRETT M. GRAFF

The First Campaign: Globalization, the Web,
and the Race for the White House

THE
THREAT
MATRIX

The FBI at War

GARRETT M. GRAFF

BACK BAY BOOKS
Little, Brown and Company
New York   Boston   London

Back Bay Books / Little, Brown and Company
Hachette Book Group
237 Park Avenue, New York, NY 10017
www.hachettebookgroup.com

Originally published in hardcover by Little, Brown and Company, March 2011
First Back Bay paperback edition, February 2012

Back Bay Books is an imprint of Little, Brown and Company. The Back Bay Books name and logo are trademarks of Hachette Book Group, Inc.

The publisher is not responsible for websites (or their content) that are not owned by the publisher.

The Hachette Speakers Bureau provides a wide range of authors for speaking events. To find out more, go to www.hachettespeakersbureau.com or call (866) 376-6591.

Library of Congress Cataloging-in-Publication Data
Graff, Garrett M.,
    The threat matrix : the FBI at war / Garrett M. Graff.—1st ed.
       p. cm.
    Includes bibliographical references and index.
    ISBN 978-0-316-06861-1 (hc) / 978-0-316-06860-4 (pb)
    1. Terrorism—United States—Prevention.   2. War on Terrorism, 2001–2009.   3. United States. Federal Bureau of Investigation.   4. Intelligence service—United States.   I. Title.
    HV6432.G714 2011
    363.325'1650973—dc22   2010053237

10 9 8 7 6 5 4 3 2 1

RRD-C

Printed in the United States of America

For my grandfathers: Bert McCord, who started my family in journalism and whose name I'm proud to carry forward, and John Price, who got my family interested in technology and died just hours before this book was completed

CONTENTS

THE
THREAT
MATRIX

INTRODUCTION
Public Enemy #1

I shall wage vigorous warfare against the enemies of
my country, of its laws, and of its principles.... I shall
always be loyal to my duty, my organization, and
my country.

> — *From J. Edgar Hoover's FBI Pledge for*
> *Law Enforcement Officers*

The final minutes of George W. Bush's eight years as president
ticked away as Bob Mueller stepped down onto the inaugural
platform. Despite weeks of wall-to-wall news coverage warning
of overcrowding for the inauguration—millions of people who might
clog the Washington Beltway and the Metro system for hours—the
chilly January day had deterred few inaugural-goers. More than perhaps anyone else on the inaugural platform, Mueller, the director of
the FBI, was responsible for keeping everyone safe for the day.

The previous twenty-four hours had been nerve-racking, like so
many of the days and nights of the past seven years. A threat out of the
Middle East, sketchy at best. Reports of a man barreling down the
Jersey Turnpike with a bomb. Agents from the FBI, the CIA, and a
dozen other agencies fanned across country and several continents,
hoping to run down the information before noon Tuesday, H-Hour

for the handover of government, democracy's greatest rite—the peaceful and amicable transfer of power from one party to another with nearly diametrically opposed views.

The last time the nation had gathered to do this, in January 2001, the world had been a different place. That was, as everyone now said, *before.* This was the first transfer of power *after. Before,* the Clinton administration had balked at targeting a shadowy terrorist named Osama bin Laden in a faraway place called Afghanistan. *Before,* the argument had been, What had bin Laden ever done to deserve assassination? The United States didn't do that type of thing. Now, *after,* everything was different.

Just days prior to the inauguration of Barack Obama, Hellfire missiles launched from a Predator drone half a world away from Washington had killed two Kenyans suspected in the 1998 attacks on the U.S. embassies in Tanzania and Kenya. Usama al-Kini, also known as Fahid Mohammed Ally Msalam, and Sheikh Ahmed Salim Swedan likely never saw the missiles closing on them at speeds topping Mach 1.3 and likely never felt the twenty-pound warheads explode. Although the FBI's global footprint had expanded considerably, the United States had no other practical means to eliminate this pair of terrorists. The two men, living in South Waziristan—a remote tribal part of Pakistan most Americans would be hard-pressed to locate on a map—were unreachable. The CIA drones and their Hellfire missiles were a different type of justice, an outside-the-courtroom, permanent justice— one that, *after,* the U.S. government had decided was more than appropriate to mete out but had been off the table *before.* (The precise term for such measures—*extralegal*—had become all too familiar to the American people *after.*)

Al-Kini and Swedan were both on the Bureau's "Most Wanted Terrorist" list, making the attacks a big victory for the United States, yet, since the United States didn't acknowledge these covert missile strikes, it didn't officially consider them dead. Months later, both men's names would still be on the FBI's public list; inside the government, though, no one was looking too hard for them.

The minutes ticked away on inaugural day. Of the government men onstage, only a few had been in the fateful national security meeting the morning of September 12, 2001, the day *after* everything had changed. Now, in just two hours, most of them would depart government. A green-and-white Marine helicopter from HMX-1, the presidential helicopter squadron, sat on the East Front Plaza of the Capitol, waiting to ferry George W. Bush back to private life. Vice President Dick Cheney, confined to a wheelchair after straining his back moving boxes the weekend before, would also depart—only to appear in the coming months as a vocal opponent of the new administration's approach to terrorism. Of the entire national security team, those departures would leave only Mueller still in the position he had held on September 11, 2001, that brilliant and crisp fall day when the planes had come.

Only one other member of the national security team would be carrying over from Bush to Obama—and his absence today was intentional. Hidden in a secure location outside Washington, Robert Gates—the wizened secretary of defense who on 9/11 had been a dean at Texas A&M—was, in the bland parlance of bureaucracy, the "designated successor," part of the elaborate continuity-of-government plans created during the Cold War to ensure the United States would survive even the most catastrophic assault. Originally designed to protect against surprise Soviet intercontinental ballistic missiles coming in over the North Pole, the continuity-of-government operation now mostly guarded against terrorists with a smuggled nuclear weapon stuffed in a suitcase. In the coming hours, a new national security team would begin to flow into the federal apparatus across the city and move into the White House, where air pressure is always kept elevated to ensure biological or chemical agents can't penetrate inside. Only Mueller would be left among the security team to recall the fear, tension, and shock of September 12, 2001, the uncertainty of the day *after.* The soldiers in the streets; the smoke, visible from his office, rising from the Pentagon across the Potomac River; the concrete barriers that sprang up everywhere overnight like some sort of ugly, aggressive species of weed; that smell—part burning jet fuel, part burning paper, part burning flesh.

Mueller, wrapped in long overcoat and scarf, his gloved hands protected from the cold, walked to the front of the stage, his longtime wife and companion, Ann, by his side. On 9/11, just days after moving to Washington, she had sat through that historic day alone, watching the television in their temporary apartment six blocks from where they now stood. Her husband hadn't returned until long after she'd gone to sleep.

From the banister, they could survey the largest crowd ever assembled for a presidential inauguration. It spread out for over a mile, the length of the National Mall, the nation's so-called backyard. Somewhere out in the crowd were 155 teams of Mueller's agents in plainclothes, watching for anything unusual. A few blocks away, the FBI Hostage Rescue Team, created thirty years earlier as the nation's elite antiterror strike force, sat poised to react. To back them up, SWAT teams, hazardous-material units, bomb squads, and even weapons of mass destruction response teams were located at strategic points around the crowded city. Armored military-like vehicles topped with flashing lights were hidden just out of sight, ready for action. Police helicopters circled the city, their expensive sensors and surveillance gear hard at work. Gas masks hung from the waists of thousands of law enforcement personnel, as well as the National Guard troops who stood on every street corner for miles. Fighter jets bristling with missiles slung under their wings waited to respond to trouble from above, while deep beneath the city Secret Service agents searched tunnels and sewers for trouble below. Most military coups in the world were carried out with less firepower, materiel, and personnel than were deployed to the streets of Washington for what everyone hoped would be a peaceful and uneventful transition of power.

The early-morning crowd before Mueller was ecstatic despite the hour, the security hassles, and the bone-chilling cold. While the crowd on the Mall and in the Capitol complex was swept up in the euphoric moment of hope and the promise of change brought about by the election of the nation's first black president and a team representing a youthful new generation of leadership, Mueller knew the fear that prevailed behind the scenes.

Until hours earlier, it had seemed possible that the day would go very differently. Three different threads of intelligence had indicated that al-Shabaab, one of the many Islamic jihadist groups that formed the international web of al-Qaeda affiliates, had dispatched attackers from its base in Somalia to slip across the Canadian border and explode bombs on the Mall during the inauguration. The government had been tracking the intelligence for weeks, but only recently had new information moved the threat onto a different tier of seriousness.

Harakat al-Shabaab al-Mujahideen—the "Movement of Warrior Youth"—was still relatively new to the terrorism game; it wouldn't even formally be declared a "Foreign Terrorist Organization" by the State Department for another month, yet its capabilities were already well-known enough to seriously worry the government officials in the days leading up to the inauguration. (Kenya, the president's ancestral country and the site of the 1998 embassy attack that had helped usher in the age of al-Qaeda, was also under threat, according to the available intelligence.)

The national security teams of President Bush and President-elect Obama had been gathering repeatedly in the White House and at the guest residence, Blair House, for the week leading up to the inauguration to track the latest intelligence. The rooms pulsed with a sense of nervous energy on the part of the new Obama staff and a world-weariness on the part of the Bush officials who had only days left to go in their public service.

While the two national security teams didn't have much history working together, sitting on one side was a face familiar to everyone: John Brennan, one of the nation's most skilled counterterrorism leaders who had led the newly formed National Counterterrorism Center after 9/11, only to part ways with the Bush administration over its handling of the Iraq war. Brennan had become a close adviser to the Democratic nominee and had been the top candidate to take over the CIA until concerns about his role in the Agency's enhanced-interrogation program earlier in the decade had forced him into a position that didn't require Senate confirmation. Now Brennan served as the calming force on the Obama team in the room. He'd been through this sort of thing before.

A week before, the two national security teams had teased out a mock scenario imagining multiple bombs detonating simultaneously around the country—a domestic version of what had happened in East Africa in 1998, in Madrid in 2004, and twice in London in 2005. Hanging over every meeting and every discussion was a question spoken only in whispers: How real did the threat have to be before the government should consider canceling the ceremony or moving it indoors to a secure location? There was some precedent: President Reagan's second inaugural had been moved to the Capitol Rotunda because of nasty cold weather. This weather was heavier.

In one meeting, incoming secretary of state Hillary Clinton had asked a pointed question: "So what should Barack Obama do if he's in the middle of his Inaugural Address and a bomb goes off way in the back of the crowd on the Mall? What does he do? Is the Secret Service going to whisk him off the podium, so the American people see their incoming president disappear in the middle of the Inaugural Address? I don't think so." But was that truly credible?

The decision was made: Obama would continue the speech, if at all possible.

Nearly every passing hour brought new information. One terrorist suspect was chased through Heathrow Airport—British police officers literally running, their radios and utility belts banging against their hips as they charged through the heavy crowds—only, after further investigation, to be deemed harmless, a false alarm. An interrogation team in Uganda was calling Washington regularly as one source was hooked up to a polygraph machine to test his trustworthiness. The U.S. polygrapher was under intense pressure: *Is this guy legit? Are you sure?* The inauguration could hang on the answer.

On inauguration eve, the president-elect had canceled the final run-through of his Inaugural Address to go over the latest intelligence one more time at Blair House. His aides could tell the pressure was weighing on him. Since just after the election, he'd been getting the presidential daily threat briefings from the CIA and the rest of the U.S. security apparatus. After one pre-election briefing by Director of National Intelligence Mike McConnell, then-Senator Obama had said wryly, "You know, I've been worried about losing this election. After talking to you guys, I'm worried about winning the election." Now, with the heavy crown poised to rest on his head, each day seemed to bring new threats and causes of concern for President-elect Obama.

The Inauguration Day threat provided a key lesson for the new administration: No matter what else President Obama hoped to accomplish during his tenure in office, no matter if the most pressing issue seemed to be an economy teetering on the brink of complete collapse, no matter if he hoped to pass a game-changing health care bill in his first year in office, or if he hoped to change the nation's direction by closing the Guantánamo Bay prison and withdrawing troops from Iraq and Afghanistan, he didn't get to dictate when and where the terrorists engaged. Al-Qaeda and its affiliates might have been on the defensive, but the advantage on the field was still theirs. The government, after all, had set itself a standard of being successful in stopping attacks 100 percent of the time. The bad guys only had to get lucky once.

The next morning, the soon-to-be leader of the free world had marked the day by attending the traditional service at St. John's Church. Bishop T. D. Jakes read from the Book of Daniel, explaining, "In times of crisis, good men must stand up. God always sends the best men into the worst times." Across the street, the two national security teams huddled for a final round of meetings. For Mueller, it would be the last time he sat in conference with many of the colleagues he'd spent years working alongside. Condoleezza Rice had been in that meeting the day *after*. Mike Hayden, only hours left in his tenure as CIA director, had been head of the National Security Agency on 9/11. Attorney General Michael Mukasey had been a federal judge in New York, where he'd helped set major legal precedents in the unfolding war on terror. Then there were the new folks, including one man who made the normally stoic Mueller smile: Eric Holder, the incoming attorney general, was one of his longtime colleagues; the two men had been prosecutors in the District of Columbia a decade before.

The joint meeting, poignant for many in the room, had left everyone feeling more at ease. After all the worry, the al-Shabaab threat was amounting to nothing. Before it had even taken office, the Obama administration had survived its first false alarm; for the outgoing Bush administration, the fizzled plot was the last of thousands of such false alarms since that morning in September 2001.

On that day, Barack Obama had been an Illinois state senator, evacuating the Illinois legislative offices as ordered during the moments when everyone believed everything and everywhere was a target. Years later, he had run for president partly on a platform of ending the most morally troubling aspects of his predecessor's approach to terror. "It's time to turn the page," he'd said in one 2007 speech. Now, as the president-elect climbed into his new limo, the reminders of the era *after* literally surrounded him — his new ride, nicknamed "the Beast," was a freshly upgraded version of the presidential limo custom-built by GM that could withstand rocket attacks, seal off the interior from outside air, and deploy tear gas. The man who would soon pledge to "the best of my ability, preserve, protect, and defend the Constitution of the United States" would redefine in the coming years his own fight in the age of global terror. His first executive orders after being sworn in — documents that were already drafted and prepared for his signature as he rode down Pennsylvania Avenue toward the Capitol — banned torture in interrogations and committed to closing the Guantánamo Bay prison within a year (a deadline that would slip and later be almost abandoned entirely).

As Obama reclined in "the Beast," flipping through papers while passing the crowds lining the streets, Mueller looked over the crowd on the Mall. The FBI director was confident — or at least as confident as one could be these days — that the event would proceed as scheduled. Yet the huge behind-the-scenes security apparatus still churned away. The al-Shabaab threat might have been averted, but there were all sorts of other things to worry about.

Eight blocks from the Mall, in the FBI's Washington Field Office (WFO in Bureau parlance), more than a hundred agents and representatives from other agencies monitored the inaugural scene by remote camera in the top-floor Command and Tactical Operations Center (CTOC). Down the hall, a team of linguists listened to live SIGINT intercepts — that is, signals intelligence, like phone taps — for any sign of trouble. The WFO command center featured scores of workstations, each tasked with a specific role, spread out in a room packed with computers, ringing telephones, and giant wall screens. One projector screen scrolled live intelligence combed from all of the assembled agencies. Maps showed the location of countersniper teams around the event and the parade route. Every possibility had been gamed out, every response calculated. Across the street from the Washington Field Office, the Secret Service was working to secure the National Building Museum, the site of one of the more than a dozen inaugural balls set for that evening. It would be a long day.

Luckily for Mueller, as the moment of handover neared, he was confident in the Bureau's knowledge, planning, and response, and he was able to worry about other things. At 10:32 A.M., with eighty-eight minutes to go until the reign of George W. Bush entered the history books, he wanted to know: "Where's Melissa?" Somewhere in the million-person crowd below were his daughter and her boyfriend, fresh in from New York. Even with the most sophisticated surveillance gear ever assembled in American history for this event, some things would remain a mystery.

For almost five years after 9/11, Bob Mueller and the attorney general— first John Ashcroft, later Alberto Gonzales—met every morning in the FBI's Strategic Information and Operations Center (SIOC, pronounced "sigh-awk," in FBI jargon) and then shortly after 8 A.M., piled into their armored Suburbans in the basement of the Hoover Building for the short run up Pennsylvania Avenue to the White House. Weaving at high speed through the barriers around the executive complex, the motorcade, bristling with tense, heavily armed agents, would pull up just outside the West Wing. They carried with them a copy of the day's "Threat Matrix," a printed spreadsheet of all the various terrorist plots and worrisome intelligence the government was currently tracking. At 8:30, the duo, joined by a few aides, would be ushered into the Oval Office to update the president on the Threat Matrix just as the CIA was wrapping up its morning intelligence briefing. Trying to lighten the tension on one of those scary early days, President Bush, an avid sports fan, summarized the 8 A.M. CIA briefing and the following 8:30 FBI briefing as "first offense, then defense." He was basically right.

Since J. Edgar Hoover took over the Bureau in the late 1920s, the FBI had led the nation's defense, blocking and tackling an ever-evolving set of criminals and evildoers who sought to harm the United States. For seven decades, we have turned to the FBI to protect us from that which we fear the most. The forms our fears have taken have dictated their ever-changing set of priorities, requiring a constantly changing set of skills and specialties.

The sheer breadth of what is forced onto the FBI's plate each year is staggering. In the summer of 2008, the FBI investigated claims of an NBA referee that the basketball playoffs were rigged. That fall, as the economy collapsed under a wave of bad mortgages, the FBI launched mortgage fraud task forces across the country, building off the financial expertise it developed earlier in the decade when it was called upon to investigate the string of collapses of Enron, Global Crossing, and other corporate whirlpools. The threat of Somali pirates meant agents were off to the Horn of Africa. All the while, they investigated some hundred thousand other crimes, ranging from bank robberies to kidnappings to corrupt public officials, and worked to keep foreign spies from stealing our secrets. That's more or less how we want it. We expect that the morning after something bad happens—whatever it is, whatever American value is threatened—the news headlines will begin "FBI launches investigation into X," or "FBI arrives on scene of Y." *Everything will be okay,* we're told; *the FBI is here.* when Congresswoman Gabrielle Giffords was shot in January 2011, President Obama underscored his concern by immediately dispatching Mueller to Tucson to head the investigation personally.

That belief that the FBI is all that stands between decent, hardworking, law-abiding, taxpaying Americans and those who seek to do us harm was precisely the construct J. Edgar Hoover worked fanatically to create for half a century. As Hoover biographer Richard Gid Powers once explained, "Because of [Hoover's] success in turning the FBI into a symbol of justice, the public had come to expect the dispatch of FBI agents as an indication of the concern of the Federal Government."

In 1924, Hoover had been handed control of the Bureau, a corrupt investigatory backwater used by the government for whatever purposes suited it; the 441 agents were mostly political cronies or investigators who had washed out of jobs elsewhere. They had little power and even less respect. Hoover was a progressive of the first rank. With the backing of the attorney general, Harlan Fiske Stone, he changed promotion rules, fired or sidelined the worst of the political patrons, and instituted a formal training program. As his efforts succeeded, the quality of the Bureau began to rise—although he still needed something dramatic to prove that to the country.

He found it at Union Station in Kansas City, Missouri, the "Gateway to the West."

The FBI's myth starts with the capture of a notorious escaped convict named Frank Nash, in Hot Springs, Arkansas, a dangerous organized crime center during the 1930s. Because FBI agents didn't yet have the power to arrest people or carry firearms, the Bureau had taken a local police chief along with them to make Nash's capture marginally legal.* Then came the challenge of getting Nash five hundred miles back to Leavenworth Penitentiary in Kansas while staying one step ahead of the friends who would seek to rescue Nash before he was safely locked up again. After a hair-raising high-speed escape from Hot Springs by car, during which the two agents and the police chief talked their way through two roadblocks set up by corrupt Arkansas police set on freeing Nash, the team boarded the overnight train to Kansas City and hunkered down in a cabin to wait.

The cavernous Union Station in Kansas City was one of the busiest train stations in the country during its heyday in the teens and twenties. On some days more than 250 trains rolled through the station. Even at 7 A.M. on the Saturday morning of June 17, 1933, the station was busy—a half-dozen trains were due in that hour alone. The Travelers Aid station was just opening in the T-shaped main hall as two Kansas City police officers and two local FBI agents pulled up and parked illegally outside the east doors. They hurried down to the tracks, meeting the overnight Missouri Pacific train from Arkansas as it pulled up.

After hearing a prearranged knock on their cabin door, the nervous lawmen emerged with their prisoner. They knew trouble was possible and had arranged to drive him the last leg rather than wait the hour for the train to continue north on to Leavenworth Penitentiary. There was no time to waste—in this region, at this time in history, Nash had more friends around than the FBI did.

Witnesses would later vividly recall the flying wedge of lawmen that sliced through the morning travelers, escorting Nash through the hall toward the curb. The group was just settling Nash into the front seat of the FBI's Chevrolet when a group of gunmen emerged out of the bustling crowd on the curb and ambushed them.

---

* At this point in its history, the FBI was actually known as the Bureau of Investigation, then later as the United States Bureau of Investigation before it officially became the FBI in 1935. For clarity, I refer to it as the FBI even during times it was known by an earlier name.

As the story goes, a gangster appeared brandishing a machine gun and shouted, "Up, up!" Then another gunman yelled, "Let 'em have it!" In the Bureau's official retelling of the story, lead ripped into the police cars from nearly every direction as three (or perhaps four or maybe it was seven) gunmen slaughtered the group of Bureau agents and Kansas City lawmen. Machine gun bullets riddled the front of Union Station—some scars of which are still visible today in the granite facade. When the smoke cleared, the two Kansas City policemen who had met the group at the station were dead, as was the police chief who had accompanied the FBI agents to Arkansas to capture Nash. One Bureau agent was killed, two other agents were wounded; only one agent escaped harm. And, most recklessly, as the Bureau's official history concludes, "The prisoner, Frank Nash, was also killed by a misdirected gunshot that entered his skull, thereby defeating the very purpose of the conspiracy to gain his freedom."

The horror of the scene was quickly telegraphed to Washington and from coast to coast. Hoover immediately ordered every Bureau resource available to hunt for the killers who had embarrassed his fledgling agency. In the coming weeks, the FBI would track down and capture or kill in the process all three men they believed responsible for the rampage: bank robber and Nash friend Verne Miller, notorious killer Charles "Pretty Boy" Floyd, and Floyd's sidekick, Adam Richetti.

The bloody shootout at Union Station forever changed the American public's perception of crime. The senseless and immoral slaughter of the supposedly unarmed public servants in full view of the Kansas City public was an outrage to the rule of law, the nation, and American values. While colorful bank-robbing gangsters had been the toast of the country in the midst of the Depression, the Kansas City Massacre instantly united public opinion against them. Within a year, Hoover had used the incident to justify nine strict anticrime laws that professionalized the Bureau—granting it rights to arrest suspects anywhere in the country, to execute warrants, and to carry firearms—and federalizing crimes including transporting stolen goods or fleeing across state lines, robbing banks, and killing or injuring federal agents. Thanks to the events of that Saturday morning in June, the FBI would have the power to search the country for criminals and bring them to heel. A national police force had been born, Hoover was its head, and—as the Kansas City investigation would prove—it always got its man.

Or so goes the myth. The reality of the Kansas City Massacre bears little resemblance to the story sold to the public. True, friends of Frank Nash certainly did try to free him from the Bureau outside Union Station. True, four lawmen died needlessly in the Kansas City dawn. The rest is fiction.

The truth, uncovered by journalist Robert Unger decades later from the FBI's own case files, shows that what likely happened is that three of the four lawmen killed, and perhaps even all four, were killed by friendly fire—a so-called blue-on-blue shooting. Far from unarmed, all but one of the agents and police at Union Station that day were armed with a mix of shotguns and revolvers. It was Special Agent Joe Lackey, tired and sleep-deprived from the forty-eight-hour trek to capture and return Nash, who, stuck in the backseat of the car as the ambush started, panicked and opened fire with an unfamiliar shotgun—mistakenly killing Nash, his fellow agent Caffrey, and one of the Kansas City policemen with two wild shots. While gangster Verne Miller was certainly at the scene, there's no definitive proof that either Floyd or Richetti was involved in the ambush, and in fact, but for investigative missteps at the case's beginning, any of a dozen local gangsters might have emerged as the actual suspects. Miller's intention had been to execute the rescue without firing a shot, and had Lackey not opened fire first, Miller would not have used his machine gun at all. As Unger wrote, "Empires aren't built on failed missions and panicked agents and bungled investigations. Young John Edgar Hoover and his FBI needed a cause, a crusade. He needed good and evil. And he needed victory. The truth would offer none of that. But the legend provided it all."

The Kansas City Massacre would touch off J. Edgar Hoover's multi-year cross-country battle between good and evil and galvanize the Depression-era American public. According to the FBI's mythology, just months after the massacre, George "Machine Gun" Kelly shouted, "Don't shoot, G-men! Don't shoot, G-men!" as agents closed in on him, coining the slang phrase that became shorthand for Bureau agents in the years to come. Over the next two years, a rotating series of "Public Enemies," most with colorful nicknames, would face the FBI's unrelenting pressure.

Outlaws Bonnie Parker and Clyde Barrow—violent, sexually adventurous kids barely out of their teens—died in a police ambush in Bienville Parish, Louisiana, on May 23, 1934. There was John Dillinger, gunned down by FBI agents in an alley beside the Biograph Theater in Lincoln Park, Chicago, on July 22, 1934, after a multi-state robbery spree and numerous shootouts with police. That fall, "Baby Face" Nelson died following a shootout in which he killed FBI special agents Herman Hollis and Samuel P. Cowley. The Barker Gang, led by matriarch Ma Barker, cut a bloody path of kidnappings and robberies across the country until, one by one, they were hunted down by the newly empowered FBI. Ma and her son Fred died in a 1935 shootout in Ocklawaha, Florida; another son, Arthur "Doc" Barker, died while trying to escape from Alcatraz.

The first Public Enemy period ended in New Orleans when the FBI ran to ground Alvin "Creepy" Karpis—so named for his disturbing smile—who, the story goes, was captured by Hoover himself. Unfortunately, no one on the arrest team had remembered to bring handcuffs to the bust, so agents tied Karpis's hands with a necktie. When no one knew how to get to the Federal Building to put Karpis in jail, the helpful outlaw provided turn-by-turn directions.

Over the coming decades, an ever-evolving definition of "Public Enemy #1" would keep Hoover and the Bureau busy—and the nation as a whole on edge. There were the kidnappers of the 1930s, the Nazi saboteurs of the 1940s, the Communist spies of the 1950s, the Ku Klux Klan and later the student radicals of the 1960s, violent extremist groups like the Black Panthers, the Symbionese Liberation Army, and the Weather Underground in the 1970s, the Mafia and La Cosa Nostra in the 1980s, right-wing American militias and "deadbeat dads" in the 1990s, and so on. Along the way, there were hundreds of less-memorable investigations brought about by what Bureau officials call in private the "flavor of the day": the Enrons, mortgage frauds, pirates, run-of-the-mill bank robberies, public corruption cases, cyber scams, child pornographers, corrupt congressmen, and whatever else came along. As immortalized by the iconic "Ten Most Wanted" list, the FBI, given time, has continued to always get its man—of the nearly five hundred fugitives who have been on the list since its inception in 1950, only thirty have never been located.

Anyone Hoover perceived as a threat to "the American Way" found himself—or herself—in the Bureau's crosshairs, even, unfortunately, "radicals" we now celebrate, such as the Reverend Martin Luther King Jr. In the 1960s, John Lennon was considered a possible threat by Hoover's FBI. Yet when the FBI inaugurated its new visitor entrance at the Hoover Building in the fall of 2008, if you listened carefully to the lobby background music you could catch John Lennon piped over the speakers—a sign of just how far the FBI had come since its Hoover days.

Each morning, waiting in Mueller's SUV as it idles at the curb of his house in Georgetown is a two-to-three-inch-thick blue binder labeled "Director's Briefing." Across the bottom, in small type, appears the line TOP SECRET/NOFORN/SCI, meaning that the contents include some of the most sensitive information in the U.S. government and that it shouldn't be shared with any foreign countries.

Inside the front cover, appearing even before the daily Threat Matrix, is a spreadsheet that captures just how far the Bureau has come since that terrible day at Kansas City's Union Station. Pages long, the spreadsheet lists each FBI agent currently detailed overseas, what case he or she is working on, where the agent is normally based, and how long the agent is expected to be overseas. On many days, the list includes well over three hundred personnel—not counting the hundreds of legal attachés permanently stationed in foreign countries. The Bureau that once didn't even have the power to arrest anyone anywhere now oversees operations that span the globe and annually searches for suspects on six of the seven continents. Once during Mueller's time as director, it even worked a computer-hacking case in Antarctica, eventually arresting the suspected hackers in Romania. As was formerly true of the British Empire, the sun never sets on today's FBI.

Mueller's binder is the daily summary of the product of the multibillion-dollar (perhaps even trillion-dollar) antiterrorist apparatus that has emerged since 9/11. Beyond the global agent breakdown are a variety of different threat assessments, materials gathered by agents and analysts from thousands of websites, interviews, and leads tracked each day. The rise, maturation, and evolution of the contents of that binder in many ways mark the rise, maturation, and evolution of Bob Mueller himself as FBI director. When he started in the job, he thought that his main task would be to modernize the FBI's computer system. His confirmation hearing in the summer of 2001 barely even mentioned the subject of terrorism. All that changed. Just minutes after President Bush, reading to schoolchildren in Florida, heard about the attacks on the World Trade Center, he called the newly installed FBI head: "This is what we pay you for." And one week after he'd entered the Hoover Building as director for the first time, Mueller's term, President Bush's term, the FBI, and the nation were transformed.

For Mueller, the intensity of the new environment is evident from the first moments of his day. Tight security around the FBI director isn't new; the position has long been a focus of criminals and the mentally unbalanced. Long before the security culture in Washington reached the extremes of today—when unrecognizable junior cabinet officials race through town in black SUVs with security personnel adopting the iconic look of Secret Service agents—J. Edgar Hoover was the only person other than the president in Washington to travel in an armored limousine. Yet as late as the 1990s, the then director Louis Freeh often drove himself and his family around. On official duty, only a single driver—an FBI legend and former varsity football player named John Griglione—accompanied him. As Freeh instructed Griglione, "If anything happens, you drive. I'll shoot." (For his part, in those more innocent days of the first nine months of 2001, Attorney General John Ashcroft tried to decline a security detail because of the tax implications—government officials with drivers are taxed on the estimated value of the car and driver.)

Mueller is picked up each morning by Griglione, who leads an armored multi-vehicle motorcade. Gone is J. Edgar Hoover's sleek bulletproof Cadillac. Today's government-issue Suburbans, weighing in at five tons, are closer to tanks than cars and include defenses against nuclear, biological, and chemical assaults. Mueller emerges from one of these vehicles in the basement of the Hoover Building shortly after 6 A.M. and is whisked by elevator to the seventh-floor director's suite, where a friendly man from the Office of the Director of National Intelligence is waiting to talk Mueller through the thick blue briefing binder. What the day brings from that moment forward is anyone's guess.

The binder is the product of the night shift and, most likely, a few gallons of government-issue coffee. While the rest of Washington sleeps, a tiny group at the National Counterterrorism Center and the Office of the Director of National Intelligence—staffed with some of the top minds from the FBI, the CIA, Homeland Security, and the Pentagon, among others—catalogs the world's terrorist "chatter." At 1 A.M., they convene via Secure Video Conference Teleconference (SVTC, pronounced "sivutz," in government-speak), assembling the men and women from sixteen agencies responsible for the Threat Matrix and the Presidential Daily Briefing, to talk through what will be "briefed" that morning, which of the day's four thousand new reports, leads, and possible threats warrant high-level attention.

Then, an hour before dawn, they fan out across the city equipped with so much information and so many top secret briefing binders that they wheel the oversized, locked briefcases behind them on luggage carriers. They scatter at the White House, the CIA's Langley headquarters, the massive trapezoidal Greek Revival structure known as "Main Justice" that serves as the headquarters for the Justice Department and the attorney general, and the Department of Homeland Security's sprawling complex off Nebraska Avenue in upper Washington, as well as the Hoover Building.

The DNI briefers hand-deliver the daily terrorist Threat Matrix to the few dozen people in the U.S. government privileged to see it. As the sun begins to rise over the Capitol dome, they review the document in detail with their assigned principals, listen carefully to any questions, and jot down issues for follow-up. They then reconvene with their counterparts to hand over their unique responsibility to the day shift. Then the process begins anew for another day. Of course, *privilege* might not be the right word for those who see the daily briefing. The listing of dozens of threats to the homeland and Americans overseas, large and small, is a catalogue of horrors. The threats, according to those who get the document delivered each morning, have a profound impact on one's thinking—it's hard to ever see the world in the same way after witnessing the worst that humans can imagine doing to others. It hangs over you all day and each night. You go to bed wondering if the world will be safe until you awake. What type of day will tomorrow bring?

*　　*　　*

Since Hoover, no FBI director has served as long as Mueller. He has reshaped the FBI in profound ways, remaking in short order an agency not known for changing with alacrity. For Mueller, those early days at the FBI were a rude awakening. A Marine platoon commander–turned–prosecutor, he was accustomed to being his own boss and moving as fast as he wanted. The Bureau was different; as people at the FBI lament, "Bureaucracy is literally our middle name." At a graduation for new agents at Quantico in the spring of 2008, the class speaker, new agent Eric Boyce, joked that the training taught the recruits that the Bureau has a form for everything and that he had to fill out five forms just to speak at graduation. It was a joke that rang so true in the Bureau that even Mueller's stone-faced security detail standing by the door cracked a smile. Mueller shot back that Boyce was lucky—it used to be twenty forms to speak at graduation but they'd streamlined it to five.

In more than nine years as director, Mueller has presided over a transformation of the FBI unlike anything since Hoover took over more than eighty years ago. What Hoover made national, linking cases and agents across state lines, Mueller has made international. To combat global terror, the FBI, the nation's top domestic law enforcement agency, has had to push out far beyond U.S. borders. Whereas Hoover in his lifetime never crossed either the Pacific Ocean or the Atlantic Ocean, Mueller has become a global diplomat, journeying far from the U.S. shore to advance the nation's security. A world map in the deputy director's office shows more than sixty locations abroad where agents are posted, and Bureau leaders talk of its reach "from Indianapolis to Islamabad." In 2008, Mueller traveled to Phnom Penh, Cambodia, to open what was then the newest overseas FBI office—a presence that since then has expanded to include Algiers. Any given year sees him touch down in more than a score of countries. To explain why the Bureau is engaging so heavily overseas, leaders point out that the 9/11 plot was planned in three countries—Germany, Malaysia, and Afghanistan—and executed in a fourth. "Criminals and terrorists don't respect borders," says former deputy director John Pistole, "and neither can our efforts."

To a certain extent, the rise of the FBI is the story of the rise of technology. It was, after all, the invention of the Model T that allowed criminals to range farther afield and launched the interstate bank robbery sprees of "Public Enemies" like John Dillinger, Bonnie and Clyde, and Alvin Karpis. The end of the horse era meant that a sheriff's posse could no longer stem a criminal tide if someone could rob a bank in one state in the morning and another in a different state in the afternoon. The advent of commercial aviation only accelerated the speed at which criminals could move from coast to coast. A more national approach to crime fighting was required. Today, the ease of communication via the internet and the huge interlocking network of international flights, commerce, trade, and financial transactions mean that it can be just as easy to direct an attack from Pakistan as it is from within the United States. As Phil Mudd, who served as an executive in the FBI's post-9/11 National Security Branch, explains, "Until I go home at night and purchase something on Amazon.com, the internet is my enemy."

Despite the scores of books written about the Bush administration and the "War on Terror," few mention Mueller as more than a sideline character. Since his appointment as director, few articles have examined his role in the Bureau, even though he's the only member of the president's national security team still in place from 9/11. He only reluctantly speaks in public or submits to interviews. As his former Justice Department chief of staff Dennis Saylor says, "I can't think of a greater tribute to his personality than the fact that he's relatively unknown."

Figures like George Tenet, Tom Ridge, and Michael Chertoff may have figured more highly in the national news over the past decade, yet it is Mueller who brings the domestic threats of the world to the president in the Oval Office, and it is Mueller's 13,500 agents, now serving in more than 60 countries around the world and 56 field offices and 400 satellite resident agency offices around the country, who perhaps will determine whether "the Next One" happens. Those in law enforcement circles understand that Mueller is leading the most significant makeover ever of the world's premier law enforcement and intelligence agency. In doing so, he has revealed an independent streak that has at times annoyed and angered the two administrations that he's served since the Bureau's post-9/11 role has put both it and him in the middle of some uncomfortable situations.

Post-Hoover reforms were designed to keep the Bureau free from political pressure and interference. No director before Mueller has lasted for a full ten-year term, a length sufficient in theory to outlast whichever president appointed him (and they have all been "hims" thus far). Those terms have often been rocky. During the Clinton era, Director Louis Freeh had such a sour relationship with President Clinton that the two barely spoke. (It was, in hindsight, a luxury of the pre-9/11 world that the FBI could operate so freely from the president.)

Every six weeks or so, Mueller makes the short forty-five-minute trip to the FBI Academy, south of Washington on the grounds of the Quantico Marine Corps Base, to administer the oath of office to a new crop of FBI agents. Roughly half of the Bureau's agents are new since 9/11, meaning they've joined a Bureau radically different from the one that J. Edgar Hoover headed until the 1970s.

In the 2010 *Businessweek* ranking of the "Hottest Employers," some 57,000 college students named the FBI the third most desirable employer in the country—just behind Google and Disney. "We may never crack the top two—we do not offer free food or spa treatments, nor do we have a theme park," Mueller joked in a rare moment of levity, "but we did manage to bump Apple out of the number three spot to number four. Even I could not believe that the FBI somehow trumped the iPhone."

There are few corners of government as well-educated as the FBI; nearly half the agents possess an advanced degree of one kind or another. Many are lawyers or CPAs, some are MDs, scores have PhDs. In 2009, one new agents' class at the Quantico FBI Academy even had a rocket scientist. Many of these agents take pay cuts to come to the FBI, where their salaries start at around $61,000. For all of them, the Bureau is a cause rather than a job.

Culture, history, and tradition matter a lot in this world. In the walk-in gun vaults that now exist in every field office, Capone-era Thompson submachine guns still sit side by side with high-tech M4s and MP5s. The "Tommy guns" are mostly for show—no FBI SWAT ever deploys with them—though for an organization steeped in its own history, they are an important link to the generations of agents who have worn the badge before.

The training and mind-set of agents is evident from the Hoover Building parking garage—one can walk the rows of cars (mostly Ford Crown Victorias or Dodge Chargers) and tell almost immediately which belong to agents and which belong to civilian staff. The ones that belong to agents are parked as they are trained to park at Quantico—that is, facing front out, ready for action at a moment's notice—and the civilian cars are parked facing in, as nearly everyone else regularly parks.

During Bob Mueller's Senate confirmation hearing in 2001, Alabama senator Jeff Sessions, a former prosecutor, recalled an exchange during one of the trials he prosecuted in Alabama. An FBI special agent who, Sessions said, "had worked her heart out" on the case, was on the stand facing cross-examination.

"Well, who all are special agents of the FBI? You call yourself a special agent," the defense lawyer asked.

"Basically the agents of the FBI," she replied.

"All of them?" the lawyer asked incredulously.

"Virtually all of them," the agent replied.

"Well, it's not too special, is it?" he said jokingly.

The special agent fixed the defense attorney with an icy stare: "It is to me, sir."

While *terrorism* has become the watchword of the past decade, acts of terror have always been a regular part of the FBI's and our nation's history. America certainly faces threats more advanced and more deadly than before, but the attempt to gain political advantage through acts of terror is hardly new or unique to the modern era. One of the nascent Bureau's first cases involved the bombing of Attorney General A. Mitchell Palmer's house in 1919, an act that left the front stoop of Palmer's neighbor, the then secretary of the navy Franklin D. Roosevelt, strewn with the bomber's body parts. A year later, police and agents went door to door among New York blacksmiths after a bomb targeted Wall Street, asking if anyone recognized the horseshoe recovered from the unlucky animal who had pulled the explosive cart down Wall Street.

Long before the rest of the nation wised up to the transnational threats of the twenty-first century, a small group of prosecutors, FBI agents and analysts, and others in the intelligence community were wrestling with how to bring down criminals and terrorists far from U.S. shores. Long before he was FBI director, Louis Freeh learned about the international reach of organized crime as a junior assistant U.S. attorney when a Mafia case took him from the streets of Queens to the streets of Palermo, Sicily. Long before controversies over terrorist renditions became a regular topic on the nightly news, FBI deputy director Buck Revell stood on the bridge of a U.S. Navy ship in the Mediterranean anxiously awaiting the first terrorist to be captured by the United States overseas. Long before he oversaw the FBI's response to 9/11, Robert Mueller found himself thrust into the Pan Am 103 bombing investigation—then the deadliest terrorist attack ever on American civilians—a complicated case some 3,600 miles away from his office in the Justice Department in Washington. Long before he was killed as the World Trade Center collapsed around him on 9/11, Special Agent John O'Neill had been ringing the bell on the rising threat of al-Qaeda and Islamic terrorism.

This is the story of the world these men and others created, the precedents they set, and the cases they worked that together established the groundwork for how we combat terrorism and international crime today.

Al-Qaeda and its affiliate groups may be the enemy du jour, yet history demonstrates that such groups, driven by religious extremism, fanaticism, and the politics of the moment, have regularly come and gone. The only constant in our nation's battle against terrorism, in fact, has been the FBI, whose powers, skills, and capabilities have evolved across generations to meet new threats in new places. Founded four decades before the CIA, the FBI has fought terrorism in varying forms since its earliest days. Radical labor activists, anarchists, student radicals, right-wing extremists, left-wing extremists, Puerto Rican nationalists, Croatian separatists, Muslim extremists, the IRA, the PLO, the Red Brigade, Galleanists, the Weather Underground, Libyans, Iranians, Italian mobsters, antigovernment loners, white supremacists, black extremists, and now al-Qaeda—the FBI has been through it all.

Groups whose motives and stories are largely lost to history once were front-burner cases for the FBI. For almost a decade, under three different FBI directors, agents tracked Abu Nidal's organization through more than sixteen U.S. cities, using wiretaps, informants, and indictments to dismantle a group that at the time was considered highly dangerous and is today effectively lost to the historical scrap pile of failed ideologies.* Domestically, the FBI has, in recent decades, battled anti-abortion "terrorists" who have bombed abortion clinics, white supremacists like Timothy McVeigh, survivalists like the Unabomber, and environmental extremists like Daniel Andreas San Diego, who in 2009 became the first domestic terror suspect to make the FBI's "Most Wanted Terrorist" list. For thirty years before Mohamed Atta passed through airport security in Portland, Maine, the Bureau had been developing its response to an ever-changing group of airplane hijackers—some violent, many just disturbed or desperate.

While the vast majority of its agents still work domestically, the FBI has become, without notice or attention from the public, the world's first global law enforcement agency. The Bureau has teams specially stationed and equipped to respond anywhere in the world within hours; FBI "forward staging areas" overseas contain all the equipment necessary for the Bureau's "Fly Teams" to run crime scenes anywhere on the planet. The FBI is becoming one of the nation's lead overseas representatives and has become as recognizable a global brand as just about any U.S. export. In Valencia, Spain, I found FBI T-shirts prominently displayed outside a small store near the city's main cathedral. In Paris, France, sitting at a café near Notre Dame, I spotted a man wearing an "FBI: Famous Beer Inspector" T-shirt, and a nearby

---

*The National Security Act of 1947 had first given the FBI authority to plant listening devices to eavesdrop on Communist gatherings, yet at the time there was no mechanism for doing it in criminal cases. Such "technicalities" though, didn't slow Hoover down: Within years, he had agents tapping phones in criminal cases, even though the information wasn't admissible in court. Only in 1968 did the Bureau get for the first time the ability legally to tap telephones as part of criminal matters.

tourist trap offered T-shirts saying "FBI: Fort Beau Intelligent" ("Strong Beautiful Intelligent"). Then of course there's the more crass "Federal Boobie Inspector" badges offered for sale in many spring break destinations. Onetime deputy director Tom Pickard recalls running across FBI shirts for sale at a rural Hungarian gas station. Mike Bonner, who served a four-year stint in Africa with the FBI in the early 2000s, recalls, "I've been to shantytowns in Nigeria, South Africa, and Ghana where kids are wearing FBI hats and T-shirts. It certainly gets the brand out there."

For overseas visits by FBI executives, the effect of the Bureau's brand is even more exaggerated. Short of the secretary of state, vice president, or president, there are few visitors considered more prestigious for a host government than the FBI director. In some countries, the figurative red carpet is literally a red carpet at the bottom of the plane's stairs. Each year, the National Academy, the Bureau's training facility at Quantico, Virginia, brings hundreds of foreign police officers through for lessons in modern crime fighting, forensics, and terrorism. The yellow bricks given as a reward for completing the Academy's intense program stand on the desks or in the trophy cabinets of many top law enforcement officials across the world.

Everybody knows the G-men.

Yet despite its public presence and brand recognition, the modern FBI remains a mystery to many. Getting the vast Bureau apparatus to open up for the purposes of this book wasn't always easy. My background, prior to this book, was mostly in technology issues, writing on how the internet and globalization were reshaping the way that businesses and politics operated. When I began researching the FBI, on assignment for *The Washingtonian,* I was surprised by how often the subject of globalization came up in conversations with agents and FBI leaders. The first time I met Bob Mueller, he grilled me about an article I'd written on Tom Friedman's *The World Is Flat,* which turned out to be one of Mueller's favorite books and one that has influenced greatly his thinking about the Bureau. Over the next two years, I traveled tens of thousands of miles tracing the evolution of the FBI into a global investigative force. I spoke with well over 150 current and former FBI agents, analysts, and staff, including nearly all of the living FBI directors, as well as agents and officials of other U.S. and foreign intelligence agencies. I visited FBI field offices small and large, scattered across the United States, journeyed by airplane to Sicily and by Amtrak to Queens with Bureau agents to understand Mafia cases started before I was born, spent afternoons with the secretive Hostage Rescue Team at Quantico, and interviewed retired agents in their homes surrounded by decades of memorabilia from their careers. I spent many hours with Director Mueller and scores of hours interviewing his senior leadership team—more than any other journalist. I traveled to facilities that had never before been open to the public and spoke with agents who had never before spoken to the public (and some who, to be frank, cooperated with me only because they had been told to do so). And yet at no time was I asked to tailor my research and reporting or submit my conclusions to the FBI for approval.

This book is, at its heart, a journalistic undertaking—an attempt to understand better the central agency in America's fight against terrorism. In order to complete it, I pored over more than a hundred thousand pages of reports, case files, and books concerning the Bureau, including thousands of pages of material never before seen by the public. In a very few instances, I have decided, after much discussion with sources, to withhold information that could compromise what the intelligence community refers to as "sources and methods." Nowhere have I created composites of agents. I have spoken with most of the agents and other players named in this book, although not all of them agreed to speak on the record.

As a historian is wont to do, I have tried with the benefit of hindsight to create a coherent thread out of an incoherent time. The agents who experienced these events and launched these investigations didn't know where they would lead. Likewise, the six directors of the FBI and the half-dozen presidential administrations involved in this story couldn't foresee all of the effects of their decisions. This story unfolded on multiple fronts among the case agents in the field, the executives at FBI headquarters, and the halls of power in Washington at the White House, the Pentagon, Main Justice, and CIA Headquarters at Langley, Virginia. Yet, at the same time, this story is more linear than one might imagine. The scandals of Hoover's era contributed directly to the intelligence failures that led to 9/11 a generation later; the cases and bureaucratic disputes of the 1980s helped lay the groundwork for how we choose to respond to terrorism in the twenty-first century; the response after 9/11 depended heavily on work done by agents before the attacks. Inevitably, not every player is mentioned; not every investigation is discussed; not every relevant case study or example is cited. I've followed a single thread, even as the Bureau today wrestles with more complex challenges than ever before. The work of thousands of agents on public corruption, violent crime, gangs, drugs, and white-collar and cyber crime for the most part is left aside in this telling. The scandal that was the Robert Hanssen spy case, perhaps the most devastating espionage incident in the nation's history, receives only a glancing mention, as does the Wen Ho Lee matter, Ruby Ridge, Waco, and even the years-long hunt for the Unabomber and the mailer of the 2001 anthrax letters. Only two of the FBI's Ten Most Wanted Fugitives, as of mid-2010, are mentioned at all. Those compelling stories, told so well by other journalists, and many cases still untold, simply fall outside the scope of this project.

Like the directors who came before him, Mueller has spent years in the post trying to get what he calls "ground truth," an actual understanding of what the FBI does and how it does it. Fighting terrorism especially has been a learning process for the FBI and the United States. This is the story of how—and what—the FBI learned.

PART I
1972–1992

CHAPTER I
1972

The year, 1972, was a memory, like it or not....
The future was calling us, and no matter what,
there was no turning back now.

—The Wonder Years

The year 1972 was officially the longest year in recorded history. To ensure the time on earth kept up with its orbit of the sun, the official world timekeepers—the International Time Bureau at the Paris Observatory—added two leap seconds to the leap year, something that had never happened before and hasn't been repeated since. There was certainly enough history to fill the year—among many other notable events, Nixon visited China, a hapless gang of burglars was caught in the Watergate, Jane Fonda toured North Vietnam, Bobby Fischer defeated Boris Spassky to become the first American world chess champion, and the last manned mission to the moon, *Apollo 17*, returned safely to earth. But 1972 turned out to be an especially important year in the history of the Federal Bureau of Investigation, perhaps the most important of all.

J. Edgar Hoover, it is said, never took a vacation, but he often spent weekends in Manhattan, the home of the FBI's largest and most politically powerful field office, staying with his aide Clyde Tolson in a suite at the Waldorf Astoria that the hotel comped the legendary FBI director—without a doubt the most famous man in American law enforcement and arguably the second most powerful man in the government. As much as he liked the escapes, Hoover never liked being away from his desk at the Justice Department in Washington and would every few hours call his deputy at the Bureau, Mark Felt. On one such weekend getaway he'd received that panicked phone call at 2:30 P.M. on December 7, 1941, from Robert Shivers, the special agent in charge of the FBI's Honolulu Field Office, informing him of a surprise attack on the naval base at Pearl Harbor. Hoover had heard the explosions in the background, across the thousands of miles of scratchy copper telephone wire—the sounds of the worst intelligence failure in U.S. history. Sixty years after that phone call, New York would be the scene of the next catastrophic U.S. intelligence failure, but Hoover would be long gone by then.

His calls back to Washington were not the only predictable elements of Hoover's Manhattan excursions. In fact, he was a man of intense routine—his workday began precisely at 9:05 and ended with exactly one bourbon and soda. But 1970s New York was less amenable to his routine. The Stork Club, just off Fifth Avenue, where he'd spent many an evening sipping Jack Daniel's, had closed in 1965, its building demolished to become a tiny pocket park. The cozy postwar café society that had thrived in New York, where Hoover had rubbed elbows with movie stars and politicians (even the occasional gangster), was giving way across Manhattan to new signs of progress. America's largest city was still an unrivaled center of energy, celebrity, and glamour, but now with more of a radical beat than someone like Hoover—*especially* Hoover—could stomach. Once he had been a fulcrum; now he was merely off balance.

On Hoover's final trip to New York, in April 1972, the south tower of the new World Trade Center was welcoming its first tenants: Morgan Stanley, the law firm Thacher Proffitt & Wood, Dow Jones, and the New York Stock Exchange. Hoover never lived to see the towers officially open a few months later, debuting as the tallest buildings in the world and a physical incarnation of America's growing financial and commercial dominance on the world stage. Perhaps that was for the best: New York always made Hoover a bit uncomfortable.

On his last day in the Big Apple, Hoover walked out of the new home of the FBI New York Field Office—26 Federal Plaza, the recently completed Jacob Javits Federal Building—his bulldog-like jaw set firmly against the spring cold. The towers loomed over southern Manhattan just a few blocks away. When Hoover arrived in New York the day before, their tops had been shrouded in the clouds of an overcast and rainy Monday, but the storm had blown through. Now, resplendent in their enormity, the twin towers reached toward the blue above, casting their shadows north toward 26 Federal Plaza, which by comparison was no architectural triumph. The *New York Times*'s architectural critic labeled the forty-story Javits structure upon opening "one of the most monumentally mediocre Federal buildings in history." Yet these two edifices, in their own way, would come to play defining roles in the drama that unfolded for the FBI over the next generation—a drama that Hoover himself could never have imagined that April morning but one that would shape the future of his beloved Bureau.

You will hear FBI agents of a certain vintage, all of them retired now, refer to "the Funeral." When they say it, there's no doubt that it's capitalized and there's no doubt about what event they're referencing. The phrase is also always uttered with a vague wistfulness. The Funeral refers, of course, to the death of "the Director"—also always capitalized—J. Edgar Hoover.

The day that Hoover died, agents of that era argue, a big part of the Bureau died too. Never again would it be as powerful, as omnipotent, as flawless (at least in the eyes of the public). The era that followed was tumultuous—three directors in just fourteen months, infectious politicking, broken careers, and the scandalous airing of all too much dirty laundry. The fawning press disappeared and the scaffold of public esteem collapsed. The Funeral, these agents say, was the end of the good times.

The good times had an incredible run, to be sure. It's hard to capture the sweep of history that Hoover observed. He'd been director for three years before Charles Lindbergh flew across the Atlantic in 1927 and he was director three years after Neil Armstrong landed on the moon in 1969. The forty-eight years of J. Edgar's reign as director of the FBI saw the Great Depression, World War II and the Cold War, the Atomic Age and the Space Race, the Korean War and Vietnam; he witnessed the rise of the automobile, commercial aviation, the telephone, television, and the suburbs. His Bureau battled bank robbers, kidnappers, Nazis, deserters, Commies, the KGB, student radicals, the mob, and the Klan—the last two perhaps not as hard as it could have. He started under another, unrelated Hoover—Herbert Hoover—and served straight through to Richard Nixon, fully a quarter of the history of his beloved country, amassing along the way power and reach that would far exceed the comfort level of most democratic systems.

There was one thing J. Edgar didn't see in his impressive life. If he had lived through the summer of 1972, he would have seen the terrifying arrival of a new breed of criminal unlike anything the world had witnessed—the truly international, ideologically driven, borderless, and stateless terrorist. And if he had lived through that fall of '72, he would have seen that his daring G-men weren't trained for what would come next.

Oh, what a funeral it was!

John Edgar Hoover was nothing if not a man of habit. Never married, he lived in his childhood home with his mother until she died in 1938, and only after her death did he move to the house he'd occupy for the rest of his life. He lunched promptly at noon, left the office promptly each night at 4:30 P.M., and even amid the swirling social circuit of Washington, Hoover only attended events hosted by his bosses—the attorney general or the president.

And so it was immediately strange when he didn't meet his Bureau chauffeur the Tuesday morning of May 2, 1972. Shortly after 8:30 A.M., his housekeeper went upstairs and found the director dead of a heart ailment. The news flew through the Bureau: "The king is dead." The acting attorney general announced Hoover's passing to the world at 11 A.M., and a few hours later his regular table at the Mayflower Hotel, where for decades he lunched nearly every day with Clyde Tolson, dining on a ritual meal of chicken soup and cottage cheese, sat empty.

Hoover's death was front-page news throughout the country. Editorials praised him in terms reserved more for emperors than appointed government officials.* Washington nearly came to a standstill. Congress quickly voted to commemorate Hoover by having him lie in state at the Capitol, the first civil servant ever so honored—but of course Hoover was no ordinary civil servant. Paranoid in death as he had been in life, the director was, by his instructions, buried in a half-ton lead-lined coffin to discourage would-be grave desecrators. After eight military pallbearers successfully navigated the thousand-pound coffin up the steps of the Capitol, it sat for a day on the catafalque originally built for President Lincoln's body. Thousands of mourners filed past. Addressing the crowd in the Rotunda during the first of two funeral services, Chief Justice Warren Burger said, "From modest beginnings he rose to the pinnacle of his profession and established a worldwide reputation that was without equal among those to whom societies entrust the difficult tasks relating to enforcement of the law.... If the great institution he created is faithful to his standards of professional excellence, fidelity to law, and dedication to the public interest, it will survive and go on in a world of conflict and turmoil."

The following day Hoover's body was taken from the Capitol to the National Presbyterian Church on Nebraska Avenue for the second funeral service. In what one observer labeled a "television spectacle" carried to a live audience nationwide, two thousand mourners, including Mamie Eisenhower, congressional leaders, and law enforcement personnel from across the country, packed the church. Reverend Edward Elson, who had ministered regularly to Hoover through his life, led the congregation in Psalm 46 and Psalm 23, and prayed, "We thank thee for thy servant Edgar... for his invincible fidelity to the moral law and the laws derived therefrom, for the strength of his manhood, his elevated patriotism, his kindness and generosity, his reverence for life and his warmhearted friendship." The U.S. Army Chorus sang "How Firm a Foundation."

Eulogizing Hoover as "the peace officer without peer," President

---

* The *Press-Chronicle* in Tennessee provided a typical treatment, writing, "J. Edgar Hoover was America's symbol of tough law enforcement. There he stood granite-like through the vicissitudes of half a century protecting his country against all enemies—be they internal gangsters or external predators."

Nixon echoed the chief justice's remarks of the day before. "There is a belief that a changing of the guard will also mean a changing of the rules," Nixon told the crowd. "This will not happen. The FBI will carry on in the future, true to the finest traditions in the past, because regardless of what the snipers and detractors would have us believe, the fact is that Director Hoover built the Bureau totally on principle, not on personality. He built well. He built to last. For that reason, the FBI will remain as a memorial to him, a living memorial, continuing to create a climate of protection, security, and impartial justice that benefits every American."

Afterward, Hoover's funeral motorcade wound through three of the four quadrants of Washington, past the Mayflower, the White House, and his childhood home in Seward Square, to the Congressional Cemetery, where his body would rest near those of his parents; the entire nine-mile route was closed to traffic, and police from across the country stood almost shoulder to shoulder in salute. The Senate chaplain, Edward Elson, tossed the first handful of dirt onto the casket.

The debate over where the Bureau would go after Hoover began immediately. The *Philadelphia Inquirer* wrote, "How do you replace an American institution in what could be the second most powerful job in the nation?" Of course, not everyone had viewed Hoover positively: Syndicated columnists Robert Novak and Rowland Evans wrote, "It was fitting that the director died in his sleep. That was the way the Bureau was run lately." Recalled *Time* magazine, "With a genius for administration and popular myth, [Hoover] fashioned his career as an improbable bureaucratic morality play peopled by bad guys and G-men. The drama worked well enough when everyone agreed on the villains—'Pretty Boy' Floyd, John Dillinger, Nazi agents—but finally curdled somewhat in more ambiguous days." Those "ambiguous days" toward the end were when the nonpartisan FBI seemed to be creeping more toward pursuing an ideological agenda driven by what Hoover saw as excessive permissiveness in American society. In Hoover's final decade, the Bureau harassed student radicals, civil rights leaders such as Martin Luther King Jr. (whom Hoover once labeled "the most notorious liar in the country"), and other political opponents whose views differed from the strict code by which Hoover abided.

In the wake of Hoover's death, President Nixon proclaimed that the FBI's new headquarters, still rising on Pennsylvania Avenue, would henceforth be known as the J. Edgar Hoover Building. A generation later, perhaps there's no stronger metaphor for the Bureau's tough position than that headquarters building in downtown Washington—ugly, worn, and outdated, plastered at every corner with the name J. Edgar Hoover. The block-sized concrete monstrosity is one of the best examples of the blessedly brief Brutalist era of architecture. Bureau analysts today have estimated that the government could tear down the eleven-story nightmare and sell the emptied lot for some $700 million. (No one, they recognize, would ever want the building.) The thousands of staff who spend their days wandering the depressingly drab corridors inside certainly would love a fresh start somewhere else, a building perhaps filled with light and a whole lot less linoleum. And yet the Bureau is centrally located, halfway between the Capitol at one end of Pennsylvania Avenue and the White House at the other, and is within walking distance of every one of Washington's Metro lines, making it accessible to workers from all corners of the region. Perhaps someday the FBI will be able to move, but for now it's stuck where it is. Just as, nearly forty years after Hoover's death, the Bureau remains in the Hoover Building, it is still fighting to overcome the legacy left it in 1972.

In a 1937 *New Yorker* profile, Jack Anderson had warned, "There is, in fact, so much of John Edgar Hoover in the FBI as it is organized and operated today that if he were lost to it, its effectiveness would sag, possibly with disastrous results." Fast-forward thirty-five years, through five administrations, World War II, and the Cold War, and Anderson's words would prove all too true.

On several occasions, presidents had contemplated replacing Hoover. Lesser public servants—in fact, every single one not named John Edgar Hoover—were required by statute to retire at age seventy. President Kennedy was said to have wanted Hoover to retire at that then-mandatory federal retirement age in 1965, and when Lyndon Johnson privately considered urging Hoover into retirement, the satirical British news show *That Was the Week That Was,* hosted by David

Frost, reported, "President Johnson has declared that he does not intend to replace J. Edgar Hoover. However, J. Edgar Hoover has not disclosed whether he plans to replace President Johnson."

In the end, Lyndon Johnson caved and signed an executive order in 1964 saying that the FBI chief didn't need to worry about such petty rules. As LBJ said at the Rose Garden ceremony, "Edgar, the law says that you must retire next January when you reach your seventieth birthday, and I know you wouldn't want to break the law. But the nation cannot afford to lose you."

In a whirlwind two days following Hoover's death, L. Patrick Gray III, an ex-navy man known for his loyalty to Richard Nixon, became acting director—an outsider walking into a culture known for its hostility to outsiders. Driving back to the Justice Department from the White House, where the announcement of his appointment had been made, Gray expressed some reservations to Acting Attorney General Richard Kleindienst. "Pat, there is no more important position in our government than the director of the FBI," Kleindienst replied. "Everyone knows the director of the FBI."

Gray walked into the fifth-floor offices of the FBI and found himself in the midst of the House Hoover Built. "This was Hoover's preserve and visitors from the Justice Department were neither encouraged nor welcomed," he recalled years later. The anteroom was packed with grim mementoes of Hoover's fifty-year fight against crime. There was John Dillinger's death mask; the submachine gun favored by Clyde Barrow; the black hood used in the hanging of an obscure murderer named Carl Panzram. His agents reflected Hoover's own unrelenting conservative patriotism. Even during a time of social unrest, 75 percent of the FBI's new agents had served in Vietnam.

Met inside by W. Mark Felt, the Bureau's associate director and the man who would later become famous as Bob Woodward's "Deep Throat" in Watergate, Gray shook hands and proceeded into what he called "the center ring of the Hoover extravaganza," the ornate conference room where the fifteen leaders of the FBI were assembled. "I noted their chiseled faces, their impeccable dress, their clean, crisp appearance overall. These were the assistant directors of the Federal Bureau of Investigation, men molded by Hoover, advanced by Hoover, and occupying their present positions by his mandate," Gray recalled.

"I had before me an almost impossible task. I had to learn all there was to know about the FBI as fast as possible and without the benefit of a no-holds-barred briefing from the man whom I had been appointed to succeed."

From the start, Gray's tenure marked a major shift from the reclusive, moralistic days of Hoover's reign. Whereas Hoover had dined either alone or with his chief aide, Gray lunched at Washington's fashionable Sans Souci restaurant. Beyond power dining choices, though, the FBI was undergoing monumental changes. Four months after Hoover's death, halfway around the globe, a new world would be announced in flickering black-and-white TV images, and the Bureau would never be the same.

Nothing bad was supposed to happen at the Munich Olympics—bad things didn't fit with the happy-go-lucky image that the West German government had worked so hard to create for the "Carefree Games." With the intention of hosting an Olympics wholly different from the militaristic Hitler-led Berlin Games of 1936, the 1972 host committee had decided that security would take a backseat for the Olympics' return to German soil. The athletes' village was open to nearly anyone, and many competitors chose just to jump the low fences rather than make their way through the official entrances; security personnel, the "Olys," were unarmed, and when early in the Games several hundred demonstrators appeared on a nearby hill, security persuaded them to disperse by offering them candy.

Indeed, looking back today from an era when the Olympics are as much about tight security as they are about athletics, it's hard to imagine just how easy it was for Black September to attack the Munich Games. The total security budget then was some $2 million ($10 million in 2010 dollars), whereas by comparison, the post-9/11 security budget for the Sydney Olympics amounted to a billion dollars.

Black September, a Palestinian terrorist group, had no problems executing its plan at the Munich Olympics. Posing as Brazilians, the attackers talked their way into the athletes' village to scout the Israeli compound in the days leading up to the attack, and were invited inside for a tour of the athletes' apartments by an Israeli athlete. On the night of Black September's assault, drunk, carousing American athletes actually helped the terrorists, who were disguised as fellow Olympians, scale the fence around the village and carry their gym bags filled with AK-47s and submachine guns.

It's not as if the attack was entirely unforeseen—in fact, Dr. Georg Sieber, a West German police psychologist, had walked through twenty-six different scenarios for possible trouble. Situation 21 had focused on Palestinian terrorists storming the Israeli compound, killing hostages, and demanding the release of their counterparts in Israeli jails and a plane to make their escape to an Arab country. The West German authorities, though, weren't thrilled with Sieber's worst-case scenarios and had asked him to come up with less-scary alternatives. It would turn out that Sieber had gotten only one significant detail of the plan wrong: His imaginary Situation 21 had the Palestinians storming the compound at 5 A.M. In reality, they stormed the compound at 4:10 A.M., fifty minutes "early."*

The eight terrorists began their September 5 attack by jimmying the door to the Israeli rooms at 31 Connollystrasse. Sieber had envisioned them using a blasting cap, but the door wasn't even secure enough to require that. Chaos reigned for a few minutes as the terrorists moved from room to room. Some athletes resisted—two were killed while trying to wrestle guns from their attackers—and others wandered sleepily from their rooms into the midst of the horror. A cleaning lady outside called the Olympic security office at 4:47 A.M. to report gunfire. The first unarmed Oly to arrive on the scene marched up to the hooded terrorist standing guard outside the Israeli dorm and demanded, "What is the meaning of this?" Minutes later the terrorists released their first set of demands—free 234 Palestinians held in Israeli jails—and rolled the dead body of wrestling coach Moshe Weinberg into the street as proof of their determination. Black September announced that beginning at 9 A.M., its members would execute one hostage every hour until their demands were met. They knew Israel didn't negotiate with terrorists, and indeed, within a few hours, word

---

*Another of Sieber's twenty-six scenarios imagined a hijacked airliner crashing into the crowded Olympic Stadium. Unfortunately, he'd live to see a version of that scenario come true on another September morning nearly three decades later.

came that Israeli prime minister Golda Meir would not consider freeing even a single prisoner as "the slightest concession to terrorist blackmail."

The terrorists gradually extended their deadline through the day, realizing that the longer the situation unfolded the greater the audience became. TV cameras were trained live on the compound, and the world was captivated by the grainy images of hooded terrorists watching from the balconies; inside the compound, those TV images provided a great opportunity for the terrorists to watch themselves live. The West German police quickly invented and discarded plan after plan. One idea to use police disguised as food deliverymen was abandoned after Black September insisted the food be left outside; another idea to storm the building by sneaking police through the ventilation ducts was canceled when the ten police, in tracksuits and carrying submachine guns, were shown on live TV climbing onto the building. At 5 P.M., Black September issued new demands: a plane to take them and the Israeli hostages to Egypt. If the Palestinian prisoners weren't waiting at the Cairo airport, all of the Israelis would be executed.

As the deadline of 9 P.M. neared, West German officials prepped two Iroquois helicopters for the short flight to Fürstenfeldbruck Air Base, where authorities swore that the situation must come to an end. Still reeling from the legacy of the Holocaust, the German government could never allow Jewish hostages to be taken off German soil by terrorists. Two plans were put in place: An ambush team of police would hide on the plane and take the terrorists down when they boarded, or a separate team of snipers would try to pick the Palestinian terrorists off as they crossed the tarmac before they boarded.

A few minutes after ten, the helicopters took off. Two carried assortments of hostages and terrorists; a third, ferrying frantic West German officials, raced ahead. The terror unfolding was so new and unforeseen that no specialized units stood ready to respond. West Germany had no elite special forces like the U.S. Navy SEALs or Israel's own Sayerat Matkal. And there was no way to reason with the unreasonable. Barring a miracle, there was effectively no chance of a successful outcome.

The hole became even deeper when the onboard ambush team of police en route to the airport voted to abandon what they saw as a "suicide mission," leaving the snipers as the only line of defense. The chosen snipers themselves weren't specially trained—they simply enjoyed shooting competitively in their free time. Meanwhile, no one had bothered to count the terrorists, so the snipers didn't know how many awaited them. Not issued night-vision equipment or even two-way radios so that they could coordinate their attack, the snipers, in remote locations on the airfield, had been told simply to open fire when they heard gunfire. Meanwhile, armored personnel carriers had gotten stuck in traffic on their way to the airport, and many police units were incorrectly dispatched to Riem, Munich's main airport. A helicopter ferrying one of the few special police assault teams to the airport landed at the wrong end of the airfield, leaving the team more than two kilometers from the action.

Police snipers felled two terrorists in their opening volley and fatally wounded a third, leaving five unharmed. The surviving Black Septembrists proceeded to shoot out many of the airport's lights. An hour passed with just the occasional shot back and forth. As midnight neared, the long-awaited armored vehicles arrived and advanced on the helicopters. A terrorist opened fire into the belly of one helicopter as the ugly behemoths neared, shooting all the hostages inside before tossing a grenade through the open door. The once-dark airport tarmac was suddenly bathed in light from the flames. A shootout at the other helicopter left two terrorists and all of the other hostages dead too. Three Black Septembrists were captured. Shortly after 12:30 A.M. on September 6, nearly twenty hours after the hostage situation began and some two hours after the helicopters arrived at the airport, West German police tracked the last remaining terrorist to where he was hiding beneath a railroad car on the airfield's edge, ending what was to become a wake-up call to governments around the world.

Mistake after mistake had piled up through the night, an unfortunate testament to the novelty of the terror the police faced. As morning broke, the results of those mistakes were spread gruesomely across the tarmac—the burned skeleton of a helicopter surrounded by fifteen dead: Nine Israeli hostages, one police officer, and five terrorists. West German intelligence had overlooked at least three reports of Black September agents entering the country in the two weeks before the attack on the "Carefree Games"—an oversight all the more glaring considering that the group had launched five attacks in Europe within the past year, including three in West Germany. Something would have to change. Within two weeks, Germany launched GSG-9, its first counterterrorism special forces unit.

On September 15, 1972, in the United States, the CIA produced its first weekly summary of international terrorist activity—an initial draft of the Threat Matrix that decades later would greet the nation's top intelligence officials each morning. President Nixon called to check what the FBI's contingency plans were for terrorist attacks on major U.S. cities; the short answer: There weren't any.

The thirty-first U.S. skyjacking of 1972 started off like all of the others that year—basically peaceful and random. Hijackings weren't new; all told, between 1960 and 1972 some 17,000 U.S. passengers and crew had been hijacked—about 1,400 Americans a year on average. At a certain level, hijackings had become an almost accepted inconvenience of air travel—much like afternoon thunderstorms at Chicago's O'Hare Airport. But the events of 11/11 proved a wake-up call that the FBI was ill equipped to respond to the new threat of violent terrorism from the skies.

Much like Munich's "Carefree Games," Atlanta-based Southern Airways was supposed to be the "happy" airline. The blue-and-yellow planes that crisscrossed the nation daily during the early 1970s had smiley faces painted on their noses underneath the inscription "Have a Nice Day."

Southern Airways Flight 49 had originated in Memphis and was on its second leg, a short fifteen-minute hop from Birmingham to Montgomery, when just before landing a man barreled his way into the cockpit—one arm around the neck of flight attendant Donna Holman, the other brandishing a .38 caliber Smith & Wesson revolver. His command was clear: "Head north, Captain—this is a hijacking."

Captain William R. Haas hesitated only a moment before he answered, "You've got it." As he transmitted a hijack code to air traffic control, he turned on the "Fasten Seat Belt" sign. First Officer Harold Johnson began to turn the airplane. On the ground, Birmingham air traffic controllers began their normal procedures—they notified the FBI in Washington and the FAA's special hijacking command post.

There had been enough hijackings that the procedures were well-known and widely used. Yet one thing was puzzling: Nearly every hijacker demanded to be flown south to Cuba. As air traffic controllers watched Flight 49's heading swing north, they realized something different was happening here.

Security procedures, lax as they were, had worked—sort of. The airline had pegged Lewis Moore as a possible security risk and asked him whether he'd be willing to undergo screening. He readily agreed. Security officers patted him down but never checked the contents of the overcoat he held, inside of which was the arsenal he'd soon use against Flight 49. His two partners, Henry Jackson and Melvin Cale, unscreened, had no problems boarding. The trio intended to hijack the plane in response to Moore and Jackson's latest run-in with Detroit police—they'd been arrested on October 13 and accused of a series of rapes and assaults. Earlier, after a previous incident in which Moore and Jackson had accused the police of beating them outside a bar, the city had tried to settle their $4 million police brutality lawsuit for $25. It was an insult, made worse in their minds by the follow-up arrest. The two men skipped bond, missed a planned October 30 hearing on the charges against them, recruited Moore's half brother, Melvin, and headed for Memphis.

After a quick refueling stop in Jackson, Mississippi, the plane headed toward Detroit, where Moore and his compatriots planned to settle their score with city officials. The two flight attendants served dinner to the worried passengers, and the three hijackers began helping themselves to the plentiful supply of onboard liquor.

On the ground, FBI agents arrived at the Detroit control tower and phoned the mayor to relay the hijackers' $10 million ransom demand. Other agents passed the hijackers' request along to Southern's headquarters in Atlanta. Southern's Chicago station manager was dispatched to a local bank, where he met with FBI agents and, under escort, signed for a briefcase full of ransom money—nowhere close to the full amount but enough, the airline hoped, to buy them more time. At Chicago's Midway Airport, the official and agents boarded another Southern jet and began to give chase. At the insistence of the Southern captain, the agents left behind their heavy weapons and carried only their sidearms.

As bad weather descended on Detroit, Flight 49 diverted to Cleveland, where it refueled and then took off for Toronto to avoid sitting idle. In Toronto, the hijackers learned that Southern had gathered only $500,000 in ransom and, insulted by the paltry amount, refused to take the money or release the passengers. Instead the plane refueled and took off once again, heading back to the States. The hijacking had been under way for almost twelve hours already, and as the plane ascended, a scary new element was added to the equation. Haas radioed that unless their ransom demands were met, the hijackers intended to crash the plane into the Oak Ridge nuclear facility in Tennessee. This was something the nation had never seen before. Skyjacking was one thing—nuclear terrorism was something else.

On the ground, the hijacking response proceeded on multiple fronts. Officials at Oak Ridge scrambled to shut down the systems and minimize potential damage. The Southern Airways chase plane was still tailing the hijacked flight, and the navy had also launched a plane loaded with FBI agents, heavy weapons, and gear. After talking over the situation with airline and technical personnel, the responding agents had decided that their best option would be to shoot out the airliner's tires when it was on the ground. No one believed the plane could take off with flat tires, and with the aircraft disabled, it would be possible to better negotiate or, if need be, take more aggressive action. By now, the Atomic Energy Commission, the White House, and the Pentagon were all involved.

After another refueling stop in Lexington, Kentucky, Flight 49 returned to circling above Oak Ridge. As the morning haze burned off and the flight's passengers caught glimpses of their intended target below, Moore made a chilling threat: "I was born to die and if I have to take all of you with me, that's all right with me. We're gonna make this thing look worse than Munich."

Ground controllers connected Flight 49 to the White House, and a voice came over the cockpit intercom. "This is John Ehrlichman," said the president's top domestic aide. "And who am I speaking with?"

"I'm up over Oak Ridge, where I'll either throw a grenade or I'll put this plane down nose first," Jackson barked. "We want a letter signed by the president declaring that our $10 million ransom demand is to be a grant from the federal government and that we won't be prosecuted."

Ehrlichman demurred, saying such a request would take some time, and Jackson exploded. "If you don't, I'm gonna show you the Olympics wasn't anything—the Munich incident wasn't shit."

The hijackers, initially instructed to head to Knoxville, where FBI agents and airline officials had gathered, directed the plane instead to Chattanooga, setting off a rush to get the response team there. In an age when interstate communication was still limited, the repeated hops were wreaking havoc with the FBI's plans. Acting Director Pat Gray was home in Connecticut, so while he was in touch with headquarters, it fell to Assistant Director Robert Gebhardt, the head of the criminal division, to coordinate much of the response.

At Chattanooga, FBI agents flooded the airport and prepared to deliver the ransom via a refueling truck. Local police blocked off nearby roads and tried to control the crowds that had assembled as word spread that the dramatic headline-grabbing skyjacking was coming to town. Even peanut and popcorn vendors showed up to feed the spectators. Agents gathered food and beer to put aboard the plane, since it had been nearly a day since those on Flight 49 had eaten. Although the FBI lacked a critical response team, some Bureau sharpshooters hid themselves at strategic points around the airport in case they were needed. However, the response plan was far from perfect: No one at Chattanooga thought to summon even a single ambulance in case medical attention was required.

The fuel truck made its way slowly out on the runway toward the hijacked DC-9. The sacks of ransom money in the cabin made it impossible for the driver to shift into a higher gear. The money, food, and other supplies were passed through a cockpit window and then the truck began to refuel the jet. The flight attendants began the laborious process of counting the money. Although the hijackers had demanded $10 million, Southern Airways had been able to assemble only $2 million—but because it would take hours to count it all, they gambled on the hijackers' not being able to tell the difference. Indeed, the trio of hijackers, unaware that they'd been swindled out of the bulk of their ransom payment, celebrated, declaring happily that they were millionaires, and began passing out cash to the passengers "for your inconvenience." (They also gave the pilot and first officer some $300,000, stuffing it in crevices all over the cockpit.)

As Captain Haas negotiated to get the passengers off the plane, another wave of panic swept through airport officials—no one had thought to have a bus or other transport available, so a Chattanooga police car was dispatched to search the roads around the airport for the closest municipal bus. But it was too late. Southern Airways Flight 49 revved up and began taxiing down the runway. "Southern 49—advise intentions," the tower interrogated.

"Going to Cuba—they want to talk to Castro," First Officer Johnson replied.

So many hijackers fled south during the 1960s and early 1970s, after the United States broke off diplomatic relations with Cuba, that Fidel Castro, despite his pleasure at the aggravation such incidents caused his neighbor to the north, didn't exactly roll out the welcome mat for arriving criminals. Indeed, he had set aside a shabby aging mansion in Havana's Siboney district nicknamed the "Casa de Transitos," the "Hijackers' House," for them to live in under twenty-four-hour guard. The score of hijackers residing there received a forty-pesos-a-month living stipend, yet were only rarely permitted to venture outside to spend it. Most passed their time working in sugarcane fields under Castro's orders. More than a dozen had fled back to the United States; others tried to commit suicide, some successfully. Now, despite the dire living condition of most hijackers in Castro's orbit, Moore, Jackson, and Cale hoped their millions in U.S. currency could buy them a better life, free from the hassle of "the Man."

As the plane winged south down the Florida peninsula, a new worry developed: President Nixon was at his "Winter White House" retreat in Key Biscayne, off the coast of Miami. Given the hijackers' demonstrated willingness to turn their craft into a missile, he could become a target. Sure, the single-floor concrete ranch-style house at 500 Bay Lane would be difficult to even spot from the air, but the Secret Service and the military couldn't take that chance. Pentagon officials contacted the nearby Homestead Air Reserve Base and placed on alert F-106 "Delta Dart" fighters from the 48th Interceptor Squadron.

Luckily, the decision never had to be made—Flight 49 touched down in Havana at 4:50 P.M. Believing that, like so many other hijackings before it, the incident was over as soon as the hijacked plane arrived in Cuba, the two chase aircraft—packed with materiel, FBI agents, and Southern Airways corporate officials—set down at Tampa's MacDill Air Force Base for the personnel to eat dinner and for the planes to refuel before beginning their journey homeward.

Except that it wasn't over. To Moore and Jackson's surprise, the Cubans weren't thrilled to see them and, far from welcoming their millions in greenbacks, surrounded the plane with soldiers. Castro himself watched from afar, refusing to greet the hijackers as heroes. José Abrantes, Castro's security chief, personally explained the situation to Jackson: "The matter is one that will have to be considered by the proper political authorities."

"You people sound like a bunch of Washington bureaucrats," Jackson spat back.

"I'm sorry, señor. There are certain procedures that must be followed, whether you're in Washington or Havana."

"I thought this was supposed to be a free country," Jackson sputtered.

"There is freedom here for the Cuban people, but the admission of foreigners addresses itself to proper authorities. Otherwise," Abrantes said with a laugh, "you must understand our tiny island couldn't hold all of the people who might want to come here."

The hijackers retreated back into the plane and held a grenade to Captain Haas's head, demanding more fuel; the Cuban government, not altogether unhappy to be rid of the situation, complied. As Flight 49 took off, heading north again, frantic calls crisscrossed the United States. The FBI agents at MacDill—about to sit down for a well-deserved meal at a nearby motel—were readied for action, the FAA and FBI hijacking command posts in Washington were reactivated, and Acting Director Gray got on the phone with Southern Airways' general manager in Atlanta. This situation had to end, Gray announced.

Assistant Director Robert Gebhardt radioed the agents aboard the navy chase plane, circling over Florida, with the plan: "Instructions are that the hijacked craft be disabled when next on the ground."

"Roger," replied an agent from the Detroit Field Office who had spent a long day following Flight 49 across the country.

"Over and out. That's the completion of our transmission and instructions," Gebhardt concluded.

Without much discussion and with even less planning, Gray had overruled Hoover's long-standing rule that no action would be taken by the Bureau against a hijacked airliner unless the pilot of the craft had been informed and had consented. As Gray later explained to Congress, in his thinking, "the pilot was not a free agent; there was no way of getting word to him."

Nerves on all sides were frayed as the dramatic situation converged on Orlando Airport shortly after 9 P.M. Saturday night, November 11, 1972. FBI agents from the Orlando Resident Agency arrived first, taking control of the airport. Local police began to close the roads around the airport. On its side of the shared civilian-military airport, the air force shut down the massive floodlights, plunging the tarmac into darkness. When Southern Airways Flight 49 landed, its exhausted pilots, passengers, and hijackers had no idea that, three miles behind them in the approach pattern, two planes packed with FBI agents were readying for a showdown. "This plane isn't getting off the ground," Knoxville special agent in charge (SAC) Wallace Estill announced to the chase plane team.

Gebhardt spoke by radio with one of the FBI agents in the airport control tower. "I have given [the other agents] instructions to go out there and shoot the goddamn tires out and disable the plane. What we wanted to do is rush the plane at the same time.... Mr. Gray says disable the plane and to storm the plane."

"That's ten-four. I copy. Disable and storm," the agent replied.

The hijackers had been afraid of just such an encounter from their first stop. Haas later recalled that the hijackers believed each person they spotted outside was "an FBI man with a high-powered telescopic rifle ready to pick them off at any minute." If only the hijackers had been aware of the FBI's actual capabilities at that point—the agents on the ground and on the chase plane who would execute the plan lacked heavy weapons and weren't specially trained for such hostage rescue missions. The FBI agents at the Orlando Resident Agency, a suboffice of the Tampa Field Office, didn't have a single rifle—their request earlier that year for such heavy weapons had been held up because their safe wasn't large enough to hold long rifles. (The current safe held a single shotgun.) Furthermore, the agents on the ground had no way to contact the FBI team on board the chase aircraft, and as a result the latter executed the plan to end the standoff before the other local agents even knew what would happen. On board the chase aircraft, far from his home territory, Knoxville SAC Estill divided the sixteen FBI agents into four-man teams; they only had enough shoulder weapons—four shotguns and two rifles—to give one or two to each team. On the ground, the agents ran nearly a mile across the airport, approaching the hijacked craft from the rear.*

The first volley of rifle shots from the FBI failed to penetrate the thick tires, so another team of agents with shotguns began firing heavy slugs into the main tires. All told, according to the number of shell casings gathered at the scene afterward, the FBI agents fired twenty-six shots at the plane's landing gear. As the first tires deflated and the plane began to tilt left, those on board figured out what was happening. Underneath, one team of agents approached the external latch to open the rear stairs. As the hijackers ordered Captain Haas to rev the engines, Jackson and Moore leaned out the cockpit window and shot blindly into the dark. The injured plane lurched twenty-five to fifty yards down the runway, with agents giving chase.

Then Jackson ordered First Officer Johnson to his feet, thinking the copilot had somehow approved the attack during his conversations on the radio. "We're gonna shoot you," Jackson screamed. "Stand up on the seat: I'm gonna kill you!" The shot from Jackson's revolver caught Johnson in the arm as terrified passengers looked on. Cale interceded and insisted they get moving. The hijackers, panicked and confused, moved the now injured copilot back toward the cockpit. "Get your ass back in the cockpit or I will kill you," Cale barked. The order was given to take off.

The revving engines sent the FBI team underneath rolling head over heels. The hot exhaust burned two agents and shredded their suits as it pushed them some seventy-five yards back down the runway. One agent's clothes were mostly ripped off. Flight 49 began to scrape along the runway, picking up speed. The agents had disabled only two

---

*The report later from the assaulting agents explained, "Due to the fact that all Agents in a fire team were not equally fleet, we arrived under the plan somewhat scattered and not according to the original organizational plan. The roar of the jets was deafening and it was impossible to communicate with one another.... Those Agents in a position to do so and each acting on his own opened fire with the weapon he was carrying."

of the eight tires. In the darkness, sparks and debris from the damaged plane trailed the DC-9 as it prepared to take off. A flash lit the night as a piece of rubber cast off by the landing gear was sucked into the left engine. After initially giving chase on foot, the FBI teams now stood helpless on the runway, watching the hijacked craft gather speed. There would be no following it. By using the emergency exits, they'd rendered their own chase aircraft inoperable.*

Miraculously, at the very last possible moment, an air pocket underneath the plane gave a tiny bit of lift, raising the intact tires and wounded landing gear just enough off the ground. A second later and the plane would have crashed through the airport's boundary fence with catastrophic results.

The plane gained altitude, and Jackson ordered it south to Cuba again. Haas, though, couldn't fly above 11,000 feet, since the damaged plane's systems couldn't pressurize the cabin.† More than twenty-four hours after it was first hijacked, after thousands of miles and nearly a dozen stops in three countries, Flight 49 was on its last legs. Two million dollars in ransom cluttered the aisles, garbage overflowed, and the injured copilot tried to perform his flight duties with his one good arm. The hostages, exhausted and low on blood sugar and adrenaline after the long ordeal, dozed fitfully, stared out the windows, or watched the hijackers talk among themselves at the front of the cabin. With the engines running constantly since the hijacking had begun, there was at best another couple of hours of flight time before the engines ran out of oil and began to seize up. Their only hope was to land quickly, yet with their landing gear shot up and damaged, that itself wouldn't prove easy. Knowing the situation aboard Flight 49, all the would-be rescuers could do was mobilize the Coast Guard for a possible recovery operation. One passenger, engineer Alex Halberstadt, later related, "Before we landed at Orlando, we were just on a hijacked aircraft. After the FBI acted, we were on a crippled hijacked

---

*The second chase aircraft—the navy C-118 with another team of agents on board—landed during the shoot-out, but after the assault on the ground, Bureau officials decided not to give any further pursuit.
†A later examination of Flight 49 found that no bullets had penetrated the plane's exterior. The systems damage came from the ill-advised takeoff.

aircraft with three gunmen going mad." Halberstadt added, "They turned a bad trip into an immediate emergency."

As Flight 49 headed south, Castro returned to the Havana airport. He put out a call to gather all available emergency vehicles; ambulances and fire engines from around Havana raced toward the airport, sirens screaming. Normal protocol would call for the runway to be covered in fire retardant foam, but there wasn't enough foam in all of Cuba to do that. Planning for the worst, doctors and crews gathered at the closest Havana hospital to treat crash victims.

Meanwhile, the flight attendants did their best to clear the aisles of ransom money and garbage, review safety procedures with the passengers, and demonstrate crash positions. The hijackers, suddenly docile in the face of the gravity of the situation, took seats next to the window emergency exits with bags of ransom money gathered at their feet and in their laps. Worried about what would happen to the hijackers' weapons in a hard landing, the flight attendants stepped up and demanded that the hijackers surrender them. With barely a word, Jackson, Moore, and Cale handed over grenades, guns, and ammunition. "There'll be no more shooting," Jackson said, exhaustion evident in his voice.

Five miles out from the runway, as the plane rapidly closed the distance to the airport and the Cuban countryside passed by just hundreds of feet away, the crew opened the emergency exits, sending a roaring gust of wind through the cabin. Garbage flew around the interior like debris ahead of a thunderstorm.

With a lurch and a horrific screech, the plane hit the runway hard. Sparks and smoke poured from the damaged landing gear as it disintegrated at speeds over a hundred miles per hour. Captain Haas slammed on the brakes and reversed the engines to slow the plane. After the plane slid to a halt, the flight attendants began evacuating passengers from the smoky cabin. Within minutes, everyone stood on the tarmac, miraculously alive and safe. The hijackers ran for the nearby high grass but didn't make it far. Cuban soldiers were waiting, and the last the passengers saw of the trio of hijackers, they were being marched into the terminal. Castro later told Haas, "They'll be kept in boxes four by four by four."

The press conference the next morning at FBI Headquarters in Washington wasn't pretty. Questions about the shooting and accusations of recklessness kept FBI spokesperson Thomas Bishop on the defensive. The Bureau declined to comment on almost any aspect of the decision-making process that led to their attempt to storm the aircraft. The fact that Southern Airways Flight 49's passengers had escaped unharmed and that only one person—First Officer Johnson—had been wounded during the ordeal was more luck (and a testament to Captain Haas's skill and patience under duress) than anything else. But, comment or not, it was clear that multiple times through the incident, the entire airliner had almost been lost. There had been no team specially trained to deal with hostage situations. Hostage negotiation training barely existed. As in Munich, the FBI's sharpshooters considered their skill more a hobby than a professional requirement. Communications equipment had made coordination and planning difficult. The weaponry available was a joke. This idea of "terrorism," inflicting terror for political means, was something new to U.S. shores and to the U.S. government.

Up until then, no one had ever died in a U.S. hijacking, and the government's impractical idea to make every passenger walk through a metal detector had seemed an inconvenience that the traveling public would never tolerate. "It's an impossible problem short of searching every passenger," an FAA spokesman had been quoted saying in the years prior to Flight 49.

That all changed after 11/11. Within two months, the FAA initiated the first-ever mandatory screening for all aviation passengers. The results proved the program's worth: During the first year alone, some 1,600 guns, 1,200 explosive devices, and 15,000 knives were confiscated by the new security screeners. More important, not a single U.S. commercial airliner was hijacked in 1973 after the new measures were implemented. There was also talk of armoring and locking cockpit doors, giving pilots the opportunity to carry weapons, and centralizing airport security nationwide under a single agency. It would take another three decades for those measures to be implemented.

The FBI, meanwhile, realized that the events surrounding Flight 49 wouldn't fade into the past.* There were pluses—the American

---

* The Bureau made a multitude of changes to its own policies in the wake of Flight 49, perhaps most significant being that in a November 23 memo, Mark Felt allowed

public for the first time began to take the question of terrorism seriously and began to accept trade-offs of civil liberties in exchange for greater security. Yet there were also major minuses—the image of the seemingly invincible G-man was beginning to take a beating. Richard Marquise, then a special agent in Detroit who would go on to head the investigation of the Pan Am 103 bombing, remembers boarding a Southern Airways flight a few months after the hostage incident. Upon hearing that an armed FBI agent was on board, the pilot came back to talk to Marquise and demanded that the young agent hand over his weapon.

"I'm sorry, sir, I can't do that," Marquise replied sheepishly, knowing the full level of distrust pilots now had for the FBI.

"What about your bullets, can you take out your bullets and give them to me?"

"No. Sorry, sir."

"Well, don't shoot anyone on my plane unless I give you permission," the pilot said warily.

The encounter was unnerving for the young agent, whose father had spent his career in Hoover's FBI and knew the high regard with which the Bureau had been held by the American people. Now, for the first time, there were fundamental questions as to whether the FBI could do its job.

It took just six months after Munich for the Black September terror campaign to arrive in the United States. In March 1973, just a week after Black September assassinated the U.S. ambassador in Sudan, the FBI in New York—after being tipped off by a National Security Agency intercept of a communiqué by the Iraqi Mission at the United Nations—began a frantic search for three car bombs placed around the city by Black September leader Khalid Al-Jawary. Of the three explosive devices, two were parked on Fifth Avenue and the third was

---

agents who were responsible for responding to hijacking to take Bureau vehicles home with them on nights and weekends in case they were needed while off duty. Its own reports were scathing: "Radio communications are inadequate.... Shoulder weapons normally assigned to such agencies are inadequate...." and so on.

supposed to target El Al's cargo terminal at Kennedy Airport. Amazingly, the two cars containing the Fifth Avenue bombs had been illegally parked and thus towed by the city to an impound lot before anyone discovered their deadly contents.

As the FBI investigation unfolded, agents discovered that the devices had been set to go off during a Big Apple visit by Israel's Golda Meir on March 4—two days *before* the NSA intercept led officials even to begin the search. All three powerful bombs, which would have killed anyone within a hundred yards of the explosion, had, fortunately, been improperly wired and thus failed to explode. Once again, the nation and the FBI had gotten lucky.

CHAPTER 2
COINTELPRO

> Great peace have they which love thy law.
> — *Psalm 119, read by President Nixon*
> *at J. Edgar Hoover's funeral*

The decade from 1973 to 1983 was perhaps the most tumultuous in the history of the FBI—and repeatedly raised questions about whether the organization could or should continue to exist.

Much as the country passed the Twenty-second Amendment, limiting a president to two terms, in the wake of FDR's unprecedented four terms, Congress quickly decided that in a democracy no one should be able to amass the power that Hoover had: It decreed that future FBI directors would serve ten-year terms—long enough to outlast whatever president appointed them and thus provide some political cover, yet not long enough to establish a separate power base.

The first acting director, L. Patrick Gray, began the process of modernizing Hoover's Bureau. Against the wishes of the rest of the FBI executive conference, he lifted the prohibition on hiring female agents almost immediately—although he tried briefly to keep the same height requirements for both males and females, thus ensuring that any female agents would be of Amazonian proportions. Gray relaxed the severe weight restrictions Hoover had set on agents and allowed agents for the first time to take their Bureau-issued cars home after work, rather than dropping them every night at a central garage.

Originally, Nixon had said that Gray was just a temporary place-holder until after the election, and he kept everyone (including Gray) guessing about who would be nominated to serve as the permanent director. Meanwhile, Gray dutifully plugged away, not just by day but by night: He always went home with two full briefcases of reading about the Bureau and its various components. The learning curve was steep. "I didn't know how to ask the right questions," Gray later said. It was a refrain that future directors would repeat in private moments during their first years in the job.

Despite his good intentions, Gray's year as acting director was marked by constant infighting and controversy. It quickly proved impossible to muffle the ambitions of a generation of budding leaders who had hoped to lead the FBI after Hoover, and decades of repressed office politics held in check as long as Hoover lived burst out into the open.

The tensions were aggravated by Gray's constant travel schedule, which kept him out of many decisions and led to the moniker "Three-Day Gray" in reference to how much time he spent at headquarters each week. Afraid of being captured during one of the era's regular hijackings, Gray traveled on military aircraft whenever possible. The $200,000 in charges he racked up during a year of constant visits to FBI field offices—he made it to all fifty-six except Honolulu during his short tenure—overwhelmed the positive intent and dogged him inside and outside the Bureau.

The crop of agents that existed in the beginning of the 1970s was heavily Catholic, primarily of Irish or Italian descent, almost exclusively white, and entirely male. Many hailed from the Northeast—Boston, Queens, New Jersey. At the time, out of some 8,600 agents, only 120 were black or Hispanic. Gray immediately set out to boost the number of black and Spanish-speaking agents.

As director, Gray began refocusing the policies guiding the "brick agents" in the field, chief among them deemphasizing statistics for statistics' sake. Unfortunately for an agency that ostensibly prides itself on its independence and nonpartisanship, Gray found himself drawn into the defining political battle of the age: the Watergate break-in, which occurred just a month after Hoover's death and a week into

Gray's tenure, and which came to consume much of the FBI's time and resources. By the end, every field office in the country would be actively engaged in the investigation, chasing leads and sending reports to Washington. Although Gray was involved in the investigation early on, he turned over control to his deputy, Mark Felt, when the focus narrowed to White House misdeeds.

Gray clashed repeatedly, sometimes publicly, with Felt, who the White House believed (correctly, as it turned out) was leaking information about the investigation to Bob Woodward and Carl Bernstein of the *Washington Post*. Felt, who had aspirations of being named director both before and after Gray, remarked later, "The record amply demonstrates that President Nixon made Pat Gray the Acting Director of the FBI because he wanted a politician in J. Edgar Hoover's position who would convert the Bureau into an adjunct of the White House machine." Nixon's White House capitalized on the disorder in the post-Hoover FBI to politicize the Bureau in ways that Hoover never would have allowed. The longtime FBI leader had resisted Nixon's political agenda (one of the reasons the infamous "Plumbers" unit was created at the White House was to tackle political-intelligence tasks that Hoover would refuse), yet after his death and Gray's arrival, many of these walls fell down.

Felt had joined the FBI during World War II, as the Bureau underwent a tremendous expansion from 600 agents at the time of the attack on Pearl Harbor to 4,000 by the time the first atomic bomb was dropped on Hiroshima. The war transformed the Bureau at home and overseas, pushing it beyond U.S. shores in a major way for the first time. The Bureau's "Special Intelligence Service" had overseen U.S. intelligence operations in South America through the war; 360 agents, working undercover in the neutral countries of the Western Hemisphere, had been responsible for uncovering scores of Axis spy networks and propaganda agents. At home, the FBI investigated German saboteurs (and notably excused itself from any part in the Japanese American relocation operations). As the war ended and Nazi spies and provocateurs were no longer a threat, the FBI shifted and expanded its domestic security investigations to focus on possible Communist influence in the United States. Over time, this anti-Communist effort would become a driving focus of Hoover's life, and thus the Bureau's.

Tall, athletic, and square-jawed, Felt was a recruiting-poster example of a Hoover-era G-man—perhaps not an insignificant career booster in a Bureau where appearances mattered to the extent that Hoover personally approved the actor who would star in ABC's TV series *The F.B.I.* After a career that spanned chasing Nazis during World War II, battling organized crime in Kansas City and later the New Left radicals in the 1960s, as well as a lengthy period working in the FBI's inspection division—its internal watchdog group—Felt had risen to become Hoover's day-to-day right hand. He was a by-the-book agent who, like his boss, had little tolerance for those in the Bureau who stepped outside of the narrow boundaries prescribed for them. When one top agent in Oklahoma City went too far in his womanizing, Felt transferred or disciplined forty-three out of the office's fifty agents.

"It's impossible to exaggerate how high the stakes were in Watergate," recalled Felt, who, of course, as Deep Throat was far from a disinterested observer of the power struggle between the FBI and the White House. "We faced no simple burglary, but an assault on government institutions, an attack on the FBI's integrity, and unrelenting pressure to unravel one of the greatest political scandals in our nation's history."

In the first three months of a multi-year investigation, the FBI interviewed some 1,500 people and tracked 1,900 leads. CIA and FBI tension ran high, as leads from Watergate—money trails, employment records, covert programs, and so on—kept dead-ending at the CIA. Distrust between the White House and the FBI was even more intense, with both doubting Gray's loyalty.

After the 1972 election, Gray was finally nominated for the permanent director position—yet his nomination was quickly derailed as Nixon's popularity plummeted with evidence of further administration misdeeds coming to light. Under intense congressional questioning during his confirmation hearing, Gray admitted that he'd provided documents to the White House and that White House officials had "probably" lied to Congress in discussing the incident. When it became clear that Gray wasn't going to get confirmed, he asked that his nomination be withdrawn—then bitterly confessed to Senator Lowell Weicker that he had been given documents by White House aide E. Howard Hunt during a meeting in June 1972 and told to make them disappear. Gray said he burned them in his home fireplace without reading them.

The idea that the head of the FBI had been involved in obstruction of justice was more than the capital could bear. Within days, Gray was gone from the FBI.

By May 2, 1973, just a year after Hoover's death, another acting FBI director was occupying Hoover's suite. William Ruckelshaus had been appointed specifically as a caretaker. In response, the FBI's entire senior leadership sent an unprecedented telegram to the White House asking for an insider to be named as the permanent director. The Bureau, it seemed, was disintegrating.

During Gray's brief tenure, terrorism had figured high on the FBI's agenda. He had struggled to reassure the government that the United States would handle a Munich situation better than the Germans, and he had struggled to answer for the botched hijacking intervention on Southern Airways Flight 49. Set against a backdrop of social unrest and still deeply influenced by Hoover's sense of patriotism and moral code, the FBI was emphatic that it would do whatever was necessary to prevent further disasters.

Felt believed he had the go-ahead to continue the Bureau's long-standing tradition of "extralegal" methods when it came to preserving domestic security. In one "black bag job," an extralegal break-in, agents covertly entered the offices of a Palestinian organization suspected of terrorist ties. Agents gathered scads of material, including the names of many of the group's sympathizers in the United States. Across the country, other agents quickly set out to interview and fingerprint those potential suspects—thus putting them on notice that the FBI knew who they were and would be watching them. The break-in seemed to have worked: Even as it aggressively attacked around the world, Palestinian terror in the United States was the dog that didn't bark. "Convinced that the FBI was all-knowing and ever-present, terrorists refused to accept assignments in the United States," Felt explained later.

While the Palestinians seemed the biggest international threat in 1972, back home Felt and FBI executives were clear that their target was the Weather Underground. The Weathermen—named for the line in Bob Dylan's "Subterranean Homesick Blues": "You don't need a weatherman to know which way the wind blows"—were markedly more violent and radical than many other of the New Left groups of the late 1960s, targeting police, defense installations, and other symbols of the government. They recruited heavily, established international ties to countries such as the Soviet Union, Cuba, North Vietnam, Algeria, and Lebanon, and trained extensively. In a two-year period from 1970 to 1972, there were sixty-three bomb attacks on federal buildings in the United States, most likely the responsibility of the Weathermen.

President Nixon had told the FBI he wanted "aggressive action" against the extremists, and the FBI, carefully tracking the Weathermen's meetings with foreign governments and agents, believed it could (and should) pursue them with every tool at its disposal. One note to Felt from Gray on July 18, 1972, carried the notation, "Hunt to ground. No holds barred." Numerous Bureau black bag jobs targeted the group. As Felt recalled, "These terrorists openly bragged of their Communist beliefs, their ties to unfriendly foreign countries, and of their intentions to bring down our government by force and violence."

Then COINTELPRO broke.

In 1973, after the FBI had been under the interim management of Acting Director William Ruckelshaus for ten weeks, the White House made Kansas City police chief Clarence Kelley, a retired former FBI special agent, the first permanent director since Hoover's death the year before.★ Initially, things looked promising. Kelley knew law enforcement, both inside and outside the FBI. For the agents who had lived through the Funeral, Kelley's era was something of a renaissance. Perhaps the biggest breath of fresh air was that for the first time in

---

★Deep in the midst of Watergate, President Nixon wanted the swearing-in of a new FBI director to garner some good headlines—so, since Kelley's wife was ill, he proposed holding it at the police chief's house in Kansas City. "You mean the president would come here? To my house?" Kelley asked the White House advance team. In the end, the Kansas City chief's house was too small, so when *Air Force One* touched down in Missouri, the president and Kelley conducted the swearing-in on the grounds of the Federal Building.

nearly twenty years, senior agents could sit down with the director and discuss problems openly. Admitting failure or a stumbling block didn't automatically lead to banishment, as it often had under Hoover.

During Kelley's tenure, he worked hard to modernize the Bureau and establish basic business practices that had been lacking under Hoover. "Hoover undoubtedly stayed in office too long. He personally suffered for it, as did the FBI," Kelley concluded. No change was more critical than shifting the Bureau's official priorities. Under Hoover, the FBI had tracked its success through five measures: stolen property recovered, money saved, fines levied, fugitives located, and convictions obtained. While Hoover loved to trumpet the annual growth in the statistics—and, of course, argue that the only way to increase them would be to get a bigger budget—the system over time corrupted the FBI's priorities. In Hoover's annual reporting, a single major case, such as the investigation of Martin Luther King's assassination, would be considered equal in the Bureau's accounting to the arrest of a bank robber or the recovery of a stolen automobile. This provided a huge disincentive for agents to embark on complicated investigations, such as political corruption or white-collar crime, that might lead to only a handful of arrests. Special Agent Oliver "Buck" Revell, who would rise to be one of the FBI's top executives in the 1980s, recalled, "The Bureau's statistical measurement of success was as fallacious as the military's use of the body count method in Vietnam."

Kelley's new "quality over quantity" efforts made a tremendous difference in the Bureau's focus and casework. In a single year, the number of cases investigated by the FBI fell by almost half, with the Bureau shedding more than 135,000 unimportant cases. Yet in the reform efforts that followed President Nixon's August 1974 resignation, revelations of the FBI's "dirty laundry" brought a quick end to the seeming Kelley renaissance.

The controversy that would later explode during Kelley's tenure actually began with a burglary in March 1971 at the FBI's tiny resident agency in sleepy Media, Pennsylvania. The leftist activist group Citizens Committee to Investigate the Federal Bureau of Investigation stole more than a thousand poorly secured documents, many of which dealt with a little-known FBI initiative known as COINTELPRO (short for "counterintelligence program"). Started in the 1950s and focused on the Communist Party USA, COINTELPRO gradually expanded to encompass just about every activist group whose agenda or motivations were suspect in Hoover's increasingly paranoid view of the world. FBI agents used disinformation, inappropriate and sometimes illegal surveillance, and other shadowy tactics to target and harass those Hoover deemed a threat to "order." Specific programs focused on the Ku Klux Klan, the Black Panthers, and the Socialist Workers Party, as well as numerous groups on what the FBI called the New Left—the anti-war, free-love student movements that sprang up in the shadow of Vietnam. In total, seven different COINTELPRO programs operated at various points, five domestically focused, two tracking foreign groups. All told, the FBI had proposed 3,247 counterintelligence actions and implemented 2,370; 1 percent, investigators later concluded, were judged to be methodologically illegal or improper. There was intense debate about whether the Bureau's vigorous efforts to spy on so many groups and individuals—from top civil rights leaders to low-level anti-war protesters—was chilling even if done with legal methods. Much of the work was sanctioned at some level, albeit often ambiguously, by the upper circles of government, up to and including presidential sanction and backing, but in the end it was the FBI that had carried the bag.

By and large, the COINTELPRO programs were shut down in the early 1970s as agents started to fear public exposure. When Kelley began dealing with the controversy, most programs had been closed for years. Even Hoover, whose efforts in the waning years of his life departed more and more from mainstream American values, had realized that COINTELPRO was a bridge too far and begun to wind its programs down.* As his biographer Richard Gid Powers explains, "Hoover's political sense told him the Bureau was going to have to

---

* In addition to winding down the COINTELPRO programs, Hoover had coincidentally been in the middle of upgrading office security at the small resident agencies in 1971, fearful of just the type of break-in that occurred in Media. That particular RA, though, had not yet received the new tamper-proof office safes that Hoover was having installed before its burglary. In the wake of the Media theft, he closed one hundred of the smallest and most insecure Bureau RAs. Most were never reopened.

operate far more openly than ever in the past. Like it or not, the public and the Congress were going to be looking over the FBI's shoulder from now on."

Kelley argued that the efforts had been launched with the best of intentions during times of unrest and worry. "FBI employees in these programs had acted in good faith and within the bounds of what was expected of them by the president, the attorney general, Congress, and, I believe, a majority of the American people," he told a press conference. Riots had been tearing apart U.S. cities; Puerto Rican nationalists had opened fire on the U.S. House, and the Weather Underground had exploded a bomb at the U.S. Capitol; assassinations had targeted the president, presidential candidates, and civil rights leaders. To second-guess the decisions made in the heat of those moments in the relative calm of the 1970s was unfair, he argued.

COINTELPRO's exposure, following on the heels of the Gray scandal, helped usher in a new era of congressional oversight of the FBI. Apart from his highly choreographed annual appearance in front of the appropriations committees to discuss the FBI's budget, Hoover hadn't faced much grilling on the Hill—his power, after all, greatly exceeded that of most members of Congress. Kelley didn't have that luxury: In his fifty-five months as director, he spent more time testifying in front of Congress than Hoover had in his entire forty-eight years as director. In 1975, to ensure that the Bureau was prepared for greater scrutiny, he established the FBI's first congressional affairs office.

Domestic security efforts came to a stop as agents realized that the wrong investigation could quickly end their careers—and possibly send them to jail. "The counterterrorism program ground to a halt," Revell recalls. "People in the Bureau didn't want to work that stuff."

Despite the wake-up call Munich and Southern Airways had provided, the Bureau calculatedly returned to a dormant state. Terrorism became a vacated backwater. Darkly, agents circulated a joke that would be familiar for decades to come: "Big cases, big problems; small cases, small problems; no cases, no problems." For the few agents who cared about terrorism, a lack of resources made their efforts nearly futile. In Detroit, where Richard Marquise was stationed through most of the 1970s, none of the five domestic security squads specifically focused on terrorism—this despite the fact that in the wake of the Munich attack, the CIA had passed along some intelligence to Marquise's squad in the Motor City that a local terrorist cell was planning a similar hostage-taking event in Michigan. For days, members of Marquise's squad sat outside a convenience store where the group was thought to congregate, watching a crowd of Middle Eastern men come and go. "We didn't know anything about them. We didn't know anything about Shiites or Sunnis, their habits, their religion, or anything," Marquise recalls. Nor, for that matter, did almost anyone in the FBI. Over time, Marquise's team determined that nothing was amiss. Yet it was doubtful that if something nefarious had been going on, those young agents would have had adequate support to stop it.

Two years later, Marquise ended up interviewing an actual terrorist, a lapsed member of the Black September movement. The suspect's brother had turned him in, calling the FBI to report that his sibling had extremist views and had recently arrived in Michigan. Marquise and his partner interviewed the brother at length, though they had little else to go on and no resources overseas on which to draw for more information. The informant had provided a copy of the suspect's overseas college transcript, and using it, Marquise decided his best bet was to bluff.

Under questioning, the suspect initially denied everything. Then Marquise dropped in front of him a huge pile of paper topped by the college transcript. The agent had typed his own name across the top of the document, as if the school had sent it directly to the FBI. "Look at this. We've conducted a worldwide investigation. We know everything about you," Marquise bluffed. The suspect immediately cracked, admitting that he'd attended Black September training camps and pleading that he'd left that life behind to come live peacefully in America and raise a family. Information gushed forth about Black September's recruiting, training, and techniques. By the end of the lengthy interview, Marquise and his partner were convinced that the man, like the earlier convenience store group, meant no harm.

Following protocol, Marquise wrote up the interview and the voluminous information that he'd gathered about Black September and gave the report to his supervisor, who sent it on to Washington. Recalls Marquise, "Nothing came of it as far as I knew."

Despite such official indifference, a small group of agents across the FBI was forging ahead—learning about the growth of international terrorism and how the Bureau should respond even as the political environment became more untenable every passing month. Buck Revell, like many of the loyal and patriotic company men who dot the upper reaches of the FBI, comes from a family that served: His grandfather, an army cavalryman, chased Pancho Villa through Mexico; his father and uncles served in World War II; he promptly joined the Marines after college. He flew helicopters, and in the midst of the terrifying days of the Cuban Missile Crisis served as part of the flotilla that sought to blockade Cuba. After the assassination of John F. Kennedy in 1963, Revell left the corps and joined Hoover's Bureau; he spent time in Kansas City and Philadelphia, chasing criminals by day and pursuing a graduate degree at Temple University on the GI Bill by night. The FBI had fascinated the gregarious Oklahoma native since the Boy Scouts, when he'd done a fingerprint merit badge as one rung on the ladder toward achieving his Eagle Scout rank. After a stint in Philadelphia too short for his taste, Revell was informed, in the stilted language of Hoover, that he was being transferred to "the seat of government."

"Headquarters was a very different place from where I had come," he recalls. "It thrived on office politics and bristled with rumor." The fastidiousness of that culture stifled Revell—known to everyone but his family as Buck, from an old football nickname. Hoover denied him an early pay raise and issued a formal letter of censure for misspelling *apprise* in a memo to a Justice Department office. In his own way, under the oppressive structure of headquarters, Revell quickly came to be an understated rebel—he brought his coffee back to his desk and wore colored shirts.

In the fall of 1973, during a turn on the Bureau's inspection division, Revell got his first overseas assignment: a lengthy tour of the FBI's Asian operations in Tokyo, Hong Kong, Manila, and Singapore. For a rising agent, the tour of the overseas Legal Attachés—"legats" in Bureau-speak—proved an eye-opening experience: Intrigue unimaginable to a street agent in Kansas City seemed to be a natural part of life overseas. In Toyko, Bill Childs, a legendary agent who had spent twenty years liaising with the Japanese National Police Agency, described the rise of the Yakuza organized crime group. In Hong Kong, Revell learned that the previous legat agent had been transferred out of Asia after rumors that he'd uncovered embarrassing information about Nixon's trip to China. In Manila, the legat informed the inspectors that as corrupt as the regime of Ferdinand Marcos was, the U.S. government had no choice but to engage with him because the dictator had total control of the country.

At the time, legat positions were staffed exclusively by agents who spent most of their time focused on foreign counterintelligence, with little background in criminal matters. There was hardly any notion that the overseas offices could be used to further criminal investigations back home or that foreign police agencies had much to teach the U.S. law enforcement community. The legats were intelligence assets only. These geopolitics were a revelation to Revell.

Beyond opening his eyes to an increasingly vital part of the Bureau, the legat trip overseas had an added advantage for Revell: He and his wife, Sharon, had been hoping to adopt a child from Korea, and the process had become bogged down in red tape. With the help of embassy officials in Seoul, Revell stopped in Korea on his way home and arrived back at Washington's Dulles Airport after a nineteen-hour trip carrying a little bundle wrapped in an orange blanket.

As the 1970s wore on, Kelley had to rebuild a domestic security initiative almost from scratch, imbuing it with new authority and legitimacy. As part of the program, Kelley moved domestic security investigations from the foreign counterintelligence division to the criminal division. Working with Attorney General Edward Levi, the FBI established new guidelines for future investigations. A classified version of the guidelines governed the criteria under which foreign groups could be investigated; an unclassified version focused on investigative guidelines pertaining to domestic groups. The reforms limited the FBI to investigating crimes; political motives were now irrelevant. "It had to be a program that the American people saw as legitimate," says Revell, who at the time was serving as the director's chief inspector, his lead internal watchdog. The reactive stance outlined by the Levi guidelines would have profound implications in the years before 9/11. At the time, though, it allowed the FBI a middle ground that prevented further erosion of the Bureau's authority.

Previously, FBI agents had drawn little distinction between domestic terrorist groups like the Weather Underground and foreign groups like Black September. The Justice Department, however, had seen things differently: The Weather Underground, as a domestic group, was given First and Fourth Amendment protections that allowed free speech and prohibited unreasonable search and seizure. The Justice Department's unrelenting post-Watergate gaze fell on more than 125 current and former FBI agents.

Caught in that glare, Felt, Gray, and FBI deputy director Edward Miller were all indicted for their roles in the anti–Weather Underground operations. Some 1,200 current and former agents packed the plaza outside the D.C. courtroom for the arraignment on April 20, 1978. Inside, while they were being fingerprinted after pleading not guilty, Felt, who had little love for Gray, said to the former acting director, "Pat, how many years of service have you given your country?"

"Twenty-six years. Twenty years in the navy and six years with the government," replied Gray, his fingers still stained with black ink.

"This is the reward which your country has for you," Felt replied, stepping forward for his own turn at the fingerprint stand.

"To not take action against these people and know of a bombing in advance would simply be to stick your fingers in your ears and protect your eardrums when the explosion went off and then start the investigation," Felt said later. In his mind, and that of many agents during that era, they had been protecting the country by targeting terroristic elements that threatened American democracy. Yes, the break-ins were "extralegal," but they were necessary for the country's "greater good," Felt argued. But, said Felt, "All this was brushed aside by Attorney General Bell in his need to play up to the national media which were howling for FBI blood."

Felt (who alone ran up some $600,000 in legal defense bills) and Miller were convicted during a trial in 1980 in which President Nixon and numerous former attorneys general appeared as defense witnesses. Though not sentenced to jail, both men faced fines of several thousand dollars. President Reagan pardoned them both the following year. "Their convictions...grew out of their good-faith belief that their actions were necessary to preserve the security interests of our country," Reagan said. He continued, "America was at war in 1972...[and]

four years ago, thousands of draft evaders and others who violated the Selective Service laws were unconditionally pardoned by my predecessor. America was generous to those who refused to serve their country in the Vietnam War. We can be no less generous to two men who acted on high principle to bring an end to the terrorism that was threatening our nation."

Felt was unapologetic: "You're either going to have an FBI that tries to stop violence before it happens or you are not," he said. "Personally, I think this is justified, and I'd do it again tomorrow."

As Felt had lamentably predicted, under the new rules the FBI would only launch an investigation once "the dust had cleared" from a bombing. Bitterness ran through the ranks. Agents mocked Kelley's passive caretaker approach to being director, joking, "The FBI wouldn't be in this predicament if Clarence Kelley were alive." For the first time in its history, the FBI saw its budget reduced—nearly a thousand agents fell off the rolls between 1973 and 1978. The next year Felt warned, "Because terrorism in the United States was largely contained and we have been relatively free from it for several years, complacency has developed." That complacency was rooted in an inability to detect and investigate, a weakness that, when combined with the failures of the CIA and other American intelligence agencies, would lead to disaster. This was not a case of the FBI missing the forest for the trees—it was a case of the Bureau having nobody looking at the roots. The path to 9/11 begins here in the rubble of COINTELPRO.

After the high-profile scandals and abuses came to light, as allegations and indictments swirled around the upper levels of the FBI, the government set about creating a new system to govern how its lead domestic investigative agency handled national security cases.

The man who, more than anyone, developed those guidelines was an authoritarian former FBI agent named Allan Kornblum. Kornblum had worked a series of civil rights cases in Mississippi during the end of the 1960s, including the murder of Ben Chester White, a black sharecropper, by a Klansman, Ernest Avants—one of the many civil rights cases that languished for decades before Avants was finally convicted in a federal trial in 2003. Ethics had always been a central facet of Kornblum's life; he wrote his PhD dissertation at Princeton in the 1970s on corruption and ethics in the New York City Police Department, where he had worked as a patrolman for a few years before joining the FBI. In 1975, he was chosen by the Justice Department to investigate the appropriate response to the still-unfolding fallout of J. Edgar Hoover's illegal activities. Kornblum worked diligently for years, piecing together new rules for domestic intelligence investigations. Eventually, under Presidents Ford and Carter, Kornblum was tasked with implementing the guidelines he'd helped create at the Justice Department. For the next twenty years, Kornblum would become the government's own domestic surveillance watchdog.

One of the reforms enacted in COINTELPRO's wake was the 1978 Foreign Intelligence Surveillance Act (FISA). The FISA statute, in Congress's explicit terms, was the "exclusive means" by which the federal government could gather intelligence domestically. It allowed the FBI—and the FBI alone, not the CIA or any other agency—to gain special warrants through a new, specialized body, the U.S. Foreign Intelligence Surveillance Court. The FISA warrants had a lower burden of proof than typical criminal wiretap requests (so-called Title III wiretaps), but they required a higher level of approval: Usually the attorney general himself (or later, herself) had to approve a FISA request before it could be submitted to the court. This meant prosecutors had to be very careful not to poison their own cases by mixing information gleaned from one type of wiretap with that from another.

Some on the inside worried that the new post-Hoover and post-Nixon guidelines on national security investigations seemed to handicap the investigative efforts of the FBI. A young Justice official, Rudolph W. Giuliani, became a key player on the Working Group/Cabinet Committee to Combat Terrorism. The Justice Department, he said at one meeting in May 1976, "must take a more active position in combating terrorism." "Under the new guidelines, there's difficulty in collecting domestic intelligence unless there's some indication that there had been a violation of law," he worried. Although Giuliani noted in the meeting that the guidelines could be amended, if needed, the FBI didn't feel it was in a position to ask for more power. "The FBI was too cowed by its recent public thrashing," historian Timothy Naftali recounts.

Over the coming decades, those guidelines would eventually con-
strict investigations in precisely the way Giuliani feared. Twenty-three
years later, the threads of the reaction to the FBI's illegal investigations, Kornblum's surveillance restrictions, and Giuliani's fears would
all come together in the single greatest U.S. intelligence failure since
Pearl Harbor. Rudy Giuliani, of course, by then would be the mayor
of the city under attack; Allan Kornblum would still be acting as the
court watchdog; and the FBI agents who had been thwarted by the
restrictions would be standing under the doomed World Trade Center.

Ronald Reagan's 1981 inaugural marked two historic firsts: It was the
first ceremony held on the West Front of the Capitol—a move made
partly to save money on construction costs and partly to allow more
spectators to stretch down the Mall to the Washington Monument. It
was also the first inaugural address to mention terrorism. "As for the
enemies of freedom, those who are potential adversaries, they will be
reminded that peace is the highest aspiration of the American people.
We will negotiate for it, sacrifice for it; we will not surrender for it—
now or ever," Reagan promised. "Above all, we must realize that no
arsenal, or no weapon in the arsenals of the world, is so formidable as
the will and moral courage of free men and women. It is a weapon our
adversaries in today's world do not have. It is a weapon that we as
Americans do have. Let that be understood by those who practice terrorism and prey upon their neighbors."

Despite that warning, the first years of the 1980s saw a rise in terrorism in the United States, from twenty-nine incidents in 1980 to
forty-two in 1981 to fifty-one in 1983, the worst year since the unrest
of Vietnam. The attacks, for the most part, were small-scale—the
fifty-one incidents in 1983 killed seven and wounded twenty-six.
Revell, though, still saw what he described as a "psychological funk"
among agents. They wanted nothing to do with terrorism.

During his tenure, Kelley had identified three national priorities
for the FBI—counterintelligence, organized crime, and white-collar
crime—and when Kelley's successor, federal judge William Webster,
took office in 1978, Revell began to push for a fourth: counterterrorism. But the high-profile prosecutions of Felt and Miller had hardly

convinced agents that counterterrorism was a successful and worthwhile career path. Webster, initially resistant, came around as the FBI began to plan for the high-profile Los Angeles Olympics of 1984. The United States could not afford a Munich.

Watching the Munich Olympics debacle unfold on a flickering television screen with his partner, Special Agent Danny O. Coulson recognized that terrorism, at one level, wasn't new—but the strain was changing. He spent his early FBI years in New York tracking the Black Liberation Army (BLA), a domestic terrorist group that had been assassinating NYPD officers. By the time they were brought to heel, the BLA was suspected in the murders of at least thirteen police officers coast to coast.

One night, knowing that the BLA had been using the 1966 film *The Battle of Algiers* for training, Coulson and his fellow investigators watched the cinematic depiction of the Algerian insurgency against the occupying French Foreign Legion and gendarmes. "You did not have to know or care about the Algerian revolution to be intoxicated by its raw energy and righteous fury at the cruelties of a callous state," Coulson recalled years later.*

As part of his work, Coulson had joined the fledgling New York FBI SWAT team, learning tactical skills in upstate New York and at the FBI Academy, yet the SWAT team knew they couldn't handle the really bad stuff. Watching the Munich situation go from bad to worse, Coulson commented to his partner, "If it were going down here, you know who'd get the ticket."

"Yep, us, and we aren't ready for it."

In 1977, the United States had its first serious domestic hostage incident since Southern Airways Flight 49, and the government real-

---

*The film was a how-to guide for insurgents and a frightening foretelling of the tactics the BLA used to ambush unsuspecting cops. Yet the defensive tactics revealed in the movie helped save Coulson's life one night on the streets of the Bronx. The movie taught the agents that pairs of French gendarmes walked thirty feet apart, ensuring that an ambush couldn't kill both officers; Coulson's team adopted the same tactic. When the FBI finally caught one of the BLA killers, he described watching Coulson and his partner investigate a suspected hideout and how the killer had decided against attacking them because they were too far apart to both be killed in the same attack. Chills went down Coulson's neck.

ized it wasn't much better prepared. Members of the Hanafi Muslim sect seized control of city hall in Washington, D.C., as part of a coordinated attack that also included the B'nai B'rith headquarters and a mosque near Embassy Row. They shot Washington's future mayor Marion Barry, killed a radio reporter, and had more than 150 hostages as police arrived on the scene. The attack paralyzed the city for thirty-eight hours—every member of Congress was offered a police guard, and British prime minister James Callaghan, arriving for a summit with Jimmy Carter, did not receive the customary nineteen-gun salute due to worries that the terrorists would misinterpret the cannon fire.

The FBI's Washington SWAT team arrived on the scene, and firearms investigators quickly began to train additional agents how to use M16 automatic rifles. (The FBI's standard weapon was still the six-shooter revolver and would remain so until nearly 1990, long after criminals had switched to automatic pistols with high-capacity magazines.) "It was the worst situation we've ever had," one FBI official told reporters at the time. Luckily for everyone involved, a group of Muslim ambassadors was able to negotiate a peaceful end to the siege. Officials watched the scene knowing that the United States had dodged its own Munich by luck, not skill. "We would have made a good stand," Coulson recalls, "but if we'd had to go in, it would have been messy." During the intensive monthslong follow-up investigation of the incident—one of the first major "domestic security investigations" since COINTELPRO broke—Bureau officials became increasingly disturbed by the sect's violent propensities. (One memo from the Washington Field Office to FBI Headquarters recommended suspending tours of the Hoover Building for security reasons.) Sensitive to the legacy of COINTELPRO, the Bureau carefully outlined the investigation's scope, with dozens of memos whipping back and forth among headquarters and the field offices to determine which suspects were eligible to be investigated.

Also in the wake of the Hanafi siege, the United States created two teams. The first was the Special Forces Operational Detachment–Delta—the ultra-secret Delta Force that would later be used in the attempted rescue of the Iranian embassy hostages. After Delta's disastrous Desert One mission, the Naval Special Warfare Development Group, more commonly known as SEAL Team Six, was launched. As the U.S. forces trained, it became apparent that these two elite units weren't right for domestic situations. Beyond the legal restrictions of the Posse Comitatus Act, which limited the ability of the military to operate within the United States, the military mind-set wasn't right for law enforcement operations. Delta and the SEALs were ultra-trained killers, not much interested in warrants or *Miranda* warnings.

As a result, the FBI's newly constituted Special Operations and Research Unit (SOARU) began to train alongside Delta and study its tactics. Delta Force soon realized, however, that it didn't want any part of the FBI's operations. The legal restraints and use-of-force investigations that inevitably were a part of law enforcement operations domestically didn't jibe with Delta's secret profile. The FBI would need to figure out how to do this stuff itself.

In response, Director William Webster and other Bureau executives toured Delta's secret training facility at Fort Bragg. Webster watched as commandos stormed a group of "terrorists" in a training exercise; later, as he walked through the Delta compound, the FBI officials pointed out all the fancy gear that FBI SWAT teams lacked: night vision equipment, maritime assault capabilities, explosive breaching materials for going through walls, secure communications.

There was one thing, though, Delta didn't have.

"I don't see any handcuffs," Webster commented to Major General Richard Scholtes, the commander of the special forces team.

"We don't have handcuffs," the general replied. "It's not my job to arrest people."

Warning bells went off in the director's head.

By the time Webster returned to the Hoover Building, the FBI had a new mission, and when Coulson heard that the FBI was starting an elite counterterrorism force, he wanted to be a part of it.

Despite his SWAT background, however, Coulson was an odd choice. He had no military training, only a law degree and his time on the streets as an agent. Since investigating the BLA assassins, Coulson had spent years working congressional affairs at FBI headquarters—answering questions about the COINTELPRO scandal and Watergate, and working with the Church and Pike Committees. Having been on the firing line during one of the Bureau's darkest hours, he understood better than just about anyone the high moral standard the country expected from the FBI. "My experience on the Hill showed me, as no abstraction could, how immensely destructive the Bureau could be when it sacrificed law to what its leaders falsely imagined to be order," he recalls. "Anybody who read the Hoover files, including me, came away with a healthy distrust of giving the FBI too much power." Over time, he says, "I became intimately familiar with nearly every stupid, mean, illegal, immoral act perpetrated by the Bureau in the name of patriotism and righteousness."

Webster and Buck Revell decided Coulson was perfect to lead the FBI's new elite counterterrorism force. As Coulson says, "They didn't see a sniper, they saw a lawyer in a three-piece suit."

The FBI's newly constituted Hostage Rescue Team (HRT) was going to have to be different from anything else in the United States. "The Delta guys didn't want to go through grand juries, get their weapons seized," Coulson recalls. "They wanted to fly their helicopters off into the sunset." So while Delta and SEAL Team Six were trained, as one operator put it, "to kill people and break things," HRT was going to have to learn how *not* to kill people. Its motto, right from the start, underscored its difference: *"Servare Vitas,"* to save lives.

Coulson arrived at the FBI Academy at Quantico as the head of a unit that didn't exist. "No budget, no bullets, no radio, no car, no building," Coulson recalls. "Our first office was a cardboard box retrieved from a dumpster."

HRT's first class of fifty "operators" was chosen with the help of SOARU trainers, psychiatrists, and Delta Force commander Charlie Beckwith. Applicants spent a week going through various mental, physical, and psychiatric tests before being offered a slot. Many didn't make it. "In a way," Coulson says with a laugh, "I'm the father of every guy who's ever joined HRT, because the guys I picked picked all the operators who followed."

Then the new team was off for months of intense training. "My plan from the start was to do anything," Coulson says. Airplane hijackings, "tubular assaults" on subways, stronghold assaults, maritime assaults, snipers, urban capabilities, rural capabilities, mountain capabilities, and desert capabilities—HRT needed to be prepared to operate anywhere and needed to go light-years beyond the traditional training of SWAT teams, which practiced slow and stealthy assaults rather than the overwhelming and violent "close-quarters battle" (CQB) tactics practiced by special forces. After training with Delta and U.S. special forces, HRT's budding operators headed overseas — training alongside the British SAS, the German GSG-9, and the French GIGN. They even conducted secret operations overseas with foreign special ops forces. "We had a lot of things going for us," Coulson said. "There are a lot of countries that would let HRT in that wouldn't let the military in because we had a law enforcement mission."

The training was not only intense but dangerous. In one live-fire demonstration, Buck Revell played a hostage and found bullets smacking into targets inches from his head. ("As I waited for them to come through the door, I hoped I hadn't ever disciplined any of these guys," Revell recalls.) The next day, another HRT operator summoned Coulson for an ominous telephone call: "Revell's on the phone." He was surprised to find Revell's wife, Sharon, on the line rather than the Bureau executive. Coulson was told in no uncertain terms that Buck was now a grandfather and was prohibited from participating in any live-fire demonstrations.

Revell was making his own waves on the counterterrorism front. As he rose through the ranks of the FBI, he kept coming back to that early swing through Asia visiting the legats, and how critical those international relationships would be as transnational crime and terrorism came to the fore. In 1938, the FBI had joined Interpol, the international coordinating police body, yet it had stayed on the sidelines until after World War II because of Nazi involvement in the organization, then later withdrew entirely in 1950, when Hoover feared a strong Communist influence. Since then, the FBI's international perspective had atrophied. By the early 1980s, the DEA and Customs had more agents overseas than the Bureau. Revell set out to change that, pushing in 1980 for the Bureau to reengage in Interpol. The FBI soon had an agent heading the international organization's new counterterrorism program. They were playing catch-up — but at least they were playing.

Then came Beirut. The U.S. embassy there had long been a target of snipers, rocket attacks, and even the occasional grenade — and would be for decades to come—but no one was prepared for its total destruction at the hands of the Iranian terrorist group Hezbollah. On April 18, 1983, a pickup loaded with a solid ton of ammonium fertilizer explosive crashed through the gate of the U.S. embassy. The explosion was so massive that the seven-story embassy was literally lifted off its foundation. The Red Cross would later use buckets to gather the human remains; more than sixty people died, including a high-ranking visiting CIA officer and the entire Beirut CIA station—the deadliest attack in the CIA's history. Six months later, at dawn on October 23, a similar attack destroyed the barracks that held the U.S. Marines contingent of the multinational force occupying the country. That bomb—the equivalent of six tons of TNT—was, according to the FBI Laboratory, the "largest conventional blast ever seen by the explosive experts community." More than 70 percent of the building's mostly sleeping occupants were killed; 220 Marines died in the service's greatest single-day loss of life since the battle of Iwo Jima. Combined with army, navy, and civilian casualties, as well as a related attack the same day on the French paratroopers' barracks nearby, Hezbollah killed more than three hundred people.

America had never seen anything like it. In the wake of the Beirut bombings, Marine Corps commandant General Paul X. Kelley called Revell, concerned about the military's ability to respond to what was in essence a large-scale crime scene: "I'm not satisfied that our team can do this."

"We don't have any jurisdiction," Revell protested.

"Bullshit. I want to know who did this," the general responded.

In the end, after an official interagency request for assistance, the FBI sent a crime scene team and investigators to Beirut to comb through the rubble. It was the first time the FBI had deployed investigators overseas for such an incident. Operating abroad put them squarely on the turf of the CIA—and that initial encounter didn't go well. Within a few days, the FBI team dispatched to Beirut returned to the United States; the CIA had blocked them. The message was clear: *Thanks, but we've got this covered.* That clash had not been restricted to terse international phone calls: The FBI's liaison to the CIA recalled physical altercations in the team's hotel rooms.

It took careful negotiations between the Hoover Building and

Langley before the FBI team was allowed to return and continue its work. Eventually the Bureau pieced together the responsibility of the Popular Front for the Liberation of Palestine, a well-known terrorist group, and linked it to an Iranian-backed terrorist named Imad Mughniyeh, who would become a ghost and a hunted man for the next two decades.

As traumatizing as the attacks on the Beirut embassy and barracks were for the United States, the government learned little from them: When, seven weeks later as part of a coordinated attack on six different targets, terrorists struck the U.S. embassy in Kuwait, it hadn't even taken the basic security step of blocking the approach to the building.

Yet the Beirut bombings and the lead-up to the 1984 Olympics marked a turning point in the FBI's history. Agents began to see counterterrorism as something other than a career backwater. This stuff was real, it was happening, and it was taking American lives.

CHAPTER 3
The Pizza Connection

The paths of glory lead but to the grave.
— *Thomas Gray, "Elegy Written
in a Country Churchyard"*

The story of the FBI's rise as an international crime-fighting organization begins, appropriately, far from the shores of the United States. In the 1970s and 1980s, the Italian mob and all its various tentacles were barely understood by investigators or the public. In fact, it was unclear whether the Mafia existed at all—many politicians, police officials, and prosecutors doubted that there was any coordination between local mobsters and racketeers. At a time when technology was scarce and even interstate cooperation among investigators rare, the idea that there was an international crime syndicate—with strict hierarchies and local, regional, and national governing bodies— was almost unfathomable.

Hoover had long maintained there was "no proof of the existence of a national syndicate or organized crime network." Two theories have risen to explain why Hoover, a keen observer of the national landscape, ignored the rise of organized crime. The first, more conspiratorial, theory holds that organized crime had something it could use to blackmail Hoover through his half-century of leadership—perhaps evidence of a less-than-moral liaison. The second theory, more likely given Hoover's personality, held that the director tacitly acknowledged the problem of organized crime but avoided confronting it because of just how difficult it would be to uproot. Throughout his career, he preferred smaller, shorter investigations with a high likelihood of success—such as car thefts—that would help bolster the statistics he reported to Congress every year.★

In typical Hoover fashion, the Bureau focused its anti–organized crime efforts on individuals. Hoover wrapped them into his "Top Hoodlum Program," the famous "Ten Most Wanted" efforts that had borne such fruit since the 1930s. However, much like the terrorist groups that would follow it in later decades, the Mafia was insidious precisely because it was larger than any single person. It could never be taken down one kingpin or one racketeer at a time.

After Hoover's death, after the Funeral, the Bureau began to reprioritize, and Director Kelley put organized crime at the top of that new list. During the 1970s, the Bureau began to dispatch surveillance squads to follow suspected Mafia members and to piece together their mysterious world—one of the first times that such squads were used outside of the counterintelligence investigations. For months at a time—and later for years—agents tracked mobsters around New York, snapped pictures, staked out apartments and social clubs, and watched from the shadows. What they found was something larger and more complex than could have been imagined. Though the FBI was often able to close small, isolated cases through the 1970s, it made little major progress against New York's so-called Five Families—the Bonnano, Gambino, Genovese, Colombo, and Lucchese organized crime organizations that ruled the city's underworld.

★ This is, coincidentally, one of the reasons for the existence of the modern-day Drug Enforcement Agency. Hoover realized that fighting drugs was a losing battle and so, even as he grasped for more authority and crimes to investigate in the late 1920s and early 1930s, he refused to involve the FBI in drug crimes—leading to the creation of the separate Federal Bureau of Narcotics in the Department of the Treasury, the forerunner of today's DEA. It wasn't until 1982 that the FBI received concurrent jurisdiction over drug-related crimes. Thus, the Pizza Connection would also prove to be one of the FBI's first major drug investigations.

★   ★   ★

The global investigation that would become known as "the Pizza Connection" grew out of two apparently unrelated murders on different continents in July 1979.

On July 12, shortly after 2:45 P.M., a blue Mercury Montego double-parked outside Joe and Mary's Italian-American Restaurant on Knickerbocker Avenue in Bushwick, Brooklyn, a once-prosperous neighborhood of Germans and Italians that had given way in recent years to a poorer class of Puerto Ricans and blacks. The riots during the New York City blackout exactly two years earlier had left chunks of the neighborhood looking, as one resident described it, like Dresden after World War II. Knickerbocker Avenue had largely survived the unrest because the shop owners there used force to defend their stores, and so a small Italian enclave still existed on the street. Three men in ski masks exited the Mercury and charged inside the restaurant, past the sign that promised "We Give Special Attention to Outgoing Orders," past the print hanging on the wall of Leonardo da Vinci's *The Last Supper,* past the restaurant counter where a Frank Sinatra album was propped up, and right into the garden out back, where Bonanno family boss Carmine Galante was dining with a friend, Leonardo Coppola, and two bodyguards. Galante, the son of a fisherman from Sicily's Castellammare del Golfo, was a vicious killer and lifelong criminal; he'd formed his first street gang at age eleven, been involved in his first shootout with police at age twenty and spent much of the next decade behind bars, and become a hit man for Vito Genovese by age thirty before joining the Bonnano family and rising to boss.

Shotgun blasts echoed through the neighborhood. When police arrived moments later, Galante and Coppola, along with the restaurant owner's son, were dead. Surprisingly, though, Galante's two bodyguards, Cesare Bonventre and Baldassare "Baldo" Amato, were nowhere to be found. Far from giving their lives for their boss, they appeared to have survived unharmed. Agents were even more puzzled when they found spent shell casings that didn't match the weapons used by the killers near where Bonventre and Amato had been standing.

More than two years would pass before the FBI's organized crime teams came to understand exactly what was at stake in the Italian restaurant's garden and how it was connected to what happened after.

Across the Atlantic, some 4,200 miles away, Palermo police captain Boris Giuliano was deep into an investigation about money laundering and the Sicilian heroin trade. The case was one of the first worked with U.S. authorities—a DEA agent had even been providing crucial help in Palermo until his bosses decided that it was too dangerous for a U.S. agent to operate in Sicily. Giuliano, the head of the Palermo police's Squadra Mobile, "Flying Squad," investigative team, didn't have the luxury of leaving his hometown.

That spring of 1979, he had had a unique opportunity to attend the FBI's National Academy, which brought handpicked international police officers to Quantico for ten weeks of intensive training. Since its founding in 1935, the National Academy had become one of the FBI's most important tools for recruiting and fostering law enforcement allies globally, an elite international brotherhood of the best law enforcement personnel. Each year about a thousand police from across the country and across the world learn procedures and investigative techniques, and get what amounts to a ten-week pep rally for policing as FBI agents reassure beleaguered law enforcement officers from foreign countries that they're not alone in their efforts.

Back home, the capture of a cash-filled suitcase at the Palermo airport launched Giuliano into the money-laundering investigation. Yet the investigation ran into a roadblock almost immediately, when the Mafia gunned down his colleague. Ten days later, Giuliano was waiting in a café for his driver when an assassin snuck up and shot him in the back. In the next day's newspaper, no article carried a byline— none of the journalists wanted the Mafia to know who had written about Giuliano's death.

As with the Galante murder in New York, it would be more than a year before the Italian police figured out the significance of what Giuliano had uncovered. Both murders, it would turn out, were part of what was becoming the Sicilian Mafia's key cash cow: a transAtlantic pipeline of literally tons of heroin from Sicily to New York. Launched in 1977, it had taken the place of the "French Connection" heroin trade of the early 1970s made famous by Gene Hackman's classic movie.

What we consider "the Mafia" is actually known to its members as "La Cosa Nostra," "this thing of ours." It is subdivided in the United States among "the Arm" in Buffalo, "the Outfit" in Chicago, and the famed "Five Families" in New York City, among others. LCN's members are almost exclusively of Italian or Sicilian descent; traditionally, each new member must be sponsored by an existing member and, after a test (which often means murder), must swear his allegiance to the family. Mafiosi abide by a strict set of rules that govern their behavior, from telling the truth to family members at all times to refraining from messing around with any members' wives or girlfriends. The only way to leave the Mafia is by dying. But none of this compares to the situation in Italy. "The extent of Mafia control of daily life in Sicily is something that people outside of Italy cannot quite fathom," writes Alexander Stille, who has reported on the issue for years. "The American Mafia is a parasitic phenomenon operating at the margins of society. In southern Italy it plays a central role in almost every phase of economic and political life." In addition to the Sicilian-based Cosa Nostra, southern Italy is also terrorized by the Camorra, based in Naples, and the 'Ndrangheta, based around Calabria. Around Apulia there's also the Sacra Corona Unita, the United Sacred Crown, which broke off from the Camorra in the 1970s. Each unit has separate families or clans—upwards of 150 in Sicily alone—separate dialects, traditions, and rackets that together have made penetrating and dismantling them a long, bloody, and exhaustive effort. What in the United States is considered a criminal enterprise is in Italy very much a terrorist organization—sowing seeds of unrest and fear and advancing a political agenda through targeted assassinations, not-so-veiled threats, and public bombings.

When Giuliano was gunned down, two men who would transform the anti-Mafia fight in Palermo were settling into their new jobs across town as magistrates, the investigative prosecutors in Italy's sometimes chaotic justice system. After growing up in middle-class Sicilian families led by domineering fathers, childhood friends Giovanni Falcone and Paolo Borsellino had decided to join the magistrature together. Although he began his career dealing with bankruptcies, Falcone was drawn into the anti-Mafia battle. In the fall of 1979, Cesare Terranova, a tough anti-Mafia investigator who hadn't even had a chance to start his new job as head of the Palermo Palace of Justice, was killed. In January 1980, the Mafia—fat from heroin profits—assassinated the president of the Sicilian region. In May 1980, three killers took out police captain Emanuele Basile, who had picked up Giuliano's drug investigation following his death. In retaliation, the Italian police arrested fifty-five Mafiosi in the days after Basile's killing, busting a major drug operation with links to the Gambino crime family in New York. That case, a mess from the start, landed on the desk of Falcone.

The Mafia grossly underestimated Falcone, especially when he immediately released eighteen out of twenty-eight accused Mafiosi. The defense lawyers wrongly saw weakness where Falcone, with a strong sense of civil liberties, diligently intended to focus his attention on those facing overwhelming evidence of their guilt. Their overconfidence eroded as he carefully began to assemble cases, uncover files and incriminating money transfers, and interview witnesses. Within weeks, Falcone was under the police protection that would follow him for twelve years. On August 6, 1980, the Mafia gunned down Gaetano Costa, the prosecutor who had signed the fifty-five arrest warrants in the wake of Basile's death. Falcone rushed to his fallen comrade.

At the scene, a colleague said to him, "Imagine—I was sure it was you."

J. Edgar Hoover didn't conduct many background investigations personally, yet for Charlie Rooney he made an exception. In the waning days of the Hoover era, the Brooklyn native had applied for a part-time position with the FBI, filling out the fifteen-page, double-sided application, including the question that asked whether the federal government employed any relatives. Rooney listed his second cousin, John, though he didn't realize the significance of his relative. "Uncle John" was the powerful Brooklyn congressman John J. Rooney, the chair of the House appropriations subcommittee that oversaw the FBI's budget. Hoover had called the congressman personally to check up on the young Rooney's credentials. Charlie soon started at the FBI as a file clerk and, after Hoover's death, became a night clerk and later a surveillance specialist before applying to be a special agent in 1976.

Rooney worked corruption cases, foreign counterintelligence, and, during one harried period in 1978, investigated the Jonestown massacre, in Georgetown, Guyana, one of the first international cases the FBI had ever worked. Rooney's squad in the New York Field Office sat next to an aggressive rising-star agent named Louis Freeh, although the two rarely exchanged much more than pleasantries—one learned quickly in the FBI never to ask a colleague what he was working on. If you needed to know, you'd be told.

In those days, agents were assigned cases via a big filing cabinet. Each agent had a mail folder in the cabinet, and cases, as handed out by supervisors and delivered by the field office's "rotor girls," were deposited in the folder. *Find a case in your folder and it was yours.* When Rooney left the office on Friday, February 1, 1980, his squad had been dedicated to public corruption; on Monday morning, his supervisor announced they were now focusing on organized crime—part of the Bureau's gradual shift to combating the problem. That day, Rooney opened his folder to discover a few sheets of paper profiling Mafia associate Salvatore Catalano. His partner, Carmine Russo, was assigned two other associates named Cesare Bonventre and Baldassare "Baldo" Amato. Little was known about any of the men except they had ties to the Bonnano family. Unlike in some cases, there were no specific allegations of criminal activity. The agents' role was to develop intelligence on the assigned figures, map their daily routines, their associations, and their jobs, and learn the details of their lives. In FBI protocol, each investigation had to have a code name, and cases involving the Bonnano family all had to begin with the code word "Genus," so Rooney's investigation started as "Operation Genus Cattails." Those few sheets of paper on February 2, 1980, would grow into the biggest case the FBI had ever tackled.

"We always started with the basics: who, what, where, when, why, and how," Rooney explains. They quickly began to perceive that something was amiss. There seemed to be a group of Sicilians operating with the highest levels of the Bonnano family. Rooney and Russo both knew the neighborhoods they were investigating and recognized that a certain group didn't fit in—this handful of Sicilians wore capes and fedoras and greeted each other with elaborate kisses on the cheeks. "Carmine, these guys look like they're right off the boat," Rooney said.

Carmine Russo had an advantage shared by few other FBI agents at the time: He was born and bred Sicilian. In 1955, at age nine, Russo had stepped off "the boat" at Pier 92, arriving in the United States with his family for a new life after sailing weeks earlier from Palermo harbor.* Raised with a strong ethic of service, he'd wanted to enter the priesthood. Instead, he joined the navy, serving four years as a radioman, where he developed the nickname "Golden Ears" for his proficiency at interpreting Morse code. Later, that skill would help him during the long months of deciphering Sicilian wiretaps in the Pizza case. After being discharged at the Brooklyn Navy Yard just as the Vietnam War was escalating, he joined the NYPD, working surveillance and intelligence, where he was introduced to the seedy underworld of New York organized crime. Still later, he worked as an investigator for the state prosecutor, all the while applying with various federal agencies, hoping to use his language skills. To his surprise and despite his foreign ancestry, which normally posed problems for the Bureau's intense background checks, the FBI eventually hired him.

To help the agents understand what was unfolding before their surveillance cars and telephoto lenses, the Bureau was aided by an especially novel and dangerous venture: An FBI agent, embedded undercover deeper than any had ever been allowed during Hoover's days, was working his way into the Bonnano family. For five years, Joseph Pistone, using the cover of a Florida jewel thief named Donnie Brasco, had been ingratiating himself as a low-level mobster.†

After years of working the sidelines, Pistone was taken under the family's wing and began in 1979 to get confusing tips about this new branch of the New York Mafia. "They're Zips," one mobster told him. "The Zips are into drugs. Drugs is their business." Pistone later figured out that "Zips" was a pejorative for Sicilians, although the exact origin of the word was always mysterious. A different night, while he

---

*Russo learned later that one of the Sicilian heroin traffickers that he was investigating had actually arrived in New York on June 15, 1955, aboard the same ship as Russo and his family.

†Buck Revell had actually recruited Pistone, a former naval investigator, to the Bureau when they were both working in Philadelphia.

and another mobster guarded a restaurant meeting of their boss, Galante, his companion said offhandedly, "Galante and Carlo Gambino were the first ones to bring the Zips over from Sicily to this country—and what they did is when they brought them over, they set them up in various businesses like pizza parlors." Over time the FBI would come to understand that since the 1950s, the Sicilian Mafia had infiltrated at least fifty-four American cities and towns, establishing a network of pizza parlors they used to launder money and distribute heroin. Pizza places were perfect cover: They were high-traffic businesses rich in cash. Over time, Sicilians took over almost the entire supply chain, creating lucrative side businesses that sold tomato sauce, cheese, oils, Italian meats, and other pizza ingredients. They even had a "Mafia bank" to loan recent immigrants the start-up money for their own franchises, which in turn extended the network even further.

When Galante was murdered in July 1979, Pistone got another tip: Sal Catalano was taking over. As a mobster told him, "The Zips are part of the Bonnano family, but they're the Sicilian faction. They're separate from the Americans." Such fragments of information were confusing, but there was nothing else to go on.

Meanwhile, Rooney, Russo, and other investigators tailed the Mafiosi when they had free time—in between other investigations, court prep, and when a car was available. It would be years before the surveillance operation became a priority.

On October 6, 1980, an NYPD team watched Giuseppe Ganci and Salvatore Catalano ride in a Cadillac from Knickerbocker Avenue to Bay Ridge, Brooklyn. The cops' eyes widened as an almost unmistakable figure joined the two Sicilians at Martini's Seafood Restaurant: Paul Castellano, the Gambino family boss, along with his top adviser, Tom Bilotti. *What on earth were two seemingly low-level street guys doing meeting with one of the most powerful mobsters in America?* Only years later would investigators understand that they had witnessed the meeting in which the American Cosa Nostra and the Sicilian Mafia worked out payment terms for the heroin trade.

Another FBI agent, Robert Paquette, from the New Rochelle Resident Agency, uncovered another clue later that month. Paquette specialized in white-collar crime and money laundering, but he had volunteered to be on the FBI SWAT team. In the wake of Munich and

Southern Airways, the Bureau had begun regular realistic counterterrorism exercises. Paquette, in his full SWAT gear, was practicing rappelling from a helicopter in rural Pennsylvania when he was summoned to the phone for an informant's tip. He landed on the ground and was told, "I know a guy who's looking to move a large sum of money out to Switzerland."

"How large?" Paquette asked distractedly, his adrenaline still pumping from the exercise.

"Sixty."

"Sixty what?"

"Million." That snapped him to attention. The sum was baffling. He'd spent years investigating Wall Street scams and multimillion-dollar frauds, yet $60 million in cash meant something else entirely.

A few days later, an FBI surveillance van, old, blue, and beat up—indistinguishable from any of the thousands of old delivery vans clogging New York's streets—sat at the curb of Third Avenue and 42nd Street, where the informant had sent the Bureau. A silver Audi driven by the suspect pulled up, and a passenger emerged with a bag that Paquette later confirmed held $200,000 in cash. Three weeks later, the routine was repeated. This time a suspect carried into a nearby office building an obviously heavy box labeled "Gordon's Vodka"—too heavy, though, to have just held bottles of vodka.

Intrigued, Paquette tried to learn more and eventually hit pay dirt: The silver Audi in question belonged to Frank Castronovo, who, according to the Bureau's index files, had been recently tailed by a Queens agent named Rooney. Paquette called the Queens office and explained his nascent case. Rooney picked up on the significance quickly: "We got to get together."

Following his strange sighting at the Castellano meeting, Ganci had been targeted for more intense surveillance. In November, he carried a suitcase into a fancy hotel on New York's Upper East Side and later was photographed with a short, balding man eating pizza in Little Italy. Only much later would Italian authorities figure out that the pizza eater was Sicilian crime boss Giuseppe Bono.

The investigation's first months found the FBI drowning in incomprehensible information: Leads led to new leads, surveillance led to new surveillance—all eventually totaling thousands of photographs, scores of faces, endless lists of license plate numbers and addresses, travel records and receipts. Rooney and Russo hunted through the guest lists of hotels on the East Side, looking for any name they recognized and zeroing in on anyone who made long-distance phone calls to Sicily. "Every day, we'd find another piece of the puzzle, and that kept us going," Rooney recalls. Still, many colleagues doubted the agents had a case. Although the other agents would never have said a word to Russo, who was known for his temper, the quieter Rooney often would hear complaints.

The agents passed some of the most promising leads to Special Agent Leone Flossi, the assistant legal attaché in Rome, who followed up with Italian authorities. Those leads started to trickle down to Falcone's team in Palermo.

The Italian magistrate made his first trip to the United States in December 1980. In what was to be the first of scores of meetings with U.S. officials over the next twelve years, he acquired important evidence that would prove key in his later prosecutions. Rooney, Russo, and the U.S. investigators sat with Falcone and laid out their case, weak and circumstantial as it was. There seemed to be money moving back and forth between the United States and Italy. The investigators didn't know why. Intelligence gathered in New York and in Italy had picked up confusing conversations about fish, tangerines, and lemons, but it was inconceivable that the Mafia cared that much about seafood imports and produce quality. *What, then, were they really discussing?*

Business concluded, the magistrate wanted to see the Big Apple. He was relaxed and happy to be away from the pressures of the Palermo streets. "I'm not afraid here," he told his FBI colleagues. He went shopping for blue jeans in the afternoons and then held court through the evening over dinner. On another visit, Falcone, free from his bodyguards and isolated Palermo existence, announced at the end of the day's meetings in his thick Sicilian accent, "I want to go dancing." The team headed out.

Mafia investigations had traditionally stopped at the ocean's edge. Until the beginning of the 1980s, there had been virtually no coordination between police agencies across international boundaries. Even as late as a year after Falcone's first visit to New York, cooperation between the Italians and the U.S. government was haphazard at best.

In 1981, Italian police issued warrants for three of the Sicilians under FBI surveillance on Knickerbocker Avenue, word of which never trickled down to Rooney, Russo, and their colleagues.

Gradually, after months of gathering puzzle pieces, investigators began to get a clearer picture. Paquette had spent almost half a year trying to identify the man who had been dropping off boxes the previous November. He'd gone through hundreds of corporate records trying to identify the office where the money had been taken. Finally he broke down and took the gamble of visiting the office in question personally. Paquette's heart was pounding as he walked in. He might run into the suspect at any second and would need a cover story at the ready. The office rental manager immediately identified the man in the photograph as Sal Amendolito and explained that Amendolito had skipped without paying rent some time ago. *At last, a name!* The name led to more phone records, which led to a list of Amendolito's "employees" at his front company, Overseas Business Services, which led to a big score: One former employee still had a copy of Amendolito's personal address book, packed with phone numbers.

With the assistance of Special Agent James Kallstrom, a former Marine who headed the New York Field Office's special operations command, the tools at the agents' disposal expanded. More surveillance teams were tasked to the investigation. In May 1981, agents set up a surveillance post overlooking Catalano's bakery and installed a covert video camera to observe Giuseppe Ganci's house nearby. The sprawling case was eating up more and more of the agents' time. In a not so subtle hint about her feelings, Rooney's wife, Jane, hung on the family refrigerator a picture of Charlie for their two kids—ages five and three—with the caption, "This is your father." On the rare weekends when he didn't go to the office, Rooney would go to a rail museum in Riverhead and help other enthusiasts restore an old steam locomotive. Working with his hands was a welcome distraction after an exhausting week of piecing together the heroin ring.

For Russo, the case was an equal driving passion. Several times in 1981 and 1982, supervisors stopped by his desk and said, "You've done a great job on this case, got lots of information; feel free to shut it down." Russo refused.

"Stopping wasn't in my nature," he explains.

On May 6, 1981, Rooney was at his desk in the Queens FBI office when all of the investigation's pen registers—devices that could be installed on phones to record the numbers dialed—started going off at once. Several calls were international. Something had obviously happened.

With Pistone's undercover help, it became clear that the night before, three Bonnano capos had been lured into an ambush and killed. The news spread like wildfire even though none of the bodies had turned up.★ One assassin, Santo Giordano, had been wounded in the attack. Russo spent May 7, his thirty-fifth birthday, visiting the mobster in a Queens hospital.

"How'd it happen, Santo?" Russo asked.

"Argument over a parking spot," the gangster replied casually, despite a wound so severe that it would leave him partially paralyzed.

"Where?"

"I don't remember."

The two men, investigator and instigator, exchanged a knowing look and smiled.

In the aftermath of the assassinations, it became obvious to investigators that a power struggle had developed at the upper levels of the Bonnano family, driven by profits from the incredible amount of heroin flowing through the system. The Galante killing on the restaurant terrace in July 1979 had been just the beginning.

In late May, Rooney and his team encountered a name they hadn't yet heard: Giuseppe Bono. Surveillance had shot a couple of pictures of the guy at Catalano's bakery and followed him back to an enormous mansion in Pelham that he evidently owned. Rooney called the Italians: Had they ever heard of him? Falcone's team didn't believe the

---

★ The body of Alphonse "Sonny Red" Indelicato was located several weeks after the murders in a vacant lot on the Brooklyn-Queens border. The remains of Dominick "Sonny Black" Napolitano and Dominick "Big Trin" Trinchera were not recovered until 2004.

question at first. Bono was, according to Falcone's investigation, one of the most powerful mobsters in the world and a leader of the global heroin trade. Bono had dropped off the Italian map and was presumed to be in hiding in South America. He was number one on the 162-person list of Italian organized crime figures—the equivalent of Hoover's Public Enemy #1—and he was just walking the streets of Queens? To a later generation of FBI agents, a find of this importance would be like discovering that Osama bin Laden had been living in a London flat.

An informant soon brought agents an even bigger surprise: Evidently, just days after he'd been photographed eating pizza with Ganci the previous November, Bono had been married at St. Patrick's Cathedral and held an elaborate reception at the Pierre Hotel. The gala, featuring three hundred mobsters from the United States and Sicily, was probably the largest gathering of La Cosa Nostra in history (and a testament to how safe they felt operating in the United States). The bill for the evening came to over $64,000. Amazingly, Bono had had all the guests photographed at the reception, and with the help of the DEA's Anthony Petrucci, investigators managed to put their hands on copies of the photos. If they could figure out who all these people were, they would have a dramatis personae for their case. To avoid identifying the portraits' source, Rooney and his wife, Jane—also an FBI employee—spent long nights cutting the head shots out of the pictures and pasting them onto sheets of paper. The "Pumpkin Heads," as the photo arrays came to be known, were a hit on both sides of the Atlantic—Falcone and the Italians were fascinated to discover how many locals had traveled to New York; the New Yorkers, for their part, were just thankful that someone recognized some of the hundreds of mystery faces. "To us, these names meant nothing, but to Falcone these were international players," Rooney recalls.

Special Agent Paquette made his first trip overseas as part of tracing his end of the money trail. International travel was still a rarity for FBI agents, so he took a lot of teasing: "Hey, Bobby, what European spa are you touring now?" But the trip proved fruitful, providing more names and companies, and revealing some tactics.

Late in 1981, Russo was waiting outside the Suffolk County jail as two of the original investigation targets—Bonventre and Amato—

were released after serving eight months on gun charges. He handed the newly free men subpoenas to appear before a grand jury investigating the Bonnano capo murders.

"Have a good time on Thirteenth Avenue," Russo said.

"Thanks," Bonventre replied.

That same month, a new boss arrived at the FBI office. Special Agent Frank Storey, transferred from Philadelphia to head the organized crime unit in New York, quickly brought a new focus to the investigation: "If you're not working on Title IIIs," Storey said, using the FBI language for a wiretap, "you're spinning your wheels. You could follow these guys around forever and not know what the hell they were doing."

In 1982, the FBI investigators went to the prosecutors at the Eastern District of New York, which covered Brooklyn, and were rebuffed for wiretap requests—the evidence wasn't there yet, the U.S. Attorney's Office said. Rooney had another avenue to pursue: His onetime colleague in the New York Field Office, Louis Freeh, had left the Bureau and moved to the Southern District U.S. Attorney's Office. In the fall of 1982, Freeh wrapped up his work on the cases that had come out of Joseph Pistone's undercover work. He asked to review the evidence Rooney and Russo had accumulated. "I'll take over this stuff," he told them.

In October, both sides gathered at the FBI compound in Quantico for a major consultation. For the first time, Falcone met Freeh, and the two men recognized in each other a common drive. Over a week of meetings that would prove a key turning point, the two sides shared information and bonded.

A month after the Quantico meeting, Russo, who had earlier made a fruitless investigative trip to Italy, was told, "Go back to Italy. They'll give you everything they can." After lengthy meetings with Falcone and the Italian National Police's Gianni de Gennaro, he came back with bags stuffed with wiretap recordings, bank records, photos, and intelligence of all sorts. "We were proving to the other agents— you've got to trust people," Russo says. "It all comes down to people." The comparatively small team of Rooney, Russo, Freeh, and fellow prosecutor Richard Martin on the American side and Falcone's team on the Italian side, including Borsellino, Rocco Chinnici, and Antonino Cassarà, were deep in uncharted territory.

The case had taken over the agents' lives. Many nights, after tucking his children into bed, Russo would head back out for more surveillance, never bothering officially to clock in. The agents found they couldn't let their guard down anywhere. In the fall of 1982, Russo and his wife, pregnant with the couple's fifth child, were at her obstetrician's office when the agent recognized one of the other couples in the waiting room.

"Hi, Mr. Russo, how're you?" asked Baldo Amato, sitting next to his own pregnant wife.

"How's the deli doing?" Russo shot back.

"Oh, you know about that?" Amato responded.

As they were leaving, Russo's wife, Carmela, inquired, "Who was that couple?"

"A guy I know from work," Russo said as casually as he could.

Toward the end of 1982, FBI supervisors centralized the investigation in the Manhattan office. By the end of February, working with Freeh, they'd amassed a 101-page affidavit—vastly longer than a traditional Title III application. In March, a judge approved their first wiretap request on Ganci's phone. Over the next year, agents would intercept nearly a hundred thousand telephone conversations—including many that turned out to be just ordinary citizens ordering pizza.

Scores of agents in several agencies, including Customs, the Internal Revenue Service (IRS), the NYPD, the Immigration and Naturalization Service (INS), and the DEA were now involved. Yet rather than getting closer to a conclusion, the case only seemed to grow more complicated, involving more players, more unknown leads, and more countries. One night in May 1983, Special Agent in Charge Tom Sheer, the head of the FBI's Criminal Division in New York, stopped by the squad's bullpen: "What are you guys waiting for? The case to solve itself? How's it coming?" he asked jokingly.

Rooney fixed the boss with a stare: "It sucks, pal."

Later, Rooney's supervisor chided him: "You can't talk to the SAC like that."

"Well, he asked me," Rooney said defensively.

That spring the case reached another major turning point: President Reagan appointed an ambitious Justice Department official, Rudolph Giuliani, as the new U.S. attorney for the Southern District—Freeh's new boss. Giuliani, a native New Yorker of Italian descent, arrived from Washington set on dismantling the Mafia; he'd overseen national anti–organized crime efforts and helped establish joint government "strike forces" in many East Coast cities. As associate attorney general, the Justice Department's third-highest position, Giuliani had been briefed regularly by the FBI on the evolving case, still known to the Bureau as Operation Genus Cattails. An individual with less drive and ambition would have seen the U.S. attorney's post as a demotion—it was organizationally many rungs beneath Justice's number-three post—but Giuliani saw it as a career-making perch. Indeed, he, Freeh, and Tom Sheer would make a formidable team.

Earlier attempts by the Justice Department and the FBI to crack down on the Mafia had been hindered by weak laws. In a pattern that would repeat itself as the threat of terrorism rose in the 1970s, the criminal code didn't accurately reflect the dangers of organized crime. Until the 1970s, mob-related murders were considered state or local offenses, so the Bureau couldn't even investigate the killings that flared up during periods of internal Mafia turmoil. The Bureau's only two relevant federal laws—an anti-racketeering statute and an anti-gambling statute—both required interstate travel by the suspects, so any mobster who kept his business within state lines couldn't be pursued. The Mafia had come to understand that the courts generally treated crimes like racketeering and loan-sharking lightly as long as they remained violence free. Thus mobsters, even when convicted, often drew at most a few years in jail, which the organization saw as merely the price of doing business. Mobsters were assured that their families would be financially taken care of while they were behind bars, and their jobs would be waiting for them when they got out.

Thus the Bureau and prosecutors quickly realized that they needed a stronger tool if their efforts were to have any impact on the mob. Innovative prosecutors had begun to rely on an obscure 1970 law, the Racketeer Influenced and Corrupt Organizations Act (RICO), which made it a federal crime for members of an "organization" or "association in fact" to commit crimes in the furtherance of their organization. Thinking in terms of organizations rather than individuals was a revolution in the FBI mind-set—one that would prove crucial decades later as it began to move against terrorist organizations like al-Qaeda.

In the spring and summer of 1983, Falcone's team got a big break: The magistrate located Francesco Gasparini, an Italian courier bringing drugs to Palermo from Bangkok en route to New York, and arrested him in Paris. Weeks later, Egyptian police seized a Greek vessel in the Suez Canal with 233 kilos of heroin aboard and found it guarded by a Sicilian Mafioso. After Italian police located the dealer, Thai police arrested him in Bangkok.

While Falcone was in Thailand interviewing the trafficker, back home in Sicily, Falcone's boss, Rocco Chinnici, along with two bodyguards, was killed by a car bomb outside his home.* Chinnici's assassination revolutionized how Italy pursued Mafia crimes. Instead of assigning cases to a single prosecutor, who could be felled at any time to stall the investigation, the Italian government established an "anti-Mafia pool." The ten-person pool, led by Falcone with Paolo Borsellini at his side, was meant to lessen the threat against any single individual. Each person in the pool would be involved in all the investigations, mitigating the risk of assassination for any single person.

That same summer, DEA agent Anthony Petrucci, who had been working with Russo, Rooney, and the FBI New York team, received a call from a colleague in Philadelphia: Could he investigate a telephone number that had come up in an undercover drug buy in the City of Brotherly Love, 894-4739? Neither Petrucci nor any other agent on the New York case needed to look up the number; Giuseppe Ganci's had been the first phone they'd wiretapped. "We're working different ends of the same case," Petrucci exclaimed. As it turned out, the Philly team, with an informant's help, had infiltrated a chain of

---

*The assassination had a major impact on the New York FBI team—Chinnici's doorman, who also died in the blast, was named Russo. These weren't just Carmine Russo's countrymen—the victims of the Mafia's reign of terror were Russo's own blood.

Sicilian pizzerias in Philadelphia that were being used to help move large quantities of heroin. It had successfully negotiated the purchase of a half-kilo of extremely high-quality heroin, a buy that—unbeknownst to the DEA or the Sicilians—Russo had overheard on the wiretaps of Ganci's phone. While the FBI had amassed plenty of evidence of cash transfers and coded conversations, this particular conversation provided the first hard evidence confirming that the Sicilians were moving drugs. After much discussion, everyone agreed that the Philadelphia case would be put on hold. Despite having a solid narcotics case, the investigators knew they were onto something bigger.

The DEA investigation helped the Genus Cattails team crack the code, because for the first time the FBI eavesdroppers knew, from the Philadelphia DEA side, how much money and how much heroin was being exchanged. Conversations about "chocolates" and "papers" suddenly made more sense. Now the agents needed proof of what was inside the bags that the surveillance teams watched being exchanged. FBI supervisor Lew Schiliro hatched a plan—after a delivery, the NYPD would stop one of the Sicilians on a seemingly routine traffic infraction. Then they'd search the car, discover the package, and, later, drop the charges before having to admit in court that the intelligence came from wiretaps. Despite Freeh's objections, a surveillance team was carefully positioned on August 7, but the operation fell apart when agents lost the target during a chase through Brooklyn. Three weeks later, Schiliro had another chance. Again Freeh worried that they'd be prematurely showing their hand, though by the time he learned about it, it was a moot point: Schiliro had already ordered one of the Sicilians stopped.

The NYPD pulled over Giuseppe Baldinucci in a Howard Beach parking lot. The Sicilian, who never asked why he had been stopped, possessed a number of different car registrations and IDs, as well as a packet of heroin and $40,000 in cash. Furthermore, a computer database check found that the Sicilian was wanted by the Secret Service on a fugitive warrant stemming from counterfeiting and mail theft charges in 1980. The outstanding warrant gave them cover for stopping Baldinucci and meant the FBI wouldn't have to tip its hand to the extensive surveillance and wiretap operation. Schiliro thought they'd won the lottery—but Freeh was still furious.

The pace of the investigation continued to accelerate. In mid-September, Falcone and his team landed in New York for a conference at Governors Island with the ever-expanding cast of agencies, prosecutors, and agents involved in the case. At the same time, with the help of the DEA and Customs, FBI agents intercepted a major drug shipment passing through Port Elizabeth in New Jersey. The Buffalo-bound shipment was hidden in pallets containing boxes of tiles. When agents drilled into a pallet, a stream of white power came pouring out. "Would you like a test kit or can you guess what it is?" Rooney asked the accompanying Customs agent, Mike Fahy.

After much negotiation between field offices and after trading the nearly pure heroin for a fake look-alike, the drug shipment was allowed to continue on to Buffalo. Agents made seven arrests in the Buffalo shipment, pretending that it was a routine drug bust even as it allowed them to take down Andrea Aiello, a major Mafia figure in Buffalo. Curiously, the Buffalo arrests led a Philadelphia Mafioso to comment to the DEA's undercover agent that he feared arrest for the shipment too—the FBI had never before suspected that the Philadelphia and Buffalo branches were connected. *Just how interlinked and coordinated were these Sicilians?*

In October, with the help of Falcone's Italian team, Brazilian police located and captured Tommaso Buscetta, a major Mafia assassin. The Brazilian end of the investigation quickly took off, as the Brazilians arrested other Sicilians under surveillance—phone records promptly linked them to others, and the son of Gaetano Badalamenti, one of the most powerful organized crime figures in the world, was caught up in the sweep. Unfortunately for investigators, Badalamenti fled after the Brazilians released him prematurely. The Mafioso loomed large over the investigation on both sides of the Atlantic—Falcone badly wanted to get his hands on the at-large Mafia leader, as evidently did other members of the Mafia: Two of Badalamenti's great-nephews had been murdered recently in New Jersey.

Now the mosaic began to fill. Through informants and surveillance, agents learned of flights to the Bahamas and clandestine meetings in New York hotel rooms involving millions in cash, as well as more names and more phone numbers. By November 1983, Rooney and Russo began to feel the pressure from FBI Headquarters. They'd been up on the wiretaps for months, thousands of man-hours were disappearing in the surveillance, and not insignificant international travel bills were being racked up. "This was much bigger than anything the Bureau had ever seen," Rooney says. "This wasn't your typical case of a drug deal at the corner of Walk and Don't Walk."

However, the FBI needed more help—by the end of 1983, it had more wires going than it had Italian and Sicilian speakers. What about asking the Italians to come listen to the wires? Antonio Cassarà, the assistant chief of Palermo's Squadra Mobile, took a plane to New York. He sat down with Rooney, Russo, and a few other investigators, and they laid out where their investigation stood before they broke the big news. "We believe we have Badalamenti on the phone," Russo explained. Impossible, the Italian police officer protested. There was no way that the FBI's drug investigation had somehow managed to stumble onto the head of all the Italian Mafia, the onetime head of the Cupola, the Sicilian Mafia's governing organization—arguably the most powerful criminal in the world. There was no hard evidence, only coded conversations and obscure references, yet the FBI case agents had a gut feeling they'd located the big fish. After all, the agents' instincts had driven the case this far. The more emphatic Russo became that they had the Mafia kingpin, the more Cassarà protested: No way, nohow do you have Badalamenti on the phone. The afternoon ended in an impasse.

That night, Rooney took the Italian magistrate out to dinner at a New York pub and Cassarà ate his first hamburger; he was dubious of the American staple too. "Still to this day I believe he thought that we were crazy on two counts—the identification of Badalamenti and that we ate hamburgers," Rooney recalls.

The visit, though, bore fruit: A handful of Italian National Police officers soon arrived in New York City and, moving the investigation even deeper into uncharted territory, were deputized as U.S. marshals so they could participate in the wiretaps and evidence collection.

Through an unusually cold winter, more than a hundred agents and FBI staff pulled long hours monitoring the wiretaps and conducting surveillance. Russo, sitting in the secret surveillance room overlooking one of the target pizzerias, shivered on the 3 P.M. to 11 P.M. shift, since the building's heat was turned off after hours. To combat the cold, he wore a navy peacoat and cap. He spent his shift hunched over a legal pad, frantically transcribing a day's worth of calls and double-checking the work of the day shift—he'd seen them miss too many calls in the highly nuanced Sicilian dialect to fully trust their efforts. In the morning, as Russo slept, Agent Patrick Luzio would deliver the previous day's calls to Freeh's office for review.

In an intercepted telephone call on February 8, Badalamenti promised to deliver "containers" of what he said, in code, was 90 percent pure heroin for $60,000 apiece. Over the next day, follow-up calls confirmed the terms and delivery at a Fort Lauderdale Howard Johnson hotel. The FBI quickly dispatched agents to Florida, and a Coast Guard transport plane was packed full of Bureau equipment—almost a score of agents, six surveillance cars, and lots of high-tech tools. The Tampa SAC called up to Sheer in New York: "I don't mean to be impertinent, but what are you doing down here with your own army?"

As much as he wanted to stop the drugs from entering the United States, Freeh saw getting Badalamenti and dismantling the whole operation as a more important catch. Giuliani agreed—they'd let the drugs enter and hope to catch the whale himself.

A little over a month later, the FBI's technical wizards succeeded for the first time in tracing an international call in real time: They discovered that Badalamenti—or at least the person speaking in the voice they suspected belonged to the Mafioso leader—was using a pay phone in Rio. An FBI agent and Brazilian police arrived at the scene within half an hour and found nothing.

On April 5, the FBI agents heard again from Badalamenti. The boss called Pietro Alfano, a Chicago Mafioso, with an order: "All right. Listen to me. Next week you have to be there. Listen to me.... Make it . . . for Madrid." *Boom: Target in sight.* Alfano promptly arranged for a flight to Madrid. The next day's afternoon KLM flight to Madrid via Amsterdam carried the Sicilian mobster and, unbeknownst to him, a DEA agent and an FBI agent too. The following morning, a team of undercover Spanish antidrug police met the party at Madrid-Barajas Airport. For more than a day, the FBI, the DEA, and Spanish police waited nervously outside the apartment Alfano had been spotted entering.

Then, around lunchtime, Alfano walked out with an older man. A block later, authorities pounced, guns drawn. Inside a nearby police station, the questioning started.

"Are you Gaetano Badalamenti?" Spanish deputy police chief José María Rodríguez Merino asked.

"No, I am Paulo Alves Barbosa," the man replied.

"Where do you live?"

"I don't know."

The trap snapped shut across two continents. Swiss authorities, with the help of the FBI, brought in a suspected money launderer. In New York, agents took down another Mafioso as he tried to board a plane to Sicily. Louis Freeh, Rooney, and Customs agent Mike Fahy holed up for a long night, preparing warrants and readying evidence and affidavits, as investigators and officers from other agencies gathered at the FBI command post for the predawn raid that would end Operation Genus Cattails. For three years, investigators had known that the suspects were involved in massive amounts of drug trafficking and money laundering; the suspects had been targeted by intense surveillance involving round-the-clock details of more than a hundred agents and police, as well as extensive electronic wiretaps, and yet the government had still barely cracked the organization.

A little before 6 A.M. on April 9, Tom Sheer gave the green light to the more than four hundred agents and police scattered across the United States: "Let's go." Amazingly, in busting the biggest drug-smuggling operation ever uncovered in the United States, the agents at the end of the day had seized just one ounce of cocaine, taken off a suspect in Temperance, Michigan. But only two suspects had escaped the day's dragnet—the two Galante bodyguards, Cesare Bonventre and Baldo Amato. The coming weeks, though, made it clear that their luck had run out too: Bonventre's body was found hacked in half and stuffed in two drums of glue. Amato turned himself in after his *compare*'s body was found.

"Do yourself a favor and talk to us," Russo said to the target he'd once run into at his wife's doctor's office. "We can protect you."

"I appreciate that, Mr. Russo, but I have no enemies," Amato replied.

Seven years after he arrived in the United States from Italy, Alfredo Principe was fed up with teaching high school Spanish and Italian in Albany, New York. The father of one of his students, an FBI agent, encouraged him to join the Bureau—the FBI always needed language specialists, he said. Principe visited the local resident agency in Albany and filled out an application. A year passed with no word before his wife finally convinced him to call. "We don't need any Spanish speakers," a distracted agent on the phone told Principe in mid-1983. He protested that his native languages actually were Italian and Sicilian and got an immediate reaction—he could almost hear the agent sit up straight on the other end of the phone: "I'll call you back in ten minutes." With the next phone call, Principe was summoned for an interview—the FBI desperately needed more Italian and Sicilian speakers—and a year later, after a background check that involved agents walking the streets of his Calabrian hometown at the toe of Italy, Principe was thrown into the deep end of the Pizza Connection.

For a while, a Sicilian-born Catholic priest in Washington had helped the Bureau translate the tapes, as did the handful of agents who had learned the language from their immigrant parents. It wasn't enough. In 1963, the U.S. Army Language School had hired a Sicilian to launch a new nine-month program for the FBI split equally between Italian and Sicilian, but in a pattern that would repeat itself in the first years of this century as the FBI found itself desperately short of Arabic and Persian speakers, by the 1980s there were still very few FBI employees who could understand the Mafia's native tongues. Thus one of Principe's main tasks was helping the trans-Atlantic prosecutors put their cases together. When Rudy Giuliani needed to call Italy, he called Principe first to translate, and when the cooperating Mafiosi or the case's defendants needed to be debriefed, that task fell to Principe too. It was Principe who was waiting at the Metropolitan Correctional Center (MCC), across from the federal courthouse in New York, the night Badalamenti arrived from Spain. Principe and a federal prosecutor spent the evening interrogating the Mafia head, who continued to protest that he was nothing but a peasant farmer.

When, back in Italy, Falcone was finished with Buscetta (who'd been extradited from Brazil), Principe and other FBI investigators spent months in rural New Jersey, sequestered at an isolated estate rented by the government to house the Mafia killer, debriefing him and preparing him for trial. The mornings would begin with the hit man knocking at Principe's door: "Professor"—Buscetta used the honorific as a nod to Principe's former teaching career—"let's go for a walk." The two men would wander the grounds, bantering in Sicilian about the case, and Principe would pass along some English lessons. ("Buscetta was always trying to better himself," Principe recalls.) Then, after the walk, Buscetta would hand one of the security agents a list of groceries before he settled in with prosecutors Richard Martin and Bob Bucknam. Each night Buscetta cooked everyone at the estate a giant Italian meal.

Meanwhile Freeh, Rooney, and the team crisscrossed the globe, collecting testimony and running down more leads. A half-dozen Italian police officers had to be prepped for trial and taught the differences between U.S. courts and Italian courts. (For one thing, in Italian courts at the time, there was no such thing as cross-examination. The Italians were baffled as to why they'd have to face questions from the defendants—*wasn't their word as police officers trustworthy?*) One trip took the team to Switzerland to talk money laundering with bankers there, then on to Turkey to talk heroin transportation methods. In Switzerland, a retired U.S. federal judge presided side by side with a Swiss judge to ensure that the interviews met the standards of law and evidence for both countries. In Turkey, cultural differences didn't mesh smoothly: Rooney asked Turkish authorities whether the men Turkey had arrested for transporting morphine base—a key heroin ingredient—would cooperate. "How do we know that they will talk to us?"

"Of course they will talk—otherwise we will cut off their heads," replied a Turkish official. Knowing that testimony under such circumstances could never be admissible in a U.S. courtroom, the Americans suggested another approach.

The case's toll continued to rise. In the summer of 1985, just two years after the assassination of Rocco Chinnici, Magistrate Antonio Cassarà, the Italian police investigator who had doubted that the FBI had found Badalamenti as well as the wisdom of the American hamburger, called his wife to say he was coming home from work early. As his motorcade pulled up minutes later and his wife stepped out of the house to scan the street for trouble, a battalion of more than a dozen Mafia gunmen opened fire from a second-story balcony overlooking the house. Cassarà's security detail never had a chance. His wife watched in horror as more than two hundred shots tore her husband and his entourage apart. Days later, Falcone, Borsellino, and their families were hustled out of their houses in the middle of the night and whisked to the Italian island prison of Asinara. For more than a month, the prosecutors lived in the fortress there, an isolated outpost known as the Alcatraz of Italy, to ensure their safety as they finished what became known as the "maxi-indictment." When finished, their work indicted a total of 452 defendants, filling 40 volumes and 8,607 pages—not counting appendices—and was considered the most complete history of La Cosa Nostra ever written.

That fall, the Pizza Connection "maxi-trial" opened in New York. The thirty-five original defendants had been whittled down to twenty-two who would stand trial together in the largest case ever prosecuted in the United States. In Italy, Falcone's maxi-trial would dwarf that.

In New York, when Louis Freeh, Richard Martin, Bob Bucknam, and a team of other prosecutors sat down to lay out a strategy, they realized the hurdles ahead: Most of the evidence lay in stale and boring transcripts of coded conversations. How could they make the wiretap transcripts come alive? In the end, Freeh's team settled on a novel approach: They hired actors, who would come to be known as the "Pizza Players," to read the transcripts aloud in the courtroom.

Over the coming seventeen-month Pizza trial—by comparison nearly twice as long as the seemingly endless O. J. Simpson trial of 1995—hundreds of witnesses, including nearly two hundred different federal agents, passed through the courtroom while fall turned to winter, then spring, then summer, then fall, then winter again, and so on.

When the jury was finally given the case, the judge supplied a 59-page verdict sheet to complete, as well as the nearly 250 pages of the original indictment and his own instructions, a 410-page "summary" by the government, and even more pages from the various defense attorneys with their explanations of innocence.

At the same time, another team of Giuliani's prosecutors—led by a young rising star named Michael Chertoff—were prosecuting a separate major organized crime case targeting the leaders of New York's Five Families. The government argued that the families ran organized crime through a multi-family governing body called "the Commission."★ In November 1986, all the Commission defendants were found guilty of a variety of charges ranging from extortion to loan sharking to racketeering to murder (including the murder of Carmine Galante on the Italian restaurant patio in July 1979 that had helped launch the original Pizza investigation). Between the Pizza Connection and the Commission case, Giuliani had certainly achieved what he wanted when he came to New York—Italian organized crime would never be the same.

Meanwhile, for its own "maxi-trial," the Italian government had spent some $18 million to create a special bunker near Palermo's notorious Ucciardone prison. Thirty cages for prisoners ringed the back wall of the *aula-bunker,* the bunker hall. More stadium than courtroom, it had seats and desks for some one thousand defense attorneys and witnesses and another thousand seats for spectators in a gallery above. The building was built to withstand rocket fire, the barred windows were made of thick bulletproof glass, and more than three thousand soldiers stood guard outside for the beginning of the trial.

With so many defendants, the trial that started on February 16, 1986, was a circus. Defendants stripped, threw water, and smoked cigarettes inside their cages. One defendant was placed in a straitjacket after feigning madness. The courtroom fell fully silent, though, as the verdicts were read on the evening of December 16, 1987. The process took hours. All told, 338 of the 452 defendants were found guilty. Nineteen of the top bosses were sentenced to life in prison. But the

---

★ "The Commission" included Paul Castellano of the Gambino family, who had been observed years earlier by surveillance agents at Martini's Seafood Restaurant meeting with the Sicilians to establish the payment terms for the heroin smuggling. Like some of the defendants in the Pizza Connection case, he was murdered before the Commission trial began.

Mafia also had its own justice to dole out: Of the 114 defendants who were acquitted in the courtroom, one was killed even before he made it from prison back to his house with celebratory champagne—the first of at least 18 to die in the coming months.

Falcone and Borsellino had only a brief moment to celebrate their success. Already, the prosecutors were moving forward, issuing a new indictment of eighty Mafiosi that came to be known as "Maxi II." In March 1988, U.S. federal agents launched a sweeping raid that came to be known as "Pizza II," taking down sixty-four more Mafiosi in almost half a dozen states. The Italian team rounded up over two hundred more. In December, in Operation Iron Tower, the FBI arrested another 75 Mafiosi in the United States, and the Italians arrested 133 in Italy. The number of arrests stunned even the investigators themselves: In the United States, this had virtually all grown out of a few pieces of paper handed to Russo and Rooney in 1980; in Italy, Falcone's efforts were remedying a generation of neglect that had allowed the Mafia to grow more powerful than ever.

Time and again, Freeh and Falcone teamed up—pursuing the same case on different sides of the Atlantic, each lending resources to the other's leads. The partnership had a profound effect on the New York prosecutor; he was grasping that no major case stopped at the water's edge. Yet one major difference remained between the two: While Freeh had enjoyed the full support of his boss, Rudolph Giuliani, and was rewarded for his efforts with an appointment in 1991 as a federal judge in the Southern District of New York, Falcone's success only isolated him in the Italian power structure—his amazing track record threatened too many people. The magistrate could read the writing on the wall, confiding to a friend: "I'm a dead man." He was rejected for a promotion, and his supportive boss was replaced with a less understanding official who slowly dismantled much of the work that Falcone's team had done. Recognizing that he needed to change approaches, Falcone ran for the Consiglio Superiore della Magistratura, the judicial system's governing body, to try to nationalize the anti-Mafia efforts. Unbelievably, he lost. Abandoning his native Sicily in March 1990, he took a job as director of penal affairs, an obscure government position that he'd quickly turn into one of the most powerful Italian posts. Amid a political crisis that had paralyzed government and stalled reforms once again, Falcone gave an interview to *La Repubblica* on Tuesday, May 19, 1992. "Cosa Nostra never forgets," he told the newspaper. "The enemy is always there, ready to strike."

At the end of the week, on Saturday afternoon, May 23, 1992, he set off for Palermo. Falcone was in a good mood as he got off the plane and approached his three-car motorcade. He asked to drive himself, so he and his wife, Francesa, sat up front, and his bodyguard climbed in back. They pulled out of the airport, racing down the highway. The security profile had seemed to be improving, so there was no escort helicopter watching overhead and the route hadn't been scouted in advance with the thoroughness that typically proceeded his travel. If it had, perhaps the advance team would have noticed some unusual construction around a highway culvert near Capice, where Mafiosi had buried a seven-hundred-kilogram bomb under the road. Observing from a nearby hill, the Mafiosi triggered the bomb as the lead car passed over, obliterating it and killing all three bodyguards inside instantly. Falcone's car, which had slowed momentarily while Falcone and his driver exchanged car keys, plowed into the debris, fatally injuring the crusading judge and his wife. The bodyguard in the backseat lived.★

News of the explosion interrupted all broadcast television in Italy. Claudio Magris, writing in *Corriere della Sera,* said, "No one more than he embodied the state. The fact that we have been unable or unwilling to protect him means that the state does not exist." Banners throughout Palermo proclaimed "Falcone Lives."

Falcone's partner, Borsellino, sat in silence in his house for days, knowing that Falcone's death meant a similar sentence for him. He'd often said darkly, "They will kill him first, then they will kill me." Two months later, the Mafia did just that when Borsellino went to his mother's apartment for his regular Sunday afternoon visit.† As he rang the intercom for her high-rise building, a parked car next to him

---

★Underscoring what Falcone had been up against throughout his career, one of the Mafiosi watching from the hill above was talking on his cell phone with an Italian member of Parliament as the bomb went off.

†Borsellino's security detail had asked him to vary his routine, but Sundays with his mother were sacred, so they'd persuaded the city to declare the street outside his mother's building a no-parking zone. However, the rule hadn't yet taken effect.

exploded, killing him and all of his bodyguards. (The explosion was so powerful that the body of one of his guards, who was on her first day on the job, was found on the second floor of the building across the street.) At Borsellino's funeral, a near-riot broke out when the crowd, led by hundreds of police bodyguards who had protected the prosecutors and felt their efforts had been in vain, attacked the Italian president and the head of the National Police. The government got the message: Within days, seven thousand Italian troops landed on Sicily to wage a campaign against the Mafia unlike any seen since World War II. The investigations after Falcone's death would eventually expand to include one third of the Italian Parliament. Governments of more than seventy cities and towns were dissolved due to Mafia influence. Within the next two years, the murder rate in all of Italy fell by almost half, underscoring just how much crime in the country was Mafia related.

Falcone's prosecutions and eventual assassination shaped a generation of FBI agents and executives. Every year a team from the Bureau, joined by other U.S. agencies like the DEA, returns to Palermo on May 23 to remember Falcone, Borsellino, and the others who lost their lives fighting the Mafia, in a citywide ceremony. The first Italian memorial ceremony in 1994 the two governments jointly decided was too risky for Freeh, by then the FBI director, to attend; every year but one since, he has led the U.S. delegation. On this side of the Atlantic, new agents training at the FBI Academy in Quantico walk by a small garden named for Falcone, not far from where Freeh and the Italian magistrate first met—a quiet testament to the groundbreaking case that began the transformation of the FBI into an international crime fighter a generation ago.

Yet even as the joint FBI-Italian effort made progress against the Mafia, another danger was on the rise—one that would, over time, exact a much bigger toll and expand the FBI's powers and jurisdiction in ways that J. Edgar Hoover could have never imagined. The Pizza Connection, in the end, had all the elements of the terrorism cases that would unfold over the coming decades—the huge language barriers faced in foreign investigations, the sprawling international scope of modern criminal enterprises, and the challenges of collecting, processing, and preserving evidence far from U.S. courtrooms.

CHAPTER 4
Operation Goldenrod

Hey boss, it's him and we got him.
— *FBI special agent Woody Johnson*

Long before the U.S. public focused on the terrorist threat of al-Qaeda, the Libyans and the Iranians were Public Enemy #1.

Fred Stremmel, who would become one of the FBI's lead terrorism analysts, first came to the FBI's counterterror beat to investigate 1981 rumors that Libyan "hit teams" had arrived in the United States to target President Ronald Reagan and other senior officials. Libyan leader Muammar Qaddafi had purportedly dispatched assassins to avenge the U.S. downing of two Libyan military aircraft over the Gulf of Sidra in August 1981. "Most of us had no experience in international terrorism and possessed a paucity of knowledge regarding Islam and the Middle East," Stremmel recalls. "We all were very much behind the curve." Despite extensive investigation, no proof arose that such hit teams had ever existed. Stremmel, though, sensed the winds and decided to remain on the terror beat.* He'd end up working counterterrorism for almost twenty-five years.

---

* The FBI Task Force also focused on the aid that two former CIA officers, Edwin Wilson and Frank Terpil, as well as other U.S. Army Special Forces members, had

Just after Christmas 1985, terrorists simultaneously attacked the airports in Vienna and Rome, throwing grenades and opening fire with submachine guns. By the time police and security guards responded and killed most of the terrorists, twenty civilians were dead, including five Americans, and more than a hundred travelers were wounded. Blame first fell on the Palestinian Liberation Organization (PLO), but Abu Nidal, a vicious Palestinian militant who led his own terrorist splinter group, soon claimed responsibility. Nidal, who had explained earlier that year in a *Der Spiegel* interview, "I am the evil spirit which moves around only at night causing...nightmares," would be a thorn for Western intelligence agencies for more than two decades.* The Libyan government officially denied any responsibility, yet it praised the attacks. President Reagan announced that U.S. sanctions against Libya would be expanded and assets held in the United States frozen.

In March 1986, a brief clash between the U.S. and Libyan navies ended with the sinking of four Libyan patrol boats. Days later, Libyan intelligence agents bombed U.S. servicemen at the La Belle discotheque in West Berlin, killing two army sergeants and a Turkish woman, and injuring some seventy-nine Americans, along with nearly two hundred others. Subsequently, U.S. intelligence intercepted messages from Libya to its diplomats in East Berlin ordering the attack. Ten days after the disco bombing, more than one hundred U.S. fighters and bombers swept over Libya, pounding sites in Tripoli and Banghazi. Targeting what the United States said were "terrorist centers" and key facilities for Qaddafi, Operation El Dorado Canyon ended up killing Qaddafi's fifteen-month-old adopted daughter, injuring two of his sons, and possibly even wounding the Libyan leader himself.† Within minutes of the attack, President Reagan addressed the nation:

provided to the Libyan regime in the 1970s. Wilson was indicted, convicted, and spent twenty-seven years in jail; Terpil is still a fugitive.

* Nidal was never captured by Western governments. He eventually died in Baghdad, Iraq, in August 2002. Whether he was killed in a shoot-out with Saddam Hussein's intelligence service or committed suicide has never been definitively established.

† One U.S. F-111 bomber and its two-person crew were lost amid the heavy fire from antiaircraft batteries. Several residential buildings and the French embassy were hit by errant bombs, killing more than a dozen Libyan civilians.

"When our citizens are abused or attacked anywhere in the world, we will respond in self-defense. Today we have done what we had to do," he declared. "If necessary, we shall do it again." Qaddafi, for his part, promised to "pursue U.S. citizens in their country and streets."

On October 7, 1985, four Palestinian terrorists seized control of the cruise ship *Achille Lauro* just off the coast of Alexandria, Egypt, during a Mediterranean vacation cruise. Opening fire with Soviet-made submachine guns, they ordered all the passengers to the dining room. Almost as soon as they had boarded in Genoa, the attackers had attracted attention. (All Arabs, they improbably gave their nationality as Norwegian, and carried attaché cases everywhere they went outside their cabins.) They now demanded that in exchange for releasing the passengers unharmed, fifty Palestinian prisoners be freed from Israeli jails. The American and British passengers were separated from the rest of the 125 passengers and 315 crew and told they'd be killed if the demands weren't met.

Back in Washington, the incident became one of the first missions for President Reagan's new Terrorist Incident Working Group, which had been created in 1982 for such incidents and included personnel from State, Defense, the Joint Chiefs, the White House, and the National Security Council (represented in this case in part by an operations officer named Lieutenant Colonel Oliver North). Meeting regularly through the crisis, the group deployed Delta Force teams to the Mediterranean just in case. With the recent passage of so-called long arm statutes in the United States, the dozen or so Americans on board the *Achille Lauro* made the incident an official FBI matter. A crime had been committed.

The terrorists had actually launched their attack earlier than planned after a waiter spotted them cleaning their weapons. Now, off the coast of Egypt and with the ship under their control, no government seemed willing to let them enter its territorial waters. As one deadline came and went without action by Israel, the terrorists singled out Leon Klinghoffer, a sixty-nine-year-old retired New York appliance manufacturer who, after two strokes, was confined to a wheelchair. They rolled his wheelchair to the side of the ship, fired a single shot to his head, and pushed him into the sea. His body washed up a week later in Syria.

Working with Egyptian officials, the secretary general of the Palestinian Liberation Front (the group claiming responsibility for the attack) negotiated an end to the hostage drama: If the terrorists surrendered, they would be guaranteed safe passage out of Egypt. Hearing from their commander onshore, the terrorists aboard the *Achille Lauro* motored in. Meanwhile the U.S. ambassador to Egypt, Nicholas Veliotes, visited the ship and, confirming that the only casualty of the incident was American, promptly radioed a blunt message to the Egyptian foreign minister: "We insist that they prosecute those sons of bitches." The Italians, too, insisted on extradition of the terrorists to stand trial for the hijacking of the Italian vessel.

Hours later, word leaked to the U.S. government that Egypt was preparing to fly the terrorists to Tunis, accompanied by assorted officials and diplomats—including Mohammed Abul Abbas, the PLF secretary-general who had helped negotiate the end of the hostage situation. President Reagan, at a Sara Lee bakery in Deerfield, Illinois, to talk tax reform, ordered action—fast. The aircraft carrier USS *Saratoga,* steaming toward Yugoslavia, was ordered south, and a plan hastily came together: The *Saratoga*'s planes would force the EgyptAir jet down at a NATO base on Sicily, where the terrorists would be taken into custody by Delta operatives.

Buck Revell recalls that he was driving home on the evening of October 10, 1985, when his car radio buzzed with a message to call the White House switchboard for Colonel North. Revell picked up the primitive, bulky car phone and called. "Get over here," North said. "I can't say anything else on an open line."

For the only time in his career, Revell raced up to the White House with his lights flashing and the siren on his Bureau car wailing. When Revell entered the Situation Room, North exclaimed, "Buck, we've got these guys!" As Revell realized what was about to go down in the skies over the Mediterranean, his eyes widened. The Bureau was knee-deep in the Pizza Connection work with magistrate Giovanni Falcone and his team, and Revell knew better than almost anyone that the police in Sicily weren't to be trifled with.

"Damn it, Ollie!" Buck exploded. "You can't force the plane down in Italian territory. They have jurisdiction. Their laws don't give them any discretion. They'll have to arrest the terrorists."

North said, "Don't worry. Carl Stiner [the Delta commander] will have those guys out before the Italians even know they were there."

Revell, seeing the Bureau's years of close Italian cooperation unravel before his eyes, was desperate: "The Carabinieri are practically an occupation force in Sicily. They won't back down. It's their country! It was their ship that was hijacked." According to Revell, North remained unconcerned.

As evening descended on Washington, the U.S. planes moved into position in the Mediterranean. Traveling at more than four hundred knots, four F-14s took up positions around the EgyptAir transport about two hours into its flight, as three other fighters waited above the NATO base at Sigonella, flying elliptical combat air patrols to ensure the skies stayed open and safe. The American interceptors flashed their lights and dipped their wings—the message was clear: land or be shot down.

In the Situation Room, Revell and Assistant Attorney General Steve Trott took aside Admiral John Poindexter, the deputy national security advisor, and strongly urged him to bring the plane down anywhere but in Italy. It was too late: The Delta team was already in place, and the F-14s were already escorting the jetliner toward shore.

Anxious, Revell and the others listened to reports that began trickling back from Sigonella: The EgyptAir plane was safely on the tarmac. Delta had the plane surrounded. The Carabinieri had barged onto the base and now had Delta encircled. It appeared an armed showdown was imminent between NATO allies.

Fearing further escalation, Poindexter ordered Delta to stand down, and the Italian paramilitary police took the terrorists into custody. Behind the scenes, the Italian and American governments were livid at one another—and both were furious at the Egyptians, who had been ready to free the terrorists. Publicly, though, the U.S. government proclaimed the Italians' capture of the terrorists a victory. Unaware of what had transpired on the ground, the press was puzzled by the White House's seemingly muted response to the Italian capture of the terrorists.*

---

*Dispatched to Italy, FBI special agent Gary Noesner, working with other agents from the Washington Field Office's extraterritorial squad, questioned Youssef Majed al-Molqi, one of the hijackers. Noesner was a pioneer of the still-nascent

"Thank God we finally won one," said Senator Patrick Moynihan, who represented New York, Klinghoffer's home. *USA Today*'s front page trumpeted the American pride: "We Got 'Em." The *New York Daily News* was more direct: "We Bag the Bums." Echoing Joe Louis, President Reagan proclaimed the incident a "message to terrorists everywhere": "You can run, but you can't hide."

Back in the United States, public jubilation over the hijackers' capture was short-lived. Within days, the Italians—afraid, for the moment, that a prosecution would only bring more attacks on Italians at home and abroad—released hijacking ringleader Abu Abbas. Within months, Attorney General Ed Meese and Revell were on a plane to Italy to meet with the interior minister, Oscar Luigi Scalfaro. "How could the Americans have forced down a plane in Italian territory without the authority of the Italians?" Scalfaro asked the delegation during a meeting at the ministry in Rome, his emotion-filled eyes underscoring the depth of the betrayal he felt from his American "friends."

"How could the Italians have released a terrorist directly responsible for killing an American?" Meese shot back. It would be eighteen years, April 2003, when Abu Abbas was captured outside Baghdad by the U.S. military invading Iraq, until he'd again be in U.S. hands.

Following World War II, when the U.S. government set up the modern national security apparatus and delineated responsibilities, the CIA got everything overseas, and the FBI got everything domestically. At the time, the line between the two was clear and easy to follow. Over the coming decades, particularly with the rapid development of the

---

field of hostage negotiation and tried out some of his rapport-building techniques on the terrorist, who had thus far resisted the Italians' intense interrogations. Within hours, Molqi surprised the agents; when asked about what led to Klinghoffer's death, the terrorist explained his reasoning and finished by saying, "So I wheeled him to the side of the ship and shot him, then threw him overboard for all to see." Noesner was surprised: "This was an important moment for me, when I began to think about the distinction between interrogation and interviewing," he recalled later. "If the goal was to find out useful information, there were at least times when it made more sense to use a nonthreatening and relaxed manner and try to project some sense that we were trying to understand him."

internet and technology, the line between foreign and domestic would almost disappear. It was the passage of the Hostage Taking Act in 1984 and the Anti-Terrorism Act in 1986—the first so-called long-arm statutes, which made overseas attacks prosecutable in the United States—that put the FBI squarely on the CIA's foreign turf.

Well before then, though, the CIA and the FBI had a long and troubled history that dated back to the tense relationship between Hoover and "Wild Bill" Donovan, the founder of the World War II–era CIA predecessor, the Office of Strategic Services (OSS). In fact, if it wasn't for Hoover's legendary stubbornness, the CIA may never have even come into existence. At the outbreak of World War II, British intelligence pushed the U.S. government to establish a counterespionage force that could work in Europe and Asia; the FBI was at the time already handling all of the Western Hemisphere. The lead FBI counterintelligence official, Percy "Sam" Foxworth, who headed the New York Field Office, was floated as the Brits' preferred choice for the top spook. But Hoover didn't trust the British (the FBI had caught British agents breaking into friendly embassies in Washington), and he didn't trust Foxworth, who for all of his many professional accomplishments and talents was a problem case in Hoover's eyes. Explains historian Timothy Naftali, "Pudgy and a poor shot, Foxworth did not match the ideal picture of the model G-Man, and despite a series of cautionary letters accumulating in his personnel file, Foxworth seemed unwilling to lose his excess weight and appear regularly at the shooting range."

There are few more potent examples in U.S. history of a government official cutting off his nose to spite his face. Hoover's dogged stubbornness—and his vision of what an FBI agent should be—created the opening that allowed "Wild Bill" Donovan (the so-called father of U.S. intelligence) to slip in, gain power with the OSS, and eventually, after the war, convert it into the modern-day Central Intelligence Agency.

For decades, CIA station chiefs and the few overseas FBI legal attachés worked largely independently—in many cases, neither fully trusting the motives of the other. Further tension came from the fact that because domestic counterintelligence fell under the FBI's jurisdiction, it was the Bureau's responsibility to investigate the CIA for possible spies. FBI director William Webster and CIA director Admiral Stansfield Turner had some rapport—they had been freshmen together at Amherst College—but that only went so far. Later, Webster left the FBI to run the CIA, and while he retained a soft spot for the Bureau, it didn't make much difference on the operational level given the then-entrenched service rivalry.

That rivalry would only get worse after *Achille Lauro*. When the CIA came up empty in its quest for a terrorist scalp soon after the hijacking, the FBI stepped in and became the first U.S. agency to count coup in the still-obscure war on terror. The Bureau was taking down enemies—and in Langley, making them too.

Fawaz Younis, as one terrorism expert explained, was just a "second-tier hijacker." He wasn't the leader of a group; he wasn't particularly notorious; he hadn't even, as far as the United States knew at the time, been involved in the death of a single U.S. citizen. Dewey Clarridge, one of the pioneers of the CIA's antiterrorism efforts, recalled, "In all honesty, from one to ten on a scale of terrorism, Fawaz Younis was at best a three." But while the masterminds were still beyond the reach of the government in the war-torn Lebanon capital of Beirut, Younis was foolish enough to leave the besieged city.

The events that put Younis in the spotlight began on the morning of June 11, 1985, as a yellow Mercedes taxi screeched to a halt on the tarmac in Beirut, just feet from the stairs, as seventy-four passengers and crew were settling into a Royal Jordanian Boeing 727. Five hijackers got out and sprang into action. The ringleader, known on board as "Nazeeh," rushed the cockpit while his comrades went after the eight Jordanian air marshals on board. Surprised and quickly overpowered, the guards were bound, and a flight attendant showed the terrorists where the marshals' machine guns had been secretly stashed.

Nazeeh, whose real name was Fawaz Younis, belonged to a generation that had seen the Lebanon civil war for nearly half their lives. The long-running civil war between rival Palestinian factions, as well as Shiite, Sunni, and Christian militias, had taken tens of thousands of lives and turned Beirut, once a shining gem of the Middle East, into one of the worst cities on the planet. In 1979, at age twenty, Younis joined the militant Shiite Lebanese Amal group, yet he continued working as a used car salesman until 1984, when Amal seized full control of western Beirut. At that point, his active involvement with the most militant fringes kicked into higher gear. By the following year, he was gathering his four fellow terrorists, loading them up with weapons and ammunition, and setting out for the airport.

Younis ordered the pilot to fly to Tunis. He intended to land the plane during the ongoing Arab League meeting in Tunisia and demand the banishment of Palestinians from his home country — Palestinian refugees were a key source of tension amid the warring factions in Lebanon. As the hijacked plane winged across the Mediterranean, the terrorists tortured the Jordanian air marshals, burning them with cigarettes and striking them with bayonets. Their horrible screams filled the mostly silent airplane.

Caught off guard when the Tunisian government refused the plane permission to land, Younis directed the plane to Palermo, Sicily, where it refueled and authorities provided food. Then, again blocked from landing in Tunis, the plane returned to Beirut, where Younis demanded a meeting with the head of the Arab League and threatened to "deliver the corpses to him" if refused. The Boeing jet then took off for Syria, which also refused to let it land, before finally returning to Beirut. In the chaos that was Beirut at the time, additional terrorists joined Younis's team and planted explosives on board.

For his part, Younis disembarked and allowed the rest of the passengers, crew, and battered air marshals off, too. He read a statement to the press, after which his colleagues set off the onboard explosives. By the time the explosions and flames ceased, little was left of the plane. All seventy-four people survived the incident; yet, unfortunately for Younis, four of the passengers were American citizens. Under the recently passed long-arm statutes, that made his hijacking the FBI's problem.

Nearly a year passed before the United States began in earnest to investigate the incident. By that point, investigators had been repeatedly frustrated in another attempt to combat international terrorism. Just days after the Beirut hijacking, Hezbollah militants hijacked TWA Flight 847, en route from Athens to Rome, and murdered an American. The terrorists, having their demands for the release of Palestinian

118 • GARRETT M. GRAFF

prisoners rejected, tortured U.S. Navy Seabee Robert Stethem, shot him, and finally dumped his body on the tarmac of the Beirut airport, not far from the burned-out hulk of Younis's Royal Jordanian flight. Unsuccessful in its attempts to arrest the perpetrators of that incident, the United States would still be searching for three of the ringleaders after 9/11.★

In January 1986, President Reagan issued a classified "finding," allowing the CIA for the first time to kidnap terrorists overseas and bring them to face justice in the United States. With its new powers, the CIA attempted to capture Imad Mughniyeh, a notorious Hezbollah intelligence officer who went by the name Abu Dokhan, "Father of Smoke." He was believed to be responsible not just for the Flight 847 incident but also for the bombing of the U.S. embassy and Marine barracks in Beirut and the taking of some of the dozens of U.S. hostages being held in Beirut. After tracing him to Paris, the CIA tried to kidnap Mughniyeh from his hotel room—yet when agents burst in, they found instead of the terrorist mastermind an innocent, unrelated family.†

The CIA's efforts having failed, the FBI stepped ahead. "They had their shot, and they blew it," a Bureau official said at the time. The FBI would take a more realistic approach—and aim lower. With leaders like Mughniyeh proving beyond reach, it would try for a less important operative—Fawaz Younis. "He was a target because of opportunity," Revell says. For months, the FBI painstakingly assem-

---

★ Three of the alleged Flight 847 hijackers were named to the first iteration of the FBI's Most Wanted Terrorists list in 2002.

† For the next two decades, Mughniyeh would remain an elusive target of the FBI's international terrorism search. During that time, he would add to his demonic legend via his involvement in the Khobar Towers attack in Saudi Arabia in 1996, which killed nineteen Americans. Mughniyeh would eventually be killed by a car bomb in Damascus, Syria, in 2008. While the United States suggested that he was targeted by rival factions, evidence suggests the attack was likely the work of the Israeli Mossad. Either way, the United States was happy to see him finally go—said State Department spokesman Sean McCormack: "The world is a better place without this man in it. He was a cold-blooded killer, a mass murderer, and a terrorist responsible for countless innocent lives lost. One way or another, he was brought to justice."

bled evidence for a warrant. By the fall of 1986, the high-level working group composed of representatives from the CIA, FBI, DEA, and the National Security Council was ready. Now came the hard part: After the *Achille Lauro* debacle, the FBI knew it had to snatch Younis in international waters and transport him back to the United States through international territory; he couldn't set foot on any foreign territory between his capture and his arrival in the United States, lest a foreign government demand the right to prosecute him. Nobody wanted a repeat of the Sicilian fiasco.

After previous operations had bogged down partially because of the chain of approval and bureaucracy, the Younis takedown would be handled at the highest levels. In early 1987, Secretary of State George Shultz, CIA director William Casey, and the FBI's William Webster signed a secret authorization for the FBI to go after Younis. The plan was dubbed Operation Goldenrod.

Jamal Hamdan, a DEA informant in Lebanon, would be the bait. He had been a mentor to the used-car-salesman-turned-terrorist, at one time hiring Younis as his driver. Their relationship had been interrupted when Hamdan went to jail for killing his own sister-in-law in a fit of rage after suspecting her of being a prostitute. When he was released and moved to Cyprus, Hamdan had been recruited by the DEA, which, on learning of his affiliation with Younis, turned him over to the CIA in a rare act of interagency cooperation. From March to September 1987, Hamdan and Younis had more than sixty telephone conversations and three in-person meetings. U.S. investigators were surprised to learn during a covertly recorded July meeting that Younis had also been involved in the TWA Flight 847 hijacking. Hamdan asked Younis why he'd taken part in the hijackings. The disillusioned young terrorist replied, "Because I'm a donkey," implying that he was stupid for accepting the offer.

The following month, after listening to yet another complaint from Younis about his lack of money, Hamdan offered Younis the opportunity to join him in a drug-smuggling scheme—the trap decided on by the FBI. Younis eagerly accepted. Unlike domestic fugitive captures, which the FBI executes daily, this operation would have to be run four thousand miles from U.S. soil. The CIA, while better versed in foreign operations, shared the logistical challenge:

Their planes lacked the ability to fly the required distances without a refueling stop. As a result, there was only one option, an aircraft carrier. Buck Revell began to call around—would the navy mind if the FBI borrowed a $200 million ship, complete with ninety aircraft and five thousand sailors and Marines?

For the USS *Saratoga,* landing a role in Operation Goldenrod came with the hope of some delicious payback, since F-14s from the ship had earlier forced the *Achille Lauro* hijackers to land, only to have them slip away afterward. Now the ship's crew had a chance to ensure Younis wouldn't be so lucky.

As the first days of September ticked by, Hamdan held off the eager Younis, who was desperate for money and wanted to get the deal under way. On September 8, Revell was on his way to the airport when he got the final call from Attorney General Ed Meese. "It's a go, it's a go!" the attorney general said excitedly after meeting with President Reagan, adding, "Don't come back without him."

Revell flew to Italy and helicoptered aboard the aircraft carrier battle group's command ship, the USS *Butte.* He was joined by the case agents, a CIA officer, and a quick reaction force from the Hostage Rescue Team—the first time Danny Coulson's elite group had been sent overseas as part of a U.S. operation.

In Athens, a CIA front company rented a pleasure yacht, *Skunk Kilo,* and a team of FBI agents sailed into international waters off Cyprus. It was one of the stranger assignments in FBI history: On board were HRT operators, including Woody Johnson, the new team commander who had taken Coulson's place, as well as an FBI agent who was a licensed sailor and two female agents from the Washington Field Office whose main role was to look alluring as Younis approached. On the morning of September 13, Hamdan and Younis, along with Hamdan's brother, set out from the Sheraton Marina—tardy because Younis had been up late partying the night before. The *Butte* was idling just off the twelve-mile international limit, and as the minutes ticked by, Revell grew even more anxious. "He was no show, no show, no show," the FBI executive recalls. "I almost caused another international incident. If it came down to it, if they didn't come all the way out, I told the navy commodore we were going to go in and get him." From shore, a massive CIA operation was watching the whole thing go down from an executive suite at the local Sheraton Hotel, a few floors above where Younis and Hamdan had been staying.

As Younis's launch finally approached, the two female agents lounged on deck in halter tops and shorts. (The FBI had vetoed the CIA's suggestion of bikinis.) Younis was frisked as he was brought aboard, offered a beer, and led to the back of the eighty-one-foot yacht. Then, standing on either side of him, Special Agents Donald Glasser and George Gast knocked Younis's legs out from under him and brought him crashing to the deck. (Agents later learned that that fall broke both Younis's wrists—a fact that would become a point of contention in subsequent court proceedings, as the hijacker's lawyers argued he had been mistreated and abused as a prisoner.) Special Agent Dimitry Droujinsky, who was fluent in Arabic, advised Younis of his rights and told him he was under arrest. "When we told him we were FBI and not the Israelis, he was relieved," Revell recalls.

Johnson radioed the *Butte:* "Hey boss, it's him and we got him." Everyone whooped. Within moments, Revell and a support team were rocketing across the water as quickly as the admiral's launch could carry them. A dejected and surprised Younis was placed in the bow and offered a soda and some melon.

As the navy crew raised the launch back on board, carrying Revell, Younis, and other agents, the winch motor burned out. For several long minutes, the launch hung over the Mediterranean, swinging back and forth in suspended animation. The day's events, coupled probably with a hangover from his previous night of partying and nervousness about what lay ahead, finally hit Younis. With his hands cuffed behind him, he leaned over the side of the launch and vomited.

After a doctor's checkup, agents again advised Younis in Arabic of his *Miranda* rights. Younis began to talk, figuring he had little to lose. For four days, the FBI agents debriefed Younis on board the *Butte* as it steamed west to meet the *Saratoga.* Younis explained he had become quite disillusioned with Amal, especially after the organization refused to help him out with his medical expenses following a motorcycle accident. Younis, additionally, was annoyed that he hadn't received as a thank-you one of the machine guns taken from the sky marshals in the Royal Jordanian hijacking—everyone else in the hijacking team had gotten one. Never asking to see an attorney, Younis quickly admitted his role in the hijackings and then proceeded to give the FBI and the CIA some of the most valuable intelligence on terrorist operations in Beirut that they had ever acquired. Agents questioned him closely about the hostages, the hostage takers, and daily life in Beirut, as well as about the hierarchy and leadership of the various terrorist groups in Lebanon, such as Hezbollah and Amal.

The agents and Younis developed an almost regular routine: Younis would wake up, have breakfast, go for a walk or sit outside with the agents taking in the sea air, then talk for a while until he got tired or hungry, then after a nap or a meal—liver was a particular favorite—they'd continue the interview. On one of the final afternoons before arriving at the *Saratoga,* while sitting on deck in the fresh air, an agent declared what a beautiful day it was. "Not for me," Younis said sullenly.

At the conclusion of the interviews on the fourth day, after fingerprinting and photographing Younis, the two FBI agents—Tom Hansen and Droujinsky—presented Younis with a summary of his comments written in Arabic. He carefully read through them, made a single change to the document, initialed it, and handed it back to the FBI.

At 5 A.M. on September 17, the final phase of Operation Goldenrod began. Philip Voss, commander of the *Saratoga's* antisubmarine wing, had been informed, much to his dismay, that he would personally be flying the long-haul mission. And the FBI planned to fill every other seat in the jet—with a flight surgeon, a heavily sedated Younis, and two HRT operators—so Voss wouldn't have a copilot or navigator for the longest flight an S-3 Viking had ever attempted. Revell, a former Marine aviator, knew the pain of the long journey ahead: He'd once flown for twelve straight hours in his helicopter during a mission and on landing had to be carried from the cockpit. Voss was in for an even longer ride.

CH-46 helicopters shuttled the FBI team and its prisoner to the deck of the *Saratoga* as Voss strapped himself into his $40 million jet. High overhead was a KC-10 tanker that had flown thirteen hours nonstop from Seymour Johnson Air Force Base in North Carolina to accompany Voss across the Atlantic. The catapult launch off the carrier, where steam pressure propelled the plane to a speed of more than 150 miles per hour in just the length of a football field, left the FBI agents gasping.

After a midair refuel over the carrier, Voss set off west; two F-14s flew escort for the first hundred miles. After that, the two planes would be defenseless until they reached the U.S. coast. Flying through the Strait of Gilbraltar, Voss followed a carefully planned path through international waters. At various points across the Atlantic, other tankers met the two planes, since the midair refueling tanker required its own midair refueling. To evade radar in the final stretch—secrecy was such that the FAA hadn't even been told of the flight—Voss expertly flew in the shadow of the tanker, mere yards off the giant plane's fuselage.

Just before 3:45 P.M., the good news came: "Diamond 702, you are clear to make an approach into Andrews Air Force Base," the radio cackled. By the time Voss touched down on one of the wide runways, the trip had set three world records: the longest flight ever by an S-3 Viking jet, the longest flight ever off an aircraft carrier, and the longest flight ever by a KC-10 refueling plane.★

On September 17, at 4:45 P.M. Washington local time, a freshly showered Younis stood in a Washington, D.C., courtroom, under heavy guard of U.S. marshals, facing charges of hostage taking, conspiracy, and destruction of an aircraft. The five-count indictment, filed by the U.S. attorney for the District of Columbia, Joseph diGenova, and under seal for nearly a year, was a dry read compared to the dramatic operation that had led to Younis standing on American soil. "It is a major policy goal of the United States Government that we bring to justice those who are accused of being responsible for terrorist crimes," Ed Meese told journalists at a press conference after the surprise capture and arraignment. "It is the first such operation, but it will most certainly not be the last."

Lebanon vigorously protested Younis's arrest, but the United States ignored the complaints. The arrest had the desired impact: For months afterward, other terrorist leaders refused to leave Lebanon, fearing American capture. While the operation proved the United States

---

★ After the mission's end, the navy tried to bill the FBI for the use of its resources in the capture. The Bureau told the service to take up the matter with the president. "The air refueling alone would have blown our budget for years," Revell said, laughing.

could go anywhere to get international terrorists, it also demonstrated to the FBI how unprepared the U.S. legal system was for the new era of terrorism. The court initially threw out Younis's confession, arguing that the four days of interrogation aboard the *Butte* was excessive. The FBI and government appealed, and an appeals court upheld the confession, even though it chastised the FBI for the lengthy questioning sessions. "The court just had no concept of intelligence," Revell says ruefully. Younis would end up serving roughly half of his thirty-year sentence in federal prison. In March 2005, U.S. Immigration and Customs Enforcement (ICE) deported him to Lebanon.

Over the coming years, the Justice Department would regularly flex the muscles it began to develop with Younis's case. In 1989, Robert Mueller, then the assistant attorney general in charge of the Justice Department's criminal division, helped lead the team that went after Panamanian dictator Manuel Noriega. In that case, known as Operation Just Cause, the entire weight of the U.S. military was brought to bear in arresting Noriega. For the first time, the military was used to capture an indicted criminal for prosecution in the United States. Much of the controversy over Noriega's capture and subsequent detention, trial, and sentencing foreshadowed the debate over al-Qaeda detainees years later.

Noriega repeatedly pled that he should be considered a prisoner of war and that his treatment violated the Geneva Convention. The U.S. government agreed to certain provisions in his care and treatment, consistent with his rights as a prisoner of war, but still considered him a criminal defendant. This view put the Justice Department at odds with groups like Human Rights Watch, which argued that because the U.S. military had been deployed to effect his arrest, Noriega was eligible for prisoner-of-war status. "It is, moreover, irrelevant whether or not the entire invasion of Panama was conceived, for U.S. purposes, as merely a gigantic posse undertaking an arrest," Human Rights Watch argued in court. "The fact remains that it was an international armed conflict."

Mueller, responding on the president's behalf to Noriega's lawyer, rejected the pleas. "Your client is in civilian custody for violations of domestic criminal law," Mueller wrote. "The Geneva Convention was not designed to resolve issues of domestic criminal pretrial detainees. Moreover, we believe that no provision of the Convention has been violated and that your client's detention comports with all appropriate laws and standards."

Through the 1980s, the FBI's new focus on counterterrorism paid dividends. At Buck Revell's urging, new legal attachés were assigned overseas, and salaries were raised to attract more qualified agents. By the end of President Reagan's second term, the FBI was able to point to at least fifty-three terrorist operations it had stopped or disrupted during the 1980s—incidents that underscored terrorism's clear and present danger to the United States, even if most of the public remained blissfully unaware of the shadow war playing out across the country and around the world. In 1982, the same year that terrorism was officially elevated to an FBI national priority, agents had arrested three members of the Armenian Secret Army for the Liberation of Armenia as they attempted to plant a bomb in the Air Canada cargo area at Los Angeles International Airport. The following year, in 1983, the FBI had interrupted a plot by Ayatollah Khomeini sympathizers to firebomb a movie theater in Seattle, Washington. Surveilling the group, FBI agents found it had already assembled the explosives and gasoline necessary for the attack and mapped out how to execute it. Two years later, agents in New Orleans had brought down a cell of Sikhs who planned to assassinate Indian prime minister Rajiv Gandhi during a visit to the Big Easy; the case proved particularly disturbing to agents because the plotters were U.S. residents—a rare issue at the time. The same radical group was suspected in two Air India bombings that had killed hundreds of passengers, as well as a thwarted attempt at a third.

Perhaps the most disturbing of the plots was the 1985 investigation of the El Rukn Street Gang, a Chicago group that had broken away from the Black Panthers and had attempted to purchase a shoulder-fired surface-to-air rocket. Further FBI investigation uncovered that the group had been subcontracted by Libyan intelligence to shoot down an airliner as it departed Chicago's O'Hare Airport. But what really spooked the Bureau was that the plot was far enough along that by the time the five group members were arrested, they had already chosen the specific flight to destroy. Agents in the counterterrorism section realized just how close they'd come to a major disaster on U.S. soil.

If the El Rukn investigation came to define everything that went right in the FBI's budding war against international terrorism, the investigation of the Committee in Solidarity with the People of El Salvador (CISPES) came to define what would happen when an FBI investigation ran amok. CISPES, a version of which continues to this day, started in the fall of 1980 to provide international support to the movement in El Salvador to overthrow the U.S.-backed government. By backing the guerilla organization known as the FMLN—the Farabundo Martí National Liberation Front—CISPES showed up on the FBI's radar. FMLN had been involved in kidnappings and murders and was suspected of assassinating at least one U.S. official in El Salvador. In the summer of 1981, the Department of Justice requested that the FBI determine whether CISPES was required to register as a foreign agent.

Within two years, the FBI had begun to investigate whether the group was facilitating or funding terrorism abroad. Thanks to a quirk of U.S. law, any group that supported revolutionary activity abroad was considered a "terrorist" group—even if it was a prodemocracy movement against a cruel, autocratic dictator. Thus, no matter how well meaning or munificent the goal of FMLN, any American backing to it was considered terrorist support. The original investigation had come soon after three bombings in the Washington area, including one at the U.S. Capitol and another at a military installation near Washington where a group claimed responsibility in solidarity with the people of El Salvador. Initially, the focus was primarily on the group's Washington headquarters and the Dallas chapter, where a Central American expat named Frank Varelli was operating as an informant to the FBI, in an investigation run by Special Agent Daniel Flanagan. In October 1983, the scope greatly expanded to include all local CISPES chapters. As was required by the guidelines governing foreign intelligence investigations, the Department of Justice twice signed off on continuing the case. In June 1983, the Justice Department ruled that the CISPES case no longer met the requirements to continue investigation, and the FBI shuttered the case.

A year later, El Salvador remained a hot-button political topic, and the FBI reopened the case amid nebulous threats to President Reagan and a commercial airliner. In July 1984, FBI Headquarters sent out a directive emphasizing how critical it was that the investigation be "closely supervised" to ensure that it didn't go off the rails or spread too wide. "Political activities or political lobbying by CISPES... are not, repeat not, targets of this investigation," the memo instructed. Unfortunately, the strict language sent by headquarters didn't match the actions. For some two years, the CISPES investigation continued, though it lacked intensity and made little progress. While thousands of possible suspects (almost all of whom were innocent) and hundreds of leads were wrapped up in the files, none led to a criminal prosecution. All told, nearly two hundred different spin-off investigations grew out of the original CISPES focus.*

The investigation didn't come to the attention of top-level Bureau executives until Flanagan's car was burglarized. When he reported a set of files had been stolen, the extent of the problems with the CISPES case began to come clear. At headquarters, Revell ordered a quick investigation to determine what was in the missing files and was horrified to learn the extent of the disorganized, poorly coordinated, and wide-ranging wild goose chase.

FBI officials involved in the matter still get worked up discussing the investigation. "Everything that could go wrong did go wrong," says Steve Pomerantz, a Bureau executive who ran the after-the-fact investigation for the FBI's inspection division. "It was a bad investigation with a bad informant with a bad agent with bad supervision."

The FBI's follow-up inspection of the file cost some $800,000, roughly as much as the entire original investigation. The chief informant, Varelli, had slipped through a series of holes: His background wasn't checked, his contradictory claims weren't reconciled, and his information wasn't fully vetted. "Mr. Varelli provided a mixed bag of information. Some of his information has proven to be correct. Some

---

*Some of these spin-offs later made headlines: A Xavier University professor was investigated after a final exam question in one of his classes asked about students' opinions of Central American policy; the name of the Maryknoll Sisters appeared in FBI files, prompting derision when the story broke that the FBI could consider a peaceful group of missionary nuns a threat to national security.

of his information was blatantly false. Some of it was concocted out of his own mind, and some of it was fabricated on the basis of contacts that he had initiated in El Salvador," Revell recalled later.

Varelli's agent contact had his own set of problems. In fact, in reviewing the case, FBI officials found to their dismay that the only criminality uncovered by the multi-year investigation was by Daniel Flanagan himself. Flanagan, the FBI inspectors determined, had both improperly given Varelli classified documents as well as withheld payments—that is, he'd stolen money from his own informant. The focus on CISPES, which, whatever the FBI claimed, appeared to be motivated by political pressure from the White House, was at best a colossal waste of time and money, and at worst evidence of an agency driven by a right-wing vendetta.

As the story exploded in the press and allegations swirled, the FBI tried to defend its actions while admitting mistakes. "When the information we have points toward even a remote possibility of terrorism on these shores, it is the Bureau's sworn duty to investigate the matter fully," William Sessions said. "At the same time, the mistakes of judgment that took place during the CISPES investigation were serious ones."

One of the most damaging charges to Bureau morale publicly, and privately, was that FBI agents had been breaking into CISPES offices for "black bag jobs" like those of Hoover's day. Even though Bureau officials swore that the FBI had never broken into any CISPES office— and no proof ever surfaced—it was a damaging allegation. Critics found it easy to point to COINTELPRO and CISPES and say the FBI was out of control. Fred Stremmel, the FBI analyst, recalls the case's "demoralizing impact on the counterterrorism program." He says, "After CISPES, it was much harder to open a full investigation on U.S. persons."

In the end, three FBI agents were censured and suspended for fourteen days, three others received censures, and Flanagan resigned rather than face dismissal. Critics said the domestic security and intelligence portfolio should be permanently separated from the FBI's criminal investigations. Critics announced it was time to break off those areas from the FBI and start a new agency—just as Canada was in the process of doing right then. Most other Western countries had the same split; Britain had New Scotland Yard for criminal matters and MI5 for domestic security issues. Perhaps it was time to do the same thing in the United States.

The United States has always struggled with the balance of free speech and liberty, particularly during times of war. Often, under duress, the Constitution has temporarily given way. During the Civil War, Abraham Lincoln fought a running battle over his power to suspend the Constitution's habeas corpus provision. The Alien and Sedition Acts of the late 1700s and the Sedition Act of 1918 focused on whether the government could halt or punish speech because of its likelihood to harm the United States. During World War I, in a case called *Schenck v. United States,* Justice Oliver Wendell Holmes provided the standard on which future incursions of free speech would be judged. The particular case focused on whether Congress could restrict speech against the draft, considered crucial to the U.S. war effort. Holmes wrote,

> The question in every case is whether the words used are used in such circumstances and are of such a nature as to create a *clear and present danger* that they will bring about the substantive evils that the United States Congress has a right to prevent. It is a question of proximity and degree. When a nation is at war, many things that might be said in time of peace are such a hindrance to its effort that their utterance will not be endured so long as men fight, and that no Court could regard them as protected by any constitutional right.

In a later decision, *Brandenburg v. Ohio,* the "clear and present danger" standard evolved further to focus on whether speech would likely provoke an "imminent lawless action."

Revell found himself, in the press and in front of Congress, defending not just the FBI's investigation into CISPES, but also the FBI's entire counterterrorism and domestic security program. Since it is always easier for the human mind to focus on the one thing that happened rather than on the fifty-three incidents that didn't, Revell was in the hot seat. Pointing to the interdicted incidents—the El Rukn gang's planned shoot-down, the Air India bombing, the assassination plot against Rajiv Gandhi, and so on—Revell tried to explain that the FBI and U.S. agencies had a near-perfect record. "If these incidents had indeed occurred, then the United States would be seen as a center for terrorism," he said to Congress. "We have been able to put together a coalition of our intelligence services, our law enforcement agencies, and acted, under law, to prevent terrorism before the bomb went off."

However, when it came to civil liberties in a democracy, near perfection was rarely good enough. A heated back-and-forth with Republican senator Arlen Specter in one congressional hearing revealed the divide between more aggressive FBI agents and those who feared that the CISPES investigation had uncovered a Bureau that considered itself exempt from constitutional restraints. When the Bureau had initiated the CISPES investigation, Revell explained, the FBI agents in the CISPES matter had good intentions—an echo of what Mark Felt had argued a decade before. "All I can try and do is explain what was in their minds. There is a subjective basis to this analysis process in meeting certain standards. I can't say that in every instance they were correct in their analysis," Revell explained.

"I have grave problems with that. If you talk about a state of mind of a witness in a trial, that's one thing. When you are talking about trained investigators in the FBI, I think you have to be proceeding on the basis of tangible hard facts," Specter replied.

Revell tried to point out that everything started as intelligence— the FBI was obligated to investigate leads as they came in, unsure what would pan out and what wouldn't. The FBI investigated hundreds of leads that never led to criminal activity. The key was to shut the wrong investigations down quickly, before trampling on an innocent suspect's civil liberties.

Specter wasn't having any of it.

"In a democratic society such as ours, perhaps we should wait until a bomb goes off before we act," he said.

"In that case, Senator, there's going to be a lot of blood in the street," Revell shot back.

The FBI had made its own mess, but as animosity toward its actions evolved into profound skepticism of its motives, it was easy for the Bureau to shift its perception of blame to those shining the spotlights.

Hadn't the agency—from then director William Sessions on down— admitted fault? If the CISPES investigation had been an extreme, did it really make sense to swing to another? "The counterterrorism section was effectively neutralized," Revell concluded later. "Agents would be only too happy to work noncontroversial cases, such as bank robberies and kidnappings. To work counterterrorism was to become a target for the wildest and cruelest of accusations a law enforcement officer could possibly endure."

The New York Field Office, seeing what had happened to the agents and supervisors who became wrapped up in CISPES, balked at investigating a group with suspected terrorists in New York. In November 1990, Rabbi Meir Kahane, an American-born Israeli politician and the founder of the Jewish Defense League, was assassinated after a speech at a New York City Marriott. Police chased down the suspect, El Sayyid A. Nosair, blocks away, after he also tried to kill a postal police officer.

Despite the urgings of other Bureau leaders for a more thorough investigation—the suspect seemed to have ties to a sketchy group of Middle Easterners who were training with firearms in military-like settings around the greater New York City area—the case was quickly shut down. The post-CISPES environment left little room for error. Nosair's compatriots would become, years later, the terror cell that attacked the World Trade Center in 1993. In fact, the suspect who drove the bomb truck into the basement was Nosair's roommate.

"You can't draw a straight line from CISPES to 9/11," concludes Steve Pomerantz, "but you can certainly draw a jagged dotted line from CISPES to 9/11." Added another FBI counterterrorism official, "Without CISPES, would the first World Trade Center attack have ever happened? I'm not sure. Without the first World Trade Center attack, would the second one have ever happened? I don't think so."

CHAPTER 5
SCOTBOM

Where, I ask, is the justice?
— *Robert Mueller*

For three generations, dating from the beginning of commercial flight in the 1920s until the end of the 1990s, and long before discount airlines such as JetBlue, Southwest, and Virgin America plied the skies, Pan American World Airways was unofficially "America's airline." It emanated American strength and dominance — its headquarters in New York, the Pan Am Building, and its terminal at John F. Kennedy International Airport, on Long Island, were the largest buildings of their kind in the world — and its planes, with their iconic blue-globe logo, touched down daily on every continent but Antarctica. The airline was so confident that Pan Am even established, at the height of the space race in the 1960s, a "waiting list" for passengers who wanted to sign up for the first commercial flights to the moon. Pan Am's powerful planes carried the Beatles to the United States, ferried James Bond around on his missions, and were a daily reminder to passengers worldwide of the rising hegemony of the United States. It was almost natural that it would be on board a Pan Am flight that the United States would experience its first massive civilian casualties as a result of international terrorism.

On December 21, 1988, Flight 103, Pan Am's regularly scheduled London–New York flight, carrying 243 passengers and 16 crew, closed its doors for departure. Within an hour, the 747, nicknamed Maid of the Seas, had settled into a routine late-night flight over the Scottish border. Fully loaded, the plane weighed more than 600,000 pounds. The bomb that brought the plane down weighed less than a pound.

Some six miles above the Scottish village of Lockerbie, the explosion punched a hole in the side of the airplane, cracking the fuselage and sucking passengers out into the freezing darkness of the Scottish night. Within three seconds, the nose of the plane had torn off. Wreckage spewed from the doomed airliner, filling the night sky for miles as the plane hurtled forward at 500 miles per hour. It took some of the victims as long as three minutes to fall to earth; investigators were never able to determine whether they were conscious for the interminable fall, although many were most certainly alive.

As this happened, a controller at the North Atlantic's Shanwick Oceanic Area Air Traffic Control watched with confusion as the radar blip labeled PA103 suddenly became hundreds of smaller blips, much like a starburst, and then disappeared entirely. The main section of the plane, with its fuel-packed wings, hit the earth and exploded with a force large enough to register at a British Geological Survey seismic monitoring station. The machine's needle marked the time as 36.5 seconds after 7:03 P.M.

As they wandered out of their houses into a landscape dotted with fire, bodies, and wreckage, the thirty-five hundred inhabitants of Lockerbie quickly realized something terrible had transpired. As resident Mike Carnahan later told a local TV reporter, "The whole sky was lit up with flames. It was actually raining, liquid fire. You could see several houses on the skyline with the roofs totally off and all you could see was flaming timbers."

At 7:33, Britain's Channel Four interrupted its programming to announce the crash. Chief Constable John Boyd, the head of the Dumfries and Galloway police, was at the local station by 8:15 P.M. The scale of the calamity almost immediately overwhelmed him. While no jurisdiction in the world would have been fully prepared for a disaster the magnitude of Pan Am 103's bombing, Lockerbie on December 21, 1988, was perhaps uniquely unsuited. The Dumfries and Galloway Constabulary, which was responsible for the unforgiving surrounding landscape of moors, lakes, and valleys, was the smallest police force in Britain. It was the darkest day of the year in a part of the world where winter daylight filled only eight hours of the day. For the investigators, there was only one piece of luck: If the explosion had come just a few minutes later, the wreckage would have fallen into the Atlantic, forever burying it below miles of ocean.

That first night, there was nothing but chaos. Fires burned fiercely as police and citizens searched for survivors. There were none from the plane, and eleven Lockerbie residents had been killed by falling wreckage. At the local headquarters, Boyd plotted on maps the reports of debris and bodies. By 9 P.M., the first victim arrived: A farmer from the nearby village of Tundergarth came to town hall with the body of a baby he'd carefully placed in a sack. The rules of collecting evidence and careful investigation were set aside by necessity.

Since Pan Am 103 had been a U.S.-flagged carrier bound for home, American officials were involved from the start, yet despite the huge resources of the multibillion-dollar U.S. government intelligence operation, the FBI first learned of the bombing from CNN. Buck Revell, sitting in his office doing paperwork before taking off for the holidays, looked up from his desk to see the first sketchy reports of trouble from Lockerbie. He immediately called FBI director William Sessions. "It was a seven forty-seven," Revell told him, predicting major casualties. "Usually, this time of year, they're full." At its headquarters, Pan Am scrambled to respond too. The first draft of the passenger list was incomplete and inaccurate; days would pass before the airline could answer fully who had boarded the plane in London. Officials quickly came to believe a bomb had brought the plane down for the simple reason that modern airliners didn't just break up in midair on their own.

From the start, the FBI investigators engaged in Lockerbie had a guiding refrain: "Not another Zia." Just four months earlier, the plane of Pakistani president Muhammad Zia-ul-Haq had crashed after takeoff, killing the American ambassador to Pakistan, a U.S. Army brigadier general, and other members of the U.S. delegation. It had taken more than ten days for the FBI to get approval to send a team to Pakistan—the big holdup was the new U.S. ambassador, Robert Oakley, who thought the FBI would "complicate" the situation—and by the time investigators arrived, the evidence had been collected and destroyed.*

The Pan Am 103 case, investigators hoped, wouldn't be the same. A special U.S. Air Force jet whisked the American ambassador to Great Britain and Special Agent Tim Dorch, the assistant legal attaché in London, to Lockerbie, the first wave of a veritable deluge of U.S. aid that would descend on the small Scottish town in the coming weeks. At 2 A.M. in Lockerbie, less than seven hours after the wreckage of Pan Am 103 had begun to fall from the sky, Scottish investigator Boyd announced during his first staff meeting, "The FBI is here and they are fully operational."

Back home, the FBI's top explosives technician left for Scotland. Special Agent James Thurman, who had a master's degree in forensic science and had graduated from the navy's Explosive Ordnance Disposal school before joining the FBI, had more than a decade of experience investigating the most difficult explosives cases for the Bureau. Over the coming months, two FBI agents would remain permanently stationed at Lockerbie as the nascent investigation grew into a formal command center; they stayed, eventually, for three years. The FBI even installed an encrypted telephone link in the Lockerbie command post to make possible secure conversations with Washington.

The next morning, more help flooded into Lockerbie, even as police realized the daunting task ahead: Searching the countryside for clues would take months, retrieving the bodies alone might take weeks. By afternoon, amazingly, police had uncovered the first evidence of a bomb—wreckage found near Tundergarth had obvious signs of scorching consistent with a detonation. Field-testing of the wreckage detected traces of PETN and RDX, two key ingredients of Semtex explosive. The response to Pan Am 103 was officially becoming a criminal matter. That same day, Detective Chief Inspector Harry Bell, one of Scotland's most accomplished investigators, arrived to

---

* While the final theory of the case involved mechanical problems in the C-130, it's hard to say whether an earlier arrival by the FBI would have led to a different conclusion. The Pakistanis insisted, without obvious evidence, that a mysterious gas had rendered everyone aboard unconscious and led to the plane's crash.

help. Bell, with John Orr, detective chief superintendent of the nearby Strathclyde police force, and Stuart Henderson—who later replaced John Boyd—would lead the investigation in the coming years.

During the brief stretches of daylight, much of it punctuated by the cold rain and fog that mark Scottish winters, investigators began to divide the search area into regions—the smallest, Sector B, alone covered 58 square miles. Every inch of some 845 square miles would have to be scoured by investigators, most of it more than once. Tens of thousands of pieces of evidence were collected, enough that over time investigators were able to rebuild more than 85 percent of the plane on a metal scaffold in Longtown, Scotland. The thoroughness of the search was underscored to investigators when, in the early days of the investigation, a Federal Aviation Administration official had lost his hearing aid during a preliminary search of a bog. It turned up days later in a bag of evidence collected during a subsequent search. The last items wouldn't be found until early spring 1990, more than sixteen months after the crash.

The Lockerbie crash was then and remains today the single largest crime scene ever investigated. By the end, investigators would follow nearly 10,000 independent leads and interview some 16,000 witnesses in more than 50 countries. The passengers and crew on Pan Am 103 alone came from 21 countries, and investigators fanned out across the world to gather dental records, fingerprints, and other information that would help identify the bodies.

If a bomb had brought down the flight, investigators reasoned, there were three possible ways that the device might have been brought on board. First, it might have been carried on by a suicide bomber, and while no such attack had previously targeted civil aviation, the rise of Palestinian suicide bombings validated the possibility. The second theory proposed a "mule"—an otherwise innocent passenger who had carried aboard an explosive device provided by someone else, perhaps hidden in a gift, as had happened in the 1986 attempted bombing of an El Al flight, when a Syrian intelligence agent working undercover persuaded his fiancée to carry a bomb aboard the flight unknowingly. Third was the "inside man" theory, that an airport employee of some kind had exploited security loopholes to smuggle the bomb on board.

Investigators began by exploring the first two possibilities, identifying all the passengers, their backgrounds, their ties, and their habits, searching for anything that would indicate either a possible terrorist or a mule. The initial investigations led to many uncomfortable conversations with victims' families in the early days after the crash. One by one, victims were eliminated as possible suspects. At the same time, several victims turned out to be U.S. government personnel, including several involved in the high-stakes Beirut hostage negotiations. Were any of them targeted because of this connection?

On Christmas Eve, a constable working in the Newcastleton Forest found a piece of a luggage pallet with obvious scorching—a sign that the bomb had been in the luggage compartment below the passenger cabin. Tagged as evidence, the luggage frame was a key clue; police shut down the motorway so that it could be rushed at full speed to the laboratory at the Royal Armament Research and Development Establishment. The British equivalent, in forensics terms, of the FBI's storied lab, RARDE had a much older pedigree: It dated its founding to the Guy Fawkes Gunpowder Plot to blow up Parliament and kill King James I in 1605. On December 26, the British government called L. Paul Bremer III, the State Department ambassador-at-large for combating terrorism, with the news that everyone had been waiting for: RARDE officially thought a bomb had caused the explosion.*

While the FBI had been involved in the crash investigation from the first hours, the explosive residue officially activated one of the long-arm statutes, which made it the FBI's responsibility to investigate any terrorism that killed American citizens. The Pan Am 103 investigation quickly pulled in agents from around the country. Special Agent Neil Herman—who would later lead the FBI's counterterrorism efforts in New York before 9/11—was tasked with interviewing some of the victims' families. New Year's Eve found him heading up a long, winding driveway to visit the parents of one student victim (a group from Syracuse University had been aboard the flight). Herman and his partner found the house dark; their knocks at the front and the back doors went unanswered. They were about to slip their cards into the door and head back to New York when Herman spied a darkened

---

* Bremer would go on to be President George W. Bush's viceroy in Baghdad after the 2003 invasion of Iraq.

figure through the window in the living room. The grieving mother was sitting in the dark alone, with no support network, no friends or family to keep her company. The agents ended up talking to her for more than four hours, late into the night, piecing together her child's life, gathering descriptions of his luggage and so on, but mostly just listening to a heartbroken mother. No one from the government had spoken to her in the ten days since the holiday attack. "It really struck me how ill equipped we were to deal with this," Herman says. "Multiply her by two hundred and seventy victims and families."

As more wreckage was painstakingly recovered, investigators zeroed in on luggage pallet AVE4041, which, according to loading records, had been placed at station 14L on the left side of the forward cargo hold. The bomb had evidently been right behind the "P" in the Pan Am logo on the side of the plane. Further wreckage, pieced together and examined by RARDE, pointed to a recovered Japanese-manufactured Toshiba cassette recorder as the likely containment device for the bomb. By the end of January, investigators had begun to locate wreckage belonging to the suitcase that had held the bomb. After determining that it was a Samsonite bag, police flew to the company's headquarters and narrowed the search further: That specific case had been made for only three years, 1985 to 1988, and sold only in the Middle East, although with 3,500 such suitcases in circulation, that knowledge didn't help much.

The early months of the investigation were filled with dead ends, wild theories, and intriguing possibilities. Within hours of the crash, a man with a thick accent phoned the Associated Press and UPI offices in London and read a short statement referring to the accidental shoot-down of an Iranian airliner by the USS *Vincennes* in the summer of 1988 that had killed 290 civilians: "We, the Guardians of the Islamic Revolution, are undertaking this heroic execution in revenge of blowing the Iran Air plane by America a few months ago and keeping the Shah's family in America." But the U.S. intelligence community, which had its own state-of-the-art computer system and database on terrorist groups and threats, could locate no previous mention of the Guardians of the Islamic Revolution. The CIA's Counterterrorism Center noted that, in the year before Pan Am 103, some 830 terrorist operations had targeted people in 84 countries, killing more than 600 and wounding over 2,000. It was a long list of possible suspects and possible motives.

Desperate to avoid culpability, Pan Am launched its own parallel investigation. The airline had been targeted before. On August 11, 1982, a bomb underneath a seat on a Tokyo-to-Honolulu flight had killed one passenger and injured others, though it didn't down the plane. A similar bomb two weeks later was found and disarmed aboard a plane in Rio de Janeiro. Two years later, in January 1984, Alitalia staff discovered a bomb before it was transferred to a connecting Pan Am flight.* Yet despite these previous incidents, Pan Am seemed to remain uninterested in security procedures. "Pan Am is highly vulnerable to most forms of terrorist attack," an outside security consultant warned in a report to the airline two years before the bombing of Flight 103. "It must be regarded as good fortune that, for the time being, no disastrous act of terrorism has struck the corporation."†

All told, the initial suspect list was over 1,200 people, ranging from the passengers and crew on board to ground personnel who helped ready the plane in London. At Heathrow, Pan Am used the same area of the airport as IranAir—did any of its personnel sneak over and plant the bomb? Investigators joked darkly, though seriously, that the only people who could be eliminated immediately as suspects were the citizens of Lockerbie who died from the falling wreckage.

One early theory suggested that an American student had served as an unwitting mule after investigators identified her suitcase as having been carried in the targeted container and found that she'd befriended a mysterious Middle Eastern man in Germany named Bilbassi. Investigators also looked seriously at a threat phoned in to the American embassy in Helsinki in early December saying a Pan Am flight would

---

*Airport rules strictly prohibited checked bags from being loaded unless the passenger had boarded as well, though many airlines rarely honored the policy in practice.

†When, after the bombing, the company's report from two years earlier surfaced, victims' families were outraged. In the end, Pan Am's own investigators, trying to defend themselves from the pending lawsuits for negligence, pointed to two baggage handlers in Frankfurt—neither of whom government investigators believed was involved.

be targeted for a bombing, and weighed the likelihood of a conspiratorial alliance of the CIA, Mossad, and heroin smugglers.

Many of the most promising leads seemed to stem from Germany, where Flight 103 had originated before touching down in London, and because authorities there had interrupted a bomb plot earlier that year by the Popular Front for the Liberation of Palestine—General Command. Yet the West Germans and the Scots didn't get along from the very start. Each was out to prove that the other failed to protect Pan Am 103. British translators pored through more than forty binders of case files from Germany's Operation Autumn Leaves (Operation Herbstlaub, in German), which had uncovered a cell that had employed bomb maker Marwan Khreesat to fashion explosive devices contained in a cassette recorder similar to the suspected bomb vehicle in Flight 103. The Scottish team suspected that the German reluctance to cooperate fully was fueled by its own cover-up—the Germans had released Khreesat, who had ties to Jordanian intelligence, and knew more about the emerging prime suspect than they wanted to let on.

Within the United States, the international investigation had its own set of rivalries and intraservice disputes. Even though at least one CIA operative had died on the flight and four other people on board had U.S. intelligence or special forces links, rumors swirled that the CIA had played a role in the bombing. Because of the allegations, the CIA refused to participate in any of the coordinating conferences held in Lockerbie—it wanted to be able to say publicly that it had never sent anyone to Lockerbie, ever.★

While the CIA and FBI technically cooperated—an FBI agent was assigned to Langley headquarters as liaison on the case—the two agencies had difficulty working together. For its part, the CIA was increasingly frustrated about the extension of the long-arm statutes and the FBI's growing overseas jurisdiction. This wasn't, Langley felt, how the two agencies were supposed to operate. The success of Oper-

---

★ One promising lead did bring investigators back to the Agency: A Spanish passport in the wreckage for an individual whose name didn't appear on the passenger manifests seemed likely link to the bomber until the CIA eventually confessed that it was the name used as a cover identity of one of its operatives who died on board.

ation Goldenrod, after the CIA's own failure to capture Imad Mughniyeh in Paris, only underscored how the FBI's law enforcement jurisdiction was creeping onto the CIA's playing field. Like a slow-acting poison, doubts began to circulate among the investigatory team. The CIA canceled a meeting in Washington to discuss Khreesat's Jordanian ties, leading to speculation that it too was involved in the cover-up. In a moment of pique, an FBI agent who couldn't get an important piece of information out of a CIA officer during a Langley visit pulled out his handcuffs and threatened to arrest the officer for obstruction of justice.

By late spring, investigators had identified 14 of the total of 66 baggage items in the AVE4041 container; each bore telltale signs of the explosion. The investigation was narrowing, yet the theories continued to multiply. Hundreds of hours were devoted to recreating the movement of luggage through the Heathrow and Frankfurt airports. The bags on the bottom row of the container had come from transferring passengers in London. At the end of tireless inquiries, the team determined that the bags on the second and third rows of AVE4041 had been the last bags loaded onto the Frankfurt leg—and that those final bags had been the "interline" luggage claimed by other transferring passengers. None of the bags had been X-rayed, nor had they been "reconciled" with a passenger on board; that is, no one had ensured that the passengers whose luggage came interline had ever boarded Pan Am 103.

RARDE was also piecing together fragments of clothing from the wreckage that contained traces of explosives and thus likely originated in the bomb-carrying suitcase. It was an odd mix: two herringbone skirts, a man's pajamas, tartan trousers made by Yorkie Clothing Company, and so on. The most promising fragment was a blue infant's onesie that carried the label Malta Trading Company and that was determined to have been inside the explosive case. In March, two detectives took off for Malta, where they met the manufacturer, who told them five hundred such outfits had been made there on the island, most of them sent to Ireland. The rest went locally to Maltese outlets or to continental Europe.

Yet for all the leads and theories, there was precious little actual evidence. The Lord Advocate, Peter Fraser, even considered shutting down the investigation entirely in early summer, explaining later, "We don't want to kid people that there is an active investigation if really policemen are just shuffling files around." The summer case conference in Tysons Corner, Virginia, which brought together investigators from all the affected countries, was frustrating for the lack of progress.

In August, nearly nine months after the bombing, investigators got the break for which they'd been patiently waiting: The British team was finally given a computer printout of the baggage loading list from Pan Am 103. (Mistakenly stapled to the top of the list were two German intelligence memos showing the West Germans had had the list by early February and failed to turn it over.) Over time, investigators came to focus on bag B8849, which appeared to have traveled from Malta to Frankfurt on December 21 aboard Air Malta Flight 180, even though there was no record of any of that flight's forty-seven passengers transferring to Pan Am 103. Investigators immediately remembered the Maltese clothing found in the suspect Samsonite bag that contained the bomb.

On September 1, Inspector Bell was back in Malta at the offices of Yorkie Clothing. The manufacturer quickly identified the tartan trouser fragments as belonging to pants and said the factory had records of who had ordered them. According to the office's files, the clothing in question had been shipped on November 18, 1988, to a local store owned by a man named Tony Gauci. After Bell arrived at the one-room store owned by Edward Gauci and his two sons, Anthony and Paul, the shopkeepers quickly identified every piece of clothing in question—and were even able in several cases to produce identical items still for sale in the store.

As Bell recorded in his statement, "Anthony Gauci interjected and stated that he could recall selling a pair of the checked trousers, size 34, and three pairs of the pajamas to a male person. [Gauci] informed me that the man had also purchased the following items: one imitation Harris Tweed jacket; one woolen cardigan; one black umbrella; one blue colored 'Baby Gro' with a motif described by the witness as a 'sheep's face' on the front; and one pair of gents' brown herring-bone material trousers, size 36." Gauci had perfectly described the clothing fragments found by RARDE technicians to contain traces of explosive. The investigators snapped to attention—*did they finally have a suspect in their sights?* The purchase, Gauci explained, stood out in his mind because the customer, whom he identified as speaking the "Libyan language," had entered the store on November 23, 1988, and gathered items without regard to size, style, or color. It had been raining that day and Gauci had also sold the man an umbrella. Back in Scotland, investigators dove into the nearly four million pieces of recovered wreckage to see if any umbrellas were among them. Of the five umbrellas carried aboard Pan Am 103, one, under careful examination, was found to have fibers from the blue baby onesie embedded in it; forensics had independently backed up Gauci's story.

Keeping as low a profile as they could, investigators from Lockerbie, the FBI, and the Bunderkriminalamt (a German national police agency), flooded the tiny island of Malta. (Secrecy didn't last long: A local paper reported in late September that FBI agents had been interviewing clothing manufacturers; the British papers followed up with more reporting. So much for a low profile, agents thought.) After Gauci reported in follow-up interviews that the same man had returned twice to his store since November—including once since Bell had interviewed him—the store was put under surveillance; the Gaucis were themselves put under police guard. An FBI sketch artist worked to come up with a composite of the suspect, described by Gauci as well dressed, about five foot ten inches tall, fifty years of age, with a high forehead set off by dark hair. It also didn't escape notice by investigators that the Libyans' local embassy was on the same street as Gauci's shop. Had they been focused on the wrong terrorists this whole time?

At Malta's Luqa airport, investigators found the baggage records didn't produce any leads, so the bomb must have gotten on board the plane through abnormal means—most likely the bomb was brought on by a baggage handler or some other ground personnel at Luqa who wasn't routinely searched when entering or leaving work, and thus could have easily carried a suitcase into the airport.

Orr scheduled the next international coordinating conference almost immediately. For the first time, the inside-man theory dominated conversation: Rather than a passenger, an airline employee had smuggled the bomb on board. The Scots pulled the FBI team aside and told them they were investigating a tiny piece of a circuit board found in the wreckage. For now, they refused to share it with the FBI. The six-month wait as the Scottish police circled the world trying to match the circuit board would prove to be one of the case's most frustrating delays.

All around, in fact, frustration continued to build. Jordanian investigators, drawn in because of Operation Autumn Leaves, insisted that the FBI not share valuable intelligence with the Scots; the Germans likewise demanded that none of the information it shared with the FBI on the Popular Front for the Liberation of Palestine—General Command (PFLP–GC), which had hired Khreesat, be shown to the Scots. With the number of games other agencies were playing with the U.S. investigators, the FBI could only imagine what was happening behind its back around the world. Things were moving slowly; the FBI had dispatched a team of analysts to Malta to compile a database by hand of immigration records, a process that would take nearly a year to complete—although it ultimately yielded crucial evidence. Returning from one conference, the Bureau's lead agent, Richard Marquise, vented to his boss, Neil Gallagher, that the FBI seemed to be losing interest. The Scots still had more than eighty investigators assigned to Lockerbie; the FBI had far fewer and was rotating agents in and out of Malta with little regard for their investigative value.

On June 11, 1990, the international team arrived again in the United States for another meeting. The gathering at the FBI Academy in Quantico seemed unlikely to be fruitful. There was little new to report, and goodwill seemed to be in increasingly short supply. The Scots finally presented to the whole group news of the PT-35 circuit board and their unsuccessful global search for a manufacturer. All told, the Scots had gone through fifty-five companies around the world who made circuit boards; none could identify the fragment. Puzzled, FBI explosives specialist James Thurman asked for pictures of the tiny piece of evidence, which he took to a CIA contact. Within two days, the CIA contact identified it as a circuit board similar to one seized in Africa a couple of years earlier. Thurman, near ecstatic with excitement, asked to examine the seized timer more carefully. Using a magnifying glass, he began to go over it and then shouted, in triumph, "I have you now!"

The tiny piece of circuit board, smaller than a fingernail and found pressed into the clothing from the bomb suitcase on Pan Am 103, matched timers seized in two West African countries—Togo and Senegal—in the late 1980s. In 1986, the Togolese government had put down a coup attempt supposedly backed by the Libyan government, seizing explosive timers that were later turned over to the CIA and then the FBI. In February 1988, meanwhile, two Libyans had been arrested in Dakar, Senegal, in possession of nineteen pounds of Semtex explosives, as well as timers, fuses, detonators, weapons, and ammunition. While the men had been released four months later and most of the evidence had long disappeared, the CIA had kept photographs of the timers. Thus it could prove that ten months before the bombing at Lockerbie, a known Libyan intelligence officer had possessed an identical explosive timer. The FBI-created Maltese database revealed that a man using the same alias as one of the men arrested in Senegal had departed from Malta on October 19, 1988—just two months before the bombing. (As the Pan Am 103 case zeroed in on Libya, it merged with another FBI investigation, into the September 1989 bombing of a French airliner over Niger, which had killed eight Americans, including the wife of the U.S. ambassador to Chad. That bombing also pointed toward Libyan agents.)

The Lockerbie timer also helped solve another puzzle: It was time based, not barometric based, helping to answer why the explosive baggage had seemed to be able to take off and land repeatedly without going off. The timing device, Marquise recalls, helped investigators conclude that Khreesat and the PFLP–GC had not been involved after all, since his radio bombs had been barometric rather than time based.

Thurman found another clue on the circuit board: Further examination of the timer yielded the tiny letters "MEBO" inside the timer from Togo. The FBI, MI5, and CIA were, after months of work, able to trace the letters back to a Swiss company, Meister et Bollier, adding another country to the ever-expanding investigative circle.

In November 1990, Marquise, for the first time placed in charge of all aspects of the investigation and assigned on special duty to the WFO, reported to his new task force. At the Justice Department, he sat down with Robert Mueller, who, as assistant attorney general in charge of the criminal division, was overseeing the prosecution of the case. In front of Mueller and the rest of the prosecutorial team—Brian Murtagh and Dana Biehl—Marquise laid out the latest evidence. Mueller's orders were clear: "Proceed toward indictment." *Let's get this case moving.*

WFO was located far from the Hoover Building, in a run-down neighborhood known by the thoroughly unromantic moniker of Buzzard Point. SCOTBOM, as the FBI had dubbed the case, had been allotted three tiny windowless rooms with dark wood paneling, which were soon covered floor to ceiling with 747 diagrams, crime-scene photographs, maps, and other clues. By the door of the office, the team kept two photographs to remind themselves of the stakes: one, a tiny baby shoe recovered from the fields of Lockerbie; the other, a picture of the American flag on the tail of Pan Am 103.

On November 14, 1990, Marquise was on a plane to Lockerbie, where he waited anxiously for word from the Swiss interview of Mebo's three-person staff: Edwin Bollier, Erwin Meister, and Ueli Lumpert. Hal Hendershot represented the FBI at the interview. Lumpert, examining photos of the tiny circuit board fragment, recognized it as one he built in 1985. Bollier had handled the account in question; he testified that he'd begun working with the Libyan government in the 1970s and in 1985 had been approached by an intelligence officer who asked Mebo to provide timers for Libya's war in Chad. All together, Mebo had built twenty prototypes, and Libya promised that if they proved satisfactory, it would order up to ten thousand more. A rush order three years later—in December 1988—fell through at the last minute. Following the Pan Am bombing, Bollier had tried to reach his Libyan contacts, to no avail. They had all gone suspiciously silent.

In a subsequent interview with the FBI in the United States in early 1991, Bollier was shown the FBI's sketch of the suspect from the shop in Malta. Bollier commented that it looked like a Libyan agent he'd dealt with before, Abdelbaset Ali Mohmed Al Megrahi. The FBI's database of Malta's immigration records showed that Al Megrahi had been present in Malta the day the clothing was purchased; his passport photo, in fact, closely matched the FBI sketch. For his part, Gauci picked the Libyan agent out of a British-style twelve-photo lineup, saying that of all the pictures he'd been shown, this one most closely resembled the man who bought the clothing. Al Megrahi had appeared on the investigators' radar months before, but there was nothing specific to link him to the bombing. Now that appeared to be changing.

With more than a half-dozen countries involved—the United States, Britain, Scotland, Switzerland, Germany, France, and Malta— putting together a case that met everyone's standards was difficult. "We talked through everything, and everything was always done to the higher standard," Marquise explains. In the United States, for instance, the legal standard for a photo array—the selection of possible suspects' photos that police used instead of an in-person lineup—was six photos; in Scotland, though, it was twelve. Nor did the international scope of the investigation make life easy for the witnesses; for example, after being interviewed by a magistrate in Switzerland and by FBI agents in America, Bollier had to be interviewed by Scottish officials in Scotland in order for his testimony to be usable there.

As the case neared an indictment, the international investigators and prosecutors found themselves focusing on the fine print of their respective legal codes and engaging in deep philosophical debates. The discussions, Marquise recalled, were pure gray: "I know what murder means: *I kill you.* Well, then you start going through the details and the standards are just a little different. It may mean five factors in one country, three in another. Was Megrahi guilty of murder? Depends on the country."

Additionally, with international terrorism being such a new threat, there were no mechanisms in place to allow for intelligence information to be used in court. The investigators would for the first time have to devise a system to enter such information into evidence. At every meeting, the international team danced around the question of where a prosecution would ultimately take place. "Jurisdiction was an eggshell problem," Marquise says. "It was always there but no one wanted to talk about it. It was always the elephant in the room." In their private discussions, the Scottish Lord Advocate and Bob Mueller tried to deflect the debate for as long as possible, arguing there was more investigation to do first. As Mueller explained his position, "I recognize that Scotland has significant equities which support trial of the case in your country. However, the primary target of this act of terrorism was the United States. The majority of the victims were Americans and the Pan American aircraft was targeted precisely because it was of United States registry."

To help settle the issue for now, Mueller traveled to London to meet with the Scottish Lord Advocate and agreed to announce indictments simultaneously by November 15, 1991. The joint indictment, Mueller believed, would benefit both countries. "It adds credibility to both our investigations," he said. Who would get their hands on the suspects first was a question for down the road. Mueller and the FBI still wanted to pursue an "irregular rendition" à la Operation Goldenrod; for themselves, the Scots didn't see that as an option.

Al Megrahi had evidently bought the clothing, but investigators had determined that another Libyan agent in Malta had put the bomb suitcase aboard Air Malta; still others had been involved in procuring the timers from Mebo. Investigators began to zero in on Al Amin Khalifa Fhimah, who had been serving as the station manager for Libyan Arab Airlines in Malta on December 21, 1988. After locating Fhimah's diary, found with his Malta airport access badge, investigators saw a notation stating that on December 15 "AB" would come to Malta to pick up "TAGGS" from the airport. Investigators guessed that "AB" meant Abdelbaset Al Megrahi, while "TAGGS" might be a reference to the luggage tags necessary to get a piece of baggage on board a plane (in the days before computerized luggage tags, the bag tags were just pieces of cardboard, sometimes preprinted, sometimes handwritten). Now the investigators had to get a warrant to officially make the diary part of the evidence chain.

In June 1991, the FBI and Justice teams sat down for a presentation by the CIA about Libya and Libyan intelligence. The case outlines seemed to be getting clearer, yet the evidence was still mostly circumstantial. After years of distrust, the parties seemed to be working together well on both sides of the Atlantic. MI5 had completed a critical handwriting analysis of Maltese immigration and hotel records that had helped the Scottish police. The CIA had identified the critical timer clue. Now it was helping to fill in some information gaps. Mueller put forward the theory that the Libyans had executed the bombing in retaliation for U.S. air strikes against Qaddafi's regime in 1986. It seemed as good a theory as any.

A key witness appeared in that summer of 1991; the FBI first interviewed him aboard a U.S. Navy ship in the Mediterranean before bringing him back to Washington for further debriefing. Abdul Majid

Giaka, a former Libyan intelligence officer who had worked in the Libyan Arab Airlines Malta office, provided critical tips regarding Al Megrahi's handling of Semtex explosives and confirmed that Fhimah and Al Megrahi had visited Malta together on December 20, 1988. Fhimah, at the time, was carrying a brown, hard-sided suitcase—just like the luggage that had held the bomb. Giaka quickly became lonely in the United States under heavy protection and asked to rendezvous with his wife in London; before he left, Mueller met with Giaka at the Department of Justice to underscore to the Libyan how important his testimony was to the case. They couldn't afford to lose him. Mueller was getting ready to move forward; the federal grand jury would begin work in early September. Prosecutors and other investigators were already preparing background, prepping evidence, and piecing together information to be included in the forthcoming indictment.

The case for Mueller was a personal one. He'd traveled repeatedly to the United Kingdom for meetings and trekked the fields of Lockerbie himself. On one trip, Mueller walked through the ramshackle warehouse that held the thousands of pieces of evidence collected from the lochs, moors, and forests of Scotland. The signs of lives interrupted struck him: the numerous Syracuse University T-shirts, the single sneaker sitting on a shelf, a white teddy bear. "The Scots just did a phenomenal job with the crime scene," he recalls.

Mueller constantly pushed the investigators forward, getting involved in the case to a level that a high-ranking Justice Department official almost never does, right down to instructing Marquise on specific avenues for further investigation. Marquise turned to him in one meeting, after yet another set of assignments, and sighed. "Geez," he said to Mueller, "if I didn't know better, I'd think you want to be FBI director."

The White House and the National Security Council closely monitored the case. The Reagan administration had been surprised in February 1988 by the indictment on drug smuggling charges of its close ally Panamanian dictator Manuel Noriega, and a general rule of thumb had been developed: Give the White House a heads-up anytime you're going to indict a foreign agent. ("If you tag Libya with Pan Am 103, that's fair to say it's going to disrupt our relationship with Libya," Mueller deadpans.) As a result, Mueller would regularly visit the Cabinet Room at the White House, charts and pictures in hand, to explain to President Bush and his team what Justice had in mind.

To Mueller, the process underscored why such complex investigations needed a law enforcement eye. A few months after Lockerbie, he sat through a CIA briefing pointing toward Syria, Khreesat, and the PFLP–GC as the culprits behind the attack. "That's always stuck with me as a lesson in the difference between intelligence and evidence. I always try to remember that," he recalls today. "What if we had gone and attacked Syria based on that initial intelligence? Then, after the attack, it came out that Libya had been behind it? What could we have done?" Added Mueller, "Intelligence is benefited by the rigor that comes from an investigative standpoint."

Marquise was the last witness for the secret federal grand jury on Friday, November 8, 1991, leaving the SCOTBOM case in the hands of twenty-three grand jurors. On November 14, Mueller, Sessions, U.S. Attorney Jay Stephens, and Attorney General William Barr made the stunning public announcement: "We charge that two Libyan officials, acting as operatives of the Libyan intelligence agency, along with other co-conspirators, planted and detonated the bomb that destroyed Pan Am 103." Scottish investigators simultaneously announced the same indictments.

From there, the case would drag on for years. *ABC News* interviewed the two suspects in Libya later that month; both denied any responsibility for the bombing. With the men safely in Libya, there was no chance for an Operation Goldenrod–like capture and extradition. Marquise was reassigned within six months; the other investigators moved along, too. The tenth anniversary of the bombing came and went without justice. Then, in April 1999, prolonged negotiations led to Qaddafi turning over the two suspects; the international economic sanctions imposed on Libya were taking a toll on his country, and the leader wanted to put the incident behind him.

The final negotiated agreement said that a panel of Scottish judges would try the two men under Scottish law in the Netherlands. Distinct from the international court in The Hague, the Scottish court would ensure that the men faced justice from the country where the crime they were charged with had been committed.

Allowing the Scots to move forward meant some compromises

from the United States, primarily taking the death penalty, which was prohibited in Scotland, off the table for the bombers. Mueller badly wanted the death penalty. For him, for a crime to be punishable by death it had "to be especially heinous and you have to be 100 percent sure he's guilty." In his mind, this case clearly met his criteria. As he says, "There's never closure. If there can't be closure, there should be justice—both for the victims as well as the society at large."

The trial began in May 2000. For nine months, the court held testimony from around the world. In what many observers saw as a political verdict by the Scottish judges, Al Megrahi was convicted and Fhimah was found not guilty. Marquise was in the courtroom, having caught an overnight flight from Oklahoma, where he was stationed at the time with the FBI; Mueller, just days into his tenure as acting deputy U.S. attorney general under the new administration of President George W. Bush, watched with victims' families and other officials via satellite hookup in Washington.

The world may never know what truly transpired in the case of Pan Am 103. Al Megrahi was undeniably involved, although he wasn't the mastermind and certainly wasn't the highest-ranking official in on the plot; Fhimah, too, was probably involved, though it's possible he didn't know that his activities would contribute to the bombing. Libya was definitely involved, though who knew what within the Libyan government is still open to speculation. One theory, still subscribed to by some investigators, is that Libya was primarily acting as a subcontractor for the USS *Vincennes*–obsessed Iranians. The Iranians, this theory holds, had arranged for the PFLP–GC cell in Germany to bomb Pan Am 103, but when that effort was busted by the German police, they turned to the Libyans to carry out the bombing. Another scenario is that Libya was retaliating for the 1986 attacks on Qaddafi's infrastructure. Absent some deathbed revelation or the opening of secret government archives, we may never know for sure.

The case, though, remains significant to a generation of U.S. officials. Buck Revell, who had been the Bureau's number three at the time of the bombing, says, "The legacy of Pan Am 103 can't be overstated. It was the FBI's first large-scale cooperative international investigation resulting in indictments being handed down against officers of a foreign government engaged in acts of terrorism against the

United States. It solidified the Bureau's ability to work extraterritorially and created a wealth of legal precedents in the unwieldy pursuit of international justice."

Even as evidence had accrued through the 1980s, terrorism had been seen as a secondary threat, a "small crime" set against the threats of counterintelligence and espionage that the Bureau dealt with much of the time. SCOTBOM, despite its state sponsorship, began to change that perception. A small cell could still wreak havoc and kill hundreds of Americans.

For Mueller, walking through Lockerbie was the equivalent of what walking through the rubble of 9/11 at Ground Zero would be for a later generation of U.S. leaders: It was the moment when he knew that what lay ahead was not what had happened in the past; it was the moment when he rededicated himself to the pursuit of justice and to fighting for the United States in the courtroom. Just as the death of Giovanni Falcone and his Italian colleagues had helped define for Louis Freeh what was at stake, the warehouse at Lockerbie was Mueller's moment of dedication, the consecration of hallowed ground and sacrifice spoken of at Gettysburg by Lincoln a century and a half before.

The case set a significant precedent, too, for there was never a military reaction to the terrorist attack. The international response to Pan Am 103 has been handled entirely through the legal justice system and through economic sanctions. It took over a decade, with a verdict that felt to many involved to have been a fizzled-out compromise, but to the FBI and the Justice Department, the SCOTBOM prosecution showed that America could punish wrongdoing in a manner that was thoroughly compatible with the best of the nation's traditions. As Mueller had written in a perhaps too hopeful private note to the Scottish Lord Advocate in 1990, "If all civilized nations join together to apply the rules of law to international terrorists, certainly we will be successful in ridding the world of the scourge of terrorism."

Not everyone would agree with that approach, however, as Mueller would learn firsthand soon after the Lockerbie verdict was delivered in 2001.

PART II

1992–2002

CHAPTER 6
JTTF New York

The New York Office has always been the "flagship"
of the Bureau because of the best work, in the
greatest city, by the finest people.
— *Plaque at 26 Federal Plaza,*
New York, commemorating the Bureau's
one hundredth anniversary in 2008

According to Bureau lore, there are two different ways to do things: the Bureau way and the New York way. For decades, the New York Field Office, the largest and most politically powerful in the nation, has had its own set of rules. While technically the Southern District of New York, according to the Justice Department's organizational chart, the area is known by FBI agents as the Sovereign District of New York. For years it was the only field office headed not by a special agent in charge — the Bureau's typical top field position — but by a more senior assistant director aided by a team of SACs. It ran its own rules and its own team.

Agents have long referred to the "New York attitude," a brashness that has marked the many highly talented individuals who have passed through the New York office and as a result handled many of the nation's highest-profile cases. "It was not unusual that those agents sometimes thought of themselves as superior and somehow apart from the rest of the Bureau," explained Mark Felt years ago.

Responsible for the safety and security of upwards of twelve million Americans living in New York City, Long Island, and the five counties immediately north of the city, the New York Field Office, housed for the past forty years in the massive Jacob Javits Federal Building at 26 Federal Plaza, has more than two thousand FBI personnel and some five hundred officers from other agencies assigned to its joint task forces. The Long Island Resident Agency alone, one of the five New York suboffices spread out across its territory, is larger than nearly half the field offices in the country.

A half-dozen special agents in charge lead divisions dealing with foreign counterintelligence, domestic terrorism, international terrorism, criminal activity, and administration as well as New York's fabled Special Operations Group, founded by James Kallstrom, which provides surveillance equipment and high-tech wizardry to investigators and proved so key surveillance-wise in the Pizza Connection. Indeed, New York is, its agents argue, the only field office that deals with every single type of crime confronting the FBI. As Special Agent Joe Valiquette, who spent nearly two decades as the field office's spokesperson, says, "New York encompasses every priority of the Bureau."

For many years, the personnel needs of the New York office were so great that the Bureau's official policy was to send all single agents coming out of Quantico to the Big Apple. (The explanation was economic: Until fairly recently, there was no cost-of-living adjustment for FBI agents living in New York, so they were paid the same salary as any agent in the rest of the country—meaning that it was nearly impossible to support a family on an agent's salary.)

To understand the FBI's struggle to confront terrorism and international threats in the 1990s, one has to understand the Sovereign District of New York, because never has a field office held more sway in the FBI than New York did in the 1990s under Director Louis Freeh, himself a graduate of the city's mean streets. The bonds formed during investigations of violent and organized crime during the 1980s—during big cases like the Pizza Connection and the thousands of smaller cases that overran New York City amid its skyrocketing crime rate in the Reagan years—went a long way in determining friendships, loyalty, and promotions throughout the Bureau in the following decade. New York was the epicenter of terrorism in the 1990s as well as the epicenter of the FBI's power, which meant that those united by their work in the 1980s had a tremendous impact on all that went right and wrong.

The NYPD and the FBI have always had a tense relationship—each considers the other agency ineffectual—but it was never worse than in the late 1970s. Bombing investigations were a particular sore spot. It's hard to imagine now, but in the 1970s New York saw dozens of relatively major bombings each year by terrorist groups—almost all of them domestic groups like the Weather Underground and the Black Panthers or anti-Castro groups like Omega 7. The FBI didn't have a specific squad that handled bombings, so investigating agents were just pulled from the criminal division. Four days after Christmas 1975, a major bombing at La Guardia Airport (which remains unsolved to this day), killed eleven people, leading the Bureau to designate an ad hoc special squad to handle bombings. Yet at each bomb scene, the FBI and the NYPD's Arson and Explosives Unit still interviewed witnesses separately and collected their own forensics. "We'd respond to these crime scenes and be fighting over evidence and witnesses," recalls Neil Herman, one of the first agents assigned to the FBI squad—known as M-9—that focused on terrorism in the Big Apple after the La Guardia bombing.

Herman, the son of a noted midwestern sportswriter, had planned to follow his father into journalism before being swept up in the Bureau's huge Nixon-era expansion, a push by the paranoid president to combat the rising anti-war unrest on college campuses. He arrived at his first office assignment in New York, one of the freshly minted agents nicknamed "Nixon's 1000," on the day in August 1974 when President Nixon resigned. What followed over the next decade for Herman was a crash course in dealing with bombings and infighting between the FBI and the NYPD. "The agents who came to New York in the seventies, we grew up with this," Herman recalls.

Special Agent Joe Valiquette also witnessed these tensions first-hand, having been the case agent on the August 3, 1977, bombing of the Mobil Oil office building by the Puerto Rican nationalist group FALN, which had simultaneously targeted a Defense Department building and threatened to explode bombs in thirteen other buildings. More than 100,000 people had been evacuated because of the threats, including the occupants of the World Trade Center and the Empire State Building. At the Mobil Oil building crime scene, where one person had died and many others had been wounded, the NYPD had found the bomb evidence and the FBI had walked away with the bomber's fingerprints. At an NYPD raid the following year on FALN's Queens bomb factory, the police stopped arriving FBI agents at the door, barring them from the scene. With no ranking FBI agent to force the issue—the squad supervisor was on vacation—the Bureau was shut out of the investigation.

The debate over who was in control at a crime scene wasn't academic, but at times the FBI's claims were made on tenuous grounds. Even when the Bureau won the right to investigate a crime scene, there wasn't always much it could do on its own. The military's Picatinny Arsenal in New Jersey actually handled the forensic evidence from the La Guardia bombing, because the FBI's own facilities weren't up to snuff at the time. "The Bureau wasn't really equipped to handle these cases," Neil Herman recalls. The infighting also depleted the already scarce resources for investigations. Often agents who lived outside Manhattan took the Bureau's cars (known as "bucars" in FBI parlance) home at night, so those such as Herman who lived in the city were forced to take subways, buses, or taxis to investigate bombings that occurred during off-hours.

Joe McFarland, the special agent in charge of administration for the New York Field Office, decided something had to be done. The FBI and the NYPD had started a very successful joint bank robbery task force in the 1970s by agreeing to pool resources, and the two organizations decided to expand that model into terrorism cases: Twelve FBI agents and twelve cops would work side by side, sharing everything. Helping to get the NYPD aboard, the FBI offered to pick up all the overtime bills for the cops. With the city hard-pressed for money (New York City had almost gone bankrupt in 1975), that extra cash was enough to overcome the NYPD's natural reluctance to cooperate with the FBI. "If the Bureau hadn't paid those monies, it never would have got off the ground," Herman says. In fact, all of the task force's vehicles, supplies, and office space would come from the federal government, and in return for the federal government's generosity, all of the cases investigated by the Joint Terrorism Task Force would go to federal court. Valiquette was assigned as one of the first FBI agents on the JTTF, which went operational in May 1980.

The first major JTTF case involved a 1981 armored car robbery in Nyack, New York, about forty miles up the Hudson River from New York City. An alliance of domestic terrorists including the Black Panthers and former Weathermen machine-gunned down a Brinks guard and two police officers. The subsequent wide-ranging investigation tracked down the killers one by one and proved the team's effectiveness. "That really solidified [the JTTF] in New York, but it still took twenty years to realize that this was a concept that was important nationwide," Herman explains. Over the next two decades, the JTTF became the Bureau's primary counterterrorism vehicle. Today the New York JTTF encompasses some 500 personnel from 44 different local, state, and federal agencies, including approximately 130 NYPD detectives as well as agents and analysts from the CIA, NSA, ATF, Immigration and Customs Enforcement (ICE), TSA, Secret Service, Defense Intelligence Agency, Department of State Diplomatic Security Service, U.S. Park Police, U.S. Marshals, Port Authority Police, even the New York City Fire Department. By 2001, the JTTF model had spread to 35 cities. Today, in the wake of 9/11 and after a directive from Mueller to expand further, there are more than 100 FBI JTTFs nationwide.

Within years of its founding, the New York JTTF was a powerhouse investigative force. After assembling over a two-year period— via wiretaps, informants, and other evidence—what the FBI thought was an ironclad case that a cell of the New Afrikan Freedom Fighters, an organization made up of remnants of the group that carried out the Nyack Brinks robbery, was planning another armored car stick-up as well as an assault on the courthouse to free one of the group's leaders, the JTTF swept in. On the eve of the planned attacks, the task force raided four houses, arresting ten participants and uncovering a trove of weapons and seemingly incriminating evidence, including an Uzi submachine gun and drawings of the layout of the courtrooms.

Jurors at the subsequent trial were unconvinced. All of the defendants were acquitted on the most serious conspiracy charges, and while some were convicted of minor weapons charges, the jury's message was clear: If it hasn't happened yet, it's not a crime.

"There was a signal," Herman recalls. "You almost had to let the conspiracy commit the crime. People were dubious: 'Were these guys capable of doing what they say?'" It was only a year later that the CISPES matter would lead to the heated exchange between Senator Arlen Specter and the FBI's Buck Revell in which the Pennsylvania senator would challenge the FBI, saying, "In a democratic society such as ours, perhaps we should wait until a bomb goes off before we act." The legacy of the FBI's past abuses, Herman realized, was now hindering its ability to prosecute new cases going forward. "The government overreached in an attempt to combat what it thought was a threat," Herman recalls. "The Bureau had to live with abuses from the past."

The JTTF model proved so effective in a short period of time that by the end of the 1990s, with the exception of the Pan Am 103 bombing, terrorism seemed to be falling off the Bureau's radar. The murder of the rabbi Meir Kahane in November 1990 could have provided a first glimpse of the growing threat of Islamic radicals in the United States, but after CISPES, agents showed little interest in pressing the investigation.

Kahane's assassin had been a person of interest to the JTTF. He'd been photographed, along with others from his mosque, participating in small-arms training at a shooting range in Calverton, Long Island, just off Exit 71 on the Long Island Expressway. JTTF intelligence had indicated a possible threat against Atlantic City casinos, so agents from the Special Operations Group tailed the group multiple times in the summer of 1989 as they practiced with assault weapons. Special Agent James Fogle crouched near the shooting range with a camera and a huge zoom lens, snapping pictures as they fired their weapons. Militant training in and of itself wasn't a crime, and more radical mosques had been offering similar training to members who wanted to travel to Afghanistan and fight in the U.S.-backed war against the Soviets there. The idea of launching jihad in the United States itself was still so foreign that the shooting-range trips didn't set off any warning bells. Nor did anyone understand the significance of the T-shirt worn by one of the trainees, which showed a map of Afghanistan with the name Services Office on it, denoting a shadowy group in the mountains of Afghanistan and Pakistan that was morphing into something called al-Qaeda—"the base."

.If it ever occurred to the agents to ask why the Middle Easterners were still doing weapons training five months after the Soviet Army had pulled out of Afghanistan, evidence of such curiosity went unrecorded. Indeed, the JTTF, which since the early 1980s had doubled in size, to some forty investigators, didn't even bother to identify the people training at the shooting range. Once the casino threat passed, the SOG surveillance ended.

Despite uncovering piles of troubling evidence after Kahane's assassination, including copies of the army's special forces training manual, the FBI wrapped up the investigation quickly. Two agents from the JTTF, FBI agent John Anticev and NYPD detective Louis Napoli, had dug out the Calverton shooting-range photos and immediately recognized the assassin. But the FBI wasn't interested. The Manhattan district attorney had already claimed the case, so it was no longer a federal priority. Locally, the NYPD, already on edge over the assassination of a leading rabbi, didn't seem interested in uncovering a wider Muslim conspiracy. Thousands of documents in Arabic hauled away from the assassin's apartment were never examined; investigators later said that the looming Gulf War had tied up most of the Arabic translation resources.

The case was of particular interest to someone, however. A wealthy Saudi contributed $20,000 to the assassin's defense fund—the first time the donor's name, Osama bin Laden, ever came to the attention of the FBI.

Three years later, the JTTF would regret dismissing the case so casually. Just a year after the Calverton target practice, one of the shooters met Sheikh Omar Abdel Rahman, aka the Blind Sheikh, at Kennedy Airport and welcomed him to the United States. The sheikh, who had memorized the Koran in Braille as a child after losing his sight and been radicalized in his native Egypt during the 1970s, later became a leading spiritual leader with the Egyptian Islamic Jihad and by 1988 was in Pakistan, supporting the Afghan war. In 1990, despite being on a U.S. terrorist watch list, he managed to obtain a U.S. visa and arrived in New York from Sudan. (The State Department would later reveal that the CIA in Sudan had granted Rahman's visa, probably as thanks for his work in supporting the Afghan war against the Soviets.) Among the documents in the possession of investigators after Rabbi Kahane's assassination was a fatwa by Rahman against U.S. targets such as the "pillars" and "edifices of capitalism." These would only come to light after the first World Trade Center attack.

Had they been more inclined or encouraged, investigators wouldn't have had to go far to uncover a wider conspiracy. It was the roommate of Kahane's assassin who climbed into a rental van on February 26, 1993, in New Jersey and drove toward the World Trade Center with bomb maker Ramzi Yousef.

In the months leading up to the World Trade Center attack, even as the street agents pushed ahead into unfamiliar territory, the FBI's bureaucratic reluctance to involve itself in sensitive, preemptive national security research shut down the only source who might have warned of the bombing. When Carson Dunbar, a longtime administrative supervisor, became the assistant special agent in charge of the FBI's New York terrorism division in April 1992, he cut ties with the Bureau's only effective source within the Blind Sheikh's circles.

Emad Salem had first ended up on the FBI's radar in a Russian counterintelligence investigation; Salem, as head of security at a Times Square hotel, had been helpful in identifying guests who might be Russian spies. He later confided to his handler, Special Agent Nancy Floyd, that a dangerous Egyptian cleric was setting up shop in New York. Over time, Rahman's influence spread to three mosques, two in Brooklyn, one in Jersey City. "I tell you, the sheikh and his followers— it's a nest of vipers," he told Floyd.

Salem quickly became a key intelligence asset for the Bureau, meaning that, with the FBI's distinction between "intelligence investigations" and "criminal investigations," his work and information could never be used in a criminal case. Intelligence investigations, mostly focused on foreign spies, had a lower burden of proof, because they were not designed to lead to court prosecutions; in most instances, at the conclusion of an intelligence case, the targeted foreign spy or agent would be declared persona non grata and expelled from the United States by the State Department rather than face a prison sentence. Considering that many terrorism cases at the time still focused on state-sponsored terrorists, like the long-running cat-and-mouse game with the Libyans, most were considered intelligence cases.

Over time, Salem worked his way into the heart of the Blind Sheikh's circle, becoming a trusted bodyguard and once being invited to help assassinate Egyptian president Hosni Mubarak. Dunbar, who had never worked terrorism cases before but as an administrator knew the Bureau's bureaucracy and rules well, didn't trust Salem. He recklessly summoned the Bureau's source to the New York Field Office, risking possible exposure if anyone saw the sheikh's confidant walk into a federal office building, and pushed the informant both to begin wearing a wire and to testify in open court and thus reveal his identity publicly. Such a deal would transform Salem into a criminal informant rather than an intelligence informant, but it was an odd demand, because a clear criminal case wasn't even being investigated. After months of back-and-forth among the informant, investigators, and FBI supervisors, Salem, who had been earning $500 a week as an informant, stopped cooperating, in July 1992. Knowing of nothing specific but believing that he could see where the sheikh's activity was leading, Salem said something to his FBI handlers that would haunt them in the coming months: "Don't call me when the bombs go off."

The New York JTTF duo of Napoli and Anticev, also believing that something was afoot, made one final attempt to squeeze information from the sheikh's inner circle, subpoenaing twenty-six members of the mosque—including, to avoid casting suspicion, their source, Salem. Nothing.

Acting out of the abundance of caution inherent in the Bureau's administrative management after COINTELPRO and CISPES, Dunbar also shut down a parallel investigation of other cell members. Surveillance on the second group, which had been undergoing paramilitary training outside Harrisburg, Pennsylvania, ended in January 1993.

Dunbar's decision to end the ongoing investigations—in hindsight a stunning mistake—probably was the right one from the Bureau hierarchy's perspective. From a management standpoint, the Rahman case seemed particularly fraught with peril. The Bureau was particularly sensitive to investigating religious figures like the Blind Sheikh after the fallout of CISPES, and besides, his breed of extremism didn't jibe with how the FBI then approached terrorism. In a landscape dominated by Libyan and Iranian terrorists backed by their intelligence services, the Egyptian extremist cleric didn't seem to be connected to any government. Explains Fred Stremmel, who worked on the sheikh's case in Washington, "It was difficult to articulate what foreign power or terrorist group he was working on behalf of." Chris Voss, then a New York JTTF agent, adds, "Carson's heart was in the right place. His job was to keep things from going awry. A high percentage shot in counterterrorism is ninety percent. Well, he's overseeing a hundred cases, so even at those odds, ten of the cases are going to blow up in his face."

In September 1992, just weeks after Salem drifted away from the FBI, Ramzi Yousef came to the United States. Arriving at Kennedy Airport, he asked for asylum and pretended to be an Iraqi refugee. An INS agent at the airport interviewed him and recommended that he be detained until a hearing could be scheduled; the INS lockup area was full, so he was released. Yousef took a taxi directly to one of the Blind Sheikh's mosques. In the coming months, working with many veterans of the Calverton target practice sessions, he busied himself assembling the makings of a powerful truck bomb.

In January 1993, the *New York Times* profiled Sheikh Rahman and his activities to support jihad abroad and revealed that the FBI was actively investigating the cleric for his involvement in Kahane's murder as well as other acts of violence. Wrote the *Times*'s Chris Hedges, "The F.B.I. is also investigating the cleric in connection with three slayings in the United States, and Egyptian authorities contend that he is behind dozens of violent attacks in Egypt, including a spate of shootings against foreign tourists." Yet the investigation still wasn't a top priority. After working with Rahman and his allies in Afghanistan through the 1980s against the Soviets, many government officials didn't understand the monster they had created with the mujahideen they had funded and armed. Several weeks after the *Times* piece, the FBI finally obtained a FISA warrant to tape the sheikh's telephone calls after counterterrorism section chief Neil Gallagher convinced the Justice Department that it needed "to stretch" on the sheikh.* Yet it never conducted on-the-ground surveillance, which might have led to uncovering the bomb factory and the World Trade Center plot. Beyond that, Yousef had missed his immigration hearing by nearly two months, but no warning bells went off, either at INS or elsewhere in the government.

Indeed, as Yousef and the roommate of Kahane's assassin, Mohammed Salameh, climbed into their Ryder rental van on February 26, 1993, the JTTF, so successful in the 1980s, was in danger of being shut down. Getting resources consistently had long been a problem. Both the Bureau and the NYPD had a tendency to scale back on agents when things got quiet — and now, to those above ground level, things were almost silent. The JTTF had been a bit too successful for its own good.

The spate of terrorism in the 1970s and early 1980s had trailed off by the end of the decade. Concerted efforts by federal, state, and local law enforcement at home and intelligence agencies abroad had largely brought to an end the hijackings that had plagued civil aviation. Groups such as the Black Panthers, Omega 7, Black September, the Croatian separatists, and Puerto Rican nationalists had been weakened and mostly rendered nonoperational. The CIA's decade-long campaign against Abu Nidal had borne fruit, causing the group to fall apart. To bureaucrats reviewing budgets, it seemed as if the terror threat might have peaked — which was exactly the wrong way of looking at terrorism.

The after-the-fact cases, when hundreds of agents and detectives flooded the zone, were huge resource drains on the Bureau and the JTTF. "The only way to make these investigations cost-effective was to stop the attack before it happened," Herman explains. "When it's a quiet time, when it's a lull, that's when you should worry the most. The Bureau and the NYPD always told us that they'd give us five

---

*Again, a FISA warrant was designed for intelligence investigations, not criminal prosecutions, so whatever the FBI found in the wiretap would not easily be available for use in court.

hundred agents and detectives after a bombing, but the whole point was that you wanted to stop it before the bomb goes off."

Herman understood the sinister dynamic in a way his higher-ups did not: "Terrorism is cyclical. Left alone, it will always come back, usually in a bolder and more lethal form than before." In the weeks before the bombing of the World Trade Center in 1993, the NYPD was moving to disband its participation in the JTTF. "They'd put just about every domestic group out of business for all intents and purposes," recalls then special agent Chris Voss. "Most of those groups were years away from being operational again. We hadn't had a crime we could prosecute in years." Transfer orders came through for the NYPD's JTTF commander: It was time to move on.

The bombers would have gotten an earlier start, but Ramzi Yousef overslept and his companions didn't want to wake him. It was nearly noon before their three-car convoy arrived at the parking garage underneath the World Trade Center. Yousef finished the bomb assembly and lit a twelve-minute fuse. Leaving the van behind, he got in another of the group's vehicles and barely made it out of the garage in time, as the exit was blocked by another departing van for four minutes. At 12:17 P.M., February 26, 1993, the 600-pound bomb—a unique mix of urea nitrate unlike anything the FBI had seen in studying some 70,000 bombings—exploded. The bomb carved a crater more than 100 feet wide several stories deep in the complex and tossed about enormous concrete pillars like pick-up sticks. Amazingly, only six people died; five of them were part of the small staff that worked in the underground maze of the towers.*

The word back at 26 Federal Plaza was that a transformer had exploded. Within an hour, the first investigators had made it far enough into the garage to recognize the work of a bomb. Even though more than 750 pieces of emergency apparatus, both fire and EMS, swarmed in the streets around the Trade Center—the largest emergency response New York had ever seen—the FBI's initial reaction

---

* The sixth victim was a dental salesman who had just parked in the garage near the explosion.

was relatively basic. Special Agent Chuck Stern, who would become the case agent for the bombing, was just blocks away getting a sandwich when he heard the explosion. He walked to the scene and later transmitted the first word of the attack back to FBI Headquarters, using the heading "NONMIDEAST TERRORISM." The idea that the attack was Mideast-related was barely considered.

Yousef, who had changed into a designer suit and intended to fly back to Pakistan from Kennedy Airport, didn't want to miss out on the credit. Soon after TV news pointed toward a group called the Serbian Liberation Army, he called the NYPD tip line from the first-class lounge of Pakistan International Airlines and offered the name of his own group as the bombers before he boarded the plane and safely escaped. Yousef outlined the reasoning behind his attack in a letter a month later, in which he claimed that the "Fifth Battalion in the Liberation Army" was responsible. He demanded that the United States halt support for Israel and leave Middle Eastern countries alone.

No one had heard of the Fifth Battalion, and the press and investigators first suspected a connection to the former Yugoslavia, then racked by ethnic violence (Croatian separatists, for example, had a long history of violence in the United States, including a 1980 bombing inside the Statue of Liberty). By Friday evening, teams of agents from the JTTF were camped outside the homes of known Balkan activists in the New York City area, while agents back in the New York command center began to check phone records for suspicious activity.★

However, Salem and the FBI agents who had dealt with him had other suspicions. At a 1:00 A.M. briefing in the office of Assistant Director Jim Fox, U.S. Attorney Mary Jo White heard for the first time from Louis Napoli and the JTTF that the FBI had had a source who might be able to help them. "Get him in here," said White, fired up and not entirely pleased to be hearing that the FBI might have had material evidence of the attack's planning.

★ In the following week's cover story, "Who Could Have Done It?," *Time* magazine focused on "Balkan factions," then gave a nod to Palestinian groups, Iranian Hezbollah, Iraqis, Libyans, Russians, and even what the magazine called "a psychotic, mad-as-hell American." There was no mention of Egyptian jihadists or non-state-sponsored Mideast groups.

"Well, we were paying him, like, five hundred a week. This time, you know, considering what's happened, he's probably gonna want a million dollars," Napoli said.

"I don't give a damn what he wants. If he can deliver, give it to him," White replied.

Down in Washington, the new national security advisor, Anthony Lake, who had been on the job for barely a month, called staffer Richard Clarke, a rare holdover from the George H. W. Bush administration. "Did the Serbs do it?" he asked. As Clarke pursued that question, the navy officer handling the Situation Room asked if the National Security Council even dealt with domestic attacks. The idea of foreign terrorists attacking the homeland was still so hard to imagine that there wasn't a clear policy for such incidents. President Bush had made it through his four-year term without ever formulating a policy on terror. The single attack during his tenure, on Pan Am 103, while creating an important precedent for the FBI and international investigations, had not involved the military and hadn't elevated terrorism to a national issue. So Clarke made up the policy as he went along, replying quickly to the navy officer, "Yes, yes, we do."

As information flowed in, the attackers seemed mysterious. In the White House, the NSC's Clarke turned to the FBI's Bob Blitzer in a briefing: "What is this group?"

"Nobody we know. New York thinks there may be some links to the guy who shot a rabbi up there last fall. They all seem to be related to a Muslim preacher from Egypt, a guy in Brooklyn or Jersey City," Blitzer said, puzzled himself.

The CIA's representative chimed in: "They are not known members of Hezbollah or Abu Nidal or Palestinian Islamic Jihad or any other terrorist group."

In the coming months, the FBI and the White House would argue over who ran the show when it came to terrorism. In a meeting with FBI officials and Attorney General Janet Reno, Lake and other NSC staff members argued that as the coordinators of counterterrorism policy, they needed more access to the FBI's investigation. For its part, the FBI argued that the evidence gathered as part of a criminal matter

ЧЧ#

couldn't be shared with "civilians" prior to an indictment. Reno finally weighed in: "If it's terrorism that involves foreign powers or groups, or it could be, the Bureau will tell a few senior NSC officials what it knows." The FBI agreed reluctantly—it and the Justice Department dragged their feet on a promised "memorandum of understanding" between the DOJ and the NSC for years. Information sharing didn't come naturally. "Usually," Clarke recalled years later, "the FBI acted like Lake-Reno was a resort in Nevada."

Herman worked until 4:00 A.M. the first night, drove home, showered, and returned to the office at 6:00. By the end of the weekend, more than seventy agents would be working the case full-time, with hundreds more tracking leads across the country. Yet it was almost purely by luck that in the hours after the attack, working from a command post in the nearby Vista Hotel at 3 World Trade, investigators quickly caught a break.★ Alert bomb techs from the ATF and NYPD found a piece of wreckage, almost indistinguishable amid the chaotic, smoky, eerily lit scene on the garage's B-2 level, that they recognized as coming from the exploding van itself. A veteran of the NYPD car theft task force working the bomb scene had the foresight to check whether it happened to contain a VIN number, the unique identifier used by manufacturers to track vehicles. It did, and they quickly traced the identifier to a yellow E-50 Ford Econoline van owned by the Ryder rental company. On Sunday morning, Jim Fox announced at the morning multi-agency briefing that forensic analysis confirmed the presence of explosives at the scene; the Trade Center was now officially a bombing and thus officially an FBI investigation, which would come to be known in Bureau parlance as TRADEBOM.

Mohammed Salameh will not go down as one of history's shrewdest terrorists. After he called to report the theft of the Ryder van the night before the attack, he returned to the rental agency to request his

---

★ In 2001, the Vista Hotel, which dated back to 1836 and was Lower Manhattan's first hotel, was again used as a staging area by emergency responders on 9/11. Some forty people, mostly firefighters, were killed inside when the building was destroyed by the towers' collapse.

$400 deposit back. Luckily, Ryder's bureaucracy kept him waiting for a week, by which point investigators had established the link to the truck bomb. When Salameh went back on Thursday, March 4, Special Agent Bill Atkinson was present, playing a Ryder "loss prevention analyst," and told Salameh that he had some paperwork to fill out. Enjoying the role, Atkinson negotiated what refund Salameh would get and grilled Salameh on why he'd rented the truck and what he'd done with the truck. Atkinson even told him he doubted that the truck had actually been stolen. During one exchange, Salameh promised, "I'm a Muslim. I'm honest." When Salameh left, $200 in hand, FBI agents pounced.*

Agents quickly rounded up more of the cell, raiding building after building. In a Staten Island apartment, the address to which Salameh had told Agent Atkinson that he'd planned to help move his friend, the FBI found Abdul Rahman Yasin. Yasin, a native of Bloomington, Indiana, initially fooled investigators by proving very cooperative and showing them Yousef's bomb factory on Parampo Avenue. Agents labeled him a "cooperating witness" and allowed him to go free, not even thinking to hold his passport. Yasin fled the next day to the Mideast, landing in Amman, then traveling to Baghdad. By August, he would be indicted for his involvement in the bomb cell; when the FBI created its Most Wanted Terrorists list in the wake of 9/11, he was one of the twenty-two initial fugitives named. As of 2011, Abdul Rahman Yasin, aka Abdul Rahman Said Yasin, aka Aboud Yasin, aka Abdul Rahman S. Taha, aka Abdul Rahman S. Taher, was still free despite a $5 million reward on his head.

Safe in Pakistan, Ramzi Yousef would become the focus of a multi-year, transcontinental FBI manhunt, and by the time he was caught, he would have laid the groundwork for the 9/11 plot.

Emad Salem didn't waste any time after the first attack. A $500-a-week hotel clerk when he was discovered by the Bureau and

---

*The FBI had hoped to be able to follow Salameh, unraveling more of the plot, but media leaks made them worried he'd flee. Had Salameh read *Newsday* that morning, he would have seen that the FBI had traced the blast vehicle.

a $500-a-week informant when he fell out with the Bureau, Salem now convinced the Bureau that his information was worth a cool $1.5 million. Mary Jo White was right: If he could deliver, it was worth it.

Over the coming months, as other agents worked the TRADE-BOM plot, Salem revealed that the threat from Muslim radicals in Brooklyn was both bigger and more dangerous than anyone imagined. Just two months after the explosion at the World Trade Center, he was approached by supporters of Sheikh Rahman and asked to participate in what came to be known as the "Day of Terror" plot. In coordinated attacks, the jihadists planned to bomb the UN, the Holland and Lincoln Tunnels, the George Washington Bridge, and other buildings—even the FBI's 26 Federal Plaza office. Having been tipped off, the FBI watched the plot develop with a mix of caution, amazement, and horror. Thanks to Salem's guidance, the militants' bomb factory in Queens was under constant video surveillance. The images of the cell's members mixing chemicals in giant trash barrels just a few blocks from the Van Wyck Expressway and around the corner from Public School 117 provided an awesome view of a new kind of terrorism in the homeland. In June, the cell conducted its first test explosion in a rural part of Connecticut. Meanwhile, Salem was audaciously able to tape Sheikh Rahman issuing a fatwa against the American military and advocating its destruction.

Early on the morning of June 24, FBI SWAT teams sneaked into the warehouse as "the subjects were actually mixing the witch's brew," Jim Fox said later. The FBI moved quickly, arresting supposed mastermind Siddig Ibrahim Siddig Ali and seven others. In the coming weeks, the Blind Sheikh himself and others would be indicted as well. All would be convicted at trial. (Presiding over the case was Judge Michael Mukasey, who would become attorney general under President George W. Bush.)

The case's Bureau code name, TERRSTOP, underscored the new approach to terrorism: If the FBI had intelligence on an unfolding plot, it would bust it. In this area at least, the hesitancy inspired by the FBI's previous excesses and political suspicion evaporated. With lives on the line, after-the-fact prosecution was no longer an option. The terror groups that had truly worried the United States in the 1980s—Libyans, Iranians, Palestinians—were fading away, and the New York

Field Office was for the first time realizing at a deep level that it was confronting a complicated geopolitical situation, one with international and local implications. This new enemy—radical Islamic terror, separate from any state sponsorship and operating in the U.S. homeland—wasn't going to be content with a single attack. Stremmel told his supervisor, Special Agent Dave Williams, after reviewing the TERRSTOP file, "My God—I thought the Libyans were dangerous, but they don't hold a candle to these guys. Rahman and his guys scare the shit out of me."

But not everyone in Washington agreed. The wider U.S. government had been focused elsewhere, on the collapse of the Soviet Union and the Persian Gulf War. So while Rahman's fatwas weren't just empty words—he had become the global spiritual leader of the burgeoning radical Islamic movement, particularly Egyptian Islamic Jihad and Al Gama' al-Islamiyya, two groups overseas that had killed scores of Egyptians—his leadership didn't much concern the intelligence community. Neither group had killed Americans, so they weren't designated terrorism groups by the State Department. Extensive pressure from the Egyptian government didn't change that. In one January 1993 briefing, Stremmel had been interrupted by an intelligence official who asked, "How can a blind, crippled, old guy pose a threat to us?"

"I've always thought that the twenty-six months between the Kahane assassination and the first World Trade Center bombing was a key period," Neil Herman told a journalist years later. "A time when we really could have made a statement. But that time was just lost. I'm not saying we could have prevented everything that followed, but it would have given us a fighting chance."

Ever since the installation of the FISA restrictions, the line between national security investigations and criminal investigations had been hard to establish. The law, mostly established in 1978 with the FISA statute, had not kept up with the times. National security investigations were meant for counterintelligence work, foreign agents conducting espionage or terrorism on U.S. soil—a system that had worked fine when most terrorist groups were state-sponsored. Now, as the first waves of non-state-sponsored terrorists came along, the government was unsure precisely how to proceed.

Legally, the challenge was that the burden of proof for a FISA warrant was lower than what was known as a Title III warrant for a wiretap in a criminal case. (The authority for such wiretaps was first established in Title III of President Johnson's Omnibus Crime Control and Safe Streets Act of 1968.) That meant that the judges on the FISA court, and specifically the Office of Intelligence Policy Review at the Justice Department, were wary of evidence gathered under a FISA warrant being used to further a criminal prosecution. Allan Kornblum, the one-time FBI agent who had investigated civil rights cases in the South in the 1960s before being appointed to write the surveillance regulations in the 1970s, was a critical eye in OIPR. He required endless rewrites of warrant applications, always asking for more proof, higher burdens of evidence, and more run-arounds; his sense of caution bordered on the absurd. "Allan could be a real pain in the neck," recalls Fred Stremmel. "I saw him beat the bejesus out of some of his attorneys."

The idea of erecting a "Chinese wall" between the intelligence side of an investigation and the parallel criminal investigation had been floated early in the 1990s under George H. W. Bush's administration. Now that model seemed appropriate to respond to the Blind Sheikh case. Kornblum had singled out his concerns over the Southern District's FISA applications, so Mary Jo White's office put together a memo drawing a line between the intelligence agents, who were still working on tracking active, new threats, and the criminal agents prosecuting the existing case and indictments. During an all-day meeting in New York, the Southern District prosecutors and Justice Department lawyers hammered out a formula covering how to proceed. They passed their conclusion up the chain to the Justice Department for approval—to demonstrate to the FISA court, in Jamie Gorelick's words, that "there was a grown-up watching too." Gorelick, who was the deputy attorney general under Janet Reno at the time, recalls, "It was a nonissue when it came up." However, what was supposed to be a one-time memo dealing with the particular circumstances of a complicated, unique case became official Justice Department and FBI policy. The Chinese wall had been built.

The wall was never supposed to be a barrier to sharing information

174 • GARRETT M. GRAFF

within the government—between the CIA and the FBI, for instance—or among intelligence and criminal agents at the FBI. It was only supposed to cover sharing information between the FBI and prosecutors. In short, it was meant to prevent information gathered under a FISA warrant from appearing in a courtroom. Anything short of that was completely acceptable—and in fact encouraged.

Yet no one wanted to run afoul of the rules, so over the coming years, FBI agents concerned about what they could and could not discuss with prosecutors would continually query Kornblum at OIPR, who became in effect the keeper of the wall. Over time, interpreted and reinterpreted, each time leading to a slightly more cautious approach, the so-called wall between intelligence and criminal investigations would eventually calcify into a hard-and-fast, inviolate policy. It became the excuse for agents (and particularly other agencies) to avoid sharing information. If they shared information across the wall, agents feared they could end up being criminally prosecuted themselves. More than any other policy or action, the wall would create the environment that led to the failure to stop the 9/11 attacks.

The year 1993 wasn't shaping up to be a good one in FBI history. Aside from dealing with the first major terror attack on the homeland, the FBI leadership was being consumed from within by allegations of abuse of power by Director William Sessions—or, more specifically, abuse of power by Sessions's wife, Alice, who had come to be known in the Bureau as the "codirector." The wife of the FBI director has no formal role in government, and in fact there was little precedent for directors' spouses in general; Hoover never had a wife, and Clarence Kelley's wife had been sick and thus had never moved to Washington from Kansas City. Alice Sessions repeatedly clashed with FBI officials over her access to headquarters, over a fence that the Bureau wanted to install at the Sessionses' house for security purposes, and over the use of Bureau vehicles for personal errands. She even accused the FBI on occasion of bugging her house.

Sessions, who had taken over the Bureau in 1987 when William Webster became the director of the CIA, proved something of an odd duck within the FBI's conformist culture. He wore his FBI badge on his dress shirt—out of pride, he said; to avoid the possible tax implications of using his motorcade for personal errands, he kept an unloaded gun in the trunk of his vehicle so he could claim it was being used for law enforcement. He managed to finagle a "business trip" back to his home state of Texas almost every other month. During crucial moments, he displayed a bizarre lack of interest in crises, and according to agents around him, he sang or hummed during briefings when he got bored.

After an investigation, the Justice Department's Office of Professional Responsibility issued a 161-page report detailing a laundry list of allegations, including claims that the director had used an FBI jet to transport firewood from New York to Washington. The report struck a nerve with veterans of the Bureau and the Justice Department, leading to open warfare in the press, on Capitol Hill, and in the FBI executive suites between Sessions and his deputies. Former attorney general William Barr accused Sessions of "a clear pattern of your taking advantage of the government." Buck Revell openly attacked the director. The press loved every outburst.

As the FBI leadership team became increasingly distracted by the investigations and sniping in the executive suite, two poorly managed situations unfolded that would bedevil the Bureau for years to come. The first took place in August 1992, in Ruby Ridge, Idaho, when U.S. marshals attempting to arrest the white separatist Randy Weaver engaged in a firefight with his family, which killed one federal agent and one member of Weaver's group. Law enforcement, including the FBI's Hostage Rescue Team, descended on the mountain in the hours following the initial firefight. Unclear and probably inappropriate rules of engagement for the agents on the scene encouraged further escalation, and a day later an FBI sniper fired on the Weaver cabin, mistakenly killing the separatist's wife, Vicki. The situation dragged on for more than a week before a negotiated surrender brought the matter to a peaceful end. Congressional investigations and internal FBI inquiries into the "Ruby Ridge massacre," as Weaver's supporters dubbed it, would preoccupy the FBI leadership, upend careers, and cause discord between agents and management through the rest of the decade.

Just six months after Ruby Ridge—and only two days after the February 26, 1993, World Trade Center bombing—the FBI was called upon after the ATF bungled a raid on the Waco, Texas, compound of David Koresh's Branch Davidian sect. After blowing a chance to surprise Koresh, ATF agents had engaged in a brutal firefight with compound residents. Four ATF agents were killed, setting off a dramatic federal response. Even as the Bureau was busy deploying investigators and resources to the fiery cavern of the Trade Center parking garage in New York, hundreds more law enforcement officers poured into Waco. The FBI took control and brought military Bradley Fighting Vehicles to the compound, since the Branch Davidians' .50-caliber weaponry could tear apart unarmored vehicles. On April 19, 1993, after the standoff had lasted fifty-one days, Justice Department officials decided to use tanks to deploy tear gas into the compound and bring the situation to a close. Officials watched with horror as wind-whipped fire spread throughout the building and consumed the entire structure, killing seventy-six Branch Davidians, including Koresh and twenty young children.

The newly installed attorney general, Janet Reno, near tears, took full responsibility for the decision to use the gas. Later analysis determined, though, that the sect probably intentionally set the fire. Numerous investigations, both federal and congressional, picked over both incidents, finding numerous flaws in the ATF's and FBI's actions. Several agents and supervisors saw their careers effectively ended as a result of the mess. The incineration of so many people haunted many of those involved and became a rallying point for extremists convinced that the federal government was a dictatorial monster. One of those inspired by the events of Ruby Ridge and Waco, Timothy McVeigh, would choose to blow up the Oklahoma City federal building on April 19, 1995, partly to commemorate the Branch Davidian siege.

Amid these public scandals, the Bureau's internal scandal over the leadership and effectiveness of Director Sessions continued. "I've never seen an organization come as close to ceasing to function as the FBI did during that period," recalls then FBI executive Steven Pomerantz. In the end, President Bush kicked the Sessions problem on to the next administration. On July 19, 1993, President Clinton phoned Sessions at 3:50 P.M. to say that because he refused to resign, he was being fired—the first time a president had ever invoked his right to remove the FBI head. Deputy Attorney General Philip Heymann was waiting in Sessions's office to receive his badge and credentials. Adding insult to injury, Clinton called back nine minutes later to make sure that Sessions understood that the firing took effect immediately. The FBI director was escorted from the Hoover Building.

Clinton had hoped to appoint a friend from Oxford University, Massachusetts judge Richard Stearns, as the new director of the FBI, but after Stearns withdrew, only one serious candidate remained: the scrappy former racket-busting FBI agent turned Pizza Connection prosecutor turned federal judge, Louis Freeh. On August 6, 1993, just two weeks after President Clinton sent his nomination to the Senate, Freeh became the fifth director of the FBI.

Louis Freeh's father, a World War II veteran, had always told him to serve his country — and he had, as an agent, a prosecutor, and a judge. His Italian maternal grandparents had taught themselves English by reading undeliverable magazines, catalogues, and comic books discarded from the New York Post Office, where his grandfather worked. A product of Catholic schools, Freeh had made Eagle Scout in the Boy Scouts, and yet his school counselor didn't think much of his prospects, telling him, "You're not really college material. Go to trade school. Plumbers do very well these days."

In the end, Freeh had attended Rutgers, working several hours a day at a variety of odd jobs, before moving on to law school. In the midst of the unrest surrounding Vietnam, law school classes were frequently canceled, and both his classmates and his professors thought Freeh was crazy for even considering joining the FBI, the ultimate oppressive tool of the establishment. Freeh didn't care what they thought.

For Freeh, the first "brick agent" to head the FBI, the job was the treat of a lifetime, a position that more than made up for relinquishing the lifetime tenure of the federal judgeship he currently held. Just a day after Sessions's firing, President Clinton stood next to Freeh in the Rose Garden and announced his choice to lead the Bureau, calling Freeh a "law enforcement legend" and "the best possible person to head the FBI as it faces new challenges and a new century." After an easy Senate confirmation and the swearing-in ceremony, Freeh, following his old friend and Pizza Connection case agent Charlie Rooney in his Buick, drove his family Volvo up to the gates of the Hoover Building. When the guard tried to bar Freeh from entering because he didn't have an FBI ID, Rooney laughed: "Don't you have him on your list? He's your new boss."

Freeh's time as director would come to be defined by two dominant themes, the rise of international terrorism and the investigations into presidential misconduct under President Clinton. As prescient as he was in recognizing the rising threat of international terror and global criminal enterprises, he would leave the Bureau with a mixed legacy. In remarks his first day as director, Freeh cited the need to expand the Bureau's overseas relationships with foreign police agencies. "They have the intelligence bases that we don't have with respect to some of these emerging groups, and I think working closer with them is going to aid us greatly in preventing these events," he said, referring to the World Trade Center attack. But at the same time he was blind for too long to the rise of technology, something in which he had very little interest—and that blindness would turn out to be costly.

Ironically for the FBI, which has struggled so badly in the past decade with computers and technology, the Bureau's filing system has traditionally been one of its sources of strength. Hoover built a repository of millions of fingerprints; investigative paper files, stored in floor-to-ceiling cabinets called "rotors," were meticulously cross-referenced and indexed. Everything was carefully labeled, ordered, and marked. Intelligence squads were denoted with an *I;* criminal squads were denoted with a *C.** Later on, as the Bureau evolved, additional designations were added: *IT* for international terrorism, *DT* for domestic terrorism, and later *CT* (counterterrorism), encompassing both. The squad that began in New York in the early 1990s as I-22 would evolve to I-49, then later IT-1 and still later CT-1. By the end of its many name changes, CT-1 would be one of the most storied squads in the annals of FBI history.

In the early 1990s, though, it was almost in a backwater: a foreign counterintelligence team that focused primarily on the Sudanese and Egyptians—which, as had been made clear to its members, was not

---

*FBI squads generally consist of about twenty agents.

exactly the sexiest, front-burner investigation in the Bureau. Squad I-22 spent the first part of the 1990s building cases against Sudanese diplomats attached to the United Nations, particularly Siraj Yousef and Ahmed Yousef, who were becoming something of a terror network themselves, meeting with shady groups, introducing one international terrorist to another—definitely not the type of people the U.S. government wanted living in New York under diplomatic cover. With a solid case, the agents worked with the State Department to declare Siraj and Ahmed Yousef persona non grata and expel them from the country, but when Mike Anticev (who had joined his brother, John, on the FBI JTTF squad) called Washington to work out the details, headquarters wasn't that interested. "Back then, nobody cared," Anticev recalls.

After the Sudanese diplomat episode, squad supervisor Tom Lange summoned Jack Cloonan, Danny Coleman, and Mike Anticev to his office: "Some rich Saudi is financing terrorism," he told them. The guy, someone named Osama bin Laden, was living in Khartoum, Sudan, at the time, so the case fell within the domain of the Bureau's New York Sudanese squad. The CIA was starting an investigation too, and Coleman would be appointed the liaison.

Lange closed the meeting with an aside: "This should last no longer than six months."

Ramzi Yousef, the FBI's new Public Enemy #1, was unlike anything the world had seen since the days of assassin-for-hire Carlos the Jackal, who had waged attacks across the globe through the 1970s. Yousef had used his own passport to enter the United States, so his picture was readily at hand. On April 2, 1993, the Bureau made an exception to its normal policy, expanding to eleven the Ten Most Wanted list to include him. The U.S. government promised $2 million to anyone who helped bring him to justice. Once Yousef made the top-ten list, it would just be a matter of time and hundreds of man-hours before he was captured. And thanks to the long-arm statutes of the 1980s and renditions like Operation Goldenrod, the Bureau was beginning to get pretty good at the overseas snatch.

Two weeks after Yousef's name was added to the Most Wanted

list, the first joint team of FBI and CIA agents landed in Islamabad, Pakistan. Some 37,000 matchboxes with Yousef's picture, name, and reward information were air-dropped over Baluchistan, the rural area of Pakistan where he was suspected of hiding out. Yousef, however, wasn't going to lie low. He attempted to assassinate Pakistani leader Benazir Bhutto, helped bomb Iran's Imam Reza Shrine, and even plotted to destroy the Israeli embassy in Bangkok. With each attack he became more sophisticated, perfecting techniques and honing his tradecraft.*

Tracking Yousef as best they could, increasingly anxious CIA and FBI officials began to understand that many of the new terror suspects were former Afghan allies—and that they didn't appear to be working in isolation. Something seemed to be coalescing. In the midst of his plots, Yousef joined up with his uncle, a shadowy and until then unknown radical named Khalid Sheikh Mohammed. "For two years, [Yousef] wasn't hiding out. He was traveling, out and about planning more events. It's rather remarkable. He had money. He traveled extensively," Neil Herman says. "We always felt there was a network, an organization out there."

By the end of 1993, Yousef was well along in planning the biggest terror attack the world had ever seen, a complicated and coordinated aerial attack with sophisticated bombs on a dozen airliners over the Pacific. He code-named the plot Bojinka, Serbo-Croatian for "the explosion." If successful, Bojinka would have killed thousands and possibly halted international commerce for weeks. Yousef spent months carefully perfecting the bomb recipe, but then Osama bin Laden's emissaries recruited him to help assassinate President Clinton during a visit to the Philippines in November 1994. After studying the feasibility of murdering Clinton with everything from a Stinger missile to phosgene gas, Yousef decided the attack would be too difficult and returned to planning his original attack. On the night of December 1, 1994, Yousef's associate Wali Khan Amin Shah planted the first test explosive in a Manila theater; it exploded exactly as Yousef had hoped,

---

*In one attack, for instance, Yousef carried his bomb in a stolen truck rather than a rented one, realizing that the paper trail created by the Ryder rental had helped the FBI find the World Trade Center cell quickly.

although, luckily, no one in the theater was killed. A week later, Yousef rented a flat in Manila's Dona Josefa apartment building to house the bomb factory. Even as he plotted the Bojinka operation, he thought that he would assassinate Pope John Paul II during a January visit by the pontiff to Manila; the new apartment overlooked the main route the pontiff would take to move around the city.

On December 11, Yousef boarded a Philippines Airlines flight from Manila to Cebu and, midflight, assembled a bomb whose parts he'd hidden on various parts of his body and left it under seat 26K in economy class. He disembarked in Cebu and the flight continued on to Tokyo; the bomb exploded two hours later, killing a twenty-four-year-old Japanese engineer who'd been unlucky enough to sit in Yousef's former seat. Heavily damaged, the plane could barely make an emergency landing in Okinawa. Yousef was thrilled with the results. A little tweaking and he'd have a fatal weapon.

Less than a month later, though, everything unexpectedly unraveled. A fire started while Yousef and his accomplice Abdul Hakim Murad were mixing chemicals. The responding firefighters summoned police, who summoned specialized antiterror police after seeing the contents of the smoky, chemical-filled apartment. Police arrested Murad when he tried to sneak back into the apartment to reclaim the terrorists' computer, files, and manuals. Yousef quickly escaped back into Pakistan, melting away before law enforcement figured out he was involved. (Khan, the third member of the cell, was arrested by the Filipinos days after the apartment fire tipped them off to the Manila cell; he also escaped but was recaptured in Malaysia at the end of 1995.)

Fingerprints in the apartment matched Yousef's, and the FBI arrived quickly. This time, it was soon evident that Yousef was up to something far, far worse than even the TRADEBOM attack. Agents fanned out across Manila to investigate the plot; an FBI computer expert arrived to decipher the laptop. The files on the captured computer revealed just how close the plot had come to fruition: Yousef and his associates, including his uncle Khalid Sheikh Mohammed, planned to attack on January 21, 1994, just two weeks after the fire. The bomb maker's glee was evident: Agents found a draft business card with Yousef's name and the title "International Terrorist." Yousef had also created a fake wanted poster for his accomplice, offering a reward of

$100,000,000,000 for Murad, whose occupation was listed as "Int. Terrorist and Fugitive."

Murad's time as a fugitive, though, was over. After he had spent two months in the custody of the Filipino police, Murad was handed over to the FBI at Manila's Ninoy Aquino International Airport on April 13, 1995. Special Agents Frank Pellegrino and Thomas Donlon were among those waiting to take custody. During the long flight back to the U.S., which required a refueling stop in Alaska, the New York FBI agents began to get frightening details from Murad. The three men chatted in English. On the flight back and in subsequent interrogations, Murad unveiled a complicated, transnational, and highly coordinated plot against the United States, dropping such details as the fact that the terrorists had considered crashing a plane into CIA Headquarters in Langley, Virginia. Step by step, he walked Pellegrino and Donlon through the Bojinka plot—how the bombs were constructed, where the terrorists had purchased the ingredients, how they had paid for their travel. Murad outlined extensive flight training that he and others had undergone in the United States in 1991. Personal details came out too: From Murad, the FBI agents for the first time learned that Ramzi Yousef was married and had two daughters.

While Murad claimed that the "Liberation Army" consisted only of him and Yousef, it was clear to the agents that something more was in the works. All of this globe-trotting was too much for just two guys to put together alone. Perhaps the most chilling detail of the in-flight interrogation, though, was that Yousef intended to attack the Trade Center a second time; he felt that he should have been able to bring it down the first time, but lack of money had left him unable to build a bomb of sufficient size.

The capture of Ramzi Yousef marked a passing of the torch from a generation of agents who had investigated the emergence of this shadowy new terrorist network to a team of agents who would ride the investigation through September 11 and beyond. That handoff began one Sunday morning in February 1995.

It was partly fear of the long arms and long memory of the FBI that prompted Ishtiaque Parker to contact the U.S. embassy in Islamabad a few weeks after Yousef escaped from the Philippines. Parker, who had been recruited to help with Yousef's attacks, was concerned that his name could be found on the captured Manila laptop. He told the embassy's security officer he knew the bomb maker's hideout, a tip that made it back to the desk of National Security Council counterterrorism guru Richard Clarke, who called the FBI early on February 12, 1995.

"O'Neill," barked the unfamiliar agent answering Clarke's call.

"Who are you?" Clarke asked.

"I'm John O'Neill. Who the fuck are you?" the agent replied.

O'Neill, who had just been appointed head of the FBI's counterterrorism section, had driven straight to the Hoover Building from his former post in Chicago; he was scheduled to start work the following Tuesday but had come to the office early to sort through some matters.

Clarke explained that the Pakistan tip seemed legit and the United States didn't have much time before Yousef disappeared back into the wilds of Peshawar. Thus O'Neill's first assignment in the new job would be one of the biggest operations the FBI had undertaken since Operation Goldenrod in 1987.

The FBI needed two teams: one to make the snatch on the ground, the other to do the rendition out of Pakistan. O'Neill began calling around. Within hours, a team led by Chuck Stern was in the air en route to Islamabad. FBI agent Brad Garrett was coincidentally already heading to Islamabad by commercial airliners, as part of his ongoing investigation into Mir Kasi's 1993 attack on CIA employees waiting to enter the Agency's Langley headquarters.* Garrett was pressed into service for the Bureau's Yousef operation. O'Neill remained at the Hoover Building, as he would without interruption for the next three days. Director Louis Freeh and Attorney General Reno closely monitored the operation as well.

There was just a single FBI legat on the ground in Pakistan, as well as several Diplomatic Security Service agents at the embassy and a few

---

*Kasi's shooting rampage had killed two CIA employees and wounded three others on January 25, 1993. He, like Yousef, escaped into rural parts of Pakistan. Captured in 1997, he stood trial in the United States, was convicted, and was executed in 2002.

DEA agents. Luckily, Benazir Bhutto, Pakistan's prime minister, had herself been a target of Yousef's bomb-making and fully understood the threat that he posed as long as he was free. The Pakistani government was ready to help get Yousef off the street and out of the country. The small team of U.S. agents joined forces with the Pakistani military to storm Yousef's hideout on Monday afternoon about 4:30 P.M. local time, 6:30 A.M. back in Washington, less than twenty-four hours after the first word of Yousef's location had arrived in the capital. The target location, the two-story Su Casa Guest House, was a favorite stopover for "freedom fighters" heading to Afghanistan; only later would the FBI figure out that a group controlled by Osama bin Laden owned it. Pakistani troops and undercover intelligence agents took up positions around the building as the informant, Parker, walked inside to double-check that Yousef was still there. He walked back outside and ran his hands through his hair, the sign to go ahead with the bust. Pakistani forces stormed into room 16, AK-47s at the ready.

The bomb maker, who was lying on the bed when troops kicked in his door, seemed calm initially; he evidently believed this was a routine immigration matter. Then the makeshift U.S. grab team entered the room, DSS agent Bill Miller greeting him with, "What's up, Ramzi?" Only then did the bomb maker realize he was in much bigger trouble. Arriving minutes after the bust, Brad Garrett fingerprinted Yousef and, with Miller, began the interrogation at a Pakistani intelligence base.

Their first question was supposed to be simple: "What's your name?"

"Ali Baloch. Well, I have many," Yousef replied, smiling broadly.

Garrett produced a copy of the Most Wanted poster and held it up to the terrorist. "Is Ramzi Ahmed Yousef one of them?"

"Oh, yeah, that's me," Yousef said, still smiling.

"Well, good, good." A pause, then: "Did you blow up the World Trade Center or have any involvement in that?"

Yousef leaned back in his chair and a beat passed. "Well, I masterminded blowing up the World Trade Center."

Yousef was hustled aboard a private jet borrowed by the government and flown back to the United States. On board, he changed into an orange prison-issue jumpsuit and was examined by a doctor. The bomb maker explained to Stern and others that he'd hoped to topple one tower into the other, bringing them both down and killing everyone inside. After the plane landed at Stewart Air Force Base, just north of New York City, agents moved Yousef to a waiting helicopter for the quick ride to the courthouse in downtown Manhattan.

As the Sikorsky helicopter glided down the Hudson in the middle of the night, Chuck Stern leaned over and undid Yousef's blindfold and pointed across to the glittering World Trade Center towers. "They're still standing," he shouted into the terrorist's ear above the copter's engine noise.

"They wouldn't be if I'd gotten a little more money," Yousef replied.

Over the next three years—culminating in a sentence that would confine the bomb maker to the federal supermax prison in Florence, Colorado, for the rest of his life—Yousef's prosecution proved how law enforcement was evolving to meet a new threat. The FBI Lab conducted some five thousand different examinations as part of the trial preparation; prosecutors and agents put together a thousand different exhibits outlining various parts of the plot. Though the proceedings were held in New York, Yousef was also charged with the deeds thousands of miles away targeting non-Americans, the pope, and the airliners over the Pacific. His first trial focused on the World Trade Center bombing; a second trial focused on the Bojinka plot.

Counterterrorism and intelligence officials trooped through the trial. Special Agent Tom Pickard, who supervised New York's National Security Division, often sat in the back, watching the bright, articulate terrorist represent himself in the proceedings. During breaks, Pickard would introduce him to visiting officials. Everyone left with a greater understanding of just how dangerous the new threat was. Yousef was the opposite of almost everything the Bureau had dealt with in the 1980s—smart, organized, detail-driven, charismatic, and compelling. "To me, it was a real eye-opener," Pickard says.

However, the case also demonstrated just how long a road the FBI and the U.S. government still had before them. *Time's* article on Yousef's arrest quoted a "Karachi businessman" who had been staying at the guesthouse, a floor below. *Time* identified the man as Khalid Sheikh, but he was known to U.S. intelligence as Khalid Sheikh Mohammed—Yousef's uncle, who was quickly becoming Osama bin Laden's right-hand man. "It was like a hurricane, a big panic," Khalid

Sheikh told the *Time* reporters, without apparent concern for being identified. In describing Yousef's capture, he said, "They were dragging him downstairs. He was blindfolded, barefoot and had his hands and legs bound, and was shouting, 'I'm innocent; why are you taking me?' and 'Show me the arrest warrant.'" It would be some seven years before the United States next got its hands on KSM—only after he masterminded the 9/11 plots.

The specter of terror put the Bureau in a challenging position. Since the field was still mostly new to the FBI, most Bureau bosses had never worked terror cases as agents before they had become supervisors. Even John O'Neill, who would go on to be the primary driver of the FBI's counterterrorism mission, had never worked a terrorism case himself before arriving at the Hoover Building on the day Yousef was located in Pakistan. "It's hard to manage something you've never worked," Herman explains.

"The national security agents were a distinct minority," says Marion "Spike" Bowman, who was recruited from the navy and the National Security Agency in 1995 to head up the Bureau's new National Security Law Unit. "At a basic level, how do you tell one agent from another? The easiest way to do that is to look at cases opened, arrests made, and conviction numbers. On the national security side, you don't get any of that." Thus, Bowman explains, the agents in the 1990s who went into areas such as counterterrorism generally stayed for a while, if for no other reason than they were hard-pressed professionally to compete with fellow criminal agents with better statistics.

Even as prosecutors began to build their case against Yousef, the FBI JTTF and TRADEBOM investigators continued their quest to bring all the World Trade Center bombers to justice. U.S. intelligence had long believed Eyad Mahmoud Ismail Najim, a suspected driver in the New York operation, was hiding in Jordan, but the United States did not have an operative extradition treaty with that Mideast country. As the treaty was negotiated and ultimately signed in March 1995, the United States pushed for Najim's return to face trial.

Special Agent Thomas Pickard got the assignment to bring him back in August. Pickard, who eventually became the deputy director of the FBI and led the investigation of the 9/11 attacks from headquarters, told his wife that he was leaving on a trip but he couldn't tell her where or when he would be coming back. Despite nearly two decades in the Bureau, Pickard rarely traveled overseas. In fact, when he'd joined the Bureau, agents rarely even crossed state lines. During his first posting in New York, following a lead into New Jersey required asking a New York Field Office supervisor to call a Newark Field Office supervisor for permission to cross the Hudson.

After refueling over the Mediterranean, the rendition team settled into a holding pattern over the ocean when Jordanian officials asked the team to postpone landing until nightfall. The Amman airport handled both military and commercial traffic, and there was no need to advertise the American presence. After the plane taxied to a remote part of the runway, Pickard alone was allowed off the plane, and emerged from the aircraft with a stack of documents from the Justice Department and the State Department, some tied up elaborately with red ribbons, to make the handoff official. A doctor, a fingerprint expert, and a handful of Hostage Rescue Team operators had to stay behind.

A Jordanian government official met the New York agent and escorted him to a small blockhouse nearby. "Would you like to have some tea?" the official asked, inviting Pickard to sit down. Confused as to the protocol, Pickard agreed, and the two men sat making small talk for what seemed an eternity to the nervous agent. Slowly, the conversation drifted toward the prisoner. "I hear," the official began, "that you Americans often like to use handcuffs. Will you use handcuffs on this prisoner?"

Pickard paused, his mind racing with possible answers. FBI agents learn early—and are reminded in the field often—of the unpredictability of unrestrained suspects. He hesitantly answered, "I am a guest in your country. I will observe whatever your customs dictate."

"Good," the official answered. "No handcuffs. More tea?"

The conversation circled away from the matter at hand before drifting back. "I hear you Americans often cover prisoners with a hood."

Pickard offered the same answer. "Oh good," the Jordanian said. "No hood." And as if some magical answer had been given, he snapped his fingers, and two guards entered, escorting an uncuffed, unhooded

Najim. Najim didn't blink or look disconcerted at all during the hand-over. The official introduced the two men as if they were aspiring business partners. Unsure precisely what to say, Pickard said only, "I'm from the FBI, and I'm here to take you back to America." The official gestured Najim forward and then began to say goodbye to Pickard; out of his element and again uncertain of the protocol, Pickard watched as Najim, the man he'd traveled six thousand miles to capture, set off across the tarmac toward the waiting jet, unescorted, unsearched, and unrestrained. As Najim approached the plane alone, Pickard, who still had paperwork to complete, grabbed his radio and warned the team inside that the prisoner was about to appear in the doorway alone. The surprised HRT operators, themselves unsure of the protocol, knocked Najim to the ground as he came on board and searched him.

After Pickard reboarded the plane and the door closed, the pilot began to rev the engines for takeoff. Before the plane began to move, though, the pilot summoned Pickard to the cockpit with a problem: A Jordanian military half-track with soldiers on board had rumbled out onto the tarmac and parked in front of the U.S. Air Force jet. The Amman air traffic controllers announced that the FBI team was pro-hibited from leaving with Najim. If agents handed the TRADEBOM suspect back, they would be allowed to leave without further incident.

Pickard, tired, stressed, and now more confused than ever, consid-ered his options. In the darkness of the Amman night, pierced by the airport's floodlights, the Jordanian military appeared to hold most of the cards. The last time such an incident had occurred, a decade before, the standoff came at Sigonella air base in Sicily, after the United States had forced down the Egyptian airliner carrying the escaping hijackers of the *Achille Lauro*. That had been a showdown between Delta Force commandos and a friendly NATO government. This situation was entirely different. Pickard, the air force crew, the doctor, the finger-print examiner, and the HRT operators were on their own.

The FBI team was armed, but they'd be no match for any sizable force if the Jordanians decided to take the plane. On the other hand, the team had flown halfway around the world to get Najim, and FBI agents are taught never to release a prisoner until he makes it before a judge. The Jordanians weren't getting this guy back, Pickard swore.

As the stalemate festered and time passed, Pickard finally played his best card: "We're going to sit right here until dawn comes, and then we're going to put a big American flag up in the window for all to see," he announced to the nervous Jordanians. A few minutes later, the half-track rumbled away, and the Air Force pilots throttled the engines back up. Denied overflight rights by other countries because of its cargo, the plane—just like Fawaz Younis's flight some fifteen years before—threaded its way through the Strait of Gibraltar and nonstop back across the Atlantic before landing in upstate New York.*

That November, Pickard was called upon to bring Wali Khan Aman Shah to the United States after the Malaysian police had run the Bojinka suspect to ground. For the second rendition, Pickard tried to recruit many of the same team; they'd proven themselves capable under the extreme stress of the Amman incident. The fingerprint examiner, though, just laughed at Pickard. "You don't need me to come along," he said. "Even you could make this examination—he only has three fingers!" One of the professional hazards of being a bomb maker was that your own creations would bite you.

Agents often explain that Louis Freeh began his term as director with a "GS-14 mentality," referring to the civil service rank of a midlevel field supervisor. While he'd served for years in the FBI, he'd never risen to the leadership ranks of headquarters, where he would have gotten a broader perspective on the Bureau's problems and structure. Thus, as director, he seemed disproportionally focused on the everyday problems of street agents, as opposed to the bigger structural issues that are usually the purview of the director. An agent who worked alongside him explains, "He didn't have the big picture. Louis started and was trying to fix all the problems of the last forty years."

---

*A few weeks later, Pickard learned that his tarmac threat hadn't been quite as effective as he'd thought. When he was visiting another intelligence agency in Washington, a friend played him the radio transmissions between Pickard and the Amman tower, picked up by U.S. eavesdropping equipment. "This is the point where we're lucky we had an aircraft carrier offshore and scrambled fighter jets to come help you," his contact said. As the American carrier fighter jets screamed toward shore, the Jordanians had evidently decided that discretion was the better part of valor.

Thus, depending on whether one was a street agent or a Bureau executive, Freeh's tenure was either a glorious period for the FBI or a mockery of all the post-Hoover reforms. When Freeh visited field offices as director, he often demanded to meet privately with the "brick agents" and exiled their supervisors during his stay. Then, during the ride back to the airport with the office's special agent in charge, Freeh would tick off the problems street agents had identified and demand a quick fix. Such moves made him extremely popular with the street agents but infuriated the supervisory agent corps. Once, a recently widowed Houston agent was denied a transfer to Memphis to raise his child near his late wife's family. Freeh heard about it and word came down: "Put that agent on a plane to Memphis tomorrow."

Louis Freeh led as one of the guys. One of his most famous demonstrations of his commitment to agents was jogging. He jogged with FBI classes at Quantico; he jogged overseas with embassy Marine Corps guards and local agents; he jogged with National Academy classes; he even jogged with Patrick Leahy, the top Democrat on the Senate Judiciary Committee, at the senator's farm in Vermont. He literally pounded the pavement to remind all that he was not one to be permanently lodged in an office or eternally wearing loafers. Freeh ran with people because it said something about his priorities, his style of leadership, and his allegiance. Louis Freeh missed only two new agent class graduations, and agents still brag good-naturedly about which class he liked most: "Oh, he only jogged with you once? He jogged with us twice." And it wasn't just about the running—he seemed to remember everyone he met. One agent recalls that after shaking the director's hand following a run, he headed for the showers; moments later he turned around, water jetting onto his body, and came face-to-face with the naked director, who greeted him by name.

Freeh tore through the Hoover Building, eliminating layers of what he saw as unnecessary supervisors and bureaucracy. Agents were asked to transfer back to the field, but as an incentive were told that they could keep their headquarters-level pay; hundreds jumped at the opportunity. One specific management decision infuriated Bureau purists: A reorganization by Freeh led to the appointment in the same day of three new assistant directors—a female, a Hispanic male, and a black male. The female agent, the former special agent in charge of

Anchorage, skipped several levels to become assistant director; elevating the Hispanic agent, a junior assistant special agent in charge (ASAC) in Miami, was the equivalent of promoting a military colonel to a three-star general. "These moves quickly established that Freeh was going to return to a system of promotion by favoritism, cronyism, and political correctness," says Buck Revell, who had retired from the FBI by that time.

Moreover, Freeh, as a former agent, took a different view of his investigative role as FBI director. He'd worked these cases before; he'd prosecuted the biggest mob case the nation had ever seen; he knew how to run an investigation. Agents first saw this tendency play out in the wake of the bombing of the Alfred P. Murrah Federal Building in Oklahoma City, where Freeh personally approved the photo arrays used to help identify the suspects, normally a decision that occurs a dozen layers below the director's office. A similar trait would show in future investigations: In the 1996 Atlanta Olympic Park bombing, he dictated questions to be asked in the interrogation of the lead suspect, Richard Jewell, who turned out to be innocent.

Even though the Oklahoma City bombing turned out to be entirely of domestic origin, it was part of a convergence of four major events in the first half of 1995 that helped raise the profile of counterterrorism in the Bureau and the wider government apparatus. First came the capture of Ramzi Yousef, whose interrogation underlined just how ambitious this new wave of terrorists were. This was also the moment when the chatter about a certain Saudi financier took a significant uptick. "It was then you began to hear the name Osama bin Laden — it became critical," says Fred Stremmel, the longtime FBI analyst who had been working terrorism ever since the Libyans threatened assassinations during the 1980 presidential election.

Coinciding with Yousef's capture was the arrival of John O'Neill as the new section chief of counterterrorism for the FBI. O'Neill would make sounding the alert about terrorism within the Bureau his mission for the next six years. "He energized us. He had a lot of foresight," Stremmel recalls. "He liaisoned with our counterparts here and overseas. He brought in a lot of analysts. He had a vision." O'Neill and his team would fight a lonely fight for too long. It remained hard to get Bureau-wide attention for the matter. Even Richard Marquise, the case agent from SCOTBOM, recalls that he never heard of al-Qaeda during his time leading counterterrorism squads in the 1990s. "I was an SAC before I heard of al-Qaeda," he recalls, meaning sometime after 1999.

Third was the Oklahoma City bombing, OKBOMB (as it was referred to), the first major terrorist attack of Freeh's tenure. Agents close to him say it was highly formative in focusing his attention on the threat of terrorism. Coming just weeks after the Yousef capture, when Freeh was finally putting the fiascoes at Waco and Ruby Ridge behind him, the Oklahoma City attack had Freeh's full attention. In fact, in the weeks between Yousef's February capture and the April Oklahoma City bombing, Freeh gave a speech listing his top priorities as director, and terrorism wasn't mentioned at all. It took the one-two punch of Yousef and OKBOMB to bring the director around. ("He didn't open his eyes until the Yousef rendition," Stremmel says.)

Freeh stood in Oklahoma City atop the debris of the ruined building and proclaimed to the crowd of officials around him, "*Hostes humani generis*. Enemies of mankind. You cannot slaughter innocent men, women, and America's kids and get away with it. We will not rest or have peace until this crime against humanity is adjudged and punished."

The fourth factor in elevating counterterrorism as a priority took place secretly. On June 21, 1995, President Clinton signed the classified Presidential Decision Directive 39, titled "United States Policy on Counterterrorism." It stated, in part, that the United States should "deter, defeat and respond vigorously to all terrorist attacks on our territory and against our citizens." Simultaneously deeming terror both a national security threat and a criminal law enforcement matter, it was the first presidential decision directive to deal with the subject since the Reagan years had reaffirmed the FBI as the nation's primary counterterrorism agency. As Freeh had said to Congress, "Somebody ought to be in charge when the bomb goes off. We think it should be the FBI." Clinton agreed.

The FBI first used its new authority under PDD 39 just thirteen days later, when an American, Donald Hutchings, was kidnapped, along with five other tourists, in the disputed Kashmir corner of the Himalayas.★ Within hours, an FBI team was en route to India. From that point forward, thanks to PDD 39, the FBI's global powers would make it the most far-reaching, capable, and powerful law enforcement agency in the world. Investigating international kidnappings of Americans quickly became a major task for the Bureau; by 2003 it had helped out on more than 120 cases. Interpol might work mainly as a coordinating policy body and central repository for police agencies, but the FBI was becoming, step by step, the world's police force.

For every victory, such as capturing Ramzi Yousef, there were setbacks. On March 20, 1995, the Japanese cult Aum Shinrikyo released sarin nerve gas into the Tokyo subway, sickening more than a thousand people and killing twelve. Only some minor tactical mistakes by the group prevented the death toll from reaching into the hundreds. In the wake of the attack, the NSC's Richard Clarke asked the FBI's John O'Neill for the Bureau's file on the cult, which was supposed to have operations around the world. The FBI had nothing to share.

Sitting in the White House Situation Room coordinating the U.S. response, Clarke asked in frustration, "How can you be sure that there are no Aum here, John, just because you don't have an FBI file on them? Did you look them up in the Manhattan phone book?"

O'Neill dispatched another agent to call the New York Field Office. When the agent returned to the Situation Room and handed O'Neill a note, the hard-charging FBI agent swore and turned to Clarke: "Fuck. They're in the phone book. East Forty-eighth Street at Fifth."

The FBI was well on its way to figuring out the new wave of terrorism, but it still had a lot to learn about the new enemies it faced.

★The agents ultimately came back empty-handed. The FBI believes the tourists were executed sometime in December 1995; their bodies have never been found. The suspected group of terrorists was later suspected to be linked to the abduction and murder of *Wall Street Journal* reporter Daniel Pearl after 9/11.

CHAPTER 7
Pax Americana

Our comfortable routine is no eternal necessity
of things, but merely a little space of calm in
the midst of the tempestuous untamed
streaming of the world.

— *Oliver Wendell Holmes*

Powerful U.S. attorneys such as Rudy Giuliani and Mary Jo White had given New York's law enforcement agencies sovereignty from Washington oversight; aggressive, no-nonsense prosecutors like Louis Freeh and Pat Fitzgerald had been willing and able to take on unprecedented cases. Agents such as Carmine Russo and Charlie Rooney could chase seemingly unpromising leads for months, fitting together puzzle pieces as they attempted to sniff out a larger case. As a result, arguably the most visionary legal work in the country was churning out of a small corner of the Southern District U.S. Attorney's Office and the FBI's New York Field Office, led by people who saw a new threat emerging and saw a new place on the world stage for the United States and the FBI.

Special Agent Jack Cloonan had been on the FBI team that traveled to Germany in 1985 to investigate the Bureau's first extraterritorial case, the TWA Flight 847 hijacking, during which U.S. Navy diver Robert Stethem was murdered. He had subsequently been sent to the Newark Field Office for several years, where he worked an undercover investigation into corrupt towing contracts with the city. Now back in New York, Cloonan was assigned to Squad I-49, a new team tasked with looking specifically at radical Egyptian jihad movements, a target inspired by the Blind Sheikh's terror cells.

After the World Trade Center bombing, Neil Gallagher, then the FBI's counterterrorism section chief, convened some of the Bureau's experts to try to imagine what would come next. The consensus was clear: Attacks were going to be more spectacular—multiple hijackings, bigger bombs, maybe even a weapon of mass destruction. "It dawned on everyone after the World Trade Center and the Sheikh trial; you get the first inclination that there's a radical Islamic movement that extends far beyond Egypt and the Middle East," Cloonan says. "It appeared to extend big into the United States. Thousands of people subscribed to these beliefs. This was not just rhetoric from these groups. To some extent, the Bureau was slow to pick up on that." The motivations behind the attacks were not so much political as nihilistic, couched in theology. As analyst Fred Stremmel says, "You're going from the political to the religious. That's a real benchmark."

Nationally, the counterterrorism program was still off the radar. When it did engage, the Bureau was jumping from case to case, missing the new trend that was changing the threats. "You get so focused on the criminal aspect that it can be myopic. You lose the big picture," Cloonan reflected. "Beyond the law enforcement angle, do we have the analytic resources to look at this? It's hard. You're forced to pick and choose." As Stremmel says, "It was a priority program, but it still wasn't a priority for resources. Your hours were getting longer, your briefings were getting longer, the list of threats was also getting longer, and there were fewer people to help." In fact, out of more than 20,000 personnel in the Bureau nationwide, only about 125 people worked CT. But if in Washington the Bureau was treading backward, in New York, Squad I-49, a team of fewer than 20 agents under supervisor Tom Lange, was going to play offense. For better or worse, they were almost entirely on their own.

"The people on the squad had to learn about this movement, and we quickly realized there was not a lot of material for us to look at,"

Cloonan recalls. As it evolved, I-49's focus soon came to be assembling a prosecutable case against Osama bin Laden. At the time, bin Laden was somewhat of a mystery—a name, not a case. "We thought it was an unusual assignment. It didn't really seem possible," Cloonan says. But, he added, "When you hang around Pat Fitzgerald for any length, you realize that it's possible."

Pat Fitzgerald, a hard-charging, meticulous, and brilliant assistant U.S. attorney working in the Southern District who would become the famous investigator of the Valerie Plame leak investigation a decade later, was unique. He worked terrorism cases like a street agent, doing intense interviews, making huge case files. Perhaps more than anyone, Fitzgerald would use his intense focus to turn the Southern District under Mary Jo White into ground zero for the legal battle against terror.

The case against bin Laden began slowly. Many of the FBI's leads came from "overhears," intercepts that were hard to interpret or understand. If this was all they had, the case was a dead end. But the CIA, long at odds with the Bureau, would jump-start Squad I-49's investigation in a big way.

It was almost pure coincidence that the CIA had targeted resources at bin Laden. As the Agency's resources dwindled and atrophied after the Cold War, Director John Deutch wanted to create a "virtual station" in Washington that focused attention on a single issue rather than a geographic region. The problem the CIA chose—from many that it considered—was terrorist financing, which gradually evolved into a specific focus on bin Laden. The first head of the "terrorist financial links" unit, veteran CIA officer Michael Scheuer, named it after his son, Alec.

In a way, Danny Coleman was the perfect FBI agent to be posted to Alec Station. "Danny was a natural-born spook," explains his colleague Chris Voss, who worked the TERRSTOP case with Coleman in New York. "He understood them. He spoke their language. He knew how to move." At the nondescript office building in northern Virginia where Alec Station was based, Coleman began to pore over more than forty boxes of material the CIA had collected on the Saudi terrorist leader. The depth of the CIA's information astounded him. During one meeting at the Agency, Coleman blew his top regarding the intelligence that the CIA hadn't shared with the Bureau. "I ought to arrest you all for obstruction of justice," he snapped, echoing frustrations expressed by an agent during the SCOTBOM case years earlier. When he traveled back to New York, though, he tried to convey to his squad that the Agency just operated under a different set of principles. "Look, they don't tell each other shit. It's not personal," he told his colleagues. "It's the way they are."

In the spring of 1996, the CIA passed along news that it had found a valuable informer from the obscure network of the Saudi financier. A man had walked into the U.S. embassy in Eritrea, the tiny African country sandwiched between the Sudan and Ethiopia on the Red Sea, and explained that he was a member of al-Qaeda. Fitzgerald, fellow prosecutor Ken Karas, and a team of FBI agents—including Frank Pellegrino and Coleman, who just weeks earlier had begun his Alec Station posting—traveled to Ramstein Air Force Base in Germany to meet Jamal al-Fadl, whom they came to nickname "Junior." Over the course of more than a week of conversations, al-Fadl claimed he'd been a key operations person in bin Laden's movement and skimmed off some of the Saudi's money. Then, afraid he would be caught, he turned to the United States as an escape route.

Junior had been living in Brooklyn and been radicalized at the Al-Farooq Mosque, the onetime home of the Blind Sheikh and a hotbed of extremism well known to the FBI JTTF from the investigations of Kahane's assassination and the 1993 World Trade Center bombing. Al-Fadl had evidently been the third person to join bin Laden's group and now poured out details of its growth. "You found out what a day in the life of al-Qaeda was like—what time bin Laden got up, where they went, what they ate," Cloonan says. For some on the U.S. team, the discussions with al-Fadl were the first time they'd heard that bin Laden's network, which had previously been under the umbrella of a group called Special Services, was morphing into something greater.

The new information was heart-stopping for the investigators. The Libyans, as threatening as they'd seemed in the 1980s, were kind of the Keystone Kops of terror. They had what some agents joked was a stereotypical Middle Eastern sense of time, and thus regularly missed deadlines and meetings; they embezzled their own operations funds; they had big mouths. Recalls Stremmel, "That all changed with the new group. They're disciplined, they're not corrupt, they're well trained. They're true believers. They had very good information security—a lot better than ours."

At almost the same time Junior was spilling to the FBI team, Osama bin Laden's group was undergoing its next permutation. After years of being harbored by the Sudanese, bin Laden was encouraged to take his operation elsewhere after a series of actions angered his hosts. He found a willing new ally and home among the Taliban in Afghanistan, where much of the Islamic jihad movement had originally gotten off the ground in the battle against the Soviet invasion of the 1980s. The move to Afghanistan coincided with a shift in rhetoric: Osama bin Laden's extremism deepened, his willingness to attack the West grew, and he began to speak more openly of violence against the United States. In a series of declarations and statements, bin Laden declared that al-Qaeda would expel the West from Islamic lands, especially Saudi Arabia, which retained large U.S. military bases from the Gulf War.

In the fifties and sixties, John O'Neill grew up in Atlantic City on a steady dose of the popular TV series *The F.B.I.,* part of J. Edgar Hoover's huge propaganda machine. O'Neill always wanted to be an agent. He applied to American University in Washington for its proximity to the Bureau and almost immediately signed up as a part-time fingerprint clerk. Soon thereafter, he married his high school sweetheart, Christine—who was at the time still in high school—and they had a son two years later. After college, O'Neill became a tour guide at FBI Headquarters, taking night classes toward a master of science degree in forensics sciences at George Washington University. In July 1976, as the country celebrated its bicentennial, he started new agent's training at Quantico—a dream come true. His first post was Baltimore.

O'Neill was a complicated individual. He and Christine grew apart, but he never divorced her, despite having several long-term girlfriends in other cities over the years. (He'd explain away the matter as "It's a Catholic thing," yet friends later assumed it had something to do with ensuring that his family remained eligible for his government health insurance and pension.) While working at headquarters

THE THREAT MATRIX • 199

on white-collar crime, he met Mary Lynn Stevens, a credit union executive, with whom he would have a relationship for the rest of his life. In July 1991, O'Neill became the criminal division ASAC in Chicago, responsible for violent crime, white-collar crime, and organized crime. Imbued by his parents with a tireless work ethic—his parents drove a cab, his mother taking the day shift, his father the night shift— he became legendary for his long hours. Often he'd be the first one in the office in the morning and the last one to leave at night.

O'Neill believed deeply in appearances and official protocol. He ranted about the FBI's frumpy blue raid jackets, which he thought were demeaning and unattractive. "You ever see a Secret Service agent walk around in a vinyl jacket reading 'Secret Service'?" he'd complain. "Whether it's freezing cold or burning hot, whether they're carrying a machine gun or running alongside a limo, they always look great—crisp shirt, tie perfectly done, dark suit." O'Neill thought the Bureau had gone soft, gotten away from the sharp appearance it had had under Hoover. "You never saw him underdressed," recalls one of his agents, Steve Gaudin. "He had the panache."

In December 1994, O'Neill was appointed the chief of counterterrorism at FBI Headquarters, and in February, he drove his silver Buick Regal straight from Chicago to the Hoover Building to begin. He was just settling into his office that Sunday when Richard Clarke called with the news that Ramzi Yousef had been located in Pakistan.

Over the coming months, O'Neill became fixated on the rise of bin Laden. At one point, talking with Clarke, he compared bin Laden to the young Adolf Hitler—someone no one took seriously until it was too late. "It's like *Mein Kampf,*" O'Neill would explain. "Bin Laden's just like this. When you read what this guy says he's going to do, he's serious. There are a lot of people who support him."

Yet it was often hard to tell where bin Laden's movement stopped and started. In October 1993, when U.S. special forces in Mogadishu, Somalia, engaged in a fierce battle (chronicled by the book and the film *Black Hawk Down*), bin Laden's organization later claimed credit for helping to shoot down the American helicopters and killing eighteen U.S. troops. When President Clinton ordered American troops to withdraw from the country after the attack, the Islamists declared a victory and proclaimed the Americans "cowards."

Beginning in January 1996, a year after the Oklahoma City bombing, O'Neill pushed for the FBI to separate its terrorism division into two parts, domestic and international. His interest was in what was coming from overseas. Someone else should be looking at the homeland, he argued. The world was getting more complicated, and the FBI needed to recognize that domestic threats were often very different from international ones. "O'Neill was the face of terrorism, always clawing for attention," Fred Stremmel reflects. "After he left, it wasn't as aggressive."

Indeed, O'Neill became something of a one-man marketing machine for terrorism, as Buck Revell had been for the FBI the decade before. During a speech in Chicago, O'Neill outlined how the Bureau was marshaling a response to the new threat against the United States. "At the time of the World Trade Center bombing, the FBI and most of the intelligence community was putting most of its eggs, if you will, in the basket of investigating states that sponsor terrorism. We still do that. Iran, Iraq, Libya, Syria, Sudan. The World Trade Center case made us painfully aware that there is this new realm that's out there that's growing at a pretty fast pace, and that is religious extremism," he told the crowd. "Almost all of the groups today, if they choose to, have the ability to strike us here in the United States."

Whereas the 1970s and early 1980s had seen hundreds of small attacks—pipe bombs, incendiary attacks, and the like—the 1990s were an era in which the total number of terrorist attacks had fallen but the attacks were much larger and deadlier and more far-reaching. Terrorists, O'Neill argued, relied on fear to accomplish their goal, which required news attention; they'd figured out that hitting an embassy with a rocket, while terrifying and even deadly for those at the target, didn't have the profile necessary to focus the media. Oklahoma City had interrupted the wall-to-wall coverage of the O. J. Simpson trial as few other stories would have.

Exhibit A came during a rare moment of warmth between the FBI and CIA. On June 25, 1996, John O'Neill hosted a big barbecue at the Quantico academy to help the FBI and CIA counterterrorism teams to mend fences and to encourage more cooperation between the agencies. The highlight of the day was supposed to be time at the weapons range. (CIA analyst positions are mostly desk jobs, so the Langley guests were excited about the chance to spend some time on the firing line.) Then, in midafternoon, everyone's beeper started to go off.

The participants soon learned that a gigantic truck bomb had obliterated the Khobar Towers housing complex in Riyadh, Saudi Arabia. Since it was just six months since a December 1995 car bomb attack on U.S. personnel in Saudi Arabia, security had been on alert at the compound, which housed military personnel from a number of countries, and a sentry had noticed the suspiciously parked truck and begun an evacuation. It was too late: 19 Americans were killed and more than 370 people were injured by the blast, the explosive equivalent of some ten tons of TNT. The building was almost entirely gone, and the blast concussion broke windows up to a mile away.

O'Neill stayed at the barbecue—this was an important bonding opportunity—but he dispatched John Lipka and other agents back to Washington to begin planning the FBI's response. That response would become the FBI's largest overseas deployment to date, including forensics specialists, investigators, the Hostage Rescue Team, and other units. The agents worked long hours at the crime scene and were under orders to drink a pint of water every fifteen minutes. (After several agents began to suffer from heat exhaustion, the FBI moved its operations to nighttime.) Injured military personnel worked side by side, helping the investigation and underscoring its importance.

The Saudis weren't inclined to cooperate. "Saudi Arabia was just a void that wasn't being dealt with," Neil Herman recalls. Throughout the 1990s, the Saudi government was afraid to upset the delicate balance of power in the kingdom between the royal family and the clerics. At best, it was only a vaguely willing participant in counterterrorism efforts. In 1997, the FBI had a chance to snatch Imad Mughniyeh, who had long eluded U.S. intelligence. Mughniyeh was supposed to be on board a flight that would have a layover in Saudi Arabia, but as the Bureau prepared a team to snatch him when he landed, the Saudi government waved the flight off, warning that the terrorist leader was at risk of capture if he landed.

After the car bombing in December 1995 had killed five Americans and two Indians, the Saudi government claimed that its agents had interrogated the suspects, tried them, and executed them before informing the FBI. The Bureau remained dubious that the men represented the full extent of the plot, although those arrested had cited bin Laden's influence in their decision to launch the attack. Now, by Saudi government order, agents couldn't leave the Khobar Towers crime scene to investigate leads; they couldn't access phone records or other basic investigative tools; they couldn't interview witnesses or talk with possible suspects.

Louis Freeh had developed a close friendship with Prince Bandar bin Sultan, the powerful Saudi ambassador to the United States, and thought himself capable of smoothing over the situation. During a trip to Khobar Towers, Freeh, accompanied by O'Neill, had a series of late-night meetings with Saudi officials. On the flight back to the States, Freeh said, "Wasn't that a great trip? I think they're really going to help us."

O'Neill, never shy, couldn't hold back: "You're kidding. They didn't give us anything. They were just shining sunshine up your ass."

The rest of the flight passed in icy silence.

Khobar Towers would be one of the last major cases O'Neill worked from headquarters. Tom Pickard, who had been the special agent in charge of national security in New York and had worked the renditions on the TRADEBOM case, had become one of Freeh's most trusted agents. When Freeh promoted Pickard to head the Washington Field Office, an assistant-director-level position, O'Neill got the nod to replace him in New York. Overseeing some four hundred agents working both counterterrorism and counterintelligence, O'Neill was in heaven. His office on the twenty-sixth floor of the Federal Building seemingly overlooked all of New York, from Harlem to Brooklyn. When O'Neill arrived, he asked his assistant to set up meetings with everyone from the mayor to the fire commissioner, the police commissioner, even Archbishop John O'Connor. He became a regular at Elaine's, the establishment bar on the Upper East Side, and was often seen there late into the night, sipping Chivas and holding court. The Jersey boy would own New York.

The Saudis might have gotten one over on Louis Freeh, but not many others did. After several initial missteps, Freeh quickly proved himself an excellent political player. He installed the FBI's first chief of staff, Bob Bucknam, an old friend from the Pizza Connection and the Southern District U.S. Attorney's Office, to be his political watchdog. He also befriended congressional Republicans (who, coincidentally, controlled the FBI's budget) against what he saw as endemic corruption in the White House. As warm as they'd been in the Rose Garden at his nomination, Louis Freeh and President Clinton soon soured on each other.

Freeh's relationship with the president and the White House deteriorated quickly, beginning with the 1996 disclosure that FBI clerks had inappropriately sent private personnel files to the White House, a scandal that came to be known as Filegate. Despite its being an innocent clerical mix-up on the Bureau's end, Freeh—without notifying the Justice Department—released a statement blaming the White House, saying, "The FBI and I were victimized." He regularly encouraged investigations into Clinton administration misdeeds, and that antagonism permeated Freeh's leadership circle, which came to be known as "Friends of Louis," or FOLs. During one conference call, Deputy Director Robert "Bear" Bryant argued against providing the White House with background information on the FBI's investigation into illegal Chinese campaign financing before Secretary of State Madeleine Albright's trip to China. "Why should we brief him?" Bryant said of the president. "He's a crook. He's no better than a bank robber. Would we tell a bank robber about our investigation?" Freeh, for his part, turned in his White House gate pass, preferring to sign in and out during each visit so there was a public record of his trips.

Given the way Washington plays power games, Freeh's persecution of the president made the FBI director more powerful. The only person who could fire him was the president, and Freeh had neutralized that enemy. "The president felt the director was way out of control," then deputy attorney general Jamie Gorelick recalls. "It was terrible. [Freeh's] accusations of corruption meant that the president taking action to address a dysfunctional relationship would only feed the allegation of corruption. The director became bulletproof."

Privately, President Clinton expressed his frustration with the FBI's investigations into his administration. Historian Taylor Branch, who had a series of secret conversations with Bill Clinton during his presidency, recalled, "When I asked about his duty to hold the Bureau accountable anyway, or at least try, he said such an effort would backfire." Clinton similarly came to loathe the man he'd nominated to lead the Bureau: "Louis Freeh is a goddamn fucking asshole," he reportedly said behind closed doors.

Freeh's focus on scoring political points against the president made the nation less safe. Post-9/11—when FBI director Mueller met daily with President Bush for more than three years—it seems an oddity and a luxury that the United States existed in a world where the FBI director and the president didn't speak. But that became the situation with Clinton and Freeh. One night the FBI director was speaking at a cocktail party with a reporter and told him candidly that it had been three and a half years since he'd spoken to the president. "It was like Louis didn't want to debase himself by talking to the president of the United States," one Bureau executive explains.

Had President Clinton maintained a closer relationship with his head of domestic law enforcement, perhaps he would have felt more empowered to take action against the rising threats overseas. Instead, the FBI director's disgust and actions isolated the president from the very structures meant to inform his decision-making. "An FBI director should be able to go to the president, sit down, and say, 'You should know about this.' I wish that I had been able to do that. We had vital business to discuss," Freeh recalled. "There was always some new investigation brewing."

For the majority of Clinton's second term, beginning when the FBI launched its campaign finance investigation of President Clinton in late 1997—before the first sealed bin Laden indictment and the al-Qaeda leader's fatwa against the United States, through the East Africa embassy bombings, the missile strikes against bin Laden in Afghanistan, and the millennium plots, and up past the bombing of the USS *Cole* in October 2000—the FBI director and the president of the United States never spoke personally.

By early 1998, Squad I-49 was close to accomplishing what just years earlier had seemed an impossible task: It had a sealed indictment against Osama bin Laden for financing terrorism. Junior al-Fadl had opened the floodgates. After the agents in Germany had realized Junior's value, they'd flown him on a government plane to New York's Stewart Air Force Base and then helicoptered him to a Residence Inn in New Jersey, the first of many safe houses. What had seemed an impossible mission when Lange first announced the bin Laden investigation now quickly moved forward. "Less than two years [after starting], we got a sealed indictment on someone who's never set foot in the United States," Mike Anticev recalls in amazement. "We were doing stuff that nobody understood."

The indictment coincided roughly with a troubling new development in bin Laden's organization. Now allied with Egyptian Islamic Jihad leader Ayman al-Zawahiri, bin Laden in February 1998 issued an official fatwa—a binding religious document—calling on Muslims to wage war against the United States. Later that spring bin Laden directly threatened the United States in an interview with *ABC News*'s John Miller (who would become the head of the FBI's public affairs division a few years later). "The call to wage war against America was made because America has spearheaded the crusade against the Islamic nation, sending tens of thousands of its troops to the land of the two holy mosques over and above its meddling in its affairs and its politics, and its support of the oppressive, corrupt and tyrannical regime that is in control," he told Miller in Afghanistan. "Nothing could stop you except perhaps retaliation in kind. We do not have to differentiate between military or civilian. As far as we are concerned, they are all targets, and this is what the fatwa says."

In hindsight, Squad I-49's work was some of the most important going on in the Bureau in the late 1990s, but at the time its members certainly didn't feel that way. Less than two years before the 9/11 attacks, just two squads were working al-Qaeda and "OBL"; Squad I-49 focused on bin Laden and al-Qaeda's central command, while Squad I-45 focused on the suspects who participated in embassy bombings. By the end of the 1990s, the Bureau leadership in New York and Washington rotated with such regularity that the team grew tired trying to explain its work to new bosses. "I didn't want to be walking in to talk to a boss who didn't know what al-Qaeda was. From the ground agent's perspective, it doesn't give you as much confidence," Cloonan says. The bosses didn't seem all that interested anyhow, and moved the squad's workspace to the eighth floor at 290 Broadway, the satellite FBI office across the street from 26 Federal Plaza. The agents were alone on the floor, about as far removed as a team could get from the bosses. Neither of the two assistant directors who led the New York Office during this period, Barry Mawn and Jim Kallstrom, ever visited the squad's office. "For the rest of the office, for the rest of the counterterrorism squads, we were on our own. It wasn't by design; it just evolved," Cloonan says. The setup, as isolating as it was, gave the team incredible freedom. "We didn't have to justify or sell anything," Mike Anticev says, echoing Cloonan's words: "We were on our own."

For the squad, the evolving case became life-defining. Cloonan, much to his wife's dismay, kept a wanted poster of Osama bin Laden in his bedroom; it was the first thing he saw in the morning and the last thing he saw at night. Mike Anticev spent hours talking on the phone with Junior, counseling him about the case and about life in the United States. Altogether, the FBI and the U.S. government spent more than $1 million on Junior and his family, keeping them happy and willing to cooperate during more than a decade in U.S. custody, first with the Bureau and then later in the U.S. Marshals' Witness Protection Program. At the beginning, agents were with Junior twenty-four hours a day as they moved from location to location in New Jersey. At one hotel stop, Anticev and Cloonan sat poolside as Junior splashed in the water, paddling around on a neon-colored foam noodle, dodging families and other hotel guests and flirting with the young lifeguard. "Geez, Jack, if those people had any idea who that was in the pool with them..." Anticev mused.

The al-Qaeda turncoat quickly came to love American food. He'd wake up most days asking the team first about breakfast: "We gonna get pancakes today?" He also loved Big Macs and happily ballooned under the FBI's watch. Agents spent long afternoons in between debriefings and interrogations playing Junior in basketball and another game he came to love in the United States, Ping-Pong. "It was quiet moments when you weren't doing the formal session that were really interesting," Cloonan says. Late at night, unable to sleep, Junior would open up to the agents on watch.

Junior led an isolated existence. The agents tried to limit his contact with newspapers and television to ensure he wasn't being influenced by outside events. He couldn't make friends easily because he was undercover. As part of the FBI's deal with him, the team had smuggled his wife and family out of Sudan and brought then to New York, and then helped his wife through the culture shock. "One day she's in the Sudan, then the next day she's in Cairo, and the next day she's in the U.S. Can you imagine how disconcerting that is? Look, we're the unbelievers, the bloodsuckers, and here we are saying, 'Don't worry, you're safe'?" Cloonan explains. Before she arrived in the States, she had never cooked on a stove, and she hadn't seen her husband in more than two years. Taking her and the family food shopping, the agents tried to explain American grocery stores. Junior's wife punched a frozen turkey, trying to ascertain what this mysterious thing was.

For the team's Fourth of July party, agents decided to get some lobsters too. Junior's wife's eyes grew wide as the agents plunged their hands into the tank to pick out the writhing crustaceans with the giant claws. "She thought we were trying to feed her children waterborne spiders," Cloonan recalls.

As they checked out, the cashier clerk asked about the strange group—a handful of white, tough-looking Americans and a large African family shopping together. "Oh, we're missionaries," Cloonan replied, thinking fast.

As they walked out, Mike Anticev burst out laughing: "What a line of bullshit, Jack."

"Well, we are on a mission," Cloonan, deadpan, shot back.

Even as Osama bin Laden built an Islamist network in the Middle East, recruiting followers by preaching that the West was at war with Muslims, another team of FBI agents began investigating the worst massacre of Muslims in recent history. In the summer of 1999, the international tribunal studying atrocities during the brutal civil war in the former Yugoslavia asked for help excavating mass graves. The United Nations, which was in charge of the efforts in Kosovo, asked Director Freeh for forensic help.

Kosovo was one of the most challenging missions the FBI had

undertaken, and yet transnational investigations seemed increasingly to be where the Bureau was heading. Kosovo was the FBI's third genocide investigation in six years; agents had assisted investigations in Bosnia-Herzegovina in 1993 and in Rwanda in 1994. Knowing that the UN forces, code-named KFOR for Kosovo Force, were consumed with peacekeeping, the FBI team left Andrews Air Force Base with some 95,000 pounds of equipment—everything it would need to be self-sufficient for months. In an era before digital photography, film and cameras alone filled half of a tractor-trailer. The FBI settled into a corner of the Italian NATO peacekeepers' camp. The nights were filled with the sounds of distant gunfire and artillery fire.

The first team of sixty-five FBI agents and forensics experts was unprepared for the horrors its members began to uncover in Dja-kovica, one of the flashpoints of the war. At one scene searched by the Bureau, Serbian troops had herded twenty Muslims into a home's basement, opened fire, and then burned the building down. Most of the victims were children. Relatives watched quietly as the FBI team exhumed bodies and laid them under white tarps in the fields nearby. At another house, they found the body of a baby still wrapped in his mother's arms. North of Pristina, the FBI uncovered twenty-three members of one family buried in shallow graves where they'd been caught after hiding in the forest; one young boy was still dressed in a red snowsuit and had his baby bottle with him. "We were trying to work a sensitive investigation in the midst of a civil war," recalls HRT operator Jim Yacone, who would later command the Hostage Rescue Team. Even for Yacone, a veteran of the army's operations in Somalia, Yugoslavia was a terrible environment. "You had to do everything. We went from being knee-deep in graves to running convoy escort between warring factions."

Almost month by month, the FBI's overseas presence grew. Legats opened at a rapid pace under Freeh, who kept up a busy schedule of foreign trips, courting presidents, prime ministers, and law enforcement officials. During one trip through the former Soviet Union, the behemoth whose spies the FBI had spent decades tracking (and whose most damaging spy, Robert Hanssen, was still employed by the FBI at the time), Freeh opened the first legat in Moscow, headed by Special Agent Michael di Pretoro, who had spent his career chasing Soviet spies. In a way, the appointment made sense—di Pretoro spoke Russian fluently—but it was an odd turnabout for the counterintelligence agent to sit across conference tables from his old KGB adversaries. At each stop during the trip—in Slovakia, the Czech Republic, Hungary, Poland, Lithuania, the Ukraine, and Russia—Freeh hammered home his motto: "The world has become a very small and dangerous place." He saw firsthand the legacy of state-run terror—the industrialization of Auschwitz and the bloodstained walls of a former Lithuanian prison that had headquartered the KGB. Deeply moved, he argued that protecting civil liberties was an important part of building a nation of laws, and cited in his speeches the FBI's own abuses in COINTELPRO and CISPES. This was a new era of foreign affairs. "The trip symbolizes the transition from Cold War politics to the far more difficult issues of the postwar world," Assistant Secretary of State Richard Holbrooke said in a speech during Freeh's trip at a stop in Berlin. "The CIA and Defense Department issues that predominated during the Cold War have receded. Let me state clearly here and now: We are in a new phase of foreign policy. The FBI is moving to the forefront of this new foreign policy." Back in Washington, a stop at the Hoover Building on Pennsylvania Avenue became almost as de rigueur for visiting foreign leaders as stops at the two ends of the broad street, the White House and Capitol Hill.

The expanding mission and global footprint weren't universally welcomed. Former secretary of state Al Haig, for one, was a vocal opponent. "The FBI has more than enough to do at home and a great deal of work to do to achieve our law enforcement objectives at home to a better degree than we have in the past," he complained. "To pervert the mission of the FBI to become an external, international law enforcement agency is wrongheaded."

The powerful House Appropriations chair, Bob Livingston, was also troubled, but following a tradition dating back to Hoover's tenure, few members wanted to be seen as denying the Bureau the resources it said it needed. Livingston succeeded in shutting off new funding for legats in 1998. "I just did not feel, and still do not feel, that the FBI, whose charter is to be our domestic and paramount federal law enforcement agency, has any business spreading themselves so thin all over the world," Livingston said. But by 1999, thanks to Louis

Freeh's force of personality and his close relationship with other House Republicans, the money was back and the FBI was back on the march, opening offices in Brasilia, Budapest, and Amman.

While the FBI was blossoming, the CIA was lost in the years following the fall of the Soviet Union. Since William Webster, the one-time FBI director, had left as CIA director in 1991, four directors and four interim acting directors had cycled through in six years. "The trouble is there's too much to do," said John Deutch, who spent eighteen months as CIA director in the mid-1990s under President Clinton. George Tenet, who replaced Deutch as director, phrased it more bluntly: The CIA was stretched far beyond its ability to answer the central questions posed by the new world and hadn't made the transition to a post-Soviet world. The 1993 discovery of a major Russian spy deep within the CIA, Aldrich Ames—who since 1985 had turned over most of the CIA's and FBI's most important secrets to the Russians, leading to the arrest and execution of nearly every major U.S. source in the Kremlin—led to years of investigations, recriminations, and even an FBI-led purge of some three hundred CIA officials (all of whom were later found to be innocent). Budgets were shrinking, stations were closing, veteran analysts were retiring. "The atrophy was tremendous," Tenet recalled during a speech in 2005. "We were nearly bankrupt."

The so-called peace dividend, the savings that foreign policy experts decided should come with the end of the Cold War, meant that Congress was regularly hacking money from the intelligence community's budget. From 1991 to 1997, every single year the CIA's budget was smaller than the year before—and the FBI's budget grew. The Bureau gained more than 1,300 new special agents between 1993 and 1998. Proving the old adage that power abhors a vacuum, Freeh forged ahead into the openings provided by the Agency's atrophy: During the 1990s, the CIA closed twenty overseas stations while the FBI opened twenty-two new ones.

Freeh was leading the FBI abroad—and other nations were loving it. President Clinton, in his private conversations with historian Taylor Branch, remarked after returning from a tour of the Baltic states that everyone was asking for Louis Freeh. "No kidding," the president said. Freeh was the king: From Poland on through all the former

Soviet republics, people spoke of the FBI director as if he were a rock star, Clinton explained. As Branch recounted the conversation, "Clinton said their yearning reflected deep social fears where the birth of liberty brought disorder, meaning freedom to steal or be stolen from, and people clamored for the FBI because organized crime preyed on their wobbly institutions."

Freeh told reporters back in Washington, "It's not a question of taking over anybody's turf. It's now our turf because it's a law enforcement arena." Freeh was so dominant that when George Tenet was appointed CIA director, he even asked the FBI director to swear him in, hoping to send a message that the two agencies should be good friends.

Mike Rolince, who headed the international counterterrorism mission toward the end of the 1990s, described the Bureau's position as it evolved in the decade after the fall of the Berlin Wall: "If you harm an American, we're coming." It was a throwback, in its own way, to the Pax Romana, the era of relative peace begun under the Roman emperor Augustus Caesar, during which a system of law and order matured and granted Roman citizens safety anywhere in the known world. For the first time since, a country's police force had developed to the point where it could attempt to enforce a similar global peace; no corner on earth existed where the FBI wouldn't go or couldn't go to track down criminals who harmed Americans.

In March 1999, eight tourists, including two Americans, on an expedition to see gorillas were ambushed and killed by Hutu rebels in a Ugandan nature park. Within two days, a team of FBI agents landed in Uganda's capital, Kampala, to begin the hunt. FBI agent Jennifer Snell spent the better part of four years running the killers down. Eventually she located three of them, arrested them, and brought them to the United States for trial. In announcing the 2003 arrests, Michael Chertoff, the head of the Justice Department's Criminal Division, declared, "Those who commit acts of terror against Americans, whenever and wherever, will be hunted, captured, and brought to justice."

Yet there were still lines the Bureau wouldn't cross. Two decades after it began hunting Imad Mughniyeh, the Hezbollah bomb maker who was believed to have killed more Americans than any other terrorist before 9/11, agents located him in the Middle East. Court officials warned that the FBI's plan to extract him "shocked the conscience of the court" because it involved administering sedatives to the terrorist to effect the snatch. "We would have got him, but we would have had to drug him to get him out. Otherwise, we were going to make a lot of noise," an FBI executive recalls.

That was at least the third attempt by the U.S. government to grab Mughniyeh in the 1990s. An effort to kidnap him off a ship in the Mediterranean was canceled when the United States couldn't confirm that he was on board. Later, the Saudis had spoiled an attempt to capture him during a flight through the kingdom. It would be another decade before Israeli agents in Syria assassinated him by planting a bomb in his car's headrest.

While Louis Freeh was the driving force behind the Bureau's expansion, Deputy Director Bryant had the vision. Since its inception in the years preceding World War II, the legat program had been mostly a quiet backwater in the Bureau, its members known internally as the Mormon Mafia, because the agents selected for the program were disproportionally Mormon. (Their time as missionaries gave them language training and a comfort level with life overseas in an era before globalization made international travel the norm.) Too often, Bryant felt, the agents sent overseas, particularly those deployed to civilized Western European capitals, were conservative diplomats, formal liaisons who spent most of their time filling out reports, attending meetings, and working the reception circuit. When Louis Freeh arrived as director, only eight of the FBI's twenty-one legats were outside Western Europe and North America—in Colombia, Panama, Japan, Hong Kong, Australia, the Philippines, Thailand, and Venezuela. "It was very frustrating to send leads overseas," recalls Neil Herman. "These guys had responsibility sometimes for dozens of countries—Rome covered something like twenty-seven countries across the Mideast and Africa—and they spent much of their time on the wine-and-cheese circuit, attending receptions." If the FBI was going to succeed in its expansion, it needed more operational agents—cops who wouldn't be afraid to ruffle feathers to get stuff done.

One of the first agents in Bryant's new mold was Tom Knowles. It had actually been the FBI's nascent international efforts that had attracted Knowles to the Bureau in the late 1980s. "From everything I knew, when you're with the CIA and you screw up overseas, they leave you. Well, I tend to screw up a lot, so I wanted an agency that would own me and try to get me back," Knowles recalls with a laugh. He'd spent three years as a military police officer in Stuttgart, Germany, working a protection detail for an air force general, then seven years as a street cop in the rough neighborhoods of his native Fresno, California.

While working a two-man resident agency in Oklahoma, he received a threat against his life following a public corruption case against a local sheriff; one witness was killed, a cooperating cop was shot up, and the Bureau decided it was time to get its agent out. Knowles first went to Los Angeles, then on to the Hoover Building. He arrived at headquarters in February 1993 to work international terrorism. "People told me as I was leaving drugs in Los Angeles, 'Knowles, your career is over if you go to counterterrorism,' he recalls. "It was considered a showstopper." Two weeks after Knowles started, Ramzi Yousef and his crew attacked the World Trade Center.

Knowles ended up in the middle of the Blind Sheikh investigation, dashing back and forth to the FISA court, coordinating between headquarters and the TERRSTOP agents on the ground in New York. "We were constantly running into things we'd never seen before," he recalls. Within two years, Bryant summoned him and asked him to go overseas, to Legat Athens, which had operational responsibility for a dozen countries throughout the Middle East.

Bryant gave the new legat tough marching orders. "I want you to break the back of Seventeen November," he told Knowles as the agent prepared to depart. The terrorist group 17N, little known in the United States, had assassinated the CIA's station chief in 1975, and over the coming years claimed responsibility for dozens of rocket attacks on American and Greek targets as well as the assassination of local prosecutors, journalists, Greek government officials, and U.S. military personnel. Two months after Knowles arrived in Athens, 17N launched a single antitank rocket into the rear of the embassy, damaging three U.S. vehicles. The group released a statement: "To the American FBI, welcome to Greece, and to its chief, Thomas Knowles, let the hunters see what it feels like to be hunted." Knowles recalls, "I started to get a real bad vibe about my new assignment." The 17N investigation became a driving force of his assignment; at its peak, the investigation occupied seventeen FBI agents and personnel in Athens working under dangerous conditions.

While the Greek embassy had the second largest security budget and was considered to have the second highest threat profile of any U.S. embassy, the dozen countries that Knowles covered also included the top target: Lebanon. Beirut was just about as hostile a territory as the FBI had ever operated in, and Knowles spent nearly a third of his time in the frontierlike city. Just getting into Lebanon involved a fast, 120-mile sea-level ride in the jumpseat of an army Black Hawk helicopter known as the Beirut Air Bridge—the BAB, for short—from Cyprus across the Mediterranean into Lebanon, dodging Syrian air defense radar. (Sometimes the Israeli Air Force would toy with the U.S. helicopters just for fun, necessitating an abort.) The helicopter would drop down into the heavily guarded hilltop embassy compound, stay no more than a few minutes on the ground, and then race back out to sea. The bombed-out hulk of the old embassy, the remnant of the 1983 attack that killed sixty-three and heralded the arrival of Islamic terrorism, stood next to the helipad as a constant reminder of the region's dangers. Now the building shell was just used as high ground on which to perch heavy machine gun nests manned by security forces. From the embassy, ringed by three rounds of fences, Lebanese tanks, checkpoints, and perimeter guard posts at every twenty-five yards, Knowles could look down into southern Beirut, which was controlled by Hezbollah. Mortar nets and antirocket fences covered the few buildings not dug into the hillside.

Leaving the compound for official visits involved armored motorcades manned with mounted rooftop .50-caliber machine guns; unofficial trips out meant that Knowles and a member of the local CIA station drove in an unmarked car under cover of night, staying in constant radio contact with the embassy. The two men would sneak through Beirut, conducting surveillance, tracking terrorists, and doing their best to remain undetected. Investigating wasn't easy; even tracking down a telephone number handed over by Washington as a potential lead meant conducting surveillance to figure out who owned the telephone line, as no computerized database could answer the question. Hezbollah had a standing $1 million bounty for the capture or murder of any FBI or CIA agent in Lebanon; Knowles knew that capture meant a painful death, and he traveled with his sidearm, as much to ensure that he wasn't captured alive as to defend himself. As they pulled back up to the outer embassy gate late at night, the duo would finally radio in, "We're home—thanks."

The Athens assignment took its toll. During one scare, when Knowles had been following a lead in Beirut and the usual helicopter exfiltration was grounded because of terrorist threats, he spent twenty-one days holed up in the Beirut embassy compound with little to do but play pool, lift weights, and drink. At the Athens embassy, his secretary teased him that when he arrived in Greece in 1995 she'd never seen a legat who looked so young and so blond. By the time he left three years later, his hair had gone mostly gray.

One of Knowles's priorities was to round up the remaining members of the Hezbollah cell that had hijacked TWA 847 a decade before. Imad Mughniyeh remained forever elusive, but the FBI had located Hasan Izz-Al-Din, one of the leaders of the attack. FBI counterterrorism chief Dale Watson sneaked into Lebanon to meet with President Rafic Hariri and ask that the Hezbollah terrorist be turned over to the United States. It was a strange meeting. Hariri looked at Watson for a long while, knowing both that he couldn't be seen to help the United States and that Hezbollah already had its sights on him as well. He finally asked if the United States would be satisfied if his own security forces removed the terrorist from the picture. "We'll take care of it," he promised.

"We really want to try this guy ourselves," Watson said earnestly. "He deserves U.S. justice."

"I just can't," Hariri said, sighing.*

Just as the FBI had developed an advanced system for bringing terrorists and criminals to justice back in the United States after Operation Goldenrod, the CIA had been running its own rendition program since the mid-1990s. While the FBI focused on returning suspects for open trials in U.S. courts, the CIA's program was more a rental fleet for hire—specifically Egyptian hire. After determining that much of

---

*In 2005, Hariri was assassinated when a one-ton car bomb exploded next to his motorcade; Hasan Izz-Al-Din, a charter member of the FBI's post-9/11 Most Wanted Terrorists list, remains at large, with a $5 million U.S. bounty on his head.

al-Qaeda's leadership was Egyptian, the Agency had made its air fleet available to transport any captured terrorist wanted by Egypt back to face that country's unique justice system. Many of those transported by the CIA to Egypt disappeared without further word. In the summer of 1998, as Knowles was heading back to Washington, the CIA located Mohammed al-Zawahiri, the brother of Ayman al-Zawahiri, al-Qaeda's second in command, in Albania. Since he wasn't part of the sealed al-Qaeda indictment in the United States put together by I-49, there was no way to bring him back to face U.S. justice. Instead, the CIA abducted him and a number of his companions from Tirana and handed them over to Egypt, where, according to human rights groups, the men were tortured.

Through his allies at Egyptian Islamic Jihad, the al-Qaeda operations chief released a statement on August 5 to a London paper concerning his brother's disappearance: "We should like to inform the Americans that, in short, their message has been received and that they should read carefully the reply that will, with God's help, be written in the language that they understand."

Two days later, on August 7, 1998, al-Qaeda's reply came.

Steve Gaudin wanted desperately to get off the Joint Terrorism Task Force. He'd joined the FBI for some action, and yet he constantly seemed about as far from the center as he could be. Following six years in the army's 82nd Airborne Division as an infantry officer, Gaudin had signed on to the FBI in part because he didn't know what else to do. Where he'd grown up, in the North End of Boston, the city's Italian section, his friends and neighbors were more likely to become the subject of an FBI investigation than they were to join in one. But the Bureau seemed to promise the sort of adrenaline rush—legal adrenaline rush, that is—that Gaudin craved, and so Quantico it was.

On the fateful day when new agents received their first office orders, he tore open the envelope and read, "Kingston." *Awesome,* he thought. *I'm going to Jamaica to join some sort of super-duper, high-impact drug task force.* Then someone clarified: Kingston, New York. His heart sank.

The two-man Kingston RA, part of the Albany Field Office, was above a Dunkin' Donuts in a strip mall. The floor sloped noticeably to one side; the office didn't even have a working typewriter, so Gaudin mostly had to handwrite reports—and there were a lot of reports to write. As the new agent, Gaudin was expected to do anything the senior agent—the only other agent—didn't want to do, including processing the mail, writing up reports, and handling all the walk-ins. As far as Gaudin could determine, most walk-ins wanted to talk about some tinfoil government conspiracy or another, but they all required paperwork. Making things even less pleasant, Gaudin and the senior agent never developed a particularly close relationship. In four years of working together and sharing an office, they went to lunch exactly once. Gaudin paid.

When the opportunity arose, Gaudin seized a transfer to Albany, then volunteered for a transfer to New York in 1997, where he was assigned to the Joint Terrorism Task Force. *Fantastic, terrorism's where it's at,* he thought. There too, though, he languished, never getting a big case. The only redeeming fact was that at least he'd made it onto the New York SWAT team. JTTF, Gaudin concluded, was a dead end, and by the summer of 1998 he wanted out.

That summer the Goodwill Games came to New York. The games were a sort of athletic mini-Olympics backed by Ted Turner, involving some one hundred countries, thousands of athletes, and tens of thousands of spectators. Gaudin's supervisor, John O'Neill, told him that if he did a good job overseeing the Bureau's involvement in the games, O'Neill would get him a transfer to a fugitive task force afterward. That was more like it, Gaudin thought—criss-crossing the city, warrants in hand, kicking in doors and hauling bad guys to jail. The Goodwill Games were a huge responsibility, yet in the end it mostly amounted to lots of coordinating meetings and long hours in the command post waiting for something to happen. Nothing did. On August 2, Gaudin wrapped up the games and headed down to the Jersey shore for a vacation before he moved to the fugitive squad.

Early on August 7, 1998, his pager went off. Then it went off again and again. Gaudin called in. "Just get here," supervisor Chuck Frahm said. There wasn't time for elaboration.

Not bothering to change out of his bathing suit, tank top, and flip-flops, Gaudin raced back to the JTTF offices in New York. He spotted O'Neill, Frahm, and Pat D'Amuro standing together as he walked in. The trio looked at the vacationing agent. "At least you got dressed," O'Neill cracked.

O'Neill explained that the embassies in Nairobi and Dar es Salaam had been bombed that morning. Casualties were extensive in Kenya; Tanzania, luckily, happened to be celebrating a national holiday, and the U.S. embassy had been closed. "Where do you want to go, Nairobi or Dar es Salaam?" O'Neill asked.

"Nairobi. I don't even know where Dar es Salaam is," Gaudin replied, echoing a sentiment shared across the United States that morning. "Why me?"

"Pat's going to be the team leader in Nairobi. You're going to be his bodyguard. Keep him safe," O'Neill said. Freeh was concerned that al-Qaeda, knowing that an enormous U.S. deployment would follow the attacks, was planning a second wave of strikes targeting the response team. The Bureau would go in well armed and prepared for a fight. To secure access to the bomb site and workspace for the FBI team, Louis Freeh had called a senior Kenyan police officer who had attended the FBI National Academy.

Before the FBI team could leave the United States, though, there was a debate about who would be in charge. Headquarters had first assigned the Washington Field Office the primary response (as the so-called office of origin), and O'Neill was not happy. "You know we've been working this," he argued to Freeh. "You need New York agents working this." Eventually headquarters relented and 26 Federal Plaza got the green light, though Tom Pickard drew a line at O'Neill's participation. The New York counterterrorism leader desperately wanted to go—this was a big one, and he'd seen it coming—and yet for the sake of internal politics he was told to stay home. The on-scene commander for the bombings would be a Washington agent. O'Neill's friend Fran Townsend, who was then at the Justice Department, later explained, "This is the World Series and he's gotten benched. That's exactly how he felt about it. He was very, very upset about it, and bitter."

As the team assembled hours later, O'Neill told them that the NYPD had provided a bus for the ride to Washington's Andrews Air Force Base. Yet when the bus showed up—a regular New York City Transit bus with hard blue plastic seats—the FBI team discovered to

J. Edgar Hoover, center, shown here in the 1940s at the Stork Club in New York during one of his rare trips away from Washington, shaped the FBI over nearly half a century as director.

The then-new, enormous FBI Headquarters was named in honor of Hoover by President Nixon the day after Hoover died in May 1972.

The haunting live TV images of Black September militants holding hostage Israeli Olympians in Munich ushered in a new era of terrorism. (Photo courtesy of Getty Images)

Italian magistrates Giovanni Falcone (right) and Paolo Borsellino both lost their lives fighting the Mafia in Sicily.

The hijacking of Southern Airways Flight 49, shown here at the Toronto airport in the ordeal's first hours, was a turning point in aviation terror. (Photo by UPI)

Carmine Russo, Louis Freeh, Charlie Rooney, and Pat Luzio helped lead the groundbreaking Mafia investigation that came to be known as the "Pizza Connection."

Oliver "Buck" Revell, who more than any other FBI leader in the 1980s helped advance the Bureau's counter-terrorism efforts, led Operation Goldenrod.

The FBI surveilled a suspected terror cell doing target practice in Calverton, Long Island, but gave up following them before the group targeted the World Trade Center for a bomb attack in 1993.

The TERRSTOP investigation by the FBI broke up a plot to bomb major New York landmarks. Agents burst in on the plotters as they mixed the bomb materials.

The "Blind Sheikh," Omar Abdel-Rahman, led one of the first Islamic extremist terror networks from his Brooklyn mosque before his arrest in 1993.

Ramzi Yousef, the mastermind of the World Trade Center bombing and other planned terror attacks, was hunted to ground by U.S. authorities in Pakistan in 1995.

Louis Freeh (center left) and Dale Watson (center right) pushed the FBI to engage more internationally. In this photo, they are examining evidence in Yemen from the bombing of the USS *Cole*.

John O'Neill, an outsized personality within the traditional Bureau, tried to move terrorism to the fore of the FBI's priorities.

Bob Mueller was a star hockey player at St. Paul's School during high school.

ROBERT SWAN MUELLER

Bob is the son of Mr. and Mrs. Robert S. Mueller, born oń August 7, 1944, in New York City. He graduated rom St. Paul's School in Concord, New Hampshire after playing soccer, hockey and lacrosse, and distinguishing himself on the student council.

Bob majored in Princeton's politics department and, assisted by Professor Falk, wrote a thesis entitled *The Case Between the Union of South Africa and Liberia Before the International Court of Justice*. He lived with Bill Larson and Bob Bedell his senior year in 342 Foulke, and joined Cottage Club. Bob played varsity hockey and lacrosse for Princeton. After a year of teaching he intends to go to medical school. Bob considers himself a Republican, and lives at 810 Mt. Moro Road in Villanova, Pennsylvania.

At Princeton, Mueller wrote a senior thesis about international justice—a subject about which he would get expansive firsthand knowledge during his career. (Photo courtesy of Princeton University Library)

Mueller's time as a marine, during which he led a platoon in Vietnam and was awarded a Bronze Star and a Purple Heart, was seminal in shaping his personality. In this photo, he's receiving an award from Colonel Martin "Stormy" Sexton, his regimental commander, in Dong Ha, South Vietnam, in 1969.

their horror that the bus had a speed governor installed and couldn't top 50 miles per hour. The police escort seemed laughable as the agents crept south in the slow lane of the Jersey Turnpike, cars whizzing by. Gaudin, who was on board for the long ride to Washington, felt his army Ranger experience kick in: He pulled out his poncho liner, lay down in the aisle, and went to sleep. Who knew when he'd next have a chance?

At Andrews Air Force Base, the team boarded an air force C-5 Galaxy, one of the largest military aircraft in the world, for the long flight to Africa. On the more than fourteen-hour flight, agents napped or read books, and midflight they were offered the chance to buy military-issue sandwiches. After years in the Bureau, Gaudin felt a momentary surge of comfort as he settled into a rear seat on the plane's upper deck and the plane's four enormous GE engines pushed the Galaxy through the sky. This life he understood. "For the army, this was common. I knew these procedures, knew these people. From the FBI perspective, it was unheard of," he recalls.

In addition to the seventy or so FBI personnel in the first deployment, the air force plane carried a heavy rescue truck belonging to the Fairfax County Urban Search and Rescue Team, an elite group from northern Virginia funded in part by the U.S. government that was one of the designated first responders to major incidents such as embassy bombings. Most of that rescue team was ahead of the FBI, already digging through the wreckage. When the C-5 touched down, rescue personnel were eagerly awaiting their truck; the FBI team, though, found no one to meet them.

The agents disembarked, looking to the right into the low-slung, smoggy city of Nairobi and to the left into a neighboring nature preserve of African savanna filled with giraffes. Minutes passed as the team stood alone in the morning sun, the temperature already rising.

Eventually a series of Kenyan trucks appeared; only one agent on the team, Megan Miller, spoke Swahili and was able to communicate with the drivers. The FBI team clambered onto the trucks and headed downtown. As the convoy drove, the agents not sure at all what awaited them, the trucks passed from major roads to smaller ones and eventually into side streets so narrow they could barely squeeze through. They inched forward slowly—much too slowly for the FBI agents, who were realizing what an enormous, unprotected target they presented. Up front, Gaudin turned around and locked eyes with D'Amuro in the back of the truck. D'Amuro nodded. Tense, Gaudin hefted his MP5 submachine gun from the floor onto his lap, ready for whatever came next.

The first glimpse of the bomb site stopped them in their tracks. Smoke still rose from the mound of rubble; the embassy had largely escaped serious damage, though the explosion had leveled a nearby secretarial school. Gaudin had a single thought: *Thank God I don't have to solve this — I'm only here to protect Pat.* Then he began to look around, taking in for the first time the size of the crowd. Kenyans stretched as far as the eye could see, pressing up against the bomb scene, twenty or thirty deep even on the edge of the crater; there was noise everywhere, screams rising above everything else. Suddenly protecting Pat seemed more than mission enough. If al-Qaeda was going to come after the team in Kenya, there was going to be very little Gaudin or the rest of the team could do.

A guy wearing a safari vest came up to the group. "You the guys from New York?"

Gaudin, out of his element, immediately reverted to a more familiar New York approach: "Depends. Who the fuck are you?"

"I'm the legat from Pretoria," explained Bob Wright, who until a day before had been the lone FBI agent covering the entire continent of Africa. Gaudin blanched and saw his FBI career, which had just seemed to be getting exciting, flash before his eyes. One didn't talk to a GS-15 FBI supervisor the way he just had. The exchange, though, was quickly forgotten as everyone got down to business, and Wright and Gaudin, along with other agents from Squads I-45 and I-49, would spend much of the next two years working together across Africa.

Nearby, Special Agent Abby Perkins surveyed the chaos of the embassy ruins. She'd never wanted to end up in the New York Field Office; on her preference form at new agents' training in Quantico, she'd ranked New York as her fifty-second choice out of the fifty-six field offices. Yet her assignment there as a new agent had proven a perfect fit. She always volunteered for any special assignment, any new task force, any big new project — and in New York, there was no shortage of big new challenges. "I was single, flexible, and excited," she recalls. By the summer of 1998, she'd spent the better part of two years on the New York JTTF's Irish terrorism squad, working against the IRA. Initially her boss, Chuck Stern, didn't want her to be part of the squad heading to Nairobi, as he believed she'd never go back to the IRA squad, but after some pleading, she boarded the slow-moving bus to Washington. Like Gaudin, she was too new to the Bureau to understand fully how unique the circumstances in which she now found herself were. Now, looking at the embassy, she began to break down the case in her mind: Start from the rubble and work out.

The FBI team eventually settled into the lunchroom of the nearby Canadian consulate, the agents sitting almost on top of each other and answering a tip line set up by the Kenyan government, writing down leads by hand and making carbon copies. Everyone in Kenya seemed to have information and a personal theory: It was ninjas from Somalia who had flown in on helicopters and fast-roped down to attack the embassy; it was a disgruntled pizza maker who had packed his pizza oven full of explosives. Kenyan police began rounding up suspects left and right, arresting them based on one tip or another and then waiting to sort out the information later.

On the night of August 11, D'Amuro summoned Gaudin and handed him a lead: "Debbie took a call. There's a guy who doesn't fit in at a hotel." Agent Debbie Doren was a good investigator, well prepared and on her game. If she thought this lead was worth following up, it probably was.

"Why me?" Gaudin asked. "I'm supposed to stick by you."

"Look around, Steve. You can't protect me here," D'Amuro replied.

Gaudin laughed. "Glad you recognized that. I realized that as soon as we stepped off the bus." He paused. "So what's our guy look like? What nationality? What's his name? Got anything else to go on?"

"Nope. If you don't like this one, I've got a huge stack here for you," D'Amuro said, gesturing to his foot-high pile of lead sheets.

The next morning, Gaudin, Special Agent Steve Bongardt, and NYPD JTTF detective Wayne Parola teamed up with two Kenyan police officers to track down the lead. The whole situation suddenly seemed less promising, though, as Kenyans loaded the three FBI agents into the back of a white police paddywagon and locked them in. Gaudin exchanged a glance with Bongardt and Parola as the police wagon accelerated. Parola was a tough, old-school NYPD detective and Bongardt was a powerfully built Naval Academy grad who had spent more than a decade as an F-14 fighter pilot. If attacked, they'd at least be able to put up a good fight—if they could get out of the wagon.

They drove and drove—fifteen minutes, twenty minutes, thirty minutes. Then the wagon veered off the main roads and onto smaller roads. It was like the trip from the airport all over again. Where were they heading? Gaudin doubted they were supposed to be this far away. He tried to raise D'Amuro on the FBI radio. Nothing but static. They were on their own.

He pounded on the wall divider and the wagon pulled over. The Kenyan police sergeant came around back and opened the door so they could converse.

"Where are you taking us?"

"Somalitown," the Kenyan replied matter-of-factly.

"No, no, no—we're supposed to go to Eastleigh."

"Yes, of course, Mr. Steve. Somalitown is Eastleigh. All the Somalis live there."

Silently, Gaudin cursed.

Then the Kenyan officer added, "That's why we put you in back. They don't like *mazungas* there. The white guys." With that, he closed the door, locking the agents back inside, and set off again.

The wagon continued through smaller villages, creeping along through crowds of pedestrians, into what the agents had always imagined rural Africa looked like. As they rolled forward, it began to dawn on Gaudin that he'd made a mistake: In the dazed condition the tired and out-of-place FBI team was working under, he'd assumed that the hotel mentioned in the tip was a Ramada. But now, as they went farther and farther out of the city, he realized the unlikelihood that a Western chain would locate way out in Eastleigh. He reread the tip. Not Ramada, he saw: *Ramadah*.

The police wagon came to a stop in front of the Ramadah Hotel, far from anywhere, and the Kenyans proceeded inside. A crowd gathered. There weren't many vehicles in town; a large police van from Nairobi was definitely worth gawking at. There was no escape for the agents, locked in from the outside. Gaudin looked around and began to run some calculations. He had his MP5 and his sidearm. Bongardt and Parola both had their sidearms. Maybe 150, 200 rounds total between the three of them. Would that be enough to get them out of trouble? Outside, a pedestrian sidled up to the wagon and leaned against it, his back to the agents inside, who could only peer through the vehicle's barred slats. "You're going to get killed here," the man whispered out of the corner of his mouth in broken English. When the agents inside realized what was happening, they snapped to full alert. "I told the girl on the phone not to send you," the man outside continued.

"Why? What's going on?" Gaudin asked, trying not to sound too nervous.

"I told them not to send you. You're going to get me killed."

Trying to build some rapport, Gaudin asked, "What's your name, buddy?"

"I won't tell you. This is not good. You should leave now."

Parola spoke up. "Everybody likes Michael Jordan. What if we call you Michael Jordan?"

The informant laughed. "Yes, you may call me Michael Jordan." The FBI team breathed a sigh of relief; they had a connection now. The informant went on to explain that the man who didn't fit in had checked out of the Ramadah Hotel and gone down the street to the Iftan Lodge, where he was now staying. Then Michael Jordan disappeared into the crowd again.

When the Kenyan officers came out of the hotel empty-handed and opened the back of the wagon, Gaudin passed along the informant's new tip. The wagon crept down the street to the Iftan Lodge, the growing crowd walking alongside. The mission wasn't exactly covert. Bongardt pointed out a narrow window slit in a corner building on the street: "If we're ambushed, let's meet up there. It's the only building I see made of brick." Left unsaid was how, if the agents were ambushed, they would get out of the back of a vehicle specifically designed to prevent people inside from escaping.

After arriving in front of the Iftan Lodge, the Kenyan officer came around again and opened the back. "Mr. Steve, before I go in and get this man, please—I'm only a sergeant."

Gaudin, thinking the officer lacked the authority to arrest someone on his own, replied, "Sure. Who do we need to get to arrest someone? Should we call a lieutenant? A colonel?"

"No, Mr. Steve, I'm only a sergeant. I'm not senior enough to have a gun."

Gaudin paused. Then, disobeying every instinct drilled into an FBI agent in his career, he reached to his waistband and handed over his sidearm: "Here, take mine." His mind flashed through the answer he'd provide down the road at some career-ending, internal misconduct investigation back at headquarters: "And, Agent Gaudin, why did you think that handing your service weapon to a foreign national was a good idea?" Now, however, it seemed like the only idea.

"Mr. Steve, may I have some extra bullets?" Gaudin, in for a penny, in for a pound, handed the Kenyan extra magazines, mentally subtracting the weapon and the ammunition from the FBI team's escape plan.

"Mr. Steve, I don't have any handcuffs."

Gaudin handed over his handcuffs. Then the door slammed shut and the agents were left alone with the still-growing crowd of curious onlookers. Bongardt and Parola arched their eyebrows.

Within minutes, the Kenyan sergeant was back. The suspect was inside the hotel. Injured and without any identification, he had, astonishingly, $800 in American currency and an admission slip from the M. P. Shah Hospital in Nairobi, where many of the bombing victims had been treated. Gaudin looked at the currency; it was eight crisp new $100 bills. The new design, with the oversized Ben Franklin, had been released just eighteen months or so earlier. The bills were still rare in circulation. Apparently the man had huge bandages wrapped around his hands, with fresh blood still seeping through. His forehead bore a series of enormous, poorly executed stitches, with threads still hanging off. "It was obvious this work wasn't done at the Massachusetts General Hospital," Gaudin recalls. "These weren't weeks-old wounds. These were days-old wounds." The admission slip was stamped 7 August 1998, the day of the bombing.

Gaudin's mind flashed back to the senior agent in the Kingston RA. One of the things the other agent, unfriendly as he may have been, had drilled into the newbie while they sat over the Dunkin' Donuts was the phrase "JDLR." Always, he instructed, be on the lookout for someone who "just doesn't look right." What was an injured guy doing far from downtown Nairobi with a medical slip showing he'd been treated at the hospital where most bombing victims had been taken, his only possession eight crisp American bills that were so new that the ATM Gaudin had used in New York before heading to Africa wasn't even handing them out yet?

"What do we do with this guy?" Gaudin asked.

"Mr. Steve," the Kenyan officer explained, "in Kenya we can hold someone for two days if they don't have identification on them."

"So is this guy under arrest?"

"Yes, as of now, this man is under arrest."

"Then get him and let's get out of here," Gaudin said, eyeing the crowd.

On the ride back to Nairobi, Gaudin, Bongardt, and Parola warily eyed their uncuffed suspect. It was close confines; the FBI team had all the weapons, but a struggle in the cramped back of the paddywagon probably wouldn't end well for anyone involved. Gaudin patted the man on the leg and offered some butterscotch candies he had in his pocket. He then showed his FBI credentials and advised the suspect of his Miranda rights, using the FBI's standard FD-395 Advice of Rights card, out of habit more than anything. The suspect, who told the agents his name was Khaled Saleem bin Rasheed, didn't seem particularly concerned; he appeared to think this was all some sort of immigration mix-up. He kept repeating in English, "Okay, okay, close my file."*

At police headquarters, the agents began to question their JDLR suspect. The rest of the investigating team ignored them, because intelligence agents in Pakistan had already arrested another suspect, Mohammed Odeh, and the investigation was rapidly focusing on him. "No one could care less about [bin Rasheed]," Gaudin recalls.

The suspect's initial story from the field seemed credible enough: While visiting a friend from Yemen, he had been in the vicinity of the blast and had woken up in the hospital; he had lost his briefcase

---

*Later, Gaudin ran into a Justice Department prosecutor back at Kenya police headquarters who told him that the Miranda warning didn't apply in Kenya. There was a separate form the Justice Department used for international interrogations, basically a "Toto, we're not in Kansas anymore" form that explains that the suspect would have certain rights if he or she were in the United States, but that these rights may not apply in the current situation.

containing all his papers and ID in the confusion, and he now assumed his friend was dead. Bin Rasheed insisted that the clothes on his back were what he had worn into the country and were the only possessions he had left. But when Bongardt and Gaudin, along with two Kenyan police officers, began to question him with the help of a CIA linguist, within moments the linguist signaled that she wanted to speak with the agents in private. The suspect, she explained to the agents outside the room, was speaking the Fusha dialect of Arabic — a phrase that at the time meant nothing to either agent. Fusha, the linguist explained, was classical Arabic, the equivalent, perhaps, of Shakespearean English; this immediately told the agents that the suspect was a wealthy, well-educated individual, making it even stranger that he was in the far suburbs of Nairobi. JDLR, Gaudin thought as he walked back into the room.

The more the FBI team pressed, the less sense the story made. Bin Rasheed told Gaudin and Bongardt that he hadn't picked the remote Ramadah Hotel himself; a cabdriver at the airport had delivered him there because it was apparent the traveler didn't speak Swahili and the hotel was a regular destination for Arab visitors. Over the following hours, the story became even more complicated, but for every evolving detail, the suspect had another explanation. Gaudin kept studying the man's clothes — crisp green denim jeans and a light shirt. Everything was perfect. Everything was clean. *Too clean.*

Gaudin, an army guy, decided quickly that the man he was questioning had had military training, perhaps even counterintelligence and counterinterrogation training. A key facet of such training, he recalled, was that when captured and questioned, you were supposed to tell a logical lie, one that was straightforward and easy to remember, while dragging out the process for as long as possible. The value of information degrades quickly once you're off the battlefield, so delaying for a few hours or a few days before giving up valuable intelligence can make a big difference.

The next day, Gaudin sat down to question bin Rasheed again. He asked the suspect to look him over. "Look at how dirty I am. I've been in the city for just a few days. Now look at you, look at your clothes."

"American men are pigs," the suspect explained. "Arab men are clean."

"I'll give you that," Gaudin said.

He nodded and began to explain his own time in the army, how he'd had training in resisting interrogations when captured and so on. Then he dropped the punch line. "I think you got the same training," he told the suspect. "If you remember your instruction, you're supposed to tell a logical lie. You said one thing that was illogical."

The suspect's reaction sealed the deal. Rather than dismissing Gaudin's speech, laughing, or protesting, bin Rasheed grabbed his chair and pulled it up close to the table, close to Gaudin. "Where was I illogical?" he asked.

Gaudin stared down at the suspect's shoes as he began to talk. "I'm willing to give you that after the explosion you returned to the Ramadah Hotel and you have in your room the magic cleaning solution that gets blood and dirt out of your jeans."

Bin Rasheed nodded. Gaudin then turned to the suspect's crisp, untorn shirt and the large cut down his back that had been treated and bandaged at the hospital.

"I'm willing to grant you that in the explosion, a piece of glass fell down the back of your shirt, between your neck and your collar, and scraped your back without damaging your shirt in any way. Then you used your magic solution to get all the blood out of your shirt back at the hotel."

"God controls the universe. Anything's possible." Bin Rasheed shrugged.

"But there are two things you don't wash," Gaudin said, still staring at the shoes.

Bin Rasheed's mind was obviously spinning, working overtime to figure out the FBI agent's line of questioning. He said, "Mr. Steve, of course I don't wash my shoes."

"I don't care about your shoes. No, but I said two things," Gaudin said, standing and grasping his own belt. "You don't wash a belt. Look at yours—it's pristine." Gaudin slapped both his hands down on the table hard, the smack reverberating through the small room. "Get up," he commanded in his best army drill sergeant voice. The suspect snapped to attention.

"I knew as soon as he stood, rigid and robotlike, that he was certainly ex-military," Gaudin recalls.

"Undo your belt," Gaudin commanded. The suspect did so, and the heavy belt buckle immediately fell to the side, exposing the inside of the belt. The FBI agents and the suspect saw the incriminating evidence at the same moment: a price tag—a price tag in Kenyan shillings. The belt wasn't old; it had been purchased inside the country. The suspect closed his eyes for a moment. Then he locked eyes with Gaudin. "You were good," he said. "But I have to pray now."

A week after the embassy bombings, the national security team described the incident to President Clinton. The FBI and the CIA were on the same page: "This one is a slam-dunk," declared George Tenet, using the phrase that would become synonymous with the Agency's failures after the Iraq invasion. "There is no doubt this was an al-Qaeda operation. Both we and the Bureau have plenty of evidence." Over the coming days, the government would hotly debate how to respond. Yet when it did, the political implications greatly overshadowed the response.

Meanwhile the FBI team continued its investigation, trying to prove or disprove the suspect's story. Bongardt spent much of the coming days working with "Michael Jordan," who became a key source for the investigators. On August 14, Gaudin and others headed to the M. P. Shah Hospital to find someone—a doctor, nurse, anyone—who had a memory of their suspect. As they made their way through the hospital, Gaudin noticed a janitor who seemed to follow them around, always pushing his mop distractedly across the floor while the FBI showed bin Rasheed's picture to staff members. Finally Gaudin said to the others, "That guy wants to tell us something." He went up to the janitor and introduced himself as an FBI agent.

"Are you here for the keys and the bullets?" the janitor asked.

Having absolutely no idea what the janitor meant but playing a hunch, Gaudin replied excitedly, "Yes! Are you the guy with the bullets and the keys? We've been looking for you."

"I gave them to the police. Would you like to see where I found them?"

The janitor led them to a dismal men's bathroom in the center of the hospital, pointed to a window, and explained that he had found several bullets and a set of keys on the ledge in the hours after the bombing. He had handed them over to some of the Kenyan police swarming the hospital. The FBI agents found that in the postblast confusion, the keys and bullets had miraculously been properly retained as evidence by the police. The FBI took custody of them. It would turn out to be one of the luckiest breaks of the case.

At the airport, the FBI team found bin Rasheed's landing card, on which he'd clearly written, before even going through customs, that he was planning to stay at the Ramadah Hotel. He had been lying about the cabdriver choosing the hotel for him. The trap was snapping shut on bin Rasheed fast.

Life for the FBI agents in Kenya was hard. They boarded buses at their hotel each morning for a secure trip to the Kenyan police headquarters, where they worked all day, eating little more than bland military MRE rations. A parade of dignitaries came through to visit the bomb site—Madeleine Albright came, as did Louis Freeh, visiting his troops.

On August 21, just hours after Freeh left, Pat D'Amuro called the team together with alarming news: The White House, without much warning to the FBI, had decided to strike both bin Laden's camps in Afghanistan and a factory in the Sudan with cruise missiles. The FBI was going to evacuate nearly everyone from Africa. "We immediately started to gather up evidence as quickly as we could, figuring that we had just hours left in country," recalls Abby Perkins.

The good news/bad news for Gaudin was that since he had lucked onto a suspect—even one considered secondary by many involved in the investigation—his work was too important for him to evacuate with the rest. He'd be part of the skeleton crew left behind in Nairobi. The remaining team would increase its level of security. If there had been one al-Qaeda cell here, chances were good there was a second.

The retaliation for the embassy bombings came at an odd moment in American history. On August 17, just four days before the cruise missile attack, President Clinton had testified before the grand jury investigating his relationship with Monica Lewinsky. The agents manning the FBI's operations center that night paused for a moment during their investigation of the bombing to watch the president confess on live TV that he'd had "a relationship with Miss Lewinsky that was not appropriate." While those within the government realized that the al-Qaeda threat was real, some pundits and critics saw the launch of seventy-five Tomahawk missiles into Sudan and Afghanistan as an attempt to distract public attention from the president's scandal at home. Unfortunately, that real threat was being overshadowed by domestic politics.

President Clinton went back on TV as the dust from the missiles cleared. "Let our actions today send this message loud and clear: There are no expendable American targets," he said. "There will be no sanctuary for terrorists. We will defend our people, our interests, and our values." President Clinton's Executive Order 13099 imposed sanctions on al-Qaeda in general and Osama bin Laden specifically, and was later expanded to include the Taliban. The government's so-called Pol-Mil Plan, a political and military strategy document for combating al-Qaeda, was dubbed Operation Delenda, a reference to the Roman saying *"Carthage delenda est"* (Carthage must be destroyed). For his part, Osama bin Laden didn't take well to President Clinton's missile attack and turned the tables, offering a $9 million reward for the assassination of Louis Freeh, George Tenet, Madeleine Albright, or Secretary of Defense William Cohen.

Not everyone in the United States was pleased about the missile attacks. John O'Neill believed the strike was a dumb move, one that elevated Osama bin Laden in the eyes of the world, gave hope to his followers that they were having an impact on the Great Satan, and served as a recruiting tool for new followers. The head of the New York Field Office, Jim Kallstrom, went a step further: The missile strike, he said, was "fucking stupid." In a bizarre moment of international diplomacy, even the Taliban's leader, Mullah Omar, contacted the State Department to warn that the attacks would only arouse more sympathy for bin Laden's cause.

The CIA and the military, in contrast, strongly favored more lethal action. Mike Scheuer, the head of the virtual Alec Station, which focused on bin Laden, vehemently encouraged targeting the al-Qaeda leader for death, but the six layers of supervisors and executives between Scheuer and Tenet all recommended against it. Despite their interest in arresting bin Laden and seeing him face justice, top Bureau officials weren't averse to the idea of more direct means either. "Let's put it this way: We were in favor of removing bin Laden from the picture," Dale Watson recalls years later, diplomatically.

In the coming months, the CIA and other government agencies would debate a variety of ways to solve the Osama bin Laden problem. They considered inserting a strike team to capture him and recruiting locals in Afghanistan or Pakistan to do their dirty work. They reviewed maps and conceived plans, but nothing ever got off the drawing board. George Tenet repeatedly rejected the Agency's more ambitious plans; in May 1998, just a few months before the embassy bombings, Afghan allies had conducted a four-day dress rehearsal of a plan to kidnap bin Laden for trial back in the United States, but the green light for the actual operation never came, either before or after the embassy bombings.

Logistics were often the main issue. John MacGaffin, the CIA's number-two clandestine service officer during the 1990s, told the *New York Times*'s Tim Weiner, "The CIA knew bin Laden's location almost every day—sometimes within fifty miles, sometimes within fifty feet." For one reason or another, despite numerous plans, the Agency never moved against him. Its operational capability to snatch bin Laden, even if it knew where he was, just wasn't there. When, during a presentation by the CIA about the plan to grab him, Danny Coleman asked what chance of success the plan held, the CIA briefer was blunt: "Slim to none."

Beyond lacking the capability, the CIA appeared to lack the authority. Janet Reno and John O'Neill, among others, argued that a targeted assassination was legally out of bounds. Since 1976, Gerald Ford's Executive Order 11905 had prohibited the U.S. government from assassinating foreign leaders.* That was a line many were still wary to cross. President Clinton would authorize the Agency only to kill bin Laden in "self-defense," but the only way to provoke the chance to kill in imminent self-defense would be to get boots on the ground in Afghanistan.

As had been the case for decades, some of the reluctance to risk U.S. lives in pursuit of someone like bin Laden came from terrorism's

---

* The executive order had come after the Church and Pike Commissions uncovered the CIA's varied assassination programs during the 1960s and had been kept in effect by every president since Ford, although it had been amended repeatedly.

intangibility. Most Americans didn't know anyone personally affected by a terrorist attack. For all of the drama, Yousef's World Trade Center bomb hadn't proved a catalyzing moment for the nation. Bojinka never happened. The most visible and deadly attack of the decade, Oklahoma City, had been the action of domestic extremists, not militant Islamic radicals. Combating international terrorism was certainly a U.S. priority, but through the 1990s there were priorities that ranked higher. The politics of national security meant that action against bin Laden's training camps was constantly weighed against the need to maintain good relations with the nuclear-armed Pakistani government next door. The Pakistani government already saw the United States as siding with India in the two nations' long-running border disputes, and so attacking bin Laden would further upset his powerful allies and friends in the Pakistani Inter-Services Intelligence (ISI). For a threat so far off the radar of most Americans, U.S. leaders did not find it worthwhile to upset a violent region of the world.

On and off until 9/11, Operation Afghan Eyes targeted bin Laden, tracking him, watching, waiting for some kind of final action that never came. Some two years after the missile attacks, on September 7, 2000—just a little over a month before the attack on the USS *Cole*—State Department counterterrorism chief Michael Sheehan was summoned at 2 A.M. by Richard Clarke to the Agency's operations center at Langley. The two men, along with Cofer Black, the CIA's counterterrorism chief, watched silently by satellite video linkup as bin Laden wandered outside in midday Afghanistan, half a world away. An unarmed Predator drone circled miles above bin Laden's compound at Tarnak Farm, making lazy figure eights out of sight of the ground. Its powerful camera, though, left no doubt as to what it observed. Bin Laden's white robe flowed out behind him as he moved around the compound, oblivious of the American eyes faraway.★

After watching bin Laden remotely, the military and the CIA prepared to move ahead with an armed version of the drone. In June 2001, a prototype attacked a Tarnak Farm mockup built in the Nevada

---

★ When the drone crashed in Uzbekistan weeks later, the Agency and the Pentagon couldn't agree on who should pay the $3 million to replace it, so the program wasn't restarted until after 9/11.

desert. In February of that year the first armed Predator had successfully hit a target within 6 inches of its intended mark. Now the Hellfire missile, tipped by a twenty-pound warhead, slammed into the fake bin Laden camp at close to a thousand miles per hour. No one would have survived. But the Bush administration kept its gloves on. Bin Laden was allowed to live.

Left behind in Kenya as the rest of the FBI contingent evacuated, Gaudin and the more senior John Anticev further interrogated their suspect, who now admitted that his real name was Mohamed Rashed Daoud al-'Owhali. The agents were particularly interested in who he had called after being injured. "You must have told someone," Anticev said. Bin Rasheed provided a telephone number, 967-1-200-578, that would prove to be perhaps the single most valuable piece of intelligence collected by the United States in the years before 9/11. The phone number, U.S. intelligence later determined, led to a safe house in Yemen run by a man named Ahmed al-Hada.* The safe house turned out to be a central clearinghouse for al-Qaeda information, and more than 220 incoming and outgoing calls from that location had helped organize and execute the embassy bombings. Osama bin Laden himself was a regular caller. In fact, closer monitoring of the number in subsequent years could well have led to the unraveling of both the USS *Cole* and 9/11 plots. But that was all down the road; for the moment, the agents had to figure out the phone number's importance.

The FBI agents took the number to the Kenyan phone company. In contrast to the procedure in the United States, where agents had to prepare a warrant, get it signed by a judge, and then present it to the phone company, in Kenya they only had to convince the single police officer assigned to the phone company that they needed information. Reviewing a list of every incoming and outgoing call for 967-1-200-578, agents zeroed in on a single call from a pay phone near the Iftan Lodge after the bombing. That agreed with what al-'Owhali was

---

*Proving how small the terrorist circles were, agents later determined that al-Hada's daughter was married to Khalid al-Mihdhar, one of the eventual 9/11 hijackers.

telling them. More curious, though, was a series of telephone calls from a Kenyan landline to a number in Yemen in the weeks leading up to the bombing. The last call was at 9:19 A.M. on August 7, just thirty minutes before the attack. What were the chances that their suspect was innocently checking in with a friend back in Yemen who just happened to have other friends in Nairobi who called right up until the bombing? Suddenly the interest in Gaudin and Bongardt's suspect grew dramatically.

Working with the Kenyan police, the FBI traced the landline to 43 Rundu Estates, on the outskirts of Nairobi, a fancy villa in a neighborhood called home by many of the city's wealthy and by many foreign diplomats.* Inside Nairobi's premier equivalent of a gated community, complete with twelve-times-a-month garbage collection, special fire protection, and clean running water, number 43 was an imposing building with a terracotta roof, a two-car garage, and a high fence. It was not the likely guest home of someone who would end up out at the Iftan Lodge in Somalitown.

Agents obtained a warrant to search the premises after the landlord explained that a group of Arab men had rented the estate for several months, paying cash, and then moved out the day of the bombing. As an evidence technician began his search, he shouted from the garage, "We don't even need to swab for explosive residue." The floor of the garage was thick with TNT powder. He had found where the bomb had been assembled.

On August 20, Gaudin began the morning interrogation session by laying down a series of horrific pictures of the Kenyan bombing victims, including a haunting photograph of a woman and child on a passing bus, fused together in the flash and fire that followed the explosion. "Why did these people have to die?" Gaudin asked. "I understand targeting the Americans, but what did these people ever do?"

Al-'Owhali looked away. "That's not the way it was supposed to happen," he said.

Then Gaudin laid on the table a photo of 43 Rundu Estates.

Al-'Owhali's face fell. "You know the whole story."

---

*In the U.S. government exhibits and prosecution, Rundu is misspelled as "Rhundu." I've used the home association's spelling.

The terror suspect proceeded to rant for a few minutes, explaining that the bombing wasn't his fault—the Americans had brought it on themselves; the Americans were responsible for the deaths of the hundreds of Kenyans. He stated, "America is my enemy, not Kenya." Quickly they entered a negotiation. Al-'Owhali proffered that, given a guarantee by President Clinton that he could be tried in the United States, he'd reveal his whole story, telling the FBI all about someone named Osama bin Laden and this thing called al-Qaeda. It was the first time the New York FBI agent had ever heard the name al-Qaeda, translated by the linguist as "the base."

Gaudin almost missed the opportunity; he left the interrogation room to pretend to call Clinton, planning to reenter later and say that he'd talked to the president to secure the guarantee. But while he was killing time washing his hands in the bathroom, he decided to double-check with the Justice Department prosecutors. He went upstairs to find Pat Fitzgerald, who was running the Justice Department's end of the embassy bombing investigation, and explained what al-'Owhali had said. Fitzgerald, who knew all about Osama bin Laden, al-Qaeda, and the sealed indictment (so secret that Gaudin and most of the JTTF wasn't aware of it), immediately grasped the significance of what was unfolding in the room below.

Over the course of three intense days, August 22 to 25, the agents quizzed the suspect at length. Al-'Owhali, twenty-one years old, was Saudi, rich, and privileged. He'd been radicalized as a teenager, after listening to sermons about the Americans and the Jews. Al-'Owhali had subsequently traveled to Afghanistan for training in bin Laden's camps, where he had excelled, and eventually he volunteered to be a martyr. When told that his operation would take place in Africa, he was disappointed: He wanted to strike Americans in America.

The agent and the terrorist quickly developed a good rapport. One morning, just after President Clinton's grand jury testimony back in the States, al-'Owhali, smiling mischievously, wagged his finger at Gaudin: "Mr. Steve, your president. Tsk, tsk, tsk. Him and Monica, shame, shame, shame. No good." Another time, as the prisoner and the FBI agent passed a window overlooking the front entrance of the Kenyan police headquarters, where a team of FBI agents had gathered to board a bus for the day's trip to the bomb scene, he cautioned, "One grenade would take out all those guys. You like to make yourselves a soft target." It was, Gaudin recalls, not a typical combative interrogation. "We were like two soldiers talking about a battle that's already over in a war that's still going on," he says. They often shared a single bottle of water through the day; Gaudin provided tips from his own army experience on how to make the military MREs as palatable as possible. The terrorist held back little, answering each question thoroughly. The unfolding story—the details of the bomb plot, the planning, the execution—perfectly matched the information Debbie Doren and John Anticev were getting out of Mohammed Odeh, the bomber captured in Pakistan.

Al-'Owhali's role had been to ride with the bomb, then, upon reaching the compound, throw grenades to overpower and confuse the guards. He'd argued that the bomb should be driven to the front of the embassy, where the only building affected would be the American compound; instead the planners had decided to drive to the back entrance, which was hemmed in on all sides by Kenyan buildings. In the event that the bomb failed to ignite, al-'Owhali was supposed to unlock the back of the truck and toss in a grenade to detonate the bomb himself. Gaudin, listening intently, paused, his mind churning: Unlock the truck? He excused himself from the room, dug through the evidence locker, and returned minutes later to toss the keys found in the M. P. Shah Hospital onto the table. Al-'Owhali's eyes went wide. These FBI agents were magic; they knew everything.

When the embassy guards refused to open the gate for the bombers, al-'Owhali had tried to get away. Sure, he'd signed up to be a martyr, but he hadn't become a martyr to die in a poorly executed operation in Africa that mostly killed Africans. He'd live, hoping to fulfill his dream of killing Americans on their own soil.

Meanwhile, details from the interrogation spread throughout the government and the U.S. intelligence community, even though the wall prevented additional information from aiding Gaudin in return. One afternoon, Pat D'Amuro pulled Gaudin aside: "Steve, you did good. I can't tell you what, but you got the right guy." As Gaudin recalls, "I could tell this was causing excitement on the other side of the wall, but it couldn't come back to me."

Even during the Mirandized FBI interviews, good intelligence poured out of the suspect. Al-'Owhali claimed that al-Qaeda was planning an attack on a U.S. naval ship when it refueled in Yemen, a threat Gaudin conveyed back to FBI headquarters and then passed on to the intelligence community. (Two years later, when bombers struck the USS *Cole,* Gaudin was chastised for not sharing the tip; he dug out of his files his message to headquarters and the subsequent memo that had gone out to the whole intelligence community.) More chilling, though, was al-'Owhali's tip that al-Qaeda was actively planning an attack inside the United States. "The big attack is coming, and there's nothing you can do to stop it," the suspect told the FBI interrogator.

The decision to bring the bombing suspects back to the United States for trial wasn't a foregone conclusion. Pat Fitzgerald spent long hours debating the topic with Janet Reno and Mary Jo White on the phone before deciding to deliver Odeh and al-'Owhali to the United States. When the FBI jet landed at Stewart Air Force Base, now a familiar stop for Bureau rendition teams, John O'Neill stood triumphant on the tarmac. As the team moved from the plane to a waiting helicopter for the final leg to downtown New York, a beaming O'Neill threw his arm around Gaudin, who had been such a reluctant member of the JTTF just weeks before. "A little better than working up in Albany, huh?" O'Neill said, laughing with pride.

The East Africa bombing team spent the better part of a year putting the case together and running down suspects. For weeks and months, often with little notice and no idea how long they'd be gone, the squad members would have to grab their passports and wish friends and family farewell. Agents took to leaving piles of blank checks in their desk drawers so that colleagues could pay their rent, utilities, and credit card bills during unexpected trips. In Kenya, the JTTF agents spent their days in pairs—one FBI agent, one Kenyan officer—following leads around the country. The work took them to small villages, far off the track, beaten or otherwise. In some villages they became so well known that they'd bring presents for the local children—marbles or perhaps a small Nerf football. Abby Perkins's Kenyan partner carefully guided her through their daily meals, figuring out where the safest places to eat were.

The work on the East Africa bombings reaped immediate dividends. Intelligence gathered in Kenya and Nairobi convinced the British to mount a major counterterrorism sweep in September 1998 that targeted al-Qaeda's operations coordinators in the U.K., including its media and public affairs shop, which helped distribute the group's press releases and messages. As Squad I-49's investigation into al-Qaeda deepened, even with all the intelligence from intercepts, documents, and forensics, they found themselves still relying on Junior, the informer who had escaped Sudan with some of bin Laden's money. "We also realized that no matter how many reams of evidence you collect, nothing beats a live, walking, talking witness," Jack Cloonan says. "So we wanted another one."

They soon got their wish when a phone call came in from Morocco: There's a guy here who wants to talk. L'Houssaine Kherchtou, aka Abu Talal, had a complicated relationship as an intelligence source. An al-Qaeda operative, he'd been in Nairobi on August 7 when the embassies were bombed. While he claimed to be uninvolved, he tried to flee the country, knowing that being in proximity to the attack looked bad. British intelligence stopped him at the Nairobi airport, debriefed him, and held him as the bombing investigation unfolded, determining as best they could that his presence in Kenya was indeed only a coincidence. Nevertheless, the British had never told the U.S. government or the hundreds of FBI agents swarming through Nairobi that they had detained an al-Qaeda operative. Later, when I-49 learned of his presence, it pushed the British to resurrect the source. "We realized this is a guy we need to find," Cloonan says.

After much encouragement and pressure, the Moroccans lured Kherchtou, whom agents came to dub "Joe the Moroccan," to Rabat by telling him he had to sort out some immigration issues with his children. Soon thereafter, O'Neill, Cloonan, and the rest of the FBI team arrived.

Fitzgerald hadn't bothered to make the trip, figuring that the Bureau was wasting its time with Joe. Within a few hours, it became clear to the agents that they weren't. Cloonan called the prosecutor and laid out some of the initial information they'd gathered. Fitzgerald, who had a staccato-like stutter when he got really excited, was jubilant at the news: "What-what-what-what are you saying?" He was on his way to North Africa as quickly as possible.

The Moroccan intelligence agency, the Direction de la Surveil-lance du Territoire (DST), had stashed Kherchtou in a giant, luxuri-ous compound outside Rabat. A private chef cooked meals for the U.S. team as it debriefed the al-Qaeda informer. While waiting for "Fitzy," as Fitzgerald was known to the team, Ali Soufan, a young Arabic-speaking FBI agent who had spent extensive time studying al-Qaeda's ideology, tried to bond with Joe. After Fitzgerald arrived, O'Neill spent much of the interrogation session talking on his cell phone back to the United States, coordinating Bureau business thou-sands of miles away. At times Fitzgerald seemed ready to throttle the talkative FBI agent—couldn't he see they were having critical con-versations here? When they wrapped up the first day's interrogation, Fitzgerald and Cloonan walked out to the compound's corral and Fitzgerald, leaning against the fence, called Mary Jo White back in New York to give a positive report. He handed the phone to Cloonan.

"What do you think?" White asked.

"I think he's the real deal, Mary," Cloonan said.

"Well, it's your ass if you're wrong," she said, only half jokingly.

Not long afterward, O'Neill offered Cloonan an intelligence assessment of a lower order. He told his fellow FBI agent, "We're in Morocco. We've got to have a party." Cloonan was skeptical: "Party or dinner?" "Dinner," O'Neill replied definitively. "John, we don't have any money," Cloonan explained, but he called in a debt with the local CIA station chief, an old friend, and the whole team—Moroccans, CIA, and FBI—dined out big. O'Neill got up and gave a toast: "Two hundred years ago, the United States came to the aid of Morocco as the Marines attacked the Barbary pirates. Today Morocco is returning the favor."

Thereafter, sticking the CIA with the bill for John O'Neill's over-seas entertaining became something of a tradition.* During dinner in Amman later in the case, O'Neill, puffing on his favored Davidoff cigar, held court well into the night at a Lebanese restaurant and ulti-mately charged the whole thing to Langley. "There was no one better

---

*The Agency, because of its "black budget" and lack of spending oversight by Congress, traditionally is able to open purse strings for luxuries the Bureau can't afford.

at schmoozing," Cloonan recalls with a laugh. "When he was on, he was the best." During another visit to Jordan, O'Neill decided he wanted to see the Gulf of Aqaba, sandwiched between Jordan and the Sinai Peninsula. Led by Jordanian intelligence, with O'Neill riding in his own Mercedes with a smartly dressed driver, the rest of the team following in another Mercedes, the group arrived at a resort in Aqaba to find the Jordanian agency's boat pulled up to take them out onto the storied body of water. O'Neill squeezed in a massage at the hotel, but not before turning to Cloonan with an important final order: "Go out and buy me a bathing suit."

Once the FBI team determined that Joe the Moroccan was the real deal, it had to get him out of the country. The flight back to the United States was odd and tense. The Moroccan government put the al-Qaeda informer and the FBI agents on Royal Air Maroc's once-a-day flight from Casablanca to New York's JFK Airport, filling the entire first-class cabin. In New York, they were met by more FBI agents and escorted off the plane by Port Authority police before the rest of the passengers had any clue what was going on. "He looked like, pardon the expression, any other Joe coming out of Morocco," Cloonan recalls. Then the debriefing began in earnest. Kherchtou's information led to the indictments of six more al-Qaeda operatives in the embassy bombing case, and he ended up being the star witness in the bombing trial—the witness whom jurors afterward said they trusted the most.

As investigators talked to al-'Owhali, Kherchtou, and Junior al-Fadl, Pat Fitzgerald had a troubling realization: Al-Qaeda, in his words, "thinks in a much longer time frame than we do." Al-Qaeda wasn't just any terrorist group; it was the most sophisticated, advanced, and methodical group the FBI had ever seen. The embassy plot had originally involved as many as five U.S. embassies; a variety of reasons had led al-Qaeda to zero in on just two, but even this was chilling, both because it showed a kind of restraint associated with grander strategic ambitions and because the surveillance on the embassies had apparently been conducted as early as 1994. As the investigators did the math in their heads, that meant, if al-Qaeda was still working on the same time horizon, they were planning attacks as far ahead as 2003. (Indeed, unbeknown to investigators, the planning for the 9/11 plot was already under way.) Pat D'Amuro told the team back in New York, "This isn't over. There's going to be more of this."

As the Nairobi investigation came together, the New York JTTF team headed south to assume control over operations in Tanzania. After the initial tug-of-war over which field office would be the office of origin for the East Africa embassy bombings, New York's al-Qaeda expertise had won out over the Washington Field Office. When Abby Perkins met up with Steve Bongardt in Dar es Salaam, she brought with her ten copies of the FBI's carefully constructed photo books, showing each of the possible suspects for KENBOM. As one of the case agents for TANBOM (as the Tanzania investigation was labeled by the FBI), she recognized from the beginning the overlap with the KENBOM investigation: the same names, the same places, the same logistics, the same issues. "We turned over every rock. You kept going until you ran out of things to look at," she says.

In Tanzania, Special Agent Mike Forsi spent weeks tracking down the Dar es Salaam bomb factory. He called Perkins close to her October birthday to say, "I have a present for you." They'd found the bomb factory, complete with a leftover blasting cap still sitting on a windowsill. Other agents traveled to Zanzibar, one of many stops they made across the African continent, to interview suspects' family members.

Before the East African bombings, it had been a big deal for FBI agents to travel overseas, yet those on Squad I-49 had worked out a special travel system that allowed them nearly a blank check for foreign travel. "Across the Maghreb, across southern Africa, Europe, there probably wasn't a country we didn't touch," Cloonan says. "In some cases, we didn't have legats that even covered those countries, so this was the first time those countries had ever dealt with the FBI." Numerous colleagues back in New York joked that the whole case was one big junket. I-49 member Russ Fincher recalls other agents asking, "What kind of boondoggle are you trying to work here?"

It most certainly was not a boondoggle. On a visit to Mauritania, chasing a lead as the squad sought to develop its case against bin Laden's organization, the team landed in Nouakchott, at one of the West African country's half-dozen airports with paved runways, on board a commercial Air Afrique flight. "You get off the plane and there's sand blowing through the door from the Sahara," Cloonan recalls. The first person the team spotted, standing at the base of the airplane stairs, was a retired CIA officer, carrying out some unmentioned mission. They stayed at the guesthouse of a former French Foreign Legion officer to keep a low profile in the capital, a sprawling city of perhaps a million largely nomadic people whose name translates from Berber as "the place of the winds." Across the street was what locals called a hospital, with open, unscreened windows and sanitary conditions that any Westerner would reject. Nevertheless, each morning when the team left the residence, they passed a long line of mothers with children waiting to see doctors. One day Cloonan walked alone up to the next cross street, John F. Kennedy Avenue, and was accosted by one of the mothers; he handed her a few ougiya, the local currency. The next morning, half a dozen women were waiting for the FBI team when they left the house. The trip, though, yielded valuable information, and then the FBI was off to the next country.

Each KENBOM or TANBOM fugitive had an agent assigned to run him to ground. Special Agent Aaron Zebley had the task of tracking down Ali Mandela, a suspect who, as his nickname implied, looked much like a younger Nelson Mandela.

Despite Steve Gaudin's international travel, in the year since the embassy bombings he had managed to settle down with a girlfriend. They were planning to depart for a brief summer vacation one morning in August 1999 when a call came at 3 A.M. "I've found Ali Mandela," Zebley said. The fugitive appeared to be in South Africa. Gaudin's girlfriend, angry at yet another sleepless night and vacation ruined by the Bureau's demands, gave some parting advice to the FBI agent: When you come back, don't bother coming back.

The news in South Africa, though, wasn't good. It was nearly immediately apparent that the suspect they assumed to be Ali Mandela in fact wasn't. Nevertheless, Gaudin and Zebley found themselves in a small conference room in Cape Town with the South African legat, Bob Wright, and officers from the country's immigration and refugee asylum service, who insisted that the visiting FBI guests at least review some immigration records while they were there. The South Africans pulled out boxes stuffed with immigration cards and dumped them on the table. Gaudin and Zebley groaned and agreed to peruse the cards for a little while before their evening flight back to the States. Miraculously, the second card Gaudin picked up to examine bore fruit.

"Zeb, where do I know this name from? Who is Zahran Nasser Maulid?" Gaudin asked, holding up the picture with the name written across the top of the card.

"That's KKM!" Aaron almost shouted.

"Who the fuck is KKM?" a South African official asked. "That's not your guy."

"What's going on here?" Bob Wright asked, also confused.

Gaudin pulled the South African aside; they couldn't risk a leak. "Who do you trust? This is important." In May agents had discovered that bombing suspect Khalfan Khamis Mohamed had used the name as an alias to get a Tanzanian passport. The police officer shooed a few people from the room and assembled five officers, four men and one woman. "These people, these are the best. What's going on? Who's KKM? I thought we were looking for Ali Mandela."

"No, you don't understand," Gaudin said, holding up the picture. "This guy is Khalfan Khamis Mohamed. There's already an indictment for him—he's one of the bombers. If we can get him, there's a five-million-dollar reward on his head."

Gaudin called New York and received two disparate responses from his supervisors. They either didn't believe he'd stumbled upon one of the country's most wanted terrorists or, if they did believe him, they wanted to send the whole FBI cavalry. "We're going to send the whole FBI circus tent," one told Gaudin. HRT, negotiators, bomb techs, evidence search teams, street agents—they'd saturate South Africa. With O'Neill's help, Gaudin and Zebley convinced the higher-ups that their best bet was to wait. Every forty-two days, like clockwork, Mohamed had been coming back to the refugee office to get his visa renewed. As long as he wasn't scared off, there was no reason to think he wouldn't walk right into the FBI's arms if they were patient. A small team of backup agents, including Perkins and Mike Forsi, left for Cape Town.

During the day, some of the FBI agents set out undercover with the South African immigration authorities to raid known immigrant residences and check documents. Zebley and Gaudin waited at the immigration facility, with Gaudin posing as a South African colonel. Refugees seeking asylum queued each morning, and in typical bureaucratic fashion, not everyone got his or her visa stamped. Latecomers were turned away, forced to return some other day or risk arrest if the authorities found that they'd overstayed their forty-two-day visas. Tensions ran high in the queue, with the crowd becoming more frantic as the day wore on and hopes of getting visas renewed successfully dwindled. Zebley and Gaudin watched in horror as the authorities wheeled out a firehose and blasted the crowd in the afternoon to keep it under control.

The two agents realized that given the line's chaos, the only practical thing to do was somehow to get to the applicants early. The team hatched a plan. Gaudin, dressed in his full colonel's uniform, complete with epaulets and medals, and looking vaguely like a character from a Gilbert and Sullivan operetta, went out each morning with a basket to collect the refugees' immigration cards. Then all the cards were brought inside and stamped. The refugees waited peacefully outside for their documents, which were returned in the afternoon. This meant not only that the FBI had a first, calm look at the documents, but also that the South Africans suddenly had a much more efficient mechanism for processing immigration claims.

The system worked smoothly—a little too smoothly, actually. The crowds got larger as word spread in the refugee community that a new policy meant everyone was getting a stamp. No more wasted days! The head of refugee services, who had no idea that an American FBI team was operating undercover in his agency, asked to meet this innovative new colonel who had so streamlined and revolutionized his agency's process. Gaudin, nervous that he'd blow the whole operation, was summoned and thanked for his contribution. "We haven't had to use the firehose all week," the head of refugee services announced, without any idea of Gaudin's real identity.

The weeks ticked by as KKM's forty-two-day deadline approached. October 5, 1999, arrived. The small team of FBI agents and South African immigration officers stationed themselves strategically around the building. Perkins and her counterpart anxiously sat in a car across an empty dirt field from the front of the building. Forsi and Zebley were in another car around the corner.

Gaudin went out with his basket. After weeks of the dulling routine, he searched each refugee's face with renewed enthusiasm, his energy mounting as he worked his way down the line. KKM was here somewhere. Yet Gaudin made it to the end of the morning line without any luck.

Then came a shout from his South African partner at the front door of the office: "Steve, the boss wants to see you."

"Not now, Sully. I'm busy."

"No, Steve, the boss *really* needs you. You need to come right now."

Walking inside, dejected, Gaudin boarded the elevator and found himself standing just inches away from Khalfan Khamis Mohamed. Sully, the South African officer, had seen the terrorist suspect walk up to the end of the line and, unaware of the new policy that ensured everyone a stamp, turn away after mentally calculating that he was unlikely to reach the front of the line that day. The officer had approached him and, thinking quickly, quietly told Mohamed that for some money, he would take him to the head of the line and get him a stamp. The Tanzanian bomb maker happily forked over a few hundred rand—getting the stamp that day meant that he wouldn't have to miss another day at the Burger World franchise where he had worked since the attack. The South African officer then led him up to the front and sent his partner to grab the FBI agent.

As the elevator ascended, Gaudin cracked a joke about how he was probably in trouble and was being summoned to the boss's office. The group disembarked on the top floor, still laughing. The two South African police went first, KKM second, and Gaudin brought up the rear, the police acting as casual as they could. Ten feet passed. Twenty feet passed. Gaudin, last in the line, was getting nervous. The building was cavernous; if KKM got spooked and escaped down a hallway or made it to a stairwell, it was possible that they would never see him again. Finally Gaudin's anxiety overcame him. He broke into a full sprint and slammed into the bomber from behind, his arms encircling KKM and pinning his arms. The two men dropped hard, like a linebacker sacking a quarterback in a high school football game.

Gaudin handcuffed the dazed and confused suspect and rolled him over, growling, "FBI. Don't even bother telling me you're not KKM." Zebley, Forsi, and Perkins were pounding up the stairs and into the hallway, with South African officers close behind. Perkins grabbed Gaudin in a big hug, and then the agents hustled the terrorist down to the basement, into a waiting car, and off to the airport for the long flight to Washington.

In a dormlike holding cell at the airport, as the team waited for the FBI plane to arrive, Perkins and Forsi advised Mohamed, who had learned English in primary school, of his rights.

"Does this mean I'm going to see America?" he asked after signing the advice-of-rights form.

"Yes, there's a good chance you will," Perkins said.

A pleased Mohamed explained that he wanted to tell the American people why he'd attacked their nation, how it was his obligation and duty to kill Americans. In fact, he explained, if the FBI hadn't found him, he had planned to continue launching attacks against Americans around the world. As the agents recorded in their report, "KKM stated that America is a superpower with the ability to change the world. KKM stated that only bombings will make America listen to them." His matter-of-fact manner was chilling, but as he explained, "You found me in Cape Town. You must already know everything. There's no reason for me to tell you one thing if you already know in fact another was true."

The interrogation continued on the flight back to Stewart Air Force Base, ranging from KKM's weapons training in Somalia and Afghanistan during the 1990s to the specifics of the Kenya plot. KKM identified a number of fellow suspects and plotters in the FBI's photo books, writing on the back of each picture the name by which he knew the individual. He said that bin Laden was the leader of "his people" but acknowledged that he'd never met the Saudi terrorist leader. Though he was handcuffed for the flight, at one point the agents handed Mohamed a pen to draw a diagram. Perkins's spider sense went off as she watched the terrorist with the sharp pen sitting next to her. "Why don't I take that back?" she said, reaching for it. Her intuition was well founded. A year later, Mohamed and another East Africa bombing suspect, Mamdouh Mahmud Salim, attacked a guard in prison, blinding him with hot sauce and then stabbing him in the eye with a sharpened comb, causing him to lose his eye and suffer severe brain damage.

★   ★   ★

Dale Watson was part of a generation of FBI agents left floundering after the end of the Cold War. After growing up in Alabama, he joined the army right out of college, specializing in counterintelligence. Discharged from the military on a Saturday, he was sworn into the FBI the following Monday. He'd spent most of his first decade as an agent chasing Soviet bloc spies, recruiting informants, and even landing himself one top-level source considered so sensitive that the case is still classified today. By the end of the 1980s, he was probably the world's leading expert on Lithuanian intelligence. Then the Soviet Union broke up.

Watson ended up in D.C., heading the team watching the Iranian-backed terrorist group Hezbollah. It wasn't until he returned to the field, though, that he got his first on-the-ground experience with terrorism, when as assistant special agent in charge of the Kansas City Field Office, he headed an OKBOMB task force in 1995. "That was probably one of the most fulfilling times for me in the Bureau," Watson recalls.

Later that year, Watson got a telephone call from Bear Bryant asking him to return to Washington and become, as part of a new exchange program, the number-two official in the CIA's Counterterrorism Center. After listening to Bryant explain how the Bureau wanted to step up its CT capability and change the way it handled such cases, and how key it was to have a good working understanding of the Agency and terrorism cases from their viewpoint, Watson politely declined.

Bryant called again just before Christmas, and Watson again declined, expanding on his views of the Agency bluntly: "I don't like those people. I don't know those people." Then, in the office late one evening just before New Year's, Watson answered the phone to hear a growl from Bryant's Washington office: "I put you out there. I'll take you back anytime." Then Bryant hung up.

Watson didn't hear another word from Washington until the January day when a glassine envelope showed up in Kansas City with his name on it. "Those envelopes only came from headquarters, and they never had good news in them—it meant you were being disciplined, transferred, or worse," he explains. The envelope contained orders to report to the CIA Counterterrorism Center pronto.

Watson dragged his feet leaving Kansas City, hoping the whole thing would blow over and headquarters would change its mind. He knew the career risk the CIA job meant. "Normally, being detailed out of the Bureau is a career-killer. You're out of sight, you're out of mind. You're not working cases, not rising through a field office, not on the calls with the executives," he recalls. Then another call from Bryant in the spring settled the situation. "Dale," Bryant warned him, "if you're not at the CIA by June twelfth, I'm putting you on leave without pay."

The job would transform Watson's career and place him at the center of the Bureau's counterterrorism program during its most formative period. For one thing, the CIA position gave him a new appreciation for the constraints under which the CIA operated. In a way, the FBI turned out to have more freedom to operate overseas, since in most cases it worked hand-in-hand with local law enforcement and with the support of the host government. The CIA had to play the politics of ambassadors, the host government, local leaders, its own headquarters at Langley, and the State Department in Foggy Bottom, which for the most part provided the cover for CIA agents operating overseas.

Yet the Bureau wasn't free of politics by any stretch. At the top of Watson's agenda was the FBI's sensitive investigation into the Khobar Towers bombing, which continued to drag on without resolution because the White House didn't want to hear the answer the FBI had found. In Freeh's deteriorating relationship with the Clinton administration, the Saudi Arabia bombing was becoming another flashpoint. "Khobar Towers was a political nightmare. The administration looked at terrorism as a criminal matter, yet these were hard political problems," Watson says. "The president's on record saying, 'We're going to get these guys,' and yet, as more comes out, the White House doesn't want the case solved. They'd accept three guys from Saudi Arabia, but as we're saying it was the Lebanese Hezbollah with the backing of the Iranian government, what in the world are you going to do with that?"

The months leading up to the millennium were a scary time for authorities, as the much-hyped "Y2K bug" threatened computer havoc in banking, power plants, and government systems and terrorism fears increased. It seemed that every Friday through the fall of 1999 some piece of incoming intelligence would result in the staff working through the weekend. (Clarke, Watson, and Watson's CIA counterpart, Cofer Black, came to call the weekly crises "Friday follies.") The fear, in retrospect, was well placed, even more than was clear to the U.S. government or the U.S. public at the time.

The first threat, a plot by a sixteen-member al-Qaeda cell to attack the Radisson Hotel in Amman, was discovered by Jordanian intelligence. The Jordanian cell leader, who helped assemble the bombs, had only recently returned to the Middle East after quitting his job as a cabdriver in Boston, a known infiltration point for Islamic extremists. (The FBI was already tracking reports of Algerians sneaking into Boston harbor onboard tankers, including liquid natural gas tankers that, if exploded in the harbor, would level most of Massachusetts's largest city.) As the investigation into the plot evolved, Ali Soufan spent weeks in Amman, working side by side with the Jordanians. Single and dedicated, he agreed to miss the holidays; Thanksgiving, Christmas, and New Year's all passed during his deployment. One of the plotters turned out to be Abu Musab al-Zarqawi, the senior al-Qaeda leader, who escaped capture. Elsewhere in the region, shortly after New Year's, another Boston cabdriver, Bassam Kanj, who had been through bin Laden's Khalden training camp, was among a score of attackers killed in a five-day rebellion against the Lebanese Army that the militants hoped would spark a global Islamic uprising.

Back home in the United States, at 6 P.M. on December 14, customs inspector Diana Dean stopped the last car off the Port Angeles ferry, coming from Vancouver to Washington State. "She's one of the real heroes of the war on terror," Dale Watson relates today. "It's raining, her husband is calling, asking when she'll be home for dinner, and she's got just one last car to check before she leaves. Yet she took the time to realize something was off." The driver was nervous; at one point in the questioning, he handed over his Costco card rather than his ID. "So you like to shop in bulk?" another customs inspector teased. When a third customs inspector noticed something unusual in the car's trunk, the driver bolted. Customs officers chased him for four blocks before they caught him trying to carjack a woman at a red light.

As they investigated further back at the inspection station, shaking the bottles of liquid found in the suspect's trunk, he got ever more nervous and ducked down to the floor. If they'd known that they were fiddling with liquid nitroglycerin, which is unstable on its best day, they'd probably have been nervous too.

Seattle FBI agent Fred Humphries got a call around eleven that night from an agent in Port Angeles, who needed someone to read the suspect his *Miranda* rights *en français*. On the phone with Humphries, the suspect declined in French to speak further. Humphries immediately asked the suspect to put the Port Angeles FBI agent back on the phone. "There is no way this guy is who he says he is," Humphries said. "There's no way he's from Montreal." The suspect was speaking Algerian French, not Québécois French. By the next day, the legat in Ottawa, after talking with the Canadian Security Intelligence Service about the suspect, called Humphries: "If this is your guy, you've got trouble." The suspicious ferry passenger, it turned out, was an Algerian named Ahmed Ressam, who had spent the better part of a decade living in Canada and had attended terrorist training camps in Afghanistan.

Ressam's arrest was a gut punch to Squad I-49. Another plot was evidently unfolding right in the United States, even as they continued work on the embassy bombing cases overseas—and it came at a time when the Y2K bug already had the nation on edge. The Bureau dove into action. (Only years later would the government figure out that the terrorist's goal had been to explode a bomb at Los Angeles International Airport on New Year's Eve.) Ressam had been carrying a piece of paper with a telephone number and the name Ghani. Thinking first that the scribbled number was a 318 area code, Jack Cloonan traced the number to a child in Monroe, Louisiana. Studying further, he surmised that it was a 718 number: Brooklyn. Research quickly revealed that the number belonged to another Algerian, Abdulghani Meskini. Coast to coast, thousands of FBI agents began working through lists of suspected Islamic radicals, conducting early morning "knock and talks" designed to surprise and unnerve the interview subjects. According to Fran Townsend, the head of Justice's intelligence office, and Mike Rolince, then section chief of international terrorism, the Bureau promptly set up a record number of FISA warrants for eavesdropping on immigrants who had ties to Meskini in

New York, Boston, and elsewhere. Meskini himself was put under a blanket of surveillance so heavy it seemed impossible for him not to notice; agents monitored every movement and, thanks to FISA wiretaps, every phone call.

During a performance of *The Nutcracker* at Lincoln Center that O'Neill was attending with his longtime girlfriend, Valerie James, his pager went off twenty times. "We were running around like maniacs," recalls David Kelley, one of the federal prosecutors on Pat Fitzgerald's team. "Everyone is warning that your ATM will stop working, that planes will fall from the sky, and on top of all of that we've got threat information jumping all over the place. I felt like the little Dutch boy standing before the dike." Townsend, in her office at Justice, held up a Grinch doll at a staff meeting and said, "Christmas is canceled."

Then the blue van surfaced. In the wake of the Ressam arrest, which had made national news, tips had been pouring in from concerned citizens. This one seemed legit: A gas station attendant in Texas reported a group of Middle Easterners in a van loaded with boxes. After tracing the van, the FBI picked up the trail and followed it north and east with increasing apprehension. Then the surveillance crew lost track of the van somewhere around Washington, D.C. No one knew the final destination. "The pucker factor was through the roof," Mike Rolince remembers.

Warning bells went off up and down the system the following day, when Meskini walked into a Brooklyn restaurant and a few moments later the blue van arrived. The occupants got out and went in—for lunch, or a rendezvous with their fellow cell terrorists? The surveillance agents called O'Neill from the scene: "Boss, you'll never believe what just happened." SWAT personnel moved into position in case an assault was required. After thirty minutes, their meal concluded, the van's occupants came out and drove off. The surveillance blanket now extended to them too. Over the following two days, the van just kept circling New York, seemingly with no real destination in mind.

Then the team had a brainstorm: Nothing like a routine traffic stop to enable them to poke around without raising suspicion. An investigator walked by the parked van in the middle of the night and with a quick hit broke the van's taillight. The next morning, as soon as the van pulled out of its parking spot, an NYPD patrol car pulled it over. A large contingent of SWAT personnel and nervous agents waited nearby. Amazingly, it was all just a coincidence. The men had no knowledge of Meskini or Ressam; they had come to New York to sell Korans. The back of the van was filled with religious CDs.

That got them off, but not Meskini. On December 30, before dawn, JTTF agents crashed through Meskini's door and took him into custody. "Don't move or I'll shoot you in the head," an agent told Meskini as he was forced to the floor. After the arrest, as O'Neill and counterterrorism supervisor Ken Maxwell stood outside the apartment, O'Neill's cell phone rang. He passed it to Maxwell. Janet Reno was on the line. "I want to thank you and your team," she told Maxwell. "I know you guys have worked hard through Christmas and New Year's. I want you to know the president and I appreciate it." Louis Freeh later said that the whole case, code-named BORDER-BOM, was "the template of how that is supposed to work."

If Ahmed Ressam had been just a little calmer as he crossed the border, or if he had crossed the porous and unguarded Canadian border illegally anywhere along its multi-thousand-mile length, he would probably have succeeded in his plot. Once again the United States had gotten lucky. But nervousness remained. Authorities never satisfactorily uncovered the extent of Ressam's domestic support network, if he had one. Much of the case unraveled later. It is always a challenge to take down a case before the suspects have executed their plot, but in the FBI's view, this one kept the country safe for New Year's.

The United States didn't learn about the final part of the so-called millennium plot until a year later. Al-Qaeda had planned to attack the navy's Aegis destroyer *The Sullivans* as it refueled in Yemen around New Year's. The attacker overloaded the skiff, however, replacing the extra flotation devices with explosives in order to maximize the boat's firepower, and it sank as soon as it was pushed into the water.

The period between the embassy bombings and the end of the Clinton administration saw little government movement on the terrorism front, even as the millennium plot underscored al-Qaeda's seriousness. "That two years there was a lost time," remembers Neil Herman. In December 1998, George Tenet had made an attempt to rally the government to confront terrorism seriously. "We are at war," he wrote in a memo to top CIA leaders. "I want no resources or people spared in this effort." Yet his words weren't followed by action, despite the best efforts of the small counterterrorism teams.

The FBI's international expansion continued, but the Bureau split over how and where resources should be focused. After his stint in Legat Athens and the many trips into the war zone of Beirut had turned his hair gray, Tom Knowles returned to the Hoover Building in 1998 to help supervise the FBI's international operations section, including all the new offices that had opened just in the three years he'd been overseas: Germany, Pakistan, Poland, Saudi Arabia, Estonia, Israel, Argentina, and the Ukraine, as well as the FBI's first two offices in Africa—Egypt and Bob Wright's legat in South Africa.

At the top of Knowles's agenda, after living with the tension and risks of Athens, was assembling a comprehensive training program for agents heading overseas. Agents were arriving in country before the embassy had lined up a place for them to live; one new legat arrived to find that his office was literally a janitor's closet. In conversations on Capitol Hill, Freeh and his chief of staff, Bob Bucknam—the Pizza Connection prosecutor whom Freeh had recruited to help run the Bureau—would promise congressional officials, "Give us a laptop and a cell phone and we can put an agent anywhere." Knowles balked at the tough talk. "Bullshit," he said. "You can, sure, but he's at risk from the moment he lands overseas. That's great for the movies, but you need an infrastructure. You've got to figure out housing, schools, embassy workspace, all sorts of things." He had been frustrated as he headed to Athens by the Bureau's scattershot training, and he had paid personally for his wife to attend a tactical driving course and a countersurveillance course before she joined him in Greece. "I figured the fastest way to get to me was for someone to get to her," he says. "Overseas, the spouse is just as much a target as the agent." As 17N had warned him, overseas the hunters could become the hunted.

Each new overseas deployment of agents meant new discussions, new strategies, and new debates. When the embassy bombings sent huge teams of FBI agents abroad for the first time, the FBI's position was that HRT should have a high-profile, force-protection role. The State Department wanted the FBI to put its weapons away. As Knowles

254 • GARRETT M. GRAFF

explained it within the Hoover Building, "If the French consulate was bombed in New York, would we want French military walking the streets of Manhattan carrying M-16s?"

Beyond such challenges of training, funding, and logistics, Knowles found guiding the Bureau's international expansion at headquarters a political minefield. There were ambassadors to woo and cajole; there were Hill aides and wary congressmen like Bob Livingston to be convinced; and there was the State Department's traditional, conservative nature to navigate. The number-two man in the Singapore embassy resisted the posting of an agent to the island city-state, dragging his feet and delaying a deployment for years. "In their eyes, we were a bunch of cowboys," Knowles recalls of the State Department. "They looked at us as a bunch of knuckle-draggers who weren't capable of diplomacy."

While Congress controlled the funding for overseas operations, the State Department's ambassadors personally oversaw who could work out of a given country—and both they and Congress were often dubious of the need for an FBI agent to be stationed overseas. Knowles got used to meetings where other U.S. officials asked him to justify the need for a new FBI foreign post: What exactly was the agent going to do? What type of cases originated from that region? What leads did the FBI need to track in that country? Freeh's force of personality could only get the FBI so far. Capitol Hill and the State Department wanted real justifications for each new overseas post.

But there was no larger problem than the CIA, which was nervous about the FBI's continued growth during an era when it was busy shuttering overseas stations. During a secret meeting in Rome of every European legat and CIA station chief, the leadership of the two agencies tried to ease growing tensions. "The American people deserve better," the CIA and FBI leaders told the assembled operatives. "If you can't get along, pack your shit and go home." The underlying message, though, was more subtle: The CIA had to get used to having the FBI operate on its turf.

In an attempt to provide greater focus for the FBI's international team, Knowles had begun to divide the headquarters support staff into country desks, much as the State Department handles the world. He had also begun a comprehensive project to research where the program's resources should be directed, asking the analysts to compile every overseas lead from the past three years. Where were the leads coming from? What level of crime did the leads refer to? Was the FBI finding a lot of motor vehicle theft traced to the Balkans? Or a lot of public corruption out of Africa? The result, he hoped, would help the program concentrate on what it should be concentrating on. There'd been little matching of leads to legats thus far; the Bureau's expansion had come opportunistically, for the most part.

When Bucknam told Knowles in mid-2000 that Freeh wanted a dozen new legats, Knowles was ready with a detailed list, heavily researched, the product of hundreds of hours of work by a team of analysts. Topping it, surprisingly, was a recommendation for a new suboffice in Vancouver. Hundreds of leads each year ended in the British Columbian capital, and it was a pain for the legats in Ottawa to travel there. Beyond that there were capitals such as Dublin, which had seen seventy-five important leads in the previous year, and Abu Dhabi, which had seen seventy-two.

When Knowles met with Bucknam to present his findings, the chief of staff scanned the list and then drew a line through the entire recommendation. "This isn't where we need to be," Bucknam told Knowles. "Louie wants to be in Tbilisi."

Freeh had a close relationship with the Georgian president, yet Knowles also knew that the FBI had followed only six leads to the former Soviet republic in the past year. It hardly seemed to Knowles a good use of three agents and $1 million annually to open a legat there. Freeh, though, had his own agenda. He wasn't concentrating on where the investigations had been; he was looking ahead to where the threats could be.

"It's geopolitics," Bucknam explained, ticking off other countries where the director wanted an FBI presence—places such as Hanoi, Vietnam, and Tashkent, Uzbekistan—most of which didn't register at the top of the Bureau's list of research. Hanoi had seen just a single lead in the previous year, Tashkent only three. "Give me a memo that justifies those." This wasn't about criminal leads, Bucknam argued. No one cared about following bank robbers or stolen car cases overseas. The FBI's efforts abroad should focus on countering rising threats and backing friendly governments. It's not about stats, Bucknam said. It's about international diplomacy.

Knowles balked. The research and facts said what they said;

Congress wanted facts and now they would get them. How could that be challenged? Facts can be manipulated, Bucknam replied. Both men's tempers rose quickly. Before Knowles stormed out, he angrily said, "You're a puny fat fuck!" Within a few months, Deputy Director Tom Pickard reassigned Knowles to a violent crime task force at Quantico, and much of the structure of the overseas training program that Knowles had worked so hard to institute was discarded. Freeh's plan to open a legat in Tbilisi moved forward.*

"I was so disappointed, in me and the FBI," Knowles remembers.

By the end of Freeh's reign in 2001, the FBI had expanded to more than forty countries. Bin Laden's operation, meanwhile, had been traced to some sixty countries. The two groups were locked in an international cat-and-mouse game.

An effort to arrest the al-Qaeda leader Khalid Sheikh Mohammed in Qatar, where he was supposed to be working for the water ministry, went awry after someone in the Qatari government leaked word to him ahead of time, enabling him to flee before the agents' arrival. But the FBI was ready for wherever he would next appear. Frank Pellegrino, who was leading the case against Mohammed (known in U.S. circles as KSM), established a network of safe houses around the world so that wherever agents could find him, they could nab him.

On September 11, 1999, a year after the embassy bombings, Neil Herman and many members of the FBI's counterterrorism team gathered at the World Trade Center's Windows on the World restaurant to toast his retirement. He had spent a quarter century working international counterterrorism in the Big Apple and watching the Bureau learn and grow as it worked terror cases. What had begun with just an ad hoc squad in New York had morphed into a worldwide enterprise, with agents now fanned out across the globe to bring bombers and terrorists to justice. There was much to celebrate. The following September, in 2000, the JTTF threw itself a twentieth birthday party in the space;

---

* The FBI legat in Tbilisi took years more to work through the various governmental processes and didn't open until 2004. As of 2011, the FBI still hasn't opened offices in Hanoi or Tashkent.

it too had come a long way since its founding from interagency squabbling over the crime scenes of Omega 7, the FALN, and the Weather Underground. For the large black-tie gala, hundreds of current and former members of the JTTF packed Windows on the World; original commanders came back from retirement, and historical displays covering the task force's most famous (and infamous) cases decorated the walls. Just the day before the JTTF birthday party, Osama bin Laden had appeared on Al Jazeera with his latest threat: "Enough of words! It is time to take action against this iniquitous and faithless force that has spread troops through Egypt, Yemen, and Saudi Arabia."

That fall, as the nation took sides in the heated presidential race between Al Gore and George W. Bush, the FBI's Squad I-49 busied itself preparing for the embassy bombings trial. "We had witnesses who had never been on an escalator or an elevator," Gaudin recalls. "The amount of the logistics involved in it was overwhelming." Witnesses flew with an FBI escort from Africa, via Europe, to Kennedy Airport. Other agents waited at the airport with winter clothes donated by Vermont's Killington ski resort, which was only too happy to get rid of the previous season's puffy purple ski patrol jackets. The foreigners were then taken to their hotel and given an orientation tutorial. Nothing could be assumed. One of the first witnesses was scalded by the hot water in the hotel bathroom, so all future witnesses were carefully told which faucet handle denoted hot and which denoted cold.

When a delegation of Tanzanian police officials was taken to the Hoover Building for meetings, Gaudin, Perkins, and Bongardt treated them to a lunch at the McDonald's across from headquarters. Standing in line to order, the Tanzanians chattered away in Swahili until one turned to Gaudin and asked, "Where do you keep the animals? I didn't see any pasture or grass nearby."

Gaudin tried to explain. "Oh, there are no animals here. It's all frozen."

"What? You freeze the cows?" came the puzzled response.

"Just order the Big Mac. You'll love it," Gaudin said.

When Maxwell was promoted to ASAC on the JTTF, O'Neill pulled him aside and said, "This is a one-mistake job. You make one and they'll kill you. In baseball, if you make .300, you're great. In basketball, if you shoot fifty percent from the field, you're a hero. Here, you've got to bat a thousand every day. The risk is tremendous." Most of those hunting the terrorists were single, and those who weren't often ended up dumped or divorced. Soufan, like everyone on the squad, pulled long hours. Over dinner one night at Sette, a favorite JTTF hangout nicknamed "the fifty-first precinct," O'Neill told Soufan, "Ali, this job is like a mistress. It has to consume you. You have to operate with the bad guys' schedule. You have to live like them."

Gaudin and other members of the squad were repeatedly awakened late at night by calls from O'Neill: "Whatcha doin'?"

"God, John, I'm sleeping. We gotta be at work in seven hours," Gaudin complained.

"Get up. The Jordanians are in town tonight and we've got to spend time with them."

O'Neill had a unique approach to what's known in the FBI as "liaison": meeting and wooing other foreign and domestic services. He sometimes referred to his evening entertaining as his night job; often it would literally keep him up most of the night. He became legendary for partying until two or three in the morning and then showing up at the office by eight looking fresh, pressed, and as dapper as always. "You know, John, all these guys think you're a vampire—you just hang upside-down under a bridge for a few hours and then come in fresh the next day," Maxwell joked one night.

The long hours of personal conversation, drinks, and meals paid off in spades when O'Neill's agents traveled the world. They tapped into a network of foreign law enforcement and intelligence officials who worshipped O'Neill and smoothed their way into hostile countries, helped them gain access to suspects in foreign prisons, and aided them in getting tips out of normally reluctant allies.

In late 1998, O'Neill was horrified to hear that a Saudi delegation of intelligence officials visiting Washington had not received any special treatment; the Mukhabarat team, infuriated by the way they'd been disrespected in Washington, called him and threatened to cancel the New York leg of their visit to discuss the embassy bombings. O'Neill insisted that they come, telling the officials, "Just trust me." He arranged an NYPD motorcycle escort on the airport tarmac, then whisked the Saudi delegation into New York in a large motorcade packed with armed SWAT officers. When the motorcade pulled up at the Plaza Hotel, the Saudi flag was draped over the hotel entrance. Inside, the Saudis were whisked to their rooms without having to check in. At the restaurant for dinner, O'Neill pulled his squad together. "Not one of you better fucking talk work. Tonight we eat and become friends," he instructed. At the end of the lengthy, extravagant dinner, the Saudi intelligence chief stood and offered a toast: "Tomorrow, we start business." The trip was saved.

As the embassy trial proceeded, mostly out of the limelight, down Center Street from the federal Southern District Courthouse in Foley Square, a line of TV trucks and reporters waited anxiously for a glimpse of Sean "Puff Daddy" Combs, who was facing charges stemming from a December 1999 nightclub shooting. One day as the FBI agents walked down the courthouse steps in the midst of the nearly five-month-long trial, Mike Anticev looked up the street, shook his head in puzzlement, and gestured toward the municipal court. "That's where all the cameras are," he noted. "No one cares what's going on at the federal courthouse."

The lack of interest wasn't limited to the public. A few weeks after the verdicts came down in the spring of 2001, just months before the 9/11 attacks, New York's assistant director Barry Mawn boarded the elevator at 26 Federal Plaza with Gaudin and a few other agents. Just making conversation, he cheerily asked, "How's everybody doing today?"

Years of exhausting globe-trotting and countless hours in the courtroom, cold dinners, and late nights came to the fore. In his thick Boston accent, Gaudin replied, "Not well, sir. We just had a big case over here and no bosses have come by to say congratulations."

The elevator fell silent.

After the trial was over, John O'Neill went to Gaudin and told the young agent that he was being sent to Arabic language school at Middlebury College in Vermont for the summer of 2001. Gaudin protested: "The case is over."

O'Neill didn't mince words: "No—there's more coming."

O'Neill was fighting his own battles. In the late spring of 2000, New York's assistant director Lew Schiliro announced his retirement.

O'Neill was a step closer to his life's dream: becoming head of the New York office. For now, he was the acting assistant director in charge. The final decision had come down to him or Mawn, the cofounder of the JTTF in the 1980s, who had already led the field offices in Newark and Boston. Ultimately, it was a close call, everyone agreed, but Mawn didn't have nearly as much baggage hanging around his neck. O'Neill's oversized personality had made a lot of enemies within the Bureau and the U.S. government, and despite powerful allies such as Richard Clarke, he had two major blemishes on his record, in the eyes of the FBI, at least. As Mike Rolince, who did like O'Neill, explains, "The Bureau doesn't like A-Rods on its team—.300 hitters do the best."

When he attended a mandatory retirement planning seminar in Orlando in June 2000, O'Neill took along paperwork to complete. His pager went off during the seminar, and he left to return the telephone call, leaving his work and briefcase behind. When he returned, the seminar had ended, the room was empty, and his briefcase had been stolen. Inside his briefcase, against every Bureau policy, was a copy of the New York Field Office's annual national security report, listing every ongoing investigation, sources, informants, wiretaps, and theory. It was the crown jewel of an FBI office; in the wrong hands, it would undo years of the entire division's work.

O'Neill immediately reported the loss—a report that quickly ricocheted straight up to Louis Freeh, who then briefed Janet Reno. Within hours, the briefcase was recovered at a nearby hotel. It turned out that O'Neill hadn't been targeted by a sneaky foreign power; a petty thief had just gotten lucky and taken only his cigar cutter, lighter, and Montblanc pen. No one had touched the documents. FBI fingerprint examiners dusted them to be sure. But the damage was done. The FBI opened an internal investigation, which had the potential to grow into a criminal probe.

It wasn't O'Neill's first transgression. Earlier, during a trip south with Valerie James, he had experienced engine trouble in New Jersey. Because the FBI is sensitive about allowing civilians into Bureau cars, he often just drove his personal vehicle all the time, on duty and off. His trusty Buick, though, ran into trouble close to a secret garage where the Bureau kept its undercover vehicles—the fake utility trucks, taxis, unmarked cars, vans, and other vehicles that it used for surveillance. The location of the garage and the fleet inside were closely held secrets for the Bureau. Nevertheless, O'Neill drove his longtime girlfriend up to the garage to exchange his Buick for a Bureau car. Just taking her to the location was a violation of security protocols, but he might have escaped that incident without notice if he hadn't also allowed her to go into the garage to use the bathroom. The subsequent investigation led to a three-year block on any promotions and a month's suspension without pay. For someone whose personal identity was so tied up in the Bureau—and someone who already lived financially close to or over the line, supporting multiple relationships and all of his unofficial FBI "liaison" activity—the month's suspension was devastating, even though it was eventually shortened to just fifteen days.

In the end, Freeh chose Mawn to head the New York office. During a trip to New York, before Mawn began, Freeh tried to make amends to O'Neill. Standing outside the ADIC's office, Freeh said, "Let's go into your office."

"That's not my office and I don't sit there," O'Neill said coldly.

From the moment John O'Neill was passed over for the promotion, it was clear that his time in the FBI was coming to a close.

CHAPTER 8
The Wall

What is called "foreknowledge" cannot be elicited
from spirits, nor from gods, not by analogy with past
events, nor from calculations. It must be obtained
from men who know the enemy situation.

— *Sun Tzu,* The Art of War

Just a year after the arrest of KKM, the FBI deployed back overseas,
this time with the full cavalry. On October 12, 2000, three weeks
after the JTTF's shiny twentieth birthday party at Windows on the
World, two men in a fiberglass skiff pulled alongside the USS *Cole,* a
billion-dollar guided-missile destroyer. The destroyer had been in
port barely two hours. The men waved and then snapped to attention
just before triggering an enormous explosion that took their lives and
those of seventeen American sailors. Even though the *Cole* was well
armored and built to withstand missile strikes, it was seriously damaged by the suicide attack; the bomb tore a 1,600-square-foot hole in
its side, and flooding overwhelmed the ship's pumps, leading to fears
that it might sink entirely. The government had had indications that
al-Qaeda hoped to attack a U.S. Navy ship as it refueled in Yemen,
going back as far as Steve Gaudin's interview with al-'Owhali in the
days after the East Africa bombings. (American intelligence did not

know yet that al-Qaeda had failed in its attempt on the USS *The Sulli-vans* in the days after the new millennium.) While this attack had suc-ceeded, once again the United States had gotten lucky—the *Cole's* magazines and fuel hadn't exploded, and engineers staved off the sink-ing. Meanwhile, al-Qaeda had screwed up again: The videographer it assigned to capture the attack from shore for later propaganda use had fallen asleep before the attack.

Within hours, O'Neill and a team of agents from New York were en route to Yemen. Some hundred agents and FBI personnel boarded a C-17 military transport. The trip was a challenge from the start: France and Saudi Arabia denied overflight rights for the U.S. mission, and in an ominous sign of what was to come, the U.S. ambassador to Yemen, Bar-bara Bodine, tried to waylay the team, forcing them to kill time at the air base in Ramstein, Germany, where they were at least able to interview injured members of the *Cole* crew as they arrived by medevac.

Yemen was unlike any environment the FBI had ever worked in before. NPR journalist Dina Temple-Raston, who reported from Yemen, once recounted a common joke she heard in the country: God decides to return to earth and have an up-close look at how his cre-ation is faring. He lands first in the United States. He tours Times Square and then alights on the Hollywood Hills. He throws up his hands in disgust. "This is not at all what I had in mind," he says. He decides to take a look at Europe, hoping for a happier result. Instead all he sees is pollution and scantily clad women on billboards. Then God goes to Yemen. He looks around, nods, and smiles: "This is exactly the way I left it."

Most of the major terrorism incidents of the previous dozen years had occurred in friendly territories. The bombing of Pan Am 103 had occurred over America's closest ally. The bombings in East Africa had happened in two countries uniquely inclined to be cooperative. Even Saudi Arabia, the site of the Khobar Towers attack, was nominally a U.S. ally. The bombing of the USS *Cole* was something else entirely. "We got spoiled by Kenya and Tanzania," Ali Soufan says.

Challenges started as soon as the FBI's contingent touched down in Aden. A group of Yemeni soldiers surrounded the plane when it came to a stop on the tarmac; as they did so, the Hostage Rescue Team, in charge of force protection, prepared for a possible shoot-out.

Under the hot sun—daytime highs in October are still over 100 degrees—Special Agent Tim Clemente decided to walk out onto the tarmac with an armful of bottled water as a peace offering. Before he left the plane, he handed his camera to a fellow agent: "Get some pictures. Either way this turns out, it'll be interesting."

The water bottles did the trick, but as the agents pulled out for the ride downtown, they received their next unwelcome surprise: A sign announced that the airport had been built by the Bin Laden Group, the family construction firm from which Osama had broken away. Throughout the coming investigation, the relationship with the locals would be tense. For starters, the Yemeni government didn't understand the point of the investigation. The bombers were dead, right?

Beyond the problems with the host government, though, the American ambassador quickly became John O'Neill's personal nemesis. Like some of her diplomatic colleagues, Barbara Bodine thought the FBI agents were cowboys out to ruin her developing relationship with the Yemenis; she'd requested that the FBI team be kept small, perhaps in the neighborhood of two dozen agents. O'Neill had brought around 150—smaller, yes, than the teams that had investigated the embassy bombings, but still large enough to cause Bodine to rant about the U.S. "invasion" of Yemen. On a personal level, things got off to a bad start when O'Neill said he was happy to be in "Yay-man," rhyming it with *Cayman.* Bodine corrected him icily: "Ye-*men.*" More seriously, she tried to prohibit the FBI team from carrying heavy weapons, in a country O'Neill described as containing "eighteen million citizens and fifty million machine guns." O'Neill tried to put his team up at one hotel that provided good protection for it, but Bodine insisted on another hotel, which backed up against the ocean—meaning that the team was trapped if attacked. Her orders about how to work in Yemen came across to the FBI team not as diplomatic counsel but as petty spite. She chastised female agents for their outfits, stalking up to one agent, yanking out her tucked-in polo shirt, and saying, "Cover your butt."

As the investigation proceeded, the FBI faced the reality that Yemen was the most hostile environment in which the Bureau had ever operated. John O'Neill often called to update Fran Townsend back at Main Justice while hiding under his bed as gunfire rattled in the background. One night, gunfire got close enough that the HRT took up defensive positions, as did the Marine contingent that helped with security at the hotel. En route back from the ship the next day, the team's helicopter undertook evasive maneuvers when a surface-to-air missile attempted to lock onto it. Nowhere was safe. Inside the hotel, O'Neill's team discovered that the Yemenis had been bugging the FBI's rooms. Outside the hotel, U.S. intelligence noticed al-Qaeda sympathizers surveilling the FBI operations for a possible follow-up attack. Not even the local provisions could be trusted. "You couldn't drink the water. We were cooking our own food," agent Russ Fincher recalls. "It was like a siege."

O'Neill asked to move his men out to the U.S. naval flotilla that had gradually accumulated in Aden harbor to aid in the recovery operation. Ambassador Bodine at first refused, saying that she didn't want to slight the Yemenis; but for the agents in Yemen, each day's motorcade from the hotel was nerve-racking. "It was just like that ambush scene in *Clear and Present Danger*. You always had a feeling a child would be sent out into the road, stop the convoy, and then they'd hit us," Fincher says. In the end, Freeh backed O'Neill and the agents moved offshore. Concerned for their safety, NYPD commissioner Bernard Kerik and Rudy Giuliani ordered the NYPD JTTF detectives home. The NYPD leadership didn't see what the JTTF was doing halfway around the world anyway. Bill Allee, the NYPD's chief of detectives, asked in one meeting, "What's this got to do with New York?"

The *Cole* crime scene was like a scene out of a horror movie. Much of the crew had been sleeping on deck since the attack, since their quarters had been ruined by the bomb. The stench of their dead comrades, whose bodies had yet to be removed from the twisted metal underneath, hung over everything. "The crime scene of the *Cole* was one you'd never forget," Soufan recalls. "The floor was just gone. The metal was tangled. The smell. It was a sad and sorrowful scene." The sailors bravely continued on, yet by the time the FBI arrived, many seemed close to an emotional breakdown. Clad in plastic suits, the FBI and Naval Criminal Investigative Service (NCIS) investigation teams somehow managed to work in 110-degree heat.

In the months following the attack, the government, the FBI, and

John O'Neill went to great lengths to court the Yemenis. President Ali Abdullah Saleh came to the United States and, as part of his trip, visited the FBI Laboratory at Quantico, which briefly improved cooperation, but nearly every aspect of the investigation still required negotiation. When the Yemeni government wouldn't allow the U.S. investigators to dredge the harbor for sunken evidence, the United States ended up "buying" the harbor's mud for $1 million, dredging it, and shipping it elsewhere for processing. The Yemenis held in custody more than one hundred people tied to the bombings, most of them just lucky (or unlucky) enough to be witnesses. "If this is how they treat their cooperating witnesses, imagine how they treat the more difficult ones," O'Neill said, only half joking, to his team one night. The FBI was allowed to witness interrogations but could only submit questions for the Yemenis to ask.

Two days before Thanksgiving, O'Neill headed back to the United States, having lost twenty-five pounds since he had set foot in the New York Field Office. His relationship with Bodine hadn't improved at all. In fact, it marked a new milestone for the FBI's overseas operations: When Ambassador Bodine barred him from returning to continue the investigation, O'Neill became the first FBI agent to be labeled persona non grata in a foreign country by his own government.

The crime-scene evidence quickly began to point toward bin Laden. A witness directed agents to what turned out to be the bomb factory, a walled-off estate that looked much like those used in Nairobi and Dar es Salaam. "By November 2000, we had no doubt that al-Qaeda was behind the *Cole*," Soufan says. Over the coming months, the case agents, Soufan and Steve Bongardt, led teams back and forth to Yemen in a frustrating exercise of two steps forward, one step back. The two men were some of the most aggressive agents in the squad, but there was only so much they could do under such difficult working conditions.

Working relationships further deteriorated over the spring. When American authorities uncovered a plot for eight al-Qaeda terrorists to scale the embassy's wall and attack with three rocket-propelled grenades, Bodine was nonplussed. "How much damage can three grenades do?" she asked. "They can do a lot of damage if it involves people," snapped Mary Galligan, the FBI's on-scene commander at the time.

On June 16, 2001, Father's Day—just days after Squad I-49 had won the convictions back in New York in the East Africa embassy bombing trial—the FBI prepared to pull out of Yemen, against the ambassador's wishes. There was a final tense showdown at the gates of the embassy compound. Marine guards refused to let the agents exit, as the ambassador maintained that they couldn't leave without her permission. Back in Washington, Mike Rolince's family counted forty-six phone calls from the Bureau, tracking the unfolding situation at the Yemen embassy.

As the FBI's O'Neill, Ambassador Bodine, and the Yemeni government locked horns, President Clinton, getting reports on the investigation's progress, remarked with a sigh, "Look, I've had a lot of trouble with the FBI myself."

Even though there was convincing evidence by November 2000 that al-Qaeda was behind the attack on the naval ship, there was little hunger in the Clinton administration to retaliate. The military response to the East Africa bombings had, it seemed, hurt Clinton more than it had hurt bin Laden. As Ali Soufan recalls, "People told us that they didn't want al-Qaeda to be involved in the attack—as if we had anything to do with where the case led us." Michael Sheehan, who had worked counterterrorism issues at the National Security Council, told Richard Clarke, "Who the shit do they think attacked the *Cole*? Fucking Martians? Does al-Qaeda have to attack the Pentagon to get their attention?"

It's easy to look back and wonder why the United States didn't act sooner, bringing al-Qaeda to heel under a hail of cruise missiles, a stream of covert SEAL missions, and the relentless pressure of the most powerful government in the history of the world. Yet right up until about nine o'clock on the morning of September 11, the global network of al-Qaeda hadn't yet proven itself a huge threat to the United States. Al-Qaeda had managed just a single attack on the homeland, if one was generously to give it credit for the first World Trade Center attack. It had been more successful overseas, where it had attacked the *Cole* and the embassies, but the attacks were focused on government targets, not the American public. It was hard to convince elected leaders, let alone the broader public, that it was imperative to bring the full resources of the U.S. government to bear on such a peripheral target, no matter how ambitious those watching it believed the group to be.

Freeh would tell the 9/11 Commission that he'd pushed for more resources to be dedicated to terrorism, yet those within the FBI counterterrorism section and at the Justice Department disputed his claim—with good reason. Terrorism might technically have been labeled a priority, but that message had a hard time breaking through to the FBI ranks, where the Criminal Division traditionally held sway. Inside the U.S. government, terrorism up until 9/11 was always secondary to foreign policy issues with countries such as Russia, China, Israel and Palestine, and India and Pakistan, and to standard FBI investigations such as organized crime, white-collar crime, and public corruption. At times even "deadbeat dads," that great media- and politician-generated scourge of the mid-1990s, when high-profile attention was focused on the problem of fathers who failed to pay child support, seemed a higher priority for FBI resources than terrorism. Given such a low public profile, it was hard to convince others of counterterrorism's importance—and the secretive nature of the intelligence world made it even harder. "The Bureau isn't very good at describing the threat in foreign counterintelligence. Terrorism gets mixed up in that. It was a squishy tomato," Dale Watson says. "You can't just come out and say that you're launching a terrorist war in Afghanistan."

At every meeting Janet Reno had with the fiercely independent and often contentious FBI director, she asked Freeh, "Do you have the money you need to do what you need to do?" Every time, Freeh said yes, but that wasn't the view of those working the terrorism cases. Says Stremmel, "Freeh would see the same people, worn out, and we were never able to get more people." Repeatedly the counterterrorism team got pulled into unrelated incidents. The mysterious crashes of TWA Flight 800 and EgyptAir Flight 990 consumed much-needed counterterrorism resources. The EgyptAir flight was quickly blamed on a copilot's personal desire for suicide and was unrelated to terrorism. As for Flight 800, as Neil Herman explains, "We recognized it wasn't a crime, but we couldn't prove it wasn't a crime." It took more than two years—and advanced computer modeling by the CIA—to prove beyond a reasonable doubt to investigators that the flight's center fuel tank had exploded because of a mechanical problem. Throughout the investigation, the New York counterterrorism team worked the case.

All the while, resources kept getting thinner. On the day that Mike Rolince took over international counterterrorism at the Bureau, the group had 635 staff members nationwide. On the day Rolince left two years later—after the bombings in Kenya and Tanzania, after the attack on the USS *Cole,* after the crash of EgyptAir Flight 990, after the TWA Flight 800 investigation—he had only 530 personnel. As the threat grew, as the network of Islamic radicals grew in scope and capability, the FBI's counterterrorism staff had actually dwindled by 20 percent. Fresh staff was especially needed as the job took such a great personal toll. "There weren't many people who stayed with these cases," says Herman, whose marriage cracked under the strain. "The people who work these become very emotionally involved. At some point, you burn out and drop off." As Stremmel says, "These intense and long-term cases really age you. One is never the same."

In 1998 and 1999, the New York JTTF made a push against the informal representatives of the Taliban who were operating in the city. There was only one problem: Herman couldn't find anyone who could understand their conversations. The FBI severely lacked Arabic speakers in the New York office—Soufan was the only agent who spoke the language—and so the JTTF asked for help from the military. No luck. The CIA didn't have anyone who could help either. The investigation languished.

The government was still trying to figure out how to balance past civil liberties scandals such as CISPES and COINTELPRO with the need to investigate a religiously motivated terror network. "We'd have these conversations with the legal people about how we could only wire certain rooms in a mosque, as if people would only discuss a plot in one room but not another," Herman says. But even with a tap, there was nobody to translate it. "You really had to wait until the crime was committed."

Watson, for his part, sat at his desk in the Hoover Building and most days realized that he'd done nothing to combat the long-term threat of terrorism. "I had an in-box, an out-box, and a calendar. I'm just sitting here waiting," he recalls. Frustrated, he began work on an initiative to push the FBI away from a case-oriented perspective toward a threat-oriented approach. His strategic plan, dubbed MAXCAP05, set a goal of having the FBI achieve its "maximum feasible capacity" in counterterrorism by 2005. Its first steps weren't pretty. Watson's first "Director's Report on Terrorism" opened with a map showing the capabilities of the nation's fifty-six field offices. It was a sea of red: every single field office was rated as dangerously below required capabilities. Much of the MAXCAP05 process involved documenting FBI shortfalls so that they could be fixed in the years ahead. Watson recalls the response from the field offices and SACs: "I was attacked viciously."

He argued to Freeh: "We've got two thousand agents working narcotics. Cocaine is cheaper today than it was when we started. We're working meth cases in Kentucky now. That's not high-level stuff. That's not our business. We've got to give it back to DEA and get out."

"You're nuts," Freeh replied.

"Let's get out of drugs. Let's get out of doing note-job bank robberies in St. Louis. The local cops can investigate that as well as we can. We need to dedicate resources to terror," Watson argued.

"That's our bread-and-butter," Freeh said.

The Bureau wasn't used to strategic planning and strategic thinking; the Criminal Division was trained to be reactive. People committed crimes and the Bureau solved them. It dealt in cases, not threats. It was good at tactics, not strategy. Perhaps the FBI's greatest strength is its ability to redirect resources, "surging" agents toward a problem or a case. In the wake of the Oklahoma City bombing, the number of FBI agents in western Kansas went from 2 to 150 in forty-eight hours. Many agents, executives, and observers will say in unguarded moments that the Bureau solves what it wants to solve. The momentum and resources a Bureau surge brings—man-hours, forensics, databases, technology, cars, helicopters, planes, and guns—are almost unstoppable. "No one can withstand that pressure," Watson says. "It's just a matter of what you want to do."

The Bureau wasn't alone in the reactive mind-set. The first real threat-based programs in law enforcement were just a few years old. Under Commissioner William Bratton, the NYPD earlier in the decade had revolutionized policing with its COMPSTAT program, tracking crimes and redirecting police resources to high-threat areas. In Boston, concentrated efforts by local, state, and federal law enforcement had dramatically dropped the city's murder rate by an intense focus on the small group of gang members who had a history of violence. Such efforts at the time were still localized and novel.

The USS *Cole* attack did little to jolt the government into recognizing the threats ahead. At the presidential candidate debate in St. Louis on October 17, 2000, just five days after the bombing, the focus was on the plane crash that had killed Governor Mel Carnahan the day before. Jim Lehrer, the moderator, started with a moment of silence for the late governor, not for the U.S. sailors; George W. Bush offered his condolences to the families whose lives had been upended by the plane crash; only Al Gore mentioned the families of the *Cole* victims as well as Carnahan's family. Al-Qaeda never came up in the debate. Out on the campaign trail, Bush's running mate, Dick Cheney, warned terrorists, "If you're going to attack, you'll be hit very hard and very quick. It's not time for diplomacy and debate. It's time for action." But despite his comments, the issue of terrorism was far from front and center.

When the new administration arrived, counterterrorism was still considered an equal priority with counterintelligence, violent crime, and the FBI's other traditional priorities. The Bush administration in 2001 was not at all supportive of MAXCAP05. Watson recalls, "The results the FBI was trying to achieve through MAXCAP05 would have been difficult to quantify. DOJ didn't like the fact that there would be no statistical reflection of this improvement."

Richard Clarke, O'Neill, and others who saw the rising threat were getting frustrated. Under the existing guidelines for national security investigations, agents couldn't investigate anything unless there was evidence of a crime. They couldn't attend church services or mosque services to get a feel for whether extremist cells existed. Until a threat surfaced, there was nothing they could do actively. As one agent complained to Clarke, "We go for a prosecution and the U.S. attorney here isn't interested in some minor infraction for supporting terrorism. Shit, we don't even have assistant U.S. attorneys who have top-secret clearance." But there were ways to do a lot of investigation if people were inclined. The bottom line was, they weren't inclined.

When told in one meeting by a Bureau representative that there were no Islamic extremist websites in the United States, Clarke asked a journalist who had written on the domestic Islamic jihad movement, Steven Emerson, to do his own investigation. Emerson came back with a long list of such websites.

In response to the inertia and lack of interest, Watson convinced Freeh to host a meeting in Tampa involving agents from all fifty-six field offices. The gathering, later dubbed derogatorily in Bureau lore "Terrorism for Dummies," opened with Clarke's summary of al-Qaeda's aims, goals, and methods. Still feeling his way as the first assistant director for counterterrorism, Watson followed up with a strong proclamation that terrorism was the Bureau's number-one priority.* "You will find them. If you have to arrest them for jaywalking, do it. If the local U.S. attorney won't prosecute them, call me. If you can't get your FISA wiretap approved by Justice, call us. Don't just sit there and sulk. One more thing: Your bonus, your promotion, your city of assignment all depend upon how well you do on this mission," he told the agents. "I mean it. I've got Louis's backing. If you don't believe me, try me." Left unsaid: that the safety of millions of Americans depended on how well the FBI performed.

As Watson and Clarke walked through the parking lot afterward, the FBI agent explained, "The FBI is like an aircraft carrier. It takes a long time to get going in one direction and turn around and go in another. These field offices have all had their own way, little fiefdoms, for years. At least I'm starting."

Yet even Watson didn't have all the answers or as broad a strategic foundation as someone in his position would soon require. Watson, the head of the FBI's counterterrorism operations in the run-up to September 11, admitted in a deposition for an employee's lawsuit that he didn't know the difference between Sunnis and Shiites. He'd been trained, after all, as a Lithuanian intelligence expert. It would be

---

*Under the Bureau's hierarchy, the head of counterterrorism had finally been elevated to an assistant director position, equal to the head of the Criminal Division, for instance.

another generation before investigators with a solid understanding of the networks they were chasing began to arrive.

When Bill Clinton took office in 1993, Bob Mueller entered private practice as a partner in the Washington office of the white-shoe Boston law firm Hale and Dorr (now WilmerHale). He felt stifled. As William Lee, a Hale and Dorr partner, explains, "It was hard to find as many trials as he would have liked." Beyond the lack of courtroom time, when he *was* in the courtroom, he felt like he was on the wrong side of the room. As his longtime friend Tom Wilner says, "He had to defend criminals, and he just couldn't do it. He needed to be on the side of justice."

That clash within made Mueller's next step surprising only to those who didn't know him well: He called Washington's U.S. attorney, then a rising star named Eric Holder, and asked to be appointed a line homicide prosecutor—a low-level job in the largest U.S. Attorney's Office in the country.★ "That really took me aback, both because of the positions he'd had and because he was at a great firm," Holder recalls. "The decision on my side was a no-brainer. I'm getting Bob Mueller for that price?" The move meant giving up more than three quarters of the $400,000 that Mueller had been making each year at Hale and Dorr—the first stable, private-sector income he'd made in nearly twenty years. But he didn't love the work, and he'd resolved many years ago to do work that he loved.

And boy, did he love homicide. "He was just one of the guys. He didn't demand special treatment or receive it," Holder says. "He was doing what he wanted to do." Efficient, regimentally organized, and brusque, Mueller, who wore a Marine Corps lapel pin on his suit, cut a wide swath through the office. "Detectives loved him," recalls Dan Friedman, then homicide section chief. "This wasn't your usual DA." In the chaotic and cramped U.S. Attorney's Office at 555 Fourth Street

---

★In a unique setup denoting the District of Columbia's status as a federal city, the U.S. Attorney's Office there handles traditional federal crimes as well as local misdemeanors and felonies, including homicide.

NW—the "triple nickel," as it was known—Mueller was in his element, answering the phone with a half bark: "Mueller, homicide."

Washington in the mid-1990s was a very different city than it is today. Holder recalls, "It was an office that was almost under siege. D.C. was the homicide capital of the United States. We had a crack problem that had spiraled right out of control. Huge numbers of homicides that were mostly in one way or another drug-related, huge numbers of violent crimes, problems with the police, even all the way up to the mayor." The murder rate in D.C. peaked with 482 victims in 1991 and was still close to 400 homicides a year when Mueller arrived. As Friedman says, "Caseloads were heavy, detectives were swamped, and witnesses were uncooperative."

A year and a half after arriving, Mueller became the head of the homicide unit. "He loved being on the ground," explains his then colleague Lynn Leibovitz, now a widely respected judge in Washington. "His only way of politicking was to be as decent, hardworking, and upstanding as he could be and let the work stand for itself." He led a number of high-profile cases, from a horrific mass murder and robbery at a Georgetown Starbucks to a Dupont Circle accident in which a drunk Georgian diplomat killed a pedestrian. "You knew he was a guy on the rise," Friedman says.

In 1998 Eric Holder, by then the deputy attorney general under Janet Reno, made Mueller an offer he couldn't refuse. The U.S. Attorney's Office in San Francisco, where Mueller had begun two decades earlier, was in turmoil and needed someone to take over and steady the helm. Appointed a U.S. attorney and Main Justice official under Republican administrations, Mueller now had his first appointment under a Democratic one. He arrived back in San Francisco and promptly began applying his Marine-style management skills to the troubled office. Feeling that people in the office were too comfortable, he made all the attorneys reapply for their jobs. "Bob is so well respected and not a partisan person, so he was a natural fit to come in, assess, and try to get things on track," explains Beth McGarry, who eventually became his deputy in San Francisco. "He said, 'They're all up for grabs.'" As Barry Portman, who headed the San Francisco public defender's office, recalls, Mueller returned to his Vietnam experience for inspiration: "It was a good Marine Corps tactic of hit the beach every morning and wake up the troops." Intensely focused on his work, Mueller disliked what he called the staff's "California hours," that is, showing up late in the morning and taking lunch hours. He ate lunch at his desk nearly every day.

Feeling that he couldn't get the data and the details on his attorneys' cases that he needed, he worked with engineers for months to rebuild the office's case management from scratch. (The resulting program, called Alcatraz, was so well received that it was deployed nationwide for all U.S. attorneys.) The office quickly turned around. "Bob has this real rare combo of a practical day-to-day manager and a visionary at the same time," McGarry says. "Most people are one or the other." Mueller drilled into the cases, guiding strategy and even going back into court personally in ways that few U.S. attorneys ever do. The U.S. Attorney's Office and the public defender's office shared a tradition of buying lunch for whichever side lost a case, but as Portman recalls, "Nobody was buying Bob many lunches."

While administrations come and go in Washington, David Margolis is one of those officials who lives on. A onetime organized crime prosecutor, he joined Main Justice in 1965, just a year after Robert Kennedy's departure. He'd headed the organized crime unit during the Pizza Connection case and the other landmark prosecutions of the 1980s, often leading meetings in cowboy boots, jeans, and a T-shirt. By January 2001, Margolis was worn down from working yet another transition. The seemingly never-ending Florida vote recount and the resulting Supreme Court case had truncated the already short hand-off period from one president to another. George W. Bush's team had only had weeks to pull itself together. Margolis walked into his office as associate deputy attorney general at Main Justice on Monday, January 22, the first workday of the Bush administration, and immediately noticed an unsigned note on his desk: "It's 0700. Where are you?"

Margolis sat down at his desk and sighed. He knew immediately who wrote the note and what it meant: Bob Mueller was back. Mueller had been recalled to Main Justice to serve as acting deputy attorney general, the number-two official who effectively oversees the day-to-day working of Main Justice as well as the Bureau. The assignment would last until the new administration could get its own people confirmed. During his five months of setting up the Justice Department under

John Ashcroft, Mueller earned the attorney general's respect. "When I came into the department, it was already understood that he was someone who was really dedicated to law enforcement," Ashcroft recalls. "People knew they could trust his approach and instinct."

Ashcroft needed the help. In December 2000, weeks before the inauguration, President-elect Bush announced that the onetime Missouri senator would be his nominee to be the nation's seventy-ninth attorney general. Ashcroft had lost reelection weeks earlier to a dead man, Mel Carnahan, who became the first person elected posthumously to the U.S. Senate. (His wife, Jean, was appointed to fill the seat.) Given Ashcroft's high-profile and lightning-rod status, the FBI thought it better to put a security detail on the nominee sooner rather than later. Louis Freeh, knowing Ashcroft's Capitol Hill reputation for being difficult, told Deputy Director Tom Pickard to make the call. "That's fine, but they're not coming in my house," Ashcroft told Pickard. It was the first conversation in what would remain a difficult relationship throughout Ashcroft's tenure. Within months, Pickard became so fed up with Ashcroft's restrictions on the protective agents and his hostility that the FBI official offered to give up the AG's detail, turning it over to the U.S. Marshals or whatever agency Ashcroft chose. "We'll still pay for it," Pickard said. "You can have whoever you want."

Whereas Janet Reno had been remarkably popular with the agents who served on her security detail—she regularly took warm soup to the agents who sat outside her apartment on cold nights, and she attended agents' family barbecues—Ashcroft was miserable to work for. In a quirk of federal tax law, officials who receive drivers or motorcades are required to pay income tax on the service as a benefit if they use the official vehicles to commute—a not insignificant cost, often amounting to about $5,000 annually. Ashcroft refused to pay the tax, so he informed the FBI that he would walk to the office each day instead of being driven. His protective detail drove slowly alongside him the whole way from Capitol Hill to Main Justice as he walked. In July 2001, Ashcroft was caught by CBS News boarding a government jet in full fishing regalia, en route back to Missouri for a weekend trip. He accused the FBI of vindictively leaking his trip details. "If I knew you were dumb enough to wear fishing gear, I'd have called CBS myself," Pickard shot back.

The Bureau's rough spring didn't do anything to warm relations. On his first day as attorney general, Ashcroft listened as the FBI broke the news that one of its leading counterintelligence agents, Robert Hanssen, had spent decades as a Soviet spy. The revelation opened the door to perhaps the worst breach of national security since the Soviets had been given the secrets of the atomic bomb a half century before. Then it came out that FBI investigators had failed to turn over thousands of pages of documents to defense lawyers of convicted Oklahoma City bomber Timothy McVeigh, a scandal that led to the postponement of McVeigh's scheduled execution. After that, an inspector general's report found that the Bureau had misplaced 449 firearms and 184 laptop computers over the past decade, including one weapon that was subsequently used to commit a murder and at least one laptop containing classified information. During a congressional hearing, Senator Dick Durbin asked, "It is clear to me the FBI has not been starved for funds. The FBI has been starved for leadership. How did this great agency fall so far so fast? Or has this been there for such a long time that it's been carefully concealed?"

In May, Ashcroft released a budget memo outlining the priorities for the Justice Department under his watch. Whereas Janet Reno had cited counterterrorism and cybercrime as the top priorities a year before, Ashcroft's three-page missive didn't mention counterterrorism at all; instead it repeatedly emphasized combating gun violence and illegal drugs. Dale Watson, the Bureau's head of counterterrorism, walked into Pickard's office waving the memo: "Did you see this? Nothing about terrorism." He shook his head. What was going on with this new administration? Didn't anyone see the threats?

When Louis Freeh announced that he was ready to retire as FBI director in June, he didn't even bother to tell Ashcroft in advance of his announcement. Ashcroft recounted, "I didn't hear from him. Next I heard that he was leaving." Worn down by years of stress and nearing the eighth year of his term, Freeh wanted out. Personally, he couldn't afford to continue in the job; the first of his kids was nearing college age, and he could not afford to put six sons through college on a government salary. A huge payday would await him as soon as he walked out of the Hoover Building for good, and those dollar signs were tempting, especially when compared with the near-constant Capitol Hill caterwauling about the Bureau's missteps.

Freeh waited to leave office, though, until he could see one final piece of business through. He'd succeeded in convincing the new administration to pursue the Khobar Towers investigation, and on the eve of the expiration of the statute of limitations, fourteen individuals were indicted for the attack. Freeh said the indictment, led by the Eastern District of Virginia's assistant U.S. attorney, Jim Comey—later number two in John Ashcroft's Justice Department—was "a major step toward making sure that those responsible are brought to justice, as well as a testament to the value and necessity of international law enforcement cooperation to counter the danger in today's world."

The indictment was a vindication of what had turned into a years-long obsession. From the earliest days, Freeh believed that the Clinton administration didn't want to solve the Khobar bombing—it did not want the guilty party to be Iran, because it didn't want to have to retaliate against the Iranian regime, just as it had measured attacking bin Laden against its need for allies in the Pakistani government. As a result, Freeh had gone behind the commander in chief's back, calling on former president George H. W. Bush to press the Saudis (with whom the Bush family had a close friendship) for more cooperation. The move was unprecedented. Freeh made multiple trips to Saudi Arabia and in Washington aggressively courted Prince Bandar bin Sultan, the kingdom's longtime U.S. ambassador. (Bandar, a frequent cigar smoker, became the only person Freeh allowed to smoke in his Hoover Building office.) For three days in 1997, Freeh had brought the families of the Khobar victims to Quantico for briefings and discussions about the case. It was a tremendous investment of time for an FBI director. He'd told them directly, "I'm not a politician. I'm a policeman." Nothing was going to stand in his way to achieve justice. He traded forensics training with the Saudi Mabahith, the equivalent of the FBI, and made repeated entreaties to the Saudi crown prince, acknowledging that he probably wouldn't cooperate with the FBI if he were in the Saudis' shoes but promising, "We respect your laws and Sharia." In a meeting where the Saudis turned over reams of evidence, Bandar said they were doing so because "you were bugging the hell out of us." The same tenacity and willingness to break procedures and set new precedents had made Freeh such a dogged prosecutor on the Pizza Connection and other Mafia cases in New York.

Freeh clashed repeatedly with the Clinton administration about the case, arguing over evidence standards and indictable offenses. Decidedly unhappy with the way the Washington, D.C., U.S. Attorney's Office was handling the case, Freeh decided to wait out his opponents and spent the final year of the Clinton administration courting Comey to head the investigation.

Now, under the new Bush administration, Freeh pushed administration officials, including the new acting deputy attorney general, Bob Mueller, to move the case to Comey in Richmond, Virginia. When Mueller finally did so, he called Comey with a warning: "Wilma Lewis is going to be so pissed." Indeed, Lewis, who had taken over as the D.C. U.S. attorney when Eric Holder became deputy attorney general, blasted the decision, as well as both Freeh and Mueller personally. In a press release, she said the move was "ill-conceived and ill-considered." But the gambit paid off. Within weeks, Comey had pulled together the indictment. During a National Security Council briefing at the White House, under the watchful gaze of Secretary of State Colin Powell, Secretary of Defense Donald Rumsfeld, and National Security Advisor Condoleezza Rice, he presented the overwhelming evidence of Iran's involvement.

With the indictment public and amid the gathering storm of FBI scandals, Freeh retired the next day, nearly two years short of the end of his term. As director, he'd seen the Bureau grow more than 50 percent; he'd logged thousands of miles overseas, traveling to sixty-eight countries—nearly as many as the seventy-four countries Bill Clinton had visited during his presidency.

Freeh's announcement that he would step down as FBI director set off a high-stakes search for a replacement for the beaten-down agency. After initially protesting to Ashcroft that he should find someone else, Pickard stepped in to lead the Bureau while a permanent director was appointed. At their first meeting, Pickard started by reviewing the al-Qaeda threat. At their second meeting, on July 12, 2001, when Pickard began to talk counterterrorism, Ashcroft abruptly cut him off: "I don't want to hear about that anymore."

"Mr. Attorney General, I think you should sit down with George Tenet and hear right from him what's going on," Pickard said.

"I don't want you to ever talk to me about al-Qaeda," Ashcroft replied testily.

The two men argued vigorously. At one point Pickard jumped out of his chair and leaned across the table to emphasize a point. As Pickard, who like many Bureau officials regularly wore his firearm on his belt under his suit, walked out of the meeting, Ruben Garcia, Jr., the Bureau's acting deputy, said to him, only half jokingly, "You came out of your chair so fast I could see your gun. I thought you were going to use it."

Ashcroft wasn't alone. The Bush administration by and large wasn't interested in terrorism. "I was not on point," President Bush later told reporter Bob Woodward. "I didn't feel that sense of urgency."

Through the 1990s, the Justice Department, the FBI, and the special court that oversaw the Foreign Intelligence Surveillance Act were on a collision course, one set inadvertently by the now notorious Gorelick memo in the wake of TERRSTOP, the Blind Sheikh case, which drew the line between criminal investigations and intelligence operations and limited the information that could be shared in prosecutions.

At the Office of Intelligence Policy Review, the little-known office that handled FISA applications at Main Justice, Allan Kornblum had been the gateway for FBI agents seeking national security wiretaps since Jimmy Carter's presidency. He'd been appointed by Attorney General Griffin Bell in the wake of the COINTELPRO scandals and Mark Felt's prosecution to ensure that the FBI never again strayed beyond the law. He'd largely succeeded, partly by being a personal barrier to many investigations.

Kornblum still ran the office in many ways as he had in the 1970s; he worked on a Selectric typewriter whose ribbon he locked up in his safe every night. "I might as well have arrived in Pompeii," recalls Fran Townsend, the former prosecutor in New York, who began working at OIPR toward the end of President Clinton's term. The millennium plot saw the FBI and Justice Department churning out so many urgent FISA requests that Janet Reno sometimes just slept on Townsend's couch rather than going the several blocks home to her apartment, knowing that she'd only be awakened to sign off on new warrants during the night. Through her early OIPR experiences, Townsend began to feel that the FISA court was too restrained in what it would allow. She made it her personal mission to change that.

Kornblum's opponents at the Justice Department and the Bureau managed to lay some of the blame from the Wen Ho Lee debacle — in which a nuclear scientist had been charged with spying, only to be released when the case unraveled for lack of evidence — right in the administrator's lap. He'd behaved throughout the Wen Ho Lee matter, they argued, precisely as he had in all too many national security investigations: endlessly slow-rolling agents and prosecutors, sending drafts back for more research and more evidence, and handicapping the investigation. As a result of the scandal, Kornblum was finally edged out of the Justice Department, only to be hired as the FISA court's first legal adviser, which made him the official gatekeeper on the other side of the gate. According to Stewart Baker, a former general counsel for the National Security Agency and a scholar of intelligence law, Kornblum's new post was in his own eyes "a chance to make sure that the wall was enforced for real. At last even the FBI could be brought to heel."

Royce Lamberth, a Texan appointed by President Reagan, had been the head of the seven-member FISA court, which was technically known as the Foreign Intelligence Surveillance Court, since 1995. It met in a secure room deep within the Main Justice headquarters across from the Hoover Building. Being chief of the court, though, was more than a nine-to-five job. Lamberth often approved FISA warrants on the stoop of his house in the middle of the night while his cocker spaniel looked on as a witness. On the night of the embassy attacks, he'd approved five FISAs by the time dawn arrived. In a normal year, the court dealt with nearly a thousand warrant applications, virtually all of which it approved. In fact, the court is not known to have rejected any FISA application prior to 9/11, once the warrant request made it past Kornblum at OIPR.

In many cases, the wall persisted because it served the purposes of the intelligence community rather than because the court enforced it rigorously. As Fred Stremmel explains, "You could work around the wall, no matter how high they built it. You could always find a way."

But there wasn't much appetite for such maneuvers, since, helped by Kornblum's oral history, the wall had become more than anything a way for agencies to hide information and protect sources. The two strongest proponents of the wall were the other intelligence agencies; NSA and CIA liked the protection so they could avoid outing their tactics and techniques in open criminal proceedings. "We were viewed [by intelligence agencies] as trespassers or Typhoid Mary moving into their area," Pat Fitzgerald said later.

"People used the wall to protect their sources and their cases. They used it to protect their turf. I'm not talking just about the Bureau—it was across the whole intelligence community. Everybody bad-mouthed it, but everyone used it," Stremmel explains. "They should have had a come-to-Jesus meeting with Reno or the FISA court or someone. There was a lot of hand-wringing, a lot of briefings and meetings, and no one took the bull by the horns."

Throughout 2000 and early 2001, the situation grew worse. Kornblum, cozy with Lamberth, had become the physical incarnation of the wall. As Spike Bowman, of the Bureau's National Security Law Unit, explains, "Lamberth became the wall. The wall became a single judge." Kornblum's presence at the FISA court seems only to have heightened the caution. According to a government memo, "[Kornblum] had been persuading Lamberth to impose more restrictions. This became an escalating cycle." Explains Bowman, "Kornblum loved to lord it over the FBI."

Under Lamberth and with Kornblum's guidance, the court, aware of a series of mistakes in FISA applications, set up new procedures raising the wall even higher, leaving no room for honest errors or typos. "The applications were so complex that it's hard to put together a fifty- or hundred-page document without any errors," Bowman recalls. A transposed number or a misspelled street address could lead to having the whole warrant sent back. Lamberth banned one FBI agent, Michael Resnick, from ever appearing before the court again because the judge felt he'd lied on FISA applications. ("He didn't do anything wrong. He just happened to be the man in the middle," Bowman says. The FISA warrant application process was unique insofar as the agents in the field requested a warrant but then headquarters staff presented the warrant to the court; there was no direct relationship between those seeking a warrant and those granting it.) The ban upended Resnick's career; the Justice Department Office of Professional Responsibility opened an investigation into his actions that sidelined him for years. Louis Freeh personally visited Lamberth to ask him to reconsider the punishment of the agent, but as the judge later explained, "We never rescinded it. We enforced it. And we sent a message to the FBI." That message, Lamberth said, was clear: "What we found in the history of our country is you can't trust these people."

No other agent wanted to share Resnick's fate, and that new sense of caution haunted the bin Laden squad in New York. A supervisor, concerned about poisoning the broader investigation with FISA intelligence information, decided to designate a single agent on the squad as the "intel agent." That agent would see all the FISA information and wouldn't be allowed to share it with the rest of the squad without the express approval of the New York Field Office division counsel, the FBI general counsel, OIPR, and the FISA court itself. It was an incredibly cautious system, but one that the New York squad felt was justified, given the trouble Resnick and the Bureau were having with the court. That also meant that while every other agent on the squad was working the criminal side, a single intelligence agent bore responsibility—in theory—for all of the forward-looking intelligence coming in. That agent, Craig Donnachie, spent each day reading scores of reports and intercepts from the rest of the intelligence community—information he couldn't share with any of his colleagues. His supervisor, Ken Maxwell, took to asking each day, half jokingly, "Craig, anything going to blow up today?" That summer what Donnachie read was worrying: "I don't know, they're still talking about falcons, peanuts, and weddings more than usual, but no one can make sense of what they mean." Only in the summer of 2001 would a second intel agent join the squad. The Bureau dropped some twenty proposed al-Qaeda wiretaps as part of the dispute over the wall.

At the same time, the NSA, which was not supposed to have been covered by the wall but had, out of the same abundance of caution, gradually erected its own barriers, changed the way it labeled the intelligence it passed along to the FBI. Whereas in the past it had carefully reviewed each piece of information to see if it could be shared with criminal investigators before it was passed to FBI intelligence agents, the NSA switched to simply declaring that none of its intelligence could be shared with the FBI's criminal side. That simple switch saved the NSA countless hours and shifted the burden to the FBI intelligence agents to ask if they could share specific pieces of information with their colleagues. As a result, valuable intelligence never reached the bin Laden squad in New York.

In March 2001, an attempt to have Attorney General Ashcroft resurrect a series of Janet Reno's proposed reforms to the wall was punted by the acting deputy attorney general, Bob Mueller, to his permanent successor, Larry Thompson, and then never enacted. In July 2001, a General Accounting Office report became the third such document in three years to state emphatically that the procedures set up during the Blind Sheikh case were impeding investigations and not working correctly. Yet nothing was done.

Lamberth had urged Ashcroft and George W. Bush's administration to replace Fran Townsend. Independently, Ashcroft seemed to have no love for her. When she flew to Missouri to get the new attorney general to sign a request for a FISA warrant one winter night, he left her standing on the porch while he patiently reviewed the paperwork, refusing to invite her inside out of the cold, even though she was four months pregnant.

It fell to Mueller to push Townsend out the door. He knew the backstory behind the deed he had to do and told her, "It's not for cause." Nevertheless, the administration appointed her the new head of intelligence for the Coast Guard—a huge drop in prestige, and a position far from the center of the action.* Coming at about the same time as Ashcroft's decision to exclude terrorism as a priority for the Justice Department, his decision to replace Townsend—the person in

---

*Years later, in 2005, Townsend, rescued from Coast Guard banishment and promoted to be Condoleezza Rice's homeland security adviser at the National Security Council after 9/11, was surprised to get a call from John Ashcroft's office as he prepared to leave office. The attorney general wanted to host a breakfast in her honor at Main Justice. During an intimate repast in his private conference room with Jim Comey, Bob Mueller, and a few others, Ashcroft praised her work: "We've been very effective allies." Townsend just looked across at Mueller, who had a little impish twinkle in his eye. *Welcome to Washington,* she thought as she walked out of the building and headed back to the White House.

OIPR who, more than anyone else, had been fighting to modernize terrorism investigations—was just another sign to agents such as CT chief Dale Watson that the new administration didn't get it. "They're going to drive this into the ditch," he told her.

With Freeh's resignation, Ashcroft embarked on the search for a new FBI director who could bring the famously independent Bureau more tightly under the AG's control. The attorney general's office ended up interviewing just three candidates: Robert Mueller, Washington lawyer and power broker George Terwilliger, and Dan Webb, a former Chicago prosecutor and white-collar defense lawyer. Terwilliger carried a political millstone from having helped out the Bush campaign in the Florida recount; Webb removed himself from consideration. Mueller stood alone, which seemed fine, since Ashcroft liked Mueller's attitude; he had called his deputy "Square Jaw McGraw."

President Bush and Mueller, with White House deputy chief of staff Josh Bolten, met in the Oval Office for a chat. The men discussed a variety of topics and challenges the Bureau faced; terrorism came up only briefly.* The main subject was upgrading the FBI's technology. Since Hoover, there had existed a wariness of political appointees for the job of FBI director; of the four directors since Hoover, three had been federal judges and one had been a police chief, all considered beyond reproach for their judgment and political leanings. Yet both political parties respected Mueller, a consummate law enforcement professional with a track record, forged in Vietnam, of grace under fire and of getting organizations on track. "He had a lot going for him," Pickard recalls. "There are a lot of synergies between the Marines and the FBI and the U.S. attorneys and the FBI." After the Oval Office talk, President Bush told White House counsel Alberto Gonzales, "Mueller's my man."

Standing in the Rose Garden on July 5, 2001, President Bush

---

*In the midst of the conversation with the president, Mueller's wife called. Mueller, who had forgotten to silence his cell phone, knew that being interrupted by ringing phones was a particular pet peeve of the president. "I'm dead, aren't I?" Mueller said. Luckily, the president just laughed.

announced his choice, saying, "Bob Mueller's term in office will last longer than my own. And the next ten years will bring more forms of crime, new threats of terror from beyond our borders and within them. The tools of law enforcement will change as well. The FBI must be ready to protect Americans from new types of criminals who will use modern technology to defraud and disrupt our society." Continuing, Bush—more prescient than he knew at the time—said, "The Bureau must secure its rightful place as the premier counterespionage and counterterrorist organization in the United States. It must continue to serve as a resource and training center for law enforcement. And it must do all this with a firm commitment to safeguarding the constitutional rights of our citizens." Concluding, he told the assembled crowd, "Bob Mueller's experience and character convinced me that he's ready to shoulder these responsibilities. Agents of the Bureau prize three virtues above all: fidelity, bravery, and integrity. This new director is a man who exemplifies them all."

Mueller then stepped to the podium and spoke for all of forty-eight seconds—just nine sentences, a short speech by most standards, although for those who knew him, even forty-eight seconds was a long time in the spotlight.

Mueller had grown up in a wealthy corner of Philadelphia. His parents' first child—and, with four younger sisters, their only son—he developed a strong moral compass from his father. He had attended the elite St. Paul's boarding school in New Hampshire during an age when the old eastern establishment was breaking down. St. Paul's stood apart: It proudly allied itself with the Episcopal Church, and its admissions director at the time boasted of how it wasn't lowering its standards by admitting scholarship students.

St. Paul's has been described as a place where "the boys are taught to run the world but not boast about it." By the time Mueller arrived, it had a pretty solid track record: J. P. Morgan, John Jacob Astor, and William Randolph Hearst had all traversed the halls that Mueller walked. School business was conducted publicly for maximum shame to ensure conformity and enforce societal norms: grades were posted for all to see, students were reprimanded by the headmaster in front of the morning all-school meetings, chapel was held eight times each week. As Mueller's classmate Will Taft recalls, "It was a pretty predictable, stable society at that time for us without us controlling it or creating it." Explains classmate Geoffrey Douglas, the school focused on manliness and Christianity. Mueller certainly excelled at the former, leading the St. Paul's hockey team (a sport that the school claims to have brought to the U.S. in the 1870s) and playing lacrosse long before it became popular.

Even by the standards of elite private schools, Mueller's class did well for itself. John Kerry was the 2004 Democratic nominee for president; Max King went on to edit the *Philadelphia Inquirer;* Taft served as deputy secretary of defense under President Reagan and became the top lawyer for the State Department under the second President Bush. From St. Paul's, it was off to the Ivy League, which for Mueller meant Princeton, his father's alma mater. His Princeton classmate and long-time friend W. Lee Rawls, who later served as his counsel at the Bureau, explains, "He's always had a seriousness of purpose." After studying international relations, Mueller was profoundly inspired by David Hackett, a popular athlete a year ahead of him who joined the Marine Corps and died shortly thereafter in Vietnam. This model of duty and sacrifice led Mueller and a handful of his classmates to join up as well. "He was a leader on the field and pretty good friend," Mueller says today. "He was always a leader to us."

Graduating in the spring in 1966, just as Vietnam became a major issue in the United States—but before it became the cultural flashpoint it would be by '68—Mueller joined the military when enlisting carried less baggage than it would in the coming years. Mueller and his new wife, Ann, moved to Woodbridge, Virginia, in preparation for his starting Officer Candidate School. Given Mueller's old-school upbringing—the strong sense of duty woven into St. Paul's and Princeton's culture—it's no surprise that he was drawn to the Marines, the branch of the military most focused on tradition, duty, and honor. St. Paul's prayer book offers in one passage a prayer for courage: "Keep alive in our hearts, we beseech thee, that adventurous spirit which makes men scorn the way of safety, so that thy will be done. For so only, O Lord, shall we be worthy of those courageous souls who in every age have ventured all in obedience to thy call." And Mueller had just graduated from a college whose motto read, "Princeton in the nation's service and in the service of all nations." Mueller's friend Tom Wilner explains, "Bob's the best of the old prep school tradition. He stands for service, integrity, and has the confidence to never bend. He doesn't do anything for himself."

That way of thinking symbolized the Marines. As military historian Thomas Ricks observed, "The Marines are distinct even within the separate world of the U.S. military. Theirs is a culture apart. The Air Force has its planes, the Navy its ships, the Army its obsessively written and obeyed 'doctrine' that dictates how it acts. Culture—that is, the values and assumptions that shape its members—is all the Marines have." It was at Officer Candidate School at Marine Corps Base Quantico, just down the road from the future site of the FBI Academy, that Mueller first raised his right hand and swore allegiance to the Constitution, pledging to protect it against all enemies, foreign and domestic.

In highly demanding and competitive training, Mueller excelled. "Your improvement comes from the ability to maximize the embodiment of a Marine," he reflects. His only demerits were in one area, familiar to anyone who later dealt with him as FBI director: He got a D in "Delegation."

When it came time for the class's postgraduation assignments, Mueller had his heart set on going to Army Language School in Monterey Bay, California. He'd scored well enough to be near the top of his class and was cautiously optimistic. As the sergeants read off the assignments in alphabetical order, nearly every member of Mueller's class seemed headed for Vietnam. Then, when they got to the *M*'s, Mueller heard the first word of his first choice, "Army," followed by the puzzling "Ranger School."

Writing some 2,400 years ago about the soldiers who ventured forth in the Peloponnesian War, Thucydides remarked, "We must remember that one man is much the same as another, and that he is best who is trained in the severest school." Few schools are more severe in the world than the army Ranger training, a grueling sixty-one-day advanced skills and leadership program for the military's elite at Fort Benning, Georgia. The school assignment, though, wasn't good news for Mueller. Marines who survived Ranger training often became

Recon Marines—the best of the best, the Marines' special forces, yet with a life expectancy in Vietnam usually measured in weeks.

"Ranger School more than anything teaches you about how you react with no sleep and nothing to eat," Mueller recalls. "You learn who you want on point and who you don't want anywhere near point." The training, he says, saved his life more than once in the months to come.*

Rather than continuing on as a Recon Marine, Mueller found himself heading overseas as an infantry leader, helicoptering deep into the Vietnamese jungle and assuming command of a combat platoon— a twenty-person team headed nominally by a junior lieutenant and truly run by the grizzled noncommissioned officer. In Vietnam, assuming command in the field as Mueller did meant that your predecessor was dead or seriously wounded. "You land and you're at the mercy of your staff sergeant and your radioman," he recalls.

He didn't have to wait long until his first firefight. His unit came under attack on patrol and suffered casualties before it could extricate itself. Afterward, a captain came up and slapped the young lieutenant on the shoulder: "Good job, Mueller." "That vote of confidence helped me get through," he recalls. "You're standing there thinking, 'Did I do everything I could?'"

On December 11, 1968, just weeks after Mueller landed in Vietnam and just nine days after his prep school classmate Kerry earned his first Purple Heart nearby, the platoon led by now second lieutenant Mueller came under heavy fire in Quang Tri Province. The encounter that followed would earn Mueller a Bronze Star, the military's fourth highest combat award, with the special designation of a *V*, showing that the award was for combat valor. "Second Lieutenant Mueller fearlessly moved from one position to another," his citation stated. "With complete disregard for his own safety, he then skillfully supervised the evacuation of casualties from the hazardous area and, on one occasion, personally led a fire team across the fire-swept area terrain to recover a mortally wounded Marine who had fallen in a

---

*Of course Mueller, being a Marine, never got to wear the elite Ranger tab that adorns the uniforms of army graduates. Marine uniforms don't carry patches, ribbons, or the tabs popular in other services. Being a Marine, the leaders of the corps believe, is enough.

position forward of the friendly lines." The Marines praised "Mueller's courage, aggressive initiative, and unwavering devotion to duty."

On April 22, 1969, four months later, one of Mueller's squads came under attack by the Vietcong. The Marine on point for the patrol was killed immediately. Mueller led the rest of his platoon in to rescue their comrades and was shot through the thigh by an AK-47 in the ensuing battle. Despite his injury, he held his position until his men were safe. The engagement earned him the first of two Navy Commendation Medals as well as a Purple Heart. After just a month's recuperation—the through-and-through wound was a lucky one, though not what was known in the military as a "million-dollar wound," which would send him home from Vietnam—he was back on patrol. "I thought I'd at least get to go to the hospital ship," he recalls, but his injury had only landed him at an onshore field hospital.

Marine service agreed with him. During his year in Vietnam, he and Ann spoke only twice (once after he'd been wounded) and met up for five days of R&R in Hawaii. Under the tropical sun, he told her that he wanted to stay in the Marines as a career. She explained that that wasn't an option, and he eventually relented. After returning to Vietnam, he finished his active duty as an aide-de-camp to General William K. Jones, the uncle of Jim Jones, President Obama's first national security advisor. "I consider myself exceptionally lucky to have made it out of Vietnam," Mueller says. "There were many—many—who did not. And perhaps because I did survive Vietnam, I have always felt compelled to contribute."

The time in Vietnam was intensely formative for Mueller, forging his leadership skills literally under fire. Today he speaks only rarely and reluctantly of his service and experiences as a Marine, but as the saying goes, once a Marine, always a Marine.* He loves few activities in Washington more than visiting the Marine barracks at Eighth and I Streets SE for its famed evening parades. On his regular visits to Iraq and Afghanistan as FBI director, Mueller, aides say, always walked

---

* One of the only times his staff at the FBI ever heard him mention his Marine service, they were watching *We Were Soldiers,* the harrowing Mel Gibson movie of the early battles in Vietnam, on the plane home from an international trip. He looked over, saw the movie, and observed, "Pretty accurate."

with a little extra spring in his step while on the ground in-country, as if he took energy from the very air of combat.

Since staying in the Marines wasn't going to be an option, by the time he landed back in Pittsburgh, home from Vietnam for good, to meet his new daughter, he'd settled on law school, with an eye toward becoming an FBI agent. Mueller enrolled at the University of Virginia School of Law. "He was always to me a Dudley Do-Right type," explains classmate Gardner Gillespie. "You knew he'd carry his load." Unable to land a position in government after graduation, he somewhat reluctantly entered private practice with a firm in San Francisco. He was good at the law, but he hated the work. Then one morning at their small home in San Francisco, while he and Ann were making their bed, Bob uncharacteristically griped, "Don't I deserve to be doing something that makes me happy?" That something was public service.

Landing a job as an assistant U.S. attorney in San Francisco, he stood up in court for the first time as the physical embodiment of the government of the United States, a job at which he soon found he excelled, taking on tough cases and winning convictions. In its own way, that period was perhaps the happiest of their lives; their two daughters were young, San Francisco was wonderful, and Mueller enjoyed the camaraderie of the prosecutor's office. On Friday nights, Ann and the girls would pick him up after he hung out with the gang of assistant U.S. attorneys, public defenders, and cops at Harrington's Bar & Grill, the city's oldest Irish pub, down in the Embarcadero neighborhood. One year his daughter Cynthia made him a model of Harrington's out of Popsicle sticks for Christmas.

Mueller eventually rose to become chief of the office's criminal division before Joseph Russoniello was appointed U.S. attorney in 1982. Russoniello brought in his own team, and Mueller was demoted.★ Following that, Mueller jumped at the opportunity to move east and work for Boston's U.S. attorney. (Another incentive may have been

---

★When in 2008 Russoniello was appointed to a second go as U.S. attorney for the Northern District of California, Mueller singled him out publicly during a speech to the U.S. attorneys and explained that Russoniello was the only person who had ever demoted him. Mueller joked, "Joe, however many FBI agents you now have assigned to your office, it's now ten fewer."

the world-class Boston Children's Hospital, where one of his daughters, who had spina bifida, could be treated.) He made an instant impression on the Massachusetts U.S. Attorney's Office. "You cannot get the words *straight arrow* out of your head," recalls then U.S. attorney Bill Weld, who went on to become Massachusetts governor. "The agencies loved him because he knew his stuff. He didn't try to be elegant or fancy, he just put the cards on the table."

Massachusetts was also the place where Mueller's ultimate ambition first showed. After Bill Webster stepped down as FBI director, Weld passed up a chance to be considered, and Mueller was incredulous. "He already wanted to be director of the FBI so bad that he could taste it," Weld recalls. "He couldn't understand why I wouldn't want to do it." (Mueller today dismisses any early ambition on his part: "Of course it's a dream job, but there's just no way you can angle for it. The odds are so astronomical.")

After Weld departed and George H. W. Bush became president, Mueller left for private practice. It wasn't long, though, before he got a call from Richard Thornburgh, the new president's attorney general, who asked him down to Main Justice. (The call from Washington came partly because of the old boys' network: Thornburgh's chief of staff, Robert Ross, was an old St. Paul's classmate of Mueller's.) Ann protested that the timing, as their daughter was finishing high school, made such a move ill-advised: "We can't possibly do this." "You're right, it's a terrible time. Well, why don't we just go down and look at a few houses?" Bob said, his eyes twinkling. As she explains today, "When he wants to do something, he just revisits it again and again." So for two years during his first stint at the Justice Department under George H. W. Bush, they commuted back and forth from Boston to Washington while Melissa, their second daughter, finished high school, alternating weekends between the two cities.

At Main Justice, Mueller helped lead the prosecution of Manuel Noriega, one of the first major international crime prosecutions, and later worked the Pan Am 103 bombing, the first major terrorist incident involving U.S. citizens. He eventually rose to be head of the Justice Department's Criminal Division. Demonstrating an interest in technology that would continue through his career, Mueller in the early 1990s created the Department of Justice's first computer crimes unit.

After they had finally moved permanently to Washington and Mueller had left the Justice Department for private practice, Bob came home one day and told Ann he wanted to go back to being a homicide prosecutor. He'd already planned it out and spoken to Eric Holder, then the U.S. attorney. "I was shocked, but I could see what was what," Ann recalls. "The cases took a chunk out of his flesh. He was in his element."

Then, later, after his stint with Margolis as acting deputy attorney general, during which time he is rumored to have turned down the offer of the permanent DAG slot, Mueller returned to San Francisco. But Louis Freeh stepped down soon after his return to the Bay Area, and although they'd never discussed whether he'd be interested in the job, Mueller's deputy in San Francisco, Beth McGarry, said she knew the moment she heard of Freeh's departure that her boss was heading back to Washington.

Mueller's questionnaire for the Senate, which he filled out as part of his nomination as FBI director, is a document striking for its blandness.* With the exceptions of about five years in private practice spread over three different stints, during which time he'd volunteered for the public defenders' office and later served as special counsel to the war crimes prosecutor in Ethiopia, he'd worked almost continually for the government for more than thirty years. In that long career, he'd kept an abnormally low profile for normally publicity-hungry U.S. attorneys. He had, according to his Senate confirmation questionnaire, never published any significant writings or given speeches on constitutional law. Mueller listed a net worth of about $1.8 million, much of it in real estate and blue chip stocks; his and Ann's largest holdings were $126,000 in GE stock and $167,000 in IBM. About the closest thing to scandal listed anywhere on Mueller's thirty-page form was that he'd belonged to a couple of male-only country clubs in San Francisco and Boston. (He did love his golf, even though his wife generally outplayed him.)

As the country was getting its first glance at the prospective direc-

---

* There is, after all, a reason he'd earned the nickname at Main Justice of "Bobby Three Sticks," a play on the Roman numeral at the end of his name, Robert Swan Mueller III, and a reference to the three-finger Boy Scout salute.

tor, Mueller spent the summer weeks after his nomination working hard to learn about the organization he'd soon lead. As a U.S. attorney, he had worked often with FBI agents individually, but he had little sense of the larger organization, so he asked the special agent in charge of the San Francisco Field Office, Bruce Gebhardt, to brief him.

Mueller picked a good tutor. Gebhardt knew the FBI inside and out. His father, Robert, a lifelong G-man who had coordinated the FBI's response to the hijacking of Southern Airways Flight 49 a generation earlier, had been one of the Bureau's top executives post-Hoover. In addition to spending eighteen years growing up with his dad's Bureau career, during which time their family moved nine times, Bruce had spent a quarter century as a special agent by 2001, including stints as SAC in both Phoenix and San Francisco, coincidentally both field offices his father had also led. With the San Francisco ASAC, Larry Mefford, Gebhardt met with Mueller in July 2001. His first piece of advice to the prospective director: The FBI refers to the leaders of the field offices as SACs, with each letter spelled out, not as "saks" or "S-A-I-Cs," as some other agencies do. "You gotta learn the nomenclature," Gebhardt explained. He recalls, "This guy didn't know anything about the inside of the FBI. Even as a U.S. attorney, you don't know support personnel, divisions, filing systems, or any of the massive behind-the-scenes stuff in the FBI."

Vermont senator Patrick Leahy, the chair of the Senate Judiciary Committee and a former prosecutor, opened Mueller's confirmation hearing on July 30, 2001, noting, "We are at a critical juncture for the FBI. Well beyond an interview, in many ways this hearing will be a redefinition of the job of FBI director." Recent scandals and stumbles, Leahy explained, meant that the FBI had lost its ability to work as independently as it once had. "We are going to need a hands-on approach," the Senate chair explained. "Many in our country have lost some confidence in the Bureau. That is more than a PR problem, because if you erode the public trust, then you erode the ability of the FBI to do its job."

The ranking Republican, Utah's Orrin Hatch, spoke of the challenges ahead for Mueller: "One frustration that you will undoubtedly feel is that when the FBI does its job well, we will never hear about it. The newspaper headlines will never read, 'Millions of Americans Slept Safely Again Last Night.' " Little did he know how true his words would prove to be. As Hatch spoke, a group of would-be hijackers were busy making their final plans for the attack now just weeks away.

The questioning from the Senate panel over the next two days ran the gamut from securities fraud to interagency communication to the Bureau's shockingly primitive computer systems to the legacy of scandals like COINTELPRO. Arlen Specter, who on the same committee in the 1980s had argued to Buck Revell that the FBI should wait for an attack to occur rather than arrest suspected terrorists ahead of time, raised the Wen Ho Lee case. Senator Herb Kohl asked about safety locks on firearms. Delaware's Joe Biden asked about drugs. New York's senator Charles Schumer praised the nominee, saying, "Mr. Mueller has been called shy, low-key, and someone who shuns the limelight, but at the same time tough as nails and no-nonsense. For an agency in desperate need of results, not just headlines, that is exactly the right mix."

Hatch asked Mueller whether he would be willing to take the standard polygraph examination given to new agents to ensure their credibility and integrity. (Freeh, in his 1993 confirmation hearing, had promised to take it, but he had never followed up.) Mueller replied, "This may be my training from the Marine Corps, but you don't ask people to do that which you're unwilling to do yourself. I have already taken the polygraph."

"How did you do?" Hatch asked.

"I'm sitting here. That's all I've got to say," Mueller replied in his precise and obtuse speaking manner, which would become all too familiar to those whom he would testify before on the Hill.

Nearly every senator who spoke paid some sort of lip service to terrorism and the threats of a new century, yet their questions reflected no urgency or special attention to the subject. Dianne Feinstein, in fact, who served on the Select Committee on Intelligence, told Mueller directly that his new job as director of the FBI is "a job that I believe demands someone who can remain focused on the core mission of the Bureau — solving crimes and catching criminals." Over two days of hearings, only one senator, John Edwards of North Carolina, asked a question focused on terrorism.

The Senate confirmed Mueller unanimously, but before he started his new job, he quietly went to the hospital to be treated for prostate cancer. Aides joked that the famous workaholic took nearly four hours off for the operation and recovery. Not even the time in the hospital recuperating from surgery was wasted: Pickard prepared thick unclassified briefing books on Bureau procedure for Mueller to read in his hospital bed. (Later, when Mueller had a knee replaced in 2003, his aides joked that he declined anesthesia and just bit on a leather strap.)

The unclassified briefing books may have kept him company in the recovery room, but the classified material Mueller began to see and hear was the stuff of nightmares. As early as the beginning of 2001, officials and investigators had begun to believe that an attack was in the offing. In April, the FBI had issued a national alert to field offices summarizing the scant intelligence available at the time and asking for any information about "current operational activities relating to Sunni extremism." Dale Watson sent a memo to Louis Freeh noting, "Serious operational planning has been underway since late 2000, with an intended culmination in late Spring 2001.... It is not known whether there are several different parallel plans or whether all activity centers on one major operation."

By May, the threat reports seemed to be coming daily—incidents such as a walk-in to New York's FBI office who said that a three-pronged attack would soon hit London, New York, and Boston, a report that couldn't be verified. That same month, counterterrorism officials chased alleged plots in Yemen and Italy as well as a purported al-Qaeda cell in Canada. Something was coming; no one knew exactly what. On May 29, Richard Clarke e-mailed Condi Rice and her deputy, Stephen Hadley, warning, "When these attacks come, as they likely will, we will wonder what more we could have done to stop them." By that summer, as George Tenet would later tell the 9/11 Commission, "the system was blinking red." On June 28, Clarke told Rice that threats had reached a "crescendo." But nobody could put together the pieces. As Tom Pickard recalls, "Everyone was concerned, but no one had many facts."

On July 19, Pickard told a regularly scheduled conference call of SACs from across the country to double-check that their evidence response teams were ready to be deployed. But again no specifics were offered—or available.

Many threats were focused overseas. There were reports that Yemeni terrorists were planning an attack on Jordan after the previous year's operation there had failed; that another group would attack the U.S. embassy in Yemen; that a Pakistani group was targeting the American and British schools in Jeddah, Saudi Arabia; that an Iranian-backed Hezbollah cell was readying a large operation in Southeast Asia; and that an Algerian cell was casing targets in Rome. In response, the State Department stepped up security at embassies around the world, the navy's Fifth Fleet moved its ships from port out to sea as a precautionary measure, and the military's Central Command in the Middle East raised its force protection level.

At the beginning of July, the FBI sent a domestic law enforcement advisory warning of possible attacks by groups or individuals sympathetic to bin Laden; however, the information was so general and non-specific that the warning wasn't much help. In addition, the volume of threat information was so high as to be nearly impossible to process. The FBI's New York OBL unit took in more than three thousand leads over the months leading up to 9/11; Dale Watson later told the 9/11 Commission that he had wished he had "five hundred analysts looking at Osama bin Laden threat information instead of two." Watson's wish pointed to a shocking FBI weakness, decades in the making, the fault of presidential uninterest, a Bureau that had allocated resources away from terrorism, and an intelligence community that lacked cooperation and coordination.

The Bureau's antiquated technology made it even harder to process the leads agents collected. One emergency FISA warrant by the San Francisco Field Office uncovered an intriguing e-mail in a suspect's Hotmail account, but the Bureau's computer system didn't allow for a way for the e-mail to be transferred securely to the New York al-Qaeda squad. An agent finally saved the e-mail to a floppy disc and flew cross-country to deliver the disc in person.

The top-secret President's Daily Brief (PDB) for August 6, 2001, a document infamously titled "Bin Laden Determined to Strike in U.S.," reported that the "FBI is conducting approximately 70 full field investigations throughout the U.S. that it considers bin Laden–related." Through the summer, counterterrorism officials in government worked overtime to determine what was happening. They never figured it out. In fact, one of the chairs of the 9/11 Commission, Tom Kean, later said that he believed one reason the Bush administration fought so hard against releasing information relating to the attack afterward was not because of the sensitivity of that information but because of how *little* sensitive material it actually had. The August 6 PDB was striking for its generality.

Many, many rungs below the director, FBI agents were still trying to figure out what was happening with the summer's al-Qaeda threats. As Abby Perkins recalls, "Things were happening. People were on standby. It was a heavy summer. Everyone thought it'd be an international attack." In New York, Ken Maxwell, John O'Neill, and Barry Mawn met with Rudy Giuliani and Bernie Kerik to present the evidence suggesting an imminent plot. Everything points to a big attack in the works, Maxwell said. At the conclusion of the briefing, Kerik asked, "Could that happen here?"

Maxwell paused. "Well, I can't say for sure that it wouldn't, but historically al-Qaeda has always attacked us overseas. They're definitely planning something huge."

There were numerous missed opportunities that summer to get closer to the 9/11 plot, even though it seems unlikely that the FBI would have been able to unravel it in time. First on the list was the so-called Phoenix memo, written by Special Agent Kenneth Williams. Williams, a Little League coach and trained FBI SWAT sniper, was an experienced field agent with over a decade in the Phoenix Division, a high-pressure office that covers the entire state along with seven smaller resident agencies. Between the Mexican border, drug smuggling, and the numerous Native American reservations in Arizona, where the FBI served as the primary law enforcement authority, the field office had a lot on its plate. Williams was one of the only agents assigned to counterterrorism. The total annual budget for the Phoenix JTTF was just $2,060. The Bureau, Williams lamented later, was a "statistics animal," and CT just didn't provide good statistics— and so, Dale Watson's MAXCAP05 initiative notwithstanding, the Phoenix Field Office management wasn't that focused on it. Phoenix SAC Lupe Gonzalez publicly admitted that terrorism was "job four" and privately called international terrorism "mumbo-jumbo." When

Williams briefed the SAC and ASAC, he said, it "fell on deaf ears." "They wouldn't recognize al-Qaeda," Williams later explained. "They would think he was a guy named Al Kita."

In April 2000, Williams had interviewed a man who had ties to Islamic extremists and was enrolled in civil aviation courses at Arizona's Embry-Riddle Aeronautical University; the man had had a poster of Osama bin Laden hanging on his wall. Williams called around, checking in with people at FBI Headquarters, finding out what people in other parts of the country were seeing, and then wrote what was to become the most infamous memo in the history of the FBI. "Kenny's intent with his memo was to identify a trend and get a better big picture view of it," says his partner at the time, Special Agent George Piro. "When you have a pattern, the goal is always to determine whether it's a local pattern or a national pattern."

On July 10, 2001, Williams wrote in his "electronic communication" (or EC, in Bureau parlance), "Phoenix has observed an inordinate number of individuals of investigative interest who are attending or who have attended civil aviation universities and colleges in the State of Arizona. The inordinate number of these individuals attending these types of schools and fatwas issued by al-Muhajiroun spiritual leader Sheikh Omar Bakri Mohammed Fostok, an ardent supporter of OBL, gives reason to believe that a coordinated effort is underway to establish a cadre of individuals who will one day be working in the civil aviation community around the world. These individuals will be in a position in the future to conduct terror activity against civil aviation targets." His memo went on for more than four pages, outlining his evidence to support his theory, detailing the associations of suspicious individuals with local flight programs, and pointing out that one of the recently convicted East African embassy bombers had lived in Tucson, while another of Osama bin Laden's personal pilots had come to Phoenix in 1993 to procure a new jet for the terrorist leader. "Phoenix believes that it is highly probable that OBL has an established support network in place in Arizona," Williams concluded. He made a series of recommendations, suggesting that the FBI establish a national canvas of flight schools and perhaps even get the authority to review State Department visas for students coming to the United States with the intent of enrolling in flight school.

Williams's EC was, without a doubt, one of the best pieces of intelligence the FBI had seen—an excellent example of how individual law enforcement investigations can lead to big-picture intelligence theories and breakthroughs—but he later said that he wrote it without any inkling of the 9/11 attacks. In fact, he believed that the civil aviation training would primarily help smuggle explosives on board; he gave little thought to the possibility of the terrorists flying the planes themselves. He marked his memo "routine," figuring that there was nothing specific in it on which to act. (Even if such a national flight school canvas began, it would probably take over a year to complete.) In fact, the memo was considered so routine that it wasn't loaded into the FBI's online network until Friday, July 27, meaning that most people didn't read it until Monday the thirtieth.

Williams's EC went to eight FBI personnel spread across the headquarters' terrorism team, the Osama bin Laden unit, and the New York JTTF. Some of the recipients read it; some didn't. No one acted on it. In New York, it met some of the arrogance that agents outside of the Southern District say all too often marks the New York JTTF and field office. One agent in New York who read it says he quickly dismissed it, failing to believe that Osama bin Laden could have any network in Arizona and calling such a proposition a "glaring deficiency." ("New York just couldn't believe that it had anything to learn from someone in Phoenix," one agent later explained to me. "They're big, bad New York. How could someone from rinky-dink Phoenix know something they don't?") Others on the distribution list read the EC, considered it interesting, and moved on with other cases. Jack Cloonan was among them. "It was an interesting point," he reflects. "But how as a practical matter are we going to do this? We think it has merit, but we don't have the resources to do it."

The same day that the Phoenix memo was distributed, Mueller was facing questions at his confirmation hearing on the Hill about the FBI's outmoded computer system. The questioners couldn't have found a better example of its shortcomings than the Phoenix memo: The FBI's network was so antiquated that it didn't automatically notify the recipients of an EC, so none of the supervisors who were supposed to receive the memo saw it before the 9/11 attacks. Some of their careers would be ruined because they'd been cc'ed on a memo they'd never known existed.

Whatever was coming down the pike would happen without John O'Neill. After the better part of a decade ringing the bell about the rising threat of al-Qaeda, O'Neill was ready to throw in the towel. The briefcase incident and Barry Mawn's selection as head of the New York Field Office told him he had risen as far in the Bureau as he would.

At the end of June 2001, nearly a year after the briefcase theft, O'Neill took a vacation in Paris with Valerie James. They stayed at the apartment of the Paris legat, who was away at the time. They then went on to visit another FBI agent on Spain's Costa del Sol, where O'Neill read by the pool and stared across the Strait of Gibraltar at Morocco and, on July 8, marked an important milestone in his Bureau career.

"What are you smiling at?" his friend asked.

"I'm KMA," O'Neill said, beaming. "It's my KMA day."

The "Kiss My Ass" day marks the day an agent is eligible for retirement; O'Neill was free to leave the Bureau with his full pension. That same day in Spain, unbeknown to anyone in the U.S. government, Mohamed Atta was meeting in Madrid with Ramzi Binalshibh, organizing the final details of the 9/11 plot.

When O'Neill returned to the United States, he finalized an arrangement with developer Larry Silverstein to become head of security for the World Trade Center. While much was later made of O'Neill's choice of a new job—some would label him as "the man who knew"—he had no specific insight into Osama bin Laden's plans. For the FBI agent, the job was mostly coincidental, high-profile enough to offer what he now wanted more than anything. O'Neill, who'd spent his life pressed for cash yet buying round after round of drinks for everyone in sight, would finally be getting his reward—a salary of some three times his FBI's $125,000 a year. Silverstein insisted that O'Neill begin in early September.

Just days before he left the Bureau, though, on August 19, the *New York Times* published an article outlining the investigation into

O'Neill's missing briefcase. It was the only article the *Times* ever published about O'Neill's work while he was alive.*

On his final day as an FBI agent, O'Neill, who had proclaimed throughout his career, "I am the FBI," wrote a lengthy e-mail to the father of one of the sailors killed on the USS *Cole*: "In my thirty-one years of government service, my proudest moment was when I was selected to lead the investigation of the USS *Cole*. I have put my all into the investigation and truly believe that significant progress has been made." Agents toasted O'Neill that afternoon with cake; then, as his last act as an FBI agent, he signed an authorization returning FBI agents to Yemen. Al-Qaeda was still out there, and the FBI needed to stay after it.

When the embassy bombing team had wrapped up its prosecution earlier that spring, Steve Gaudin had made a comment about how glad he was the case was over.

"Over?" O'Neill roared back. "Nothing's over."

The same day that O'Neill began working at the World Trade Center, the CIA finally turned over information to the FBI that two known al-Qaeda operatives were in the country. While the intelligence community missed numerous chances in the summer of 2001 to thwart the 9/11 plot, there was probably no single bigger missed opportunity than the case of Khalid al-Mihdhar and Nawaf al-Hazmi, two of the eventual 9/11 hijackers who had already been on the U.S. radar.

The first of five oversights occurred in 2000 when the CIA realized, but neglected to tell the FBI, that al-Mihdhar had arrived in the United States just days after attending a January al-Qaeda meeting in Malaysia that included participants in the USS *Cole* plot. The CIA had even had access to al-Mihdhar's passport and recorded that he possessed a multiple-entry visa for the United States, information the Agency also didn't bother to share.

The second came when the two men were living with the FBI

---

* Tom Pickard, Dale Watson, Ambassador Bodine, and the White House's Richard Clarke were each suspected of leaking the information to the *Times*. It was never clear who did.

informant in San Diego. The informant told his FBI handler that two Saudi Arabian men were staying with him, mentioning only their first names; such guests were, according to the handler, a semiregular occurrence and the informant thought nothing of it. The FBI agent didn't ask for the visitors' full names. Of all the near misses, this was probably the closest miss, yet the one most reasonably not pursued. Informants are notorious for seizing every opportunity to milk their handlers for more money or favors; the fact that the informant himself didn't think anything of the visitors is the most powerful statement that the FBI agent did not need to be too concerned. "Look, this guy was after money. If he had the slightest inkling that his guests were worth anything, he'd have been all over us to get paid," one FBI executive concluded.

May and June of 2001 saw the most frustrating misses. Over the course of the spring and early summer, the CIA and FBI battled back and forth over the *Cole* investigation, with the CIA repeatedly stonewalling the FBI by citing the intelligence wall and refusing to share what later turned out to be valuable information. Adding to the trouble were multiple misunderstandings within the FBI, between agents and the lawyers of the National Security Law Unit, about what information was being sought, where it came from, and where it could go. Beyond that, the FBI's poor relationship with the CIA meant that it also had a poor understanding of how the Agency collected and reported information, so in some cases it didn't know the right way to ask for certain intelligence.

Not until the end of August did the CIA inform the FBI that al-Mihdhar had been visiting the United States, most recently arriving on July 4. Nevertheless, the lead received no special attention or priority; it was labeled "routine," because, as one FBI official explained later, it wasn't considered any more pressing than any of the other tips coming through the FBI units that summer. That determination might have changed if the lead had ended up with the right people in New York. Steve Bongardt, the hard-charging fighter pilot turned special agent who was the co-lead with Ali Soufan on the *Cole* investigation, says that if he'd heard the suspect was in the United States, the entire squad would have turned the country upside-down searching for him.

Even still, there were chances. Maggie Gillespie, an FBI analyst

then detailed to the CIA's Counterterrorism Center, was busy researching al-Hazmi's and al-Mihdhar's travel when she discovered their
2000 visit. She notified the State Department, Customs, the INS, and
the FBI and asked for the two to be added to their watch lists; for
unknown reasons, she didn't place them on the FAA's "no fly" list. She
also passed the information to headquarters, which passed it to New
York JTTF with the order to determine whether either man was still
in the United States. At the urging of her supervisor at the Agency,
though, she explained that this information had come from the result
of intelligence work and thus couldn't be shared with the criminal
agents.

Bongardt was accidentally forwarded an e-mail explaining that
the two men were in the country. He tried to start an investigation,
only to be told to stand down; he wasn't supposed to know that information and thus couldn't act on it. "Show me where this is written
that we can't have the intelligence," a frustrated Bongardt asked FBI
analyst Dina Corsi. "If this guy is in the country, it's not because he's
going to fucking Disneyland!" As part of the debate over the intelligence and criminal divide at the FBI and who could know about
al-Mihdhar's travel, agents and analysts missed a critical piece of evidence: The al-Qaeda operative had lied on his visa application, meaning that since he had entered the U.S. illegally, the FBI could legitimately
open a criminal investigation into his whereabouts. With that detail
overlooked and Bongardt stymied, the lead remained available only to
FBI intelligence agents.

The cruel irony of the situation was that Bongardt had been in
the lumbering Kenyan paddywagon that had collected Mohamed
al-'Owhali in Somalitown in the first days after the East Africa embassy
bombings. He'd been part of the team that researched the phone number in Yemen that the suspect had handed the FBI team—967-1-200-
578—in Nairobi, which in turn passed it along to the rest of the
intelligence community. The new information the CIA refused to
hand over from the Malaysia meeting had come about because the
NSA had overheard the details of the meeting while eavesdropping on
967-1-200-578—the same number. Now Bongardt, one of the three
agents who'd started the ball rolling, was being kept from the fruits of
his work.

All year the wall had been causing him problems. As the case agents on the *Cole* bombing, code-named ADENBOM by the FBI, Bongardt and Soufan had been back and forth to Yemen every few weeks since October 2000. The I-49 squad had been split in two to handle the ever-expanding investigations; Squad I-49 pursued bin Laden, the embassy bombers who were still at large, and the larger al-Qaeda organization, while Squad I-45 focused more on ADEN-BOM. In February 2001, Bongardt had been at dinner in Yemen with other FBI agents and the Yemeni investigators when Howard Leadbetter, the FBI's on-scene commander, needed to pass the local intelligence agency a piece of information. Leadbetter asked Bongardt, a criminal investigator, to leave the table while he talked about the intel with the locals. "Come on, Howard—if the Yemenis can know it, I can know it," Bongardt protested. No dice. Bongardt paced outside the restaurant, frustrated and disgusted.

To many of Bongardt's peers, it seemed as if the wall helped headquarters supervisors maintain closer control over field investigations; by having access to both the intelligence and the criminal evidence, they could know more than the case agents. In part, this seemed to be an extension of Louis Freeh's tendency to be the lead case agent on any large case. He liked being hands-on in a way that no director, so removed from the street, should be. It was, case agents groused, the "Jack Ryan effect," referring to the fictional Tom Clancy character who single-handedly beat back terrorists even as he rose through the series of books to be CIA director and then president. And it wasn't just Freeh: It seemed every headquarters supervisor and analyst wanted to be Jack Ryan, keeping control and pulling strings by maintaining an information monopoly over those below them on the ladder.

On August 25, al-Hazmi and al-Mihdhar—who had spent the summer in Paterson, New Jersey, a twenty-minute drive from the FBI's Newark Field Office and a thirty-minute drive from the FBI's New York Field Office—drove to William Paterson University in Wayne, New Jersey, logged on to the internet via a school computer, and purchased their plane tickets for September 11. That same day, Bongardt, after yet another request from the New York team to open a criminal investigation into al-Mihdhar's presence in the United States was denied, wrote to Dina Corsi, "Someday somebody will die—and Wall or not—the public will not understand why we are not more effective and throwing every resource we had at certain 'problems.'" Echoing the frustrations of agents over the past six years, he added, "Let's hope the National Security Law Unit will stand behind their decisions then, especially since the biggest threat to us now, OBL, is getting the most 'protection.'" Likewise, Ali Soufan wrote three memos, in November 2000, April 2001, and August 2001, asking for more information from the CIA about the *Cole* participants. They all went unanswered. He says, anger still evident in his voice years later, "They know they're here [in the United States] and we're looking for them in Yemen—they don't think that's important?"

Four days after Bongardt's outburst, the New York Field Office finally opened a formal "full field investigation" to find al-Mihdhar using intelligence resources, not criminal agents. As a "routine" request, the job was assigned to a junior agent who'd graduated from the FBI Academy just a year before and was only in his second month on the OBL squad. In fact, the al-Mihdhar investigation was the first intelligence investigation of his career. Despite sitting just feet from the desks of criminal investigators like Bongardt, Soufan, and others who knew so much about his subjects, the junior intelligence agent was prevented by the wall from asking them for help. Over the next two weeks, he checked with local hotels, checked local criminal record databases, tried to gather al-Mihdhar's travel documents, and searched the enormous ChoicePoint data-mining database to gather information. On September 10, he sat down and drafted a request for the Los Angeles Field Office to check with Sheraton hotels in the area to see whether al-Mihdhar or al-Hazmi had stayed at any of them. (Al-Mihdhar had listed a "Sheraton hotel" as his destination on his travel documents.) As the agent's request was transmitted to L.A. on the morning of 9/11, both of the hijackers were waiting at Washington's Dulles International Airport to board American Airlines Flight 77, which they would soon crash into the Pentagon.

CHAPTER 9
PENTTBOM

The winds must come from somewhere when they
blow.

> — *W. H. Auden, "Villanelle" (a poem carried by*
> *Windows on the World owner David Emil*
> *in the months after 9/11)*

John O'Neill had spent the days before he started at the World Trade Center excitedly speaking with others in the security business about his plans for the job. He was appalled at the vast complex's poor security system and had big plans to update it and make it world-class. Silverstein had nearly given him carte blanche. He had dinner the night of September 10 at his favorite haunt, Elaine's, with Ken Maxwell, his fellow veteran FBI counterterrorism agent. "We're due for something big," O'Neill told Maxwell at one point.

When September 11, 2001, dawned bright, crisp, and blue in the eastern United States, the two FBI squads that had been tracking bin Laden's organization for years were scattered around the world, chasing leads stemming from their wide-ranging investigation into al-Qaeda. Ali Soufan, the ADENBOM case agent, was leading a team in Sana'a, working through the Yemen end of the *Cole* investigation. "It was surreal," team member Jack Cloonan recalls. "We watched it all happen on the TV in the embassy. We didn't know what we were looking at." Over the course of the afternoon in Yemen, the New York JTTF squad watched helplessly as the Pentagon was attacked, United Flight 93 crashed in Pennsylvania, and the twin towers fell just blocks from the squad's offices at 290 Broadway.

Earlier that spring, Special Agent Russ Fincher, who had been working ADENBOM, had been given a new assignment when he arrived back in New York from Yemen. Abu Bilal Al Suwadi, aka the "Black Swede," was a half-Ghanaian, half-Swedish former Boston gangbanger turned radical jihadist who had targeted the Bureau team when it was staying at the Sana'a Sheraton—the threat that forced the team into the U.S. embassy compound just before it pulled out of the country entirely. Intelligence had pointed the Bureau to Al Suwadi, and now it was up to Fincher and his partner, NYPD JTTF detective Tommy Ward, to find him. They had a theory, based on Ward's years as a street cop, that gangbangers always go back to their mothers when they're on the run. Maxwell, unconvinced but willing to let their hunch play out, approved a trip to Sweden, where Al Suwadi's mother lived. In the early morning hours of September 11—just as their boss, Maxwell, sat down to dinner at Elaine's with John O'Neill six time zones earlier—special Swedish police units descended on the Black Swede's hideout. The FBI agent, NYPD detective, and Swedish forces processed the scene and interviewed the al-Qaeda terrorist until dawn. Exhausted, Fincher and Ward then collapsed at their hotel. When Fincher awoke in the late afternoon and turned on the TV, he watched for a few moments what he thought was a particularly horrible made-for-TV movie, blinking sleep from his eyes. Then he realized it wasn't a movie.

After a late night with Maxwell, who had once joked about O'Neill's uncanny ability to always appear fresh in the morning, O'Neill was at his desk on the thirty-fourth floor of the South Tower of the World Trade Center when Mohamed Atta's hijacked plane, American Airlines Flight 11—coincidentally piloted by a childhood friend of O'Neill's, Victor Saracini—crashed into the North Tower. O'Neill called his son to say that he was okay and then proceeded downstairs. His estranged wife called to check on him too. As he moved through the wreckage, he tried unsuccessfully to call Pat Patterson, an FBI colleague from the Yemen investigation. At 9:17 A.M., just minutes after United Flight 175 had crashed into the South Tower, and with both towers now heavily engulfed in flames and smoke, O'Neill reached Valerie. "Val, it's terrible. There are body parts everywhere," he said. He spoke with the third woman in his life with whom he was romantically involved, Anna DiBattista, at 9:29 A.M.: "Honey, I'm safe, I'm fine." She pleaded with him to leave the buildings. "I can't—I'm helping people and doing things. I love you. I'll be okay."

Ten minutes later, O'Neill was at the New York Fire Department command post in the North Tower, speaking with FBI agents who were streaming onto the scene. As O'Neill left the command post, Special Agent Wesley Wong yelled to him, "I owe you lunch because I missed your going-away coffee."

"I'll call you when this is over," O'Neill replied, walking toward the South Tower. Sixteen minutes later, a growing roar marked its collapse.

Steve Bongardt was often one of the first into the office even on a squad of overachievers. He drove in from New Jersey and went to the gym in the morning, so before many colleagues had even arrived, he had fired up his computer and read some of the day's intelligence. One particular lead that morning of 9/11 puzzled him: A report had Osama bin Laden reopening his large underground facility at Tora Bora in Afghanistan and sprucing it up. Huh. What the hell is he doing? Bongardt wondered.

By 8:30 A.M. most of the al-Qaeda squad had joined Bongardt in the office: Steve Gaudin, Abby Perkins, Debbie Doren, and Danny Coleman, among others from Squad I-49 and Squad I-45, were working at 290 Broadway when the first plane hit. Everyone felt the room shake as Atta's plane plowed into the World Trade Center, yet many believed it was just the building's air-conditioning system starting up. Then, from the squad supervisor's office window, it became clear that the rumble hadn't just been the AC.

Grabbing his blue FBI raid jacket, Bongardt took the elevator to the first floor with an INS agent assigned to the JTTF, only to be stopped by a man running through the building's front door. "I saw it!" he exclaimed. "I saw the plane hit the building." Bongardt pushed past him and ran down Broadway, rounding the corner onto Church Street, with the towers straight ahead. He was confused to see the second tower burning too. Then his eye fell upon a giant Pratt & Whitney jetliner engine lying on the street, five blocks or so from the World Trade Center, where it had been thrown by the impact and landed on a pedestrian. His mind quickly calculated the physics, realizing in an instant that a second plane had come from the south and hit the second tower. Thoughts came one on top of the other now, tripping over each other in his head: *This is al-Qaeda. This is why they're polishing up Tora Bora.*

Moments later, standing outside the towers, Bongardt stopped a firefighter: "What can we do?"

"You're not going in without a mask," the firefighter ordered, looking up at the inferno hundreds of feet above the street. "You qualified with an oxygen tank? You a firefighter?"

"No," Bongardt said.

"Just get people away from the building," he said, turning to go inside before stopping. "Give me your flashlight — we're going to need extras." Bongardt handed over his Maglite.

The one active-duty FBI agent who would die that day — Leonard Hatton, a distinguished bomb tech who had deployed to Khobar Towers and the *Cole* bombing, among other cases, and had once flown thirty-three hours back from Yemen to make his daughter's school dance — was a former Marine and volunteer firefighter and the only agent on the scene who would have answered yes to the question posed to Bongardt. After helping one victim away from the building, Hatton turned and went back into the towers. "Where are you going?" the victim asked the agent, according to a later account to investigators.

"Back into the building," Hatton said. He never made it out again.

Steve Bongardt stood on the plaza of the World Trade Center, watching people jump from the towers, and pledged that as hard as he had tried to push back in the weeks and months before 9/11, he would now do even more. He burned with rage. Just weeks earlier, he'd written the vitriolic e-mail about headquarters seeming more interested in protecting the terrorists' rights than in stopping a tragedy like the one he was now witnessing.

Craig Donnachie, who'd spent the summer reading all the vague but troubling intelligence barred from his colleagues' eyes, came across the airplane engine Bongardt had passed moments earlier. Incongruously, an FBI technician had set up crime tape around the hulking, smoking mass and begun to photograph it for evidence even as chaos reigned around him. The tech tried to flag Donnachie down and enlist his help in measuring it. "You've got to be kidding—not right now," the agent replied, running on toward the towers.

For Abby Perkins, the experience would exist only in snapshots, freeze frames of images screaming by: the squad running down toward the World Trade Center, blue FBI raid jackets billowing out behind them; Steve Gaudin finding a piece of the plane and putting it in his backpack; Danny Coleman holding a singed passport from a Satam al-Suqami (who would turn out to be one of the hijackers); being stopped on the streets by people saying, "I need to tell you what I saw. A plane went into the building"; hearing the rumble as the building made its final gasp; more running; ducking into the corner of a lobby with Debbie Doren. Perkins's mind raced as she remembered victims' interviews from Nairobi, about how so many of the casualties had been killed by the exploding embassy glass, about how survivors had been buried in the concrete rubble of the embassy. Now she'd know what it felt like herself. *This is how I'm going to die,* she thought as the world turned black outside. The lobby glass held; the concrete walls didn't collapse. Debbie Doren, ever the planner, headed deeper into the building and began to fill trash cans with water in case they were trapped.

Soon Doren and Perkins began to hear reports of bombings at the Supreme Court, the State Department, people shooting at Battery Park. Gradually finding one another in the chaos, the team reassembled on St. Andrews Plaza and walked north to the garage on Thirty-fourth Street that was to become the FBI's temporary New York headquarters. Dan Coleman was covered in dust, his face streaked. Perkins barely recognized her supervisor, John Liguori, his face was so black.

Squads I-49 and I-45 had visited dozens of countries in the five preceding years, tracking Osama bin Laden, al-Qaeda, and the bombers of the embassies and the USS *Cole*. Now al-Qaeda had come to them. John O'Neill had followed the terrorists everywhere he knew how. Now they'd found him.

Over the course of the day and hours that followed, the same thought came to each of the members of the squad in turn. If any of them had run into O'Neill in the morning's chaos, they would have followed him back into the burning building without a moment's thought.

David Kelley, the assistant prosecutor who had spent the previous five years circling the globe with Pat Fitzgerald and the rest of the al-Qaeda squad, had just left the North Tower with Barry Mawn, the head of the New York FBI office, when they spotted a leg lying on the plaza outside. It was wrapped in traditional Middle Eastern muslin, clothing that immediately stood out to the men because of their memories of similar clothing from Ramzi Yousef's first bombing. "We've got to grab that leg," Kelley said.

"I'm not picking that up," Mawn protested.

"No—get one of your evidence techs down here," Kelley said.

A moment after the exchange, an enormous explosion rumbled overhead. Without thinking, the two men began to sprint up Greenwich Street. As they ran, their backs were pounded by falling debris. Kelley dropped down behind cover, and the world turned black as he was covered with debris and a fine dust. "It was like being buried in a huge pile of Xerox toner," he recalls. He began to have trouble breathing. The sun disappeared. Moments passed—how many minutes, he doesn't know—and then gradually he was able to extricate himself. He looked around, still unsure exactly what had happened. "I knew I was a faster runner than Barry. I figured immediately he didn't make it," Kelley recalls. When Kelley was finally able to reach Mary Jo White that morning, he broke the news to her: "I think Barry was killed." White, relieved, only laughed: "I just talked to him. He told me *you* were dead."

Only hours after the attack, Kelley settled into the squad offices of 290 Broadway and began the work of the investigation. As he began to subpoena the airplane manifests, Michael Chertoff, the head of the Justice Department's Criminal Division, explained that Washington had already started that process. "Fuck that—it's our case," Kelley told Chertoff in Washington. That night, Kelley was driven down the

New Jersey Turnpike by an agent, the engine of the "bucar" straining, heading toward an indefinite assignment in Washington, where he would help lead the unfolding investigation.

While most of the FBI New York office assembled on Thirty-fourth Street at the temporary field office—technicians were stringing wires across the parking spots in the garage—Squad I-49 and Squad I-45 returned to 290 Broadway, where their voluminous files were suddenly in high demand.

Steve Bongardt was on a 2:30 conference call with Liguori and Maxwell. Also at the other end were Mike Rolince, headquarters supervisor Rod Middleton, and analyst Dina Corsi, whom Bongardt and Fincher had clashed with that spring.

Maxwell opened. "What do we know? Do we recognize any of the hijacker names?"

Corsi replied affirmatively and began to read some. Bongardt came alert quickly at one name in particular. "Dina!" he interrupted. "Khalid al-Mihdhar? The same one you told us about? He's on the list?"

Middleton broke in from Washington. "Steve," he said, "we did everything by the book."

Bongardt exploded. "Hope that makes you fucking feel better! Tens of thousands are dead!"

Maxwell, sitting in New York, hit the mute button on the conference call and pointed at Bongardt, saying, "Now is not the time. There will be a time for that. Now's not it."

The next day Bongardt ran a quick Lexis search on al-Mihdhar and turned up an address and phone number in San Diego. The al-Qaeda operative he'd been hunting was in the phone book. And no one had told him—and he had been denied permission to look himself.

When the first U.S. special forces units entered Afghanistan a few weeks later, every photo of an al-Qaeda leader that they carried came from the FBI's files. The al-Qaeda team, along with dozens of agents new to the case, began to scatter again. Mike Anticev headed to the Sudan, tracking bin Laden's early years. Soufan worked for weeks in Yemen interviewing al-Qaeda prisoners and then, with Gaudin, ended up in the CIA's first "black site" in Thailand, interrogating high-level detainees. Perkins headed to the United Arab Emirates to look into al-Qaeda's financing, then went on to Pakistan. For his part, Bongardt was on the first flight of the FBI's brand-new G5 Gulfstream jet, racing toward Pakistan, then on to Egypt to collect valuable pieces of evidence in the developing investigation. The counterterrorism team would come to know the G5 well; it would log hundreds of thousands of miles in the coming years ferrying FBI agents, accused terrorists, and Mueller himself to every continent in the world but Antarctica.

Mueller had officially started at the Hoover Building on September 4, the same day that National Security Council counterterrorism director Richard Clarke tapped out an e-mail to Condi Rice accusing the administration of not taking the al-Qaeda threat seriously. "Decision makers should imagine themselves on a future day when the CSG [Counterterrorism Strategy Group] has not succeeded in stopping Al-Qaeda attacks and hundreds of Americans lay dead in several countries, including the U.S.," he wrote. "What would those decision makers wish they had done earlier? That future day could happen at any time."

Mueller spent that first week as director learning the Bureau's emergency response plans—what to do in the case of a nuclear attack, how to ensure the top-secret continuity of government plans, and the like, standard operating procedure that a new director needed to know. On Friday afternoon, four days into his crash course on the Bureau, Pickard (who had returned to his post as deputy director now that Mueller had been confirmed) noted that his new boss looked a little shell-shocked. An unbelievable amount of information had been thrown at Mueller that week, much of it amounting to the nation's most sensitive secrets. As is often true of officials entering the highest levels of government, his worldview had been seriously altered, and there were few to share the burdens of his new office. "You know, the worst of it," Pickard reflected, "is you can't go home and tell your wife any of it, because it's highly classified."

The following Tuesday began like any other. Each morning the FBI leaders had gathered to bring the new director up to speed on the most important investigations. Coincidentally that morning the counterterrorism team, led by Mike Rolince, was presenting ADENBOM, the USS *Cole* bombing case. The Bureau's approach to counterterrorism was cause for concern; in his first days, Mueller had been presented with a report showing the FBI's progress on Watson's MAXCAP05 initiative in the year since its inception. Nearly every field office was still marked as operating far below "maximum capacity." The ADEN-BOM case seemed to be one of the few investigations proceeding well. Al-Qaeda was already on the lips of everyone in the room when someone interrupted to say a plane had hit the World Trade Center. "How could a plane not see the tower? It's so clear out today," Mueller wondered out loud.

Afterward, as the FBI leadership realized that the crash was intentional, the conversation migrated from Mueller's conference room to Tom Pickard's office, where a TV was on. Pickard called the FBI New York Field Office. Barry Mawn was already en route to the scene, so Pickard asked an aide in New York to hold the line open as he summoned Mueller from his own office in the seventh-floor executive wing of the Hoover Building. "Look, they've already got it on TV," said Pickard, who was watching over Mueller's shoulder as the director walked in and CNN showed video of a plane hitting the World Trade Center. A beat or two passed as both men realized that they were not witnessing a replay of the first incident but seeing a second plane and a second attack live on the news. "We've got a terrorist incident," Pickard said. The men raced to the Bureau's Strategic Information and Operations Center (SIOC), a state-of-the-art command post on the fifth floor.

Over the morning, news filtered in of the attacks at the Pentagon and in Pennsylvania, as well as of the deaths of O'Neill and Hatton in the attacks on the World Trade Center. "In circumstances like that you don't have time [to process]," Mueller recalls, saying that Pickard and counterterrorism chief Dale Watson swung into gear. "They just clicked in. The leadership mobilizes, and with that the whole organization mobilizes." Thousands of agents were dispatched to the three crime scenes.

During a pause in the morning's secure video conference, as agency heads were trying desperately to coordinate some sort of response and sharing information with the White House Situation Room, Dale Watson hailed the White House's Clarke: "Dick, call me in SIOC when you can."

When Watson's phone rang a few moments later, he had bad news to share: "We got the passenger manifests from the airlines. We recognize some names, Dick. They're al-Qaeda."

"How the fuck did they get on board, then?" Clarke, nearly sputtering, asked. His mind reeled. *There were known al-Qaeda operatives on the plane? All of the government's resources and these hijackers bought the tickets under their own names? They defeated us that easily?*

"Hey, don't shoot the messenger, friend. CIA forgot to tell us about them," Watson said, his Alabama drawl stretching out the reply. As the two men talked on the phone, they watched the second World Trade Center collapse. "Oh, dear God," Watson muttered.

President Bush learned of the attacks during a school appearance in Florida. One of his first telephone calls was to Mueller, who passed along word that the planes had been commercial airliners hijacked from Boston. Gear up, the president told his new FBI director: "This is what we pay you for."

For someone still learning where the bathrooms were in the Hoover Building, the day could have been overwhelming, but through the most intense day he would face as director, Mueller never wavered. "Bob's a good Marine," Pickard explains. "He was very cool under fire." Pickard isolated Mueller in a conference room off SIOC, restricting access to the director to help him stay focused on the decisions ahead. ("I was worried that there was going to be this string of people running into the room with news or questions, and Bob would be standing there asking them who they were," Pickard recalls.) Attorney General Ashcroft arrived later that day after returning from an aborted trip to Milwaukee; he had been to the FBI only twice since he'd started earlier that year, once for a luncheon and once to attend a briefing requested by Vice President Cheney.

As the Justice Department leadership assembled in SIOC, Executive Assistant Director Ruben Garcia, the Bureau's number three, was being whisked out of town by a motorcade full of agents nervously fingering their assault weapons. The Bureau's continuity-of-government plan automatically designated Garcia as the director-in-waiting, meaning that he had to survive an attack on Washington in order to help reconstitute the U.S. government. Rushed some forty-eight miles outside Washington to Mount Weather, near Berryville, Virginia, Garcia and his team joined much of the shadow government, including the congressional leadership that had been rushed there by helicopter. After boarding buses, they were driven deep into the mountain, passing by the bunker's thirty-four-ton, five-foot-thick door to the operations center created in the 1950s. For weeks, Garcia and a rotating team of agents would sit at Mount Weather, far below the Blue Ridge Mountains, waiting, just in case Washington disappeared. They had no specific responsibilities except to live; they passed their days in the lap of what one officials describes as 1950s-era, *Happy Days*-style luxury, but no one present was exactly relaxed.

Fred Stremmel was walking down the hall of the sprawling SIOC complex when someone told him a plane had crashed into the World Trade Center. He watched on TV minutes later as the second one crashed into the twin towers. Everyone in the operations center stood there stunned. "We probably knew it was terrorism, but we were in denial," he says. "It's like being told you have cancer. You want to deny it for as long as possible."

Then his eyes wandered around the quiet command post. His mind began to race. This place would be hopping within minutes, packed within hours, and full for weeks to come. There was a lot of work to do to get it up and running—desks had to be moved, computers set up, phone lines laid, pens and pencils located. And indeed by the end of the week, fifty-six different agencies would be working out of the FBI's SIOC as it became the headquarters of the government's response.

In fact, most of the Hoover Building was given over to the response; operations sprawled across floors, and new units sprang up out of nothing. "One day I was handed a paper and told to take it to TFOS, the Terrorist Financing Operations Section. Huh? Where's that?" Stremmel recalls. "Okay, the fourth floor? Really? Where? I go down, open this door, and overnight Dennis Lormel, the Criminal Division's financial crimes guy, has set up an entire unit—computers, agents, workspaces, the whole thing, in space that he'd just taken over from who knows where. It was like that all over the building."

Perhaps most overwhelmed in those first weeks was the newly created Threat Unit. Thousands of warnings, rumors, and allegations poured into field offices and to headquarters directly. "If there was a Muslim guy walking on Pennsylvania Avenue, suddenly that's a threat to the White House. Then there were lots of people trying to dime out their brothers-in-law, their ex-wives, their ex-boyfriends," Stremmel says.

In the wake of the attacks, the Bureau's shortcomings quickly came to the fore. The FBI's poorly named and overwhelmed Rapid-Start computer program, meant to make leads and threats easier to track, ground to a halt, earning it the moniker RapidStop. The e-mail system wasn't able to handle attachments, so agents had to FedEx photos of the hijackers to the various field offices. In fact, most of the FBI's vast stores of information were still on paper—roughly six billion pages—because the computer systems were so difficult to use; it took some twelve commands just to save a single document. Whereas the CIA had been able to conduct detailed searches for years, the FBI still couldn't sift its files for a phrase like *flight schools*. Agents and analysts would have to search for *flight* and then conduct a separate search for *schools*. The FBI, as later executives would come to say, didn't even know what it knew.

The morning after 9/11, Pickard's secretary walked into his office with a bemused look on her face and handed him a letter from Attorney General Ashcroft denying Pickard's budget request for more counterterrorism funding. The letter was dated September 10. Pickard was sure that terrorism now was finally on Ashcroft's agenda.

That same morning, Mueller joined the president and members of the cabinet and the National Security Council at the White House for a strategy session. Around the table they went, talking about paths of response and investigation. Then Mueller, who had spent most of his life as a prosecutor, spoke up.

"Wait a second. If we do some of these things, it may impair our ability to prosecute," he said.

Ashcroft responded quickly, "This is different."

With that simple exchange, ninety-three years of Bureau tradition, reinforced again and again by intelligence scandals such as CISPES and COINTELPRO and cases such as the New Afrikan Freedom Fighters, came to a halt. Since its earliest missions against German agents during World War I, the Bureau had developed an "arrest culture." It was, many argued, the world's premier after-the-fact investigation and prosecution force. As Ashcroft explains, "The history of the Department of Justice is prosecution. You deter unwanted activity by prosecuting the offenders. That falls apart when you're talking about people who kill themselves while committing the act. There's a Pyrrhic potential for prosecution. It's an empty threat."

"Prosecution is the recreation of the past," Ashcroft says. "Prevention is the anticipation of the future. That's a much more difficult task." His message, repeated regularly to the FBI and the Justice Department over the weeks after 9/11, was "think outside the box but inside the Constitution." The formal announcement of the Bureau's new role would come on November 8, 2001, but within the Bureau, Mueller made the new approach clear within hours. President Bush recalled, "I told Bob I wanted the Bureau to adopt a wartime mentality."

The message from the president to Ashcroft to Mueller was clear: "Never let this happen again." The Bureau was determined it wouldn't. In the field, agents combed each crime scene for evidence, working the largest investigation the FBI had ever tackled. Work on nearly every single other investigation in the Bureau ground to a halt. Ashcroft, who had shown so little interest in terrorism that summer, now effectively moved his staff and office into the Bureau's SIOC, which was overflowing with more than five hundred people and looked, agents recall, like Grand Central Station. So many people came in and out—prosecutors, agents, and representatives from nearly every wing of the government—that one corner of the vast complex came to be known as the mayor's office, and the sole job of the staff that worked there was to keep track of where people were.

Everyone pulled long hours. Stremmel, between his 7 A.M. to midnight shift, which never began or ended on time, would sometimes sleep in his car in the Bureau garage, afraid that he'd fall asleep driving home to northern Virginia. In the main secure conference room, Pickard led twice-daily conference calls with all fifty-six field offices to go over updates on the case quickly dubbed PENTTBOM by the Bureau.* He slept on the couch in his office; periodically his wife would drop off fresh clothes at the Hoover Building. Mueller was at the office around 5 A.M. and would work until 11 or midnight each day, but according to those around him, he never flagged. Every day he showed up pressed, clean, and ready for more. Mueller read everything the Bureau assembled for him, devouring reports and memos, and impressed the staff with his recall. ("If you put something together, you weren't wasting your time," Pickard recalls.)

On Friday of that week, September 14, Mueller and Ashcroft attended the national memorial service, along with the president and most of the leaders of the U.S. government. Earlier that morning, Congress had authorized the nation to go to war; the first CIA teams were already on their way to Afghanistan, and American troops would follow within weeks. When Mueller and Ashcroft returned to the Justice Department, they gave a short press conference to announce the names of the nineteen hijackers from the four flights and to discuss the unfolding investigation. Meanwhile, agents in all fifty-six field offices and twenty of the overseas legats were busy chasing some of the 36,000 leads and tips that had come in since the attacks. Beyond the broad details, there was little Mueller would say. He demurred on most questions about new threats, tips, and so on. A reporter asked, "Can you address the issue of intelligence failure? You didn't know anything about any of these guys. We still don't know all about them."

"That was the last question. Thank you," Mueller said, turning from the podium.

It was a question, though, that he wouldn't be able to dodge for long.

Later that afternoon, back at headquarters, Mueller wandered into Tom Pickard's office. The president had summoned him and the rest of the national security team to Camp David on Saturday for a big strategy session. "What do you do at Camp David?" he wondered out

---

*PENTTBOM stood for "Pentagon/Twin Towers Bombing," using the FBI's standard case-naming system, like ADENBOM, KENBOM, and TANBOM. It's curious that the appendage *BOM* was included, since no actual bombs were used in the attack. Agents on the case surmise that in the confusing moments after the attack, whoever opened the case file believed a bomb had been used.

loud. Over the next two days, at the president's retreat in Maryland's Cacotin Mountains, in casual outfits—President Bush wore a light parka—the national security team assembled to talk through their options. The government's response was well under way. The FBI would no longer be the lead agency in the nation's response to terrorism. As President Bush recalled, "On 9/11, it was obvious the law enforcement approach to terrorism had failed.... To protect the country, we had to wage war against the terrorists."

The new paradigm was a sea change for the role of the FBI director. Although his predecessor had gone years without meeting with the nation's commander in chief, Mueller was now in daily contact with the president, providing updates on the PENTTBOM investigation and the new threats flooding the system. When President Bush visited FBI Headquarters to attend a briefing on the 9/11 investigation and to rally the troops on September 25, the director's exhaustion and stress were evident. Over the course of that morning, he introduced himself four times to Fred Stremmel, each time politely saying, "Hello, I'm Bob Mueller," and thanking the analyst for his hard work.

Special Agent Art Cummings arrived in Washington on the night of September 11 after getting a call from Dale Watson. Watson didn't know what he wanted Cummings to do, but he knew that he needed smart people to begin reshaping the Bureau to handle counterterrorism. In fact, the FBI had three major tasks ahead: It had all the major 9/11 crime scenes to process and other sites to search, it had to figure out who bore responsibility for planning and executing the attacks, and it had to prevent any next wave of terrorism.

The first task was the easiest; after-the-fact investigations required nothing new from the FBI. "No one in the world does 'right of boom' investigation better than the FBI," Mike Rolince says. In the coming months, thousands of agents sifted for evidence at the Pentagon, in Pennsylvania, and at both Ground Zero and the Fresh Kills landfill in Staten Island, where the World Trade Center debris was taken. There were hundreds of other sites to search as well, such as al-Mihdhar and al-Hazmi's rental car, which had been found in the Dulles Airport parking lot, and there were thousands of witnesses and suspects to interview.

The second task—applying attribution—was also something the Bureau was comfortable doing. It was clear immediately after 9/11 that there would be a military response, and the FBI wanted to be extra-sure, beyond a reasonable doubt, that the country or group about to be punished with the full brunt of the U.S. military deserved the punishment. "If you're going to warm something up, you need to be sure. Not because you thought, not because of analysis—you need a level of evidence that we can be comfortable with," Cummings recalls. To some people in the Hoover Building, there was a lingering warning from the bombing of Pan Am 103: *Don't always go with your gut.* What if the United States had retaliated against Syria for the Pan Am bombing, based on a hunch, before realizing that Libya was actually the perpetrator? "The FBI's bar is one hundred percent right, one hundred percent of the time. You don't ever raise your right hand and say 'I think' to a judge," Rolince says.

The third task was the biggest evolution for the FBI. "This is phase one. What's phase two? We have nothing on a possible second wave, so we had to disrupt everything. Anyone who might be anywhere—get them off the street," Cummings recalls. That pressure across the board was enormous. For prosecutor David Kelley, the following weeks at the Justice Department were a blur of search warrants, subpoenas, and material witness warrants. "The first priority was lock everything down," he says. "If you weren't used to it, you'd have to change your underwear a couple of times a day." Leads were run down until they could go no further, until every question, every avenue, was exhausted. Mueller briefed the president each morning on all the threats the FBI was tracking, a tradition that would continue for years. "[Mueller] didn't know what he had on 9/12, 9/13—was it the beginning, the middle, or the end?" says Special Agent Michael Kortan, a longtime Mueller aide and later the Bureau's assistant director for public affairs.

One of Pickard's first questions on 9/11 was sent out across the Bureau: "What do we know that didn't make sense yesterday before the attack that now makes sense today?" The answer, it turned out, was a lot. Beyond al-Hazmi and al-Mihdhar, Pickard learned during a 3 P.M. conference call on 9/11 that the FBI had arrested a man named Zacarias Moussaoui in Minneapolis. Moussaoui had set off warning bells early in August when his flight instructor had noticed his rather strange ambitions—with little experience, Moussaoui wanted to fly a Boeing 747—and had contacted the FBI, which had launched an intelligence investigation on August 14. The Bureau quickly determined that the suspect had jihadist aspirations. During an interview with FBI agents, Moussaoui, who had arrived in the United States in February, couldn't explain the origins of $32,000 in his bank account and became agitated when asked about his travel in Pakistan. He also expressed a desire to learn martial arts. One agent, Harry Samit, concluded that Moussaoui was "an Islamic extremist preparing for some future act of violence in furtherance of radical fundamentalist goals." Samit told others that his personal hunch was Moussaoui was a would-be "suicide hijacker." Since Moussaoui had overstayed his visa, the INS prepared a deportation order, and Samit worked to obtain a special FISA warrant to examine his laptop computer. Working with impressive urgency, Samit contacted the Paris legat, as Moussaoui was a French national, who helped establish a connection between the suspect and a known rebel leader in Chechnya. As part of the warrant application, the FBI's National Security Law Unit believed, incorrectly, that it had to show that Moussaoui was a suspected agent of a foreign power. (Despite the visible trend, the FISA procedures hadn't yet been updated for the age of dispersed Islamic extremists, when terrorists weren't state-sponsored. "We couldn't articulate a concrete state or group they were agents of," Stremmel recalls.) The NSL Unit lawyers decided that the Chechen rebels didn't constitute a foreign power and declined the warrant application, not even allowing the warrant to be sent to Lamberth's FISA court.

As August ticked by, the London legat got involved and asked for British help with the case. Soon British intelligence and the CIA were involved, which brought George Tenet into the loop. Tenet, the cigar-chomping Clinton appointee who had tried with mixed results to bring order to the rudderless Agency and had turned down repeated efforts by Alec Station's Michael Scheuer to assassinate bin Laden before 9/11, had been briefing President Bush personally each day on unfolding intelligence as part of his efforts to ingratiate himself with the new administration. Believing the Moussaoui case to be an FBI investigation, Tenet never raised it with the president during their daily chats. While the case reached the highest levels of the CIA, at FBI Headquarters it never went higher than Mike Rolince, then the head of the FBI's International Terrorism Operations Section. Rolince later testified at Moussaoui's trial that the case came and went with little executive-level attention; he recalled just a few brief hallway conversations with another agent, as well as a brief discussion about whether a foreign intelligence agency (presumably British) could search the suspect's computer after Moussaoui was deported to that country. Rolince had been pulled in a million directions that summer; he'd even had to make a high-stakes August trip to Yemen as part of the *Cole* investigation to negotiate the return of FBI agents to that country with Ambassador Bodine. The Moussaoui case ended up being just one snowflake in the blizzard.

Rolince wasn't alone. FBI Headquarters, in fact, shared little of the Minneapolis Field Office's urgency. A headquarters agent complained to the Minneapolis terrorism squad supervisor that the FISA application was written dramatically to get people "spun up." The supervisor said that that was exactly his intent, adding that he was "trying to keep someone from taking a plane and crashing into the White House."* Yet the example, while prophetic, was just hyperbole; Minneapolis had no reason to believe there was a terrorist threat against the World Trade Center. No one—in Minneapolis, at FBI Headquarters, or at the CIA—drew a line from Moussaoui's case to the larger threat picture that summer.

As days passed, Pickard listened in growing horror to the things the FBI had known. But no one had had the big picture. No one had known about anyone else's investigation. One thing was clear: The proverbial Chinese wall between intelligence and criminal investigations would have to go; this was a whole new ballgame. The FBI also had to get much better about what came to be known as connecting the dots. And fast. No one knew how much time they had before the next attack.

---

*The Minneapolis agent's comment has also been reported as "crashing a plane into the World Trade Center." I was unable to confirm which version was accurate at the time, though the source who recollected the White House version had closer knowledge of the conversation.

★   ★   ★

The Phoenix Field Office's sole Arabic speaker, George Piro, had watched the attacks on the television from the office gym. Beyond being one of around fifty agents fluent in Arabic, Piro had firsthand knowledge of Islamic extremism that was unparalleled in the Bureau. Born in Lebanon, he lived through years of the civil war before his family moved to California's San Joaquin Valley, which has a large Assyrian population, when he was twelve. He already had a deeper understanding of the threat of groups like Hezbollah and Hamas than most counterterrorism experts develop in their entire careers. Drawn from the start to law enforcement—he worked in the air force security police, then as a local police detective in California—he became an FBI agent in 1999.

At the time, the Phoenix Field Office had a single squad working all the various threads of international terror. Working with a more experienced agent named Kenneth Williams, Piro had made some good cases in just two years, including the Bureau's first-ever prosecution of an Iranian agent for violating sanctions against that Middle Eastern country. And, of course, Williams had sent his EC warning about flight school saying that bin Laden's network extended to Arizona.

Seeing the attacks unfold just after 7 A.M. in Phoenix, Piro quickly showered, changed, and headed upstairs to meet Williams. Williams had been through big cases before—he'd helped work the Oklahoma City bombing—and he began to explain to Piro what the coming days were likely going to hold for the Phoenix office. As the attacks continued to unfold on live TV, the partners decided they didn't want to just sit around waiting for an order. From Williams's research and EC, they knew that Phoenix had the nation's second highest concentration of flight schools. Piro opened the yellow pages and scanned the listings until he found three programs that offered commercial licenses. The partners set out on their own research trip.

The first flight school they visited was Sawyer Aviation, out at Phoenix's Sky Harbor Airport. They asked the manager whether she'd had any suspicious students lately. With hardly any hesitation, she handed over the file of one such student, Hani Hanjour. Just then, Piro's cell phone started ringing. On the line was an agent who was at

326 • Garrett M. Graff

Logan Airport in Boston, calling with a name from the flight manifest for the Phoenix team to check out: Hani Hanjour. "I'm holding his file in my hands right now," Piro told the surprised Boston agent.

They raced back to the field office and Piro went to report their productive morning hunch. "I've identified one of the hijackers," Piro told his squad leader. "Get out of here—I don't have time for jokes today," his supervisor replied incredulously.

Hanjour's file was just the beginning; it turned out a second hijacker had also trained nearby. And then there were other suspicious individuals who hadn't been on the planes; were they lying in wait for a second wave? Warning bells went off as Piro and Williams examined the file of Faisal al-Salmi: He was Saudi, matched the age range of the other hijackers, had signed up for flight lessons along with Hanjour, but hadn't performed well. "If this guy ran into a cloud, he'd be dead," declared one flight instructor. He had no ties to the community, seemed to be mostly alone, and spent much of his free time working out.

On September 18, Piro and Williams knocked on al-Salmi's door. Over the next eight hours, the two FBI agents interrogated the Saudi flight student, first at his apartment and then later at the FBI field office. "I was very uncomfortable with his statement," recalls Piro, who alternated back and forth between Arabic and English in the interrogation. Initially al-Salmi denied any ties to Hanjour. By night's end, he admitted having conversations with Hanjour. (The FBI had already tracked down a witness who had seen the two men shopping at a secondhand store together. The owner had then picked al-Salmi out of a photo lineup.) Al-Salmi, indicted for lying to federal agents, became the first arrest directly tied to the 9/11 investigation.

September was just the beginning of a whirlwind for Piro and Williams, neither of whom took a day off until Thanksgiving and then kept going as soon as the turkey was done. By February, Piro was in the United Arab Emirates as the FBI's temporary legal attaché, tracing the money and the hijackers' schedules through the Middle Eastern country. August found him in Amman, Jordan, running leads and investigating the assassination of U.S. diplomat Lawrence Foley, who was killed by al-Qaeda sympathizers. A year later, he was bound for Iraq.

★   ★   ★

As terrifying and deadly as they were, the 9/11 attacks had been local massacres, but by mid-October reports trickled in from around the country about weaponized anthrax, which threatened doom on a national scale. As news of the deadly letters sent to news organizations and congressional leaders spread, the nation's hazardous material squads were run ragged responding to suspicious powders. Over the coming weeks, Americans reported some 10,000 suspicious letters; while most turned out to be harmless, the few that didn't killed five people, sickened more than sixty, and spread fear everywhere. The letters read:

09-11-01

THIS IS NEXT
   TAKE PENACILIN NOW
   DEATH TO AMERICA
   DEATH TO ISRAEL
   ALLAH IS GREAT

The physical impact, which included the months-long closing and multimillion-dollar cleaning of an infected Senate office building and a postal sorting facility, was large, and the psychological impact on an already edgy nation was even worse. "We were just starting to have a pretty good handle on 9/11 and then this happened," Pickard says. Recalls Mueller, "The anthrax attacks were a big one-two punch."

Within the top circles of government, the anthrax threats were part of a endless treadmill of hazards. Just days after the anthrax letters surfaced, the biohazard detectors went off at the White House and the suspicious substance that triggered the alert initially tested positive for botulinum toxin. The FBI injected the substance into lab mice. If they died within twenty-four hours, the entire White House leadership, including the president, might face similar consequences. A tense day passed until Condoleezza Rice was able to report good news to President Bush: "Feet down, not feet up."

In the meantime, Mueller was still trying to adjust to his role as the leader of an enormous bureaucracy and investigative machine.

Late at night, a few days after the attack, Mueller called in to SIOC for a final update before sleep overtook him.

"This is Bob Mueller," he told the woman answering the SIOC operations line.

"Who?"

"Bob Mueller—I'm the new director. Who's in charge?" he asked, meaning who was the SIOC duty officer for the night shift.

There was a long pause. "Well, sir, you are."

John O'Neill's body was recovered ten days after 9/11. Firefighters and rescue workers found him under twelve feet of debris in the South Tower. They later estimated that he had made it to or near his office on the thirty-fourth floor in the final moments before the tower fell. A week later, on September 28, much of his hometown of Atlantic City turned out for the funeral service. An army helicopter provided a fly-over; a bagpiper played "God Bless America"; Louis Freeh, Fran Townsend, and dozens of other government officials filled the pews of St. Nicholas of Tolentine Church. The FBI's Jim Kallstrom, who had led the New York Special Operations Division during the Pizza Connection and later rose to head the field office before Barry Mawn, eulogized O'Neill. He told the overflow crowd, "When it came to fighting terrorism, John was the FBI. And John knew all too well what the general public knows today: We are at war with evil."

Special Agent James Davis, who worked in Chicago with O'Neill, recalls looking around the church, packed with hundreds of law enforcement personnel listening to the closing notes of "Danny Boy," wrapping up a two-and-a-half-hour funeral that was half memorial and half over-the-top production. "I remember thinking, 'This would have been okay with John,'" Davis recalls. "It was a big event, which was exactly what John needed." After the service, the lengthy funeral procession set off for Holy Cross Cemetery with more than a dozen police motorcycles leading the way.*

---

* There's a certain irony in the post-9/11 lionization of O'Neill by the Bureau; in death, he's much more popular than he ever was in life, especially among the FBI executive leadership. His hard-charging nature and relentless pressure had alien-

★   ★   ★

In the wake of the attacks, Vice President Cheney, an almost unparalleled expert in government's levers—he'd previously served as White House chief of staff, congressman, and defense secretary—saw an opportunity to advance his long-held views on executive power. Cheney believed the presidency had been weakened in recent decades by an unwillingness to pursue unitary government action—a mistake he wouldn't allow the Bush administration to make. President Bush could do whatever he wanted to protect the nation, Cheney believed. "He had a single-minded objective in black and white—that American security was paramount to everything," Colin Powell's chief of staff, Lawrence Wilkerson, explained to *The New Yorker*'s Jane Mayer. "He was willing to corrupt the whole country to save it." While the theories and practices that came out of 9/11 were largely of Cheney's making, and that of his lawyer, David Addington, three other key factors contributed to Cheney's ability to push his agenda forward.

First was a group of politically appointed lawyers in key positions, primarily Jim Haynes, the general counsel at the Pentagon, and Jay Bybee and John Yoo at Justice's Office of Legal Counsel (OLC). Before the Bush administration, the OLC had been a little-known group that provided legal opinions to the rest of government. If OLC signed off on a policy or action, it was nearly impossible to prosecute someone later on for following that advice—and likewise, if OLC disallowed or blocked something, it was nearly impossible to move

---

ated many colleagues. "John was the most hated guy in New York right up until his death. Then pictures of him went everywhere," one I-49 agent recalls. In 2006, the FBI named its first overseas forward staging area (FSA) for O'Neill. The program, started after 9/11, was meant to ease the FBI's increasingly regular overseas deployments by locating important investigative tools, including everything from forensic gear to power generators to trauma packs, close to where agents might need them. The first FSA, at Ramstein Air Force Base in Germany, was also where O'Neill's team had interviewed survivors of the USS *Cole* bombing. At the dedication of the Ramstein FSA, former New York supervisor Chuck Frahm recalled that O'Neill "had a presence like no other." A second FSA facility, in Guam, to handle Pacific Rim deployments, was named for Lennie Hatton, the New York bomb tech killed on 9/11.

forward. Jack Goldsmith, who took over OLC after Bybee, described an OLC opinion as a "golden shield," a "get-out-of-jail-free card."

At the time of 9/11, OLC was without a head; Bybee wasn't confirmed by the Senate to head the office until November. Thus Yoo, as deputy, was making policy himself, and Yoo was inclined to change the U.S. approach to fighting terrorism dramatically. "For decades, the United States had dealt with terrorism primarily as a crime," he wrote. "In response to previous al-Qaeda attacks, the United States dispatched FBI agents to investigate the 'crime scene' and tried to apprehend terrorist 'suspects.'" That model, he argued, had become worse than irrelevant once al-Qaeda had launched coordinated attacks against the country's financial and government centers. "A return to this state of affairs would be a huge mistake," Yoo believed. "If a nation-state had carried out the same attacks on the same targets, there would have been no question about whether a state of war would have existed." Yoo strongly believed in the political philosophy put forth by Cheney. As journalist Charlie Savage explained, "[Yoo] said Cheney was right: For the commander in chief, everything was permitted."

The second key was George Tenet, a CIA director who was under tremendous pressure to give the White House whatever it wanted and was deeply indebted to President Bush for keeping him in his post. He was by nature disinclined to say no. Propelled forward by a near blood-lust in those under him, above him, and around him, Tenet told the White House what it wanted to hear. Cofer Black, the head of the Agency's Counterterrorism Center, assured the president and the National Security Council in the Situation Room on September 13, "You give us the mission—we can get 'em. When we're through with them, they will have flies walking across their eyeballs." The plan Black and Tenet eventually persuaded the president to approve was unprecedented in scale and scope, effectively giving the CIA carte blanche to detain, kidnap, target, and kill virtually anyone it suspected of having ties to al-Qaeda. It was the exact opposite of the tentative, cautious, safe plans Tenet had backed under the Clinton administration, with the support of Janet Reno and John O'Neill. As Black explained to Congress in September 2002, "All you need to know is that there was a 'before 9/11' and there was an 'after 9/11.' After 9/11, the gloves came off."

The third key was Bob Mueller's view of the role of an FBI director. President Bush was encouraged by Cheney, as well as by aides at Justice and the National Security Council, to abandon the model of terrorism as a law enforcement issue. Putting the CIA at the fore of the U.S. response to terrorism discarded nearly two decades of precedents that favored the FBI and a law enforcement response. Under Robert Mueller, the Bureau was uniquely positioned to allow such a change. He was not a bureaucratic infighter; he was a Marine platoon commander. He took whatever hill he was ordered to take. It wasn't in his nature to argue big-picture strategy. If the president wanted to give the lead to the CIA, that was the commander in chief's prerogative and the FBI would adjust accordingly. As FBI director, Mueller didn't make policy, he executed the policy decided by others. Besides, at the time he had little subject-matter expertise on al-Qaeda and the Bureau's history on the matter. "Coming into it, I wasn't as familiar with al-Qaeda and Osama bin Laden," Mueller recalls.

Over the months following 9/11, Yoo and Bybee not only forever altered the law enforcement response to terrorism, they even undid the rules of war. Discarding two centuries of American legal and military tradition, forgoing binding international treaty commitments, and sidestepping the normal process that would have allowed their views to be challenged, Yoo and Bybee, along with Jim Haynes at the Pentagon, crafted a sloppy legal foundation for the new approach. Whereas during the Clinton administration many of the players on the National Security Council (including the president) had a legal background, the upper ranks of the Bush administration were surprisingly devoid of lawyers; President Bush, Vice President Cheney, Secretary of State Powell, Secretary of Defense Rumsfeld, National Security Advisor Rice, CIA director Tenet, and White House chief of staff Andy Card all lacked legal training. When Jack Goldsmith took over as OLC head in 2005, he was stunned as he reviewed Bybee's and Yoo's opinions. "It was the biggest legal mess I had ever seen in my life," he said later. But after 9/11, the OLC's pronouncements were enough to give the green light. Underscoring their unique role in crafting the nation's response, the few lawyers involved in the government response—Yoo, Bybee, Haynes, Addington, and White House counsel Alberto Gonzales—eventually christened themselves the War Council.

Within days of 9/11, the Justice Department pulled together a major piece of legislation that would come to redefine the legal war on terror. The Uniting and Strengthening America by Providing Appropriate Tools Required to Intercept and Obstruct Terrorism Act of 2001, more popularly known by its acronym, the USA PATRIOT Act, was based partially on work done in the previous administration by Fran Townsend's office in hopes of updating U.S. surveillance laws and authorities. The bill torpedoed many of the provisions that had existed before 9/11, such as the wall, and cleared the path for much more aggressive terrorism investigations. As Ashcroft explained, "We wanted to err on the side of inclusion."

While Cheney's War Council consolidated power that fall, up in New York, Mary Jo White, whose office had been the driving force in America's pre-9/11 battle against al-Qaeda, decided to step down as U.S. attorney. Jim Comey, the prosecutor who had helped Louis Freeh land an indictment in the Khobar Towers case, was tapped to take over the most important U.S. Attorney's Office in the country.

In many ways, Comey was a natural choice. He'd been a prosecutor in New York under Rudolph Giuliani before moving to private practice in Virginia. However, like Bob Mueller, he remained a prosecutor at heart. In 1996, he gave up being a partner at a top-tier law firm to act as an assistant U.S. attorney in crime-ridden Richmond, launching an innovative antigun program, Project Exile, that federalized gun crimes and sent felons to federal prison rather than state prisons. Backed strongly by Eric Holder, then the deputy attorney general, the program became a national model. (For Comey, gun crimes were personal. When he was a child, a man broke into his house and held him, his brother, and three neighbors hostage at gunpoint.) The New York job put him squarely in the center of the unfolding war on terror and would, over the next five years, put him on a path to being one of the most significant players in the U.S. government.

An oversized presence — six foot eight inches tall and gregarious, with a warm smile — Comey moved to New York in December 2001, ahead of his wife and five children. The night before his first day in the job, he walked over from his temporary apartment to look at Ground Zero, still smoking and lit by powerful floodlights as the round-the-clock operation continued. Then he walked the few blocks uptown to the U.S. attorney's hulking office, lit beautifully at night. "It was strange, amazing, and scary," he recalls.

As Comey settled into the U.S. attorney's suite, he felt the Justice Department's new institutional resistance to his office. "There were a lot of people at all levels of the bureaucracy who thought New York had run the show for too long," he says. The Bush administration's inclination to centralize counterterrorism was fed partly by a sense that New York got to do whatever it wanted—a sentiment that had waxed and waned over the past decade. After Giuliani left office in 1989, the Justice Department tried to rein in the Sovereign District of New York. Mary Jo White, by force of personality and reputation, had swung the pendulum back, gaining enough power for her office to stand institutionally almost as an equal to Main Justice in Washington. Coupled with Freeh's tenure as FBI director—Freeh came from New York, believed in New York, and surrounded himself with New Yorkers like Bob Bucknam—White's position resulted in unprecedented autonomy for New York's prosecutorial and investigative efforts. "Every time Mary Jo threatened to quit, Janet Reno would give her whatever she wanted," one Justice official says. The White House, the Justice Department, and Bob Mueller all wanted to centralize the response to counterterrorism, so the pendulum had swung back to Washington in a big way.

That New York–Washington battle had begun by the time prosecutor David Kelley had talked to Michael Chertoff at noon on 9/11 and they had clashed over who would lead the case. Over the next several days, a serious confrontation developed between the New York Field Office and the Hoover Building in Washington over which would be the 9/11 attack's office of origin. New to the Bureau, Mueller didn't initially understand the "office of origin" concept, known as "the O-O" in Bureau parlance. At the Thirty-fourth Street parking garage, Mueller met with Mawn, Pat D'Amuro, Maxwell, and a few other Washington staffers. The new director laid out why he wanted the office of origin to be Washington. Barry Mawn protested. New York had the expertise; it had the investigative capabilities; it had the files; it had the Ground Zero crime scene; it had been the office of origin for the entire al-Qaeda case thus far. Besides, Mawn and the New York team argued, the Hoover Building intentionally had never been an office of origin on any case in the Bureau's history; it was designed to be filled with support staff and supervisors, not investigators. "Headquarters was never an operational entity," D'Amuro explains. "It was never meant to be." Mueller cut the conversation short. He wasn't going to run counterterrorism over a conference call. "Too bad," he said. "I want to look someone in the eye."

And so it was that the FBI's efforts migrated to Washington. The 9/11 investigation, the highest-profile case the FBI had ever undertaken, would not be run by New York or by either of the al-Qaeda squads, I-49 and I-45, who had spent years chasing bin Laden's organization around the world. Instead, the case went to I-44, a New York domestic terrorism squad, which Mueller transferred whole to Washington. Mary Galligan, who had served one tour as the on-scene commander on the *Cole* case, led the specific squad, but D'Amuro, also transferred to Washington by Mueller, became the Bureau's leader of the entire case. Some of the New York JTTF team—Abby Perkins, among many others—also headed south on Interstate 95 and began to gather together the various threads of the case. Perkins had moved into a new apartment on the West Side just ten days earlier. She had a little balcony and had hosted a few barbecues. She didn't see much more of that place for months.

In a large basement room in the Hoover Building, the PENTTBOM investigators began almost from scratch. The room was enormous and cacophonous, a situation not improved by the large air-conditioning unit that sat in the middle of the space. One night, facilities workers built a little ceiling over the top of Perkins's cubicle so she could concentrate better. The case file was a mess; nearly every piece of paper generated by the FBI was being put into the 9/11 file. There were thousands of leads. While the FBI said publicly that two thousand agents were working the case full-time, realistically just about all other work in the Bureau had stopped. By the end of the investigation, seven thousand of the Bureau's eleven thousand agents would contribute something to PENTTBOM. Agents spent days culling through massive amounts of unorganized information, determining what was good and what was bad. "Everything was getting dumped in without any vetting," Perkins recalls. "Why exactly is this in the file?"

When Mueller told the New York leadership he wanted to be able to touch the counterterrorism program, they didn't realize that he had a penchant for seeking information outside the normal channels. "He wanted it right there at his disposal. He wanted to hold it, touch it, feel it," D'Amuro recalls. One Saturday, Mueller was wandering the halls and accosted a passing supervisor with a question about a possible threat; the agent provided the best information he had, which, as it turned out, was incomplete. Then, worked up over the threat, Mueller called D'Amuro. The frustrated New York agent chastised his boss. "You've got to stop wandering around and asking about things until they're analyzed and ready to be presented."

Mueller, somewhat chagrined, understood. "You're not going to kill the supervisor, are you?"

"I'm not sure yet," the exasperated New York agent replied.

Mueller's ceaseless devotion was simultaneously exhausting and inspiring. For him, every day was a workday. Six weeks after 9/11, D'Amuro, who hadn't been home since the attack, began one briefing by playing over the conference room sound system the Christmas song "I'll Be Home for Christmas." Mueller, deadpan, fixed the agent with one of his steely looks and said, "I did say you'll be home for Christmas. I just didn't specify which year."

After a decade of Freeh's doing whatever he could to dismantle or disable the headquarters bureaucracy and empower the field offices, Mueller now had to work hard (and quickly) to centralize information and decision-making at the Hoover Building. A street agent at heart, Freeh had never fully trusted headquarters and had decimated its staff in two major purges, in one of which he promised headquarters staff three years at their current salary if they moved back to the field. Hundreds had taken the transfer, leaving headquarters with as many as six hundred fewer personnel, out of some two thousand. Freeh had eliminated entire layers of supervisors. One headquarters Bureau official recalls Freeh's staff at one meeting saying, "We're the FBI—Federal Bureau of Investigation—not the FBA—Federal Bureau of Administration." (The operational impact of the severe purges became evident when the FBI Lab, also decimated by the administrative cuts, came under intense scrutiny for a series of screw-ups at the end of Freeh's tenure.)

Now Mueller began to reverse the anti-Washington trend. In reality, much of the centralization was probably needed—the field offices had too often operated as their own independent fiefdoms, with the SACs presiding over their territory like dukes — but Mueller's approach rocked the fifty-six field office heads, who had worked their entire Bureau careers to become SACs, with all the post's historic prerogatives. Focusing on headquarters better reflected the new paradigm for terror, Mueller argued. Washington had the responsibility for coordinating with other agencies, tapping into the military structure, liaisoning with the White House — all vital parts of the new war on terror. "My thinking," Mueller explains, "was shaped by previous Bureau incidents, mainly Ruby Ridge and Waco, when I think excessive deference was shown to SACs in the field to handle situations that could easily explode."

The office-of-origin model made no sense in a global, national fight, Mueller believed. The Phoenix EC, which Mueller called an "impressive piece of analysis," had come into headquarters, where people looked at it, noted that it concerned al-Qaeda, and passed it on to New York, washing their hands of it in the process. Headquarters needed to take ownership. As he says, "I saw it as the Bureau relying on a single field office to handle something that was much larger. It would have been wrong of me to tell the assistant director in New York that he was responsible for protecting the whole country," adding, with a rare impish grin, "even though he probably would have liked that."

Instead of favoring New York, Mueller actually went to the Bureau's opposite faction: a West Coaster. In February 2002, two months after Tom Pickard had retired as Mueller's deputy, the new FBI director summoned as his new number two Bruce Gebhardt, the head of the San Francisco Field Office, whom he'd come to know while U.S. attorney. Gebhardt had a good reputation in the Bureau; he was energetic, talkative, and animated, everything Mueller wasn't. Besides, few agents had had as close a personal encounter with terrorism as Gebhardt. On Easter Sunday 1976, just four years after his father commanded the FBI response to Southern Airways Flight 49, the young Special Agent Gebhardt responded to a hijacking in progress at the Denver Airport ("I knew exactly what I was going to be doing," he recalls, "I grabbed my pen and paper and prepared to interview witnesses"), only to find himself thrust into the center of the action. The mentally disturbed hijacker, who had taken two hostages, demanded a larger plane to effect his getaway; Gebhardt and his partner were put aboard the second jet in case the FBI sniper couldn't nail the hijacker as he changed planes. "Neutralize him if he gets to you," the supervisor told him. When the hijacker boarded, after hiding between his hostages to keep the sniper at bay, Gebhardt and his partner rose from their hiding place in the fifth row of the passenger cabin and opened fire from feet away. The hijacker was killed; both hostages lived.

Gebhardt had never been through the Sovereign District of New York. Neither had Mueller. Neither cared. The era of New York was over. Mueller was under tremendous pressure and wasn't much concerned with whose apple carts he upset. As one agent explains, "[Mueller] didn't know Bureau culture very well. He thought headquarters runs things and tells the field what to do. Actually, the field runs things and tells headquarters what it needs. He was the liaison for the field." Mueller did, however, realize that someone needed to make the case for reform to the agent corps. That role would be Gebhardt's. As the San Francisco agent explains, "My responsibility was to help Bob change the FBI, change the way the FBI was thinking. SACs would listen to me. I was an inspector. My dad was FBI. I was a generalist." In a matter of weeks, Gebhardt went from being an SAC to being the highest-ranking agent in the Bureau, the acting director when Mueller went out of town, and the man who filled in for the director at the morning Oval Office briefings.

In picking Gebhardt, Mueller passed over two FBI executives who had extensive terrorism experience, SCOTBOM's Dick Marquise, who then was SAC of the Oklahoma City Field Office, and TRADE-BOM's Neil Gallagher, who was then the assistant director of the Counterintelligence Division. Aides say they suspect part of Mueller's calculation in picking Gebhardt was precisely that Gebhardt, as SAC in Phoenix and San Francisco, had been reluctant to dedicate resources to counterterrorism. He became a believer only after 9/11—a late-blooming mind-set, aides theorize, that Mueller thought would help Gebhardt sell the changes to the larger Bureau.★

Indeed, change wouldn't be easy. Many agents and executives

★ Other agents from Mueller's time in San Francisco followed Gebhardt to senior positions at headquarters, including Larry Mefford, Grant Ashley, and others—

weren't even convinced that the FBI needed to change. They were proud of the FBI's record. But as Gebhardt says, "Just because we were hardest-working, had the highest standards, longest-working law enforcement agency didn't mean we were heading in the right direction."

The failure to act on and explore further the Phoenix memo pointed out another of the Bureau's shortcomings: its inadequate analytic capability. For decades, the Bureau's dirty little personnel secret was that analysts were at best second-class citizens. The FBI was the inverse of the CIA, which was staffed mostly by analysts and had only a small core of operatives. Agents are the core of the FBI, and are taught from Quantico onward that they can solve any case with just a badge, a notebook, handcuffs, and a gun. (One FBI joke had it that there were two kinds of people in the Bureau, agents and furniture.) Analysts were mostly an afterthought in Bureau culture. Whereas special agent trainees spent months at the rigorous Quantico academy, analysts received no special training and were expected to seek out training from other agencies or ad hoc FBI Academy programs on their own.

On many squads, analysts were at best glorified file clerks, the replacements for the "rotor girls" of a past generation. Gebhardt recalls the reigning philosophy when he arrived at headquarters: "It was a joke: Take a rotor clerk, give him or her a two-step grade promotion, and boom, you've got an analyst." With a few notable exceptions, such as Fred Stremmel, who had made counterterrorism analysis a career for more than two decades, ever since he was assigned to study possible Libyan assassin teams in the early 1980s, being an analyst was seen internally as a job for wannabe agents. "There was constant pressure: 'When are you going to apply to be an agent?'" one former analyst explains.

Being an FBI analyst was a thankless job, and the retention statistics reflected that. In 1996, for instance, the FBI hired thirty-six new analysts to work international terrorism. Within a year, half had quit, transferred, or been reassigned. The analyst corps continued to fall through the 1990s, even as the al-Qaeda threat grew. As the system

---

enough that behind their backs they became known as the San Francisco mafia at the Hoover Building.

geared up for millennium threats in 1999, just fifteen strategic intelligence analysts were doing counterterrorism at the FBI. A year later, when the USS *Cole* was attacked, there were just ten. When the Phoenix memo arrived at the bin Laden unit, there was no analyst assigned there to review it.

Of course, agencies such as the CIA and the NSA hadn't offered much in the way of pre-9/11 intelligence either. Indeed, there wasn't a single human source in al-Qaeda before the attacks, and in fact, both of the top al-Qaeda defectors, Junior al-Fadl and Joe the Moroccan, were informants for the FBI. "The CIA had all the latest and greatest [technology], but not a lot of information to move around," Pickard recalls. "The FBI was choking on information, but we couldn't move it around."

Through Mueller's force of personality and skill in riding the Bush administration's post-9/11 wave, the FBI evolved and changed more quickly in the coming months than it had in any period since J. Edgar Hoover's funeral. "No one expected the FBI to change as fast as it did," one agent said in 2003.

After the attacks, President Bush ordered the Office of Personnel Management to allow federal law enforcement officials who had retired in good standing in the months before 9/11 to return to service with their security clearances intact. Mueller, alone among the heads of the major law enforcement and intelligence agencies, refused to institute the order, saying in effect thanks, but no thanks. "It accelerated his ability to purge the Kremlin," one executive explained. This was going to be a new era for the FBI.

There's the old saying about how for want of a nail the kingdom was lost. Mueller, as a platoon commander, had seen the way that tiny details came to affect large events. He was not inclined to leave things to chance. He wanted to run the FBI his way. Though Mueller's organizational preferences dovetailed with the Bush administration's vision of strong executive power, they also reflected his instincts as a leader. He would command, and he would do so with relentless focus. Says Lisa Monaco, who spent years as Mueller's chief of staff, "He started each day for almost ten years now with two hours of briefings on terrorism. The organization responds to that."

As one agent put it, "The Muellerization of the Bureau had begun."

CHAPTER 10
The Dogs of War

Cry "Havoc," and let slip the dogs of war.
— *William Shakespeare,*
Julius Caesar, *Act III, Scene 1*

The pile of rubble that once was the World Trade Center still smoldered. U.S. forces were readying for the push into Afghanistan. Yet some 8,650 miles away from Ground Zero, the FBI had some unfinished business to wrap up first.

On September 28, 2001, Special Agent Brad Deardorff was standing on the tarmac in Bangkok, anxiously trying to figure out a Plan B as Zayd Hassan Abd Al-Latif Masud al-Safarini came down the airplane stairs. Deardorff's plan had gone awry; he had hoped to hustle al-Safarini off before other passengers deplaned. Now his suspect, wanted by the United States for the 1986 hijacking of Pan Am Flight 73, was mixed in with everyone else. Other agents were waiting nearby, including Hostage Rescue Team operators, but only Deardorff had seen the suspect before. They'd met face-to-face while al-Safarini was serving his jail sentence in Pakistan for the Karachi hijacking. As the passengers loaded onto buses for transport to the terminal, Deardorff ran from bus to bus, hunting. Finally he spotted his guy. "Bomer!" he called out, using the hijacker's nickname.

Al-Safarini's heart sank as, hearing his name, he turned and his eyes zeroed in on the FBI agent. He'd just been released after the lengthy Pakistan jail sentence and was now on his way back to Jordan and, in theory, freedom. The moment he saw Deardorff, though, he knew theory wasn't going to match fact.

A longtime veteran of the counterterrorism squads from the Washington Field Office, Deardorff had gotten so accustomed to unexpected overseas trips that whenever he was back in Washington he kept a suitcase with two weeks' worth of clothing in his car trunk. A onetime Marine who had done a tour in Somalia, he had been taken as an FBI agent from Yemen to Bosnia to Indonesia, where he'd worked one case that required a journey deep into the jungle to a tribe that still hunted wild pigs with poisoned darts. Ever since the U.S. government had heard that al-Safarini would soon be free, he had been spending three or four months at a stretch wandering in the nether regions of India and Pakistan, putting together the 1986 hijacking case.

Now, aboard the crowded bus en route to the Bangkok terminal, al-Safarini thought briefly about fleeing, but he realized it would be pointless. Instead, he inhaled a final free breath and proceeded toward the FBI agent. "I told you I'd see you again," Deardorff said, his cold eyes betraying a little twinkle of pleasure.

Other agents approached, and while the hot Bangkok sun hung overhead—temperatures for the day were close to a record high—they fingerprinted al-Safarini to triple-check that they had the right guy. They had his visual identification, a verbal response to his own name, and now fingerprints. When conducting a rendition overseas, you had to be absolutely sure you were correct.

Deardorff and the FBI team hustled al-Safarini across the airport to a U.S. government plane. "I don't want our work to be negatively impacted by the way this guy is handled," Deardorff told the flight crew taking the terrorist back to the States. The trip east was civilized and pleasant; it bore little resemblance to the CIA "ghost planes" renditions that would become famous in the coming years. For the flight, al-Safarini was shackled to the seat, but he talked, smiled, and laughed with Deardorff and the other agents throughout the flight. He read a *Maxim* magazine, ate a Snickers bar, and drank a cup of coffee. He appeared in court the following Monday in Anchorage, Alaska, where a judge found cause to hold him pending trial; then he was transported to Washington, D.C., where he pleaded not guilty to the hijacking charges. After the court proceedings had worked through, he was sentenced to 160 years in prison at the federal supermax facility in Florence, Colorado.

As the months passed, Deardorff developed a close relationship with the terrorist—one that provided reams of intelligence on groups and support networks in Pakistan. "To elicit the best information you have to think strategically. In college terms, do you want a relationship or do you want immediate gratification? In these complex cases, it's the courtship. It's about getting him to answer, 'What else do you know?'" Deardorff explains. "When you walk in and hand someone a warm cup of coffee, there's the opportunity to seem fair, like you're there to hear their story. In most cases, I want them to tell me their stories."

Even as Deardorff was seeing al-Safarini through the U.S. court arraignments, though, the CIA was carving a different path. The Bureau and the Agency, as it turned out, had radically different approaches to terrorist interrogations. On October 23, 2001, three weeks after al-Safarini appeared in a Washington courtroom, a Gulfstream V executive jet, tail number N379P, landed in a dark corner of the Karachi airport shortly after 1 A.M. The plane was registered to Premier Executive Transport Services Inc., a company that didn't have an office anywhere and was headed by four fake directors. Indeed, Premier Executive Transport Services, Inc., was nothing more than a series of post office boxes and phony Social Security numbers, its true management located in Langley. Within ninety minutes, the black-clad, muscular men who had disembarked returned, dragging a hooded man whose hands and feet were shackled. Jamil Qasim Saeed Mohammed, a Yemeni microbiologist wanted in connection with the bombing of the USS Cole, was on his way not to a U.S. court of law, cup of coffee in hand, but to Jordan. He has not been heard from since.

The two flights perfectly capture the post-9/11 American response to stopping terrorism. Both Mohammed's and al-Safarini's journeys started in Pakistan; one was supposed to end in Jordan, the other actually did. Both men were terrorist suspects accused of killing Americans before 9/11. Both men were ushered aboard private U.S. jets. Arguably the story didn't end happily for either terrorist—al-Sarafini will never breathe free air again—but the two tales paint two very different portraits of America's moral compass. Over the coming months, the CIA and the FBI would see their visions of how to pursue the war on terror diverge, in a schism that began with these two flights. In the wake of the terrorist attacks, the FBI tried hard to continue to operate in the light, under the long-established constitutional procedures created during a generation of fighting terrorism; the CIA, in contrast, came to operate in the literal shadows—the "dark side" as Dick Cheney called it—under a new paradigm in which it answered to no one.

As difficult as it was for Bob Mueller to be thrown into the deep end of terrorism on his second week in the job, the FBI was incredibly lucky to have him arrive when he did. By starting a week before the attacks, Mueller couldn't be blamed for the failings that preceded him, whereas longtime CIA director George Tenet found himself on the defensive for years afterward. Mueller's job was never really at risk.* The FBI had a continuity of leadership through the period of turmoil, controversy, and recriminations that followed.

In the wake of 9/11, the FBI was handed what many call an impossible task: developing a new domestic intelligence and counterterrorism capability that misses nothing while keeping all of its criminal capabilities first-rate—without inconveniencing innocent U.S. citizens, committing racial profiling, or violating any civil rights. "I don't believe the job we've given Bob Mueller is really doable, so I don't know how you measure his progress along the way," says Brookings Institution scholar Ben Wittes, perhaps the nation's keenest observer of the legal regime of the war on terror. "One way to look at this would be, 'Who would have done a better job?' and I think that the answer is no one."

---

*In the only mainstream call for Mueller's head, the *Wall Street Journal* demanded Mueller's resignation in May 2002, after the FBI director announced his first major post-9/11 round of Bureau reforms. The paper said the new procedures didn't go far enough to addressing the FBI's myriad failures and were merely the equivalent of rearranging "bureaucratic furniture." The *Journal*'s editorial was widely repudiated, even by the FBI Agents Association, not normally a friend of any director.

344 • GARRETT M. GRAFF

As 2002 dawned, Bob Mueller found himself engaged in four major fights: an outward-facing battle against a shadowy and unfamiliar foe, a hidden battle deep within the secure secret conference rooms of government, a public battle playing out in the press and on Capitol Hill, and an internal fight in the Bureau. All this he faced in a city and a political environment that struggle to deal with more than one issue at once.

First and foremost was the pull-out-all-the-stops, full-speed-ahead war on terror. In the weeks after 9/11, Mueller's mornings began earlier and earlier. The FBI, and much of the government, began to revolve around the "Threat Matrix," a spreadsheet prepared daily to track all the unfolding terrorist plots and intelligence rumors. The matrix defined agents' and executives' lives. Most of the information was junk, but there was no incentive in the system to downplay a threat. No one wanted to dismiss a possible danger; no one wanted to be "that guy," the one who failed to follow up appropriately, the one who watched a terrorist plot play out on TV and realized that something could have been done to stop it—or, almost as bad, that some appropriate higher-up hadn't been informed at all. Claims that ordinarily wouldn't have made it past the intake agent, claims that wouldn't even have been written down weeks earlier, were suddenly the subject of briefs to the president of the United States in the Oval Office. The never-ending stream of threats had a profound effect on the thinking of government leaders in the weeks and months after 9/11.

Jim Baker, who took over the Justice Department's Office of Intelligence Policy and Review from Fran Townsend, said the daily cacophony was "like being stuck in a room listening to loud Led Zeppelin music." Yet even that was a simplification. A more accurate simile would have been sitting in a room listening simultaneously to a hundred records, each played at maximum volume, and attempting to pick out the bass line from a single song. "At each session, we went over the next day's matrix, recognizing that many, perhaps most, of the threats contained in it were bogus. We just didn't know which ones," George Tenet recalled. "You could drive yourself crazy believing all of or even half of what was in it."

That first battle—the war on terror's Threat Matrix—led directly to the second fight. In the coming weeks, the United States would prove that the most powerful fighting force in the history of man could seize Afghanistan with ease—pounding it from miles above with heavy bombers, leveling targets with missiles fired hundreds of miles away, and sweeping across the ground with both unstoppable armored convoys and elite special forces on horseback. Traditional military victory was never in question. But the terrorists' battlefield is essentially metaphysical; terrorism exists to terrorize. A terrorist hopes to cause the target to overreact in a way that undermines its legitimacy and authority, and this provides a moral victory. In this regard, al-Qaeda had already triumphed. Reviewing the daily Threat Matrix, filled to the brim with whispers, rumors, and vacuous, unconfirmed information, became all-consuming and paralyzing, a seeming tidal wave of Islamic extremist anger that threatened to unhinge American society and Western democracies.

Mueller believed that the United States had a relatively well tested system for responding to terror. Vice President Cheney thought that the United States needed to throw out the rulebook. Just five days after 9/11, he'd given an interview to Tim Russert on *Meet the Press* during which he explained that the U.S. response to the attacks would involve a break with tradition. "We also have to work, though, sort of the dark side, if you will. We've got to spend time in the shadows in the intelligence world," he said coldly. "A lot of what needs to be done here will have to be done quietly, without any discussion, using sources and methods that are available to our intelligence agencies, if we're going to be successful. That's the world these folks operate in, and so it's going to be vital for us to use any means at our disposal, basically, to achieve our objective." Later that fall, in a briefing by Tenet discussing the danger of a nuclear-armed al-Qaeda, Cheney clarified his position further, elucidating for the first time what came to be known as his "one percent doctrine," which held that the U.S. response must be decisive regardless of truth and certainty. "If there's a one percent chance that Pakistani scientists are helping al-Qaeda build or develop a nuclear weapon, we have to treat it as a certainty in terms of our response. It's not about our analysis," the vice president said. "It's about our response." Years of precedent, codified under President Clinton, were to be discarded.

Over the coming months, it became clear to Mueller and others within the Justice Department that Cheney's rules meant playing fast and loose with some of the traditional constitutional restraints—restraints beaten into the Bureau in scandals like COINTELPRO and CISPES. In the decade before 9/11, Louis Freeh had drilled into the Bureau's staff seven core FBI values. First and foremost was "rigorous obedience to the Constitution of the United States."* Freeh had also pushed the idea that agents should have a moral compass beyond just "legal orders." Beginning under his tenure, each class of agents in training spent a day at the Holocaust Museum in Washington, a trip meant to underscore what can happen when law enforcement is corrupted as well as the value of questioning what are thought to be illegal orders. Simply following orders, they were taught, was no excuse for immoral or illegal behavior.

The constitutional tensions between the Bureau, the CIA, and Vice President Cheney would take years to surface publicly, for they involved the most sensitive, compartmentalized operations in the government. The destinations of those two flights, Mohammed's to Jordan and al-Safarini's to a U.S. courtroom, were emblematic of what would become a secret war within Washington.

Mueller's third battle was more public: He found himself fighting for the survival of the Bureau. Many in Congress and elsewhere in Washington were calling for the FBI to be stripped of its intelligence component. A better model, they argued, was found in Canada or Britain, each of which had split its domestic responsibilities between a law enforcement agency, beholden to the rule of law, evidence, and open operations, and a secret domestic intelligence agency, free to avoid the courtrooms and do more aggressive eavesdropping.† The FBI, almost alone among the agencies of Western democracies, had inhabited both realms, one side of the house handling counterintelli-

---

*The other six core values instituted by Freeh were "respect for the dignity of all those we protect; compassion; fairness; uncompromising personal integrity and institutional integrity; accountability by accepting responsibility for our actions and decisions and the consequences of our actions and decisions; and leadership, both personal and professional."

†Canada split its domestic security between the Royal Canadian Mounted Police and the Canadian Security Intelligence Service (CSIS); Britain had both New Scotland Yard and MI5.

gence, tracking spies and saboteurs, focusing on disruption, and expelling threats from the country without prosecution; the other side handling the traditional criminal matters that would end in a courtroom. The evolution of terrorism from state-sponsored to independent actors meant that counterterrorism had long occupied a niche in between the two. Now many publicly argued that the Bureau couldn't oversee both roles—that it needed to be carved up. Mueller, though, saw any attempt to split the Bureau's criminal and counterintelligence missions as an admission that American democracy couldn't be protected within the bounds of the Constitution—a premise he rejected outright. Domestic intelligence, Mueller believed, should report to an attorney general, a lawyer grounded in constitutional procedure, rather than an intelligence czar.

Mueller's fourth battle was within, to evolve the Bureau's culture, refocusing on terrorism and refocusing investigative techniques, creating a new emphasis on analysis, developing a "forward-leaning" operation, as well as rebuilding the anemic technological infrastructure. His success in this fourth arena would have a lot to do with whether Congress agreed to strip the Bureau of its intelligence responsibilities. Sure, Mueller didn't want to go down as the FBI director who had the Bureau carved up under him, but beyond that, he felt the Bureau was capable of evolving and adopting a new outlook. For seventy years, the FBI had adapted to fight the new Public Enemy #1, whoever and whatever that had been. It could manage this too. Any one of these battles would have been enough to fill his days. If Mueller managed to navigate all four at once, make progress, and come out the other side, he would be the most consequential director since J. Edgar Hoover.

Mueller had been under fire before and come out the other side. In fact, when he sat in the Oval Office during the early morning terrorism briefings, he was often the only one in the room who'd been through combat himself—the only one who had ever faced an enemy and fired a weapon in hostile action, the only one with a Purple Heart, the only one who had bled for his country. George W. Bush hadn't. Dick Cheney hadn't. Donald Rumsfeld hadn't. George Tenet hadn't. Condi Rice hadn't. John Ashcroft hadn't. Andy Card hadn't. Alberto Gonzales hadn't. In the threat briefings, only one other participant had ever served in combat, Homeland Security Adviser Tom Ridge.* If the nation and the Bureau were at war, well, Bob Mueller was a warrior, and his fronts would be many.

President Bush's November 13, 2001, order, "Detention, Treatment, and Trial of Certain Non-Citizens in the War Against Terrorism," was, depending on one's viewpoint, either a terribly crafted or a perfectly written document. Filled with ambiguity and as broad as the Potomac River, the order had no checks, balances, or safeguards. It effectively meant that the Department of Defense could do whatever it wanted. How that would play out on the ground became one of the defining battles of the post-9/11 world. The first question posed by the president's order was where prisoners captured in the war on terror would go. To the interagency group studying the question, it was clear that the continental United States — "CONUS" in military and Bureau parlance — was out of the question for political reasons, even before it was ruled out on legal grounds. During the brainstorming sessions, it was someone from the Department of Justice who first said, "What about Guantánamo?" The military base on the southeastern tip of Cuba seemed to fit Secretary Rumsfeld's condition of "the legal equivalent of outer space" perfectly. About two thirds the size of the District of Columbia, Guantánamo was separated from the Cuban nation by miles of fence, barbed wire, and, on the Cuban side, a minefield. It was the modern-day equivalent of Alcatraz, the twenty-first century's inescapable "rock." The oldest overseas base in the U.S. military, leased from the Cuban government in near perpetuity for about $4,000 annually (not that Castro had cashed a rent check in decades), Guantánamo Bay had twice served in the past decade as a legal no-man's-land. During crises in Haiti and Cuba, tens of thousands of fleeing Haitians and Cubans picked up at sea by the U.S. Navy and the U.S. Coast Guard had lived for extended periods of time on the base in "migrant" camps (the Defense Department had gone out of its way to ensure that

---

* Secretary of State Powell, who was part of the National Security Council but not generally part of the morning threat meetings, also served in the military with distinction.

they were called "migrants" rather than "refugees" to limit their legal options in the United States). One of the camps, which had been named using NATO's phonetic alphabet as Alpha, Bravo, Charlie, and so on, had been designated for the migrants who had a violent streak, the criminals: Camp X-Ray. Its forty open-air fenced pens still stood on a corner of the sprawling fifty-four-square-mile base.

The military announced on December 27, 2001, two days after Christmas, that the first detainees from the battlefields in Afghanistan would arrive at "Gitmo" within weeks. Air Force General Richard B. Myers said the first wave would include eight detainees from the USS *Peleliu* and thirty-seven more from the "high-value detainee" camp near the Kandahar airport. The following day, the Justice Department's Office of Legal Counsel filed an opinion providing the legal underpinning for the camp: Deputy Assistant Attorneys General Patrick Philbin and John Yoo wrote that Gitmo was outside of the purview of U.S. courts. Ten days later, on January 8, 2002, Robert Mueller's high school classmate Will Taft, the general counsel of the State Department, walked out of a White House briefing on the rules of Guantánamo and turned to his aides: "We've got trouble." Thereafter, Taft's team tried to explain that the White House's approach was "seriously flawed," "incorrect," and "fundamentally inaccurate." No one cared. Guantánamo, as Donald Rumsfeld said in his December 27 announcement, was the "least worst place." Within weeks at the base, as the first detainees settled into the "dog cages" you could buy a "Least Worst Place" T-shirt at the PX near Camp X-Ray.

As the debate over detainees began to play out in the halls of Washington and U.S. troops surged into Afghanistan, the Pentagon asked Mueller to dispatch a team of FBI agents to the battlefield. First into the battle for the Bureau would be Tom Knowles, the former Athens legat who had led the Bureau's international operations until his falling-out with Louis Freeh. On Saturday, December 1, just weeks after the first Special Operations forces had parachuted into Afghanistan, Knowles got the call. As Pat D'Amuro recalls, "There was going to be a tremendous amount of intelligence out of the war. When a site is cleared, we need to be there. We want that pocket litter, that stuff coming out of the caves."

For a gung-ho FBI agent like Knowles, it was a dream assignment, the chance to go right into the terrorists' lair even while Ground Zero was still smoking. Knowles had worked for John O'Neill on the first rumblings of Islamic extremism a decade before; now he'd be involved in cutting off the head of the snake. Hanging up the phone, Knowles joked to himself, "Either they really liked my international experience or they really want me dead." Less than a year after being iced out of headquarters, he was back in the game.

The following Monday, he met with Dale Watson and Mike Rolince at the Hoover Building. Watson asked, "So what are you going to do?" Knowles said he was hoping the two counterterrorism executives would tell him that. "At this stage, we don't know why we're going," the executives told Knowles. "We just know the military wants us there."

Within forty-eight hours, Knowles was in Tampa, Florida, the U.S. headquarters of Central Command, the military's Middle East force. Special forces raids in Afghanistan, he learned, were uncovering large caches of documents and rounding up scores of possible al-Qaeda and Taliban members. The people needed to be processed and the documents translated and read, but in order to preserve the possibility of prosecution, the military needed someone to take custody and assume responsibility for the relevant evidence, as the special forces operators couldn't risk having to appear in court down the road. It was the same conundrum that two decades earlier had led to the creation of the Hostage Rescue Team so that Delta Force would not be used for domestic situations.

The director's initial plans for a fifty-person team were quickly scaled back as everyone realized the complexity of deploying to a war zone. Knowles pulled together, with the help of Rolince and Watson, a group of eight: Steve Bongardt and George Crouch from the New York al-Qaeda squads, two other investigators, two HRT operators, and a radio tech. Everyone on the team was ex-military.

On December 8, one week after getting the call, the team was at Andrews Air Force Base with some thirty cases of equipment plus as much personal gear as each person could carry. The men looked like they were going on the ultimate camping trip: They had the best sleeping bags, winter clothing, and gadgets that the Bureau could procure. But no one had told the air force. The loadmaster looked at his list and up at the team and said, "You're not on the manifest." Knowles's eyes went wide. Besides, the loadmaster asked, why on earth was the FBI going to Afghanistan? Didn't it know there was a war on? Eventually, with the help of offering the loadmaster a souvenir FBI hat, Knowles convinced him to let them aboard.

Their first stop was the then-secret location of Central Command Forward, the military's in-theater operations base at Doha, Qatar. Sitting in the darkened video conferencing center, Knowles began to get a picture of what the FBI was getting into. He heard that the high-value detainee site was being set up outside Kandahar. The FBI agents had planned to go to Kabul, but Knowles redirected them to the new detainee facility. After a stop in Pakistan, an Agency plane ferried the FBI team under the cover of night into Kandahar. Bongardt walked off the plane and took his first look at the darkened landscape: After working al-Qaeda for so long, it was hard to believe that the Bureau was finally here, right in the terrorists' backyard.

The runway in Kandahar was still under construction by the Seabees; American bombers had besieged the airport in the weeks before, and now that it was in coalition hands, construction crews were busy undoing all the work done by the bombs. The team slept inside the airport terminal on the first night. When Bongardt awoke at dawn, he asked a soldier where the bathrooms were. Just go outside by the cylinder cans, he was told. Minutes later, unaware of the surroundings, Bongardt found himself some fifty yards inside an uncleared minefield. He'd missed the turn for the latrine. *This is how I'm going to die,* he thought. *Taking a piss on my first morning in Afghanistan.*

Knowles gathered the team on the tarmac for an orientation meeting. Along the horizon, the high peaks of Afghanistan stretched away toward the sky. It was crystal-clear. As he began to speak, the mountains in the distance erupted as a B-52 mission targeted Taliban positions; the carpet-bombing knocked out a mile or two of ridgetop in a series of earth-shaking blasts. The explosions mounted toward the sky as the delayed sound rumbled across the valley toward the airport. Knowles's team watched in awe, reliving a moment familiar to U.S. troops for half a century as the giant, four-engine flying bomb bay emptied tons of high-explosive ordnance.

"Maybe we should go inside," Knowles said finally.

Knowles's team had landed right in the heart of the command of General Jim "Mad Dog" Mattis, a fierce and intimidating leader who was overseeing the deepest land invasion by Marine forces in history. The first Marine ever to command a naval task force, he adopted for his command motto the self-chosen epitaph of the Roman dictator Sulla: "No better friend, no worse enemy."* Knowles's first impression was that the guy probably ate nails for breakfast. In their initial conversation, Mad Dog Mattis expressed skepticism about the FBI's role on his battlefield ("We don't need a bunch of cops," he professed). Knowles replied, "General, you can't kill 'em all. We've got to make sure that the ones you can't kill we still get off the streets." The general held the agent's gaze for a long moment, then laughed before gruffly switching subjects: "You're a cop. Can you build a jail?" The high-value detainee detention center they'd come to see, it turned out, didn't exist.

Mattis had been told to prepare for a half-dozen prisoners; Central Command had told Knowles two hundred to three hundred. All anyone heard was that the Afghan-led Northern Alliance forces were rounding up hundreds and thousands of prisoners on the battlefield and selling them for bounties to the United States.

The FBI team settled into what was once a rental car bay in the Kandahar Airport and duct-taped a somewhat facetious cardboard sign over the door reading "Legat Kandahar." The windows, blown out by the U.S. bombing of the airport weeks earlier, were covered with plastic. The CIA had set up down the hall in another office and

---

*Years later, in 2005, General Mattis indelicately explained to one audience, "You go into Afghanistan, you got guys who slap women around for five years because they didn't wear a veil. You know, guys like that ain't got no manhood left anyway. So it's a hell of a lot of fun to shoot them. Actually, it's a lot of fun to fight. You know, it's a hell of a hoot. It's fun to shoot some people. I'll be right upfront with you, I like brawling." The Marine commandant afterward suggested that Mattis might have phrased his explanation more diplomatically, but Mattis was never one to pull a punch. In August 2010, after General McChrystal was removed by President Obama for his own indelicate remarks to *Rolling Stone,* Mattis took over as the leader of Central Command when General David Petraeus was appointed to head the U.S. forces in Afghanistan.

hung on the door a large 9/11 poster that showed the Trade Center and the Pentagon with the slogan "We Will Never Forget." Marines burrowed in their sleeping bags filled most corners of the facility. There was almost a campground feel to the place, which fostered the easy camaraderie that comes from stressed, exhausted men at war. It was easy to distinguish between the military men, in dirty camo uniforms, and the civilians, mostly FBI and CIA, in their parkas and wraparound sunglasses.

The Kandahar detention facility (*facility* might have been too formal a name for what amounted to open-sided tents ringed by chain-link fences and barbed wire expanding across the edge of the airfield) became the central deposit point for nearly everyone rounded up on the battlefield. Although it was closed and abandoned just a few months later, at that point in the war Kandahar was a thriving hub, with heli-copters regularly dropping off prisoners—as many as fifty a day, most arriving without paperwork, names, or explanations. Mattis made it clear that he wouldn't tolerate mistreatment of prisoners by his Marines; there was no sign of the "enhanced interrogations" that would later become de rigueur. At the same time, Mattis was no softie: When a detainee attempted to stab a guard with a homemade shiv, the general berated his Marine for firing a warning shot: "Why didn't you kill that son of a bitch?"

By the beginning of January 2002, some three thousand detainees were in Afghan jails, and the U.S. government had precious little information on most of them, since they'd been brought by allied Afghan tribes who were paid cash bounties for each prisoner deliv-ered. One of the FBI's first tasks would be to try to get photos and fingerprints from each of the detainees as he arrived. (The results of the fingerprint check quickly proved interesting. Forty prisoners swept up in mountain battles, who claimed to be Afghanistan dirt farmers, turned out to have speeding tickets, arrests, and criminal records back in the United States. The FBI team turned up more than forty battle-field detainees who had U.S. criminal records.)

The IDs were not the only task. The team was regularly dispatched on missions that came to be known as "sensitive site exploitations." Once the military had secured a site, the Bureau agents would arrive to search for evidence and intelligence. Thus it was that Bongardt, his

M4 at the ready and an M1911 .45-caliber handgun strapped to his upper thigh, found himself and other members of the team following Navy SEALs through the Tarnak Farms compound. The collection of about eighty buildings three miles from the airport, surrounded by ten-foot-high mud-and-rock walls, had served as bin Laden's headquarters and had been the subject of years of Predator surveillance before 9/11. "It was surreal," he recalled. At one point, he picked up a handful of rocks from the site for the other agents from I-49 and I-45. At another al-Qaeda training camp, he asked special forces operators to fill an empty Tabasco bottle with sand to be placed on John O'Neill's grave back in the States.

There was tremendous intelligence coming off the battlefield; the FBI agents spent their first days trying to convince the special forces teams of the importance of preserving "pocket litter," the scraps of papers, tickets, and receipts taken from prisoners coming off the battlefield. "The soldiers were doing a bang-up job [collecting things]," Bongardt remembered. But the pocket litter was being dispatched by the Agency, disappearing into the dark intelligence world without a trace, and the Bureau was desperate to establish a chain of custody— to know which piece of evidence was coming off which prisoner for questioning and intelligence-gathering down the road. "We knew exactly what would happen: Someday someone would ask to trace this evidence and we'd have no record of it," Bongardt reflected.

In one call back to the United States, the agents expressed their frustration to their supervisor, Pat D'Amuro. "Don't you realize what happened?" D'Amuro said from Washington. "These guys are never going to court."

Unable to win the bureaucratic battle, the Afghan FBI team instead convinced the special forces teams to bring the day's pocket litter to them first. They explained, "If the Agency gets in the chain of custody, we're fucked." Then, using the single working copier in the Kandahar Airport, left over from its prior civilian existence, the FBI team would work in shifts through the night, copying and tagging all the day's evidence before the Agency took it away for analysis the next morning. On the ground, the CIA and the FBI eventually developed a good relationship. Over the coming years, Bongardt would spend a significant amount of time in and around Afghanistan, becoming a regular in the late Sunday night American poker games in Kabul at the Agency's secret watering hole, "the Tali-bar," and the FBI's permanent base in Afghanistan ended up as part of a CIA facility. But that friendship didn't mean there weren't intense policy debates. Even in Afghanistan, desperate requests for intelligence shaped much of the agents' day. "It became all-consuming," Knowles says. "Forget about making progress on the investigation—just get the information back to headquarters for the matrix." He recalls, "You spent hours answering questions that had little relevance to the investigation but considering who was asking—the director, the White House, the president—had to be answered."

A by-product of all this was a constant debate with headquarters over what deserved follow-up. "Just because someone was labeled 'high-value' didn't mean they were," Knowles recalls. The majority of those detained had been swept up for the bounty money, plain and simple, and questioning quickly determined that most weren't hardened terrorists. (Explains Knowles, a former street cop, "I've arrested much worse right here on the streets of Fresno.") Besides, the cell structure of al-Qaeda meant that no ordinary battlefield soldier was going to have knowledge of overseas terrorist operations.

There was also a fierce debate over whether to Mirandize the detainees immediately. "You wouldn't Mirandize an American in this situation," Knowles argued with Justice Department officials. "We would only Mirandize someone in the U.S. when they become a suspect in a crime. I don't even know that they've ever pointed a weapon at U.S. forces." Many of those swept up in the dragnets didn't even know what a lawyer was. And if someone *did* ask for a lawyer after being Mirandized, where exactly was Knowles supposed to find a public defender? "We were so conservative in wanting to do it the right way," Knowles reflects.

As the winter continued, heavily guarded transport planes loaded with military police and prisoners in a strict two-to-one ratio departed from Kandahar regularly for Guantánamo Bay and other points in a new global network of hastily erected U.S. facilities to hold detainees in its fledgling war on terror. The Defense Department had established a procedure whereby any Arab in the detainee camps was shipped to Guantánamo, regardless of his apparent intelligence value. Hundreds of prisoners, their identities still mostly unknown, their terrorist ties nebulous, were on their way to the rocky, hot shore of Cuba. Meanwhile, more than four hundred detainees filled the two main facilities, at Kandahar and at Bagram Air Force Base to the north. Thousands more occupied other facilities around the country.

As the shipments to Guantánamo began, the first FBI rotation began to ready for its own departure in early January, after five weeks in Afghanistan. The military had been impressed with the knowledge of the New York al-Qaeda agents and asked FBI Headquarters to send more. The New York JTTF had always operated as full partners — where the FBI went, so did the NYPD — and the doubts about dispatching detectives overseas expressed during the USS *Cole* investigation ("What does this have to do with New York?") had been erased after the attacks on the twin towers. Thus it was that Special Agent Russ Fincher and NYPD Detective Marty Mahon found themselves arriving on the second FBI deployment to Afghanistan, just months after Fincher had watched the 9/11 attack unfold from the U.S. embassy in Stockholm, where he had been busy pursuing the *Cole* investigation.

From the time when the Bureau G5 coasted to a stop in Kandahar, the outgoing and incoming teams had just a day to pass along tips and intelligence before it took off again. The departing agents pointed their new colleagues to one of their biggest breakthroughs: the identification in the detainee camps of Ibn al-Shakyh al-Libi, the biggest catch to date from the al-Qaeda leadership. George Crouch and Bongardt had gotten al-Libi, who had overseen the group's most notorious training camp, to admit who he was and to offer some valuable intelligence. Now it was up to Fincher and Mahon. Crouch introduced al-Libi to Fincher before he returned home, but when the New York JTTF partners went the next day to question the prisoner, they discovered that he had disappeared. Asking around the base, they were pointed to a secret new facility being set up at the then mostly unknown Bagram Air Force Base.

The Bagram base was at the far end of the long U.S. supply chain, so conditions were about as primitive as they could be. Over the coming weeks, Fincher and Mahon spent long days questioning detainees, who were held in a bombed-out hangar. Daytime highs were only in the twenties, so a coal stove kept them warm in the spartan interview room — really nothing more than an empty electrical closet with half a picnic table. The military flew in halal MREs so the detainees could eat; the alphabet soup of military and intelligence agencies at the base ate mostly nonhalal MREs themselves. In the winter, the Americans learned to sleep with their water inside their sleeping bags; otherwise, by morning it would be frozen solid. With no regular access to showers, the agents, soldiers, and prisoners were all dirty, caked with grime everywhere but on their fingers, where the dirt wore away quickly. The only regular cleaning happened when someone arriving on a resupply flight brought in a canister or two of baby wipes.

The leader of the now infamous Khalden training camp was a tough nut to crack. Fincher and Mahon turned to I-49's father figure, Jack Cloonan, the patriarch of the New York al-Qaeda squad, for advice. "Handle this as if it's right here in New York," he advised. "Do yourself a favor: Read the man his rights. It will come out if we don't and it'll hurt the Bureau's reputation." The two agents spent hours chatting with al-Libi, searching somewhere for a connection that would enable them to talk. Out of questions, Fincher asked whether al-Libi was religious. Al-Libi nodded, then asked Fincher, a boyish-looking agent despite his salt-and-pepper hair, a question back: "Are you a godly man?" The two men, Christian and Muslim together, ended up spending hours talking religion, finally finding the bridge. Conversation poured forth. In the end, the FBI agent and the terrorist developed a solid rapport.

At one point, al-Libi, an engineer, drew a schematic of a suitcase bomb. Fincher, a biochemist by training, stopped him. "That wouldn't work," he said, pointing down at the wiring diagram. "You've got your wires backward here."

"Ah, you're an engineer!" al-Libi said, smiling broadly.

Once he opened up, al-Libi turned out to be a gold mine. He would prove key in the Moussaoui and Richard Reid (the failed "shoe bomber") investigations, as both men had gone through his training camp. Al-Libi, the JTTF investigators learned, wasn't a huge fan of bin Laden's; they'd had some major policy disagreements. Al-Libi strongly argued against attacking the American homeland, believing (correctly, as it turned out) that a strike on U.S. soil would lead to an invasion of the terrorist safe haven in Afghanistan. He didn't believe in killing civilians but wanted to target just the U.S. government and the military, and he wanted to use the camp to train all Muslims for jihad, not just those who supported al-Qaeda. And, in repeated conversations at Bagram with the JTTF agents, who were under pressure from Washington to ask, al-Libi denied any ties between Saddam Hussein and al-Qaeda. The secular dictator, al-Libi said, had no interest in Osama bin Laden's holy war. Bin Laden likewise didn't favor Saddam's corrupt regime.

The results the New York JTTF agents gathered were stunning. Intelligence officials today credit al-Libi's Bagram information with thwarting seven plots, two of which—an attack on the U.S. embassy in Yemen and one on the Prince Sultan Air Base in Saudi Arabia—were in advanced planning stages. Some of al-Libi's intelligence was instrumental in helping the military launch its Afghanistan offensive, Operation Anaconda.

As Fincher and Mahon made continuing progress, planes arriving at Bagram began dropping off shadowy men in suits who had a few questions for the talkative prisoner. The well-dressed arrivals had come from Tenet's shop. The CIA—specifically one man at Bagram, "Dave," who described himself as a case officer despite Fincher's doubts that he had ever done field operations before—hadn't felt that the FBI's results were sufficient, and they'd come to rectify the problem. Tenet, according to those familiar with the discussion, had warned President Bush that al-Libi possessed knowledge of an "imminent threat" to the United States—a claim that, according to the FBI, was an outright lie. There was no evidence then, and no evidence has emerged since, that al-Libi had any knowledge of a U.S.-focused plot. Tenet wanted the gloves to come off. In Washington, Mueller's counterarguments fell on deaf ears.

As the debate played out, Dave burst into the interview room while Fincher, Mahon, and al-Libi were talking, saying that he had an urgent task from CIA headquarters in Washington. "You're going to Egypt," he told al-Libi. "Before you get there, I am going to find your mother and fuck her." Fincher, eyes wide, jumped off the picnic table, slammed into the CIA operative, and shoved him out the door with a "What the fuck are you doing?" Furious about the new plan, the Bagram FBI team, including the military and other intelligence agencies present (minus, though, the CIA), wrote a rare joint memo to

Washington, still classified today, attesting to al-Libi's forthright cooperation and urging the continuation of the FBI interrogation. But the die was cast, President Bush having ruled against the FBI. Fincher and Mahon tried desperately to save their prisoner. They were getting loads of actionable intelligence, as well as valuable information about al-Qaeda's modus operandi. The military suggested, with a wink, that if the Bureau got there first to fly al-Libi away, that would be just fine, but FBI Headquarters refused to dispatch its plane to pick up the prisoner. Mueller played fair. He wasn't going to go behind the Agency's back, even though the Agency had gone behind the Bureau's.

After the terrorist camp leader was duct-taped and placed in a plastic box for transport aboard an unmarked CIA plane, Fincher asked to speak with him alone for a moment. "I'm not part of this," the FBI agent said, leaning over the bound prisoner. "Where they're taking you, just tell the truth like you did with us." The agent then watched, fuming and frustrated, as the CIA carried al-Libi aboard the waiting plane. Al-Libi would spend years in prison under horrendous conditions in Egypt, before reportedly being turned over to Libya, where he apparently committed suicide in 2006.★

After being subjected to mock executions and other forms of torture by the Egyptians, al-Libi supposedly offered testimony of more interest to the CIA and the Bush administration. On October 7, 2002, President Bush, using material based on al-Libi's "confession," told a crowd in Cincinnati, "We've learned that Iraq has trained al-Qaeda members in bomb-making and poisons and deadly gases." A year after al-Libi was shipped out of Bagram, after denying to Fincher and Mahon that there were any ties between Iraq and al-Qaeda, Colin Powell cited information from al-Libi about Saddam's ties to bin Laden's network in his February 2003 United Nations presentation. Sitting just behind Powell during the speech, which was widely cited as

---

★Peter Bergen and Katherine Tiedemann, in work for the New America Foundation, found 117 documented "extraordinary renditions" by the CIA between September 2001 and February 2008, in 58 of which the individuals were delivered to a third country—often Egypt—for detention and, usually, torture. Only one of those 58 prisoners specifically said he had not been tortured. Nineteen prisoners disappeared entirely, never to be heard from again.

galvanizing the United States to go to war, was George Tenet. Some in government, including the Defense Intelligence Agency, doubted al-Libi's information, but that didn't stop the march to war. Perhaps, not surprisingly, the training camp leader later recanted his story. "He clearly lied," Tenet concluded. "We just don't know when."

When Robert Mueller visited New York in the fall of 2002, he held an all-staff meeting across the street from 26 Federal Plaza in the Customs Building. It was clear by that point that there was little love lost between the new director and the New York Field Office, and in a move that rubbed many agents the wrong way, they were told to leave their weapons in their desks and to pass through the Customs Building's metal detector before entering the auditorium. Mueller's remarks, inspired by the office-of-origin debates in the preceding year, which made clear that the New York office was going to have to sacrifice, didn't sit well with the New York team either. At one point, Jack Cloonan raised his hand. Still angry over the handling of the al-Libi case in Afghanistan earlier that year and over the Bureau's failure to save al-Libi when it could, the veteran agent bluntly asked whether an FBI prisoner overseas was entitled to due process. No employee directly and publicly challenged the director of the FBI like that. "You could have heard a pin drop," one agent recalls. As that agent says, "It was, 'Man, you're going to be pumping gas tomorrow.'" In contrast to his normally straightforward responses, Mueller's answer meandered. "It wasn't so much what he said, it was how he said it," Cloonan recalls. Mueller seemed to be saying that he didn't care what happened overseas under someone else's watch. His response was legalistic; it was splitting straws, hiding in loopholes—and, more important, it didn't answer the question.

As Mueller walked out of the building, piqued by the unexpected question, he turned to one of his aides: "What was that all about?" Later, in the elevator, he observed to the New York ASAC, Ken Maxwell, "They don't seem to like me very much."

The unfortunate irony of the al-Libi case was that in much of the continuing debate over detainees, the FBI was carving a path separate from that of the rest of the U.S. government. In early 2002, Ali Soufan had flown down to the temporary detainee facilities at Gitmo to provide a lesson on interrogation. The room included FBI agents, investigators from other agencies, and military personnel. Soufan cautioned those involved not to go off the reservation. He wasn't speaking abstractly. He had already helped orchestrate one of the most successful post-9/11 al-Qaeda interrogations. In Yemen working the *Cole* case in the days after the twin towers fell, he and NCIS investigator Robert McFadden had gotten bin Laden's former bodyguard Abu Jandal to give up hour after hour of valuable information during an interrogation, which included offering the diabetic Jandal sugar-free cookies. Jandal had helped identify eight of the 9/11 hijackers in the days after the attacks. "The whole world is watching what we do here," Soufan told the Gitmo crowd. "We're going to win or lose this war depending on how we do this." The reaction was chilling. As Soufan recalls, the military didn't agree: "Their attitude was, 'You guys are cops. We don't have time for this.'"

From the White House to the mountains of Afghanistan, the government was struggling to figure "this" out—that is, how to handle and treat the hundreds of prisoners, growing in number by the day, in the new global war on terror. Al-Qaeda's fighters weren't legally soldiers. They wore no uniforms, swore allegiance to no recognized nation-state. Yet al-Qaeda members weren't strictly speaking criminals either. Argued Brookings' Ben Wittes, "The laws of war offer no useful vocabulary for such people."

As Fincher and Mahon were interrogating al-Libi at Bagram, two of their I-49 colleagues, Soufan and Steve Gaudin, found themselves dispatched to the Udon Thani Royal Thai Air Force base in the northeastern reaches of Thailand. In the 1960s, the U.S. military had opened the large joint base with the Thai military to support operations in Vietnam, and even after 1975, the densely developed region was still hospitable to Americans; a Voice of America relay station still existed, and the area even had a VFW post. Now it was one of the first of what came to be known as the CIA's "black sites." The Thai government's deal was that the United States could have the run of its facility as long as there was no public acknowledgment of the Americans' presence.

Al-Qaeda leader Abu Zubaydah was being kept in an unused warehouse on the air base. He had been captured in a joint CIA-FBI-Pakistani operation in Faisalabad, a city of two million in the northern province of Punjab in Pakistan. Authorities had actually raided multiple locations simultaneously on March 22, 2002, knowing only that Zubaydah was at one of them. A fierce gunfight had broken out at one location; when authorities were cleaning up the site afterward, an FBI agent shone his flashlight on one of the wounded prisoners, lying in the back of a pickup, and recognized the al-Qaeda higher-up, who was then rushed to a local hospital. At the hospital, FBI agents and CIA officers had a difference of opinion over who would take control of Zubaydah's cell phone, which, after the search at the scene, had been placed in an evidence bag. When it began to ring later that night, the CIA officer on site, John Kiriakou, insisted on opening the bag and answering it. "We can't open the evidence bag," the FBI agent present explained. "It would break the chain of custody." Kiraikou steamed. The FBI, he felt, just didn't get it. The rules had changed.

After hearing how badly wounded Zubaydah was, CIA Headquarters flew in a top surgeon from Johns Hopkins Hospital in Baltimore to help stabilize and save the terrorist leader. Once Zubaydah was well enough to be moved, the U.S. government disappeared him off the map. According to sources familiar with the plan at the time, he was flown from country to country for days by rotating sets of pilots with constantly changing flight plans and touched down on multiple continents before finally landing in Thailand.

There, Soufan and Gaudin began interrogating Zubaydah, who was still recovering and lay strapped to a gurney and handcuffed. Soufan held ice to his lips at times so the terrorist leader could get some fluids. The two FBI agents weren't supposed to get the first crack at Zubaydah — weren't, according to two other sources, even supposed to be allowed to interview the terrorist operations chief alone. However, in the random vagaries of twenty-first-century travel, the CIA interrogation team on its way to the black site had missed its flight, leaving an unexpected and unplanned window in which the FBI had the terrorist all to itself.

It wasn't easy, but gradually, as Soufan and Gaudin demonstrated their knowledge of the al-Qaeda network, Zubaydah warmed to them. Soufan was stunned by what they learned. The U.S. intelligence community had missed a merger of two potent terrorist forces. Khalid Sheikh Mohammed, the uncle of TRADEBOM mastermind Ramzi Yousef, who had long been a free agent in the global jihad movement, had not only joined forces with al-Qaeda but risen to become one of the organization's key leaders—its paymaster and operations manager. The 9/11 plot was mostly his doing.

The FBI agent sought out a quiet moment in the insular black site and called Ken Maxwell in New York on a secure phone. "I have to be careful talking because there are CIA guys all around," he told his supervisor back at 26 Federal Plaza. "Do you know who did 9/11?"

"Al-Qaeda," Maxwell replied. It was obvious.

"That guy who Frank Pellegrino is after," Soufan replied cryptically, in case someone could overhear them, referring to the case agent who was chasing Khalid Sheikh Mohammed.

"What the fuck? He's not even al-Qaeda," Maxwell exclaimed.

"Think again."

Astonishing information continued to flow from Zubaydah to the New York squad. And then, all of a sudden, it stopped. The CIA had decided that the Bureau's approach was moving too slowly, and an Agency contractor named John Mitchell arrived to take over the interrogation.★ Back in Washington, according to contemporaneous FBI documents, George Tenet was angry that the FBI was gathering such good information, something that might make the CIA look bad. Between al-Libi and Zubaydah, the FBI had had success in two major al-Qaeda interrogations; more than six months into the war on terror, the CIA had nothing to show for its work.

Mitchell put an immediate stop to Soufan and Gaudin's work. Despite admitting to Soufan that he had hardly any background in interrogation, he argued that as a psychologist he understood better than Soufan how the human mind worked. "Science is science," he said. Zubaydah clammed up immediately when Mitchell began his allegedly scientific interrogation routine, which included denying the

---

★In the wake of 9/11, as the Agency greatly expanded its workforce and its capabilities, it relied heavily on outside contractors to perform key field roles. The outsiders also provided a level of deniability for the press-shy Agency.

al-Qaeda leader outside contact and comforts. At one point, Soufan stumbled onto a coffin constructed as part of what was rumored to be a mock burial for Zubaydah to pressure him into talking more. "I swear to God, Pat, I'm going to arrest these guys," Soufan told D'Amuro by secure phone. But all Soufan could do was stew. As he recalled later, "It was the blind leading the blind in the most important part of the global war on terror."

Pat D'Amuro, in Washington, argued to Mueller that the Bureau shouldn't play any role in the "special interrogation techniques" being proposed over at the Pentagon and up the road at Langley. D'Amuro thought the techniques wouldn't work and wouldn't produce the dramatic results that the Agency hoped for, but also saw a bigger issue for FBI personnel. "We're handing every future defense attorney *Giglio* material," D'Amuro warned Mueller, who as a prosecutor immediately understood the significance.

The Supreme Court had ruled in *Giglio v. United States* that the personal credibility of a government official was admissible in court; thus, any FBI agent or staffer who participated in an extralegal interrogation overseas could potentially have that issue raised every time he or she testified in U.S. court on any other matter, as a way to impeach the agent's credibility. It was enough to ruin any agent's investigative career, and no prosecutor would ever touch a case that involved an agent who had potent *Giglio* material in his or her background.

"This is Washington," D'Amuro argued to Mueller. "Someday people are going to be lined up at green felt tables, and we need to be able to say we didn't do this." The administration, D'Amuro believed, was taking a short-term view of the prisoners, not considering the end game. "We can't just make them walk the plank off an aircraft carrier in the Indian Ocean," D'Amuro said during one meeting. There needed to be some sort of protocol to hold and lawfully detain the new detainees—and that began with treating them with the same rules and standards the United States had obeyed since the Revolutionary War. "I just thought it was going to be a disaster," he now says. "We were just creating amazing propaganda for al-Qaeda."

As word trickled back about what the CIA and the military were doing, the Justice Department's counterterrorism team was disgusted. Pat Fitzgerald, who by this point had interviewed more members of al-Qaeda than just about anyone alive, had found that for the most part, al-Qaeda members loved appearing before grand juries. Compared to most organized crime members, they were talkative and engaging, and even tried to proselytize to the jury members. They were proud of what they did. They *wanted* to talk. "This is what the FBI does...nearly one hundred percent of the terrorists we've taken into custody have confessed. The CIA wasn't trained; they don't do interrogations," Rolince says. "You either live by the rule of law or you don't. We're a nation of laws, not men."

Based on the word coming out of the Thai air base, FBI management decided to exclude agents from the dark side. D'Amuro ordered Gaudin and Soufan home to New York.

Before the CIA curtailed Soufan's access to Zubaydah—in fact, just days after he was moved to the black site in Thailand and began talking to the FBI team—he had hinted that there was another plot in the works. The FBI interrogation team had worked to understand the story, pulling together threads of information, evidence gleaned in raids and from other conversations. Now, recently returned from Bagram, Russ Fincher answered the al-Qaeda squad's phone line late on a Friday afternoon. He needed to run down an alias: Abu Abdullah al Mujahir. Working with Tommy Ward, his longtime NYPD partner, Fincher found a matching Florida driver's license and sent its photo on to Thailand. Zubaydah looked at it: "That's the guy." Zubaydah had called him "the South American," but U.S. agents now realized the suspect was a Puerto Rican named José Padilla, using a Muslim alias. Padilla had recently come on the radar when an acquaintance of his had a run-in with Pakistani immigration officials.

As Ward and Fincher began assembling bits of information, the picture that emerged was an odd one. Padilla was an American by birth; he had grown up in the Hispanic Chicago neighborhood of Logan Square, as a teenager joined the Puerto Rican gang the Latin Disciples, and over a number of years amassed a lengthy but largely undistinguished criminal record. He spent the latter part of his teens in juvenile detention. John Dillinger he was not; in one incident, he had punched a police officer who tried to arrest him after he stole a doughnut. Over the course of a decade, Padilla had converted to Islam, was radicalized, and legally changed his first name to Ibrahim. He moved to Egypt and became involved with an Egyptian woman with whom he had two children; his wife of six years back in Florida sought a divorce. He later ended up in Pakistan, training with jihadist elements, and at age thirty-one, in the months after 9/11, met with Zubaydah to pitch the leader on a possible plot based on some information Padilla had uncovered on the internet: plans to build a nuclear bomb.

Zubaydah must have had a hard time not laughing. The plans would have required huge resources and expertise that Padilla lacked. When asked how he planned to enrich the uranium, a process that normally involves multitudes of trained scientists, millions of dollars, and sophisticated, highly calibrated centrifuges, Padilla actually said he'd put it in a bucket and swing it around his head. Zubaydah encouraged Padilla to think small. Perhaps he could start with a so-called dirty bomb, a conventional explosive laced with radioactive material that would spread nuclear pollution across the bombsite.

Once Zubaydah had positively identified Padilla, the global hunt began. The CIA tracked him from Switzerland to Egypt for a period of weeks. "We know he's a bad guy and now he's on the loose," Fincher recalls. "What he was doing or where he was going we didn't know." In its first big post-9/11 test, the intelligence community was split. No one wanted to risk letting a terrorist into the country, but that would be the only way to uncover the support network Padilla hoped to tap. The case was being briefed all the way to the Oval Office, and the decree came down from Washington: This guy goes down the moment his feet hit U.S. soil. On May 8, in Zurich, Padilla boarded a flight to Chicago. The FBI's legal attaché from Bern and members of Swiss intelligence were also aboard the plane.

It was a ten-hour trip from Zurich to Chicago, time that was spent in intense debate throughout the government. On conference calls, Ken Maxwell argued with the decision to take him down: "Don't do this. We don't know what he's doing here." It was a losing battle. "Post 9/11, the American people's appetite for risk waned," Maxwell recalls. The decisions on when to take down plots or suspects were no longer up to case agents or prosecutors; they were coming in many cases from the Oval Office itself. The Bureau by that point had gotten so used to this that the attorney general, directing even the finest points of an investigation, was mocked behind his back as "Agent Ashcroft."

In fact, the case against Padilla was so new—just weeks old—that by its traditional standards the FBI wasn't even ready to pursue a criminal warrant. New York JTTF agent Joe Ennis instead swore out an affidavit for a material witness warrant, which would allow Padilla to be taken into custody as part of the Southern District's ongoing investigation into al-Qaeda's activities. Material witness warrants had become the government's favorite new tool in the war on terror. Hundreds had been detained on such orders, allowing authorities to sweep people of interest off the streets and to build a case for prosecution later. Thousands more were detained under immigration violations, their lives cast into limbo for weeks or months as the FBI and other government agencies sought to sort out their ties to terrorism. "We have to hold these people until we find out what is going on," the Justice Department's Michael Chertoff told his deputy in one meeting. It was yet another example of the one percent doctrine at work.

The debate over how to pursue the case stretched to the final moments, but Federal Judge Michael Mukasey signed Padilla's warrant just five minutes before the flight landed in Chicago. Fincher and Craig Donnachie were on a plane from New York to Chicago just minutes ahead of Padilla's flight; they raced through the airport, meeting up with the Bern legat, who looked like he'd walked straight from his desk to the airport with no expectation of taking a long trip to the States. Agents from the FBI and other agencies were spread throughout the airport, trying to spot someone Padilla might be meeting.

Conveniently, Padilla lied to customs agents about how much money he was carrying into the country, which provided the excuse to detain him and begin questioning him. The FBI team interviewed Padilla for more than four hours. When the interrogation seemed to have run its course, Fincher stood, taking his handcuffs from the small of his back, and said, "You're under arrest."

Padilla had been through the criminal justice system so many times before that he knew he should hold out for a plea deal, but it never came. Fincher and Donnachie located overseas eyewitnesses who had knowledge of Padilla's plotting, but Ashcroft forbade the FBI to bring the witnesses to the United States to appear in court. He also forbade the witnesses to testify by video from overseas, as was later done in other cases. As one agent involved in the case recalls, "We had a case, we had eyewitnesses who'd agreed to work with prosecutors, and they wouldn't let it work. If we can't have witnesses in the U.S., that left us with no option." As Padilla was transferred from Chicago to the high-security tenth floor of the Metropolitan Correctional Center in New York, the wheels were already in motion to try a new tack.

Because the material witness warrant was due to expire, the White House decided to transfer Padilla from the Justice Department to the Defense Department. He would be held by the military as an "enemy combatant," a category that sharply limited his rights and allowed him to be held without charge.* The attorney general announced Padilla's arrest and transfer to military custody in a hastily called press conference on June 10, 2002, conducted by satellite from Moscow, where he was holding an unrelated meeting with Russian officials: "I am pleased to announce today a significant step forward in the war on terrorism," he said. "We have captured a known terrorist who was exploring a plan to build and explode a radiological dispersion device, or 'dirty bomb,' in the United States." (Agents watching the press conference shook their heads over the irony: Here was John Ashcroft announcing by video from overseas Padilla's arrest and transfer to the military, after prohibiting the FBI's eyewitnesses from doing exactly the same thing, even though it would have allowed Padilla to stay within the criminal justice system.) It was the first of what would become almost routine government announcements in the years to come: A breathless, high-profile announcement of a terrifying scheme against the United States, whose threat was gradually downgraded as more information trickled out afterward.

---

*Mukasey, the judge who had been involved since the start of the case and who would go on to become President Bush's third attorney general, had a long history in America's evolving counterterrorism approach, dating back to overseeing the trial in the Blind Sheikh case in 1993. He wrote later that the Padilla case underscored that "current institutions and statutes are not well-suited" to the fight against Islamic terrorism and that perhaps the United States should consider establishing a "National Security Court" that would deal with the legal complexities and complications such cases inevitably provoked.

Though the official statements announcing the Padilla arrest had been carefully coordinated, Mueller downplayed the plot, saying that it was only at the "discussion stage." While the media reports ran with Padilla's ties to the dirty bomb, no one on the investigation team believed that was the actual plot. "This guy was a brain transplant away from a dirty bomb," one intelligence official recalls.

In fact, agents believed that Zubaydah had crafted a more subtle plot, intending Padilla to be part of an al-Qaeda cell that would rent apartments in large high-rises across the United States, start extensive natural gas leaks, and then blow the buildings from the inside. The hope was to turn neighbor against neighbor, overwhelming the government with false leads, suspicion, and anti-Muslim bias.

To this day, the government doesn't know who José Padilla was planning to meet with in the United States, where he was planning to go, or what his agenda actually was. He is, in the words of the old organized crime investigations, a "stand-up guy"—he won't snitch. He was carrying $10,000 in cash, hidden on his person—too little to be a major smuggling effort, meaning that the money had some operational purpose. "What would it have cost to follow him around for a few days?" Maxwell laments. "We could have been on him like white on snow. It's what we do."

Instead Padilla disappeared into the government's covert war on terror. Judge Mukasey, the future attorney general, would in the coming months issue a series of rulings upholding the government's ability to hold Padilla as an enemy combatant. He argued, however, that Padilla should still have access to a lawyer. The government refused.

Amid a growing legal battle over his status, Padilla was indicted in 2005 for conspiring "to murder, kidnap and maim people overseas." Supporters believe the indictment was specifically timed to avoid an outright ruling against the government vis-à-vis his detention. His case was wrapped into an already ongoing terrorist financing prosecution in Florida, since all of the evidence surrounding his 2002 trip to Chicago was tainted by the black-site interrogations that uncovered the evidence against him; he was never prosecuted for the underlying arrest in Chicago.

Padilla was convicted on all counts during a complicated three-month trial and is now serving his sentence at the federal supermax facility in Florence, Colorado. His lawyers allege that during his imprisonment before trial, he was repeatedly subjected to "enhanced interrogation" techniques and that the government—or, more specifically, the CIA—actually bragged internally about the rough treatment Padilla received. Disrupting the Padilla plot was later used by the CIA as part of its justification for the "enhanced interrogation" procedures—but only with a key sleight of hand. In a later memo outlining the success of these techniques, Padilla's arrest was listed as having taken place in 2003, not 2002, as it did. As it was, the intelligence that led to Padilla's arrest had been gathered during an FBI interrogation before Zubaydah was handed over to the CIA to be tortured; the "enhanced interrogation" procedures weren't even officially approved until the fall of 2002, so they could not have been involved in getting the Padilla intelligence in the spring of that year, when the FBI had access to Zubaydah. Nobody at the Bureau thought that the typo was an error. By moving the arrest a year later, the CIA gained justification for its tactics.

Many of the Guantánamo detainees, wearing earmuffs, blackened goggles, and orange jumpsuits, didn't seem like hardened terrorists as they disembarked from the bellies of the air force jets onto Cuban soil. Some were so weak they had to be carried off the planes and loaded onto the yellow schoolbuses for the trip to the camp. Communication was hard, since not all the detainees spoke Arabic. (Afghan mountain languages such as Pashtun and Urdu were common too.) The International Committee of the Red Cross, which typically monitors prisoners of war, visited at the invitation of a JAG colonel who thought it made sense for the ICRC to be there—an invitation that got him upbraided by senior defense officials. As time passed, however, the detainees received harsher treatment.

In its early years, the Guantánamo Bay Naval Base was relatively primitive. While there were McDonald's and Subway franchises on the base, for the most part detainees and interrogators ate the same food: military-issue MREs. An influx of money from Washington—some estimates range as high as $2 billion—would transform the island, building twenty-seven playgrounds, a new hospital and psych ward, baseball and football fields, a Starbucks, and an ice-cream store.

All that was to come. The handful of FBI agents on the island settled into spartan two-bedroom town houses on the base. At night, rats ran through the attics. In the unofficial FBI uniform of polo shirts and khaki cargo pants, the agents spent their days interviewing detainees, beginning as early as 6 A.M., reaching the camps in an eighteen-passenger van the Bureau had purchased that lacked a working air conditioner.

Back in the United States, much of the Bureau's attention was on safeguarding the Winter Olympics in Salt Lake City, where the ceremonies opened with the carrying of a flag from the World Trade Center into the stadium. Against that backdrop, the agents in Gitmo were left much to their own devices, with the Miami Field Office, as camp commander Major General Michael Dunlavey said later, "rotating people in and out of there like it was a turnstile at Wal-Mart." Agents dispatched in the early waves reported that the Bureau was "half-stepping" at best, ignoring the investigative issues beginning to unfold on the island. "We were dabbling with it," one agent said later. Those who did dabble didn't enjoy it. "The days are long and there is no 'getting away' from things," another agent wrote back to headquarters.

Early on, the military and the CIA expressed concern that the FBI was going to "gum up the works" by collecting evidence instead of intelligence. However, over the course of the spring, the various agencies on Guantánamo began to play well with each other. Detainees were freely handed from one agency to another, passed back and forth collegially. "Tiger teams" of interrogators—a mix of FBI agents, military investigators, linguists, and analysts—proved especially effective in gaining trust and information.

Over the course of the summer, though, roadblocks began to appear. The amount of information coming from the detainees seemed to reach a plateau. As the interviews became less useful, the military's thinking on interrogation procedures diverged from the FBI's views. Dunlavey, who was placed in charge of the camps in February 2002, explained to one journalist that Rumsfeld "wanted me to 'maximize the intelligence production.' No one ever said to me, 'The gloves are off,' but I didn't need to talk about the Geneva Conventions. It was clear that they didn't apply here."

The military began to explore alternative options, techniques with names like "fear up (harsh)" and "pride and ego-down." According to later internal documents, the FBI was concerned that the new DOD methods were "stupid, demeaning, and ineffective." Far from a crack team of the nation's elite, the interrogation teams at Gitmo often seemed to the FBI agents to be amateurs. The young soldiers had been told that they were guarding the worst of the worst, the men who had killed thousands in New York, in Washington, and over Shanksville, Pennsylvania, the terrorists who had shot at their buddies back in the mountains of Afghanistan. For the most part, that wasn't the case. Indeed, upon closer inspection, the prisoners in Gitmo were largely harmless, or something close to it. At the end of the summer of 2002, a secret CIA report concluded that at least a third of the prisoners had no substantial ties to al-Qaeda; they were mostly farmers or local Afghans swept up in the dragnets and bounty hunts the coalition led after the invasion. General Dunlavey later raised that estimate to at least half. According to research led by Mark Denbeaux at Seton Hall University, of the 517 Guantánamo detainees examined, 9 out of 10 had been captured by allied tribes or Pakistani border guards and turned over to the United States in exchange for prisoner bounties. Only 45 percent of the detainees could be found to have committed hostile acts against the United States; only 8 percent appeared to have ties to al-Qaeda. Most of the detainees, in the words of Brookings' Ben Wittes, appeared to be the "cannon fodder of international jihad." Such detainees weren't harmless—the al-Qaeda attacks in East Africa and against the *Cole,* and the 1993 bombing of the World Trade Center, had relied heavily on such "cannon fodder" for support roles—but they also weren't masterminds.

Yet at the time, the military was treating every detainee as if he were the equivalent of Osama bin Laden or Mohamed Atta. Often decades younger than the FBI agents on the island, the military interrogators had gone through training at Fort Huachuca, originally in a sixteen-week course, but as the need for interrogators grew, in abbreviated sessions that became the norm. The military had only a few hundred interrogators when operations began in Afghanistan, nowhere near the number it needed to police the huge detainee population. Many of them had never conducted a real-life interrogation before arriving at Gitmo. John Anticev, who had spent nearly fifteen years hunting al-Qaeda terrorists around the world, going back to the Rabbi Kahane assassination in New York, got into a heated disagreement in early 2002 with one young military interrogator at Gitmo over the right approach to a particular prisoner. The army reservist insisted that he was an expert interrogator, but in the course of the argument it came out that he was just weeks removed from his job as a greeter at Wal-Mart.

According to those familiar with the procedures, techniques, and debates, and especially with the way the methods were implemented, intelligence didn't always appear to be the top priority. Both FBI and military sources admitted that they had observed the behavior of interrogators and prisoners, and they believed that racism and a desire for revenge motivated at least some of the harsh treatments on the ground. If the intent was to extract valuable information, the brutality was beyond counterproductive. As Tom Knowles had argued with military officials in Afghanistan, "People would keep saying, 'This is a war zone.' What difference does that make?" he recalls. "This is a human being. An interrogation is an interrogation. You modify it to fit your situation, but the basics are the same."

Agents who arrived on the island circa 2003 were shown a military orientation video that covered how the soldiers processed arriving detainees; it was far from comforting, as it involved lots of yelling and screaming at hooded detainees kneeling on the Gitmo tarmac. One FBI agent came out of an interview and heard pounding music coming from a nearby interrogation. When he entered the observation room, unbeknown to those conducting the interrogation, he could see a detainee sitting on the floor wrapped in an Israeli flag, being subjected to loud music and strobe lights. The scene was infuriating, and not just because it didn't seem likely to lead to useful information. In Osama bin Laden's 1998 fatwa against the United States, the al-Qaeda founder had accused the United States of being controlled by the Jews, saying that the United States "serv[ed] the Jews' petty state," and as the FBI agent later complained, "This act was driving that point home for al-Qaeda."

FBI agents at Guantánamo soon learned that members of other agencies—in many cases the CIA or DOD—were impersonating them. One morning, as an FBI team loaded up equipment on the ferry that ran from one side of the base to the other, the boat's captain wandered over and asked, "Don't you guys have enough stuff on this ferry already?" He pointed ahead to a group of pickup trucks that he said a team identifying themselves as FBI agents had loaded on earlier in the morning. The FBI didn't have any pickup trucks in Guantánamo. Another morning, a detainee in the interrogation room complained to arriving agents that "you guys" had kept him up all night. No FBI agents had been present the night before.

Detainee 682, an English-speaking Saudi named Ghassan Abdallah Ghazi al-Sharbi, had been captured in Pakistan in March 2002. The al-Qaeda operative explained to one of the FBI agents that he wouldn't cooperate because two men from the Bureau had tortured him in Pakistan before moving him to Guantánamo. The accusation didn't sound right. A few nights later, two CIA officers, both of whom introduced themselves simply as "Bob," informed the FBI agent that they intended to question the Saudi. Al-Sharbi's response when the two CIA officers entered the room was instant and unmistakable: "You're Joe and Phil, the guys who tortured me in Pakistan."

The FBI agents at Guantánamo spent much of the spring of 2002 figuring out who the prisoners were, based on a combination of fingerprints, photos, and interviews.* One rotation of FBI agents spent their tour ranking the detainees based on possible intelligence value. Another key activity at Guantánamo was clearing the "lead bucket," tips from agents across the globe that needed to be checked out with the detainees. If an agent in the States acquired a photo of a possible Iranian terrorist, for example, agents at Guantánamo would show the photo to every Iranian detainee to see if anyone recognized the subject. ("With no doubt, all these interviews resulted in a negative response," the agent responsible for that particular lead noted.)

None of the cases was more frustrating to the government than that of Mohammed al-Qahtani. Certain detainees had been desig-

---

*Just as the fingerprint checks in Afghanistan were turning up U.S. connections among the detainees, when the Bureau ran the fingerprints of one Gitmo detainee, it turned out he had been a University of Nebraska student.

nated "project people," which marked them for special coordinated attention from the agencies present at Guantánamo. The military's task force and the FBI would meet to develop a specific plan to get the detainee to talk over an extended period of time, not just during a single interview.

Top among the project people was al-Qahtani, known on the island as Detainee 63. (Each detainee was numbered, beginning with the so-called American Taliban, John Walker Lindh, and Australian David Hicks, 0001 and 0002, respectively.) Detainee 63 was one of the most intriguing of those taken prisoner: Nabbed on the Tora Bora battlefield in Afghanistan just weeks after 9/11, he was shuttled from place to place for some seven months in U.S. custody until he landed in Gitmo. When FBI agents fingerprinted him, Detainee 63 was found to be one of the most sought-after subjects in the system. As it turned out, Miami immigration agents had barred him from entering the United States on August 3, 2001, when it appeared he had no specific plans once he arrived in Florida. When FBI agents later looked through the airport surveillance tapes as part of the PENTTBOM follow-up investigation, it appeared that Mohamed Atta, the ringleader of the 9/11 attacks, had been waiting to pick up al-Qahtani. That meant that the prisoner, who'd originally told investigators that he'd been in Afghanistan pursuing his interest in falconry, might actually be the 9/11 plot's so-called twentieth hijacker. (Five hijackers had captured three of the hijacked planes on 9/11; United Flight 93, inexplicably, had only had four hijackers aboard, leaving officials wondering if the fifth hijacker had never arrived in the United States.)

Al-Qahtani was put in isolation on August 8, 2002, in the navy's brig, which was hard-wired by video to the FBI command post so that he was under constant surveillance. In reality, the feed proved distracting (and boring), so agents covered the screen with cardboard.

Originally the military agreed that al-Qahtani belonged to the FBI as part of its PENTTBOM investigation. Ali Soufan, fresh from Thailand, returned to Guantánamo to interview the prisoner, who initially tried to negotiate moving back to the main camp in exchange for talking. Agents pushed him on whether he was the twentieth hijacker, saying that Zacarias Moussaoui was about to go down for al-Qahtani's crime and that the jihadist should help his innocent brother out. When al-Qahtani refused, agents realized, in Ali Soufan's words, that they were "really up the creek here." Al-Qahtani wasn't going to be easy.

According to sources familiar with the internal Bureau debate, Mueller decided that same month, in August 2002, that the FBI wouldn't participate in harsh or extreme interrogations, but his policy was evidently neither communicated to the field nor codified for nearly two years, a particular oddity given that the bureaucratic FBI relies so heavily on documentation and paper trails. "I do not believe it is appropriate for the United States to use interrogation methods that are unlawful under applicable law," Mueller wrote. "It is FBI policy that all interrogations, regardless of the status of the person being interrogated, shall be conducted using methods that would be lawful if used within the United States." While Bureau executives close to Mueller maintain that his policy was clearly communicated to those who needed to know it, others argue that his reluctance to codify the decision came in part from an aversion to picking a fight with the CIA and the military. He knew enough about what was going on in the black sites, like where Zubaydah was being held, to know he didn't want to know more.★

On September 26, 2002, the Justice Department loaded a jet in Washington for a special "legal limbo" tour. Along for the ride were David Addington and Alberto Gonzales from the White House, Jim Haynes and Jack Goldsmith from the Defense Department, the CIA's John Rizzo, the Justice Department's Alice Fisher (then deputy head of the Criminal Division), and the OLC's Patrick Philbin. The group was to go first to Guantánamo to see the detainees there, then on to Charleston,

---

★ At one point, agents interviewing detainees on Guantánamo began to collect stories of how the detainees had been allegedly mistreated while in Afghanistan. Unsure of how to file such reports—every piece of paper in the Bureau is supposed to be attached to an investigative file of one sort or another—they eventually settled on filing the reports under "war crimes." Supervisors later ordered that file closed. It wasn't, they said, the FBI's mission to investigate detainee abuse and chew over what had taken place on the battlefield of the war on terrorism. No one wanted to rock the military's boat.

South Carolina, to the navy brig that held José Padilla, and Norfolk, Virginia, to see the imprisoned Yaser Hamdi, an American caught with the Taliban. Notably absent from the trip: anyone from the FBI.★ The tour marked a turning point in the war on terror. Lieutenant Colonel Jerald Phifer, the military's Gitmo intelligence officer, had hosted brainstorming sessions on the island with twenty to thirty people, including the military, CIA, and FBI, as early as August to come up with new interrogation methods. Some ideas came straight from reverse-engineering the military's own Survival, Evasion, Resistance, and Escape (SERE) course at Fort Bragg, which trains pilots, aviators, and special forces troops how to survive behind enemy lines, evade capture, resist interrogations if captured, and escape. It was an odd choice on which to base intelligence-gathering techniques: Many of the tactics taught in the class are taught specifically because the North Koreans, North Vietnamese, and Soviets used them successfully to elicit false confessions and false testimony. In fact, the army's own 177-page interrogation manual, *US Army Field Manual on Interrogation,* publication FM 34-52, clearly explains that a key reason the military prohibits torturing prisoners is that "use of torture is not only illegal but also it is a poor technique that yields unreliable results, may damage subsequent collection efforts, and can induce the source to say what he thinks the HUMINT collector wants to hear. Use of torture can also have many possible negative consequences at national and international levels." Yet on October 11, General Dunlavey issued a twelve-page request for special new forms of questioning, procedures that didn't appear in any official outline of accepted interrogation methods. In fact, under most international laws, the new methods constituted torture.†

It's significant that the usual military legal leaders didn't participate or sign off on the decision. Haynes, Rumsfeld's counsel, had

---

★Amazingly, the trip was also conducted without telling the commanding general of the Guantánamo operation. He wouldn't learn of the visit until years later.
†When he approved them, Dunlavey didn't know that the techniques were considered forms of torture, because the staff judge advocate he asked to review the decision, Lieutenant Colonel Diane Beaver, had little background in intelligence law and none whatsoever in international law and didn't flag the new techniques as violating international law.

centralized the legal decision-making under his office, circumventing the normal approval process that could have elicited differing opinions or objections. In fact, the approvals for the new techniques came from three legal offices run by political appointees: Addington and Gonzales at the White House, Haynes at the Pentagon, and Bybee at Justice.

Mere weeks after 9/11, Fox's hit series *24* had premiered, starring fictional terrorist hunter Jack Bauer, who often resorted to torturing suspects in ticking-time-bomb scenarios. Much of the public debate about harsh interrogation, including that by leading legal scholars such as Alan Dershowitz, focused on such scenarios, in which a terrorist has information about an imminent threat, and as minutes count and lives hang in the balance, the terrorist can be made to talk only by aggressive means. The second season of *24,* which premiered in October 2002 in the midst of government discussions about harsh interrogations, opened with a terrorist quickly giving up valuable information about a nuclear bomb hidden in Los Angeles after being tortured by chemicals. Most people in the room during Phifer's brainstorming sessions had seen *24* and knew its message: Torture worked. "We saw it on cable," the staff judge advocate, Diane Beaver, said years later.

There was just one problem with this scenario: It had never happened in history.★ Beyond that, the ticking time bomb certainly didn't apply to the al-Qaeda prisoners held at Guantánamo. Many of them had been in custody for ten months or longer by the time the debate about "enhanced interrogations" started. Whatever operational information they had once possessed—and because of al-Qaeda's cell structure, most had precious little anyway—was now so far removed from the real world that it was almost useless. Even al-Qaeda's own "Manchester Manual," its version of the military SERE course, required its members to withhold operational details for only forty-eight hours to allow their "brothers" to change plans.

Yet despite the dwindling hopes that the Guantánamo prisoners might reveal useful information, the leadership at the Cuban camp felt

---

★ The first ticking time bomb appeared in Jean Lartéguy's 1960 novel *Les Centurions,* a fictional account of the French experience in Algeria that became one of the country's best-selling books since World War II. The scenario Lartéguy described had no basis then in real life, and never has occurred since.

under pressure to deliver. They were on the front lines of the war on terror. Donald Rumsfeld encouraged the belief that what was happening back home was directly tied to what was happening in combat in Afghanistan. Everyone in the military, no matter his or her physical location, was now serving on the front lines. The terrorists had attacked the Pentagon, after all, and in the attack's wake Rumsfeld encouraged its staff to wear combat fatigues in place of their normal office dress uniforms. We're all in this together, he said.

Unfortunately, in addition to the specious ticking-time-bomb concept, the military's own interrogation approach didn't seem focused on delivering results quickly; it operated within seemingly self-defeating timeframes. Some of the interrogation plans built in ten days or two weeks of sleep deprivation, stress positions, and the like before serious questioning even began. And as always there was the issue of the quality of results that those torture techniques yielded. An American Bar Association report from the 1930s stated "that sleep deprivation is the most effective torture and certain to produce any confession desired." But just any confession wasn't useful to authorities. Only honest confessions would be.

The jihadists had been taught by Al-Qaeda's doctrine that America was big and terrible. Often, in the FBI's experience, their best cooperation came when detainees realized they weren't going to get tortured, that the United States wasn't the Great Satan. Interrogators were figuring out on the battlefields of the global war on terror that not playing into al-Qaeda's propaganda could produce victories. The soldier who ran interrogations for the army in Afghanistan later explained, "One of our biggest successes...came when a valuable prisoner decided to cooperate not because he had been abused (he had not), but precisely because he realized he would not be tortured. He had heard so many horror stories that when he was treated decently, his prior worldview snapped, and suddenly we had an ally." As Ali Soufan had said in the camp's first weeks, the war would be won or lost in how the detainees were treated.

Special Agent James Clemente's first glimpse of Guantánamo Bay Naval Base in October 2002 was surprising. Two powerful hurricanes,

Isidore and Lili, had churned through the Yucatán in late September and early October and dumped abnormal amounts of rain on Cuba. The rocky, dusty island had greened up considerably. As his military transport plane conducted the required last-minute, stomach-churning, hairpin turn around the southern tip of Cuba to avoid the country's airspace, Clemente had no way of knowing that he was walking into the midst of the intensifying debate, stretching to the highest levels of government, over how detainees should be treated.

Clemente had been dispatched to Guantánamo for the Bureau's third forty-five-day rotation from the Behavioral Analysis Unit (BAU) at Quantico. The group of profilers and researchers who work on big cases and develop theories aimed at solving sticky cases such as those presented by serial killers, for example, is one of the Bureau's most mythic enterprises, featured in movies such as *Silence of the Lambs*. A onetime Bronx prosecutor and graduate of Fordham Law, Clemente had spent some fifteen years in the Bureau by 9/11, during which time he had worked a three-year undercover commodities investigation (becoming the first FBI agent ever to get his broker's license) and a multiyear turn investigating President Clinton for independent counsel Kenneth Starr. He had been teaching a class at Quantico on September 11 when his sister, who worked at the World Financial Center in New York, texted him repeatedly: *911 911 911 911.* Learning of the attacks, he interrupted an in-service training for the New York Field Office's bomb technicians in the classroom next door. The bomb techs quickly took off north. They'd left only one bomb tech agent behind to deal with any crises that happened while they were off for the training at Quantico—Lennie Hatton, who died when the towers collapsed on top of him. It wasn't lost on the bomb techs that but for the serendipitous timing of the training, many of them would probably be dead along with Hatton. Clemente finished teaching his own class, then drove to New York, without orders, and spent five days working the pile at Ground Zero. "I knew so many of those guys—Port Authority, NYPD, FDNY. There were incredibly close ties," he recalls.

In the wake of 9/11, BAU shut down its criminal projects and redirected all its resources toward developing profiles, backgrounds, and workups on the nineteen hijackers. From there, the unit began to expand its focus to other al-Qaeda players. By the following spring, the BAU agents knew more about many of the al-Qaeda leaders than just about anyone outside of the terrorists' own families. Beginning in the summer of 2002, pairs of BAU profilers left for Guantánamo to assist with the interrogation plans. Rumors had already circulated among the BAU team about the harsh treatment some prisoners faced. Just days before Clemente arrived on the island, Special Agent Bob Morton and another investigator had been called over by David Becker, a civilian contractor working for the Defense Intelligence Agency. In the agents' eyes, Becker was an inexperienced goofball, yet he was to become the Bureau's arch-nemesis on the island. His main interrogation background, he admitted, was debriefing Boeing employees in Asia. Giggling, Becker said, "You guys have to come see this." He led Morton to an interrogation room where a detainee sat with his head duct-taped. The detainee, Becker said, had been repeating verses from the Koran, and the contractor had figured out a way to shut him up. "Great idea," Morton said, his eyes boring into the contractor's. "How you gonna get it off?"

Clemente, coincidentally the first lawyer and former prosecutor sent to the island by the FBI, got his own introduction to the DOD's new, questionable tactics in the coming days. He witnessed one female military interrogator apparently sexually fondling a detainee, hoping that the shame of being touched by a woman would isolate him and make him crack. In looking over the interrogation plan for Detainee 63, Clemente heard warning bells start to clang in his head. Each of the plan's four phases represented an escalation of the hostile treatment, ending with the recommendation that the detainee be delivered to a third country for an even more violent form of torture.

Don't worry, the military assured Clemente in one meeting, the BAU has signed off on this plan. That didn't sound right to Clemente, so he excused himself and called Quantico. After summarizing the document, he asked the BAU agent who had preceded him at Gitmo, "Did you sign off on this?" "No fucking way," Clemente's predecessor said. "I told them we want nothing to do with this." Clemente returned to the meeting and explained to the military officials that the Bureau absolutely had not and would not sign off on the proposed interrogation plan.

In an environment where a lieutenant colonel is rarely questioned, Clemente's insolence hit Phifer hard. Angered, he snatched the plan back from Clemente, nearly spitting in the agent's face as he shouted, "Lead, follow, or get the fuck out of the way!"

"What are you, the schoolyard bully?" Clemente shot back.

As the working environment at Guantánamo grew more tense, Tom Neer, a veteran of the FBI's international counterterrorism world, was dispatched from the Quantico BAU to figure out why Clemente was in such trouble with the military; he quickly backed up the other agent's view. The Naval Criminal Investigative Service, the only other law enforcement agency on the island, also backed the Bureau against the military and the CIA's plans.

The one prep session for al-Qahtani that the FBI was allowed to attend left little doubt about the military's true intentions. "The general says our boots can't cross the line of the torture statute," Phifer said, his voice rising, "but our shadows sure as hell can!" The dozen or so sergeants in the room cheered. "If the rule is that noises can't be over eighty decibels"—the level at which sound is considered potentially dangerous—"I want it at seventy-nine decibels." One sergeant interjected, "Seventy-nine point nine!" Everyone cheered.

Neer and Clemente left the meeting depressed. Clemente turned to Neer and said, "That was like a fucking high school pep rally." After they voiced their complaints, the FBI agents weren't invited to any more prep meetings.

The military seemed to argue that because their techniques were aimed at extracting information rather than at torturing al-Qahtani, they were legal. Clemente explained to Beaver that the law is clear: Torture is torture, regardless of intent. "Well, the general believes me and not you," Beaver replied.

In an electronic communication on November 22, 2002, one agent wrote to assorted officials at headquarters, "The use of these tactics put FBI personnel in a tenuous situation that will perhaps necessitate FBI representatives being utilized as defense witnesses in future judicial proceedings against a Detainee." As the clock ticked down and the military finalized plans to begin its harsh treatment of al-Qahtani, the FBI agents at Gitmo grew more desperate. "The big theory [of 'enhanced interrogations'] was grinding through the government, but I was saying, 'This isn't theoretical. This guy's going to get tortured tomorrow,'" Clemente recalls.

After what he'd seen working at Ground Zero in the days after the attacks, Clemente was not unsympathetic to the desire to inflict pain on the hardened terrorists. "If you'd worked on the pile, it would be easy to rationalize," he explains. "If you'd seen those body parts, if you'd smelled, if you'd seen, if you'd been in the battle. But now they're not on the battlefield. No matter what you call them—detainees, combatants, prisoners—they're in your custody. I've worked child sex cases. I've sat across from men who have raped, abused, and murdered children. The worst of the worst. If ever there was someone you wanted to hurt, I've been there. I know you can't. It's a slippery slope."

In the movie *A Few Good Men,* a gruff Marine commander, played by Jack Nicholson, lectures a young JAG lawyer, played by Tom Cruise, on the unique aspects of service at Gitmo: "I eat breakfast eighty yards away from four thousand Cubans who are trained to kill me. So don't for one second think you're gonna come down here, flash a badge, and make me nervous." The scene kept playing through the heads of Clemente and his fellow agents as they considered their options; to say they felt constrained would be an understatement. In very practical ways, they were reliant on the military's hospitality. Their guns, badges, handcuffs—the physical incarnations of an FBI agent's unique authority—were all back on the mainland. "All we had was the law and a pen," Clemente recalls, but even then they couldn't functionally arrest the military leaders for violating the torture statute. At Gitmo, they were the guests amid thousands of armed Marines. Then there was the question of how much support the agents would get from Mueller. Headquarters wanted to get along with the military and the CIA, lest the FBI be excluded entirely from the new antiterror regime. As one agent recounted, "If Department of Defense said, 'Thanks, go away,' that would not be good for the country." All Clemente and the other agents could do was raise their concerns and hope for the best. At headquarters, Spike Bowman, who after a stint in the military had spent his Bureau career working at the National Security Law Unit and intimately knew the rules and regulations governing intelligence law, tried to intercede directly with Haynes's office at the Pentagon. His calls and letters were never returned.

Two days before Clemente and Neer rotated out of Guantánamo, they were finally able to meet with Major General Geoffrey Miller, the camp's military commander, and for two hours they laid out their concerns over the al-Qahtani plan.* The major general sat impassively through the meeting. When the agents were finished, he responded gruffly: "Well, gentlemen, thank you for your time. My boys know what they're doing." An e-mail in December back to headquarters from agents in Cuba announced a stalemate: "Looks like we are stuck in the mud with the interview approach of the military vs. law enforcement."

On December 2, 2002, the military initiated its "enhanced inter-rogation" procedure on Detainee 63. Even before his special regimen began, though, the FBI team noticed that he was already showing signs of psychological trauma, talking to nonexistent people, speaking of and to jinns (a mythic Arabic ghost). By the time the military fin-ished with al-Qahtani, he was even worse. "He looks like hell," explained the army lieutenant general, Ricardo Schmidt, who investi-gated the FBI's later allegations of abuse on behalf of the military. "He's got black coals for eyes."

And, as the FBI agents had predicted, the torture of al-Qahtani resulted in no real gains in information and intelligence. Weeks later, in a meeting between FBI officials and military personnel to go over the results of the "enhanced interrogations," the FBI executive lis-tened to the military's report, then shot back: "Look, everything you've gotten thus far is what the FBI gave you."

In August 2003, Geoffrey Miller and Diane Beaver were dis-patched to Iraq, where Miller was tasked with applying the Gitmo "lessons" to the unfolding and worsening situation in Baghdad. Two weeks later, on September 14, 2003, General Ricardo Sanchez approved new interrogation techniques, based in part on Miller and Beaver's input. The first photos of abuse at Baghdad's Abu Ghraib prison were dated October 17.

In the following years, more than four hundred FBI agents would rotate through Guantánamo. More than two hundred agents saw or

---

*Miller replaced Dunlavey as camp commander in November 2002.

heard of military and CIA use of harsh techniques, and those harsh techniques continued for more than a year after the Department of Defense eventually prohibited them. The knowledge that something was terribly wrong in the government's detainee interrogation program began to trickle out. Philip Zelikow, who led the staff of the 9/11 Commission, recalled being surprised that the FBI wasn't participating in the CIA's interrogations and that it refused to explain why. Something the CIA was doing, he suspected, must be not kosher if the FBI, which had the best al-Qaeda interrogators in the government, wasn't playing along. "It was the dog that didn't bark," he said later.

The CIA knew it was on shaky ground but, having license from the Office of Legal Counsel at Justice, proceeded anyway. Ralph DiMaio, who worked for the CIA's National Clandestine Service, reported in a sworn statement later, "The requests for advice were solicited in order to prepare the CIA to defend against future criminal, civil, and administrative proceedings that the CIA considered to be virtually inevitable." Once the Office of Legal Counsel had signed off, that was all they needed. There was really only one tactic government lawyers did refuse to condone: burying detainees alive as a way to frighten them before digging them up. Nearly everything else the Agency requested was approved.

The legal protection that the OLC memos provided gave the other agencies the cover they needed to proceed. When a congresswoman later asked why the Defense Intelligence Agency acceded to the techniques, Director Lowell Jacoby tried to explain the unique situation of the military: "Madam, I received a lawful order, it came down from the National Security Council, it was an order relayed to me by the deputy secretary of defense. My job was to execute lawful orders."

Of course, one of the main differences between the military and the law enforcement teams at Guantánamo was that thanks to their legal training and interrogation training, the law enforcement agents—specifically, the FBI and the NCIS, which also pulled its agents out of the "enhanced interrogations"—were in a position to know that the orders, while appearing to be legally justified, were actually beyond legal bounds. This was a decision arrived at, remarkably, primarily, by those on the ground in the field—the Clementes, Finchers, and Soufans who were standing in the interrogation rooms when things went south.

Strangely enough, as momentous as the decision to oppose "enhanced interrogations" seemed, it was largely overlooked by headquarters, which was consumed by the day-to-day terror fight. The FBI's deputy assistant director for counterterrorism, T. J. Harrington, said later that Gitmo was "an afterthought." Partly, according to agents and FBI personnel, that afterthought status happened because the Bureau leadership didn't want to know.

According to many FBI staff members, Pat D'Amuro was "hounding" the director at the time over the reports coming from the black sites and Guantánamo, but Mueller didn't want to hear it. "They knew what was going on and were hearing about it from all sides—the CIA, the White House, and the agents on the ground in Afghanistan and Gitmo," one FBI counterterrorism official explains. "Mueller was reticent in going against the CIA on this issue."

Mueller was a good Marine: he kept his head down and did the mission assigned. Tenet was probably his closest friend in the administration. The CIA director had shown Mueller the ropes, helped him learn the ways of Washington, helped him through the tumultuous months after 9/11. Without exactly turning a blind eye to the darker tactics in the U.S. war on terror, he believed that the Bureau had a specific role to fulfill and that other agencies had different roles. All he cared about was what the FBI was doing. As he explains, "I had no full understanding of the road we were going down, so I was concerned about where the Bureau was going." Mueller explained his caution at one point by saying, "Everyone should pay particular attention to the distinctions between allegations of abuse and the use of techniques which fall outside FBI/DOJ training and policy." Just because we wouldn't do it, he meant, doesn't mean other agencies can't do it. So he allowed a lot of leeway in what other agencies were doing. In 2002, during a secret meeting of Western intelligence leaders in New Zealand, Mueller sat quietly at Tenet's elbow as one of the CIA director's aides explained to the foreign leaders, "We're going to be working with intelligence agencies that are utterly unhesitant in what they will do to get people to talk."

FBI officials insist that there was no winking and nodding. "Those who know Bob would never, ever raise that," then deputy director Gebhardt says incredulously. Bureau leaders explain that they never realized that the interrogation techniques were so poorly conceived and untested, that the CIA's work was so flawed. Gebhardt explains, "Mueller assumed the CIA had an expertise that it didn't. The guys on the ground found that out much faster and it didn't percolate up. They didn't know until Abu Ghraib that it wasn't just a few bad apples."

Indeed, only the public disclosure of Abu Ghraib abuses in March 2004—abuses the FBI had been aware of as early as January—spurred the FBI to action. It finally issued a formal policy in May 2004 that read, in part, "FBI personnel shall not participate in any treatment or use any interrogation technique that is in violation of these guidelines regardless of whether the co-interrogator is in compliance with his or her own guidelines."

Mueller says today that it was a mistake that the Bureau didn't come out more forcefully against the "enhanced interrogations," a problem of the FBI's many layers of bureaucracy swallowing up an issue that should have gotten more of his attention. Could the Bureau have done more? Did it fail in responding to its agents' concerns at Gitmo? Mueller, his gaze steady and unflinching, doesn't mince words: "Yes."★

Yet his private comments at the time showed that perhaps he was more conflicted about the behavior of the U.S. government than he let on in public. Just weeks after Special Agent James Clemente forced a showdown with General Miller over the "enhanced interrogation" of Detainee 63, Mohammed al-Qahtani, Mueller's feelings on the subject came out during a quiet dinner party in Washington. The dinner's host, Tom Greene, a top D.C. defense attorney, began to needle fellow attorney Tom Wilner, who had signed up to be one of the first lawyers to defend the Guantánamo detainees. "I was just getting terrible shit right then from everywhere," Wilner recalls. The Muellers and the three other couples present had been friends for years, but

★As the "enhanced interrogation" issue became a public firestorm, the Justice Department's inspector general set out to interview the more than one thousand agents who had participated in combat operations, documenting their complaints about the interrogation protocols. He concluded that the "FBI should be credited for its conduct and professionalism in detainee interrogations."

even among old friends the subject of Guantánamo seemed to bring out the vitriol. "Tom was just ripping into me," Wilner recalls.

Then Mueller stood and raised his glass: "A toast. To Tom, who is doing just what an American lawyer should."

The tiny gathering fell silent.

"He never speaks out on politics, so for him to do that, it was very significant. I needed that support right then," Wilner recalls. "I just had this sense, when so many people in the administration were running around panicky, that Bob had a firm sense of what our values are."

The dinner toast was a rare outside view of the FBI director's inner dialogue during the early years after the September 11 attacks. He gave almost no speeches, no press conferences, and no interviews in his first years heading the Bureau, and he almost never publicly debated policies. Years later, he was still short and clipped his speech when talking about about interrogation protocols.

In another atypical private moment during his first year as FBI director, Mueller privately expressed doubts about some of the administration's aggressive actions. He confided to a friend, "You have to understand Bush. He's not a lawyer. He doesn't know what you shouldn't do. All he cares about is doing whatever he thinks is needed to keep people safe."* But at what cost?

---

* Two years later, the president joked about the same thing during a speech in Buffalo. On April 20, 2004, in pushing for the renewal of sections of the USA PATRIOT Act, the Yale history major told a crowd: "I'm not a lawyer, so it's kind of hard for me to kind of get bogged down in the law."

PART III
2002–2010

CHAPTER 11
Threat Matrix

In trying to defend everything, he defended nothing.
— *Frederick the Great*

There were few incentives in the days, weeks, and months after 9/11 to discount a threat before passing it up the chain. No agent wanted to be the next Mike Rolince, the highest-ranking FBI official who knew about Moussaoui prior to 9/11, when the next attack came. After years during which too little information was shared between agencies in the government, there was now too much sharing. Everyone wanted to share everything with everyone. Boxcars of information left Langley for other agencies in the government; the Hoover Building spewed forth thousands of tips, leads, and reports on a daily basis. "The only way you could lose was to not share something," recalls the Justice Department's James Comey. "The mentality was, 'When the music stops, I won't be the only one with a copy.'"

Each morning, before many Washingtonians had finished their breakfasts, as kids were being packed off to school, as commuters edged into D.C. on the Beltway and I-66, as lines at the Starbucks on Pennsylvania Avenue began to back out the door, the terror council assembled in the Oval Office to review the daily Threat Matrix. President Bush and Vice President Cheney sat in striped armchairs by the fireplace beneath the large portrait of George Washington. George Tenet, Bob Mueller, Condi Rice, and Andy Card sat on the two facing couches. Tom Ridge and John Ashcroft pulled up chairs on the fourth side.

The Threat Matrix—technically a spreadsheet titled "Terrorism Threats to U.S. Interests Worldwide"—broadly outlined every piece of information the immense U.S. government intelligence operation was tracking, including many tips and threats that just weeks earlier would have been weeded out by a junior or midlevel analyst many bureaucratic steps short of the Oval Office. Most days the Threat Matrix was no fewer than fifteen to twenty pages long, outlining each piece of intelligence, any relevant updates, the responsible agency, and follow-up actions under way. Everything was written in a broad, general form so that individual sources wouldn't be compromised.

Many of the items listed on the Threat Matrix were absurd, yet given the insecure and anxious climate, it became nearly impossible to separate the real tips from the false ones. Thus the daily threats seemed larger, more threatening, more immediate than most were in hindsight. The facts that al-Qaeda had very limited operational capability, and that, if the U.S. intelligence and law enforcement systems had worked better, the 9/11 plot would have probably been interdicted before execution, took years to come out. This disconnect ended up profoundly influencing President Bush and Vice President Cheney in their decision-making, leading them to overreact in efforts to combat what seemed to be an immediate, far-ranging, and immensely dangerous global threat of epic proportions. As the saying in computer programming goes, "Garbage in, garbage out."

The impossible task that the terror council in the Oval Office faced is illustrated by an instructive story from Asa Hutchinson, the former Arkansas congressman who served as the first undersecretary for border and transportation security in the Department of Homeland Security. When he began, one briefing informed him that there were 1.3 billion U.S. border crossings of goods and people a day. Beyond those, spread across some 20,000 miles of borders, were numerous other vulnerabilities in the system that had to be monitored and protected: the U.S. economy relies on 600,000 bridges, 190,000 miles of natural gas pipelines, 170,000 miles of public water systems,

123,000 miles of railroad tracks, 75,000 dams, 28,000 daily commercial flights, 2,800 power plants (including 104 nuclear power plants), 463 skyscrapers, and 420 commercial airports, as well as hundreds and thousands of subway stations, bus terminals, hotels, and shopping malls. Add in the overseas U.S. embassies and military bases, as well as American tourists and corporations doing business in foreign countries and the infrastructure of key American allies like Britain, Germany, France, and Spain, and the number of potential terrorist targets was almost infinite. As Hutchinson sat in the briefing confronting that enormous scale for the first time, another person present slipped him a note reading, "How do you like your odds?"

Everyone in the Oval Office Threat Matrix briefings felt the same pressure: *Don't let anything through.* Few in the room took to the new mission like John Ashcroft, who began to push the administration's antiterrorism agenda with almost religious fervor. In a speech to the U.S. Conference of Mayors on October 21, 2001, he dramatically proclaimed, "The men and women of justice and law enforcement are called on to combat a terrorist threat that is both immediate and vast; a threat that resides here, at home, but whose supporters, patrons, and sympathizers form a multinational network of evil."

Over the coming years, Ashcroft would come to be almost the fearmonger in chief. He was almost always the first in front of the cameras when a terror case erupted. He took the president's message not to let something like 9/11 happen again personally. He blasted those who questioned the administration's resolve or its tactics. The same day that Tom Knowles's team left Qatar for Afghanistan, Ashcroft appeared before the Senate Judiciary Committee with an uncompromising message: "To those who pit Americans against immigrants, citizens against noncitizens, to those who scare peace-loving people with phantoms of lost liberty, my message is this: Your tactics only aid terrorists, for they erode our national unity and diminish our resolve." Yet privately, he feared for the country. One Sunday in the fall of 2001, he summoned the department's top officials to a meeting in his secure conference room. "When a patient has a heart attack, you don't know if they'll survive or not," he told the group. "America has had a heart attack, and whether we're going to survive or not is in question."

As the nation's chief law enforcement officer, Ashcroft was responsible for making sure that the United States survived. One lesson he took from Janet Reno's tenure as his predecessor at Main Justice was that the Bureau needed to be firmly controlled. He wouldn't let the Bureau achieve the independence Louis Freeh had established under Janet Reno, when Freeh had felt comfortable conducting his own budget negotiations on Capitol Hill, speaking to the press without clearing statements through Main Justice, and even, in the case of Khobar Towers, conducting his own foreign policy. From early on in his tenure, Ashcroft had prohibited acting FBI director Tom Pickard from giving any Hill or White House briefings without clearing them through his office. "You control the Bureau by constant, close contact," David Ayres, Ashcroft's chief of staff, would regularly remind Main Justice leaders. In the weeks after the September 11 attacks, John Ashcroft literally worked out of a conference room in the FBI SIOC. "People realized it was different. Twenty people from DOJ, including Michael Chertoff, moved in and never left," Mike Rolince recalls. "That forever changed the Bureau." Each morning the attorney general (or, in his absence, the deputy attorney general) escorted Mueller to the morning threat briefings at the White House, even though Ashcroft rarely had anything to add in the meetings himself. As Mueller politely says of Ashcroft, "We were in the bunker together."

Every Wednesday at 4 P.M., the attorney general had FBI leaders come to his secure sixth-floor Main Justice conference room for "deep dives" on varying specific terrorism topics. The room was always stiflingly hot, and with their post-9/11 days beginning so early, the Justice officials often struggled to stay awake. Nevertheless the briefings were an important symbolic part of Ashcroft's tactic of subordinating the Bureau—as he made abundantly clear during one briefing after asking the briefer who had approved a certain operation.

"Your people approved this," the agent replied.

"Who exactly is 'your people'?" Ashcroft replied gruffly.

"Your staff over at the Justice Department," the agent replied.

"*You,* son, are at the Department of Justice," Ashcroft said icily.

The close relationship extended to the FBI director. At the start, Mueller was stuck between Ashcroft, who had suddenly developed a deep interest in terrorism and taken a more hands-on approach to the Bureau than any attorney general in decades, and an entrenched, complicated, and sprawling bureaucracy he didn't yet understand. While Ashcroft's closest inner circle was a group of ideological aides mostly gathered during his Senate career, Mueller, who had spent nearly his entire career in the Justice Department and had served as Ashcroft's deputy in the months after the inauguration, was closer to the attorney general than any FBI director in history, much to the concern of traditional FBI executives.

That uniquely close relationship was due in part to Mueller's prosecutor mentality and in part to the specific circumstances after 9/11. As one of Mueller's aides explains, "Never in a hundred years would he go out as independently as Freeh did." Beyond Mueller's personal inclination, though, the president's message—don't let this happen again—may have been directed toward Ashcroft on September 12, but it was meant for Mueller. Each morning in the Oval Office briefings, Mueller was under tremendous pressure from Bush and his own watchful, ever-present boss. "The FBI director was seeing the president every day. That's unprecedented. It's never happened before and may never happen again," one aide explains. "That has a cascade effect that really focuses the organization."

"After 9/11, the relationship between the FBI, the department, and the White House changed dramatically," Mueller says. Before the attacks, he explains, "there wasn't the impetus for the exchange of information when it comes to national security, because national security mostly meant espionage. Now, with so many lives at stake, the president and the attorney general, entirely appropriately, I believe, demanded more accountability for the information and the follow-up."

But again, there was always the question of what deserved follow-up. "Everything is terrorism until we prove it's not," said Jim Rice, head of the FBI's Washington-area incident response team, in one 2003 interview. "Our motto is, IT—international terrorism—or DT—domestic terrorism—or men from Mars, we're going to respond to it." At the time, Rice's team and the Washington Field Office JTTF were responding to an average of one hundred "threats" a month, 80 percent of which were immediately deemed false alarms. Another agent recalls, "We'd be sitting there saying, 'Why are we opening a case on this?' 'Oh, it was on the Threat Matrix.' We used to dread it every day."

In March 2002, under Homeland Security Advisor Tom Ridge, the administration announced a color scheme denoting just how frightened the nation should be. The green-blue-yellow-orange-red system was much maligned by pundits and comedians, but the drumbeat of "orange alerts" underscored that Americans should never get too comfortable.

On Tuesday, September 10, 2002, just hours before the first anniversary of the attack, Pat D'Amuro at headquarters got a troubling telephone call. The *Palermo Senator,* a container ship arriving in Newark after ports of call in Spain, Saudi Arabia, the UAE, and Asia, had set off Geiger counters, indicating that nuclear material was aboard. "Do you want us to hold it in port or take it out to sea?" the agent in Newark asked.

D'Amuro was annoyed. "How about you just figure out whether it's a nuclear bomb?" he said. "It's already in port—it's too late."

Tense hours passed as investigative agencies from the FBI to the Coast Guard and Port Authority gathered, waiting for a specialized Department of Energy team to arrive. President Bush was due to address the country the following day from Ellis Island, just five miles across New York Harbor—well within the blast zone of a nuclear weapon. FBI agents, with nothing to do but wait, sunned themselves on the *Palermo Senator's* deck. As further tests only raised more alarm, the FBI and the Coast Guard ordered the ship back to sea before President Bush's speech could go forward. "They were getting gamma neutron surges showing up as peaks and valleys on a graph," the ship's owner's representative later explained. "The surges could have come from anything—earthenware, bananas, television screens, or ceramic tile, or a nuclear weapon." As the *Palermo Senator* headed back out, armed FBI and Coast Guard personnel patrolled the deck and maintained a security perimeter around the ship. Anyone who came inside the thousand-yard zone was to be killed; no exceptions. It wasn't until Friday, two days after President Bush's commemoration speech at Ellis Island, that the Department of Energy was able to get its specialized equipment on board the *Palermo Senator* and determine definitively that the nuclear readings were triggered by innocuous clay tiles. The delay, everyone agreed, was unacceptable.

The *Palermo Senator* incident highlighted a frequent frustration for D'Amuro and the FBI counterterrorism threat team. Many times new devices were deployed without any thought about what would have to be done once an alarm was triggered. When the newly formed Department of Homeland Security set up expensive new radiation detectors on the George Washington Bridge, D'Amuro objected: "Do you have the manpower to stop every lane if the detectors go off?" Six hours into the first night that the detectors were operational, he got a call from the New York JTTF: A truck had tripped the alarm. D'Amuro quickly determined that no one had stopped the suspicious vehicle after it set off the radiation warnings and it had passed into Manhattan without challenge. "Technology without protocols can be more trouble than it's worth," D'Amuro says.

The same was true for intelligence. In the summer of 2004, the CIA gave the president a report headlined "Al-Qaeda Is Going to Attack the U.S." President Bush tried to call the Agency's bluff, asking the Agency briefer, "This says they're coming over the wall. You must be mobilizing every resource of the federal government to counter them. What exactly are you doing in response?" There was an awkward silence in the Oval Office before the Agency began to backtrack on its dire warning.

As the major Muslim holiday of Ramadan approached in 2002, the FBI warned authorities in Houston, Chicago, San Francisco, and Washington that al-Qaeda might try to target hospitals there. Two days later, the Bureau issued a national alert, saying, "Sources suggest al-Qaeda may favor spectacular attacks that meet several criteria: high symbolic value, mass casualties, severe damage to the U.S. economy, and maximum psychological trauma." The alert was meant, officials said at the time, to compile assorted intelligence, but it put everyone on edge.

Weeks later, information from an accused Canadian smuggler led President Bush to issue a personal appeal to the nation to help locate five Pakistanis who were said to have sneaked into the United States. "We need to know why they have been smuggled into the country and what they're doing in the country," he said, as the FBI distributed the pictures of the five suspects to the media and posted them worldwide. In a chilling follow-up to the millennium plots of 2000, further intelligence hinted at a series of New Year's Eve attacks in New York and led authorities to close the city's harbor to private vessels for two days. The entire thing turned out to be a hoax, concocted by the informant to gain favor with officials in Canada. As one counterterrorism agent at the time recalls, "There were real cases and then there were Threat Matrix cases. We used to call it ghost chasing. 'What are you working on today?' 'I'm chasing ghosts.'"

One morning the Threat Matrix cited, in its standard, concise, generalized form, "a threat from the Philippines to attack the United States unless blackmail money was paid." When Jim Comey, who had been promoted in December 2003 to deputy attorney general, asked for further information, FBI agents produced an e-mail reading: "Dear America, I will attack you if you don't pay me 9999999999999999999 99999999999999999999999 dollars. MUHAHAHA." "Anyone looking at that could tell it was written by a thirteen-year-old and it wasn't serious," Comey recalls. In the post-9/11 environment of leaving no stone unturned, the FBI ran the kid down and passed the lead to its in-country legat, who handed it over to the local Philippine police, who dutifully went and knocked on his parents' door.

Another time, a New Yorker called in a tip: "I just saw bin Laden at a BP in Queens." In due course, a JTTF agent was dispatched to check it out. "People were running around with their hair on fire. Everything was revolving around that Threat Matrix. On and on, every day," Cloonan recalls. "No one had the guts to stand up and say, 'That's bullshit.' Having said that, I can understand the predicament the director is in."

At times it was the administration that seemed unable to coordinate its message. Just before Memorial Day 2004, Tom Ridge gave a morning press conference during which, answering a reporter's question, he told reporters that there were no new threats to report. Later that day, John Ashcroft announced, with Robert Mueller at his side, that al-Qaeda was close to an attack. "We do believe that al-Qaeda plans to attack the United States, and that is a result of intelligence that is corroborated on a variety of levels. But we are not aware of details of a plan," Ashcroft announced, naming seven individuals the United States wanted to find.*

---

* One of the individuals, Adam Yahiye Gadahn, aka "Azzam the American," would go on to become, in 2006, the first American charged with treason in more than fifty years.

In another incident, an NSA or CIA subcontractor (sources differed on which agency was the primary contact) provided a series of coordinates hidden in Al Jazeera images that supposedly consisted of a list of likely terrorist targets. Transatlantic flights were canceled because of the supposed intelligence. Asa Hutchinson, now the head of the Transportation Security Administration, spent the holidays on the phone, giving a personal go or no-go to individual flights based on updated information. Jim Comey, though, doubted the threat's veracity. One set of coordinates traced back to Tappahannock, Virginia, a tiny town of two thousand people that had once been part of his territory in the Richmond U.S. Attorney's Office. "If the information is so reliable, how come it's tracing out to be farmland in Tappahannock, Virginia?" Comey asked incredulously in one briefing. "How reliable could it be?" He walked out of the meeting, still fuming that some P. T. Barnum was trying to pull a hoax and profit from obviously vacuous leads. He turned to an aide and said, "Someone should get locked up for that." Nothing ever came of the Tappahannock threat, or, indeed, of nearly any of the threats that consumed the minds of the intelligence leaders. Altogether, the U.S. government was trying to chase down upwards of five thousand threats a day, more of them like the Filipino e-mail than like the Bojinka plot.

"When I started, I believed that a giant firehose of information came in the ground floor of the U.S. government and then, as it went up, floor by floor, was whittled down until at the very top the president could drink from the cool, small stream of a water fountain," Comey says. "I was shocked to find that after 9/11 the firehose was just being passed up floor by floor. The firehose every morning hit the FBI director, the attorney general, and then the president."

The director and his team weren't necessarily believers either. "Some of the plots, you'd just sit there and says there's no way [that's true]," former deputy director Gebhardt recalls. "Bob and I were real doubters." During one briefing, Comey turned to Mueller and asked, "What are we doing, Bob? Is every lead going to make it into the Threat Matrix?" The answer, for years, was yes.

The mostly vacuous Threat Matrix seemed intended to cover up one of the biggest government flaws in the period immediately after the attacks: The government had very little good information. It still

had no human sources inside al-Qaeda. It didn't have a good understanding of the group's capabilities. Everything seemed as if it could be
possible, and thus any piece of amorphous, unsubstantiated chatter
could set off panic. Every time Mueller traveled out to a field office, as
he did a handful of times each month, local elected officials and law
enforcement leaders would demand more access to threat information.
He'd come back to Washington and lament to colleagues standing
outside the Oval Office in the morning, "They think we've got something we don't have."

As George Tenet said later, "When you have been accused of failing to connect the dots, your initial reaction is to ensure that all the
dots are briefed. Until our knowledge became more refined, our inclination was to overbrief." Tenet's statement is, perhaps unintentionally,
fascinating. He meant, in essence, that in the immediate wake of 9/11,
the entire intelligence community left the connecting of the dots to the
president. The firehose hitting the Oval Office was, in some ways, the
result of what some labeled "9/11 Commission syndrome." It was in no
one's interest to be the one who culled the threats, because it was possible you'd cull the wrong threat and end up, after the next attack, at
the green felt witness table before the next congressional inquiry. Colleagues watched as careers were destroyed because someone was cc'ed
on an e-mail like the Phoenix memo. "The search for someone
responsible had tremendous collateral consequences," Comey recalls.

The twice-daily threat briefings, the flood of intelligence reports
throughout the rest of the day, the panicked lurches and fruitless raids,
had a profound effect on the principals involved. One night, after
another day spent running down a possible terrorist weapon of mass
destruction, Comey was dropped off by his security detail at his house
outside Washington. A light burned inside; upstairs his five kids were
already asleep. As he walked up the path to his front door, he paused
for a moment and tested the wind's direction, mentally calculating
whether radioactive fallout from Washington would blow toward his
family. *I wonder whether my kids will be safe until the morning,* Comey
thought; then he realized just how paranoid he had become. As he
recalls, "Your mind comes to be dominated by the horrific consequences of low-probability events."

Of course, not all tips involved sightings at local gas stations. There was a healthy industry in Eastern Europe of criminals seeking to defraud terrorist groups on the black market for nuclear weapons. As John Brennan, the CIA official who went on to be Barack Obama's counterterrorism adviser, later explained, "We know that al-Qaeda has been involved in a number of these efforts. . . . Fortunately, I think they've been scammed a number of times, but we know that they continued to pursue that." The FBI's key al-Qaeda defector, the pancake-loving Junior al-Fadl, had told Danny Coleman and other FBI agents that al-Qaeda had tried to purchase the makings for a nuclear weapon as early as 1993, when it was scammed out of $1.5 million by a Sudanese diplomat who had promised it uranium. Even though the vast majority of nuclear smuggling tips turned out to be scams, under the one percent doctrine, each threat had to be treated as real until definitively proved otherwise.

Soon after 9/11, authorities were sent into a panic after receiving a report from an FBI legat that terrorists had managed to smuggle a nuclear bomb into the United States. The supposed bomb was, according to the tip, currently on a train somewhere between Pittsburgh and Philadelphia. The vague threat was frantically run down before the source became clear: An informant had probably misheard a conversation between two men in a bathroom in the Ukraine. For weeks afterward, President Bush would ask in briefings, half annoyed, half joking, "Is this another Ukrainian urinal incident?"

A few days after the Ukraine threat, on October 11, 2001, George Tenet told President Bush that a CIA source code-named Dragonfire reported that al-Qaeda had smuggled a ten-kiloton nuclear bomb into Manhattan. While there was no second source on the information, there was also nothing that could prove Dragonfire was wrong, and Dick Cheney was dispatched to an "undisclosed location." (The threat would prove to be one of the key reasons that the vice president stayed out of sight for much of the final months of 2001.) The Dragonfire threat ultimately amounted to nothing more serious than lots of heartburn in the intelligence community. New York City leaders were never told.

However, one lead was left uncovered. During one meeting, Ashcroft heard that one of the 9/11 hijackers had used an ATM card with the PIN 67262, which spelled OSAMA on the keypad. "They're mocking us!" he yelled. "These guys are mocking us." He ordered the Bureau to track down and investigate everyone in the United States using that ATM PIN. The FBI official present in the meeting decided, after further thought, that the task was probably better left undone.

Only passing time and sheer exhaustion would allow the government to swing the pendulum back, allowing for clear thinking to prevail. At some point, somewhere, someone would wake up one morning, look at the day's leads, and say, *Screw it. I'm not following that up,* and balance would be restored to the intelligence process. Until then, "Every morning in there was September twelfth," one person who attended the briefings explains. "Each day was a jump ball."

Those morning terrorism briefs consumed the first hours of Mueller's day, beginning with the counterterrorism division's briefing of the director in his conference room at 7 A.M., followed by the 7:30 briefing with the attorney general in the FBI SIOC, and then on to the White House and the Oval Office for the 8:30 daily rundown, then back to FBI Headquarters for Mueller's 9:15 senior staff meeting. After the morning reviews, the process would begin anew. The entire Threat Matrix was reviewed again daily at 5 P.M., updating whatever information had come in during the day and answering whatever questions the principals had from the morning brief. The entire Bureau, case agents complained, seemed to exist to feed the briefing machine in the wake of 9/11. The cycle ran without regard to day or night. Terror never slept, so neither would the government. President Bush couldn't get enough information, which meant that Director Mueller couldn't get enough information.

The pressure from the Oval Office was relentless. During a week when Bruce Gebhardt was briefing the president for the Bureau, reports came in of a group of Middle Eastern men in Kansas seeking to acquire a large warehouse for cash. "We don't know what we have here," Gebhardt told the president.

"Why do they want to buy a warehouse?" the president asked from his traditional seat next to the Oval Office fireplace.

"That's what we're investigating," Gebhardt replied.

On two subsequent mornings, all the deputy director could offer was that the Bureau was working to run down leads. On the third morning, President Bush asked for an update on the Kansas threat, but there was still nothing substantive to report.

"Don't worry, Mr. President, the FBI has Kansas surrounded," Gebhardt replied.

Everyone in the room laughed—except for Vice President Cheney.*

Out in the field, agents felt that the demand to feed information upward was impeding other investigations. As one person who attended the Oval Office briefings lamented, "They're chasing things because someone's asking, not because it's important." After yet another random request came down from Washington one day, New York counterterrorism supervisor Ken Maxwell fired off an angry e-mail to headquarters in frustration about the seemingly endless requests for briefings—requests that were distracting agents from actually following leads: "Last I checked," he wrote, "the I in FBI stood for 'investigation,' not 'information.'"

And yet it never seemed that enough information from the sprawling Bureau apparatus was making its way upward. In the late fall of 2002, Mueller was blindsided by a question in the morning Threat Matrix meeting with Ashcroft about an FBI investigation that was unfolding overseas. The meeting in SIOC was the first time that Mueller had heard of it. A few days earlier, Deputy Director Gebhardt had clashed with a field supervisor who had shied away from pursuing a FISA warrant because of the workload involved. The combination of not pursuing an investigation and the information not getting up to the director seemed reminiscent of the oversights and mistakes with Zacarias Moussaoui that had led up to 9/11.

Gebhardt fired off a blistering memo to the field office heads, saying that the Bureau's efforts weren't good enough. "You need to instill a sense of urgency," he told the nation's special agents in charge. "I'm

---

*In a sign of how overblown some threats could appear without complete information, the Kansas situation quickly resolved itself when FBI agents finally tracked down the mysterious Middle Easterners. They wanted the warehouse in order to open a flea market.

amazed and astounded and at a loss to understand."* His memo to the SACs was a dressing-down almost unheralded in the FBI's annals. Mueller followed up with his own memo, ending a decades-long practice of allowing each field office to set its own local crime priorities. Mueller informed the SACs that they all now had the same single, overarching, all-consuming priority. "While every office will have different crime problems that will require varying levels of resources, the FBI has just one set of priorities," he wrote: *Stop the next attack.*

Gebhardt heard vigorous protests from the field. "The concept of terrorism hit Washington and New York but not most other places. Not everyone immediately put it at the top of the list," he explains. "SACs would howl that we were taking their 'best program'—say, white-collar crime—from thirty agents to five. 'But that's our biggest problem out here,'" Gebhardt recalls them saying. "We hear that—we have to protect the country. If someone's going to do it, it's not going to be the CIA, it's not going to be the military."

Donald Rumsfeld had a saying: "Absence of evidence is not evidence of absence." It was a corollary to Cheney's one percent doctrine. For decades, the Bureau had dealt in evidence "beyond a reasonable doubt." Now it was learning to operate on a battlefield where the fog of war meant that "actionable intelligence" was not always possible. Yet it was often the Bureau's job to prove the negative. "They've got to report it, then we've got to act," Mueller recalls. "It's a continuous tension. If it happened once after 9/11, it happened a hundred times." That tension meant that Mueller sometimes groused as he walked out of the Oval Office, after hearing a particularly useless tip from somewhere in the intelligence community, "I can't do anything with that." The FBI, he'd say over and over again, couldn't surveil every mosque, follow every Middle Easterner purchasing fertilizer and every Muslim renting a moving van, search every truck entering New York City, and so on. As one of Mueller's fellow Oval Office terrorism briefing

---

*The phrase was actually an old Bureau colloquialism, one Gebhardt had first learned at Quantico in the 1970s as a new agent. An Academy instructor was blasting him, the son of the assistant director of the Criminal Division, for breaking the rules and missing curfew: "Gebhardt, I'm amazed and astounded and at a loss to understand." He'd used the phrase ever since.

attendees recalls, "The Bureau quickly becomes exasperated with the lack of actionable, tactical intelligence."

Tenet and Mueller, while not close friends, had a long history. As staff director of the Senate Intelligence Committee from 1988 to 1993, Tenet had often grilled Mueller when he was serving in the Department of Justice under the first President Bush. In personality, the men couldn't have been much more different: Tenet the jocular back-slapper who loved chomping on unlit cigars, and Mueller the stoic, unsmiling prosecutor. (When the two men appeared on the Hill together in the years after 9/11, as they did many, many times, Tenet would always try to get Mueller to crack a smile.) The men eventually became social friends too, dining out regularly on Sundays with their wives at a small Italian restaurant near their homes. Tenet, who had taken office in 1995, had been around Washington longer and had studied politics more closely than Mueller, and after 9/11, the CIA director took the new FBI director under his wing. "He educated me in the ways of Washington," Mueller explains. (Another FBI official phrases it differently: "In a nutshell, what Tenet said was always gospel to Mueller.") But tension between the agencies increased as the war on terror continued, and friction developed between the two directors. An FBI counterterrorism supervisor described the Threat Matrix process as "doing the CIA's bidding." Every time the CIA picked up a squib of information, it tossed it into the Threat Matrix. Then it was up to the FBI to prove the negative, that the threat wasn't true.

During one National Security Council meeting in the Situation Room, Tenet presented a variety of tidbits on the Threat Matrix that seemed to point to a larger plot.

"Bob, what does the FBI have on any of these threats? What's the domestic picture look like?" the president asked.

Mueller, ever cautious, explained that he disagreed with Tenet's assessment.

"Time out," Bush said, and he asked the CIA to explain again, in more detail.

The CIA presented a number of names of al-Qaeda suspects it thought might be in the United States. Mueller, perhaps choosing his words carelessly, said, "If they don't commit a crime, it would be difficult to identify and isolate [suspects]." What he meant was that none of the people the CIA had singled out had appeared on the Bureau's radar.

Although nearly all of the top officials were present, Dick Cheney was off-site at one of his proverbial "undisclosed locations," participating by video conference. He hit the roof. That was the "same mentality," he charged, that had led to the 9/11 attacks. On screen, he bore down on the FBI director: "Bob, do we have anything domestically on any of these CIA reports?"

"Up to this point, we haven't been able to find anything to add domestically to these perceived threats," Mueller said carefully.

"Nothing?" the president asked incredulously.

"Nothing really to add, Mr. President," the FBI director said.

Cheney cut him off. "That's just not good enough. We're hearing this too much from the FBI."

As a young agent in the 1980s, Ken Maxwell had been working a major terrorism case against a group of Croatian separatists. One day, under FBI surveillance, one of the suspects left his house outside New York City and gingerly carried a shopping bag to the trunk. Then, with another Croatian separatist, they drove into the city and repeatedly circled Union Square. Their suspicious behavior set off warning bells in the New York office. The number two in New York, a colorful Hoover-era agent named Ken Walton who had once shot a rat in the hall of the field office, declared, "All hands on deck." FBI agents flooded into Union Square, and Walton met up with Maxwell in the square's park. Everyone suspected the separatists were preparing for a bombing.

Walton asked the young case agent, "What do you want to do?"

"It was amazing," Maxwell recalls today. "I was a GS-10, but since I was the case agent, Walton trusted me to do what's best for the case and the people of New York."

The two men agreed that if the separatists went toward the trunk of their car, the FBI would take them down, but as long as they stayed with the car, it was best to keep the surveillance going. Stopping these two men, the agents concurred, might mean letting their colleagues escape. Two days later, when everyone in the group was arrested, agents discovered that the shopping bag had held six sticks of dynamite; the group had been casing Manhattan for its next attack. "It was a calculated smart risk," Maxwell recalls today. "No one was willing to mediate risk after 9/11." All of that latitude and delegated authority was now long gone.

In the summer of 2002, for the first time, Bob Mueller walked into the Oval Office with the words that everyone had been waiting anxiously to hear: *Al-Qaeda was here*. The Bureau had discovered what it believed was a sleeper cell in the small upstate New York town of Lackawanna, a depressed community yet to recover from the closing of the nearby Buffalo steel mills which was home to the nation's second largest Yemeni community.

The FBI surveillance focused on six men (although others were involved) who had traveled from Lackawanna to Afghanistan in the spring of 2001 after a visiting radical preacher convinced them that big adventures were ahead. They trained in al-Qaeda's infamous al-Farouq training camp near Kandahar, learning weapon skills and the militant ideology of jihad. (They were some of the last would-be-jihadists to go through the Afghanistan camp, as all the camps were shut down in August 2001 in anticipation of the 9/11 attacks.) At al-Farouq, the six had met and chatted with Osama bin Laden. Though they later professed to have had cold feet and refused to sign up for a "martyrdom operation," none of them exactly ran to the FBI to share their experiences after they returned to the Buffalo area. Within weeks of their departure for Afghanistan, an anonymous tip to the Buffalo Field Office reported their plans, which alerted customs agents to keep an eye out for the men when they returned. Beyond that extra attention at the border, though, the men kept a low profile. The single FBI agent assigned in Buffalo to counterterrorism, Ed Needham, didn't have the time or inclination to dig too deeply.

After 9/11, the case against the men grew serious. President Bush feared that al-Qaeda sleeper cells around the country were secreted for a second wave of attacks. In June 2002, intelligence information, partly gained from a Guantánamo detainee who had been on the 2001 New York recruiting trip, linked Kamal Derwish, an American al-Qaeda recruiter, to the Lackawanna men. Agents—more conspicuous, perhaps, than they should have been with out-of-state license plates on their undercover cars—flooded the industrial town and particularly the city's first ward, which had a large Yemeni population. ("They stuck out like a sore thumb," recalled Dennis O'Hara, the Lackawanna police chief.)

The unfolding investigation became the primary focus of Mueller's morning briefings with the president. Stanley Borgia, then the assistant special agent in charge of the Buffalo FBI, recalled later, "I would look at my watch and say, 'Eight-thirty. The president is saying to the director, 'What's going on in Buffalo?'" Agents and investigators were alarmed as e-mails among the group referred to a September "wedding," often code in al-Qaeda for an attack. In a July 2002 e-mail to Derwish, one suspect, Mukhtar al-Bakri, wrote, "I would like to remind you of obeying God and keeping him in your heart because the next meal will be very huge." A big meal also seemed to refer to a pending attack. In August, Needham traveled to Washington to brief Mueller.

As the days ticked down to the first anniversary of September 11, the president got personally involved in the decision-making, asking, "Can you guarantee me that these guys won't do something?" The FBI director was fairly confident, telling Bush, "We are ninety-nine percent sure that we can stop these guys from doing something." But in the era of the one percent doctrine, that one percent was all the doubt the government needed. The Oval Office wanted the six off the streets. As President Bush later explained in his memoir, "For me, the lesson of 9/11 was simple: Don't take chances."

Vice President Cheney argued that the Lackawanna men should be taken into custody by the U.S. military and declared enemy combatants. The FBI shouldn't be involved. Terrorism wasn't for the justice system, he believed—a view advanced by David Addington, John Yoo, and others. To support their argument, Cheney and Rumsfeld cited an October 2001 memo from Yoo saying that the president had the authority to use the military against foreign terrorists within the United States, a point hotly contested by constitutional scholars but not by the increasingly powerful vice president. Mueller, Condi Rice, and Michael Chertoff strongly argued against the idea. As the Buffalo SAC, Peter Ahearn, later explained, "There was the Department of Justice and the FBI that were basically saying this was an issue of rule of law. Why would we be doing this when we are inside the borders of the United States and this is domestic? Treating them as combatants, to me, was unnecessary. They were American citizens." In the end, the president balked and the FBI remained in the picture. There were lines, Bush felt, which still shouldn't be crossed.

On September 9, commandos in Bahrain arrested Mukhtar al-Bakri on his wedding night, while he was in bed with his bride. A New York state trooper from the Buffalo JTTF picked him up with the FBI's Gulfstream jet and brought him back to the United States. Agents also descended on Lackawanna and searched homes for evidence. National TV news crews broadcast live from the neighborhood as America learned of its first suspected "sleepers."

Derwish lived free in Yemen for ten more weeks until a Predator drone found him. George Tenet personally gave the okay from Langley before a Hellfire missile disintegrated the car in which the al-Qaeda recruiter was riding. It was a landmark decision: The U.S. government had executed an American citizen without benefit of trial. Before 9/11, Tenet had argued that a democracy shouldn't place such power in the hands of the CIA director; he didn't want to be judge, jury, and executioner. Yet the United States wasn't taking any chances anymore.

The tradeoff in the case, of course, was the unanswered questions. Authorities still aren't sure what al-Qaeda may or may not have intended for the Lackawanna Six. Prosecutors carefully tried not to label them a "cell," and it was never certain that the men actually planned to engage in terrorism in the United States or elsewhere. But these men, the government had decided, were a threat and needed to be taken out of the game. Mueller, testifying later before Congress, laid out the FBI's strategy. "You don't wait until the cell becomes operational, because if you wait until the fuse is lit, you're waiting too long," he said. "A sleeper cell can become operational in the blink of an eye."

That was true, but, as Dale Watson put it later, taking the case down early meant possibly compromising other leads down the road. "A conscious decision was made: Let's get them out of here," he said. "It could have produced a lot of good intelligence. It could have produced a lot of other individuals in the United States and outside the United States—and it might not have produced anything." Living with the certainty that the men could no longer wreak havoc paired with the uncertainty of not knowing their plans was better for the officials in Washington than the unknowns of leaving them on the street. As George Piro, who had helped identify one of the 9/11 hijackers and worked with the author of the Phoenix memo, explains, "It's a catch-22 for us. If you arrest too early, you run the risk of not understanding what's taking place and who it involves, and being accused of jumping the gun. If you arrest too late, you're second-guessed for allowing a possible risk to develop or even letting an attack unfold."

The pressure Mueller felt moved from his shoulders down through the organization. Across the Bureau, and indeed throughout the government, home phones, BlackBerrys, and secure lines rang right through the night. "I heard over and over again that if the CIA didn't catch the terrorists overseas or the Pentagon didn't capture or kill them, it was up to us," explained Larry Mefford, who headed counterterrorism for the Bureau in the wake of 9/11. "Nobody was under the pressure the FBI was under."

Knowles, the onetime head of the FBI's international operations and leader of the Bureau's team in Afghanistan, watched in growing frustration as round after round of newly promoted counterterrorism staffers blew through the revolving door at headquarters, always asking questions, demanding briefings, and trying to get up to speed. People who spent their entire lives working white-collar or organized crime cases were now proclaiming themselves experts on counterterrorism. "Everyone was so green that they had no experience," he recalls. "They didn't know anything. None of them had even been in a bar fight. They overreacted again and again. You cannot continue to run around saying the sky's on fire for months on end. It was disgusting."

Special Agent Brad Doucette wasn't one of the newbies. By the time he landed at FBI Headquarters to head up the Iran-Hezbollah unit—one of the oldest of the Bureau's counterterrorism units—in September 2002, he had spent the better part of a decade working counterterrorism, including the original TRADEBOM case and the crash of EgyptAir 990. Lured by one of Director Mueller's speeches during a field office visit about how headquarters needed good agents and strong leaders, he'd taken the Hezbollah slot when it opened up.

As the Iraq war loomed in 2003, Doucette was pressed into service to lead the FBI's command post, monitoring intelligence about possible threats to the homeland. The work and the pressure consumed him. He lost more than thirty pounds during his time at headquarters. His wife convinced her now 150-pound husband to get checked out by a doctor, who diagnosed exhaustion, but Doucette went back to work at the Hoover Building the next day. The flow of intelligence and the impetus to deal with it were too pressing. In mid-April, Fred Stremmel stopped into Doucette's office to check on him. "I never had seen anyone who looked so pale or gray," Stremmel recalls. "I asked how he was doing, and he only said that he cannot believe how management puts so much stress on everyone and chews them up." Returning to his own desk, Stremmel warned his supervisor, another friend of Doucette's, that he feared the agent was a candidate for "the big one"—a heart attack.

On the morning of April 29, 2003, six months short of his twentieth anniversary at the Bureau and just a week after U.S. troops secured Tikrit in the last major push of the ground invasion of Iraq, a call from the FBI SIOC woke Doucette at 4:30. It was in retrospect, by all accounts, nothing critical, just the same kind of alarm that cropped up almost nightly, based more on panic than on solid intelligence. He tried to go back to sleep, but a second phone call came an hour later from an agent in New York. There was simply no break. As the sky began to brighten over the capital region and the briefers began their journeys across Washington to deliver the day's Threat Matrix, Doucette fetched his FBI-issued handgun. He killed himself with a single shot just behind his right ear, becoming arguably the FBI's first casualty in the war on terror since John O'Neill and Leonard Hatton had run into the burning towers on 9/11. "It was one hundred percent the job," his wife, Suzanne, herself a former FBI agent, said later. "The extreme exhaustion. The worry. Not being able to sleep. Not being able to leave Washington."

Mueller took Doucette's death hard. For him, personnel issues had always been the toughest. "It was terrible, painful," Mueller recalls. "Doucette was the ultimate example of the counterterrorism staff, who were under huge pressure, making split-second decisions on incomplete information, and who realized that every decision they made might be second-guessed by someone down the road." Mueller adds that Washington's practice of finding a scapegoat for every failure only increased the pressure throughout the process. "Everyone was working desperately to stop the next attack, but our culture believes perfection is achievable."

He visited Suzanne three times, bringing handwritten notes from the president and the attorney general. "When people get home, let them sleep," she pleaded with the FBI director.

While Doucette was an extreme example, every member of the Bureau's counterterrorism team felt the pressure. Mueller himself ground through staff in the years after 9/11. "He drives at such speed that he can burn up people around him," Comey says. "Some people burn people up because they're assholes. Bob burns them up by sheer exertion." Whereas Bob Bucknam, who served as Louis Freeh's consigliere and chief of staff, had lasted through Freeh's entire term, Mueller went through five chiefs of staff in his first four years, and his special assistants rarely lasted more than a year. It wasn't that he was cruel to his staff—just relentless and demanding. Dan Levin, one of the chiefs of staff, said that when he left, he had worked 365 days straight. One FBI official said that Mueller runs with "the energy of the sun." "He's got one speed and it's pretty relentless," explains Lisa Monaco, a former prosecutor who as his fifth chief of staff arrived after much of the initial post-9/11 crisis environment had passed and lasted three years in the job. But while the director tried to be compassionate, he was not particularly cuddly, nor did he have time for emotional exploration. When his wife, Ann, warned him that he was working his staff too hard, he called his then counsel Chuck Rosenberg. "How are you doing?" he asked when Rosenberg answered the phone. "Fine," Rosenberg said. "What can I get you, boss?" "Nothing," Mueller replied, the conversation over. He had checked in on his staff.

Such exchanges seemed to confirm Mueller's reputation as a tough-as-nails Marine. That perception had some truth but wasn't entirely accurate, aides recall. While Mueller rarely socialized with his FBI staff, continuing a tradition that dated back to his earliest days as an assistant U.S. attorney, he was never big on ceremony and even tried to get Bureau executives to call him Bob when he started.★ That informality didn't take (mostly he's known internally as "boss"), but that was primarily the fault of the FBI's hierarchical culture. Mueller's relentlessness eased up some as the Bureau's position strengthened and the response to terrorism within the Washington apparatus matured, but only in 2009, with the new Obama administration in town, did his staff convince him to stop arriving at the office at 6:00 A.M. Instead, while his alarm clock still went off at five, he worked at home for two hours before arriving at the Hoover Building at seven.

At times, Mueller's straight-arrow nature was a source of amusement and occasional befuddlement at headquarters. In one meeting, examining the schedule for a gathering of the FBI's fifty-six SACs in New Orleans, he mused that they had better not schedule anything for Sunday morning. The agents at the conference table nodded, thinking about how the FBI executives would probably party hard late into the night in the French Quarter. "You know, because I imagine most people will want to go to church," Mueller added a moment later, quite serious. It was all the other FBI executives around him could do to stifle laughs.

His daily staff meetings looked like a throwback to the days of the G-Men and J. Edgar Hoover. Mueller set the standard in his dark suits, white shirts, and red or blue ties. One wore a colored shirt around the director at one's peril, and stories abounded of agents from out of town running around Washington the night before a meeting with him in search of a white shirt. John Miller, the legendary ABC investigative reporter who interviewed Osama bin Laden in the 1990s and spent several years under Mueller as head of public affairs, was notorious for his flamboyant outfits—colored shirts, fancy ties, and handkerchiefs. Mueller would stare down the table at the 9:15 A.M. staff meeting and ask, "John, what exactly are you wearing?"

Mueller wasn't entirely without his soft side, though. Special Agent

---

★ David Margolis recalls that as head of the Criminal Division at Main Justice under George H. W. Bush, Mueller would host summer barbecues for his section chiefs from 8 to 11 P.M. "At five minutes to eleven he'd start flipping the lights to get people out of his house," Margolis says, laughing.

Jim Clemente was undergoing his first day of chemotherapy at Johns Hopkins in 2005 when he was told that he had a visitor. Mueller, who had had his second knee replacement surgery in the same hospital earlier in the day, was wheeled into the room. The director grimaced as the nurse banged his foot against the wall. "Don't get up," Mueller said. "I obviously won't be." The two men chatted for a few minutes, never talking work. "It was an incredible gesture," Clemente recalls. "Here he was getting his own treatment and he loaded into the wheelchair, got wheeled through the complex, and visited me before he went home. We'd never even met."

But such stories were rare, and Mueller took some pleasure in his stoic reputation. When David Margolis, his longtime friend from the Justice Department, suffered a heart attack in the mid-1990s, he received a handwritten note from Mueller. When he called the then U.S. attorney to thank him, Mueller teased, "Don't be telling anyone about that. It's bad for the image."

Perhaps understandably, in the midst of all the crises, it took Mueller years to get his arms fully around the Bureau. Looking back, both current and former FBI executives lament that the director got bad advice from some of his deputies in the months after 9/11. He'd made almost no personnel decisions and learned few names before the attacks, and certainly he'd had little time to figure out whom he could trust. In the years following 9/11, Mueller earned a reputation for tearing into aides he felt weren't prepared or weren't giving him straight answers. "He was a 'kill the messenger' type," one FBI executive explains.

Mostly, though, Mueller was lacerating to anyone who came before him unprepared. He has a particular dislike for "Jell-O words," recalls Special Agent Bob Casey, who became a close aide in Mueller's first years. In briefings and meetings, agents and briefers would say things like "Such and such is linked to al-Qaeda" or "is associated with terrorists." Mueller would fume: "I don't know what *linked* means. If that's all you've got, don't brief me." He wanted specifics, definitive statements, and hard facts. "There was a level of answer that was acceptable within the Bureau that didn't provide the level of detail

Bob Mueller required—and objectively probably wasn't satisfactory either," explains his friend and counselor Lee Rawls. When asked how they were responding to a threat or following up on a lead or suspect, agents, steeped in the FBI's gung-ho culture, would confidently answer with a Bureau standby: "We got it covered, boss" or the equally popular "We're all over it, boss." Mueller didn't take well to those answers either. "It's like appearing before a smart, tough judge every day," says Lisa Monaco. "He wants to get information and the right information and he wants you to be on top of your game."★

"Everyone was afraid to be negative unless you're of a retireable age," one agent explains. "People didn't feel comfortable presenting dissenting opinions." In one incident, much discussed among the agent corps, an internal investigation was opened on an agent who allegedly made insulting comments about the director. (Nothing came of the investigation, which executives attributed to an overeager internal affairs officer.)

Mueller recalls that during his first years as FBI director, he struggled to get "ground truth," to find out "what's really happening, not just what people want to tell you." As he explains, "The mistakes I've made are when I haven't gotten to the bottom of it, dug really deep down, asked all the questions."

While Mueller wanted as many facts as possible, once he'd chewed them over, he quickly made his decision. "His gift is that he's decisive without being impulsive," Jim Comey notes. "He'll sit, listen, ask questions, and make a decision. I didn't realize at the time how rare that is in Washington." Once a decision was made, though, it was no longer open for debate. In one meeting, Mueller deployed a line from the submarine action movie *Crimson Tide:* "I'm here to protect democracy, not to practice it." In another instance, he told a group of Bureau

---

★The FBI hierarchy became sensitive to ensuring that it had the answers to the questions the director would ask. At one point, the counterterrorism division tried to organize a prebriefing at 6:30 or 6:45 A.M. before being called in by the director at 7:15 so that they could be better prepared. Maureen Baginski, whom Mueller had brought to the Bureau from the NSA to oversee intelligence, objected strenuously, feeling that the "prebrief" was an attempt to limit what information flowed upward. "Intelligence means being surprised by emerging information," she argued.

subordinates, "Generals don't listen to Marines in foxholes." As one agent explained, again using a military metaphor, "The director respects you if you want to argue about which route to take up the hill, but he won't argue over which hill is the right one to take."

In the fall of 2002, Bob Mueller found himself and the Bureau on the ropes for a second time. The more information that came out after 9/11, the more it seemed that the attacks could have been averted if everyone, especially the FBI, had connected the dots. Indeed, the Bureau's "FL"—the "fuck-ups list"—seemed a litany of tragic blunders, including failures with Zacarias Moussaoui, Williams's Phoenix memo warning of Middle Easterners taking flight training, and the two hijackers known to be in the United States. The FBI certainly wasn't alone in missing clues, but it became a top target for politicians and the public, even when blame more rightly should have fallen across the intelligence community. "To a certain extent, the Bureau took the brunt of a series of institutional failures," Ben Wittes says.

Coleen Rowley, the chief division counsel in the Minneapolis Field Office, became the voice for the FBI's missteps. Stopped by repeated institutional roadblocks during the Moussaoui investigation, she wrote a thirteen-page memo to Mueller, also delivering copies to Congress, attacking the Bureau out of post-9/11 frustration. Rowley was certain that with a more aggressive investigation, unencumbered by tentative agents and risk-averse supervisors, the FBI might have cracked the case. "It's at least possible we could have gotten lucky and uncovered one or two more of the terrorists in flight training prior to Sept. 11," she wrote. But Rowley was upset not just by pre-9/11 failures; she was certain that the Bureau was covering up the evidence of its incompetence. She directly attacked Mueller and other Bureau leaders: "I have deep concerns that a delicate shading/skewing of facts by you and others at the highest levels of FBI management has occurred and is occurring." She finished by asking for federal whistle-blower protection.

Rowley became an overnight sensation. Along with two women who helped uncover misdeeds at Enron and WorldCom, she was named *Time* magazine's Person of the Year in 2002, a year dubbed "the year of the whistleblower." Inside the Bureau's insular culture, though, her comments were less welcome. The Society of Former Special Agents compared her to spy Robert Hanssen because she'd violated the unofficial number-one precept of the FBI: Don't embarrass the Bureau. Yet her outburst couldn't be easily ignored, not just because of the way she'd gone public but because in many ways she'd offered precisely that elusive "ground truth" that Bob Mueller spoke of. The FBI had dropped the ball and, like most institutions, had no great interest in publicly broadcasting its failures. Rowley had called the Bureau — and Mueller — to task.

With mounting evidence of FBI ineptness, the clamor for reform grew so loud that Congress couldn't ignore it. In November 2002, President Bush signed the Homeland Security Act, creating a new cabinet-level department to coordinate the nation's sprawling security bureaucracy better, and the 9/11 Commission Act, which created a high-level group to study the failings leading up to the attacks and make recommendations for future improvement. A separate congressional investigation into the 9/11 intelligence failures similarly tore apart the Bureau. Recalls Comey, "The sword was hanging over the FBI."

It was clear from the start that the FBI was squarely in the 9/11 Commission's sights. "It failed and it failed and it failed and it failed," said Tom Kean, cochair of the commission and a former Republican New Jersey governor. "This is an agency that does not work. It makes you angry. And I don't know how to fix it."

There was plenty of blame to go around. Ashcroft, in his testimony before the 9/11 Commission, sparked a fury by personally attacking one of the commissioners, Jamie Gorelick, Janet Reno's former deputy attorney general, who had first signed the memos delineating FBI criminal investigations and intelligence investigations and creating the wall. Ashcroft said that her creation was "the single greatest structural cause for the September 11th problem." But Commissioner Slade Gorton, a former U.S. senator who had served in that body with Ashcroft, ripped into the attorney general, pointing out that Ashcroft's office had reaffirmed the wall as late as the month before 9/11: "If the wall was so disabling, why was it not destroyed during the course of those eight months?" Meetings were tense, staff interviews with Bureau and Justice leaders often adversarial.

A key focus of the commission's ire was Louis Freeh. As prescient as he'd been with the FBI's international expansion, Freeh had missed the technological revolution that had made so many Silicon Valley entrepreneurs huge fortunes during the dot-com boom in the 1990s. The FBI's antiquated computer system was a disaster waiting to happen. Beyond technology and resources, though, there was a larger question of the agent mind-set: At a fundamental level, could the FBI become a forward-looking organization? Could an agency focused on investigating become an agency that worked to prevent attacks?

Philip Zelikow, the head of the 9/11 Commission staff, added his own searing analysis of the Bureau's efforts through the 1990s. The legacy of CISPES, COINTELPRO, and other civil liberties scandals, Zelikow said, "may have had the unintended consequence of causing agents to even avoid legitimate investigative activity that might conceivably be viewed as infringing on religious liberties or lawful political protest." But that legacy was at best a partial excuse. "The FBI determined early in the 1990s that a preventive posture was a better way to counter the growing threat from international terrorism. In its first budget request to Congress after the 1993 World Trade Center bombing, the FBI stated that 'merely solving this type of crime is not enough; it is equally important that the FBI thwart terrorism before such acts can be perpetrated,'" Zelikow recalled. "Yet the FBI's leadership confronted two fundamental challenges in countering terrorism. First, the FBI had to reconcile this new priority with its existing agenda. This immediately required choices about whether to divert experienced agents or scarce resources from criminal or other intelligence work to terrorism." Zelikow noted that during the height of Dale Watson's push to expand the FBI's counterterrorism program toward the end of the 1990s, the Bureau's counterterrorism budget remained relatively constant, noting, "When the FBI designated national and economic security as its top priority in 1998, it did not shift its human resources accordingly."

Tom Kean grilled Freeh in the hearing on the Bureau. "I read [Zelikow's report] as an indictment of the FBI over a long period of time—you know, when I read things like that 66 percent of your analysts weren't qualified, that you didn't have the translators necessary to do the job, that you had FISA difficulties, that you had all the information on the fund-raising but you couldn't find a way to use it properly to stop terrorism," he said. "Looking at this director's efforts to reform the agency, can those reforms work, or should there be some more fundamental changes to the agency and the way we get our intelligence?"

To agents in the ranks, all of the post-9/11 investigations, and especially the 9/11 Commission, arrived with an agenda: Show that the attacks were the FBI's fault. The conclusions already seemed to be written: The FBI didn't connect the dots; the FBI didn't play nice with the NYPD or the CIA; the FBI's mind-set was outdated; FBI agents didn't know how to prevent an attack before it happened.

The 9/11 Commission never interviewed the FBI's top New York leaders, Barry Mawn and Ken Maxwell, who had both helped found the JTTF; nor did it turn to longtime counterterrorism agents like Neil Herman, who had retired in 1999 after almost three decades in the field. Instead, it quickly zeroed in on the I-49 and I-45 agents and how they hadn't stopped 9/11. The commission's first question to Ali Soufan was pointed: "Why does the CIA hate you?"

When another review panel, led by General Norman Schwarzkopf, came though New York and Ken Maxwell sat through his umpteenth lecture about how the FBI didn't share information or play well with others, he had had enough. "Please give me one specific example of information we withheld in the run-up to 9/11," he said. There was silence in the room. No one could cite an example. But that didn't stop the lecturing.

And yet, amid all the finger-wagging, there was little serious discussion about accountability and culpability. It was, one case agent reflected, as if Atlas shrugged. In fact, nowhere in government did someone lose his or her job because of 9/11. Not a single person was fired. But not everyone lasted, either.

In the wake of 9/11, the FBI came to be the agency on the firing line for many of the after-action commissions and reports. The commissioners, at the start, seemed to think that the Bureau could never remake itself as an intelligence leader. "It's like talking to a dog about becoming a cat," Commissioner John Lehman said. "It was a no-brainer that we should go to an MI5." The White House signaled that it was open to the idea of dismantling the Bureau, and certain members of the 9/11 Commission agreed. It was an idea that met with a lot of support from intelligence leaders. Richard Clarke said, "Frankly, the FBI culture, the FBI organization, and the FBI personnel are not the best we could do in this country for a domestic intelligence service."

Mueller decided that the best game was to convince the commission that he was the Bureau's best chance. He believed, according to those who worked with him at the time, that he'd begun to implement many of the required changes, but as Dale Watson had noted before 9/11, the Bureau is a large ship that can't change direction on a dime. "We knew that the FBI, if given a chance to change, could function as both a law enforcement agency and an intelligence operation," recalls Bruce Gebhardt. "I don't care who you are—you can't change an agency that large that quickly." Nonetheless, the FBI put out a seventy-four-page report documenting all the reforms, changes, and organizational advances in the counterterrorism program since 9/11.

While the CIA—especially George Tenet—developed a reputation for making the commission's life difficult and Mueller himself had frequently been at odds with the earlier joint inquiry on the attacks by Congress, Mueller gave the 9/11 team work space in the Hoover Building to go over Bureau files and made himself accessible almost instantly if needed. He showed up at commission briefings elaborately prepared with relevant charts and numbers in hand. "The Mueller Show," as his efforts came to be known by bemused commissioners, signaled a maturation and mastery of the Washington game. It helped, his old friend Tom Wilner explains, that Mueller was "not threatening—people see the lack of personal ambition. He's there to do a job the best he can."

One of Mueller's arguments was that the Bureau's law enforcement responsibilities kept it in touch with the tens of thousands of local police agencies around the country—a key source of intelligence. Agents and executives pointed out that while all criminals are not necessarily terrorists, all terrorists are criminals. Keeping the intelligence and law enforcement components linked gave the Bureau access to cases that rose up on the criminal radar that might not be readily apparent as terrorist cases.* The wall had made things diffi-

---

*In fact, of the 417 terrorism indictments in the five years after 9/11, from September 2001 to September 2006, only 143 of the individuals were actually indicted on specific terrorism charges; the rest were the result of what Ashcroft called the "spit-

cult, but one didn't tear down a wall in order to split something further. "The worst thing you can do is create another agency, and then we'll be back talking about whether they can share here or there or what. Let's try to work through it," Janet Reno said in one meeting.

To help combat that pressure, Mueller enlisted in his favor the head of MI5, Dame Eliza Manningham-Buller, to lobby the commission personally. During a trip to Washington, she visited the commission to say that Britain and its approach to domestic intelligence was the wrong model. "It just wouldn't work for you," she said. "The United States is too large." She knew every police chief in Britain by name, and her organization could maintain incredibly close relationships. That could never be replicated in the sprawling U.S. law enforcement community.

Pat Fitzgerald also became a key opponent of the MI5 model. "It would be a disaster," he told the commission. Such a move "would take us back to the Stone Age," creating more barriers and divisions rather than more collaboration and sharing. Instead, he pushed for the ideal domestic intelligence agency to be "the FBI with improvements"—primarily more information sharing, new structures, and an increased focus on career paths in areas like counterterrorism.

"The Mueller Show," so aggressive that at times the commissioners found themselves turning down invitations to lunch, breakfast, and coffee with the FBI director, gradually won fans. In one hearing, Slade Gorton said with wonder, "Mr. Mueller, not only have you done a very aggressive and, I think, so far a very effective reorganization of the FBI, you've done an excellent job in preempting this commission."

The commission's final report was basically a personal vote for Bob Mueller. "Our recommendation to leave counterterrorism intelligence collection in the United States with the FBI still depends on an assessment that the FBI—if it makes an all-out effort to institutionalize change—can do the job," it wrote. "He had clearly energized the top leadership," says Lee Hamilton, the other commission cochair. "The commission was willing to give him time to make changes."

---

ting-on-sidewalks" approach: driver's license fraud, marriage fraud, wire fraud, immigration violations, and the myriad of other lesser charges that served to disrupt potential plots and get suspects off the streets.

The 9/11 Commission finally published its report in July 2004, and it became a national bestseller. The final verdict was harsh: Neither President Bush nor President Clinton had been "well served" by the CIA and the FBI. "They did not, in my opinion, have the information they needed to make the decisions they had to make," Tom Kean said. Nevertheless, Kean, who had been so critical of the Bureau throughout, had kind words for Mueller when the director testified: "The reassuring figure in it all is you, because everybody I talk to in this town, a town which seems to have a sport in basically not liking each other very much—everybody likes you, everybody respects you, everybody has great hopes that you're actually going to fix this problem."

At the end of the day, Mueller had won. The Bureau was intact.* The 9/11 Commission's report in an early draft had even said, "We defer to Director Mueller" on which reforms should be implemented at the Bureau. Commission staff, two of whom had served as FBI analysts themselves, balked, urging that the language be tightened, but at least one of them, Michael Jacobson, despite reservations, saw promise, explaining, "The best argument for the Bureau's future is Bob Mueller."

As the threat to the Bureau's mission subsided—by 2004 it was clear that the FBI would have some space to breathe and to develop its intelligence capability—Mueller grew more comfortable as director. Even if problems hadn't been fixed, the path ahead was at least understood.

When he was editor of *The New Yorker,* Harold Ross used to chew through bright new editors, each of whom, in the magazine's parlance, was named in turn "the new Jesus." As journalist James Fallows

---

* While Mueller had won the battle, the decision to create a Department of Homeland Security that excluded the country's primary domestic law enforcement agency crippled DHS from the start. DHS more accurately should have been called the Department of Border and Transportation Security. Its two main domestic law enforcement components, the Secret Service and Immigration and Customs Enforcement, have narrow responsibilities, and neither is much focused on preventing terrorism. The Secret Service is charged with investigating financial fraud and protecting national leaders, and ICE handles only immigration and customs matters. The FBI remained without peer in the law enforcement arena.

once described the phenomenon, "Everyone who has ever worked in an office will recognize the idea. The new Jesus is the guy the boss has just brought in to solve the problems that the slackers and idiots already on the staff cannot handle. Of course sooner or later the new Jesus himself turns into a slacker or idiot, and the search for the next Jesus begins."

Maureen Baginski was Bob Mueller's first "new Jesus." As Congress, the 9/11 Commission, and later the WMD Commission all breathed down his neck, Mueller desperately searched for someone who could help transform the Bureau's ninety-five-year-old approach to investigations. He settled on Baginski, a two-decade veteran of the National Security Agency who had been the right hand of NSA director Michael Hayden and developed the nickname, not altogether complimentary, of "the Vision Lady."*

"She had a vision of where we were and where we needed to be," Mueller says. The key to the Bureau's required reforms, Mueller believed, would be instituting a culture of intelligence-gathering that permeated the organization. As he says, "Intelligence should be a separate, identifiable entity within the organization so that it can't slip away when the focus turns away from it. The next time mortgage fraud becomes an issue, for example, I don't want someone to be able to shift the resources away from intelligence."

Baginski's Bureau partner in the endeavor would be one of the FBI's rising executive stars. In the wake of 9/11, Special Agent Bob Casey had been sent from headquarters to lead the Foreign Terrorist Tracking Task Force (FTTTF, or "F-triple-T-F," as it's known in government circles), one of the many entities hastily set up in the weeks after the attacks, often without much forethought or planning. Casey had spent his career on the criminal side, although he'd dabbled in intelligence as a Houston police officer before joining the FBI in 1986 and had worked a drug intelligence task force in Phoenix. The $50-million-a-year FTTTF, designed as an awkward hybrid of an FBI

---

*Mueller's reliance on Baginski to aid his reforms of the Bureau quickly became something of a joke among those investigating the FBI. "Whatever the question was, the answer was always 'Mo Baginski,'" recalls Jamie Gorelick. "Probably more often than we'd like, actually."

effort and an independent entity reporting directly to the attorney general, with both liaison roles and operational aspirations, was never one of the great success stories of the post-9/11 world. It combined resources from the FBI, CIA, Secret Service, INS, State Department, Defense Department, and other agencies aimed both at keeping terrorists out of the United States and at deporting those who were already in the country. It worked out of Defense Department space in Crystal City, Virginia, a few miles from downtown Washington. One Bureau executive describes it as the FBI's attempt to set up a mechanism by which the government could "get KSM for speeding. It's finding the unknowns." Casey had been at the task force for about six months when he was called back to headquarters in mid-2003 for a new project to be overseen by Maureen Baginski.

Baginski had been given the high-ranking title "executive assistant director for intelligence," with an office just a few doors down from Director Mueller himself, and yet her "division," the FBI's first Office of Intelligence, existed only as a sketch on a few pages of a legal pad in a seventh-floor conference room at the Hoover Building. Casey arrived in the temporary office space to help get it off the ground, looked around at a small cadre of a half-dozen staffers, and realized just how big the task would be. "We didn't even have a cost code," he recalls. "Without a cost code—the number that lets you pay for things—you can't do anything. We couldn't get a copy machine." The Office of Intelligence also didn't have the other critical component of any federal government enterprise: an FSL (funded staffing level), which enabled it to hire and recruit staff. For now, everything—and everyone—was temporary. Within days, calls started coming in from Congress asking for detailed plans and presentations about the role of the Office of Intelligence. From Capitol Hill to the White House, a lot of people were looking over Casey's shoulders. He found himself in his cubby trying to explain that there were no plans yet. As the program evolved over the next four years, Casey would become the constant in the FBI's intelligence efforts, while the leaders of the program rotated with alarming frequency.

The successful use of intelligence, Baginski began explaining to Casey, involved four major components: requirements, planning, collection, and production. The process began with determining what information was needed (the requirements), figuring out how to get those answers and then doing so (planning and collection), and then assembling and analyzing the answers before distributing them to the relevant agencies, offices, and executives (production). "She gave the Bureau a much-needed process," Fred Stremmel explains. "The Bureau finally had a system and a process to handle intelligence and the care and feeding of analysts. We had always collected intelligence—we just weren't always good at it."

Incorporating this seemingly simple process into the FBI required wholesale changes in the Bureau's approach. Top among the necessary changes were improvements in the Bureau's analytic corps. Analysts like Stremmel, who had spent two decades working counterterrorism at headquarters, were much more the exception than the rule. "The special agent is the hero of the FBI, but if you go to the domestic intelligence side, the key player is the analyst," 9/11 Commission cochair Lee Hamilton reflects. "People have to know these ethnicities, these cultures, these languages."

Individual agents in individual cases had done much of the intelligence-gathering process for years, often quite successfully. Working a major organized crime case, drug smuggling case, and terrorism case had many investigative similarities, and agents like those on Squads I-49 and I-45 in New York had been mapping organizations, compiling valuable intelligence, and then using it to disrupt ongoing endeavors. Yet now the Bureau needed to develop a new system to do that sort of thing across the entire organization and across the world. "We didn't have an enterprise-wide, actively managed intelligence collection process," Casey says. Though the FBI had been a member of the U.S. intelligence community, as it was known in government circles, since World War II, it participated only insofar as it worked on foreign counterintelligence matters. Beyond that, it had always been somewhat separate, with different goals and different responsibilities. Of the score of other agencies in the community, none had a law enforcement component. No one else carried a badge and a gun and had the power to take someone into custody and deprive him of his freedom (legally, at least). "Reasonable doubt" was just fine with the rest of the intelligence community, since those agencies never had to worry about things like trials, judges, and perjury charges. The FBI now had to figure out which standard applied where—what could be intelligence and what had to meet the higher bar of evidence. This change of approach was one of the hardest to make, Casey found as he traveled around the country doing the "road show"—pitching the new approach to conference rooms full of agents in various field offices. "The goal is get the information," he told them. "You don't have to be right, you have to be ready." The body language in most rooms where Casey spoke was hard to miss: crossed arms, scowls, eye-rolling. This, the agents were saying wordlessly, wasn't what the FBI did.

One of the first tasks of the Office of Intelligence was bringing order to the chaos that was the daily threat briefing process. The staff found an ally in the White House to help. After some two years of the nearly constant drumbeat, the Threat Matrix was being reeled in up on Pennsylvania Avenue too. When Fran Townsend arrived at the National Security Council in 2003, back from Coast Guard purga-tory, she began to try to convince the West Wing staff that they should leave the matrix to her. "When I got there, I said, 'Holy hell, you can't be showing this directly to the president,'" she recalls. She went to President Bush and chief of staff Andy Card and asked to take owner-ship of the process: "This is my job. Let me separate the wheat from the chaff instead of you looking at it each day as all wheat." Baginski, Casey, and others worked their end down at the Hoover Building too. Gradually the process matured, and it was eventually pushed off to the newly forming National Counterterrorism Center. "Now the threats that remained needed to," Townsend says.

Mueller's new approach, and particularly his repeated public com-ments admitting the Bureau's failures before 9/11, angered many of the agents. "I know he had to fall on his sword a bit afterwards, but he didn't have to go out and do it every day," laments one counterterror-ism agent. All of Mueller's talk about how the FBI wasn't in a preven-tive mode before September 11, about how the FBI needed to do better at intelligence, about how the FBI was "now" proactive, about how the FBI needed to be better about connecting the dots, made many agents—particularly those on the I-45 and I-49 squads—feel like Mueller was selling them short. The idea that the FBI wasn't in the intelligence game, that it only cared about evidence for court proceedings, particularly rankled the counterterrorism squads. "The notion that these are two separate disciplines is so specious. Intelligence and evidence are inextricably linked," Ken Maxwell says.

"The idea that we're now in some 'prevention' mode that we never were in before was just absurd," Abby Perkins adds. "Evidence is the best intelligence you're ever going to get. Yes, you're interested in getting that into court someday, but even if you never make it to court, that evidence is proof. We talk about history to get to the future." Many of the agents recalled the mantra Steve Bongardt had used when fellow agents asked why the squads were chasing al-Qaeda bombers all over Africa before 9/11. As Bongardt said, "You work the last bombing to gain insight into how the bombers operated undetected so you can detect them next time and prevent future attacks." Working the last bombing *was* stopping the next bombing.

At headquarters, Mike Rolince argued that the Bureau needed to do more to present its impressive al-Qaeda track record, dating back to the mid-1990s. All of the terrorist photos carried by the special forces teams first on the ground in Afghanistan had been gathered by the FBI. Underscoring the importance of the work that I-45 and I-49 had accomplished before 9/11, thirteen of the original twenty-two "Most Wanted Terrorists" on the U.S. government's list were suspects whose identities had surfaced during the East Africa bombing investigations. Rolince bristled later on over the view that the Bureau hadn't done prevention before 9/11. "When you catch [Unabomber] Ted Kaczynski, you're preventing people from dying. They're career criminals. Get the ones who come after you, you prevent future attacks," he says. At headquarters one day, Rolince got fed up with Mueller's constant refrains in a meeting of how broken the FBI was and griped, "We don't have a director—we have two inspectors general."

The idea that the Bureau hadn't understood what it faced especially grated on the agents who had missed so many birthdays, anniversaries, and holidays (and lost so many boyfriends, girlfriends, and marriages) chasing al-Qaeda around the world. In a view shared by many of the agents who had worked counterterrorism before 2001, it wasn't the FBI's mind-set that needed changing. "I am an intelligence agent. I believe in taking intelligence and using it to disrupt activities using criminal procedures. It's always been about prevention," Pat D'Amuro explains. "The FBI that was broken was the databases. It'd been that way long before 9/11." Examining the evidence of the missed opportunities and the "FLs" that helped lead to the surprise attacks, agents concluded that the fixes the Bureau wanted to implement were cover-ups for management's own pre-9/11 incompetence. As one agent bluntly explains, "There seemed to be a conscious decision: We're going to blame this on FBI systems. That had nothing to do with 9/11. You allowed the wall to happen. It's bullshit."

And it was true: The failing computer system and the CIA's withheld information both repeatedly hindered the FBI's hunt for al-Qaeda terrorists, contributing much more to 9/11 than anything else. In one meeting, listening to yet another lecture about how the FBI needed to be better at connecting the dots, Frank Pellegrino, who had spent years building a case against Khalid Sheikh Mohammed, exploded over the CIA's withholding of information: "What fucking dots? They had it all."

No matter. Across the Bureau, many of the agents who had worked counterterrorism through the 1990s found themselves gradually shut out of the "new Bureau." As Tom Knowles recalls, "It was like every person who had done CT before Mueller arrived was suddenly radio-active." While they were dispatched around the world to follow up leads, the New York al-Qaeda squads mostly seemed to be unwelcome in Mueller's new FBI. Morale on the team was tough. New York felt dumped upon by headquarters, by the 9/11 Commission investigation, by Congress. Tensions and tempers ran high. "After 9/11, all the great work we'd done went by the wayside," Maxwell says. "It was as if the executives said, 'You've had your chance, now it's our turn,'" John Anticev elaborated. Not a single one of the nine assistant directors of counterterrorism since 9/11 worked al-Qaeda cases before 2001. In fact, in nearly a decade since 9/11, not one of the case agents from I-45 and I-49 has risen to a supervisor job at headquarters. "You got a feeling that if you worked terror before, you were part of the problem. You were old Bureau. Not predictive. That stings," Jack Cloonan recalls. "You can't imagine what it's like to have people look at you and think, 'You're responsible for letting 9/11 happen.'"

Just as the actual facts of the 1933 Kansas City Massacre had given way to a mythical narrative that fit better with Hoover's political needs of the moment, the Bureau's true counterterrorism capabilities were shelved in the name of what was most politically expedient for Mueller after 9/11. "The Bureau had done a terrific job before 9/11, but it wasn't going to be heard," Mueller reflected later. "That wasn't the focus. It was, 'How did you blow it this time?'" The Bureau's critics weren't interested in a nuanced discussion about the knowledge and skill of the New York Field Office. When I-49 and I-45 agents visited the elaborate exhibit hall just off the visitor's lobby at headquarters that explained the FBI's mission, history, and cases, they were crushed to discover that it skipped their work entirely. The terrorism exhibit included the TERRSTOP case, the Lackawanna Six, the Portland Seven (who were arrested in 2002 for aiding al-Qaeda), and the Virginia jihad case (a group arrested in 2003 on similar charges)—four cases in which the FBI had possibly prevented terror attacks by taking down suspected cells before they became operational; four cases that had emphasized the Bureau's new watchword, prevention. For the New York agents, it was as if their cases had never even, existed.

Perhaps if Mueller had been at the Bureau longer, understood exactly the scale and scope of the New York bin Laden investigation, he might have leaned more on those agents after 9/11. After all, he'd been receiving his first briefing on the USS *Cole* investigation when the first plane hit the World Trade Center. Defending the Bureau's pre-9/11 work wouldn't have made any difference in public opinion— and digging in his heels might well have damaged the FBI's very existence. But Mueller wasn't just playing pure politics. His approach vis-à-vis New York seemed to follow his approach to taking over the troubled San Francisco U.S. Attorney's Office, where he fired everyone and made them reapply for their jobs; like a good Marine, he'd stormed the beaches and saved the office. The New York agents couldn't help but wonder—especially since he never went to the squad for an "Attaboy" after 9/11—if he'd taken a similar view of remaking the Bureau. His jokes about the independent New York Field Office and about how New York had stolen cases from him as a junior assistant U.S. attorney in Boston, his shift of the office of origin from New York to Washington, his comments in the meeting at the Customs

Building about how "New York needed to sacrifice"—all of it seemed to point to the fact that he'd fired the FBI's own best al-Qaeda experts. That hurt.

As one long-term Bureau counterterrorism official recalls, "It was as if first lieutenants, sergeants, and privates were being blamed for the misdeeds and failures of the pre-9/11 leadership."

CHAPTER 12
In the War Zone

War is the realm of uncertainty; three quarters of the
factors on which action in war is based are wrapped
in a fog of greater or lesser uncertainty. A sensitive
and discriminating judgment is called for, a skilled
intelligence to scent out the truth.

—*Carl von Clausewitz*

The FBI teams that arrived in Afghanistan beginning in the summer of 2002 found an odd surprise: They were told by officials
on the ground that the war against al-Qaeda and the Taliban
was now their second priority. The United States needed to preserve
resources for the invasion of Iraq, and their mission in Afghanistan
was now about stabilizing the country and getting it to a place where
it would be okay while the United States shifted its focus further west.

Back home, the Pentagon and the White House were assembling
the case for war. Donald Rumsfeld had begun pressing the Pentagon
to move against Iraq even as Osama bin Laden slipped out of Tora
Bora in November 2001. Through the fall of 2002 and into the winter
of 2003, the Bureau was repeatedly asked to help link Iraq and
al-Qaeda, tying the invasion of Iraq to the post-9/11 war on terror.
"We were clear with them," Mueller recalls. "It ain't there. We held to

that." Indeed, the FBI found not only that there was no link but that there was active animosity between bin Laden's group and Saddam Hussein's Iraqi regime. FBI agents had questioned detainees in Afghanistan who had belonged to extremist groups in Iraq and had journeyed to Afghanistan expressly to train so they could overthrow Hussein's government.

During the course of 2002, pro-Iraq war hawks had pushed a Czech intelligence report that Mohamed Atta, the leader of the 9/11 hijackers, had met with an Iraqi intelligence officer, Ahmed Samir al-Ani, in Prague in April 2001. Through its PENTTBOM investigation, the FBI had already determined that Atta had been in Florida just two days before the Czechs said he'd met the Iraqi in a Prague café. After agents sifted through hundreds of thousands of records, ranging from flight reservations to car rentals and from hotel receipts to bank accounts, pulled security videotapes from scores of locations, and interviewed thousands of people around the world, the FBI concluded that there was no record that Atta had journeyed across the Atlantic in the timeframe necessary to complete the trip. The CIA also disputed the Czech account. Regardless, Deputy Defense Secretary Paul Wolfowitz summoned Pat D'Amuro to the Pentagon in August 2002 to discuss Atta's meeting. D'Amuro, accompanied by another agent, firmly maintained that the meeting hadn't happened. According to people who were present, however, Wolfowitz pressed the Bureau to the point where the agents were forced to acknowledge that they couldn't *prove* the meeting hadn't happened. That conference with Wolfowitz was not the only strange entreaty from the administration: A staffer from Vice President Cheney's office put in a rare and bureaucratically inappropriate phone call to al-Qaeda expert Danny Coleman, asking the agent to go over all the FBI's intelligence tying the terrorist group to Saddam's regime. Coleman bluntly responded that he wouldn't help with the case for war: "If you came to me for a *casus belli,* you are not going to get it."

As war loomed ever larger, the FBI launched a huge operation to map the Iraqi diaspora in the United States and to monitor antiwar groups for possible acts of terror. The Bureau was deeply concerned that Saddam Hussein might have a network of sleeper agents in the States who would launch attacks if U.S. forces invaded Iraq. In a highly classified operation code-named Darkening Clouds, one of its largest data-mining projects ever, the Bureau assembled information on some 130,000 Iraqis living in the United States, hoping to uncover hidden Iraqi intelligence networks.

The Bureau's pre-war investigations caused a stir. Peace activists reported that their activities were under surveillance. In Pittsburgh, the Thomas Merton Center, a Catholic social justice group, found its leafleting being photographed by an FBI agent from the local JTTF. Under the heading "International Terrorism Matters," the JTTF distributed a report to local law enforcement agencies saying that the Merton Center was planning a peace demonstration for the start of the war. As word spread about the Bureau's surveillance, Congressman Eliot Engel wrote to Attorney General Ashcroft, "Americans are fighting and dying in Iraq so people there can be free of tyranny, yet our own FBI is investigating our fellow Americans for exercising their freedoms." The FBI argued that it was not trying to apply political pressure to antiwar groups, just monitoring possible domestic threats. "We have to have some type of predicate, some foundation, some basis for saying, 'This person poses some type of threat,'" FBI deputy director John Pistole said. "The endgame is not to collect intelligence for political purposes. The endgame is to prevent terrorism or criminal activity."

Congress was still wary. "Law enforcement officials, of course, should take necessary and reasonable steps to ensure that demonstrations are peaceful and lawful," Senator John Edwards wrote, "but this report suggests that federal law enforcement may now be targeting individuals based on activities that are peaceful, lawful and protected under our Constitution."*

All told, the vast majority of the FBI's pre-war investigations amounted to nothing. Indeed, the line between constitutionally

---

*The Justice Department's inspector general Glenn Fine, who has been critical of many Bureau efforts since 2001, issued a 209-page report in September 2010 that cleared the FBI of investigating any antiwar groups simply because of their political views. Fine's office wrote, "The evidence did not indicate that that the FBI targeted any of the groups for investigation on the basis of their First Amendment activities." Fine did say that agents and executives provided bad information to Congress in relation to some of its pre-war surveillance but did so for the most part inadvertently.

protected peaceable assembly and possible national security threats was often hard to define—but then again, the Bureau's new "proactive" stance required it to track emerging threats before they became real. One morning in the Oval Office, Mueller was briefing the room on a Texas group the FBI was following which was, in his words, espousing "anti-American sentiments." President Bush interrupted, puzzled: "Anti-American sentiment? Is that illegal?" Mueller fixed the former Texas governor with an intense stare and waited half a beat. "It is, sir, in Texas." The entire room laughed.

In the Bureau, a telephone call from an executive at headquarters you don't know isn't generally a good thing. The probability of not a good thing increases when the only message is, "Call me back on a secure line." So it was that Special Agent Steven Martinez nervously returned Chuck Frahm's call in early February 2003. The conversation was brief. "The military wants us to go into Iraq with them," Frahm said. "We're putting together a team. Will you lead it?" Just as Frahm was offering twenty-four hours to think it over, Martinez accepted.

The mission meant that the Bureau would be deploying agents to a war zone for the first time since World War II. While the military would worry about victory in Iraq, the FBI's main task related to the war back home: locate intelligence about threats to the homeland. What were Iraq's ties to terrorist groups? Were there any "forward-deployed" Iraqi operatives who would cause trouble in the United States once an invasion occurred? Scores of agents were already working such investigations in the United States as war fever mounted; now the Bureau would have an unprecedented opportunity to take the field itself.

There was little in Martinez's résumé that made him a natural for the position. He had grown up working a union job in the San Francisco port, repairing navy ships, and since joining the Bureau had developed two specialties, drugs and cyber crimes. He did, however, have two qualities that made him exceptionally attractive as a team leader: He was trained for overseas missions as a member of the FBI's Los Angeles Rapid Deployment Team—the Bureau's quick-reaction force for international investigations like embassy attacks and kidnappings—and his vaccines and passport were up-to-date, which would be useful since he was leaving in a week.

Oddly, the Bureau generally put more effort into planning a drug raid in Los Angeles than it did into the Iraq invasion team's deployment. No real manual, much less a procurement plan, existed for Martinez's operation. The days following Frahm's request brought a whirlwind of briefings and meetings at the Hoover Building and at the military's Central Command headquarters in Tampa, Florida. Rather than deploying one of the FBI's preexisting rapid deployment squads, which had trained together and had a centralized chain of command, the Bureau cobbled together a score of agents from different units, offices, and teams. As leader, Martinez had been a last-minute addition. He met the rest of his team during a brief visit at Dulles Airport as the others were leaving for Kuwait. He still had more meetings in Washington before he could join them.

Before he left the States, Martinez went to his local REI outdoor outfitter and spent a couple of hours wandering the aisles, buying whatever gadgets he thought might prove useful on the battlefield. In Kuwait, he quickly realized that the FBI's normal procurement channels wouldn't work. "I needed wads of cash right now," he says. "Cash was king." He had the Bureau wire several hundred thousand dollars via the U.S. embassy in Kuwait City and then walked out the embassy door with $100,000 in $100 bills. Martinez and his team quickly attempted to buy almost everything they needed, including a Humvee and a couple of souped-up Toyota Land Cruisers. (The Humvee quickly became the envy of other units, since it appeared to be the only one at Camp Udairi with a built-in CD player.) Agents spent long afternoons standing in line in Kuwait stores to purchase needed supplies, hoping that when they got to the front of the line, a clerk spoke English. Often Martinez found the Bureau competing with the U.S. news media for supplies; there was only a limited amount of stuff in pre-war Kuwait, and everyone had a long list of purchases. The Bureau, for example, had to acquire phones by the dozen, as no single cell company had strong network coverage across the region. "It was a mad dash," he recalls. Just ordering porta-potties for their camp was a weeks-long project. Communication back to Washington was slow at best, so much of the decision-making fell to Martinez in the field.

Camp Udairi, an old artillery range in Kuwait ten miles from the Iraq border, was the forward staging point for U.S. forces. In a matter of weeks, the camp was transformed from bare desert to a city of several hundred thousand personnel and millions of tons of materiel. The FBI set up its tents in a corner of the constantly humming facility; the barely controlled chaos around the agents was such that they quickly determined that someone had to stand watch at night to ensure that no truck or tank drove over their tents in the dark. There was always noise, always big vehicles moving, and always, always sand. Within days, everyone in the Bureau contingent had shaved heads; any hair at all would collect dust, mix with sweat, and then turn muddy.

In order to operate alongside the military, the FBI agents traded in their handguns for NATO-standard 9mm Beretta pistols. Their standard ammunition, hydroshock law enforcement rounds especially designed to minimize ricochet and the chance of harming bystanders in urban environments, were traded in for high-velocity copper-jacketed rounds designed for military targets. There was also the business of educating the military on the FBI's needs; the team created three-by-five cards outlining intelligence priorities to distribute to U.S. forces, so that when troops questioned Iraqi prisoners and citizens, they could attempt to collect intelligence quickly. With such a small team, the FBI couldn't be everywhere.

Martinez spent his first weeks in country trying to figure out the Bureau's role beyond those three-by-five cards. "We had a general assignment, but all that process—the road map, the ops orders, the plan—had to be figured out on the ground," he recalls. "Not being former military, I didn't even know half the acronyms. You just asked a dumb question from time to time." Meanwhile, the Hostage Rescue Team, with its special forces connections, zipped around Kuwait and Saudi Arabia, training with the SEALs, Delta, and other elite units. Eventually, HRT settled into the Ali Al Salem Air Base in Kuwait to await the invasion, deciding that it was the best jumping-off point for the invasion.

Martinez knew that he had only had a limited amount of time to get the FBI ready for war. He shuttled back and forth between Kuwait and Central Command in Doha, where military briefings tracked the U.S. force readiness almost hour by hour. The sprawling Central

Command headquarters was a complicated maze of camps within camps; officers bicycled the mile or two between meetings, outracing the MPs charged with maintaining traffic rules. The Bureau's G5 jet would arrive every couple of weeks with a fresh load of supplies from the States. One flight included a blender and a few Hawaiian shirts for a luau; the bored in-country team sipped virgin piña coladas at the ensuing party, since no alcohol was allowed on base.

Some days it seemed as if the war had already started. One day in Doha an industrial explosion sent up an enormous mushroom cloud near the Central Command base, leaving everyone on edge until it was determined not to be a military event. At Camp Udairi, a friendly-fire incident shot down a British fighter jet in the desert nearby. The entire region was within Scud missile range, which meant the agents had to carry around cumbersome, alienlike masks and suits to protect against chemical and biological weapons attack. False alarms were common; warnings would sound and everyone would frantically dress, then sit around, sweating profusely in the airtight outfits, until the all-clear was given.

When the invasion began, in March 2003, the Bureau formally delegated authority from Mueller to Martinez to order the FBI into Iraq. Martinez repeatedly emphasized to his team that the Bureau wasn't there to invade Iraq. The military characterization of "permissive," "semipermissive," and "nonpermissive" environments—that is secure, moderately secure, and unsecure—was new to Martinez; he knew he didn't want most of his team in anything less than a secure environment. "HRT had to stay as close to the tip of the spear as they could to establish a chain of custody," he explains. "They were able to operate in a less permissive environment." The rest of the Bureau contingent didn't need to be first across the line; they could wait to go up with the second wave. When they did, they would move into intelligence sites and locate documents, computers, and anything that could provide investigative leads.

The week after the invasion, the 101st Airborne called Martinez: it had located a site that appeared to offer relevant intelligence. Unfortunately for the HRT operators, who were chomping at the bit to be released into the war, the closest FBI unit was the Kuwait document exploitation ("Docex") team, which had been trained to sift through reams of Iraqi government files for intelligence. They had the privilege of being first into Iraq, zipping forty miles over the border by helicopter to load up boxes of possible evidence and begin to process it for leads. HRT crossed the border soon thereafter, racing north toward Baghdad, and while HRT traveled with special forces units and anonymous "other government agency" operatives (that is, the CIA), Martinez's team was mostly on its own, operating in a foreign combat environment as a tiny appendage of a vast coalition military machine, with little precedent and little guidance. "The FBI is really great at running toward gunfire," Martinez reflects. "We're all wired like that. But I don't know whether we'd done real thinking about what we were getting ourselves into."

Amazingly, no one from the FBI leadership had talked with Martinez about possible battle casualties. "This was an elephant in the room," Martinez recalls. "I knew that was riding on my shoulders," he adds. "I was pretty convinced that I was going to take the hit if something went bad for the FBI." One afternoon, he dispatched two HRT operators to check out a possible terrorist training site; British forces had uncovered a full-sized plane mock-up at a captured Iraqi military site. The U.S. government needed to determine quickly whether the place was used for instructing firefighters or as a training facility for a 9/11-style terrorist attack. En route, the Black Hawk helicopter with the HRT aboard crashed, rolling over in the desert, its rotors snapping off, spilling wreckage across the sand—"like socks in a dryer," one of the HRT operators aboard recalled later. A similar crash on April 3 had killed half a dozen army crew. Tense moments followed back at the Kuwait headquarters, where the FBI team shared its office tent with the coalition's search-and-rescue operation. When the all-clear call came, Martinez breathed a rare sigh of relief. Each day the safety of the FBI team weighed on him: "I really don't know what the process was going to be if someone had to tell a loved one that their domestic FBI husband was blown up in Iraq."

Then there was the question of rules of engagement. Domestically, the FBI had strict after-action shooting protocols; any agent-involved shooting, whether committed on or off duty, no matter how warranted and righteous it seemed, automatically triggered a criminal investigation. What did that mean for agents in a war zone? "If I was

THE THREAT MATRIX • 439

walking down a street, perceived a threat, and shot someone, would I be under investigation? What was the FBI response?" Martinez recalls wondering. If the HRT killed people in a raid in Baghdad, how would the protocol differ from a shooting during a drug raid in Los Angeles? There weren't any answers. Martinez recalls, "There was a lot of whistling through the graveyard."

As U.S. forces circled Baghdad a few weeks after the invasion, Martinez made his own crossing. Sitting in the passenger seat of the Bureau's Land Cruiser, which was painted on top to mark it as friendly for allied aircraft flying overhead, Martinez fingered his M4 as the FBI convoy passed over the ditch marking the DMZ and moved into Iraq for the first time. (The team, dressed in standard desert drab uniforms, had made custom FBI patches for their uniforms.) Their first destination was the British-controlled port of Umm Qsar. In the weeks to come, Martinez would fly into Baghdad to meet up with the HRT and the Docex team, which had secured a shack in a far corner of the Baghdad airport to serve as the FBI's Baghdad base. It was a strange home: The airport, which had once had acres of carefully maintained orchards and gardens, now had allied planes taking off and landing around the clock. The planes dumped chaff and fired flares to ward off antiaircraft missiles, and the falling debris would ignite fires around the FBI compound at the end of the runway; in the middle of the night, the FBI team would be awakened to fight the blazes bucket-brigade-style. Detached from the main military procurement system, the FBI team mostly had to fend for itself. One night, Special Agent Fred Bradford and a local Iraqi helper tackled a goat, killed it, and roasted it over an open fire. Other agents were dispatched into downtown Baghdad to procure bread, and with that mission accomplished, everyone enjoyed a night of goat sandwiches—a welcome change from MREs.

As U.S. forces had closed in on the capital, the Iraqi government had hidden document caches in private residences around Baghdad; thus, with the help of informants, coalition military units had to go door-to-door looking for intelligence. As they uncovered the caches, documents began to flood in to the FBI team. The military devoured whatever the FBI was able to uncover from the stacks of files, and twice a day situation reports tracking the latest information in the field were sent back to the Hoover Building.

Yet even by the time the FBI got settled into its Baghdad compound, "mission creep" was already taking place. One of the most distinct memories of Martinez's time in Baghdad was a series of meetings in which Bush administration leaders made it clear that the military would be in charge of the stabilization and rebuilding of Iraq. "They were surprised by that. They didn't expect to be in charge at that point," Martinez recalls. Instead, the military had expected to turn over control to local authority or the State Department, or... well, just about anybody other than themselves.

In one meeting, a general pointed at Martinez, whose FBI team was set to return to the States soon, and told him to start planning a training program geared toward reviving the Iraqi police force. "Whoa, whoa, whoa," the agent interjected. "That's not our mission. That's an act of Congress to start doing that." There was a moment of silence in the room. "We'll figure it out," the general said, and the meeting continued.

Later that afternoon, Martinez called Washington with a warning: It was already apparent that the FBI's mission in Iraq wasn't going to end soon. As the scope of the looting of Baghdad's cultural treasures became clear, for example, the military wanted help from the FBI art crime unit, and as the military's hunt for weapons of mass destruction turned increasingly frantic, it requested FBI help in searching for the big break that would uncover the hidden WMDs that everyone knew *must* be somewhere in the country. The Bureau had better start thinking about a long-term Iraq presence, warned Martinez, whose own ninety-day rotation in Iraq was nearly up. When, back home in the United States, he added up his extra "danger pay" from the Bureau—meant to compensate for the the long hours, the weeks away from his family, and the time in a war zone—it amounted to a grand total of $83.

Special Agent George Piro arrived as part of the Bureau team that replaced Martinez's invasion force and settled into a two-room shack on the edge of the Baghdad airport complex. Pulled from the FBI Headquarters' Fly Team, its elite first responders, who go anywhere in the world to respond to terrorist incidents, Piro had flown commercially to Qatar and then on to Baghdad by "mil air," the teeth-rattling, gut-churning military transport flights that were shuttling millions of pounds of supplies and materiel into the captured Iraqi capital. Wary of shoulder-fired missiles, the planes came in high and then dove for the deck, corkscrewing in sharp turns down to the runway. "You go from staying the night before at the Ritz-Carlton in Doha to locking and loading your M4 as you hit the ground. The airport was completely dark, but you could see tanks all around. It was definitely a war zone," Piro recalls. Baghdad was a shock to his senses, even though the agent had lived just five hundred miles away in Lebanon until he was twelve.

For Piro and sixteen other agents, it became clear that the tasks ahead were manifold, from training the Iraqi police to investigating the crimes of the deposed regime to searching for the supposed WMDs to helping the U.S. forces pacify the country. The American military leadership only gradually realized how hard the new operating theaters were going to be. On September 25, 2001, Air Force General Charles Holland, the head of U.S. Special Operations, met with Donald Rumsfeld and laid out a wide selection of possible targets where the U.S. could hit back against al-Qaeda, from a camp in the Philippines to a training camp in Africa and an arms transit site in Somalia. "Rumsfeld's mouth was watering," recalled one intelligence official.

At the briefing's conclusion, the defense secretary asked, "When do we go?"

"Well, we can't, because we lack actionable intelligence," Holland replied.

In the coming weeks, Rumsfeld would repeatedly ask his staff to define that annoying term: "Is there any type of intelligence that is *inactionable?*"

In fact, the military had uncovered incredible amounts of inactionable intelligence from tips, rumors, whispers, half-understood documents, and uncooperative witnesses. In the first days of the Iraqi occupation, U.S. forces dreamed that its high-tech tool chest—drones, satellite surveillance, computer networks, and other toys—would be key to outsmarting and running to ground the players in the "Deck of Cards," the Department of Defense's Most Wanted list, which had been printed on playing cards.* All the high-tech tools, though, didn't prove as useful as the basic investigative techniques honed on the streets of the United States. "The way you catch these guys is through old-fashioned police work," Special Agent James Davis says.

The commander of the Joint Special Operations Command, General Stanley McChrystal (who would go on to head U.S. forces in Afghanistan), first asked for FBI agents to be embedded with the military in Iraq, thinking that the Bureau's agents and staff could help the military focus on finding its next targets. "We saw it as a chance to get on the battlefield and find links to the United States," Davis recalls. In response, the FBI sent over primarily agents drawn from the elite Hostage Rescue Team, but then it got a clarifying message from McChrystal explaining his desire for men like the fictional street cop on *NYPD Blue:* "I got shooters. I appreciate that," he said. "I need Sipowicz. I need investigators. We can take care of killing people." The next wave of Bureau personnel would be heavy on case agents, analysts, and evidence collection teams, personnel who were not aimed at making arrests and running cases but were aimed at acquiring actionable, evidence-based intelligence. Over the coming years, some 1,500 FBI personnel would serve at least one tour in Iraq; hundreds more would serve in Afghanistan.

Piro and the sixteen members of the FBI's Iraq deployment slept in one room and worked in the other. At night, to break up the monotony of military MREs, Piro and his teammates would zip into downtown Baghdad to buy groceries, fresh-baked bread, or takeout dinners, or to run any of life's little errands. As he recalls, "That was the happy time in Iraq. Being an Arabic-speaker gave me a chance to be involved in all sorts of projects." By the time Piro went back to Baghdad in early 2004, that freedom no longer existed.

During the brief period when there was some safety and a stable environment in Baghdad, the FBI ended up operating as a default police force, albeit a very, very small one. The army and Marines had little experience policing urban areas, and the Iraqi police were mostly

---

* The ace of spades, the highest card in the deck, was Saddam Hussein; son Qusay was the ace of hearts; son Uday was the ace of clubs.

On the day that President Bush announced his nomination of Bob Mueller as FBI director during a Rose Garden press conference, Mueller thought his major task would be revamping the Bureau's computer system. (White House Photo by Eric Draper)

By the end of the day on September 11, 2001, the FBI had mobilized a massive investigation at all three crime scenes: the Pentagon, here; Shanksville, Pennsylvania; and Ground Zero in New York.

All photographs courtesy of the FBI unless otherwise noted

For weeks after 9/11, the FBI New York Field Office was relocated to a parking garage because 26 Federal Plaza, close to Ground Zero, was deemed unsafe.

Two FBI agents from the Charlotte Field Office pose before a makeshift sign during their winter deployment to Afghanistan, just some of the hundreds of FBI agents who have worked in war zones since 2001.

President Bush looks over the newly created list of Most Wanted Terrorists with Mueller at FBI Headquarters in October 2001. Dale Watson and Tom Pickard in the background, left. (White House Photo by Eric Draper)

Mueller has made repeated trips to Afghanistan since 2002, talking with FBI personnel, meeting with Afghan leaders, and visiting with local villagers. (Photo by *Leatherneck* Magazine)

Special Agents Fred Bradford and Richard Kolko raised an FBI flag on top of the Bureau's first Iraq headquarters, on the outskirts of Baghdad International Airport, in April 2003.

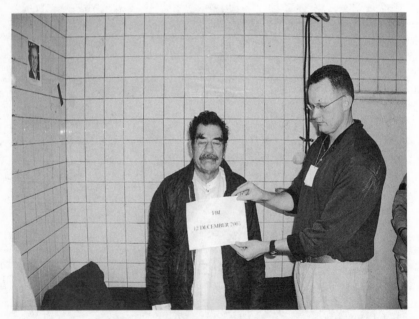

During his first stint in Baghdad, Special Agent James Davis found himself helping take mug shots of Saddam Hussein.

Special Agent George Piro interviewed the deposed Iraqi dictator over many months.

Jim Comey (left) and Mueller found themselves at odds with the president over the Terrorist Surveillance Program. (Photo courtesy of Getty Images)

President Obama, here meeting with Mueller at FBI Headquarters as Deputy Director John Pistole looks on, has been faced with a different terrorist threat than President Bush was after 9/11. (Photo by UPI)

President Obama convenes his national security staff weekly for terrorism briefings, like this one in October 2009. At lower right is the then FBI deputy director, John Pistole. (White House photo by Pete Souza)

Najibullah Zazi, being led out of his Colorado condo by Agent Eric Jorgenson, was behind one of the scariest terror plots since 9/11. (Image courtesy of KMGH)

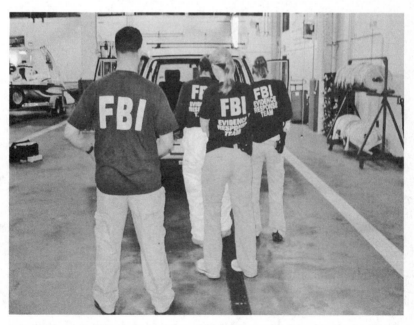

Hours after he tried to flee the country, Faisal Shahzad's car was searched by FBI evidence technicians in an empty hangar at JFK Airport.

The toll of being the longest-serving FBI director shows on Mueller, in his official portrait taken when he started in 2001 and a portrait taken in 2008, during the FBI's one hundredth anniversary. (2008 photo by Vincent Ricardel)

The one hundredth anniversary brought together all four living FBI directors: (from left) William Webster, Mueller, William Sessions, and Louis Freeh.

absent. "All the investigative techniques we use on fugitives cases work the same. Baghdad was a large, secure metropolitan area. We had a ton of experience operating under those conditions in the U.S.; the military didn't," Piro says. Agents helped train the Iraqi police force, worked kidnapping, money laundering, and terrorist financing cases, and established fingerprinting and biometric services for the occupying forces. As the FBI presence in Iraq evolved and billions in poorly monitored money flooded into Iraq, one of the agents in Baghdad was assigned solely to working on government corruption matters.

Piro's Arabic fluency was in high demand, and at odd hours he received calls from the military and other government agencies with requests to accompany them on missions. One night in August he found himself helping to capture Saddam Hussein's personal secretary, Abid Hamid Mahmud al-Tikriti, who was the highest-ranking Iraqi official captured to that point. In another instance, as the FBI was tracking a bomb maker across Baghdad, Piro dressed up as an Iraqi and was dropped off a few blocks from the suspect's apartment. He walked through the crowds, made his way into the suspect's building, and surreptitiously photographed the doors and locks in preparation for a raid. At 3:00 A.M., the military and the FBI went back in full force, just missing the suspect. It was likely that no other agent could have come close to what Piro was doing, which was both impressive and depressing.

While his Middle Eastern background gave Piro access to a host of opportunities and operations that the average American in Iraq never got, it also made him acutely aware of the doors that were closing. "The mistakes we made early on were almost irrevocable," he concludes. "It was six months and then the Iraqi people had enough." In particular, ordering the disbandment of the Iraqi military and the de-Ba'athification movement, which prevented members of Saddam Hussein's Ba'ath political party from joining the new democratic government, seemed ominous at the time to Piro. As he points out, "The military is the biggest employer." The United States took all those trained and armed employees and threw them onto the streets, he explains, dishonoring them in a culture where honor matters deeply. As he rotated out after his ninety-day stint, Piro wasn't optimistic. He wondered whether he'd return and, if so, under what conditions.

*　　*　　*

Nearly two months after the U.S. invasion, on May 12, 2003, some 27 people, including 9 Americans and 7 Saudis, were killed and more than 160 wounded by a series of attacks on Western housing compounds in Riyadh. The attacks by al-Qaeda broke an unwritten code: For the first time, the terror group was killing Saudis in Saudi Arabia. The Saudi Arabian government, which had long tacitly supported al-Qaeda with the understanding that it would leave the House of Saud alone, finally awoke to the threat. The FBI dispatched the head of the Milwaukee Field Office, Dave Mitchell, to Riyadh with a team of 75 agents and technicians.*

While Mitchell's team was working in Riyadh, Special Agent Thomas V. Fuentes, the head of the Indianapolis Field Office, was walking through the hallways of the Hoover Building. He ran into Larry Mefford, who asked him, "Will you take the next team, whatever it ends up being?" Fuentes agreed readily, not thinking too much about the conversation until the following Wednesday, when, back at home, he got a call from headquarters: He would be the FBI's first on-scene commander in post-invasion Iraq.

On July 5, he landed in Baghdad. The new FBI policy was that each on-scene incident commander should be a special agent in charge. One reason that the FBI had taken to sending SACs as incident commanders was that in the rank-conscious military environment, an SAC was the equivalent of a three-star general. (Mueller ranked as a four-star.) Thus Fuentes was given "executive" accommodations in the pool house behind the presidential palace in the U.S. occupation headquarters, known as the Green Zone, which, while bare-bones, were certainly better than those afforded to most U.S. personnel at the time. Although Piro's team had been seventeen strong, the FBI deployments were quickly growing. Eventually, each ninety-day rotation would involve no fewer than seventy people. Fuentes's trailblazing team worked incredibly long hours, and he was able to procure a nicer building in the Baghdad International Airport (BIAP) compound for

---

* The attacks and the FBI's subsequent investigation became the basis for the 2007 movie *The Kingdom*.

the Bureau. *Nicer,* though, was a relative term. The agents still had to burn their own waste, and their generators had to be taken apart and cleaned once a day to keep the pervasive desert sand at bay. The former guesthouse where the FBI set up shop had the look of having been abandoned quickly as Baghdad fell. Sheets were still on the beds; food was still in fridges. Much of Baghdad, and particularly the palace area, was still layered with debris from the coalition air strikes in the war's early days. The FBI compound was near the old zoo, so forgotten animals, freed from their enclosures by war, wandered around the area. Ibexes, gazellelike animals with distinctive corkscrew horns, became a favorite barbecue meat. "It was like an extended camping trip with twenty-five to thirty cousins," Fuentes says. Temperatures ranged as high as 140 degrees in the sun during the summer; nighttime lows often bottomed out around 115.

What the agents were supposed to do from day to day was unclear. As the second FBI rotation moved in, the Bureau was still spending much of its time vacuuming up as many remnants of information as it could. HRT operators cruised around in the Toyota Land Cruisers that Martinez's team had purchased in Kuwait before the war; the back of the SUVs were packed with breaching equipment to crack open safes. Other agents were beginning to try to make sense of the looting that had taken place in the wake of Baghdad's fall. Thousands of pieces of art and antiquities had disappeared from local museums; the Bureau's art crime unit began to try to find them.

The task list that the HRT operators had put together in the anxious days before the invasion dwindled. Intelligence sites and safe houses had been hit, key figures were being captured, the feared Iraqi terrorist cells back in the United States weren't materializing—and neither were the rumored WMDs. It seemed as if much of the FBI's energy was being spent proving negatives—proving there weren't "forward deployed" Iraqi terrorists or WMDs floating around the country. Agents began to talk openly about packing up and going home.

Then the bombs started going off.

In the course of three months on the ground in Baghdad, Fuentes watched the environment deteriorate quickly. When he had first landed, Baghdad suffered just one or two bombings a day from insurgent improvised explosive devices (IEDs), almost exclusively small stuff. By the end of July, it was closer to twenty. What had been a remarkable occurrence just a few short weeks before was now so common that when a car bomb exploded in Baghdad, people didn't even necessarily look out the window to see where it was.

As Fuentes better understood what was happening, he was particularly shocked by the state of the Iraqi National Police. Bernard Kerik, the former Giuliani NYPD commissioner, had been appointed, with his patron's backing, as the interim interior minister under viceroy L. Paul Bremer III, and he was talking up how wonderful the Iraqi police were turning out to be. Kerik was churning thousands of officers through training academies and opening new police stations across the city, yet very little progress was made in securing law and order in Baghdad. The FBI team quickly came to realize that the new Iraqi police, with a few notable exceptions, weren't worth much. "They couldn't find the ham in a ham sandwich," Fuentes recalls. Watching the rising tide of bombings and the complete lack of forensic capability among the nascent police force, Fuentes asked Washington to send explosives and forensic investigation tools. Eight big boxes soon arrived from Quantico.

On August 7, 2003, only two days after the supplies arrived, a truck bomb went off outside the Jordanian embassy in Baghdad and killed ten people. The explosion was so powerful that a car parked near the bomb ended up being flung onto the roof of a nearby building. In the chaos after the blast, crowds stormed the embassy, looting the facility and burning paintings of the Jordanian king. The Jordanian government didn't waste any time with the Iraqi police but instead filed a request with the U.S. authorities for the FBI to investigate. Bremer, after initially trying to convince the Jordanians to rely on the Iraqis, gave his permission, and four FBI explosive technicians promptly flew in from the United States. Working in the 140-degree heat, they began trying to make sense of the bombing. "Up until then, we were covert, low-profile, working to do counterterrorism and identify for the military potential high-value targets," Fuentes says. From that point forward, the FBI became a key component of the U.S. occupation in Iraq, filling in holes in the military's expertise and capabilities thousands of miles from U.S. soil.

The agents' findings proved critical to solving the embassy bombing. Eventually Jordan was able to indict the leader of al-Qaeda in Iraq, Abu Musab al-Zarqawi, and a Jordanian al-Qaeda sympathizer, Mu'amer Ahmed Yusuf al-Jaghbir, for the attack. According to the FBI's investigation, Zarqawi had ordered Jaghbir to monitor the embassy for the three days leading up to the attack. The two men, prosecutors claimed, then told a man named Nidal Arabiyat to construct the bomb, which was driven into the embassy by someone identified as Abu Ahmad. Jaghbir was captured the following spring by U.S. forces and extradited to Jordan, where he was tried, convicted, and sentenced to death.

A few days after the Jordanian bombing, one of the explosives experts from Quantico pulled Fuentes aside and said, "These things are just going to keep happening. One of us should stay permanently."

Just twelve days after the attack on the Jordanian embassy, a large truck bomb targeted the UN Headquarters in Baghdad, killing twenty-two, including the head of the UN mission in Iraq, Sérgio Viéira de Mello. Fuentes and the FBI team were out at the airport facility when they heard the news. "We grabbed people, boots, and saddles and went," he recalls. "We were on scene for three days." The FBI had found a grim new mission.

Like many U.S. officials as that year progressed, FBI convoys became targets. Once, the back window of Fuentes's Suburban was shot out. Other times, the FBI convoys narrowly missed exploding car bombs. In Afghanistan, agents came under intense fire in several ambushes, and the FBI leadership temporarily suspended participation in certain dangerous missions. While some argued that the first injuries would end the FBI's mission in Iraq, agents surmised that the FBI leaders were perversely hoping to have some casualties. "I know the director didn't want me or any other agent to die, yet it struck me that until we lost someone, we weren't players," one FBI agent recalled. "A KIA [killed in action] is an affirmation of our commitment."★

★ The wartime mission would end up costing one agent his life, though not in Iraq. Special Agent Gregory Rahoi, who had served three tours in Iraq with the Hostage Rescue Team, died in 2006 after being shot accidentally at Fort A. P. Hill in Virginia in a live-fire exercise designed to mimic conditions in Iraq and train HRT operators for missions in the war zone.

Back home, Bureau leaders recognized that casualties would probably be part of the equation, but to them, it was a necessary risk. As Mueller explains, "In my mind, the Bureau function that we're performing is precisely what we should have been doing. Sooner or later, we'll lose someone, and that'll be tragic, but it's an appropriate mission." Says James Yacone, who as the head of the Hostage Rescue Team has had dozens of his operators cycle through war zones since 9/11, "No one is ever going to argue that the single, specific mission where something goes bad was worth it. Collectively, though, the work we're doing in combat zones is making an important difference."

While the CIA, which had primacy in Iraq, was initially resistant to the Bureau's presence, the interagency squabbles soon faded in recognition of the task ahead. "It all started relatively small, but we found that we had a lot to contribute," Mueller says. "The military longed for that." Recalls Special Agent Jim Davis, "In Baghdad, there was so much shit going on, it was a target-rich environment, so as long as you were not stepping on toes, there was plenty to do."

As the Bureau got its footing, it focused on three main missions in Iraq. The first task was "document exploitation," making sense of the vast trove of documents, papers, reports, and litter that had been swept up in the invasion and occupation. There were thousands of pages to process and make sense of, many relating to the work of the Iraq Study Group, the special team tasked with locating Iraq's weapons of mass destruction.

The second mission—and to Bureau headquarters the most important one—was counterintelligence. Charged at home with protecting the United States from covert foreign influence and spies, the FBI regarded the capture of so many secret Iraq government files as a spectacular coup. "We took the Iraqi intelligence service whole," says one Bureau executive. The investigation of former Iraqi intelligence officials and their paper trails led all over the States. In one case, the FBI arrested Shaaban Hafiz Ahmad Ali Shaaban, an Indiana truck driver, for allegedly trying to scam Iraqi agents in the months running up to the war by selling them the names of fake U.S. agents.* In addition, federal prosecutors in New York, Los Angeles, Chicago, and Detroit charged a dozen people in espionage-related cases stemming from the Bureau's work in Iraq. (Additional investigations are still ongoing.)

The third mission, and the one most popular with the Bureau staff in Iraq, was to develop relationships with the Iraqi police, raise their capabilities, and then jointly locate insurgents and vet threats to the U.S. operations. Working sources, identifying targets, interrogating detainees, and developing actionable intelligence became a vital part of the mission. While the case agents, forensics investigators, and legat staff mostly stayed together in Baghdad, HRT's operators were often embedded with military special forces teams, spending days, weeks, and even months far away from the rest of the Bureau's force, tracking suspected terrorists and insurgents. "You joked that in the States we investigate a case and present it to the prosecutors to prosecute judicially. Here you investigate a case and present it to the military to prosecute kinetically," Davis recalls. In other words, the FBI found the evidence; the military killed the suspects.

They had no shortage of suspects. By late 2003, the "Al-Qaeda in Iraq" network was growing fast and foreign fighters were pouring into the area to support the insurgency. The military's tactics began to shift in response. What had started as a typical capture-or-kill operation soon began to look a lot like an organized crime investigation. The military, working with the FBI and other intelligence agencies, began to put together vast charts documenting the relationships among the terrorists and their networks. When conducting a raid on a terrorist suspect, the military — with the FBI's encouragement — began to treat the target location as a crime scene. FBI agents would descend moments after the raiding force and sweep the rooms for evidence, triaging the scene as quickly as possible, before insurgent forces could mount any retaliation. The process became ingrained quickly: Map the room,

---

*In a great moment of subterfuge, the FBI sent Shaaban and his family on a trip to Disney World—he was told he had won the trip through work—and used the family's absence to search their house surreptitiously, finding in the process documents that included an unsigned contract to recruit human shields for Iraq.

determine what came from where, bag it, tag it, and establish a chain of custody so the evidence could be used years down the road.

Intriguing leads were plentiful too: a scrap of paper with a telephone number in northern Virginia; a plane ticket leading to the United States; a name that set off warning bells when entered into databases. "Most of the leads washed out, but you couldn't be too careful. Our number-one priority was to prevent and deter hostile intent here in the U.S.," HRT commander James Yacone recalls. "When I was ASAC in Richmond, heading the JTTF, just in Richmond we were working five or six cases that had come out of Afghanistan and another three or four that had come out of Iraq."

The Bush administration had claimed from the start that it was fighting terrorists in Iraq so that the United States didn't have to fight them at home. That statement proved true in at least one of the deadliest attacks of the Iraq insurgency. A huge car bomb in Hilla, a city of some 400,000 on the Euphrates River in central Iraq, killed some 136 people and injured an equal number on February 28, 2005. Despite the carnage, it wasn't hard to figure out who the suicide bomber was: When investigators recovered the car's steering wheel, the bomber's arm was still handcuffed to it. The FBI ran his fingerprints and confirmed what jihadist propaganda sites were reporting: The latest martyr was Raed al-Banna. During his years in Rancho Cucamonga, California, Raed al-Banna, a Jordanian by birth, had been known for his hard partying. Yet he began to change his lifestyle in the months after 9/11, transforming into a strict Muslim and radicalizing before returning in 2002 to Jordan, where, according to friends, he grew unhappy and frustrated. He obtained a visa to return to the United States in July 2003, only to be denied entry by a skeptical customs official at Chicago's O'Hare Airport, who noted that he appeared to have falsified part of his visa application. After joining a cell led by al-Zarqawi, al-Banna told his family that he had taken a job as a truck driver. Within months, he was dead—along with the victims he took in his act of martyrdom.

Nearly four months before Raed al-Banna's attack, on November 18, 2004, U.S. troops fighting the second battle of Fallujah had raided an insurgent bomb factory. They quickly called the FBI in when a soldier noticed that one of the vehicles sitting in the factory, a large green Chevy Suburban waiting to be rigged with explosives, had a Texas registration sticker. It was soon discovered that other cars that must have been stolen in the United States were turning up in the Middle East in insurgent circles. A wide-ranging FBI follow-up investigation found that stolen vehicles were being smuggled out of the United States on container ships and entering the shadowy global black market. (The Texas SUV had traveled from Houston to Dubai to Iraq.) Insurgents, for their part, had figured out that the American vehicles, particularly SUVs, were perfect for bombs, because they were able to carry large amounts of explosives and blended in well with all the American military and contractor vehicles that had flooded into Iraq.

Five months after Piro noticed that the "happy time" in Iraq was starting to disappear, Jim Davis had a haunting encounter one afternoon as he traveled to Camp Ashraft, a small outpost near the Iranian border guarded by U.S. forces. Camp Ashraft held members of the Mujahideen-e-Khalq (aka the People's Mujahideen of Iraq), a refugee group Saddam had used against the Iranian regime. As was standard procedure for U.S. forces, the army Black Hawk helicopter carrying Davis traveled fast and low, skimming the surface of the desert to make the craft harder to target. Midway through the flight, Davis saw a goatherd below look up as his flock scattered at the sound of the approaching helicopter. The two men—the Arab practicing a millennium-old profession, and the FBI agent flying in a $6 million, state-of-the-art, twenty-first-century machine of war—briefly locked eyes, and the man's expression seared itself into Davis's mind. "It struck me: If the helicopter of a foreign country flies over my head while I'm on my land and scares my goats, that would piss me off. We're going to be close to wearing out our welcome," he recalls.

The son of a Michigan cop, Davis always knew that he wanted to go into law enforcement. His father, who spent years as a patrolman before becoming a detective and later rising to chief of a suburban Detroit department, told him to skip the dreary days of traffic duty and go right to the meaningful investigative stuff: Be an FBI agent. Davis never seriously considered another career. Two years after J. Edgar Hoover died, the fourteen-year-old Davis called the Detroit

Field Office and asked the agent who answered what he had to do to join the FBI. The gruff voice barked down the telephone line, "Are you white?" "Yes, I am," Davis replied, too young to find the question off-putting. "Then you need to be an accountant or a lawyer," the agent advised. So at Michigan State, Davis studied accounting. (He never figured out what the answer would have been if he'd said he wasn't white.) By age twenty-four, he was finishing new agents' training at Quantico, in the waning days of William Webster's tenure as director. He spent most of his career working financial crimes; on 9/11 he'd been heading the government fraud unit on the seventh floor of the Bureau. He was watching the TV in his office overlooking the Hoover Building's courtyard when the second plane hit. He turned around to the coworkers who had assembled in the office and said, "The Bureau will never be the same."

As the Bureau reprioritized and focused on counterterrorism in the following weeks, Davis argued that his unit should be shut down. The Bureau was looking to hand off non-terror-related investigative responsibilities to other agencies, and government fraud was one area the FBI didn't need to be in anymore. The robust inspector-general community in most of the federal government could take up the slack.

When Davis heard that the FBI was deploying agents to the Iraq war zone to go after al-Qaeda, he volunteered and was chosen as the deputy on-scene commander of Rotation 5, the fifth team of agents to head to Iraq. The team assembled at Quantico for a few days of training before heading into the war zone. During the training, the Hostage Rescue Team walked the rotation through their force protection mission (for the most part, the FBI team would travel in country via seven-ton up-armored Suburbans). Briefers provided background on Islam and Arab culture. For many of the team, pulled from the criminal ranks of the Bureau, the distinctions between Sunni and Shiite that would come to be so critical in Iraq were first laid out in the hours before departure.

From Quantico, agents boarded a leased Boeing 737 for the long trip to Doha, Qatar. To save money, the Bureau's policy was to send one rotation of agents home in the same plane that brought the new ones in — cost-effective, sure, though not great for a smooth transition. The two teams, incoming and outgoing, walked past each other on the tarmac in Doha, the weary, far-off look in the eyes of the departing team spooking the newcomers. The rotations were made up of roughly fifty FBI personnel, a mix of a dozen or so HRT shooters for security, a medic, administrative people, linguists, analysts, communications technicians, bomb technicians, and a dozen or so investigative agents. None of the men in Davis's rotation had ever been to Iraq before. After a harrowing flight via military airlift, Rotation 5 landed in the middle of the night at BIAP. For the next ninety days, BIAP, now an enormous, sprawling complex with multiple coalition camps and military facilities, would be the home for most of the team. A few agents immediately headed north to meet up with General David H. Petraeus's 101st Airborne Division.

The team drove through the complex for what seemed like an eternity before arriving at a small palace on the outskirts that Tom Fuentes had procured as the FBI's Iraq headquarters. While infinitely better than the tents in which the earlier teams had lived, the palace was still austere. There were a couple of bathrooms with running water, though nothing drinkable, and the team had be careful not to get any of the water in their eyes while showering. Most of the rooms were filled with four or more bunk beds; every FBI staffer got his or her own bunk. Gear was stored on the top bunk; the bottom one was for sleeping.

As the deputy commander, Davis had his own room, and he remembers sitting on the bed that first night wondering what the coming months had in store. *I'm far from home. I'm completely lost,* he thought, as his mind churned through the myriad of logistical issues he had to begin addressing in the morning. Chief among them: weapons. The FBI wasn't yet allowed to bring its own guns in, so there was an immediate nervousness until the team put their hands on arms the next day.

The highlight of each week was the Friday "weekly liaison event," a big party held in back of the FBI palace. There, by a festering pool of water known as "Lake Latrine," the agents would barbecue in fire pits and provide drinks for a cross-section of the local military, civilian, and government workers. The event, involving everyone from the CIA to diplomats to Coalition Provisional Authority staff, was equal parts networking and blowing off steam. Movies would be projected onto the walls of the building, and the FBI's tech team jury-rigged an outdoor sound system. Perhaps most important for making friends, the FBI, unlike the military, had access to BIAP's duty-free shops, so its staff was able to procure alcohol—although given the heightened state of alert and the need to be able to respond quickly to events, the parties only rarely became too rowdy.

Beyond the weekly liaison events, the rest of the week was long and hard, like the days for most U.S. personnel in Iraq.* Davis went for a run most mornings around seven o'clock, followed by a quick shower, and then he settled in for a day of e-mail, paperwork, and mission planning. Around 10:00 P.M., he'd place a bottle of Jim Beam on the table in the palace room the team used as a conference area and declare the day officially over. Agents and team members would trickle in, sharing news, operation details, and word from home. Phones rang through the night, coming from the United States, Afghanistan, and other bases around the world.

---

* Those long hours led to perhaps the biggest controversy over the FBI's war zone deployments: overtime pay. The Department of Justice's inspector general later found that personnel in Iraq were misstating their overtime, claiming sixteen-hour workdays for every day they were in country rather than recording actual hours worked. The argument from Bureau managers was that the sixteen-hour mark was a reasonable approximation of an agent's day: Personnel were always on call and were frequently awakened in the middle of the night. It had seemed petty to managers to make their agents clock in and out on timecards each day in a war zone. Yet as a general practice the FBI doesn't pay overtime, because built into the salaries of FBI agents is a 25 percent premium known as "availability pay," meant to cover all the extra hours they work as part of investigations, special events, or crises over the course of the year.

The Iraq overtime policies made a not insubstantial difference to agents' pay. The inspector general's report concluded that an average agent made about $31,500 extra during a ninety-day deployment. For some agents it was upwards of $45,000 extra. This large sum of money perhaps best explained overtime incentive; one agent told the IG's office that the extra chunk of money was the only reason he was able to sell the deployment to his wife.

The overtime debate, though, was also a sign of the FBI's odd culture—and the high standard to which it was held publicly. While the military was getting assailed in the press for abusing prisoners, private contractors were being criticized for killing civilians, and the CIA was running "enhanced interrogations," the FBI was getting dinged for filling out forms incorrectly.

On December 13, 2003, Davis awoke to a wildfire of rumors that Saddam had been located. Such rumors were common, and until that point always wrong, so at first it seemed like nothing more than the usual daily scuttlebutt. Then Davis's boss, on-scene commander Ed Worthington, called from the U.S. military's headquarters in the Green Zone: I can't tell you anything, but round up a fingerprint expert. "It was pretty clear to me what he's saying," Davis remembers, laughing.

In short order, the FBI found itself taking custody of the most wanted man in Iraq. Davis held the dictator while agents took his fingerprints and mugshot, as they would do for any other fugitive from justice. The coalition forces didn't immediately launch into interrogating Saddam Hussein, as the dictator was in dire physical shape following his months on the run; all efforts focused first on ensuring his health. The United States couldn't afford to have him die on its watch. Unlike most of the al-Qaeda detainees captured in the wake of the Afghanistan invasion, Saddam was immediately granted enemy-prisoner-of-war status, which meant that he was protected by the Geneva Conventions against some of the "enhanced interrogation" methods the United States had used on al-Qaeda detainees. In addition to being charged with atrocities against his own citizens, Saddam was still the object of the active U.S. investigation into the foiled plot to assassinate former president George H. W. Bush in Kuwait in April 1993.

Until his own special cell could be built, Saddam Hussein was held in the coalition's high-value detainee facility, known as Camp Cropper. Located near the airport, Camp Cropper had started out as the central booking facility for Iraq prisoners and gradually morphed into a high-profile prison for regime members such as Chemical Ali and Tariq Aziz. On one wall of Saddam's tiled cell, photos of Donald Rumsfeld and George W. Bush stood watch over the deposed dictator. On the facing wall, a poster of the military's Deck of Cards steadily tracked the capture of the Iraqi regime, so the Ace of Spades could watch each day as the net circled tighter around members of his government.

No one had expected to take Saddam alive, so there was only the barest of an outline of a program to deal with him. The CIA badly wanted to be the only agency to question the Iraqi leader, though it quickly allowed in the Bureau when it was informed that whoever questioned him might someday have to testify in court proceedings. Saddam Hussein, the government decided, would be the FBI's show to run.

On Christmas Eve 2003, George Piro was driving south on the Fairfax County Parkway outside Washington when his cell phone rang. He knew immediately it was something big. "It was my section chief—my boss's boss. He wasn't someone that I would normally have interaction with," Piro explains. The mission was quickly explained: Just months after returning from his first deployment, he was ordered back to Iraq. He'd been chosen to interrogate Saddam Hussein.

For days afterward, Piro spent long hours holed up with an intelligence analyst, developing a framework for his interrogation strategy. He met with other government agencies to discuss some of the topics, yet for the most part, he was on his own. It was standard procedure in a way: Investigate a case; break the suspect; get the confession. But what was the case? And how would the suspect react? "I was just hoping he'd talk to me," Piro says. "I don't lack for confidence, but this guy—from a distance he's larger than life. He's brought us to two wars. He's manipulated the world stage, kept the only true superpower at bay. He was an icon. Holy crap. What am I doing?"

Piro frantically devoured books and reports on Saddam and the Iraqi regime, building on the knowledge he'd acquired during his first rotation in Iraq, the summer before. He watched Dan Rather's 2003 *CBS News* interview with the Iraqi leader, read the reports by Human Rights Watch about some of the atrocities committed by the regime, and carefully paged through the classified reports on Iraq's supposed WMD programs.

Piro had been told to prepare to be gone for a year. He said an emotional goodbye to his family and arrived in Baghdad in January 2004. A thousand logistical challenges and questions awaited him. He had to understand Saddam's physical and psychological states, establish the interrogation setting, and prepare for months of intense interviewing.

To assist him, Piro had one other agent, two intelligence analysts, a profiler from the Bureau's Behavioral Analysis Unit, and a handful of linguists. Midway through the project, the second agent (who, because of the sensitive nature of his ongoing work, has still not been publicly named) rotated out and Piro was asked to help select another partner: He immediately called Todd Irinaga. While Piro was a police officer in Ceres, California, the two men had worked bank robberies and carjackings together, and Irinaga had recruited Piro into the FBI in the late 1990s. They had a close friendship, and Piro considered Irinaga a solid, well-rounded agent. Irinaga, then the head of the Modesto Resident Agency, didn't believe Piro's offer at first, but once he realized it wasn't a prank, he jumped at the chance.

Piro's team was for the most part left to itself. While more than one hundred CIA and FBI staff members were conducting interrogations in Camp Cropper, where the high-value detainees were held in what came to be known as the "petting zoo," the Saddam Hussein unit was single-minded. Though their reports were shared with the CIA and other agencies, only the FBI was involved in the interrogations from day to day. "The primary purpose was intelligence, yet we also had to be aware of his history. You couldn't ignore the atrocities that Saddam committed, and it was clear that he might face prosecution for them," Piro recalls. The question of jurisdiction hadn't yet been settled—whether the dictator could face a U.S. trial, an international trial, or an Iraqi trial. That meant that the whole team had to be able to testify in a variety of settings. ("The one agency in the U.S. government that can do both intelligence and evidence-gathering is the FBI," Piro explains.) They also interrogated other high-value Iraqi detainees, such as Chemical Ali and Tariq Aziz, to gather insights into Saddam and, as Piro says, "other information that could either corroborate or contradict what Saddam was telling us."

First, though, they needed to take control. Since Saddam was believed to speak some English, his guards were replaced with Puerto Rican National Guard troops, who were instructed to converse only in Spanish. Saddam wouldn't be able to communicate with anyone but Piro. "Every interaction had to be controlled. All of these things were imposed on him slowly, forcing him to ask me for things," Piro says.

Piro had every clock removed from Saddam's view, then walked into the interrogations wearing the most enormous watch he could find. "When you're in prison, robbed of all sense of time, day or night, you're desperate to know the time," he says. "I wanted him to know that it was easy for me to know the time. For him, it was impossible. It was all about establishing dominance." While realistically Piro had little say over what ultimately happened to Saddam—the Iraqi dictator's care and situation were top concerns for high-level U.S. officials—he projected a sense that he did.

When Piro began and the FBI team had to establish its dominance, Saddam sat on a metal chair. Piro sat in front of the door, between Saddam and freedom, while the deposed dictator literally had his back against the wall. The whole process over the ensuing months was designed to keep Saddam off balance. "If they get too comfortable, they're able to control their resistance," Piro says. Over time, as the interrogation moved to more serious topics—war crimes, atrocities, and weapons of mass destruction—Piro showed the leader more deference. "We wanted to show we respected his authority," Piro says.

At the first meeting, Piro introduced himself simply as George. Although the men would spend hundreds of hours together over the next seven months, the Iraqi dictator never knew Piro's full name or what his position was. Piro existed only as a shadowy U.S. government representative. "I told him that I was taking charge of his situation. We were going to be spending a lot of time together," Piro recalls. "He said he knew what I was there for. Every part of him said he shouldn't talk to me, but he couldn't help it."

As soon as Piro began to speak, Saddam knew that the agent was Lebanese and Christian—a good background for the interrogation. Lebanese in the Middle East are generally neutral; being a Christian meant that Piro didn't have a bone in Iraq's intense Sunni-Shiite Muslim rivalry. Saddam tried to be helpful by speaking Arabic with a Lebanese accent, while month after month Piro's Arabic acquired an Iraqi inflection.

"Of course it was a historic, unique opportunity to interview Saddam. That feeling lasted a week. Then it became work. It was incredibly intense," Piro explains. "Every day you had to prepare yourself to interact with these people. You had to prepare to listen to their crap. Tariq Aziz loved to name-drop—he was always talking about meeting U.S. leaders, kings, or the pope. I was thinking, Dude, just stop with the name-dropping. It's not going to help you." Meanwhile, the Iraqi dictator read Piro his dreadful poetry.

Piro's days began at 6:00 A.M. At 7:00 A.M. he and the doctor monitoring Saddam would examine the dictator. There was also a daily evening medical exam, meaning that Piro was the first and last person Saddam saw nearly every day. ("We could have easily made the linguist serve in that capacity, but I wanted that role. I needed to have nonthreatening interactions with Saddam and be able to see all sides of Saddam," Piro says.)

After the morning exam, Piro would return to his office in the CIA's camp and prepare for the day's interviews. Nearly every day, the team would interview one or another of the high-value detainees. As the lead agent, Piro never took notes in the interrogations. His partner took notes and jotted observations.

Over the entire interrogation, Piro conducted only twenty formal interviews; the vast majority of his daily interactions with Saddam were casual. They talked politics, history, sports, arts, the Middle East, women, and family. "For me, it was important just to get to know him," Piro explains. "I wanted to be able to understand his thought processes. It was an investment for those twenty interviews."

The hundreds of pages of interview notes with "High Value Detainee #1," declassified years later, provide fascinating reading. The conversations ranged across all aspects of life in Iraq: Saddam's rise to power, the Iraqi people and culture, the Iran-Iraq war of the 1980s, the invasion of Kuwait in 1990, the power of the ruling Ba'ath Party, Iraq's relationship with its neighbors, even Saddam's views of Osama bin Laden. The men discussed war strategy and geopolitics at length. Piro listened to a uniquely intimate, previously untold history of Iraq, offered by the man who, more than anyone else, had created the modern country. Saddam explained that he had lived in fear of U.S. attacks; he had used the telephone just twice since March 1990 and moved locations daily among a variety of settings (including his twenty palaces) to make it harder to target him. Contrary to the beliefs of Western intelligence, though, he claimed never to have used body doubles, feeling it was too hard to mimic another person. Perhaps of most immediate interest, and notably contradicting the pre-war hawks and their post-9/11 intelligence assessments, Saddam told Piro that while the Iraqi regime had had some contact with Osama bin Laden, he felt that the al-Qaeda leader was a fanatic and not to be trusted.

The dictator remained defiant throughout. At one point, when Piro referred to him as the ex-president of Iraq, Saddam quickly interjected, "I'm not the ex-president of Iraq. I am still the president of Iraq." At another point, as he felt his power slipping away in the interrogations, he even threatened a hunger strike. Several times he refused to answer questions that he felt concerned Iraqi state secrets. The 1991 Gulf War he blamed on just two causes: oil and Israel.

By March, it was clear to Piro and the head of the Iraq Survey Group, Charles Duelfer, that the country didn't actually have active WMD programs. Piro recalls, "As it became clear to Charles that [the Iraqis] didn't have WMD, it became a mission to understand why we believed they did. Why were we mistaken? What had been the intentions of the regime? What were Saddam's long-term ambitions?" They began working through the historical record, asking about specific statements, overtures, and programs to see what the regime had been trying to accomplish.

Saddam explained, over several interviews, that it was important to his national pride and national security that his neighbors believed that Iraq still possessed weapons of mass destruction. "We destroyed them. We told you, by documents," he told Piro in one interview. "By God, if I had such weapons, I would have used them in the fight against the United States." Saddam's WMD bluffs were, according to Piro, "basically a calculated, deliberate effort on his part to keep Iran, whom he considered to be his biggest threat, at bay. He planned to restart the program when sanctions were lifted, which would have been in 2002 if not for 9/11."

And yet his ego continued to lead to an arrogant form of cooperation. "Let me ask a direct question," Saddam began one interview in February. "I want to ask where, from the beginning of this interview process until now, has the information been going?" Piro explained that his reports were being passed up to senior U.S. officials, probably including President Bush. Saddam seemed satisfied with the answer.

"Going in, I had a very good understanding of Saddam the dictator. I was prepared for that Saddam. I then got to see a side of Saddam that very few people ever saw—the personal, human side," Piro recalls. "You don't expect to have someone like Saddam be, for lack of a better term, normal."

Throughout his months in prison, Saddam was desperate for news of the outside world. He asked Piro regularly about what was happening in Iraq, how the rest of the world was changing, what Russia was up to, and so on. One day he referred to *A Tale of Two Cities,* in which Charles Dickens portrays with sympathy an English prisoner in a French jail who is kept from news of the world beyond. Piro replied simply, "Over time, some things have changed. Others have not." Repeatedly, Saddam raised topics of Western culture and literature, explaining that he'd watched numerous American movies to gain an understanding of the American people. The two men watched documentaries about the Iraqi regime, which Saddam protested carried a Western bias. Piro forced him to watch video of Iraq's fall to U.S. troops and of Saddam's citizens pulling down his statue. "Iraq's the cradle of civilization, and in his mind he was the next great leader of Iraq, in the same category as great historical leaders," Piro says.

Not surprisingly, the Iraqi dictator was deeply concerned about how history would remember him. He had been offered safe passage to Saudi Arabia before the invasion if he gave up his position as Iraq's leader, but he had refused the offer because of how such a move would affect his legacy. "I hope you will be just in what history you write," the Iraqi dictator told Piro. The FBI agent replied sagely, "Fortunately or unfortunately, I will have a major impact on your history."

Over many months, Piro worked to break Saddam's spirit. One night, as they were helicoptering the Iraqi leader to a hospital for a medical checkup, Piro had Saddam's blindfold removed. "I allowed him to look out, and the lights were on. There was traffic. And it looked like any other major metropolitan city around the world," Piro recalls. He told Saddam, "Baghdad is moving forward without you."

The Iraqi dictator kept busy writing, scribbling in his nearly unintelligible handwriting poems and journals that the FBI secretly read. He tended a small flower garden outside during his rare exercise time, working with his bare hands, since he was prohibited from having access to tools. On Saddam's birthday, April 28, which was typically an Iraqi national holiday, only Piro noted the event, presenting the onetime ruler with a plate of traditional Lebanese cookies baked by

Piro's mother in California. (The Iraqi loved the cookies, though Piro's mother was not pleased to know that Saddam had been the beneficiary of her baking.)

The sparse surroundings meant that there were few escapes for Piro either. "There were two things to do, drink and work out, and I don't drink that much," he recalls. So every afternoon, Piro would put on his MP3 player and set out through the dusty landscape of the Baghdad airport, his feet powering over the flat, barren landscape of the sprawling U.S. compound to a daily soundtrack of Evanescence and Van Halen. "It was the only time I didn't have to be on—watching what I was saying, trying to interpret others' movements, reactions, and responses," he recalls. "I could just clear my mind." Even then, he could never really forget where he was; Piro had to run with his handgun strapped to his waist. "You always had to be aware of your surroundings. You didn't want to be kidnapped."

Work continued until 10:00 P.M. most days and, depending on the interview schedule, sometimes went as late as 3:00 A.M. The FBI team wrote weekly reports that were distributed to President Bush, Vice President Cheney, the CIA director, and other officials, yet for the most part it was left alone. "We were very operational, very removed from the briefings," Piro recalls. "In some ways, I'm amazed by that." Only two Washington delegations stopped by to say hello as they passed through Baghdad, the CIA's Tenet and the FBI's assistant director for counterterrorism, Gary Bald.

In July, the interrogation process came to abrupt end. The new Iraqi government issued an arrest warrant for the dictator, which instantly changed his status from prisoner of war to criminal fugitive and stopped the FBI interviews. "There was no room for negotiation," Piro recalls. For Saddam's first court appearance, Piro procured a new suit for him, and an FBI intelligence analyst cut his hair. As their time together wound down, Saddam knew that his end was near; he would probably be executed after a trial. On June 11, the Iraqi leader said that his future was in God's hands. Piro replied that God was very busy and had more important things to deal with than Saddam or Piro. Saddam quietly agreed.

At their final meeting, the Iraqi dictator actually teared up a bit. Piro had brought two Cuban cigars, and the men sat in Saddam's tiny prison garden for a final chat. Then, when Piro stood to leave, Saddam wished him goodbye in the traditional Arab manner, with three kisses, alternating on each cheek. It was a rare tender gesture, yet one that left Piro feeling awkward. "I never forgot what an evil man he was. As I would prepare for my interrogations, I would read over all the available intelligence and study the atrocities. They served as a daily reminder of who he was and what my task was," Piro recalls. "I never really lost that perspective, and it kept me focused."

Piro, exhausted, was happy to be done. In seven months, he'd never had a day off. Yet he'd made Bureau history: completing the first FBI interview of a foreign head of state and, within the Bureau, setting a record for the longest interrogation. Looking back, Piro says that although he feels he obtained most of the valuable intelligence information he could, he wishes he had had time to ask questions of historical value. "In hindsight, I would have liked to have asked more about the political landscape — Iran's role in the Middle East, Syria's role — his view of leadership, how he saw himself, his fears."

Two years later, Piro was home watching the Chicago Bears–Green Bay Packers football game on TV on New Year's Eve 2007 when news of Saddam's execution came. While the agent says he believes Saddam deserved to die, he didn't take any pleasure in the sentence. "I only watched it once," reflects Piro, who says he was appalled by the atmosphere surrounding the dictator's hanging. Iraqi officials shouted "Go to hell!" and chanted anti-Saddam slogans. "When the most dignified person at an execution is the person being executed," the interrogator concludes, "it does not speak well of the event."

Just as they had in Afghanistan, Bureau agents sometimes clashed with the military over interrogation procedures in Iraq. One agent who served in Iraq recalled, "The military folks did not like the fact that the Federal Bureau of Investigation's patient, slow, painstaking, and nonjudgmental approach was being used for people who had killed U.S. military personnel." However, as military officials came to recognize that the FBI's approach usually paid dividends, achieving "superior results" when compared to the use of harsher tactics, they "became believers." As a result, interrogators spent long days questioning local detainees in fortified interrogation rooms at Abu Ghraib, protected from the all-too-frequent mortar attacks.

While the agents at Abu Ghraib noted that the prison was overcrowded and understaffed, no one ever came forward to say he or she had witnessed torture in the facility, now infamous for the photos of abused prisoners that surfaced in 2004. That's partly because of the protocols that had developed earlier with regard to the CIA's "black sites" and Guantánamo: the FBI did what the FBI did, the military did what the military did, and each stayed out of the other's way. To a certain extent, plausible deniability reigned. The FBI couldn't complain about that which it didn't know was transpiring. "We saw some harsh treatment by our standards," Davis admits. "That was stuff you couldn't do here [in the U.S.], but we weren't [in the U.S.]. This was a war zone; things weren't going to be like they were in the U.S." The messages back and forth from Iraq at the time demonstrated the FBI agents' wariness over getting involved. "Our access to detainees at the prison is a central part of our mission and very important to our ability to get the job done," Special Agent Ed Lueckenhoff wrote on January 24, 2004, in an e-mail to headquarters after reports of mistreatment began to circulate in government circles. "The allegations...if true, or even if not true but heavily publicized, could make life difficult for us." He continued, "The FBI will not enter into an investigation of the alleged abuse.... It would be outside the scope of our mission." In the war zone, the FBI relied heavily on military resources; it needed to maintain cordial relations.

There was tremendous pressure to embed FBI agents with some of the military units—the military wanted the FBI's interrogation skills—but Bureau executives cautioned that their staff wasn't trained for a combat environment. They had a hard time saying no, though, once agents were on the ground. As James Yacone, the commander of the Hostage Rescue Team, explains, "We can't be fair-weather friends. The military needs a consistent partner. As much as we'd like to, we can't just say, 'It's too dangerous for us today, you guys go on ahead.'"

And so FBI agents, especially the HRT operators, who provide force protection for the Bureau's wartime missions and work with special forces on raids, became used to being closer to the "tip of the spear" than Bureau executives back in Washington would have liked. Agents were involved numerous times in convoys targeted by IEDs and insurgent fire. Special Agent Christopher Rigopoulos received the FBI's highest award, the Medal of Valor, for helping to save the lives of American personnel when his Combined Explosives Exploitation Cell (CEXC, pronounced "sexy") convoy came under attack. Other agents helped recover and shield injured personnel and provide medical assistance at the scene of the attack. In Afghanistan, HRT operator Jay Tabb was injured by a suicide bomber while searching a terrorist safe house.

Working with the military on the front lines for nearly a decade in Afghanistan and Iraq profoundly reshaped the FBI and its workforce. Since 9/11, thousands of FBI personnel have rotated in and out of those war-torn countries. The first teams to go to war, such as Martinez's into Iraq and Tom Knowles's team into Afghanistan, went with little preparation, no training, and no agenda. Over the following years, the training regimen improved and the mission became clearer. Agents who volunteered to go to war received weeks of specialized training in the mountains of Utah and extensive first aid training.

No part of the Bureau, though, was changed as much by the dual wars as the Hostage Rescue Team. While HRT had spent much of the 1990s sidelined by the very public failures following the fallout of Waco and Ruby Ridge—the team saw such little use that many operators left out of boredom, returning to regular agent field duties—operators after 2001 experienced near constant travel, both domestic and international. Most HRT operators have deployed to Iraq or Afghanistan between three and five times, which means they spent a total of almost a year in combat conditions overseas. Some operators are even coming up on their tenth rotation. Almost monthly, an HRT operator ends up in a combat firefight in a war zone, a major shift for an operation that can go a year domestically without any team member firing a shot in the line of duty. And whereas the military generally gives personnel a year or longer between war zone deployments, returning HRT operators get only a few days off before reentering the team's domestic operations. "There's no rest cycle," Yacone says. "It's definitely taking a toll."

In 2006, Jim Davis was headed back to Iraq, only half willingly. Given the choice between a job at headquarters and a posting in Iraq, he chose Baghdad. He landed in the Iraqi capital on New Year's Day 2007 as the FBI's second Baghdad legal attaché. In odd ways, Baghdad was the same city he'd left over two years before—the DHL Airbus hit by a surface-to-air missile in 2004 was still by the runway of the Baghdad airport, now largely stripped of parts—and yet the situation overall looked much worse. "I was unprepared mentally for the increase in the level of violence," he says. On Davis's last day in Iraq in 2004, a suicide bomber driving a truck laden with a half ton of explosives killed twenty-three people at Assassin's Gate, the main entrance to the Green Zone. It was a sign of things to come.

Mortars and rockets now targeted the embassy compound daily. "One is on a roller-coaster. Whoosh, boom, wow, you pat yourself down, that was amazing," he says. "I remember in one attack, someone later told me we took forty-five rounds. That takes forever. You're laying on the ground listening to these come in one after another. It really had an effect on people."

Despite the turmoil, Davis spent much of his second deployment working on the rule of law, helping the State Department and other U.S. officials develop the legal infrastructure and policing capabilities in Iraq. The Iraqi police had little experience, little training, and even less equipment to deal with the circumstances they faced. Getting them up to snuff was challenging on every front. (One typical training session was interrupted not just by paydays and religious holidays but by a sandstorm, two fires, and the assassination of a pair of Iraqi police officers assigned to the training facility.) Then there were the cultural issues. One of the most basic defensive moves U.S. police cadets are taught in academies is to step to the side when an assailant rushes you, push the assailant past you, and then attack him once he's off balance and facing away from you. The Iraqi recruits wouldn't do that. "Honor is very important in their culture, so they'd say, 'I have to meet his lunge, that's honorable. If someone charges me, I must meet his charge,'" Davis recalls, shaking his head. "It was tough."

Once the Iraqi police made it through training, they began to work with the FBI's Major Crimes Task Force (MCTF), which in helping with local Iraq investigations was trying to earn a reputation for fair, thorough, impartial, evidence-based policing in a region where law enforcement wasn't known for any of those adjectives.

Working almost one-on-one with Iraqi police, FBI personnel and agents saw the MCTF as the crown jewel of the rule-of-law effort. ("The good name of the FBI was attached to MCTF," Davis says.) There was certainly no shortage of work for the investigators: the body count in Iraq, civilian and military, was staggering. MCTF agents regularly visited the Rustemeyer wastewater treatment plant to help clear the traps at the plant's entrance of the many bodies that washed through down from Sadr City, the Shiite stronghold controlled by Muqtada al-Sadr. Yet prosecuting any of the Shiite "extrajudicial killings" by death squads, rogue police elements, and even the Iraqi military was difficult for political reasons.

The joint criminal investigations were a learning process for both parties. The Iraqis culturally put very little weight on DNA evidence, preferring signed statements of guilt. "The most important piece of evidence was a statement, signed with a thumbprint. Under Saddam, that worked really well," Davis recalls. The Iraqi regime, after all, had been very effective in gathering confessions regardless of a suspect's actual culpability. Under the new U.S. occupation, when suspects didn't face the same coercion, they were less willing to sign admissions, which made getting successful prosecutions harder. "We could never get [the Iraqi police] to accept the importance of physical evidence," Davis says. "They never would wrap their mind around DNA."

The rule of law was an uphill battle, like many of the Iraqi projects undertaken by the U.S. forces. "You had to focus on small successes in individual cases," Davis explains. "There weren't enough big victories to keep one motivated." He recalls frequently thinking, We're measuring progress in inches here.

One gaping hole in the coalition's efforts to respond to the ever-evolving situation in Iraq emerged as the remnants of Saddam's secret police and security forces returned to the one business they knew: making people disappear.

Special Agent Chris Voss had worked on the Joint Terrorism Task Force in New York in the early 1990s, tracking the TERRSTOP bombers in the months after the first World Trade Center bombing and taking down the suspects in a New York warehouse as they stirred the "witches' brew" that they hoped to use to blow up the Holland and Lincoln Tunnels, the FBI's New York Field Office, and other Big Apple targets. While his colleagues on the JTTF, such as Danny Coleman, began to investigate a shadowy Saudi financier named bin Laden, Voss spent two years as the co-case agent on the TWA Flight 800 investigation, proving that the flight's midair explosion was the result not of terrorism but of a terrible mechanical fluke. Then in 1998, as the rest of his squad became consumed with the East Africa embassy bombings, he began a second Bureau career as a hostage negotiator.

Globally, kidnaps for hire were increasingly a major part of the FBI's mission to protect Americans abroad, and in 2003 Voss became the Bureau's lead international hostage negotiator. Especially in places like Mexico and Colombia, the crime was a booming business. In the Philippines, the terrorist group Abu Sayyaf regularly financed its operations with ransom payments from kidnappings. All told, during his time as a negotiator, Voss worked more than 150 overseas hostage and kidnap cases.

Iraq, though, was experiencing something unlike anything the world had seen. The secret police had become experts during Saddam's regime at making people disappear and holding them securely, sometimes for years on end. Once the de-Ba'athification movement, meant to ensure that the new government was free of Saddam's influence, left them without job prospects, they went back to what they knew: kidnapping. "People never rise to the occasion," Voss explains. "They fall to their highest level of preparation." Put more simply, under stress, people revert to what they know how to do. By July 2004, fifteen months after the U.S. occupation began, the kidnappings of Western officials, employees, and contractors had started.

One of the first cases was that of twenty-six-year-old American contractor Nicholas Berg in early April 2004, some four months after de-Ba'athification became the official U.S. policy. His decapitated body was found on a Baghdad highway overpass on May 8. Three days later, a video made by his captors played on Arab television stations. The six-minute-long video became the first haunting example of a genre that would become all too common. Dressed in an orange jumpsuit like those worn by the detainees at Guantánamo, Berg read a statement: "My name is Nick Berg, my father's name is Michael, my mother's name is Susan. I have a brother and sister, David and Sarah. I live in West Chester, Pennsylvania, near Philadelphia." Five men, their faces hidden by ski masks and the traditional Arab kaffiyehs, loom over him. Abu Musab al-Zarqawi, the head of al-Qaeda in Iraq, read a long statement tying Berg's kidnapping to the American abuses at Abu Ghraib. Then the men decapitated Berg while gruesomely chanting "Allah Akbar." The video's title didn't leave much unsaid: "Sheikh Abu Musab al-Zarqawi slaughters an American infidel with his own hands."

The U.S. government's response to Berg's kidnapping was poorly thought out. The disappearance of a single contractor amid the pandemonium of 2004 Iraq didn't seem a top priority. There was no official contact from his kidnappers to respond to until the video was released. Voss's international hostage negotiation team had been left out of the FBI mission in Iraq because Mueller, worried about mission creep, was trying to keep a tight leash on the FBI's in-country operations. Despite George W. Bush's February 2002 National Security Presidential Directive 12, which designated the FBI as the lead agency in handling any Americans taken hostage overseas, Secretary of Defense Rumsfeld had made it clear that he didn't intend to abide by the directive in Iraq. The FBI's involvement with Iraq hostages would take place nearly entirely on an ad hoc basis from Quantico.

In the wake of the execution video, Berg's family blasted the U.S. government, and his father, Michael Berg, became an outspoken critic of the Bush administration. "The basic reason my son died is that George Bush and Donald Rumsfeld have taken the arrogant position that they are the leaders of the world, and that they can do anything they want to do," he said. "They've passed that attitude down to the people who work for them, who have passed it down to the people in the field, and that's why we have situations like Abu Ghraib. . . . I think what the orange jumpsuit symbolizes is that my son was a prisoner of war when the Iraqis took him. They certainly didn't treat him according to our standards for a prisoner of war, but then again, our side hasn't treated their side by the standards that we have established and agreed to for treating prisoners of war." Berg's comments handed the Iraqi insurgency an important propaganda victory and were aired widely in the Arab world.

In the wake of the Berg fiasco, the government and the FBI realized they would need to figure out a new approach. There are two halves to any kidnapping response: dealing with the kidnappers and dealing with the victim's family. The FBI had failed to engage either. Although the FBI reticently works kidnappings overseas in dangerous territories with poor local infrastructure, Iraq was an entirely new theater. "We had an operation that wasn't designed to be dropped into a war zone," Voss says. "Our approach relies on there being a local government that has some semblance of function." Iraq didn't have anything like that.

A steady stream of kidnappings began in earnest in the weeks that followed Berg's death. When a Filipino worker was seized and his kidnappers insisted that the Philippines withdraw its forces from the country in exchange for his release, the Filipino government complied. The French government paid a ransom, under the table, in exchange for two kidnapped French journalists in August 2004. Not long afterward, the Italian government secretly paid $1 million to secure the release of two Italian journalists. Parliamentary Foreign Affairs Committee leader Gustavo Selvo said in a radio interview, "In principle, we shouldn't give in to blackmail, but this time we had to." And with that, the race was on.

"It was an unprecedented kidnapping operation. It dwarfed Mexico, Colombia, everywhere else in the world. Everyone with an AK and a Toyota could get in on it," Voss recalls. "Kidnapping is a business. You really have to recognize it for what it is."

While the political effects of hostage-taking can be an important propaganda tool for terrorist groups, the ransom money is what really matters. In the wake of the U.S. invasion, the money flowing from ransom payments provided critical financial support to the remnants of Saddam's regime and aided the growing insurgency. Some companies and governments began developing reputations for paying quick ransoms, which further accelerated the process.★ As the FBI and the U.S. government began to understand the scope of the kidnapping

---

★Japan has a reputation for quickly paying ransoms without much negotiation, so some of the first hostages taken were Japanese contractors in the spring and summer of 2004. Three were released unharmed after ransoms were paid, intelligence sources believe. One was beheaded.

operation—more than two hundred foreigners and thousands of Iraqi citizens were taken in the years after the U.S. occupation began—they came to see an extensive operation on a scale far beyond that of isolated insurgents acting independently. Warehouses held large groups of hostages; a secondary underground market allowed interested parties to buy and sell hostages like goods. As the kidnapping operation matured, the growing al-Qaeda elements in Iraq realized that preexisting hostages could be a valuable propaganda resource. Former Iraqi secret police responsible for a majority of the kidnappings quickly developed a system whereby if a ransom wasn't paid in the first seventy-two hours after contact, the hostage would be sold to al-Qaeda and subsequently beheaded. "The mentality was, 'I don't care—I'm getting paid in three days one way or another,'" Voss recounts.

The flood of beheading videos threatened to be a major problem for the occupation. The State Department created a Hostage Working Group at the Baghdad embassy, which pulled together resources from across the government and concentrated attention on each case. The FBI realized, meanwhile, looking back on the Berg case, that even if it wasn't in Baghdad to negotiate with the captors, it could still do the home-front job of working with the families.

By the time the *Christian Science Monitor*'s Jill Carroll was kidnapped in 2006, the FBI had a smoother operation in place. The Berg case had taught the Bureau and the U.S. government what the hostage takers wanted to hear; if they weren't after a ransom, they wanted the propaganda victory. The first tape of Carroll, released ten days after she was kidnapped while trying to interview a Sunni leader in Baghdad, had all the markings of a pre-execution video. Her captors explained that the U.S. government had seventy-two hours to release all the female prisoners in Iraq or Carroll, who had extensively covered the Arab world, would be killed.

Ransom payments are a complicated issue in general. To discourage kidnappings, some countries had previously tried to ban ransom payments, which only had the effect of isolating and criminalizing the victims' families, who often tried to pay ransom. "When you do that, you're abandoning your citizens entirely," Voss says. Instead, the U.S. government generally removes itself from negotiations at the point where it's determined that a ransom payment will be made.

The FBI met with Carroll's family members in the United States and coached them on a response. "I, her father, and her sister are appealing directly to her captors to release this young woman who has worked so hard to show the sufferings of Iraqis to the world," her mother, Mary Beth Carroll, said on CNN two days after the video was released. The family's statements continually emphasized how Carroll had been working to tell the story of the Iraqi people; free her and she'll continue to tell your story, they said. "I wish to speak to the men holding my daughter," her father told the Arab press. "I hope that you heard the conviction in Jill's voice when speaking of your country. That was real. She is not your enemy." The appeals reached Iraq. In Baghdad, the Sunni leader Carroll had been meeting with also expressed his outrage: "I call upon the kidnappers to immediately release this reporter who came here to cover Iraq's news and defend our rights." Even a top Hamas leader from Palestine joined in the calls to free her. The Bureau, working with the government in Iraq, the State Department's Hostage Working Group, and its network of Arab sources, put out word that Carroll's kidnappers had disrespected her by allowing her to appear in Western clothes with her hair uncovered on the video. The kidnappers began to feel isolated politically. "They're trying to put themselves in a position to murder someone," Voss says. "Our goal is to stymie them without raising the threat."

The strategy appeared to be bearing fruit. Her captors went to Carroll and commented that her father was an honorable man. Thirteen days after the first video, a second video was released. Gone were the markings of the execution setup. Carroll, sobbing, now had her hair covered. Nine days after that, a third video showed her in full Islamic dress in front of a colorful backdrop of flowers, pleading with viewers to meet her captors' demands. Negotiations continued behind the scenes, but time was now on Carroll's side. Soon thereafter her captors let her go. According to multiple intelligence sources, Carroll's case is one of the only successful releases of a kidnapped Westerner in Iraq in which no cash ransom is believed to have exchanged hands.

Most of the U.S. combat casualties in Iraq were from IEDs, which month by month became a larger threat, more deadly and more common. Iraq seemed at times to have become one giant munitions stock-pile; there were countless places where old military supplies had been relocated, hidden, and reappropriated for the insurgency. The going rate to plant an IED was just $100. Even as the death toll rose, there was little to no coordination on the ground regarding the IED fight among the U.S. forces. There was no central clearinghouse of IED information; each agency or military branch collected its own intelligence and analyzed the bomb evidence as best it could.

President Bush eventually turned to Mueller for help. In response, the FBI Lab at Quantico created the Terrorist Explosive Device Analytic Center (TEDAC), which would focus on helping the U.S. effort defeat IEDs. Largely unknown outside of military circles, TEDAC, by design, existed for years off the radar. Yet its work became one of the biggest untold stories of the war in Iraq, and one with a profound impact on the FBI's resources at home. By 2011, in a shift largely unnoticed by the general public and Congress, up to 70 percent of the FBI Lab's resources were dedicated to IED investigations in Iraq and Afghanistan, which means that only about a third of the lab is currently engaged in its traditional evidence-gathering and investigation for local, county, state, and federal prosecutions across the United States.

What had been originally imagined as a small operation became the military's primary source of IED investigation (*exploitation,* in military parlance). Evidence technicians and explosives experts in Iraq and Afghanistan gathered as much as they could from the scene of nearly every IED explosion—hundreds a month—boxed it, and shipped it by military aircraft to Quantico. Over time the military and in-theater FBI evidence techs developed a three-tier system for classifying TEDAC submissions from the field. Boxes labeled "Red" received a five-day processing and evidence turnaround; "Amber" meant a thirty-day turnaround. Less pressing submissions, those least likely to provide critical forensic evidence, were labeled "Green" and, because of resource limitations, were virtually never opened. "No one imagined we'd have more than fifty to one hundred submissions a month," says Special Agent David Wilson, who served as TEDAC's director until he retired in 2010. Yet by 2010 the center was receiving upwards of eight hundred submissions a month, fewer than half of which it was able to process.*

Once opened, the IED evidence was parceled out across the FBI Lab, more than 98 percent of it going to the fingerprint lab. A lot of evidence was also processed for DNA traces. Lab techs found more than 8,840 latent fingerprints on IEDs and identified more than 206 suspects based on DNA or fingerprints. Once technicians processed the evidence, it was divided among three TEDAC teams, the first dedicated to forensics and technical exploitation, the second to intelligence, and the last to investigations. The hope was to trace the IED supply chains, examining cell phones, computer chips, plastics, and even the explosives themselves to see what matches could be found across multiple bombs. Altogether, TEDAC created a database of more than two thousand individuals linked to one IED or another—information that was sent back to the war theaters for follow-up by U.S. and NATO forces.

While the center's headquarters, located for years on the ground floor of the FBI Laboratory's parking garage, grew to be a joint operation involving more than a dozen government agencies and military units, the fact that it was based at FBI Quantico lent the effort a specific gravity: The program valued investigation and evidence collection; the military wanted actionable intelligence. It wasn't enough just to have educated guesses about how IED networks worked and developed—the military needed evidence. Explains Wilson, "You need the integrity. Your fingerprint and DNA is important to the integrity of the intelligence that it yields."

As late as the summer of 2009, TEDAC had fewer than two hundred staff members, but by 2011 that number had increased to over three hundred as the U.S. effort expanded in Afghanistan. Most of the staff came from the FBI, ATF, and CIA. (A team made up of people from the FBI, ATF, DOD, CIA, Defense Intelligence Agency, army, navy, Homeland Security, and other agencies oversees the unit.) After

---

*Unopened and unexamined, the piles of boxes in the Quantico intake room are humbling, each representing evidence from a bomb targeting U.S. forces. The cardboard piles stretch from the floor toward the ceiling, each labeled with evidence tags and notes about where it originated.

outgrowing its Quantico digs, TEDAC recently opened a second facility nearby in Lorton, Virginia, specifically focused on the Afghanistan theater, enabling the Quantico facility to concentrate on Iraq. Plans are under way to build a new facility, upgrading its capacity and staffing, in Huntsville, Alabama, by 2014. Until then, TEDAC will remain near Quantico, utilizing lab resources that have traditionally been used for domestic cases.

Distributed back to the field in the form of IIRs (Intelligence Information Reports) and FIARs (Forensics Intelligence Analysis Reports), the results of TEDAC's work have proved key to helping defeat insurgent bomb-making networks. The evidence of their success actually hung on the Quantico office wall: Using intelligence gleaned from TEDAC's work, an EA-6B Prowler electronic warfare aircraft circling over Afghanistan sent out signals on frequencies used by al-Qaeda sympathizers to detonate IEDs and managed to trigger an IED in the process of being laid. The resulting explosion killed the insurgent who had been burying the bomb. To acknowledge that achievement, the military saved some of the IED's shrapnel and mounted it on a plaque sent back to TEDAC. It was, the military believes, TEDAC's first enemy KIA.

CHAPTER 13
Showdown

Terror is not a new weapon. Throughout history it
has been used by those who could not prevail either
by persuasion or example. But inevitably they fail,
either because men are not afraid to die for a life
worth living, or because the terrorists themselves
come to realize that free men cannot be frightened.
                                      —*John F. Kennedy, 1961*

Even though the two men shared an elite upbringing, Robert
Mueller was nearly everything George W. Bush wasn't—serious,
stiff, earnest. The president appreciated that his FBI director
would say "I'll get back to you" when he didn't know the answer
rather than bluffing; those with immediate answers hadn't always done
him favors. While the president never honored Mueller with a nickname (his badge of friendship and camaraderie), they still had a warm
relationship. During slow days, when there wasn't a pressing threat or
issue on the table during their briefing, the president would fix Mueller with a twinkling eye: "Bob, how's that anthrax investigation coming along?" Mueller, touchy on the subject, would turn to stone.

The anthrax case was just one of the many unfinished pieces of
business on his desk each morning. Being FBI director had always

meant juggling a tremendous number of projects, but never more so than it did for Mueller, who was overseeing an unprecedented expansion at a time of extreme tension, simultaneously changing the culture of the Bureau and maintaining everything the Bureau has historically done well. While he had never imagined that being FBI director would be easy, he had thought it would be simpler.

When he took over on September 4, 2001, Mueller thought his major task would be remaking the Bureau's technology platform. That was a good fit for him. Beneath his stoic prosecutor façade lay just a touch of geek; he was always buying the latest gadget and figuring out how it could make life easier. Ever since reading the 1989 book *The Cuckoo's Egg: Tracking a Spy Through the Maze of Computer Espionage,* he had been ringing the bell regarding the government's ability to respond to cyber issues. At Main Justice under President George H. W. Bush and Attorney General Dick Thornburgh, Mueller had created the first cybercrime task force. Then, while at the U.S. Attorney's Office in San Francisco, he'd grown so frustrated with the government's case management system that he had overseen a team that built its own—a program so well received that the Executive Office of U.S. Attorneys in Washington took it national. By comparison, arriving at the FBI was for Mueller like stepping onto a nineteenth-century stagecoach. When he asked for some basic software to be loaded onto his Bureau computer before he started as director, he was told that the FBI system couldn't support it. Then, shocked and dismayed at the IT infrastructure during his first days on the job, Mueller ordered thousands of new Dells to replace the Bureau's aging computers. "We are way behind the curve," he lamented to Congress.

Indeed, perhaps the most damning legacy of Louis Freeh's tenure was that on 9/11, the FBI did not have a functional computer system. Freeh was a firm believer in the old maxim "Agents don't type." As one of his former executives explains, "The only things a real agent needs are a notebook, a pen, and a gun, and with those three things you can conquer the world." Freeh had had his own computer removed from his office, and in a hierarchical organization such as the Bureau, that sent a powerful message down through the ranks. In the atrophying culture of the "agent generalist," in which every division and task was supposed to be handled by a talented agent, the Bureau quickly came to lack the in-house expertise to manage major technology upgrades. Under Freeh, funds meant for technology—as much as $60 million total—had been repeatedly redirected to international projects.

In 2000, Janet Reno grew so concerned over Louis Freeh's lack of progress in modernizing the Bureau's technology infrastructure that she issued a formal memo ordering him to "immediately develop the capacity to fully assimilate and utilize intelligence information currently collected and contained in FBI files." The attorney general wrote, "I think our national security requires that we get started immediately on this effort."

Bowing to intense outside pressure, the Bureau hired Bob Dies, a former IBM executive, to overhaul the FBI computer system. It was the first time the Bureau had ever brought in a technology expert from the outside, and Dies began to make an immediate impact. He'd seen the Bureau's recent failures; his son had actually been running IBM's FBI account for three years. Dies later explained that he went to Congress and said, "All I could do was get the car out of the ditch. My goal was not to build the fanciest car—just get it out of the ditch." However, the decade of wasted effort and missed opportunities proved intensely difficult to overcome. When the last major overhaul had been done, the Bureau designed the system to work with its already outdated computers rather than investing in new machines as part of the upgrade. At a time when broadband was becoming commercially available to individual homes, some entire field offices and resident agencies were still sharing single 56k modems. The IT system had effectively not been touched since 1995, a period during which the entire dot-com boom had passed the Bureau by.

The Bureau's system, a program called Automated Case Support (ACS), was anything but automated. "The Bureau's record system was so horrendous that you could do a record search one day and get nothing, then a day later you do it again and oh my god!" Fred Stremmel recalls. It required some eleven keystrokes to complete even a basic search.* Agents were loath to load information into ACS, both because it was hard to find information once it was in the system and because

---

* The CIA, responding to a request from Congress, was able to locate in its files an FBI report that the Bureau didn't even know existed.

the system seemed to lack basic security functions; one college intern, hired to test it for vulnerabilities just before 9/11, was able to crack sensitive files by the afternoon of his first day.

The strength of the Bureau had always been its voluminous, comprehensive, and cross-referenced files. Yet Mueller reported in a congressional hearing that the FBI's paper bureaucracy, built up over ninety years, was "burdensome, if not tortuous." Many of its filing and case management systems were decades old, and the original overhaul, undertaken by Dies before Mueller started, had failed to modernize the process. For instance, the Bureau's case numbering system dated back to Hoover's days and still included notations for Prohibition, white slavery, and sedition laws from the 1920s. And then there were the new post-9/11 requirements: To handle its new intelligence responsibilities, the Bureau had to create a "top-secret" computing environment, but the overhaul plan had only budgeted for a "secret" level in addition to its traditional unclassified system. The Bureau, therefore, required a triple-tier computer system for three different investigative environments—unclassified, secret, and top-secret. (Most intelligence agencies operate only in top-secret and unclassified.)

Mueller's first attempt at righting the FBI IT ship, a program to replace ACS called the Virtual Case Management File, under the supervision of another onetime IBM executive, Wilson Lowery, failed. According to Bureau executives, Lowery was a great marketer and always seemed to have things under control. Everyone seemed to take his word that the new file would roll out in one fell swoop, smoothly and without issue. Mueller, focusing on preventing the next terrorist attack, failed to pay sufficient attention. The program was such a failure that it was scrapped almost entirely and the Bureau had to start again from scratch in 2003. "I broke my own rules—I delegated and didn't ask hard questions until it was too late," acknowledges Mueller, who, it will be recalled, had received a D in "Delegation" in Officer Candidate School as a young Marine officer. "For too long, I was convinced we were on the right track. I had no idea how far behind we were in personnel and capability. No one understood the problem," he explains. "We'd taken our existing business processes and moved those online without ever having a conversation about how moving online would change our business processes. Many of the things we were

doing on paper didn't make sense once you put them into a computer."
And separate contracts for hardware and software, mandated by government procurement systems, made for an even worse nightmare.

Thus Zalmai Azmi inherited a mess when he arrived in late 2003
as the latest in a series of FBI chief information officers (CIOs). Azmi's
relationship with Mueller stretched back to their days in San Francisco, when Azmi had been in charge of IT for all the nation's U.S.
attorneys. When Mueller's San Francisco staff received an officewide
computer upgrade and training that resulted in no downtime, the
future FBI director called Washington to offer his ultimate compli-
ment: "This operation has been run with the precision of a Marine."
With good reason: Azmi had spent seven years in the Corps working
with computers.

As he settled into the Hoover Building, Azmi couldn't believe
what he was inheriting: hundreds of different applications, networks,
platforms, and little to none of it cutting-edge. The Trilogy Project, a
half-billion-dollar upgrade to the Bureau's system, had spiraled out of
control after 9/11. Requirements for the program changed seemingly
on a daily basis. Budget overruns were being measured in the hundreds of millions.* The Bureau ran sixty-five different help desks, all
of which operated only from eight to five on weekdays—unacceptable for a Bureau now chasing terrorism threats around the clock. If
Mueller arrived at work and discovered a problem with his own computer, he had to wait an hour or more for the help desks to open.

Burned by his experiences with the Virtual Case Management
File, Mueller wasn't going to let a second chance slip by. During his
first year, he and Azmi met twice a day as they struggled to get control
of the Bureau's IT system. Day after day, Azmi was Mueller's last meeting. Mueller's wife would call to ask when he would be home, and the
refrain would be the same: "I'm here with Zal." The two men took
enormous heat as the Trilogy Project, known internally as the "Tragedy Project," went under. At one point, buffeted by criticism from

---

* One government report explained, "[Cost overruns are] not a surprise. The
attempt to make up for twenty years of neglect in two years of frenzied spending
was destined to fail."

Capitol Hill and government auditors, Mueller turned to Azmi and remarked, "Welcome to the big leagues."

In the end, two of the three sections of Trilogy were salvaged under a new technology program code-named Sentinel. The Bureau managed to build a wide-area network and upgrade its computers.* The third, a much-vaunted Virtual Case File that cost nearly $200 million, was scrapped entirely. The salvaging and reconstructing cost tens of millions of dollars, much of it money that, unlike the cash flow during Freeh's tenure, was pulled from other divisions. (Some $29 million came out of the counterterrorism budget to fund Sentinel. Mueller also drew around $40 million from other divisions and programs.) Inside the Bureau, Azmi's work drew grumbles from other managers, but Mueller never wavered in his backing; their futures were inexorably linked.

Throughout his term as director, Mueller struggled daily with the computer upgrade. In one 2010 briefing on the system, he learned that some users were experiencing a problem with "sticky keys"; that is, when they switched programs, a bug in the system would cause a specific key to stick, creating a long string of the same character, such as ggggggggggggggggggggggggggggg. In the briefing, he was told that it was a limited problem. During a field office visit a few days later in Kansas, he asked a room of agents how many were having a problem with sticky keys. Every hand went up. Later that day, at the next field office visit in Missouri, he asked again. Again every hand went up. He took a picture of the room with all the raised hands and presented it to a chagrined tech staff in the next briefing: "Is this what a limited problem looks like?"

More than nine years into Mueller's term, the program was still running behind schedule. Yet by 2010, more than a decade after the dot-com boom started and nearly a quarter century after Lotus Notes revolutionized company workplaces, after years of nine-figure development budgets, the Bureau had a partially functioning virtual case

---

* In perhaps its biggest success—beyond simply getting agents e-mail—the Bureau has deployed 13,000 BlackBerries to agents and staff in the field, which allow for both nonclassified e-mail and immediate searches of national DMV databases. An upgrade that allows criminal background checks is in field testing.

file system—even though additional overruns and failures pushed the final completion deadline past the end of Mueller's ten-year term. The hole had been so deep and the remaining strings were so taut that after a decade and nearly a billion dollars, Mueller was still not at ground level. "If you want to see what it looks like to sit out a decade of the technology revolution and then try to play catch-up, look at the FBI," one former Bureau executive laments. "It's taking another decade to catch up to the missed decade."

The sun had already been up for over an hour by the time James Comey and Bob Mueller approached the West Wing of the White House shortly after 7 A.M. on March 12, 2004. Neither had slept much in the previous week. The weather was windy and cool; the thermometer hovered just over 40 degrees as they prepared to brief the president. The two-minute ride up from the Hoover Building to the White House complex that morning hadn't left them much time to gather their thoughts, but there was still a level of calm about them as they alighted from the black Suburban on West Executive Drive, just steps from the Oval Office.

The enormous Old Executive Office Building, once home to the nation's entire State and War Departments, loomed over the back of the SUV. A stream of White House staff passed back and forth between the two buildings, their coveted ID badges slipped into shirt pockets or dangling from their necks. At that hour, many were on the way to or from the White House mess, the navy's small cafeteria in the basement of the executive mansion. Comey, introspective by instinct, paused for a moment, considering what lay ahead; Mueller, never much for reflection, did not.

As they crossed the threshold into the White House, both men fully expected it to be the last time they would enter the building, the last time they would brief the president, the last time their motorcade would pass through the White House gate without a pause, zipping past the Jersey barriers and gawking tourists straining to see through the tinted windows. Sitting in their desks at the Justice Department and the Bureau were letters of resignation, which they expected to submit over the weekend; a dozen other Justice and Bureau officials would join them. They would have submitted the letters already, except that the attorney general's chief of staff had asked them to wait until the hospitalized John Ashcroft had recuperated enough to resign as well.

By Monday, Mueller and Comey believed, their security details would be gone; they'd be left alone to face what would inevitably be a media conflagration reminiscent of the infamous Saturday Night Massacre in October 1973, when Richard Nixon had forced the dismissal of independent prosecutor Archibald Cox, which led to the resignations of Attorney General Elliot Richardson and Deputy Attorney General William Ruckelshaus, the former acting FBI director. This storm would be different: The entire leadership of the Justice Department and the FBI would go in one fell swoop over a controversy that no one would talk about and no one outside of a small group in government even knew was brewing.

In the previous weeks, the Justice Department had been consumed by debate. In the wake of 9/11, Dick Cheney, via George Tenet, had asked the National Security Agency head, General Michael Hayden, "Is there anything more you can do?" Hayden had replied with a wink and a nod: "Not with my current authorities." At the Office of Legal Counsel, John Yoo quickly provided a generic outline of the president's inherent surveillance powers, which could be used to expand the NSA's capabilities as of October 4, 2001. The result, a new NSA wiretapping program code-named Stellar Wind, was a "special access program," an extremely high level of classification that meant only a small group was even aware of it. The PATRIOT Act may have made it much easier for the FBI to get warrants for domestic eavesdropping, but it still had to get them. Cheney's office was unhappy with the restrictions on the FBI imposed over time by FISA, yet the law, perhaps the key component of the post-Hoover and post-Nixon intelligence reforms, was explicitly the "exclusive means" for intelligence wiretapping within the United States.* There was not supposed to be any wiggle room. And yet, in the haze of the weeks after 9/11, the Bush administration had launched a new program that threw

---

*David Addington told Jack Goldsmith in the midst of the 2004 debate over Stellar Wind, "We're one bomb away from getting rid of that obnoxious [FISA] court."

FISA's strict rules out the window. "I knew the Terrorist Surveillance Program would prove controversial one day. Yet I believed it was necessary," President Bush later wrote.

In fact, the Terrorist Surveillance Program (TSP) had caused consternation in the Justice Department almost since its inception. Others in government had inklings that something strange was going on. People would occasionally mention "the vice president's special program." John Bellinger, the legal adviser to the National Security Council, confronted David Addington one afternoon, saying, "I know you're up to something." Addington scowled: "If there were such a program, you'd better tell your little friends at the FBI and CIA to keep their mouths shut." Senior officials who were "read in" to the program usually received their briefing either from Addington or from Vice President Cheney himself—an odd situation, given that the vice president's office didn't officially have any surveillance oversight. Larry Thompson, Ashcroft's deputy, had refused to sign off on warrants that relied on information from the program; because he wasn't allowed to know what the program entailed, he didn't feel comfortable approving the intelligence it generated. Even in the heat of the post-9/11 world, Stellar Wind seemed a bridge too far.

When Jim Comey arrived at the Justice Department in the fall of 2003, the new head of the Office of Legal Counsel, Jack Goldsmith, pulled him aside: "I'm glad you're here. There's a lot I have to tell you." After Comey was confirmed by the Senate as Justice's number two in December, Goldsmith returned with a laundry list of programs he felt warranted more oversight. Top on Goldsmith's list was the Terrorist Surveillance Program, which required renewal by the attorney general every forty-five days. Two years after the TSP had started, though, festering doubts about it within Justice had come to the fore. The more Goldsmith and his deputy Pat Philbin learned about how the program worked, the more they worried. In fact, Goldsmith, who took over OLC from Jay Bybee just weeks before Comey's arrival at Main Justice, concluded that the surveillance program "was the biggest legal mess I'd seen in my life."

As a result, he asked for permission to let Comey into the loop. After initial administration resistance, Hayden came down to Main Justice on February 19, 2004, to meet the new deputy attorney general. "I'm so glad you're getting read in," he said, "because now I won't be alone at the table when John Kerry is elected president." Comey's internal alarms went off: What bombshell was the NSA head about to unveil? Indeed, what Hayden detailed was frightening—and even more so was the realization over the coming days that Goldsmith and Philbin seemed to understand what was going on more than Hayden and the administration did. The attorneys believed there had clearly been at least two felony violations of surveillance law.

The stressed Comey had few people he could turn to for advice; almost no one was allowed to know the program existed, and disclosing the program's existence to someone outside that circle could send him to prison. In fact, there was only one person in government whom he could confide in and trust: Bob Mueller. The two men met for a long conversation on the afternoon of March 1 to discuss the deputy attorney general's concerns; that conversation, sources say, was the first time Mueller was made aware of the pending stumbling blocks.

On Thursday, March 4, Comey met with Ashcroft for an hour to raise the legal team's myriad concerns. Though Ashcroft was in overall agreement with the notion of taking a tremendously aggressive approach to fighting terrorism, he also realized the tremendous dangers of making the Justice Department knowingly complicit in active lawbreaking. Given the department's—and the FBI's—mandate, to do so would constitute a fundamental sort of corruption. He gave his team his full backing; he would not reauthorize the program if the administration didn't agree to make substantial changes. Within hours, though, Ashcroft was struck by acute gallstone pancreatitis and rushed to the hospital. Drifting in and out of sedation over the coming days, the nation's chief law enforcement officer came close to death. With Ashcroft unable to fulfill his duties, Jim Comey suddenly found himself legally acting as attorney general. The entire weight of the decision now rested on his shoulders.

On Saturday, the Justice Department first presented its concerns to the White House. Addington was furious, but as Goldsmith acknowledged, Bush was "free to overrule [us] if he wants." On Tuesday, White House counsel Alberto Gonzales summoned Goldsmith back to 1600 Pennsylvania Avenue. The Thursday deadline for the forty-five-day reauthorization was forcing the matter; without a presidential signature, the program would come to a screeching halt. Mueller had met privately with his staff that morning to review the concerns; at noon, he and the other leaders of the intel community—Hayden and the CIA's deputy director, John McLaughlin—met privately with Cheney in the office of White House chief of staff Andy Card. That afternoon, Cheney convened the same group again, this time with the troublesome trio from the Justice Department: Comey, Goldsmith, and Philbin. There was an extensive show-and-tell by briefers from the CIA and the NSA in support of the program, including oversized chart after oversized chart, each one emphasizing how critical Stellar Wind was to the nation's security. The message was clear: If the program didn't continue, thousands would die, and it would all be Jim Comey's fault. "That's not helping me," Comey told the room while he shifted anxiously in his chair.

At one point, Comey said he couldn't find a legal basis for the program. Yoo's original memo, he explained, was specious on its face. "Others see it differently," a scowling Cheney replied.

"The analysis is flawed—in fact, fatally flawed. No lawyer reading that could reasonably rely on it," Comey said, his hand sweeping across the table dismissively.

Addington, standing in the back of the room, spoke up. "Well, I'm a lawyer," he snapped, "and I did."

Responded Comey, *"No good lawyer."*

The room went silent.

The next morning began as every day did. Comey and Mueller assembled in the FBI SIOC, reviewed the day's threat, and zipped up to the White House to brief the president. Sitting in the Oval Office, the president himself was just about the only person still in the dark over the looming showdown. In the hallway, Comey spotted Fran Townsend, who knew surveillance law better than nearly anyone in government and served on the staff of National Security Advisor Condoleezza Rice. He pulled his onetime colleague from the Southern District of New York U.S. Attorney's Office aside.

"Yesterday there was a meeting in Card's office about a surveillance program. Condi wasn't there. Is she aware of what's going on?" he asked.

"I think this is something I am not a part of," Townsend replied. She could tell that her old friend was in trouble, but she couldn't help. "I can't have this conversation."

Comey's circle of allies was shrinking fast. Riding down Pennsylvania Avenue in the back of Mueller's SUV, the FBI director and the acting attorney general sat quietly. Comey thought, *A freight train is heading down the tracks, about to derail me, my family, and my career.* He glanced to his left at his fellow passenger, thinking, *At least Bob Mueller will be standing on the tracks with me.*

That night, Mueller was at dinner with his wife and daughter when he got a call from Comey. The FBI director didn't hesitate: "I'll be right there."

The Bureau security detail at George Washington University Hospital had been under strict orders from John Ashcroft's wife not to allow any phone calls through. When Andy Card's office had called that afternoon, the caller hadn't been connected, but when President Bush himself had called the command post, the agents on duty didn't have the stomach to turn down a call from the commander in chief. At some point since that morning, Bush had learned that there was a problem with the TSP reauthorization.★ He had called Ashcroft's hospital room to say he was sending over Andy Card and Alberto Gonzales. Janet Ashcroft, the attorney general's wife, then called David Ayres, Ashcroft's chief of staff, to warn him of the imminent White House arrivals. Ayres called Comey, who at that moment was driving home on Constitution Avenue with his detail of U.S. marshals. Comey ordered his driver to the hospital; they drove Code 3 all the way, grill

---

★ In President Bush's 2010 memoir, *Decision Points,* he commented publicly about the showdown for the first time. He wrote that he knew neither that Ashcroft had been hospitalized nor that Jim Comey had stepped in as acting attorney general. According to government records, however, Comey and Mueller briefed the president as part of their regular reviews of the Threat Matrix while Ashcroft was hospitalized. The attorney general normally would have attended those briefings. It is hard to believe that the question of Ashcroft's absence was never raised during those meetings. As one senior government official explains, "Every meeting I've ever been in where a deputy unexpectedly appears in place of his principal, he offers an explanation as to the principal's absence."

lights flashing, siren wailing, engine revving. Comey's first phone call, at 7:20 P.M., was to Mueller.

After hanging up with Comey, Mueller instructed the FBI agents guarding Ashcroft not to remove Comey and the other Justice officials from the hospital room. Gonzales and Card would likely have Secret Service agents with them, and the Bureau's agents were to prevent any interference. Under no circumstances was the security detail to allow anyone to speak to Ashcroft alone. The FBI director had just ordered his agents to use force, if necessary, to prevent the Secret Service and the White House from removing Justice Department officials from a hospital room. As motorcades and officials converged on the hospital, the thought was on everyone's mind: Just how much further would this situation spiral out of control?

Comey beat Card and Gonzales to the hospital and ran up the stairs. The White House duo arrived minutes later and marched straight to Ashcroft's bedside. The FBI security detail, who moments earlier had been working one of the quietest assignments they'd ever had in an otherwise empty wing of the hospital, were suddenly very nervous.

Rallying, the drugged Ashcroft explained why he wouldn't sign off on the reauthorization and chided the administration: "You drew the circle so tight I couldn't get the advice I needed." He finished by pointing to Comey: "But that doesn't matter, because I'm not the attorney general. There is the attorney general." Jack Goldsmith said later that it was such an amazing scene he thought Ashcroft would die on the spot.

A moment of tense silence passed.

Then Card and Gonzales left, saying only, "Be well."

Mueller arrived at the hospital moments after the departure of the White House aides. He conversed briefly with Comey in the hallway and then entered Ashcroft's hospital room.

"Bob, I don't know what's happening," Ashcroft told him.

"There comes a time in every man's life when he's tested, and you passed your test tonight," Mueller replied.

A phone call came into the command post from Card, summoning Comey to the White House. Given the night's events, he refused to go without a witness, Solicitor General Ted Olson. Mueller left the

FBI detail with instructions not to allow anyone to see the attorney general without Comey's personal consent.

Frantic meetings stretched late into the night at both the Justice Department and the FBI. Senior staff had been recalled. Cars had been abandoned wherever convenient.* The core team was all on the same page; they were closely linked as friends and colleagues, and both Rosenberg and Dan Levin, Ashcroft's counselor, had done stints under Bob Mueller. These were executives familiar with the pressure of the post-9/11 Threat Matrix, the daily looming prognoses of Armageddon. Even though not all of them knew the precise details of what was unfolding, Comey and Mueller made it clear that they would not tolerate having the president continue a program that was illegal. Across the upper ranks of the Justice Department and the Bureau, letters of resignation were drafted. Comey's read, in part, "I and the Department of Justice have been asked to be part of something that is fundamentally wrong." If Comey went, Mueller went; if Comey and Mueller went, so would the top ranks of both agencies. Chris Wray, the assistant attorney general in charge of the Criminal Division—the same post Mueller had once held—stopped Comey in the hallway at Main Justice to say, "Look, I don't know what's going on, but before you guys all pull the rip cords, please give me a heads-up so I can jump with you."

By the time Comey finally made it to the White House, around 11 P.M., word had reached Andy Card that an uprising of epic proportions was under way. The news changed the dynamics of power in the room as they met. "I don't think people should try to get their way by threatening resignations," Comey said to the chief of staff in the mostly empty White House that night. "If they find themselves in a position where they're not comfortable continuing, then they should resign." At his OLC office in Main Justice that night, Jack Goldsmith found himself staring up at the painted portrait of a former attorney general that coincidentally hung over his desk: Elliot Richardson. The Saturday Night Massacre was inescapably present.

---

*Aides later joked that the wife of Chuck Rosenberg, Comey's chief of staff, was probably convinced that evening that he was having an affair. He came home late in a cab, since he couldn't recall where he had left his car.

As the leaders of the Justice Department went to bed early on the morning of the eleventh, five time zones ahead, in Madrid, a cell of al-Qaeda members fanned out across the capital region and planted thirteen bombs targeting the commuter trains. By the time the U.S. government awoke, 191 people were dead in 10 separate explosions, and some 1,800 Spanish commuters were wounded. Waking up that day, each player in the unfolding saga knew exactly what the stakes were in the unfolding showdown. *Thousands would die. It was all Jim Comey's fault.*

Thursday was D-Day and H-Hour, the final deadline to reauthorize the program. The government's response to the Madrid bombings was beginning, and Mueller, Comey, and most of the senior leaders of Justice and the Bureau were preparing to resign when a call came from Ashcroft's chief of staff with a plea: The attorney general isn't well enough to join you in resigning yet and he can't be left hanging alone; hold on until Monday, when he can join you. That delay, which ultimately gave both sides of the debate enough time to resolve their differences, was all that stopped what would have been one of the most explosive Washington scandals in recent memory.

During the disturbing terrorism briefings on Thursday, the crisis was never mentioned. President Bush left to give a speech in New York, still unclear as to the extent of the crisis unfolding among the men arrayed on his couches in the Oval Office. Mueller had become the key negotiator in the stalemate and returned to the White House within hours to meet with Andy Card. After forty minutes with the chief of staff, he stopped by Gonzales's office and then returned to Justice to meet with Comey. He then called Gonzales to update him on the situation.

Why the head of a component agency of the Justice Department, a figure several layers down the organization chart, came to be the central negotiator in the TSP scandal speaks volumes about Mueller's role in Washington. The dispute was between the Office of Legal Counsel, the attorney general, the vice president, and the National Security Agency. Mueller should not have been involved, except that Comey knew him to be honest and trustworthy to a fault; his personal integrity was beyond reproach, his sense of values and the primacy of the Constitution second to none. The White House people likewise knew and trusted him, which was why they'd opened the back channel to him in the first place. But his central role placed Mueller in a tough spot. His deputy director, Bruce Gebhardt, recalls the pain and turmoil of the week, saying, "That was probably the darkest week we spent together. You could see him agonize."

Yet Mueller's involvement drastically raised the stakes for the White House also. It could probably weather the loss of the deputy attorney general politically; no one outside of Washington knew who Jim Comey was, or even really what his position entailed. The Office of Legal Counsel was an obscure entity, powerful within the executive branch but unknown outside of it. The loss of the FBI director would be devastating, however. "No president wants the director of the FBI to resign. That's the ultimate H-bomb," former attorney general Dick Thornburgh says. The political implications would be profound.

Those who were close to Mueller at the time said that he was careful to "stay in his lane" as the crisis continued. It wasn't for him to decide whether the policy should be reauthorized. It was his job only to uphold the Justice Department's responsibility for protecting the Constitution. He had laid out his position on the tyranny of the law the year before, during a rare speech to the American Civil Liberties Union defending the Bureau's track record. "We live in dangerous times, but we are not the first generation of Americans to face threats to our security," he explained. "Like those before us, we will be judged by future generations on how we react to this crisis. And by that I mean not just whether we win the war on terrorism, because I believe we will, but also whether, as we fight that war, we safeguard for our citizens the very liberties for which we are fighting."

As the FBI director said to Jack Goldsmith in the midst of the crisis, "Your office is the expert on the law, and the president is not." If the Justice Department refused to reauthorize the Stellar Wind program and the White House proceeded anyway, he couldn't remain in his post. As Thornburgh, who has known Mueller for more than twenty years, explains, "People are smart not to test him on those issues."

In fact, Mueller overall sees little gray in the world; he's a black-or-white guy, right or wrong. His father, who was the captain of a World War II navy sub chaser, impressed on him early the importance of credibility and integrity. "You did not shade or even consider shading with him," Mueller recalls, and ever since, matters of honor and principle had been simple. "Occasionally he'll be a pain in the ass because he's so straitlaced," his counselor and old college friend Lee Rawls says. "There have been a couple of instances I've advocated cowardice and flight, and he wouldn't have it."

"The things that most of us would struggle with the most come relatively easy to him because his moral compass is so straight," one aide says with reflection and envy. "It's got to be quite comforting in its own way."

The following morning, Friday, Comey and Mueller walked into the White House for what they thought was the last time. The afternoon before, Addington had rewritten the reauthorization of the program so that it no longer had to be signed by the attorney general and instead was okayed by Gonzales's signature. The change had no true legal weight, but it allowed the administration to continue. After the morning brief wrapped up, President Bush called Comey back as he walked out of the Oval Office—in his mind, for the last time. "Jim, can I talk to you for a minute?" Bush asked.

Mueller said, "I'll wait for you downstairs."

In Bush's private dining room a moment later, the two men sat. The president was warm and kind, saying that Comey should let him take the burden of the program's reauthorization. "As Martin Luther said, 'Here I stand, I can do no other,'" Comey, who had been a religion major at the College of William and Mary, quoted, hoping to connect with the religious president. They spoke at length. Comey was shocked that Bush knew so little of what had transpired that week; his advisers had never let on.

"I think you should know that Director Mueller is going to resign today," Comey finally said.

Now it was Bush's turn to shift uncomfortably. His face made clear the shock he felt. No one had told the president that his FBI director was about to walk out.

As Comey went downstairs to meet Mueller, a Secret Service agent informed the director that the president needed to see him. Now it was Comey's turn to wait anxiously in the anteroom. Mueller and Bush met in the Oval Office, and Mueller refused to budge from his position. The Stellar Wind program as instituted was illegal. Simple as that. Black and white. The president had already reauthorized the program in Addington's memo the day before, without Justice's approval, and that meant that the president was currently on the wrong side of the law. Whereas the administration viewed the surveillance program as a necessity for the nation's security, Mueller felt just the opposite: The nation's security rested with its primacy of law. As he said in a speech he gave later, "The rule of law, civil liberties, and civil rights—these are not our burdens. They are what makes all of us safer and stronger." If President Bush didn't change course, Mueller had no choice, he said. He hadn't sworn to serve George W. Bush. He had sworn to protect the Constitution from all enemies, foreign and domestic.

President Bush blinked first. The commander in chief told the FBI director at the end of their discussion, "Tell Jim to do what Justice thinks needs to be done."

Mueller walked out of the office, his shoulders slumped from the stress, but he'd won the day. He and Comey went back to their SUV. While the FBI director's longtime driver, John Griglione, waited outside the vehicle, Comey and Mueller conversed in the back seat. Then they drove out the gate. Contrary to what they had thought just two hours earlier, they would return to the White House.

Mueller spent much of the ensuing days dealing with Stellar Wind fallout, meeting multiple times a day with various officials, including George Tenet and Vice President Cheney. In the end, President Bush signed an amended directive a week after the March 11 showdown.

The crisis over, Comey and Mueller shared a dark laugh. "This was easy," they said to each other.★

★When news of the bizarre night finally leaked in the summer of 2007 and Comey testified before Congress about the events, Congress asked Mueller for his notes from that night. By that point, though, Ashcroft had left office and Gonzales had been promoted to be Mueller's new boss. Comey had left office in the summer of 2005, seven months into Gonzales's tenure. The FBI director released a detailed

* * *

A year after the showdown over the Terrorist Surveillance Program and soon after announcing that he would leave the Justice Department in August 2005, Jim Comey ventured up the Baltimore-Washington Parkway to Fort Meade, Maryland, the headquarters of the National Security Agency, to speak to its staff in honor of Law Day. His driver was the same one who had raced him to George Washington Hospital the year before. Comey used the example of biblical exegesis (the study of texts) to explain how legal analysis and intelligence collection were closely related. "It involves a maniacal focus on the meaning of words, the history of words, the biases of historical observers, the biases of contemporary scholars," he told the assembled crowd. "Words carry great freight, words telegraph outcomes and often foreclose discussion."

As is often the case in the shadowy world of the intelligence community, there were two audiences for his speech. At the time, nearly no one in attendance knew about the crisis that had nearly put the Justice Department and the NSA on a collision course and had threatened to upend George W. Bush's presidency in the midst of his reelection campaign. Much of Comey's speech, though, was directed at the few people in the room who were quite aware of what had transpired. "It can be very, very hard to be a conscientious attorney working in the intelligence community," he told the crowd, standing at the podium and looking out at the darkened faces before him. "Hard because we are likely to hear the words, 'If we don't do this, people will die.' You can all supply your own 'this.' 'If we don't collect this type of information' or 'if we don't use this technique' or"—and here he paused for a breath—"'if we don't extend this authority.' It is

---

but heavily redacted record of some twenty-three meetings about the subject, which included his observation that Ashcroft was "feeble, barely articulate, and clearly stressed" during the hospital visit.

Gonzales, already caught up in his own scandals related to the firings of U.S. attorneys and the politicization of the Justice Department, resigned within a month of the Stellar Wind fiasco coming to light. Mueller, ever the loyal Marine, has never openly discussed his view of the showdown. When pressed by Congress, after Comey's testimony, he admitted only that the visit to the hospital was "out of the ordinary."

extraordinarily difficult to be the attorney standing in front of the freight train that is the need for 'this.'"

Comey argued that it was the responsible attorney's role to recognize the larger issues at stake. The United States was a nation of laws, not men. As public servants, all government officials had sworn the same oath, one that pointedly does not promise allegiance to the president, the government, or even the American people. The sole thing they swear to do is to protect and defend the Constitution. "We know that our actions, and those of the agencies we support, will be held up in a quiet, dignified, well-lit room, where they can be viewed with the perfect, and brutally unfair, vision of hindsight. We know they will be reviewed in hearing rooms or courtrooms where it is impossible to capture even a piece of the urgency and exigency felt during a crisis," he said in a comment all too prescient about what would unfold in the coming years. "'No' must be spoken into a storm of crisis, with loud voices all around, and with lives hanging in the balance.... It takes an understanding that, in the long run, intelligence under the law is the only sustainable intelligence in this country."

The fallout from the Iraq war resulted in yet another investigative commission — the Silberman-Robb Commission, a study of the intelligence failures that led to the decision that Iraq possessed weapons of mass destruction — which in turn resulted in more pressure on the FBI. The so-called WMD Commission had some choice words for Mueller's first five years of effort, concluding, "While the Bureau is making progress toward changing its culture, it remains a difficult task and one that we believe will require more structural change than the Bureau has instituted thus far." It added, "Many field offices are still tempted to put law enforcement ahead of intelligence-gathering, betting that 'Bin Laden is never going to Des Moines.'"

Mueller wasn't pleased that the WMD Commission was even looking at the FBI. The FBI hadn't played any role in the intelligence failures that led the U.S. into Iraq. Besides, he felt he knew what needed to be done. "His attitude was 'Why are we even involved in this?'" a source close to him recalls. Yet the commission, which examined the state of the nation's intelligence services writ large, believed that the Bureau wasn't making progress as fast as it should, and concluded that "the FBI is still far from having the strong analytic capability that is required to drive and focus the Bureau's national security work. Although the FBI's tactical analysis has made significant progress, its strategic capabilities—those that are central to guiding a long-term, systematic approach to national security issues—have lagged." It cited numerous examples of how analysts were still being treated as glorified secretaries and pointed out that of the 1,720 intelligence analysts, only 38 actually worked for the Directorate of Intelligence. Said the commission, "We conclude that the Directorate's *lack* of authority is pervasive. We asked whether the Directorate of Intelligence can ensure that intelligence collection priorities are met. It cannot. We asked whether the Directorate directly supervises most of the Bureau's analysts. It does not. We asked whether the head of the Directorate has authority to promote—or even provide personnel evaluations for—the heads of the Bureau's main intelligence-collecting arms. Again, the answer was no. Does it control the budgets or resources of units that do the Bureau's collection? No."

Vice President Cheney, too, thought that the FBI wasn't making enough progress, telling Mueller, "Don't be the pooper scooper afterwards." In Oval Office meetings, President Bush pushed Mueller to make the necessary changes to the Bureau so he wouldn't have to have Fran Townsend, his homeland security director, intercede: "Bob, you don't want her to bring this to me." Townsend recalls, "Mueller said, 'I'm dancing as fast as I can.'" Mueller responded to the commission by creating a new, unified National Security Branch, bringing together the counterterrorism and counterintelligence divisions as well as the Directorate of Intelligence. It was enough to buy the Bureau more time. "There was a lot of work still to do," Bob Casey says. "People got it in theory, but not in practice."

As the WMD Commission had phrased it, "the margin of safety is shrinking, not growing." The message from the White House was clear: "If there's another attack, you won't avoid MI5 again." Mueller took that message seriously and pushed even harder. He commissioned a major study by the consulting firm McKinsey & Company to help evaluate the FBI's reforms and recommend necessary changes for the future. "Bob had done a great job restructuring the headquarters executives, but anyone who knows the FBI knows the real changes are not happening until they're happening in the field offices," Townsend recalls.

After Baginski's attempt to lead the intelligence directorate was met with what one executive described as "organ rejection," Phil Mudd stepped in as Mueller's "new Jesus" on the intelligence front.* Mudd had spent the better part of a decade working at the CIA's Counterterrorism Center, eventually becoming the deputy director, and had come to know Mueller when the two men were briefing members of Congress in closed-door sessions. Nevertheless, he was surprised to get a series of phone calls from the FBI director asking him to join the Bureau. "I'll only do this if you're serious," Mudd said. Over several conversations, Mueller convinced the CIA veteran that he was. When Mudd arrived at the Hoover Building, he was amazed at how foreign the concept of intelligence still seemed to be to most of the FBI and decided to take a more hands-off approach to the National Security Branch, pushing ideas, concepts, and ways of thinking rather than working the levers available to the FBI's senior ranks.

Balancing the intelligence side with active investigations was an ongoing challenge. Even as Mueller and Comey's high-level drama had played out in secret, the Bureau had been racing to investigate any American links to the Madrid plot. One week after the attack, the Bureau's fingerprint unit thought it had identified a fingerprint on a bag of Madrid detonators that matched a U.S. citizen named Brandon Mayfield, an attorney in Oregon. Three different examiners signed off on the match.

The Bureau immediately began intense surveillance. Mayfield noticed vehicles following him back and forth to work. His Egyptian-born wife, for whom he'd converted to Islam, complained that the door to their house was repeatedly being dead-bolted, indicating that

---

*While Baginski was not much liked by many in the Bureau, even her critics credit her with giving Mueller the grace period from congressional and White House oversight to begin instituting changes. As one person who worked with her explains, "Sometimes Baginski was rough around the edges and one never wanted to incur her wrath, but at the end of the day she may have helped to save the Bureau."

someone else was locking (or, more accurately, relocking) their door while they were out; their son, home sick from school one day, noticed a man jiggling the doorknob. Eventually, the FBI knocked on Mayfield's door with some questions and showed up at his mother's house in Kansas, from which they took six boxes of evidence.

Back at the FBI Lab at Quantico, the fingerprint team was puzzling over their work. The Spanish police had declared that the print didn't match Mayfield's. Yet as the weeks passed and the surveillance continued, the media learned that an American suspect had come to the FBI's attention. The Bureau rushed to pull together a material witness warrant, its favorite tool after 9/11, when disruption was the watchword, and on May 6 it turned Mayfield's world upside down by arresting him and searching his home and office. There was precious little to go on other than the fingerprint match—at no point did the FBI find any other connections to the Madrid bombers or, for that matter, to any terrorist groups at all—but the Bureau, which more or less perfected fingerprinting as a manner of identification, was uniquely inclined to trust the result. Mayfield's arrest and his suspected ties to the Madrid terrorists were front-page news around the world.

Mayfield spent two weeks in jail as the FBI sorted things out. This was the MO for the new Bureau: Arrest quickly and work the case once the suspect is off the streets. Instead of building a stronger case, though, the Bureau realized too late that the Spanish authorities were right. On May 20, the Spanish police announced that the fingerprint belonged to an Algerian man; Mayfield was freed. He sued the FBI in civil court and settled with the Bureau for some $2 million in damages. It was an expensive lesson for the FBI, but one that underscored why the Bureau preferred to operate on the beyond-a-reasonable-doubt standard.* And yet the pressure—the "if you don't do this, thousands will die" pressure—coupled with the seeming avalanche of complaints about FBI hesitancy and inefficiency, meant that the Bureau

---

* As Mueller says, "One of the differences is that the intelligence community operates on speed; analysts pull together dots. We have an obligation when we disseminate information to focus on credibility because it affects people's lives here in the United States."

remained in a three-front war: against criminals, against external political muscling, and against its own culture.

By 2006, terrorist threats seemed to have settled into a numbing routine. On the first day, Justice and Homeland Security officials would trumpet that a major plot had been broken; cable news would go nuts. On the second day, court documents would lay out the precise allegations. By the third day, defense lawyers would be in on the game, arguing that there was no "there" there and that the government had entrapped the hapless talkers; the entire thing was nothing more than barroom boasting. Then the media coverage would move on to why it was that the country was so nervous about every terror alert.*

The August 2006 London airplanes plot was different. A group of possible conspirators had come under surveillance in the fall of 2005, as MI5 and New Scotland Yard redoubled their counterterrorism efforts in the wake of the July subway bombings in London. The British authorities tracked the suspects for months, not knowing initially what the plot, the potential targets, or the means of attack were. By the summer of 2006, however, it was becoming clear that a major operation was under way. For only the second time since 2001, Fran Townsend explains, "The government goes into full battle mode."

The plot emerged out of the fanatical Islamic community that had developed in and around London. Before his death in 2001, John O'Neill had repeatedly urged the British to take more seriously the rising problem of homegrown radicalization in what intelligence officials privately dubbed "Londonistan," the tightly knit, predomi-

---

* The first full-scale post-9/11 alert had been the so-called election threat, encompassing the period from the Madrid bombings to the November election, which was for many the scariest period since 2001. In August, a laptop computer found in Pakistan uncovered a possible plan to attack New York's financial district. Even though the plans were years old, the government raised the threat level to orange. Financial centers were placed on high alert. Different threads of intelligence came together to make everyone involved nervous, especially since the Madrid bombings had taken place just before a major national election, indicating al-Qaeda's desire to influence politics, but whatever had been in the offing never materialized.

nantly immigrant communities around the city. Many of these communities are poorly assimilated into the larger culture, and radical imams there are able to turn their audiences against the West. By the turn of the century, a variety of Islamic extremist groups operated in the country, including Hizb ut-Tahrir, which had been banned elsewhere, and Britain had become arguably the world's leading center of Islamists outside the Middle East and Afghanistan. Abu Hamza al-Masri, the fiery imam of the Finsbury Park Mosque, had continued to preach violence and jihad until the British arrested him in 2004 — and only then, some speculated, to avoid having to hand him over to the Americans for deportation to Guantánamo. In one meeting before 2001, O'Neill had pointedly told an MI5 executive, "If you don't take this seriously, the queen is going to end up living in Ireland."

MI5 had already received a warning from the FBI that al-Qaeda seemed to be intent on building peroxide-based bombs out of ordinary, commercially available materials. "Components of improvised explosive devices can be smuggled onto an aircraft, concealed as either clothing or personal carry-on items such as shampoo and medicine bottles, and assembled on board," the Bureau bulletin warned. As the London plot unfolded, through wiretaps, internet intercepts, and surveillance, it became clear that the would-be terrorists planned to smuggle a handful of ingredients onto airliners and assemble bombs on board that could simultaneously bring down as many as ten transatlantic flights. The attacks could have killed upward of three thousand people — the same death toll as September 11 — and was reminiscent of the Bojinka plot a decade before, when Ramzi Yousef and Khalid Sheikh Mohammed had planned to down a number of airliners over the Pacific. The deputy commissioner of the London Metropolitan Police described it as "mass murder on an unimaginable scale."

On August 6, 2006, five years to the day after the president had been presented with the CIA's Presidential Daily Brief entitled "Bin Laden Determined to Strike in U.S.," Bush and British prime minister Tony Blair spoke at length about when would be the right time to arrest the plotters. They wanted to stop the plot, but not before learning as much as they could about the plan and the reaches of the cell's support network. Before they took down the suspects, British authorities wanted to be sure that other cells weren't operating as part of the plot. Meanwhile, top national security leaders were convening three times a day to brief the latest developments; Townsend was on the phone with her British counterparts nearly constantly. Intelligence-gathering had revealed which flights were being targeted—or at least which were most likely to be targeted—but the fact there were so many and that the British and American authorities wanted to draw out the full scope of the plot meant that officials at each session were faced with an intense decision: Every day, should they let the targeted planes take off? They went around the table, each agency executive getting a simple binary question: Go or no-go? *Are you sure?*

To make matters even more stressful, vacationing White House staff members, friends, family, and colleagues were sometimes on the suspect aircraft. White House spokesperson Dana Perino and her husband boarded one plane back to the United States; the daughter of National Security Advisor Stephen Hadley was on board one of the planes on another day. The security team couldn't risk warnings that might spring the trap prematurely, so everyone, friends and strangers, boarded the flights unaware of the possibility of impending doom.

Townsend recalls, "No one would have gotten in trouble for taking the plot down, but that's not the best thing for the country." Yet it didn't make things much easier either. Townsend, who had trouble sleeping because of the stress, would go to the White House gym after the go-ahead for the planes to take off had been given and work out frenetically on the stationary bicycle until the planes had passed the point where the authorities thought they might explode. Michael Chertoff spoke for many of the principals in a phone call to Congressman Peter King, who headed the House Homeland Security Committee: "Very seldom do things get to me. This one has really gotten to me."

When the plotters began to research buying plane tickets and MI5 uncovered at least one "martyrdom video" by one suspect, the British government decided to move. An additional push came when the Pakistani government arrested one of the planners of the attacks, Rashid Rauf.★ His arrest in Pakistan might result in the plot going

---

★Rauf later "escaped" from Pakistani custody and was believed to have been involved in plots against the United States in 2008 and 2009. U.S. authorities claim

forward or the suspects escaping. Either way, something had to be done quickly.

In their first round of apprehensions the British police arrested twenty-four people, many of whom didn't seem to fit the traditional profile of terror suspects. All of them were British citizens, many were well educated, some were only recent converts to Islam. The plot had originated with senior al-Qaeda leadership in Afghanistan and Pakistan, but it also underscored the rise of a new kind of terrorist: the homegrown radical, taking orders and coordinating with terror networks overseas.

By 1:00 A.M. Washington time on August 10, 2006, all of the suspects were in custody, and travelers on both sides of the Atlantic awoke to chaos. All carry-on luggage was banned; no liquids were allowed on board except medicine and milk or juice for infants, and those liquids had to be tasted in the presence of a security official before they were allowed. Even tissues had to be taken out of their boxes. One European-bound passenger out of Dulles airport had to peel her banana.

The gamble paid off, though. The investigation resulted in a treasure trove of valuable information: Some two hundred mobile phones, four hundred computers, and thousands of DVDs, memory sticks, and other pieces of evidence were seized for analysis and tracking. In one case, a "bomb factory" was found in a public park near a suspect's apartment; he'd been mixing the chemicals in the woods so that incriminating evidence wouldn't be in his apartment.

After searching the suspects' homes and looking at how the bombs were likely to be assembled, technicians were awed. The devices were fantastically simple, easy to assemble with the right knowledge, and would have sailed right past airport security. A bottle of what appeared to be juice, a disposable camera, and a few other items were, as it turned out, all that was required to bring down an airliner.

From the start of his fatwa in the early 1990s, bin Laden had said he'd raise the level of attack with each attack. Repeatedly since 2001, al-Qaeda planners had aborted missions that didn't seem spectacular enough to follow their incredible success on 9/11. "What you have to understand is

that he was killed by a drone strike on November 22, 2008, but no proof of his death has surfaced.

the role that honor plays in these attacks," one intelligence official explains. "The blowing up of a bus lowers you to Hamas. Bin Laden doesn't want to be doing little attacks—that makes him just another Hamas, which hasn't been all that effective over time. He thinks al-Qaeda is a whole different level, thus they need to attack on a different level."

Yet ever since 2001, the group had found it harder to plan and launch those grander attacks. Al-Qaeda's financing network had been put under tremendous pressure by U.S. authorities, so the group had to wage its war without as many resources. The London planes plot, as one official involved in tracking it explains, was "9/11 on the cheap." No flight training, extended foreign residence, or first-class plane tickets were required. As the official says, "It was low-tech, low-cost, and high-yield. It provided 9/11 casualties at post-9/11 prices."

To al-Qaeda's leaders, the unraveling in London underscored that it was increasingly difficult to organize a new attack from the center. "At the time they thought they were under a lot of pressure— of course, that's nothing compared to what they face now—but they decided instead their strategy should focus on pulsing out through other groups," an intelligence official says. The ambitions changed, this official says, explaining that al-Qaeda's sights became set on delivering an attack on any level: "You got one guy? One bomb? One plane? I'll take it."

But if a bar had been lowered, the danger was still there.

Perhaps the FBI's biggest management failure since Mueller had taken over was the implementation of the National Security Letters (NSLs), an expanded authority granted under the PATRIOT Act that allowed the FBI to compel places like telephone companies and libraries to release records relating to subjects and suspects not (yet) associated with an ongoing criminal investigation. Unique among the tools in the FBI's arsenal, NSLs did not require approval by a court, a prosecutor, or the Justice Department. The FBI issued them under its own authority, and the bar for a NSL was so low as to be almost nonexistent.

NSLs generally pertained to three types of records that had previously been ruled by the courts not to be constitutionally protected: credit history, financial transactions, and "called and calling" telephone data. Unlike a wiretap, the NSL authority doesn't allow for "content" collection—the transcript of a telephone call or the text from an e-mail—but by tracing out the paths of modern life, the FBI could relatively easily figure out the movements and associations of an individual. All an FBI agent had to certify was that the requested files or records were "sought for" or "relevant" "to protect against international terrorism or clandestine intelligence activities."* Anyone who receives an NSL is gagged by the order and forbidden to mention it or warn the target of the investigation.

Lee Hamilton, the co-chair of the 9/11 Commission, says that NSLs are "awesome in their invasiveness," and he was far from the only one wary of the new power. Librarians objected strongly to the idea that the FBI could now, with minimal probable cause, subpoena records to see what books patrons had been reading. Only a few NSLs nationwide have been challenged in court, with mixed success, but when the inspector general released his first report on the FBI's use of the NSL authority in 2007, the magnitude of the Bureau's errors made front-page news. Also shocking was the scale of NSL usage: the Bureau had been requesting up to 900 a week—some 50,000 a year—since 2001, an increase of more than a hundredfold since before 9/11, when the use of NSLs was much more restricted.

The NSL nightmare was to a certain extent Mueller's doing. At the outset of the program, the Bureau's general counsel recommended that the authority to issue NSLs be immediately granted only to the SACs of the fifteen most active field offices and be expanded only after additional SACs received training on how to use the new tool properly. Mueller overruled the recommendation, immediately granting the authority to all SACs. In a November 28, 2001, "electronic communication" to the field, the National Security Law Unit attorney Michael Wood wrote that NSLs "must be used judiciously." The FBI's standard guidelines mandated "that the FBI accomplish its investigations through the 'least intrusive' means," he explained, which in turn

---

* Agents and lawyers who dealt with the authority say that it's unclear how any request could fail to meet that standard, and the Bureau has generally refused to release information about whether FBI supervisors have denied or rejected any NSLs requests.

required that "the greater availability of NSLs does not mean that they should be used in every case." Prophetically, he added, "Congress certainly will examine the manner in which the FBI exercised it." But for years after Mueller's initial decree—stunningly—both he and other headquarters executives mostly ignored the implementation and use of NSL authority in the field.

In the most expansive known operation, a start-up counterterrorism unit of the FBI tasked with "proactive data exploitation" descended on Las Vegas in the wake of a December 2003 terror alert and blanketed the city with NSLs, attempting to build a database of everyone who had visited the nation's top travel destination over a two-week period. With NSLs, they vacuumed up the hotel, airline, and car rental records of nearly a million people, none of whom, of course, were aware of the effort. Nothing came of the threat, but because of FBI policy changes after 9/11, the Bureau no longer destroyed information on innocent people it collected as part of terrorism investigations. Instead, it was constantly seeking ways to do "programmatic" collection of data, pulling together disparate data sources to seek "non-obvious relationships," linking people by shared work histories, Social Security numbers, travel patterns, and the like. The Bureau's Investigative Data Warehouse, an enormous Oracle database similar to one used by the CIA, contained close to a billion records (financial transactions, watch lists, intelligence reports, and so on) and was used more than a million times each month by Bureau agents and analysts. It would be the single largest FBI effort to connect the dots.* While casino and hotel officials in Vegas were horrified by the FBI effort— their business was built on the presumption that "what happens in Vegas stays in Vegas"—such ambitious projects were precisely what the Bureau had seemed incapable of tackling before 9/11. The 9/11

---

*According to work by *Wired,* the FBI's National Security Analysis Center contains thousands of different cross-referenced databases, ranging from international travel records of both U.S. citizens and foreigners, hotel records from Wyndham Hotels chain, Avis car rental documents, Sears credit card transactions, 200 million records from private data-mining companies like Acxiom and ChoicePoint, 696 million telephone records, lists of all private pilots in the country, and the names of the 3 million people with licenses that allow them to drive hazardous materials— among other lists.

Commission, which received a secret briefing on the data warehouse project from Gurvais Grigg, who headed the proactive data exploitation team, was full of compliments for the new system. "The efforts Grigg described reflect remarkable progress from where he was when we interviewed him [earlier]," the commission staff wrote internally. "Initiatives that then were largely aspirational are now much more concrete."

The scope of the NSL authority, coupled with the new data-mining initiatives, left many civil liberties advocates nervous. "The NSL authority was used in exactly the way the civil liberties community warned it would be," explains Mike German, a former FBI agent who joined the ACLU after becoming concerned about the FBI's handling of terrorism cases. And during congressional testimony, former attorney general William Barr complained that "simply saying that the FBI can use a National Security Letter to obtain information on any person or persons that they want so long as it is relevant to an investigation that they have determined is an appropriate one, without any review, without any accountability, without any objective standard, has rendered it meaningless."

The inspector general later concluded that there were "serious abuses" of the unprecedented power all around. Error rates ran as high as over 9 percent, meaning that as many as 20,000 incorrect National Security Letters might have been issued. All in all, the inspector general found errors (either merely improper or downright illegal) in one out of every five files his office reviewed. Many mistakes were not noticed or, if noticed, were not reported by Bureau officials. The scale of the mistakes made them hard for even the FBI's backers to stomach. "You count on them to do it right, and it's disappointing when they overreach," says Congressman Mike Rogers, a former FBI agent. "It may go beyond merely inappropriate."

To be sure, some blunders were what inspectors labeled "initial third-party errors," such as a telephone company turning over phone records for an entire family plan rather than for just a single number or turning over two months of phone records when only one was requested, but the FBI's poor procedures and oversight process compounded the errors. Alan Raul, who served as vice chair of the president's Privacy and Civil Liberties Board, which was established at the recommendation of the 9/11 Commission as an outside check on the powers granted under the PATRIOT Act, explains, "The other members and I were very surprised by the NSLs. We did perceive it as a debacle, more as a cultural and administrative one rather than an intentional one." One law professor testifying before Congress on the issue explained, "Congress has never agreed to anything like the current scale and scope of use of NSLs."*

The NSL issue was somewhat more innocuous than the headlines made it seem to be. Even the Justice Department's inspector general found no "intentional misuses," saying that most of the errors resulted from "sloppiness, mistakes, confusion, inadequate training, inadequate oversight." More than seven hundred NSLs were approved by FBI agents who lacked the authority to do so. But Mueller, aides say, took the IG's report hard, saying privately that he should have known better and paid more attention to such a critical issue. The Bureau's missteps had threatened what it saw as a crucial investigative tool in the fight against terrorism.

On the afternoon after the media broke the story in April 2007, Mueller was summoned to the White House for an off-the-schedule meeting—never a good sign in Washington—and taken through a back entrance to minimize his chances of being seen. In the meeting, Bush ripped into him: The PATRIOT Act was one of the foundations of the war on terror, and Mueller's sloppiness or inattention to NSLs threatened to undermine one of the key investigative tools the act provided. "He was furious. It was so eminently avoidable," one White House source recalls. "Now we're going to pay a political price for Bob's screw-up."

----

*Critics were shocked that something as controversial as the NSLs seemed so lost in the FBI bureaucracy, even if most, if not all, of the errors were made in good faith. As Raul explains, the debacle stemmed from the Bureau's attitude of "Get it done—we're doing the right thing for the right reasons." Perhaps most troubling among the multitude and magnitude of failures around NSLs was the fact that regular oversight reports by the inspector general were statutorily required; the Bureau knew it was going to be audited on its use of the authority, and yet it *still* failed to monitor it carefully. As Raul says, "If a private company reflected the same disregard for technical and legal compliance, the FBI and Justice would be all over them."

Alberto Gonzales, who was desperately fighting to keep his own job at the time, strongly backed Mueller. "It was an instance where Gonzales could have very easily used the distance separating Justice and the Bureau to say, 'This isn't my problem,'" the White House source explained. But Gonzales wanted to show his gravitas and stood shoulder-to-shoulder with Mueller in the meeting. "This is my fault," Mueller told the president. "I want to take care of it."

The White House meeting apparently mollified the president. Mueller took his beating. He understood what he needed to do. In the Bureau's draft statement on the issue, the genuinely frustrated Mueller toughened up his own culpability. It was, he says today, one of the examples of a time when he didn't drill down enough, push hard enough, ask the right questions, and hold the right people accountable. ("We can't afford to be sloppy like that. The American people expect that if they give us a tool, it'll be used appropriately," he says.) Mueller ended up facing harsh questioning on the Hill over the mistakes. In lobbying for the continued authority, he told Congress that if NSLs had existed before 9/11, "We could have traced Khalid al-Mihdhar to the rest of the hijackers." But the problems raised a larger question: What other Bureau problems weren't on the management's radar? "NSLs are not that complicated," general counsel Val Caproni says. "What else should we be looking at? What else out there is an NSL waiting to happen?"*

---

*In recent years, a multitude of reforms, new processes, and more substantive oversight, including a new FBI Office of Integrity and Compliance, have been implemented to address the NSL issues. Says Caproni, "Between the educational and the technical, we think we've solved about ninety-nine percent of what we saw as the substantive errors." Indeed, a follow-up inspector general report concluded that the Bureau had made "significant progress" in implementing corrective actions but that "it is too soon to say that the FBI has 'rectified' many of the problems."

CHAPTER 14
Culture Clash

We deal not with the true but with the likely.
— *Intelligence motto from*
World War II

The case of Louisiana Democratic congressman William Jefferson has to be regarded as one of the odder FBI public corruption investigations. Jefferson was caught on videotape accepting a $100,000 bribe at the Ritz-Carlton Hotel in Arlington, Virginia—a bribe he believed to be coming from a businessman interested in landing lucrative contracts in Africa but who was actually an FBI informant. When agents searched Jefferson's house four days later, they discovered the money hidden in the congressman's freezer. As the investigation unfolded, the FBI dramatically raided Jefferson's offices in the Rayburn House Office Building on a Saturday night in May 2006, barring House officials from the rooms as they searched. The raid was met with loud protests by congressional leaders in a rare moment of bipartisan unity between Republican House Speaker Dennis Hastert and Democratic leader Nancy Pelosi, who argued that under the Constitution the executive branch didn't have the authority to enter and examine files in the office space of a coequal branch of government. The president ordered the files sealed for forty-five days, preventing federal investigators from examining them, as the two branches negotiated a resolution.

Even as the rhetoric heated up—Congress threatened to take out its anger on the Justice Department's budget and even to impeach Alberto Gonzales—Mueller saw no room for negotiation. The FBI, he believed, had to be able to investigate without fear or favor. It could have no sacred cows. Mueller told White House officials he'd resign rather than order agents to return the documents they had seized. Gonzales and his deputy, Paul McNulty, both threatened to resign too.

For a second time, Mueller and the Bush administration had come to a crossroads. This time, though, two years after the hospital bedside showdown with Jim Comey, Gonzales stood with Mueller. In White House deliberations, the president was initially angry that the FBI had blindsided the administration without a prior warning that the raid was coming. (Today Mueller allows that "perhaps we could have handled that better.") Townsend, a vigorous defender of the FBI director's viewpoint, argued, "That's not the way the Justice Department works."

Mueller came out of the incident in a much stronger position, although his power came at a price. He was now seen within the administration as an independent power center in an administration that put a high price on loyalty. Having an independent FBI director such as Louis Freeh and J. Edgar Hoover had not boded well for previous presidents. Administration officials began to wonder whether Mueller was too independent. He refused to be trotted up to the Hill to lobby for the administration's agenda, and his congressional testimony often rankled. When the administration pushed FISA reform in Congress, Mueller refused to make the rounds on the Hill to advocate for it; if asked, he said, he'd express support, but he didn't see the FBI director's role as one that allowed for advocating specific policies in the political arena.

That role was supposed to belong to the attorney general, and during much of President Bush's second term, Mueller far outclassed his boss. The huge issues of the war on terror—constitutional law, criminal procedure, and intelligence law—were mostly foreign to Alberto Gonzales, and his attempts to politicize the hiring and firing of U.S. attorneys and people in other positions became a flashpoint. Just as he had been as White House counsel, Gonzales was in over his head as attorney general; he would listen intently in the morning terrorism briefings, but he rarely asked questions or expressed an interest in the larger geopolitical issues at play. Under Gonzales, for the first time in history, none of the top three officials at Justice—not even the head of the Criminal Division, Alice Fisher—had experience as criminal prosecutors. So many on the Hill had doubted Gonzales's ability to represent the government's interests separate from those of his political patron, President Bush, that he had passed Senate confirmation in 2005 by only a single vote. As one law enforcement official phrased it in the midst of Gonzales's later troubles, "He does not consider himself the chief law enforcement officer. He considers the president the chief law enforcement officer, and in that case, he is the deputy." It was a major departure from his predecessors' attitude. (One observer of Gonzales's tenure said, "The shame of it is that Al Gonzales was probably a really good Texas real estate attorney.")

Those familiar with the meetings between Gonzales and Mueller described their relationship as cordial. Mueller had a certain level of respect for Gonzales's office, but the power dynamic between the two was clear from the start: Mueller had already stared down Gonzales the year before, in the midst of the NSA wiretapping debacle. Mueller was firmly in charge of his own domain, and the Bureau remained untouched by Gonzales's efforts elsewhere to politicize hiring.

One evening in 2007, after Mueller made controversial remarks that seemed to undermine Gonzales before a Hill committee, the White House told Fran Townsend to go to his house and reel him back. Knowing the FBI director's ferocity, she demurred, and when she called him, he forbade her to show up at his Georgetown home. Despite his relentless pace, his long days, and his constant energy, Mueller had always tried to keep home as a haven, the one place he kept free from the pressure of the daily grind at the Bureau, or at least as free as he could. Agents still sometimes materialized late at night for him to sign FISA warrants, and he still exercised in the morning, long before dawn, on a stationary bike while flipping through the seemingly endless thick briefing packets that always filled his battered brown leather briefcase. (Only rarely did he make it to the bottom of the briefcase, to uncover the FBI badge that he'd carried since he became director.) Overall, though, whereas the home of his predecessor, Louis Freeh, had been filled with the energetic chaos of six young kids, Mueller's two children were grown and gone, and his residence was a quiet place where he and Ann had developed a comfortable sanctuary that slowed him down—a bit, anyway.

The couple had met at a friend's party when they were both seventeen. When Mueller started at Princeton, he invited the striking Sarah Lawrence coed to come visit for a weekend. By their senior year of college, they knew that Mueller was 1-A—that is, eligible for military service—so they wasted no time marrying. They were wed on Labor Day weekend 1966 at St. Stephen's Church, an imposing Episcopal Gothic Revival building just outside Pittsburgh, near where Ann had grown up. After a year in New York, where Ann got her teaching degree and Mueller recovered from knee surgery and got a master's in international relations before shipping out for Vietnam, they moved to Woodbridge, Virginia, for Mueller to attend Officer Candidate School at Quantico, the sprawling, rural, wooded base that would become so central to his time as a Marine and later as FBI director. Shortly after their arrival, they went out for a drink and wandered into a bar where the clock on the wall was set to Saigon time. So it would be for the next four decades: There was a clock and a Bob clock.

By the time Mueller became director of the FBI, Ann had followed her husband's career back and forth across the country, through seventeen different moves, by her count. Each time they relocated, she swore it would be the last. "Bob, the next time I move, it's into a pine box," she joked. But each time an opportunity to serve came up, she backed him—although sometimes it took some cajoling.

In the weeks after 9/11, it became clear just how dramatically the couple's lives had changed. Mueller's normally long days became nearly unending, with a stream of agents and visitors at their door through the night with urgent business. Mere days after the attacks, FBI agents had swept down on them at home, scooped the couple up, and moved them to officers' quarters at the Navy Yard after a viable threat on Mueller's life. Though they eventually settled into a town-house in Georgetown, for the next ten years they never ventured out into public alone. In an era before cell phones and before 9/11, Louis

Freeh had been able to drive himself alone up to New Jersey for over-night visits to his ailing father, and he disappeared on his own time for hours without anyone knowing where he was. Mueller's whereabouts were tracked minute to minute by the FBI SIOC and the Justice Department command post.* In one of the oddities of government service, a catastrophic attack on Washington might mean that Mueller was hustled out of the city to a secure bunker with no guarantee that his wife would be included in such an evacuation.

During their time in Washington, both Muellers had health scares. Ann barely paid attention to Bob's 2001 Senate confirmation hearings, because he was scheduled for prostate cancer surgery the day after. During his time as director, she twice underwent treatment for cancer, and he made every doctor's appointment and monitored every checkup, every dose of chemotherapy. "Everything else pales in comparison," Mueller reflects later, his voice betraying a rare chink in his typical stoicism. He even bought a grill and offered to take over the cooking while she recovered.

Their routines as a couple helped keep Mueller grounded, providing a temporary haven from the pressures of the day. As Ann notes, "His intensity and hyperfocus comes out in a trial. I always lose a piece of him. This job has been one extended trial." When Mueller traveled overseas, he almost always left on a Sunday and returned by Friday in time to take Ann out to dinner. On one Sunday morning trip to Egypt, the plane broke down before leaving Washington. He promptly called her from the airport, explained the situation, and asked, "Are we going to go to church?" Any spare moment they could seize, they did.

By the time Michael Mukasey took over as attorney general at the end of 2007, there were just fifteen months left in President Bush's term. Bob Mueller, with forty-seven months left, looked set to outlast them

---

*The constant security detail, though, did provide Mueller, who hated to stay out late, with the perfect excuse for departure. When dinner parties and events ran much past 9 P.M., he would gesture outside and explain to his hosts, "I've got to get these guys home to their families."

both. As Mueller's power consolidated in Washington during the second term of the Bush administration, the CIA, momentarily ascendant under George Tenet and Cofer Black following 9/11, after struggling so during the 1990s, had begun to see its stature erode.

Questions were raised about the Agency's post-9/11 harsh "enhanced interrogations." An Italian judge ordered the arrest of more than two dozen CIA officers, including the Rome station chief, after their sloppy tradecraft exposed an operation to kidnap a radical cleric and turn him over to Egyptian authorities. Similarly, a German court charged a baker's dozen of CIA officers for the kidnapping of a German citizen. In Sweden, Parliament launched a probe into that nation's cooperation with a CIA operation to turn over two suspected radicals, Ahmed Agiza and Muhammad Zery, to Egyptian authorities for torture.

Morale at the Agency and its public standing took a severe beating after the Iraq war revealed none of the promised weapons of mass destruction; George Tenet's "slam-dunk" comment had made him into a punch line. On Memorial Day weekend 2004, a year after the Iraq invasion, Tenet took a rare day off on the Jersey shore and stopped at the local A&P supermarket to buy some hamburger buns. Pushing a shopping cart while his security detail waited outside, he rounded one aisle and ran smack dab into Louis Freeh, who had sworn him in as CIA director in 1997. Tenet nearly broke down as he explained to the former FBI director how frustrated he was in the job: "I can't stay. Trust has been broken." "You're right, it's time to leave," Freeh replied, and he then proceeded to lay out a timetable for Tenet on how to step down and retain some respect. By Friday of that week, President Bush had accepted Tenet's resignation.

The next CIA director, Porter Goss, was a longtime and vociferous critic of the Agency. Brought in to clean house, by most accounts he failed, lasting just a year and a half. By the time the next CIA director, Michael Hayden—the air force general who had headed the National Security Agency and been a central figure in the Terrorist Surveillance Program—started, Congress had stripped the office of its role as coordinator of national intelligence. The new director of national intelligence, John Negroponte, would be the boss of the intel community. Notably, the new DNI failed in his quest to wrest control

and oversight of the FBI's National Security Branch. No one touched
Bob Mueller's Bureau.

Now that the immediate threats after 9/11, both from al-Qaeda and
from other government agencies and commissions, had passed, much
of Mueller's time was devoted to the larger structural changes he felt
the Bureau needed to make. Chief among them, he felt, was leadership development. Whereas in the military, career officers must attend
various specialized schools to advance in their field and many are sent
back to graduate school for master's degrees, MBAs, and yearlong fel-
lowships, the FBI had an almost mythic attachment to its training
division at Quantico and the idea that one-day seminars or one- or
two-week in-service training could fill any need. Recalls Phil Mudd,
who joined Mueller's Bureau after a long career with the CIA, "We'd
discuss a need and the immediate answer was always, 'How about a
two-week in-service at Quantico?' Well, how about figuring out what
we need to teach before we decide how long it should take?"

"We've always leaned toward the school of hard knocks," Special
Agent Bob Casey says. "Prove yourself on the battlefield, get a battlefield promotion. Every few battles, we'll bring you back to headquarters to smooth off the rough edges before sending you back to the field
with another promotion." Few agents had the opportunity to take
time to develop subject-matter expertise. Even years after terrorism
was supposed to be the FBI's top priority, an agent in Miami complained that the Bureau wasn't providing anywhere near enough education on terrorism and the ideology of America's enemies; "Most
people go out on their own and get books," he said. Mueller needed to
change that.

Furthermore Bureau culture deified the "agent generalist." As
John Ashcroft had once lamented privately, "If you had a heart attack
at the FBI, they wouldn't call a doctor. They would call an agent,
because they thought that agents could do everything." Field agents
ran the Bureau's departments, including IT, human resources, and
public affairs. While that tendency had made sense when the Bureau
was still small enough for Hoover to control it personally, the modern
FBI is a huge, sprawling organization. Its 2011 budget equates it to a

Fortune 300 company, larger than Eastman Kodak, Discover Card, and Campbell Soup and almost equal in size to eBay, and yet it had none of the management emphasis, training, or business practices of those similarly sized private companies. Mueller realized that the only chance he had of changing this was to hire outsiders with specific subject-matter expertise to lead FBI divisions, and in turn to push to professionalize the Bureau's processes.

One of the biggest "gets" of Mueller's tenure was Donald Packham, who headed human resources for the 50,000 employees of British Petroleum. Packham couldn't believe the FBI's mess. When he started, there wasn't even a human resources department. One section of the Bureau recruited agents; another trained them; a third took over once they were officially agents. There were no clear career paths. Packham introduced systems common in the private sector, such as "360-degree feedback," a human capital plan, summer college internships, and independent promotion boards designed to cut down on the capricious promotions that haunted the Bureau in the past. Mueller even developed a training program partnership with Chicago's Kellogg School of Management for top managers. The emphasis on business practices was clear in the executive ranks: During his stint as Mueller's deputy director, John Pistole, a career agent, talked of the Bureau's "shareholders," and one-time CIO Zal Azmi talked of his "customers" within the FBI. Over time, the makeup of Mueller's senior staff, initially constituted almost entirely of agents, would be transformed; today, nearly half of the executive leaders are Bureau outsiders.

Centralizing forces at headquarters meant filling huge personnel needs, and the needs were dire; at times, upward of three hundred positions were vacant at the Hoover Building. One of the international terrorism sections was operating in 2006 with just 62 percent of its authorized staff. One initiative helped fill some seven hundred positions at headquarters by offering the alternative of eighteen-month temporary deployments to Washington. Even that wasn't enough. Mueller's question to his staff became like a broken record: "How do you get people to put up their hands?"

In the end, Mueller figured out a way to get volunteers. All supervisors, he decreed, either had to give up their positions after five years and come to headquarters or had to move back down to the agent ranks. Mueller's so-called five-up-or-out policy (which was not actually "up or out," because supervisors could stay on as investigators; it was more of an "up or down" rule) became his most controversial HR policy as director.★ The new policy applied to about nine hundred of the Bureau's most senior supervisors scattered across the country in field offices, resident agencies, task forces, and special operations.

The move, agents groused, enabled Mueller to promote his own people more quickly. After surveying its members, the FBI Agents Association found that more than half of the affected supervisors would leave the Bureau rather than face the transfer to Washington. The numbers, as they trickled in, bore out the association's poll. In the first nine months of 2007, 576 agent supervisors across the FBI found themselves coming up against the five-year mark. Among those affected by the new policy were two New York JTTF agents, John Anticev and Russ Fincher, who were forced from their supervisory roles on the JTTF; both decided to return to the agents' ranks rather than work in the Hoover Building. They were far from the exception. Just 286 accepted the mandatory promotion and transfer to headquarters; another 150 returned to the agent ranks, taking a pay cut ranging from $10,000 to $20,000 or more in the process; and 140 left the FBI entirely, either retiring, if they had reached pension eligibility, or resigning outright. The transfers also meant that case agents in the field suddenly found themselves being supervised—more closely than in the past—by agents at headquarters who had less experience and less casework than they did.

To hear critics tell it—and there are many, inside and outside the Bureau—Mueller's inflexibility on the five-up-or-out rule has cost the Bureau hundreds of top agents with centuries of service. "I thought that was a tremendous mistake," says Congressman Rogers, the former FBI agent. "In the first go-round they lost half of the management agents. Half! I don't know how that's a success." Altogether, in the first eighteen months after the policy went into effect, more than half of the FBI's fifty-six field offices had received new SACs. After

---

★In fact, the rule had technically existed on the FBI's books for years, but it had been rarely enforced until Mueller's decree.

many rounds of complaints, Mueller amended the rule to "seven up or out," but agents groused that his flexibility came only because he had now installed his own people and wanted to keep them in the new leadership roles.

Helping to fuel the exodus from the Bureau was the lure of high-paying private security jobs. Whereas top counterterrorism and Criminal Division leaders had always been able to double or triple their Bureau salary after they retired, as John O'Neill did with his work at the World Trade Center, the need for their expertise exploded in the years after September 11. Suddenly agents could multiply their salary by four, five, six times over. The skids were further greased by a 1948 federal law that allowed law enforcement personnel to retire at age fifty and forced them to retire at age fifty-seven. "Right at the moment that these guys are reaching their peak, they're getting these incredibly good offers that are hard to refuse," says Mueller's counselor, Lee Rawls.*

The upper positions in the Bureau seemed to become a revolving door. On one Friday in April 2006, the FBI announced the departure of Gary Bald, the head of the National Security Division, who just eighteen months earlier had replaced Maureen Baginski, who had lasted only two years in her post. Bald, who had no real background in intelligence, didn't understand where the FBI fit into the pantheon of the community and was instinctively cautious as a leader, a result, perhaps, of the years he had spent working the Whitey Bulger corruption investigation in the Boston Field Office—one of the FBI's biggest black eyes in decades, because crooked agents had protected and aided the head of Boston's Irish mob.† After a challenging year leading the

---

*Many of the departing agents cited college costs as a concern. Age fifty, when agents with twenty years' service can first retire, is also the age when many of them have kids entering or close to entering college. Even Louis Freeh, when he retired, privately said that the looming costs of raising his six kids was a factor in leaving government service. Freeh's salary was $141,300 when he left office. Mueller's salary in 2010 was about $180,000. The FBI director's position is classified as a Level II government position, meaning that it is one pay rank below that of a cabinet official. Cabinet officials in 2010 were paid just under $200,000 annually.

†Bald, who had taken over the consolidated National Security Branch, once responded to a question about whether he had background knowledge about the Middle East by saying, "I wish that I had it. It would be nice."

Bureau's intelligence transformation—one marked by more setbacks than advances—Bald took a job as director of security for Royal Caribbean Cruises, which gave the FBI intelligence branch its third new head in barely as many years. That was hardly the end of the changes. The following Tuesday, the press office announced that the FBI's number-three official, Chris Swecker, was retiring to do security work at Bank of America. Swecker's predecessor, Grant Ashley, had retired just three months earlier to become head of security for Harrah's casino, just down the Las Vegas strip from two other former colleagues, Bruce Gebhardt—Mueller's former deputy director, who had left the Bureau in 2004 to be head of security for MGM Mirage—and Larry Mefford, who retired in 2004 to head up security for Wynn Resorts.

Appearing that same Tuesday before the Senate Judiciary Committee, Mueller faced a grilling by Dianne Feinstein. "In five years you have had six different heads of counterterrorism, and six different executive assistant directors overseeing counterterrorism," she noted. "What is the reason for this high turnover? What are you doing about it? And do you ask people when they join that they be required at least to stay for a period of time?"

"There are a number of factors that have contributed to the turnover," Mueller replied in the tired and respectful voice that he employs for appearances on the Hill. "The first is, you take somebody like Gary Bald, who I'll use as an example. He has thirty years of service to the FBI and to the country. He has kids in college. So the opportunities outside, particularly since September eleventh, where everyone wants a security director, and the obvious fact that many of these corporations can pay far more than the federal government, is a factor. The fact that a person has spent thirty years in the FBI in a career and still can have a second career, and has to make an earlier decision, is a factor. And the last factor is that we work twenty-four hours a day, seven days a week, and it's a lot of pressure on persons in those positions."

Feinstein wasn't buying it. "These are critical jobs at a critical time, and it would seem to me that somebody would not take a job for six months and then accept something else that came along. It would also seem to me that in terms of management practices, this ought to be advised against, counseled against, and if somebody cannot give you a commitment of time, why hire him?"

There were other reasons for the executive turnover. In Gebhardt's final speech before retiring from the Bureau in 2004, he recounted the FBI's first case ever from the South Pole, which began when the National Science Foundation's Amundsen-Scott South Pole Station science research facility received a blackmail threat, saying that its systems had been hacked and the data would be sold to the highest bidder unless the facility paid up. "Because of the subfreezing temperatures, it was impossible to send agents to the scene—no aircraft could land or take off from the site for months," Gebhardt explained. "But working from thousands of miles away, our investigators were able to trace the source of the intrusion to a server outside Pittsburgh." From there, the investigation moved to Bucharest, Romania, as the e-mails seemed to be coming from a cyber café there. This in turn helped the Bureau determine that the likely suspects were also involved in an ongoing investigation out of the Mobile, Alabama, and Los Angeles Field Offices. Romanian police working with the FBI legat in Bucharest arrested both suspects quickly. As Gebhardt concluded, "Conducting operations in Antarctica from FBI offices in D.C., Los Angeles, and Mobile, Alabama. Working hand-in-hand with police in Romania based on data from a server in Pittsburgh. It's a whole new world. Sometimes, some of us may feel like this isn't the same FBI we signed on to years ago. And we'd be right."

While terrorism had been the FBI's Public Enemy #1 since the morning of September 12, 2001, it was never the only thing on the Bureau's plate; in fact, the majority of the Bureau is still dedicated to the two hundred nonterrorism criminal and counterintelligence violations that have made up its bread and butter since the days of J. Edgar Hoover. The Bureau's organizational structure is broken down into three national security divisions—counterterrorism, counterintelligence, and cyber crime—and five criminal buckets—public corruption, civil rights, organized crime, white-collar, and violent crimes/major thefts, which includes everything from bank robberies to crimes on Indian reservations to art heists. The breadth of potential criminal violations is amazing. When FBI director Bill Webster made a mostly unsuccessful push in the 1980s to have other agencies take over some of the Bureau's work on criminal violations, he pointed out that the FBI was in charge of investigating everything from interstate transportation of unsafe refrigerators to the unauthorized display of the Civil Defense insignia. Nearly every year, Congress seemed to add more.

When John Pistole was still Mueller's deputy director (before becoming President Obama's choice to lead the Transportation Security Administration in 2010), he often asked audiences he spoke to how many FBI agents there were and provided some numbers for comparison: The NYPD had about 36,000 officers; the TSA, about 45,000 airport screeners nationwide; the Chicago police, about 13,000 officers; and the Los Angeles police and the Los Angeles county sheriffs, about 20,000 sworn personnel. Pistole's audiences generally began their guesses at about 40,000 agents and sometimes went as high as 75,000. Yet the Bureau really had just 13,500 agents, only 2,000 more than it had in 2001. At the same time, thousands of agents had been redirected to working counterterrorism cases and the FBI had started an entire new cyber crime division, which means that there are far fewer agents working the traditional pre-9/11 cases than before. Indeed, by the start of President Bush's second term, some 2,400 agents had been reassigned out of the criminal program. Fewer agents meant fewer cases. Public corruption cases declined from 2,491 in 2000 to 1,438 in 2004, violent crime cases from 32,535 to just 17,299. Organized crime cases, both domestically and internationally, fell from 7,679 to 3,685. Financial crimes went from 17,402 to 10,463. In almost every area of responsibility, the Bureau's cases were down by 40 to 50 percent. An investigation by the *Seattle Post-Intelligencer* in 2007 found that the number of cases referred to federal prosecutors by the FBI nationally had fallen by more than a third.

There were other ways, though, to measure the Bureau's new resource allocation. Sources inside and outside the FBI pointed to the worsening of the drug wars in and along the Mexican border in recent years, almost in direct correlation to the post-9/11 period during which the FBI pulled some two thousand agents away from working narcotics cases in field offices along the southern border and handed over more and more of its drug responsibilities to the DEA and other agencies. "It created a sucking chest wound on the southern border," one FBI executive says. Beyond drugs, the Bureau largely gave up even trying to pursue cases in certain categories. Fraud cases with losses of less than $150,000 virtually disappeared from the FBI's books; even cases with losses under $500,000 became hard to pursue. The situation was, in one agent's words, "triage." One source told the *Seattle Post-Intelligencer* that there were now whole categories of "risk-free" crimes—crimes that the FBI is the only organization to investigate but that it has now chosen no longer to pursue. Yet it was often criminal cases that initially helped launch terrorism investigations. One of the arguments for retaining the FBI's domestic intelligence portfolio within the FBI and not breaking it off into an MI5-style organization was that at the street level, criminals and terrorists often intersect, and these intersections remained even as the FBI abandoned many of its criminal cases. "Every single one of the terrorism cases we've investigated has had a criminal enterprise supporting it," recalls Spike Bowman, the Bureau's former longtime national security lawyer. "Often, when you're starting a case, you don't know whether you have a criminal or a terrorist." With the FBI now doing so many fewer criminal cases, Mueller laments, "We sacrifice the relationships that come from doing those cases and we sacrifice the knowledge that comes from those cases."

While the Bureau's budget roughly doubled under Mueller's tenure, compared to enormous increases in spending in other government programs and departments, the FBI's response to terrorism had been done "on the cheap," in one Bureau executive's words. Within years of its inception, the newly formed Transportation Security Administration quickly caught up with the Bureau in terms of budget. Other agencies received huge influxes of staff and resources, whereas the Bureau crept up steadily but never saw a big hiring bulge. Much of its annual increases in budget appropriations after 9/11 was used on infrastructure, especially building new secure facilities as the Bureau created almost seventy new JTTFs and outfitted them with top-secret communications systems. "The rest of the intel community already had much of that bricks-and-mortar," explains Mueller's one-time chief of staff, Lisa Monaco. The FY 2007 FBI budget, for instance, included money for only a single new agent but some $64 million to build new SCIFs (pronounced "skiffs"), the Sensitive Compartmented

Information Facilities that allow agents to read and discuss top-secret information in a secure room without fear of eavesdropping.* What agents in the field have come to call "Mueller money" has helped the Bureau open a number of new, state-of-the-art field offices—Dallas and Denver both opened expansive new facilities in 2010—but it hasn't translated to many new bodies in those new offices.

Special Agent Kenneth Williams, the author of the Phoenix memo, told the 9/11 Commission that he believed the FBI needed 50,000 agents in order to do its job properly. "We need to quadruple the number of agents we have," he said at one point. "How many of the 11,000 agents are managers?" he asked. "How many are dedicated to the war on terror? How many people are actually recruiting sources, knocking on doors? [It's] woefully inadequate."

Joe Biden, then a senator from Delaware, introduced a bill in February 2007 calling for one thousand new FBI agents. "There's no doubt that fighting terrorism should be a top priority for the FBI, but we can't forget about the risk to our neighborhoods from everyday crime," he said. "President Bush hasn't replaced the FBI agents who transitioned over from working criminal cases to counterterrorism. The FBI is at a breaking point.... They're overworked and overburdened and, frankly, they need some relief." The bill failed to pass.†

Year after year, the Bush administration whittled down the Bureau's requests. In FY 2006, when the FBI asked for up to 350 agents, the president's budget granted fewer than 75. That same year, the strategic plan regarding the need to rebuild the Criminal Division over the remaining five years of Mueller's term was declared, in one Justice Department executive's words, "dead on arrival" at Main Justice.

---

* The need for SCIFs is also making it hard for the FBI to expand counterterrorism resources in certain parts of the country. With four hundred resident agencies spread outside of the fifty-six main field offices, moving counterterrorism into the smaller RAs is prohibitively expensive. Yet consolidating into larger offices with SCIFs isn't necessarily an option either. "No congressman wants to lose his RA," one executive explained to me.

† It's notable that in the first two budgets proposed by the Obama administration, with Vice President Biden, that promise of one thousand agents never materialized. The FY 2010 budget did add several hundred new agent positions and three hundred new intelligence analysts, however.

The failure to expand the Bureau's ranks sufficiently to complete its duties was partly Mueller's own. He never made a public case for a sizable increase in the Bureau's number of agents and eschewed Louis Freeh's tactic of going straight to Capitol Hill with his budget requests. As one Bureau executive laments, "Mueller could have had anything he wanted after 9/11." But that wasn't his style. As a Marine, he made do with what he was given. And yet when asked, he would express real concern about the drain on the FBI's criminal resources. Violent crime, while at historic lows, was creeping back up. The number of homicides was down, but overall shootings were up. Mueller recognized that the decline in deaths had more to do with improvements in emergency and trauma care than it did with safer streets. "I'm not terribly optimistic about what we face down the road in terms of violent crime," he says.

When pressed on the Hill by Senator Dianne Feinstein about whether he had the staffing and resources necessary to combat violent crime, Mueller replied diplomatically, "My hope is that we will have, and get in the future, additional resources to put in that priority. But I think our priorities are appropriately aligned, although I would very much appreciate additional resources to be put into the violent crime arena."

While in many communities the FBI's anti-violent-crime efforts make a material difference in citizens' lives, holding gangs, drugs, and organized crime in check, Mueller understands that his performance—and the Bureau's performance writ large—will not be judged by the rise and fall of violent crime rates. He'll be judged only on whether he and the Bureau tackle the right threats on the Threat Matrix and stop the next plot. As Mueller says, "I'll fight tooth and nail for more criminal agents, but I'll never at the end of the day take an agent out of counterterrorism and national security."

To that end, roughly a quarter of the Bureau's new hiring after 9/11—all told, between agents and staff, about six thousand positions—came in the two areas most focused on counterterrorism. In fact, a whole new bureaucracy arose to help process the intelligence side of the house. The "rotor girls" who once dominated Bureau workspaces were long gone, as were most of the typing pools that aided agents in filling out reports. Instead, now "reports officers" examined existing and unfolding cases and mined them for larger bits of intelligence, much as Kenneth Williams's Phoenix memo had done in the summer of 2001; "all source analysts" tried to step outside the casework entirely and paint broad strategic pictures; "HUMINT (human intelligence) managers" helped understand the credibility and motivations of informants and sources. Combined, the Bureau had some 2,500 intelligence analysts, 200 reports officers, and 1,400 linguists. Each field office was given a "collection manager" and a "domain manager" to track and evaluate the local threat portfolio, and much of the Bureau's planning and budgeting had been refocused around "risk-based" strategies rather than "case-based" strategies.

However, all those new hires only went so far. Most of the new analysts and strategists were located at headquarters, and thus there haven't been nearly enough new bodies to have an impact in the field, agents say. The New York Field Office has roughly doubled its number of analysts since 2001 but still has only about 90, compared with some 1,200 agents. As one investigator explains, "Three agents can in a single day of investigation bury an analyst for weeks. For most squads, we've gone since 9/11 from one analyst supporting twelve agents to two analysts supporting twelve agents. Where are all the rest?"★

The Bureau has done only slightly better at recruiting agents who have fluency in Middle Eastern languages. As of September 2010, the FBI had 72 agents who spoke Arabic (representing about 0.5 percent of the agent population) and another 14 who spoke Farsi. While that was more than double the 33 Arabic-speaking agents in 2006, the number of Arabic translators had actually fallen over the same period, from 269 to 247. The paucity of employees with language experience wasn't due to lack of trying: Since 9/11, the Bureau had retained two

---

★The disconnect between analysts and agents still weighs heavily in the field. "We're great at strategic threat management, but we're not much better in handling tactical threat stream management," one case agent explains. "We can look down the road and anticipate where the next threat will be, where we need to concentrate resources, but at 4 P.M. on a Friday, when a tip comes in and there are two agents sitting there, are their jobs any easier? Sure, there's better technology and that's a big deal—we look more like *24* than we ever have—but the center of the world is still the two-man team, the hot lead agent who can run a threat to the ground."

recruitment firms to bring it more Middle Eastern language speakers, taken out ads in a score of publications targeting Middle Eastern communities in the United States, and partnered with various Arab American groups to recruit new agent and analyst candidates. Yet the extensive background checks necessary for a top-secret clearance (which include interviewing friends, significant others, family members, former coworkers, landlords, employers, and more) resulted in a drastic reduction of eligible prospects.*

As more water passed under the bridge after 9/11, the government's response to terror threats matured as well. There did not seem to be large numbers of al-Qaeda sleeper cells in the country; a billion people had passed back and forth over the U.S. border since the attacks without major incident; all told the FBI, Homeland Security, CIA, and other agencies seemed to have pulled a relatively secure blanket over the country. "We underestimated al-Qaeda's capabilities before 9/11 and overestimated them after," explains Michael Sheehan, the State Department's onetime ambassador at large for counterterrorism, who later worked for the NYPD. The new approach was seen in comments by New York mayor Michael Bloomberg after a 2007 plot to blow up the fuel tanks at JFK Airport was halted: "There are lots of threats to you in the world. There's the threat of a heart attack for genetic reasons. You can't sit there and worry about everything. Get a life," he instructed. "You have a much greater danger of being hit by lightning than being struck by a terrorist."

Mueller has stated repeatedly in recent years that he's unaware of any lives saved or terrorist plots blocked because of either the Terrorist Surveillance Program or the CIA's "enhanced interrogation" program. (Spike Bowman concurs, with a caveat: "I won't go so far as to say that [the TSP] saved lives, but it was an important investigative tool.") Nevertheless, there has been a general sense in the Bureau that many of the programs enacted in the heat of the moment after 9/11 weren't worth much—and certainly weren't worth the moral price paid.

Mueller had pushed back on the ones he thought were least useful.

---

*In the five years after 9/11, for example, the FBI started background checks on some 506 candidates who expressed some proficiency in a Middle Eastern language. Of those, only 162 made it through all the hoops to become an agent.

He hated one specific NSA program (the details of which are still classified) that, like the Terrorist Surveillance Program, was started after 9/11 with the strong backing of Vice President Cheney and churned out what the FBI had come to call "Pizza Hut" leads—endless lists of "suspect" telephone numbers from NSA monitoring that the FBI was left to sort through.★ Of some five thousand telephone numbers that the NSA passed along to the FBI, only ten panned out enough for the Bureau to bother to get FISAs for them. While the lists just churned out endlessly from NSA's computers, the personnel resources involved in investigating the tips on the FBI's end were tremendous. "You act like this is some treasure trove; it's a useless time suck," Mueller told NSA director Keith Alexander and Vice President Cheney in one meeting. (Mike Rolince had phrased it differently: "You know how long it takes to chase ninety-nine pieces of bullshit?")

The lack of resources available to the Bureau made the push for an intelligence culture all the more critical. Phil Mudd and other new thinkers in the Bureau used every opportunity to push an intelligence theory they called "domain management"—hunting, not gathering, as Mudd said over and over. One special agent had characterized the FBI's pre-9/11 mind-set as "a classic in-box exercise. If something showed up in your in-box on your desk, you opened a case and began an investigation." The case agents who picked up a lead could take the case anywhere it went—and sometimes, as Charlie Rooney and Carmine Russo showed in the Pizza Connection case, with great results— but cases didn't begin until there was a lead to follow. A bank robbery caused an agent to chase the bank robber and put him behind bars. The report of a Russian spy led an agent to run that spy to ground, either arresting him or expelling him from the country. Mudd's approach was different. Domain management meant knowing the landscape of the world you covered. It meant not just chasing a specific Russian organized crime case but knowing enough about that network to choose the correct target. In talking with SACs, ASACs, and task force supervisors Mudd frequently interrupted to say, "It's a good case, but is it the right case?"

★ The name comes from agents' complaints that the suspect telephone numbers are so vague they inevitably end up investigating the local pizza delivery guy.

"Rather than take the case that walks through the door, we need to focus our resources where they will have the greatest impact," Mueller says. "This means we have to do more than work our cases. We have to understand the full scope of the problem and share that intelligence." The Bureau, he hopes, is slowly moving from a case-based approach to a threat-based approach.

Unlike Freeh, who was first and foremost a street agent, Mueller, despite two decades of working with FBI agents as a prosecutor and Justice Department official and nearly a decade leading the Bureau, is first and foremost the boss. In a paramilitary agency where even close friends and colleagues refer in business conversations to "Mr." or "Ms.," where an SAC in a field office might as well be a seventeenth-century monarch in terms of respect and power, the FBI director is an almost unapproachable figure.

Whereas Freeh sent supervisors out of the room and met privately with line agents during field office visits, Mueller meets privately with supervisors and then works through a field office methodically, stopping on each floor and with each unit to pose for pictures, to give a quick pep talk, and to answer any questions agents or staffers dare to ask. Much of the time, he's met with silence. "Come on, I'm not going to send you to Yemen if I don't like your question," he pleads in the sessions. Occasionally he'll hand out an award or a service certificate. In an age when most workers change jobs every three years, and though the executive leaders of the Bureau seem to go through a revolving door at times, the number of twenty- or twenty-five-year service certificates among the Bureau's rank and file underscores how many people see the FBI as a calling.

By the nature of Mueller's position, a field office visit inevitably becomes a swirl of activity, even though he would prefer to keep a low profile and travels with only a single aide. Arriving in a U.S. city far from the Beltway, where even a casual visit by the FBI director is likely to lead the local news, Mueller's plane, one of the two executive jets owned by the FBI for prisoner renditions, dignitary travel, and counterterrorism deployments, is usually met by a not-insignificant motorcade. Local police vie for the chance to provide an escort to the visiting director without any encouragement from local SACs, and whisk him through town in a Code 3 motorcade, with motorcycles roaring and flashing lights clearing the road in front and SWAT teams watching warily from SUVs behind him. For towns unused to the thrill of a motorcade, the FBI director is a sight to behold.

Whether visiting Afghanistan or Albuquerque, Mueller travels with sophisticated secure communications gear so he can tap into the government power structure at any time, and yet for him, the value of his field visits lies in the opportunity, for once, to be disconnected. "Getting out of the Beltway is a good push for me," he says. On the return flights to Washington, he tends to be particularly introspective. Freed for the moment from the daily deluge of briefings, meetings, and requests, Mueller sees his field office trips as the primary opportunity to ask what he considers his most important question: "What's not getting through the filters?" As one of his staff good-naturedly gripes, "All the executives groan and moan when he comes back at the 9:15 [staff meeting]. He's always got a list of issues to address."

The visits haven't done much, though, to bond him with the troops in the field. He doesn't run with new agents' classes at Quantico, mostly because after two knee replacements, he can't run much at all. He's never developed the easy rapport with agents that Freeh had as director, and by and large, he hasn't tried. For Mueller, that is a reflection of his particular role; he has a drastically different portfolio than Freeh did. Freeh went years without speaking to the president, whereas Mueller for years started each day briefing President Bush in the Oval Office. "I'm sure if he could hit pause, he'd care about individual agents just as much," explains one field agent who has never met Mueller. "He's just got a lot on his plate."

In particular, Mueller remains estranged from the agent corps in New York. In his appointments since 2001, he has tried to clamp down on the strong personalities who have led the New York office in recent decades — the bulls in the FBI's china shop — and mend the contentious relationship with the NYPD. Mueller decided in 2008, when choosing a new head of the field office, that there wasn't a single agent in the FBI qualified to do what he needed done. He turned instead to Joseph M. Demarest, Jr., a former agent who had resigned earlier that year to take a top security job with Goldman Sachs. This was the first time in memory, perhaps even ever, that a former agent had been called back to serve as an assistant director. The move sent shockwaves through the agent corps. The message from Mueller couldn't have been clearer if he'd actually shown up at the New York Field Office with a broom: It was time for a clean sweep, a new start.

New York still wasn't on board.*

---

*When Demarest left in 2010, Mueller appointed the first-ever female agent to be the assistant director for New York. Janice Fedarcyk, while well respected, was not the office's choice either; many New York agents had been hoping that Detroit SAC Andy Arena, who had spent three years as the head of the New York Criminal Division, would be handed the reins. At 26 Federal Plaza, where loyalty to the Mets and the Yankees is treated with life-or-death seriousness, Fedarcyk, who had been head of the Philadelphia FBI office, had the temerity to hang a framed newspaper celebrating the 2008 World Series of the Phillies.

CHAPTER 15
The Arc of Justice

The arc of the moral universe is long, but it bends
toward justice.
                                    —*Abolitionist Theodore Parker, ca. 1850*

With counterterrorism as the Bureau's number-one priority, nearly every other unit in the FBI had been gradually starved for resources by 2008. Outside of the National Security Branch, one of the only units that hadn't seen its investigative power wither was the public corruption section, which remained on the hunt for sleazy politicians across the country. Harnessing the Bureau's resources in Illinois, U.S. attorney Patrick Fitzgerald had applied the same tenacity that he'd used to track al-Qaeda members across Africa to the endemic corruption of the Chicago political system, which on average had seen one city alderman go to jail annually since 1971.

And so it was that Fitzgerald and the FBI found themselves wrapped up in the middle of perhaps the oddest development to follow the 2008 election. A lengthy FBI public corruption investigation had been targeting Governor Rod Blagojevich when one day not long after the election an agent listening to a wiretap realized he was listening to the governor apparently setting a price on the newly elected president's Senate seat. Mueller flew to Chicago to hear the recordings and go over the evidence personally. Sitting with case supervisor Pete Cullen, he asked in wonder while listening to the wiretap recordings, "Those F-bombs are coming from the governor?"

On December 9, 2008, warrant in hand, Chicago SAC Rob Grant waited outside the gubernatorial mansion early in the morning to arrest the governor; other agents took Blagojevich's chief of staff, John Harris, into custody. Standing awkwardly with troopers from the governor's security detail, Grant called up the mansion. After several attempts to call different phone lines in the mansion, and after having the governor's wife hang up on him, Grant convinced Blagojevich to open the door. After declining an offer to change his clothes, the governor was led off to jail in a velour track suit, creating an instantly iconic perp-walk photo.

Fitzgerald and the FBI would find it hard to prove in court that Blagojevich had actually meant to auction off President Obama's Senate seat—in a 2010 trial, he was convicted on only one of twenty-three counts (the jury deadlocked on the other charges)—but that was beside the point. "It was such an egregious instance, we couldn't allow it to go forward," one Bureau executive explains. For perhaps the first time, the FBI leaders chose to apply the standard that now dominated the counterterrorism arena—disrupt and prevent—to a public corruption case. Instead of allowing the deal to possibly go forward and catching the whole thing on tape, securing an easy conviction but perhaps compromising the Senate appointment, Bureau executives decided in concert with Fitzgerald to sweep the governor off the streets, just as they would an aspiring terrorist plotter.

For Mueller, the Obama administration's arrival in Washington was cause for a reunion when Eric Holder, his old colleague from the U.S. Attorney's Office in D.C., arrived at Main Justice as his new boss. The two men get along tremendously well, having overlapped in prosecutorial circles since the early 1990s. It was Holder whom Mueller first called to become a line homicide prosecutor in 1995; then it was Holder who called Mueller in 1998 and asked him to go to San Francisco as U.S. attorney.

Holder found the department's daily routine almost unrecognizable, just eight years after having left office as deputy attorney general under President Clinton, then handing off the post to Mueller, the acting DAG at the beginning of President Bush's term. Left with the cumbersome baggage piled up by the Bush administration on its way out the door, he spent much of his first few months wrestling with whether to appoint a special prosecutor to investigate the CIA's post-9/11 "enhanced interrogations" and struggling to find a place to try Khalid Sheikh Mohammed. "So much of national security has been politicized," he lamented to a *Washington Post* reporter sixteen months into the job. "There's a lot of noise." That roar, intensified by several controversial events and individuals (some in Congress), made Mueller's job particularly challenging too.

With characteristic restrant and privacy, Mueller won't discuss whom he supported in the 2008 election, but friends noted a marked change from 2004. Then, his old St. Paul's classmate John Kerry had been the Democratic candidate, and Mueller, who had skated on the prep school hockey team with Kerry, often teased his Democratic friends about their nominee. "There was," one friend recounts, "no joking about Obama."

The Bureau and Obama had first actively interacted earlier that summer, when the Bureau informed the presidential candidate, as well as John McCain, that an unknown entity (probably Chinese or Russian) had penetrated the "Obama for America" computer network and downloaded hundreds of files. Obama's tech team had been aware of a phishing attempt, but then the Bureau, working with the Secret Service, issued a more serious warning: "You have a problem way bigger than what you understand." Reported one agent, "You have been compromised, and a serious amount of files have been loaded off your system." White House chief of staff Josh Bolten called campaign manager David Plouffe the following day to underscore the seriousness of the cyberattack. "They responded exactly how you thought they would, given their reputation for their technical prowess," a Bureau executive recalls: The Obama camp quickly dispatched two senior aides, Mark Lippert and Denis McDonough, who would play senior roles in the National Security Council under President Obama, to

Washington to deal with the problem and engaged a top-tier cyber security firm to seal the cracks.

Mueller's longtime deputy, John Pistole, provided several sanitized briefings to the junior U.S. senator from Illinois in the weeks leading up to the November 2008 election, as was customary for nominees of the major parties. (Such briefings helped ease the transition, the government believed, and establish the terrain for the man who would be president.) Mueller visited the president-elect in Chicago on November 13, 2008, just days after the election, with National Counterterrorism Center head Mike Leiter.* He liked the newly elected president immediately. He appreciated the new commander's intellectual interest and approach. The two men got along well personally. Mueller was low-key and eschewed drama and flash, as did the new president. Ivy-educated, they had both chosen public service despite lucrative other possible career choices. The new president was intensely pragmatic, a trait the Marine turned FBI director had always appreciated.

The new commander in chief quickly moved their first discussion toward a macro view. He wanted to understand things at the "30,000-foot level": What policies and strategies had to change in order to make the lives of the guys on the front lines easier? Leiter was direct on one point: The methods by which the United States had chosen to pursue the war on terror, however effective tactically, were a strategic public relations disaster around the world. As he put it, "We're doing things very well, but we're losing the messaging war. You have an opportunity to change that message, to change how the struggle is perceived." Obama replied immediately, "We're going to do that."

The 9/11 Commission had chastised the government's slow procedure for granting security clearances to new administration staff, saying that the lengthy process had left America vulnerable in 2001 in the first months of George W. Bush's term. Thus Barack Obama's campaign started submitting names of potential White House staff to the FBI before the election to speed the issuance of security clearances. The Bureau had assigned extra personnel itself, hoping to halve the

---

*Mueller met with Obama almost a month before then CIA director Michael Hayden got his audience with the new commander in chief. Hayden was quickly replaced by the new administration with Leon Panetta.

normal sixty-day process. To further assist the new president, the outgoing Bush national security team had crafted memos outlining forty worst-case crisis scenarios and possible responses for the U.S. government. National Security Advisor Stephen Hadley had told the Obama transition staff, "It's just a starting point for your own thinking if this happens, particularly early on your watch."

As the new administration was brought up to speed on the classified streams of intelligence now being fed to Barack Obama and his staff, the information quickly changed the president-elect's view of the world. "I don't think anyone can have a full understanding of the threat until you sit down each day, page through the Threat Matrix, and sit through the CIA's daily briefing," Mueller says. "He's a very fast learner."

One of Obama's first lessons came just weeks after his election, on November 26, 2008, when two dinghies went ashore under the cover of darkness in Mumbai. For someone who has never been there, it's hard to describe Mumbai, India, the second most populous city in the world. It is, like much of India, actually two cities, one that exists behind large gates and tall walls that would be instantly recognizable to any Westerner—quiet, sedate, luxurious—and one outside the walls, in the cacophonous and pollution-choked streets and slums in which most of the city's 14 million inhabitants live, with little access to sanitation, clean water, or well-maintained infrastructure. Yet even amid the bustle of the city's waterfront, fishermen noticed the two dinghies packed with ten men who came ashore at the Budhwar Park jetty shortly after dusk on November 26. They had come from a fishing trawler seized earlier at sea and had killed the boat's crew before leaving for Mumbai. Each attacker carried a backpack filled with hundreds of rounds of ammunition and grenades. Armed with AK-47s, the basic assault weapon of insurgents for a half century and now the most prevalent gun in the world, they could empty a thirty-round magazine in seconds. Shortly after landing, they struck.

Five teams of two spread across the tip of southern Mumbai, placing bombs in two taxis and attacking the city's main rail station, Chhatrapati Shivaji Terminus, where they shot travelers in the crowded station for almost an hour, killing fifty-eight people, before moving on to other sites. By the end of the night, a popular restaurant, a hospital, and a Jewish center all had been hit. Most memorable, though, was the terrorists' assault on the luxury Taj Mahal Hotel, where the final four attackers holed up for some thirty-six hours. On the top floor, South African security consultant Bob Nicholls heard the initial attack at the hotel and gathered some 150 hotel guests in a room that he barricaded against the attacks, but it took him more than two hours to reach by phone any government official who could help them. Hundreds of patrons were rescued by firefighters, who used ladders to extract the hotel guests from windows. Police and the Indian military scrambled to respond but found that their movements were being carefully tracked by the local media and broadcast live on television and radio. Several times, brave policemen, alone or in small groups, tried to slow the assaults with counterattacks, but they were severely outgunned, and many died trying.

To end the siege, Indian commandos moved methodically through the Taj Mahal Hotel, rescuing patrons and killing all four terrorists in a vicious final shootout. At another hotel, the Oberoi Trident, a team of two militants seized numerous hostages and held off government authorities for forty-two hours. By the time security forces retook the last hotel and the fires stopped burning, nearly 163 people were dead and more than 300 were injured. Only one terrorist, Ajmal Amir Qasab, was taken alive, captured after he tried to shoot it out with police at a roadblock.

India has always been a model for a pluralistic society. It had largely escaped the most radical strains of Islam; indeed, internal violence mostly involved militant Hindus, not Muslims. Whereas Guantánamo and the other prisons of the war on terror were filled with Saudi Arabians, Egyptians, and Yemenis, there was not a single Indian in Gitmo, even though the country had 138 million Muslims—a population larger than the combined total population of Egypt, Saudi Arabia, and Iraq. The attacks shattered India's calm and were described by more than one commentator as "India's 9/11." More accurately, though, they might have been called "India's Munich." The government's response found its counter-terrorism resources and special forces teams severely lacking.*

---

*Shortly afterward, the NYPD dispatched three detectives from its intelligence division to Mumbai to study the attacks. Realizing that even its specially trained Emergency Service Unit might be overwhelmed and spread too thin in a wide-

The FBI was on the scene even as the attacks unfolded. Assistant legal attaché Steve Merrill, from the FBI's New Delhi office, was on his way to Jodhpur to play on the U.S. embassy's team in the maharajah's cricket tournament—enjoying, as it were, his first day off in a month—when he learned what was happening. He immediately headed to Mumbai, arriving in the city with only his cricket gear and his BlackBerry.

Back in the Los Angeles Field Office, which bears responsibility for events around the Pacific Rim, the extraterritorial team had been watching the attacks on CNN when they received their first call. It appeared the terrorists were using a Gmail account to communicate with each other: Get a subpoena for the account. Until the magnitude of the strikes became clear, the L.A. team didn't focus much on it. "Stuff happens all around the world every day," Special Agent Geoffrey Maron says. They were used to all sorts of manmade tragedies. Life on an extraterritorial squad means spending six or seven months a year overseas; the L.A. team was used to regular excursions to the Philippines, Indonesia, and even Pakistan. Agent Michael Dehncke, who had spent more than five years on the squad and would end up spending weeks in Mumbai after the attacks, had been close to the Jakarta JW Marriott Hotel in 2003 when it was hit by a suicide bomber. "If you're on the squad long enough, you'll be in proximity to an attack," he says resignedly. India, while having an active domestic terrorism problem, had generally not been a destination for the L.A. team.

By the time the attacks were over, the investigation team included not just the Indian government but the FBI and CIA as well as New Scotland Yard and MI6 from Britain. All told, citizens from more than a score of countries died in the assaults. "Leads were going all over the place," agent Merrilee Goodwin recalls. Over the hours and days that

---

ranging assault like that in Mumbai, the NYPD began to train many more officers in the use of heavy weapons, building a supplemental force that could stop a larger group of attackers. "That scenario is here to stay," concludes James Yacone, the commander of the FBI's Hostage Rescue Team. Indeed, over the course of 2010, government officials worked to dismantle plots for Mumbai-like attacks in several Western European cities.

followed, agents flooded into Mumbai from Islamabad, New Delhi, and Los Angeles. Landing in Mumbai the day after the attacks finally ended—the hotels were still smoking and casualties were still being sorted out—the dozen agents and forensics investigators from L.A. looked like they were on an agricultural mission: As they walked across the hot tarmac, they carried shovels, rakes, sifters, and all the other odds and ends used in crime scene processing.

Agents conducted some sixty interviews, and FBI forensics specialists took hundreds of photos, pulled fingerprints from the IEDs, and pieced together one of the terrorists' broken satellite phones. The evidence leading back to Pakistan came together quickly. There was a Mountain Dew bottle packaged in Karachi as well as matchboxes and toiletries from Pakistan. A satellite phone recovered by investigators, used to help coordinate the attacks, was packed with telephone numbers of leaders of the Pakistani terror group Lashkar-e-Taiba.

To most Americans, Lashkar-e-Taiba was an unfamiliar name, and even to the FBI it was still relatively new. Begun in the mountains of Pakistan as a proxy fighter in that nation's ongoing conflict with India over the region of Kashmir, LeT is that most dangerous of terrorist groups: Wahhabi in doctrine, Islamist in ideology, and jihadist in methodology. Being Wahhabi (an ultra-conservative sect of Islam that focuses on cleansing the religion of modern cultural practices) gives it access to the huge pool of mostly Saudi Wahhabite money floating around in the extremist world; being Islamist (believing in Islam as a political force) gives it a compelling narrative with which to attract young new recruits; being jihadist (focusing on achieving its ends through violence and attacks on civilians) means the group is dangerous and seeks to be operational and offensive. Up until the Mumbai attacks, LeT had been seen as a regional threat at best; it had never attacked Americans before. "The Bureau had a passing interest in LeT, but the American intelligence community had never focused on them before," Goodwin says. "Everyone but the Indians had a pretty steep learning curve." Agents traveled around the world in the attack's wake, interviewing jailed LeT members in countries like France and Australia who could shed light on the group and its goals, members, and motivations.

In addition to tracking the Pakistani connections, the FBI agents were faced with the American victims; the injured had to be interviewed, and the identities of the five Americans killed had to be confirmed and their bodies transferred back to Dover Air Force Base in Delaware. (A Virginia father and his daughter, who were on a meditation retreat, had been killed at the Oberoi Hotel; two American rabbis died at the Chabad House, as did one of their wives.) Work proceeded almost around the clock, with leads flowing back and forth through the night. Each day the Mumbai team gathered at 6:00 P.M. to brief the L.A. Field Office as the U.S. West Coast woke up.

Like New York before 9/11, Mumbai had seen terrorism before. The same year as the first World Trade Center bombing in New York, 1993, religious fanatics had set off a series of bombs and killed more than 250 people. A decade later, in 2003, car bombs outside two hotels had killed another 50. And in 2006, a year after the London subway bombings, a series of bombs targeting railway stations and commuter trains had killed 180 individuals. But somehow all of those attacks were different: They were localized, domestically sponsored.

Within days, the FBI team was granted access to the lone survivor. Qasab, wounded and recovering from injuries, had never before met an American, the infidel that he'd been taught to hate. The tiny room where the interviews were held was packed; Indian police investigators and intelligence agents monitored the conversation, as did the minders assigned to guard the prisoner. Over the course of the interviews, the Indians mostly trickled out. "They all got fairly bored because our rapport-building took a while to establish who we were and who he was," Dehncke recalls.

The cell that had stormed Mumbai had thirty-two members who had been trained by LeT in remote portions of Pakistan. Thirteen had originally been selected to participate in the Mumbai mission, but the group was whittled down to ten. Qasab had originally linked with LeT after visiting its recruiting stall in a local Pakistani market. He needed weapons training, he explained later, in order to embark on his chosen career of being a robber. A year later, after being schooled extensively in jihad, he was on his way to Mumbai.

The government had found out that the attackers had been communicating with their handlers back in Pakistan in real time, and since further investigation revealed they'd used Voice-over-IP technology—and servers routed through New Jersey—the FBI was able to trace their calls. GPS units had helped the terrorists navigate and locate their intended targets. In at least one case, based on TV reports, the Pakistani handlers directed the team to target specific guests after hearing about their presence from news reports. "Greetings," the caller said. "There are three ministers and one secretary of the cabinet in your hotel. We don't know which room." "Oh! That's good news," one of the terrorists at the Taj replied. "It is the icing on the cake."

At the other hotel, the Oberoi, the Pakistan caller ordered, "Kill all hostages except the two Muslims. Keep your phone switched on so that we can hear the gunfire." Added another handler, "Everything is being recorded by the media. Inflict the maximum damage. Keep fighting. Don't be taken alive."

Mueller himself journeyed to India that winter to discuss the investigation, telling the press after a meeting with India's home minister, "Terrorism is not just a local issue. It is not an issue of one country; it is an issue across the world." As he said later, "It was an attack both highly coordinated and deceptively simple in its execution. This type of attack reminds us that terrorists with large agendas and little money can use rudimentary weapons to maximize their impact."

As Pakistan's culpability became clearer, the situation threatened to upset the delicate political balance with India, a relationship that all too regularly flared close to nuclear war. The region, once a united British colony, had been split awkwardly in 1947 to form Pakistan and India, and the border between the two had been the site of conflict ever since. Under the best of circumstances, the two governments had a tense relationship, so after the Mumbai attacks the FBI became the honest broker, helping to lead an investigation half a world away because it was the only agency trusted by both the Pakistanis and the Indians. "We'd be the clean team," Goodwin recalls. "India couldn't do an investigation in Pakistan and vice versa. We were looked at as being the mediators." The team in Mumbai ended up staying weeks, hoping to serve as a calming presence in an increasingly hostile environment between the two nations; war was a definite possibility.

Over the next two years, the FBI investigation into the Mumbai attacks criss-crossed continents. "Globally we've got the access and the relationships that other countries may not," Goodwin says. "We have this global presence. We've been able to follow up leads that others can't." One of the Bureau's top goals was to trace the money that funded the attack. On Saturday, November 21, 2009, just a few days before the first anniversary of the attack, Italian police in Brescia, a town east of Milan, descended on a father and son, both Pakistani, who the FBI believed had been responsible for helping to finance the assault. The day before the attacks began, according to authorities, the two, who managed a money transfer agency in Brescia, transferred the money used to open the terrorists' VOIP phone accounts.*

Separately from the FBI Mumbai team, Pat Fitzgerald in Chicago was zeroing in on an American, David Coleman Headley, who helped plan the attacks in India, traveling repeatedly to photograph and scout possible assault sites. In an independent, wide-ranging investigation that intersected quickly with the work of the L.A. agents, Fitzgerald discovered that Headley, a Chicagoan, was something of a one-man terror machine, helping to facilitate not just the Indian attacks but also a plot against a Danish cartoonist who had angered Muslims by drawing cartoons of the prophet Muhammad. Headley was arrested by FBI agents weeks before the Italian raid as he prepared to depart from Chicago's O'Hare Airport to travel to Pakistan to help plan new attacks.†

---

*In one of the oddities of globalized terrorism, northern Italy, filled with immigrants, has become a financing hub of sorts for terrorist groups. Two Tunisians from the Milan area, both captured in Afghanistan in the American invasion, had been accused of training at Ibn al-Libi's Khalden camp and helping to raise money for al-Qaeda in the years leading up to 9/11. And just weeks before the Brescia raid, a Milan judge issued warrants for seventeen people, arrested in the following days across Europe, who were accused of raising money for an Algerian terror group. The Brescia case remains ongoing.

†Headley, as it later turned out, had been on the U.S. government's radar several times before. A DEA informant in the 1990s, he had been reported in 2005 to the FBI by his ex-wife, who said he sought to engage in terrorist acts with LeT. At the time, the Bureau investigated and found nothing it could pursue; the tip seemed mostly routine at the time, one of thousands the Bureau chased from ex-lovers, spouses, business partners, and other aggrieved parties. Within months of that investigation, though, the U.S. government now alleges, Headley began active involvement with LeT. It is still unknown the extent to which the government—

Indian officials publicly credited the FBI with providing key investigative help—tracking down the terrorists' satellite phone and weaponry, tracing an outboard engine used in the attacks to Pakistan, and discovering the VOIP connections used in the attacks. The Indian government, after being criticized for its initial response, loved having the FBI's vast resources and stamp of approval for its post-attack investigation. "India wanted the FBI brand," one Justice official explains. "They wanted to demonstrate internally and externally that the investigation was professional." On India's side, a crime branch official explained to the press, "Making the FBI part of the investigation and witness will only strengthen our case. Though we have all evidence against Pakistan, we are expecting all possible cooperation from the FBI to bring the culprit to justice."

For the new administration, the Mumbai attacks were an object lesson that the FBI had become a major player in international relations. Respected overseas—even in countries like Pakistan, where the CIA had a complicated and tenuous relationship with the government—the Bureau was an esteemed brand; to other governments, it was an imprimatur of efficiency, competency, and justice-seeking.* "The Bureau really came into its own," says one Justice Department official. "It really taught the new administration the Bureau's huge role in foreign relations now. It was eye-opening for the Obama team."

---

the DEA, the FBI, the CIA, or all three—tracked Headley after the initial tip. Over the course of 2008, the U.S. government warned India three times of a possible terror attack, information that some reports attributed to the government's monitoring of Headley. Over the years, the JTTFs in both Philadelphia and New York had looked at him too, but had never found a cause to keep the surveillance going. As one former Bureau official explains, "The story of Headley is the story of resources. We can't watch everyone all the time. How long do you stay with someone, waiting for them to act?"

* The Mumbai investigation also provided yet another key example to Bureau agents of how different their work was from that of the CIA. The distinction between evidence and intelligence was underscored when CIA director Michael Hayden told the Pakistani government in the days after the Mumbai assault that there was no clear link to Pakistani intelligence officers—a theory disproved as the FBI team set to work investigating and eventually established at least two such links.

★   ★   ★

In his inaugural address, just hours after receiving the all-clear on the al-Shabaab threat, Barack Obama had promised, "We will not apologize for our way of life, nor will we waver in its defense. And for those who seek to advance their aims by inducing terror and slaughtering innocents, we say to you now that our spirit is stronger and cannot be broken—you cannot outlast us, and we will defeat you." Yet the Mumbai attacks, followed six weeks later by a threat against Obama's inauguration, underscored how the Threat Matrix he faced in 2009 was decidedly different from what had existed in President Bush's early years. Whereas the main danger to the United States leading up to and immediately following the September 11 attacks had been "core" al-Qaeda, the hierarchical and organized group headed by bin Laden and Ayman al-Zawahiri, by 2009 the group had largely given up tight control over terror activities. The pressure the al-Qaeda leadership faced from the CIA's drone program was too great to allow for operational contact with far-flung terror cells.★

"The organization switched to a greater emphasis from being the chief operator to take the role of chief motivator," Ali Soufan, who retired from the FBI in 2005 to launch his own security consulting firm, explained in 2009. "It also franchised the al-Qaeda name and encouraged other terrorist groups in places such as North Africa, Southeast Asia, the Middle East, as well as those that emerged later in places like Iraq, to operate under the al-Qaeda banner." After all, *al-Qaeda* translated as "the base"; by Obama's arrival, it was finally serving as the base of a broader, larger, global movement. As Phil Mudd explains, "They are a means to inspire a revolutionary movement."

★The Agency's drone program, code-named Sylvan-Magnolia, coordinated much-improved human intelligence sources within the terror networks to hunt and kill al-Qaeda and Taliban leaders with near abandon in the skies over Pakistan and Afghanistan. "When you're killing the operations director every couple of months, that makes it very hard to do long-term planning and continuity of operations," one intelligence official explains. When Sheik Sa'id al-Masri was killed by a drone in May 2010, he was at least the seventh operations chief al-Qaeda had had since 2001; all six of his predecessors had been killed or captured by the United States.

What most of America thought of as al-Qaeda now existed actually in three rings: the central leadership, still headed by Osama bin Laden and Ayman al-Zawahiri, who, however isolated, still maintained a strong spiritual role in the jihad; franchises like al-Qaeda in the Arabian Peninsula and other groups that had come under the banner thanks to solid propaganda efforts but that often had separate goals and targets from bin Laden's and al-Zawahiri's; and what intelligence officers called "the Kool-Aid drinkers," the homegrown extremists and terrorists radicalized via the internet—what one intelligence officials calls the "Afghanistan of the twenty-first century." Those "Kool-Aid drinkers" may never have any contact with al-Qaeda recruiters, but they still adopt the name to lend authority to their attacks. "Plots are now cooked and carried out by groups that did not grow up as al-Qaeda, even if they have now stuck the al-Qaeda name in," an FBI official explains.

After being welcomed to Washington by the al-Shaabab plot, which nearly disrupted the inauguration, the Obama administration got some breathing room on terrorism. The regular Tuesday afternoon terrorism briefings, which had replaced the daily 8:00 and 8:30 A.M. Threat Matrix briefings in the Oval Office, sometimes slipped. Some weeks they didn't happen at all. Obama faced a different existential issue for the country: When he took office, he added a daily economic brief to the schedule after the normal intelligence briefing, underscoring the seriousness with which he viewed the teetering financial system he had inherited. In some sense, the near total economic collapse of the modern financial system was his 9/11, an immediate crisis of tremendous proportions and, in the short term at least, one that directly affected far more Americans than bin Laden's attacks had.

Gradually, as spring progressed, the Threat Matrix began to fill up again, albeit with different plots from those that had troubled the Bush administration years before. The Obama White House continued the Tuesday terrorism briefings, dubbed "Terror Tuesdays," which, as the threat picture developed, became integral to the new chief executive's vision of the war on terror. Whereas the daily intelligence brief still tracked the threats of the moment, the afternoon Terror Tuesday sessions covered topics in depth, looking at the geopolitics behind various terror groups and terrorist hot spots, examining particular tactics, or working through case studies of individual plots and investigations. Gathering in the Situation Room under the White House, Obama's terror council—Mueller, CIA director Leon Panetta, National Counterterrorism Center director Mike Leiter, NSA director Keith Alexander, and the director of national intelligence, along with cabinet secretaries Robert Gates, Hillary Clinton, Janet Napolitano, and Eric Holder and various National Security Council staff—focused less on tactics than President Bush's Tuesday sessions had, a reflection of the chief executives' styles. Sometimes, as in the wake of the Christmas Day bombing attempt in Detroit, when Nigerian Umar Farouk Abdulmutallab tried to detonate a bomb hidden in his underwear and bring down a Northwest Airlines jet, the entire session would be concerned with a single case, as Mueller carefully walked the group through the forensics behind the bomb and its potential impact, but more often Obama preferred the big picture.

The key driver of the Tuesday sessions was John Brennan, who was technically assistant to the president and deputy national security advisor for homeland security and counterterrorism and who had become Obama's most trusted voice on terrorism issues.* "The president," Brennan explained to an audience at an August 2009 Center for Strategic and International Studies forum in Washington, "does not describe this as a 'war on terrorism.' That is because 'terrorism' is but a tactic—a means to an end, which in al-Qaeda's case is global domination by an Islamic caliphate. Confusing ends and means is dangerous, because by focusing on the tactic, we risk floundering among the terrorist trees while missing the growth of the extremist forest. And ultimately, confusing ends and means is self-defeating, because you can never fully defeat a tactic like terrorism, any more than you can defeat the tactic of war itself."

---

*Brennan had spent a summer in college traveling through Indonesia, where Obama had spent time growing up, and they both understood the diversity of the global Muslim community. Brennan, who played such a key role in handling the inaugural threat between the administrations in January 2009, had initially been Obama's choice to head the CIA, but his involvement during the Bush administration in the Agency's post-9/11 interrogation programs torpedoed his chances of passing Senate confirmation.

Thus, what had been called in government parlance under the Bush administration the "GWOT," the global war on terror, gave way under the Obama administration to the preferred terminology "overseas contingency operations," and then to "countering violent extremism."

Though Obama didn't consider the war against terrorists to be a united, global war, he made clear that he would take the fight wherever al-Qaeda was. As John Brennan said several months into the new administration, "We have presented President Obama with a number of actions and initiatives against al-Qaeda and other terrorist groups. Not only has he approved these operations, he has encouraged us to be even more aggressive, even more proactive, and even more innovative, to seek out new ways and new opportunities for taking down these terrorists before they can kill more innocent men, women, and children."

Obama had been influenced by the early advice from the NCTC's Mike Leiter. In his meeting with Obama and Mueller just after the election, when Leiter had told the president-elect that the United States was defeating extremist groups but losing the larger messaging war, he had said that it was critical to recast the war on terror not as a titanic struggle of the United States against the Islamic world but as a limited conflict with a specific group with a specific ideology, one that represented a distinct minority in a large, peaceful Muslim community. Brennan explained, "Why should a great and powerful nation like the United States allow its relationship with more than a billion Muslims around the world to be defined by the narrow hatred and nihilistic actions of an exceptionally small minority of Muslims? After all, this is precisely what Osama bin Laden intended with the September 11 attacks: to use al-Qaeda to foment a clash of civilizations in which the United States and Islam are seen as distinct identities that are in conflict." And yet such distinctions were not always easy to make and maintain.

In his first year in office, Obama went to great lengths to reach out to Muslim communities, giving a major address in Cairo and appointing the first U.S. special representative from the State Department to Muslim communities. During the Cairo speech, he never said *terrorist, terrorism,* or *war on terror.* Ayman al-Zawahiri blasted back in a Web video, "America has put on a new face but its heart is full of hate," while law-abiding and sometimes well-intentioned critics repeatedly conflated all of Islam with the extremist fringe.

Many a time on the campaign trail in 2007 and 2008, Barack Obama had quoted the Reverend Martin Luther King, Jr., on the subject of justice (who in turn had been quoting the abolitionist Theodore Parker). He explained on the fortieth anniversary of King's assassination, in 2008, "Dr. King once said that the arc of the moral universe is long but it bends toward justice. It bends toward justice, but here is the thing: It does not bend on its own. It bends because each of us in our own ways put our hand on that arc and we bend it in the direction of justice." Bending the arc of the war on terror toward justice was one of Obama's top priorities. Obama, who had once been a constitutional law professor, had come to office with the stated hope of putting the legal foundations of the war on terror on surer footing. He wanted to close Guantánamo, move the remaining detainees through legal proceedings, and, from a calmer time, end the extralegal measures and structures set up in the panicky period after 9/11. During the first months of his administration, he and Eric Holder quickly discovered that all of that was easier said than done.

The new president's attempt to chart a more just path that better reflected America's traditional values was on display during his first visit to FBI Headquarters, on an abnormally hot spring day in April 2009. Employees began to file into the courtyard of the Hoover Building hours before the president was expected to arrive, streaming through magnetometers manned by the Secret Service. The crowd was surprisingly black, reflecting the D.C. roots of many of the FBI's professional support staff, and younger than one would expect. Throughout the crowd, employees kept themselves cool with paper fans emblazoned with the slogan "Today's FBI. It's for you."

Most of the staff in the courtyard had blue ID badges—the basic badge for nearly all Bureau staff members. Shortly after 10:30 A.M., the Bureau's royalty—assistant directors and above, denoted by their gold badges—filed out of the Hoover Building.* They were in many ways a picture of the old Bureau: mostly male (the exception was a few officials like general counsel Val Caproni) and mostly white; only one gold badge, T. J. Harrington, in an olive suit, stood out in the crowd of blue, black, and gray suits. As the executives filled a reserved position at stage left, the crowd, whose view they were suddenly blocking, jeered and booed, only half in jest. Hearing the noise and not able to see what was happening, those at the back of the crowd began to cheer, thinking the president had appeared.

Meanwhile, up in the Bureau's seventh-floor conference room, the president met privately with Mueller, Pistole, National Security Advisor Jim Jones, counterterrorism chief John Brennan, and Deputy Attorney General David Ogden. It was a far happier briefing than it would have been in Mueller's early years. Real progress was being made. As President Obama recounted later, "By all accounts, the FBI has done an outstanding job of transitioning during an age of terrorism, cyber threats, identity theft, a whole host of new challenges. They have been able to adapt. And with the director at the helm, I have very, very great confidence that the FBI will continue to help keep the American people safe."

Their briefing complete, President Obama, marking his ninety-ninth day in office, bounded up onstage with Mueller. The men looked happy and at ease. This was a much easier visit than the one Obama had paid the week before to the CIA, just days after releasing the so-called torture memos, which documented in horrific detail the legal guidance for "enhanced interrogations" laid out by Jay Bybee and John Yoo in the months after 9/11. At the CIA, he had promised,

---

* The story of FBI ID cards, like much of the Bureau's lore, is perhaps apocryphal. One day, J. Edgar Hoover and his deputy, Clyde Tolson, were riding an elevator down in the FBI Headquarters at the Justice Department when a clerk got on, pushing a file cart, which was strictly prohibited for security reasons. Hoover barked, "Are you going to bring that into this public passenger elevator?" The clerk, not realizing or caring whom he was addressing, snapped back, "What the hell do you think I'm going to do, buddy? Tie a rope around it and drag it up the stairs?" Afterward, Hoover was never able to identify who had spoken to him so improperly, and soon thereafter, all FBI employees had to start wearing ID tags that identified them by name. Or so the story goes.

"I will be as vigorous in protecting you as you are in protecting the American people." His reception had been muted, though, by the betrayal many in the CIA felt; they'd done what they thought was necessary to protect the country in the heat of the moment after 9/11, and now, removed from the pressure and the smoke of the burning crash sites, they were being hung out to dry.

Relaxed and with a broad smile, Mueller welcomed the president and teased him. "We are not above using this occasion for recruiting purposes," the director said. "We are always looking for talented agents, but you are a wee bit past our age limit." The president's brow furrowed good-naturedly and he held up his hands in mock surrender to the crowd. However, the director continued, "It is not too early for Sasha and Malia to begin thinking about careers with the FBI." With that, he produced two FBI teddy bears from beneath the podium and handed them to the president.

Mueller also gave the president a blue FBI hat, which looked surprisingly like the ones vendors hawked to tourists near the National Mall. The president adjusted the size and then slipped it onto his head as the crowd cheered. Standing at the podium underneath a huge banner proclaiming the FBI's one hundredth birthday in 2008, the president said, "So much has changed in the last one hundred years. Thank God for change." The crowd went wild.

The president began with some standard platitudes about the FBI's unique role in American history; then, turning to a discourse on values and security, he grew more serious and more pointed. "We must always reject as false the choice between our security and our ideals," he told the quickly overheating crowd. "We know that al-Qaeda is not constrained by a constitution or by an allegiance to anything other than a hateful ideology and a determination to kill as many innocents as possible. But what makes the United States of America so special is precisely the fact that we are willing to uphold our values and ideals not just when it's easy but when it's hard, and we have been called upon to serve in such a time."

Some of the personnel in the audience knew all too well the wreckage created by the frantic months after 9/11. The Bush administration had muddled through the legal processes of the war on terror with a variety of different approaches, some of which were rejected by the courts, some of which were upheld, and created a patchwork of inconsistent outcomes. (As one foreign intelligence official who was working with the United States on processing detainees explains, "Gitmo is a system that cannot punish the guilty and free the innocent.") At the top of the new president's agenda was closing Guantánamo, tackling each detainee's case in turn, adjudicating it as well as possible, and transferring the remaining prisoners out of Cuba.

For more than three years, an FBI task force had been churning through the many leftover detainees in Guantánamo. More than three hundred agents had contributed to the "clean teams," trying to assemble workable criminal cases against the detainees. The price of the CIA's "enhanced interrogations" was becoming clear as much of the "evidence" uncovered was inadmissible in a court of law. "I think there's no surprise that they have to call in the FBI to clean up the mess left by the CIA secret detention program," Jumana Musa, advocacy director for Amnesty International, told the Los Angeles Times in 2007. "They would be smart to use evidence that did not come out of years of secret detentions, interrogations, and torture."

President Obama signed the decision to close Guantánamo within a year as one of his first orders, but that ambitious deadline soon looked hard to meet. Meanwhile, hundreds of detainees had been released or moved to other countries as it became increasingly obvious with passing time who the real bad guys in the camps were and who had been swept up in the bounty-fueled excitement after the American invasion of Afghanistan. Yet with the easy cases already taken care of, those prisoners who remained were the ones for whom there was no quick solution. Despite the number of pre-9/11 terrorists who had been held successfully, peacefully, and without incident in the federal supermax facility in Colorado, politics made it hard to find a suitable location for a new facility to hold them. The legal struggle that Obama inherited was about more than just American values, politics, and tainted evidence—it was about missed opportunities, risk management, and a maturing government process.

As the strategy for dealing with terrorism evolved, as surveillance, intelligence systems, and government procedures matured, agents came to see the José Padilla case of the spring of 2002 as the best example of "what not to do and why not to do it." While the decisions made then probably were the right ones, if José Padilla arrived in Chicago today, he would probably be admitted into the country. "He's a walking, talking collection opportunity. You follow that guy, who he's seeing, where his money is coming from and where it's going," an intelligence official explains. "You don't get any of that when you pop him coming off the plane."

The new approach meant allowing a greater degree of risk than the FBI had done before. Art Cummings, who led the National Security Branch from 2008 to 2010, argues that if you have information that a possible terrorist is coming to the United States, you want to let him in — you want to follow his every move, learn as much as you can about where he goes, who he meets, and so on. "The agent's job now isn't just to arrest bad guys. It is to understand everything in the terrorist's head, everything around him, so that we can understand his world and the world of those around him," Cummings says. "Yes, we have enough to get him off the street, but do we really want to do that? If you do that, I'm blind." Multiple times since 9/11, Cummings had issued letters to Customs and Border Protection (which has an understandably low risk tolerance) asking them to allow suspected terrorists to proceed into the United States without alerting them that authorities were watching. "I argue that not allowing him in poses the greater threat. It's counterintuitive," Cummings says.

Padilla also became another example of how the decisions made in the heat of the post-9/11 environment negatively affected justice proceedings down the road. The major evidence against him had come from Abu Zubaydah and Khalid Sheikh Mohammed, both of whom were subjected to "enhanced interrogations," which rendered their testimony impossible to use. In Zubaydah's case, even though the Padilla information had come out of questioning by Steve Gaudin and Ali Soufan, done under normal criminal interrogation procedures well before the CIA began its regimen of torture, it was now tainted. When Padilla was finally brought to trial in 2007, instead of putting him away for life for a major terrorist plot, the court convicted him of the much lesser charge of material support for terrorists and sentenced him to seventeen years in prison. With time served, he'll probably be free in 2021.

The Padilla case, unfortunately, wasn't much of an anomaly. In fact, almost across the country, prosecutors had racked up a poor track record in terrorism convictions related to cases in the period after 9/11. In Dallas, prosecutors failed to convict the leaders of the Holy Land Foundation on any of the 197 terrorism financing charges stemming from the group's alleged backing of Palestinian terror groups. Whereas by 2009 the cases involving new plots that were discovered and new suspects who were arrested seemed to be on surer ground—thanks in part to the evolving strategy whereby the FBI was waiting longer to take a case down, until the would-be terrorists had literally pushed the button—many of the earlier cases, and particularly those stemming from Guantánamo, remained a mess.

President Obama's and Eric Holder's brief attempt to try Khalid Sheikh Mohammed in Manhattan was scuttled by public outcries and a hefty theoretical court security bill. A case that did move to trial in 2010 similarly illustrated the tradeoffs inherent in the administration's new approach. Ahmed Ghailani, one of the plotters of the East Africa embassy bombings in 1998, who had been captured in July 2004 and held in the CIA's series of secret "black site" prisons for two years before he was transferred to Guantánamo, was acquitted of all but one of the 280 charges he faced in a Manhattan trial. The case against Ghailani, which veteran agent Abby Perkins had spent years building and which in 2010 brought her back from her new post in the Behavioral Analysis Unit at Quantico for one more terror trial, showed just how difficult prosecuting some of the detainees in the legal system would be; a key witness was excluded because of the Agency's "enhanced interrogations." While that one charge sent Ghailani to prison for at least twenty years, critics of the Obama administration's legal approach used the case to point out that civilian juries were an inconsistent and potentially unreliable way to ensure that terrorists stayed off the streets. "It reveals a fundamental tension between the reality that these are individuals the U.S. government will not release and the desire to hold them accountable in a criminal context in which their innocence is presumed by law," explained Juan Zarate, who had served as deputy national security advisor for counterterrorism during the Bush administration, after the verdict. "The fact that failure is an option in the criminal legal system—that acquittals are possible—raises the specter of a case in which an al-Qaeda figure can be acquitted but not be released."

Critics of the judicial system had pushed for both Bush and Obama to rely upon military commissions to bring justice to Guantánamo, but those also had an inconsistent record. (Ironically, the idea to rethink the legal constraints on the war on terror actually began with a former head of the Justice Department. Former attorney general William Barr suggested that the Bush administration consider a model he'd first thought about in the Pan Am 103 case, with Bob Mueller. "People were referring to the 9/11 attacks as criminal acts, talking about the World Trade Center as a crime scene," Barr said later. "I didn't think we should get too locked into that model. This was more of a military conflict.") The Bush administration had primarily pursued a process of trying terrorists in military tribunals rather than criminal courts, despite the impressive success that prosecutors such as Pat Fitzgerald, David Kelley, Mary Jo White, and Jim Comey had achieved before 9/11.*

Yet after many court battles just to set the rules under which such tribunals could operate, when at long last tribunals for the Guantánamo detainees got under way, they ended up providing imperfect outcomes of their own. In 2008, Salim Hamdan, whose court challenge to the Bush administration's original war-on-terror detention policy, *Hamdan v. Rumsfeld,* made it all the way to the Supreme Court, had become one of the first to face a military commission.† The al-Qaeda operative,

---

* The government had used military tribunals once before: to prosecute German saboteurs caught in the United States in the summer of 1942. Military lawyers, though, were wary of the precedent. The German trials predated the two main codes that governed warfare in the modern world, the U.S. Uniform Code of Military Justice and the international Geneva Conventions. Ironically, the FBI conference room where the military tribunals were held during World War II had come, over time, to be converted into the space for the Office of Legal Counsel, where Jack Goldsmith had tried to sort through the mess created after 9/11 by John Yoo and Jay Bybee.

† Hamdan had first come up in Squad I-49's work after 9/11 in Yemen, where Ali Soufan and NCIS agent Bob McFadden had spent weeks interviewing Abu Jandal and Jandal confirmed that Saqr al-Jedawi, aka Salim Hamdan, was bin Laden's

who had undoubtedly served as Osama bin Laden's driver, was convicted of some charges but acquitted on the most serious ones. He was freed with time served and sent back to Yemen. "If they'd sent Osama bin Laden's driver through the criminal justice system, he'd be doing a million years in jail," one member of the intelligence community lamented. "Instead we sent him back to Yemen, where he's probably making bombs to hide aboard American airliners right now."

Almost across the board, the lesson of President Obama's first year was that despite the lofty rhetoric, terrorism remained a complicated geopolitical calculus. In the summer of 2009, Scotland decided after a lengthy appeals process to release the only man convicted of the 1988 Pan Am 103 bombing. Convicted in a special Scottish court in 2001, Abdelbaset Ali Mohmed Al Megrahi had spent eight years in prison when doctors decided he was terminally ill and had only months to live. The decision to release was made, the Scottish minister of justice reported, on "compassionate grounds." Few involved on the U.S. side believed either that the terrorist deserved compassion or that the decision was based entirely on Al Megrahi's health. Just as Libya had turned over the Pan Am bombing suspects only to curry favor with the world community, the United Kingdom was now interested in currying favor with the Libyan government for business reasons.* When he was released, Al Megrahi was greeted as a hero on the tarmac in Libya, with rose petals and a cheering crowd.

The idea that Al Megrahi could walk out of prison on "compassionate grounds" made a mockery of everything that Bob Mueller had dedicated his life to fighting. Amid a series of tepid official condemnations (President Obama labeled the release "highly objectionable"),

---

driver. Much later, Soufan and New York JTTF agent George Crouch, who had been one of the first FBI teams into Afghanistan with Tom Knowles's group, wooed Hamdan to talk at Guantánamo. They fed him pizza and McDonald's Filet-o-Fish sandwiches and gave him American car and truck magazines.

* According to Scottish officials, the oil giant BP did play a role "in encouraging the U.K. government to conclude a prisoner transfer agreement with the Libyan government." Al Megrahi was not, they insisted, specifically discussed in the conversations.

Mueller's letter to Scottish minister Kenny MacAskill stood out for its pain, anger, and deep sorrow. Far from an official missive of the state to a fellow government official, Mueller's letter was personal and heartfelt, written by a man not prone to public rebukes. "Over the years I have been a prosecutor, and recently as the director of the FBI, I have made it a practice not to comment on the actions of other prosecutors, since only the prosecutor handling the case has all the facts and the law before him in reaching the appropriate decision," Mueller began. "Your decision to release Megrahi causes me to abandon that practice in this case. I do so because I am familiar with the facts, and the law, having been the Assistant Attorney General in charge of the investigation and indictment of Megrahi in 1991. And I do so because I am outraged at your decision, blithely defended on the grounds of 'compassion.'"

Few subjects were as close to Mueller's heart as the victims of Pan Am 103. He knew their families personally. He met with them regularly. He watched the victims' children grow up and watched the adults age faster than people untouched by terror age. He had, in the words of President Clinton, felt their pain. He, like Neil Herman, had seen how poorly the government was equipped to handle the victims' families. When, years later, he found the FBI facing thousands of victims' families after 9/11, he had recruited Kathryn Turman, who had moved heaven and earth in the Department of Justice's victim services' office to get Pan Am families to the trial in the Netherlands, to revamp the Bureau's own victims' programs.

For the twentieth anniversary of the bombing, in December 2008, Mueller had sat bundled up on the stage at Arlington Cemetery near the memorial cairn erected to honor the victims. The event, held on a particularly frigid Sunday, brought together a generation of men schooled in an earlier era of terror. Michael Chertoff and Mueller had greeted each other warmly, long-retired agents and intelligence officials dotted the crowd, and the families packed the seats. At the top of the hill stood the cairn, crafted of pink sandstone from the Corsehill Quarry in Dumfriesshire, which Pan Am 103 had passed over in its final seconds before exploding. A brick represented each of the victims from the flight. Relatives reached out and touched the rough-hewn sides, pausing for a moment of reflection. Mueller sat stone-faced,

556 • GARRETT M. GRAFF

flipping through the pages of his remarks with his gloved hands, his scarf wrapped tightly around his neck, until it was his turn to speak. At that moment, it seemed that some justice had been done.

That the only person behind bars for the horrid bombing would walk back onto Libyan soil a free man and be greeted with rose petals nine months later left Mueller seething. "Your action in releasing Megrahi is as inexplicable as it is detrimental to the cause of justice. Indeed your action makes a mockery of the rule of law. Your action gives comfort to terrorists around the world," Mueller wrote to MacAskill. "You could not have spent much time with the families, certainly not as much time as others involved in the investigation and prosecution. You could not have visited the small wooden warehouse where the personal items of those who perished were gathered for identification—the single sneaker belonging to a teenager; the Syracuse sweatshirt never again to be worn by a college student returning home for the holidays; the toys in a suitcase of a businessman looking forward to spending Christmas with his wife and children."

In an era when counterterrorism had become a multibillion-dollar industry and a buzzword for politicians everywhere, Mueller and the victims of Pan Am 103, who had seen the beginning of the age of terrorism directed at U.S. civilians, had been betrayed. He concluded his letter with a decidedly un-Mueller-like plea, shouted plaintively and hopelessly across the Atlantic: "Where, I ask, is the justice?" That betrayal challenged Mueller's belief in the rule of law and his faith in justice as nothing in his career had done before.

In a 2003 article for *Foreign Policy* magazine, then editor in chief Moisés Naím outlined what he called the twenty-first century's "five wars of globalization": drugs, arms, intellectual property, people, and money. What's striking is that for the most part, those wars belong more to the FBI than to the military, the traditional U.S. tool of foreign policy. Many in the Bureau continued to stress that criminal investigations were essential in the effort to destroy and to disrupt terror networks. The difference now was that those investigations were so international in focus—children, via a convoluted family tree, of the Pizza Connection case so many decades ago. "We won't go back to small drugs and smaller white-collar cases," Mueller says. "The Bureau's going to grow where no one else can do it. We're the only agency that has investigative responsibilities around the world."

In one recent FBI investigation in Charlotte, North Carolina, code-named Operation Smokescreen, the JTTF, working with the Royal Canadian Mounted Police, took down a group of cigarette smugglers who were using the proceeds to raise and launder money for Hezbollah, as well as engaging in extensive visa and marriage fraud. In fact, by Bureau estimates, only about one out of four terrorism cases ends up actually involving terrorism charges; in three out of four cases, the Justice Department ends up using simpler criminal charges to remove, disrupt, or dismantle a terrorist group. "You have a much better chance to disrupt terrorists if you find they have broken [criminal] law," one agent explained.

One reason the FBI had to take the lead in such investigations was that the systems in place to combat such global, interconnected threats, like Interpol, are often remarkably ineffective, because of a combination of underfunding and untrustworthy partners. Although the FBI participated in Interpol, Mueller didn't put much stock in it, instead seeing the Bureau's future in bilateral arrangements—not multilateral ones, since classified information is difficult to share in multilateral settings.★

In the final years of Mueller's term, Special Agent Art Cummings, who joined the Bureau in 1987 after a stint in the Navy SEALs, became one of the key drivers of the new Bureau. Cummings, who had been working counterterrorism in Richmond on 9/11 and was summoned by Mike Rolince to headquarters that day, rose quickly through the ranks, holding a variety of executive positions at the FBI and at one point serving as deputy director of the National Counterterrorism Center. Prior to Cummings's retirement to join a global financial consulting firm in Connecticut in the spring of 2010, his office as head of the National Security Branch at the Hoover Building, just a few doors

---

★ The United States does not face these challenges alone. "You cannot draw a border between the domestic and international threats," French intelligence chief Bernard Bajolet explains "It's very difficult to distinguish between inside and outside."

down from the director's, underscored how different the Bureau is today from that of Hoover's era. His metal nameplate had "Art Cummings" spelled out in both Western letters and Arabic script. Although Hoover's old globe sits around the corner in the office of Michael Kortan, the Bureau's head of public affairs, and shows the U.S.S.R., Africa still a continent filled mostly with European colonies, and India and Pakistan as a single British possession, Cummings's modern maps, including two large ones of Iraq and Afghanistan, show around 195 independent countries in the world.★ The FBI operates almost daily in at least 80 of them.

"Within our context, national borders are arbitrary. It only matters where they're standing because soil is what determines what rights they have," Cummings says. "It's not about international threats, it's about the global environment." There's still a serious question in law as to whether the FBI has jurisdiction over nonterrorism cases involving Americans overseas. "If it's terrorism, I own it," Cummings says, but that raises another question: What exactly is terrorism today? Increasingly it's hard to tell where terrorist groups end and organized crime, drug cartels, and gangs begin. The drug cartels in Mexico certainly seem to be doing a thorough job of terrorizing that country's population. Terrorism, drugs, or organized crime? Should the distinction matter?

Matthew Heron, who served as head of the FBI's organized crime section until late 2009, notes that La Cosa Nostra had slipped to number three on the Bureau's list of organized crime threats, below Russian organized crime and Asian organized crime. He spent as much of his year in Budapest or Bangkok as he did in Rome. The street gangs of a generation ago, which were limited to a single city, neighborhood, or even a few city blocks, were now just as likely to be international powerhouses. MS-13, a notoriously brutal street gang based in El Salvador and with far-reaching tentacles in the United States, led the FBI to open a new task force in Latin America to track and fight

---

★ The range depends on how one defines a sovereign state. For instance, the United Nations has 192 member countries, but that figure doesn't include the Vatican City, Kosovo, or Taiwan. The State Department recognizes, as of 2009, 194 countries, Taiwan not included.

the gang at its roots. Says one foreign counterterrorism official, "We're in the golden age of organized crime. We've let this evolve in ways we never could have imagined."

Added to such growing transnational threats, computers are making it easier for terrorists and criminals to communicate and steal. Says Special Agent Shawn Henry, who helped set up the Bureau's cyber branch, "Cyber completely changes the equation. Your possible suspects in a bank robbery had always been limited to the population of the city at the time of the bank robbery. Now you're looking at bank robberies where your pool of suspects is every person who has an internet connection anywhere in the world."

Special Agent Mike Bonner, who served four years in legats in Nigeria and South Africa, spent much of his time working internet fraud back to the United States during an overseas assignment that took him through thirty-four countries, from Angola to Mozambique to the Seychelles. Life far from the U.S. shores was filled with its own oddities, including washing fruits and vegetables in bleach and paying for a new office copier with $16,000 in cash (the copier store owner counted each bill by hand). By the time Bonner and his wife left Lagos, they were so wired into the country that one tribe inducted them as "honorary chiefs." Their family survived one coup attempt and existed at the far end of the communication and supply chain from Washington—yet the interconnectivity of the modern world meant that Bonner had full-time work tracing cases on sites like eBay and Craigslist when unsavvy Web users back in the United States found themselves done out of large chunks of money by fraudsters. "Nigerian scheme" e-mails, known in legal parlance as "419 schemes" for the part of the federal legal code they violate, but nicknamed for the African country because they provide a not insignificant chunk of the country's illegal gross domestic product, are an online constant. (The cases are notoriously difficult to prosecute because the schemes are a big business in many African countries.) Explains Mueller, "What works well for ninety-nine percent of our criminal work doesn't work all that well for counterterrorism and cyber. In cyber, the victims will be all over—and when you're starting a new operation, you don't know whether you're looking at a state sponsor, terrorists, or the high school kid across the street." Steven Martinez, who led the FBI's team into Iraq and later became head of the Los Angeles Field Office, recalls that much of his time in the cyber division was spent working with the Justice Department on educating foreign governments: "A lot of countries don't even have the laws to make this stuff illegal—that was the first step. We had to carve out relationships where the FBI had never gone before."

The world changed profoundly shortly after Mueller was sworn in as director and has continued to shift and crack in unforeseen ways. For the better part of the 1990s, Squads I-45 and I-49 toiled in relative obscurity in a distant corner of the FBI New York Field Office, working their cases on continents far removed from the five boroughs and working threats little understood by others in the FBI or elsewhere within the U.S. government. They chased Osama bin Laden long before the rest of the country was convinced he was the new Public Enemy #1.

Now that the whole government apparatus has been dedicated to combating Islamic terrorists for a decade, though, it is worth asking the question, what will be the Squad I-45 of the next decade? If there's one constant in the FBI's first century, it's that there's always another Public Enemy #1, an ever-rotating and evolving cast of characters that has included anarchists, gangsters, Nazis, Communists, the Klan, domestic terrorists, La Cosa Nostra, and Islamic militants. As Mueller thought about his final months, the international criminal on the FBI's current Ten Most Wanted list was a fugitive, like bin Laden had been before 2001, whom most Americans have never heard of: Semion Mogilevich.

The FBI set up its first Russian organized crime squad in 1994, a team that came to be known as C-24 in the New York Field Office. According to law enforcement reports, the Russian mafia is organized in more than fifty countries—roughly a quarter of the globe—and its activities range from smuggling drugs in Asia, operating casinos in Latin America, and mining diamonds in Sierra Leone to shaking down Russian NHL players in the United States and running inventive Medicare and Medicaid fraud schemes from its North American hub,

Brighton Beach, Brooklyn.★ U.S. government officials are growing more concerned with every passing year about the slipping rule of law in Russia; since 2005, the World Bank's governance indicators have showed steady deterioration, and each year has brought more corruption, less control, and more organized crime.

A native of Kiev, Mogilevich is suspected, among other things, of being the leader behind the largest money-laundering operation in U.S. history, a scheme whereby more than $7 billion—roughly the entire 2010 budget of the FBI—was laundered through the Bank of New York with the cooperation of several Russian bank officials. And this, the FBI believed, was just a small portion of billions of looted Russian dollars sloshing through the global financial system in a vast underground network. According to FBI sources, Mogilevich, a one-time Moscow fruit stand operator, had become involved in arms dealing as well as drug and alcohol smuggling, set up a transatlantic deal with the New York Genovese family to dispose of toxic waste from the Big Apple in the contaminated Chernobyl region for cut-rate prices, and helped establish an extensive international art and jewelry fraud network, partly based in Budapest, to loot Russian heritage and art collectors across the continent.

Hungary was the center of Mogilevich's operation by the end of the 1990s, when the Hungarian government first turned to the FBI for help. The Bureau and Louis Freeh had a close relationship with the former Soviet state, which was the site of an international law enforcement academy the FBI created in 1995, and the Hungarians now wanted a permanent joint task force to help combat organized crime. Even inside the Bureau, even after Louis Freeh's aggressive global expansion in the 1990s, the Budapest Project, as it's known in the FBI, was a tough sell. There were only a hundred agents in the United States working Russian organized crime; executives didn't see the need to send 4 percent of the workforce to some experiment in Hungary, and the FBI's Office of International Operations would agree

---

★ While it's often called Russian organized crime, the scope and scale of the enterprise is hardly just Russian. Law enforcement officials generally refer to it as Eurasian organized crime, lumping together all the former Iron Curtain nations.

only to six-month temporary postings. Tom Fuentes, who shepherded the program through, was able to get most of the funding out of the State Department's programs aimed at developing government institutions in Eastern Europe. (The rest he hid in various corners of his budget, an act known within the Bureau as a "weasel deal.") Mogilevich picked up and fled Hungary just days before the first FBI agents arrived in country, on April Fool's Day 2000. It took the better part of the decade, though, for the task force really to come together. Since the initial assignments were just temporary postings, the agents hardly had long enough to get oriented before they were sent home. Hungary wanted a more serious FBI commitment, so when Mueller visited Budapest for the tenth anniversary of the FBI's international law enforcement academy, he took along the first permanent agents as a present.

The agent who would become the task force's first permanent leader arrived a year later. Special Agent Mike Bobbitt, between his glasses and his subtle, easy swagger, looks precisely like what he is, a cross between an FBI agent and an accountant. He spent time working as a certified public accountant for Deloitte before joining the FBI in 1997 and conducting drug investigations on the Texas border. In Houston, he joined one of the eight squads working long hours battling big drug organizations. His cases, despite being in the heart of Texas, regularly ended up with an international angle, which got him interested in the Bureau's overseas operations. As he says, "Every case I'd be working at some point would jump overseas. If you look at the big threats—terrorism, organized crime, drug trafficking, even gangs—it's all coming from outside."

The full extent of Mogilevich's U.S. ties are still unknown. Although banned from entering the country because of his alleged criminal ties, Mogilevich has visited Boston, Philadelphia, and Miami under aliases to meet with U.S. associates, and the FBI photographed at least one of his aides attending a Republican Party fundraiser in Texas.

After a yearlong internal discussion, the FBI had put Mogilevich on its Ten Most Wanted list in the fall of 2009—an uncharacteristic addition, since unlike most of the rest of the fugitives, Mogilevich is now living more or less openly in Russia. His presence on the list is a political statement, a recognition of the threat of Russian organized crime in today's world.* There's no extradition treaty between the United States and Russia, and Mogilevich isn't likely to come to the United States to face trial—and besides, agents suspect he's operating with the support of at least some faction of the Russian government.

Just as a single FBI squad in New York led the search for the then obscure terrorist leader Osama bin Laden, "Uncle Seva," Semion (aka Semyon) Mogilevich, is a key responsibility for a small agent team, perhaps the most unique FBI force in the world. The Budapest Project is tucked away on the second floor of the century-old headquarters of the Hungarian National Investigative Office, just steps from the Central European capital's main drag, Andrassy Avenue. Comprising four FBI agents, one intelligence analyst, and an equal number of Hungarian agents, the Budapest task force is the only place in the world outside of the Iraqi and Afghanistani war zones where the FBI is fully operational on the ground in a foreign country. What started a decade ago as a focused operation against Mogilevich has gradually evolved into a "proof of concept" project for a new international law enforcement model that can effectively combat the globalization of crime. Call it, perhaps, the JTTF of the twenty-first century, the JTTF being the experimental 1980s project that grew into the model on which the entire domestic counterterrorism fight is now based.

For the most part, the FBI's overseas operations—its legal attachés—are strictly a liaison relationship. Not in Hungary. Operationally, the FBI task force works almost as if it were on U.S. soil, teaming up with its local partners, carrying weapons, conducting surveillance, making arrests, and interviewing informants.† The Budapest Project has

---

*U.S. officials have come close to nabbing Mogilevich. At one point his grandson hurt his neck in a diving accident, and thinking that he was paralyzed, Mogilevich carefully arranged for him to be flown to Turkey for treatment and planned to meet him there. Hearing of the plan, the FBI and the CIA swung into high gear and placed a grab team in Istanbul, only to find that the boy had recovered. At another point, Mogilevich and his attorney spent a day negotiating a possible surrender with U.S. officials in the Moscow embassy after being promised that he wouldn't be arrested while inside the building. The negotiations were fruitless.

†Operationally, while the original memorandum of understanding between the United States and Hungary prohibited agents from carrying weapons in country, the task force's work over time proved the necessity of firearms. Standing

proved so successful that plans are already in the works to set up three similar task forces on two continents. Forward-deploying resources for interdiction overseas is a sea change for the FBI, but it's the next logical step in a process of recognizing overseas threats, which started with the Pizza Connection in the 1980s, continued with the embassy bombings in the 1990s, and has only accelerated since 9/11. "We want Hungary to be a trip wire," says Special Agent Neil Mathison, who helped set up the task force.

Right now, the threat is Russian organized crime, something that is growing in complexity and severity with each passing year. The scope of the organizations that the task force is chasing became clear to Bobbitt following a case in late 2006 that started with a request from a Budapest district police officer for the task force's help in tracking a handful of suspicious financial transactions. What agents quickly uncovered was that the crime wasn't simply money laundering, as local police had believed, but wide-ranging financial fraud. The suspects were posting cars for sale on internet auction sites such as eBay, then e-mailing bidders off the site to arrange for a sale under the table. Dozens of English-speaking teenagers in Romania worked sweatshop-style hours posting sales and corresponding with potential buyers in the United States, Britain, Australia, and Germany. In a sophisticated operation, the group had purchased blocks of U.S. fax numbers that, thanks to the wonders of internet technology, they used to mimic legitimate U.S. bank escrow accounts while the bank accounts were actually listed in Central European countries. The buyer thought that the bank would hold the money in the escrow account until the car had been delivered, yet once the victim had wired money to the bank, a mule, called an "arrow," immediately withdrew it, before the victim had a chance to trace the wire transfer. Using fake passports from half

---

shoulder-to-shoulder on raids, conducting surveillance in questionable neighborhoods, and making high-risk arrests of organized crime figures, the Hungarian authorities and U.S. FBI agents realized it would better if both partners were armed. Similarly, the FBI began to pour resources into the firearms training for the team, since budgetary concerns didn't allow the Hungarian agents the expansive firearms training that the FBI gets. As Bobbitt says, "They're standing behind us with guns in a lot of situations, so we have a real vested interest in how well they shoot."

a dozen countries, the arrows had bank accounts across the region, in Bulgaria, Poland, Greece, Slovakia, Hungary, and the Czech Republic. As the FBI's investigation expanded, Bobbitt ended up working closely with the Slovak, Czech, Bulgarian, Romanian, and Polish financial crimes and organized crime police, all of whom turned out to be investigating various individuals in the group. However, no single investigative body, including Europol and Interpol, was investigating the entire organization and its many worldwide tentacles.

The group had operated in Slovakia for three months, then moved to the Czech Republic for three months, and then landed in Hungary, where it intended to stay for three months. Moving so frequently allowed the criminals to stay ahead of the police (the typical belief was that police would lose interest in any investigation once the criminals had left the country). They hadn't counted on the FBI's long arm and long memory. The many collaborating police entities around Europe discreetly shared with Bobbitt suspect names, bank accounts, IDs, and even electronic surveillance information, which helped lead to the arrest of Maryana Lozanova in Budapest on March 22, 2007. Agents at the scene participated in the arrest and search—something that could happen in few countries around the world—and rather than wait for the typical bureaucratic authorizations associated with a formal request to review evidence, they began interviewing witnesses and tracking down the leads in Lovanova's cell phone that same day. Her main contact, George Pletnyov, who allegedly traveled the region collecting the money from the arrows and then, after paying them 10 percent (not bad pay for what amounts to a time commitment of opening a bank account and making a single withdrawal) and keeping 10 percent for himself, passed the rest up the chain, had cell phones registered in the U.K., Austria, Slovakia, Poland, France, Germany, Bulgaria, and the Czech Republic. The text messages found in those cell phones provided names, bank accounts, withdrawal amounts, and loads of operational details. "Within eighteen months, this one of many small cells stole and laundered more than US$1.5 million from American victims. You can't help but respect them," Bobbitt says. "They're very innovative."

Bobbitt traveled back to the United States with his Hungarian NNI colleague Lieutenant Colonel Attila Szaniszlo, and they both testified before a grand jury in Washington, D.C., winning an indictment against Lozanova. Later they returned to obtain six additional indictments against other members of the organization, including three levels of leadership. Bobbitt and his partner, Special Agent Michael Brown, flew back to the United States with an NNI colleague on April 26, 2007, with Lozanova in custody and handed her over to agents from the Washington Field Office—the task force's first extradition from Hungary to the United States. As a result of the arrest and interrogation of Lozanova and various other subjects, the FBI obtained significant lead intelligence and evidence against the entire organization. That helped police in Poland make three additional arrests, including that of Pletnyov. After being coaxed by Polish authorities and the FBI into testifying at his brother's judicial hearing, Ivayloy Pletnyor, an alleged co-conspirator, was arrested by the Polish national SWAT team and by Special Agent Brown when he arrived at the court. Another suspected member of the group, Nikolay Minchev, was arrested when he arrived for a visit to Boston that the FBI had surreptitiously encouraged him to make. In a photo array, he immediately confirmed the other players. The FBI was on the right track.

Other wings of the operation have been traced to Thailand, Greece, and Spain, and the FBI's investigation is continuing further up the ladder based on evidence collected in rolling up the first several layers of the group. Such investigations are making believers even out of Hungarian officials who once doubted the task force's potential. "I didn't in the beginning believe that a case in our country could help your country," says Attila Petőfi, director of the Hungarian National Investigative Agency. "Now I see how a little piece of the puzzle can help us understand what's happening. As I've experienced, there's lots of ways we can help each other."

Three facets make scams like this one particularly troubling to U.S. investigators. First, unlike many criminals, the suspects in the new wave of auction and internet fraud are highly educated, often with graduate degrees, computer competency, and fluency in four or five languages. Second, the ease of moving across borders, particularly as new international rules constantly erode traditional border constraints, makes it ever easier for the suspects to elude law enforcement with a few hours' drive or a short airplane flight across an invisible line on a map.★ Third is the sheer scale of the money involved. This group wasn't making small change in its auction scams. One Florida physician who "purchased" four cars through the scam lost $129,000. The group is responsible, the FBI believes, for thefts of more than a $1 billion from U.S. citizens, to say nothing of their haul from Brits, Australians, and Germans.

At no point before they were arrested, though, did a single one of the suspects set foot in the United States. The internet makes it highly lucrative to rip off Americans from far away—and, at least until the task force began operating, relatively risk-free. "You just can't do this from the U.S., and if you're not looking at them from here, they're going to get away," Bobbitt says.

This single internet fraud case and the wider Mogilevich investigation indicate a fundamental transformation in the nature of criminal enterprises. Thanks to the interconnected global financial network, the international spread of technology and education, and weak foreign judicial systems, it's easier than ever to interlock legitimate business and illegitimate operations. In too many cases, today's organized crime bosses are indistinguishable from entrepreneurs in developing countries. "OC activities pose a potentially larger but less visible threat to U.S. strategic interests than in the past," an FBI report explains. "The scope and nature of OC activity and the related threat has shifted toward a more white-collar type of crime. The global economy has created an opportunity for criminals to accrue more money and power and face less scrutiny from the law enforcement agencies."

Particularly troubling to U.S. officials are the moves Eurasian organized crime has been making into the energy sector. Mogilevich's organization has close ties to the Russian energy industry and a strong influence on the Ukrainian natural gas sector, as well as owning

---

★In January 2008, Hungary joined the Schengen Agreement, a publicly obscure but critically important treaty among EU countries that spelled trouble for law enforcement. Travelers in the Schengen nations—currently twenty-five countries, stretching from Hungary on the east to Portugal in the west, Greece in the south to Finland and the Baltic states in the north—can move from country to country without border checks. "It's good for travel. It make it easy to get around Europe. It wasn't good for police. There are no borders anymore for criminals," explains Marcos J. de Miguel Luken, the Budapest liaison for the Spanish National Poice.

paper companies, timber stands, and metal companies across Eastern Europe and the former Soviet states. There's a high potential in the future, the FBI believes, for what it's beginning to call "natural resources extortion."★

The interplay between criminal organizations and governments also poses a new threat for agencies like the FBI. With strong ties to politicians, the military, and security services and a huge electronic global financial network in which to hide their assets and businesses, today's crime bosses might never be formally indicted or brought to justice. Increasingly, those ties mean FBI investigations are no longer necessarily focused on criminal indictments as an end result. Instead, the investigations are aimed at finding actionable intelligence for government decision-makers and politicians rather than evidence for grand juries.

In many ways, Budapest is a lonely outpost for the FBI personnel, as isolated and overlooked in its own way as I-49 and I-45 felt in the period leading up to 9/11. Beyond the team's physical distance from home, the dedicated focus on Eurasian organized crime is rare. Despite the growing strategic threat of Eurasian organized crime, only about thirty staff members, including the five in Budapest, in the entire Bureau are dedicated to combating it—roughly the same number of people working al-Qaeda cases before 2001.† Says Amy Stewart, the FBI's Budapest intelligence analyst, "Just because our priorities changed on 9/11 doesn't mean that the threats changed. They may have a different emphasis today, yet the rest of these things didn't just go away after 9/11."

★ The FBI suspects that Eurasian organized crime, not content only to buy overseas, is beginning to encroach on the U.S. natural resources sector and recently bought up a West Virginia mining operation and a steel mill in Oregon, among other purchases. There's so much money floating around the financial system that it's nearly impossible to label such purchases entirely dirty or entirely clean. "We can't detect where the true ownership lies," says Supervisory Special Agent Michael Bobbitt. "How far removed from dirty money are they? Even though they may be making legitimate products, that's not how we want business done in the U.S."

† In many parts of the country, virtually no attention is paid to Eurasian organized crime. In San Francisco, for instance, the Bureau's organized crime resources go to fighting Asian gangs and groups, identified in that region as the top criminal priority.

That recognition—that the next threats are likely to be different from those we face today—has been the driving force behind the Bureau's overseas expansion over the past twenty years. As Marcos J. de Miguel Luken, who as the Budapest liaison for the Spanish National Police participated in chasing down leads in the internet scam investigation, explains, the FBI's presence in Budapest is more than just a unique project—it's a powerful statement of the Bureau's ambitions and the way the FBI sees itself in the world. "We don't see ourselves as an international crime-fighting force," he says of the Spanish National Police. "It's different for the FBI. In Spain, we're not to get involved in something unless it's Spanish. The FBI has the resources, and the budget, to go further afield. The FBI considers it's a threat that someday could come to the U.S."

Even as new threats grew overseas, the Obama administration quickly discovered that technology had made it vastly easier for terrorist groups to recruit and train possible fighters and martyrs here at home as well. A sprawling and complicated FBI investigation in Minneapolis, launched after residents of the Somali community there noticed a score of young men leaving their families, uncovered a network drawing American teens east to Somalia for militant training and terrorist operations. The young Minneapolis men were being urged by extremist preachers, primarily from two local mosques, and by internet propaganda, to return to their homeland and help defend it against an invasion, begun in 2006, by Ethiopia. "The internet is giving us so much self-radicalization," Special Agent Brad Deardorff explains. Deardorff spent years chasing terrorists overseas, including the old Pan Am hijacker he caught in Thailand just days after 9/11, but with a transfer away from the Washington Field Office Fly Team, he now focuses almost exclusively on fighting terrorists here in the United States. "There are a lot of disgruntled teens and social networking online," he adds. "You just need one guy bent on death and killing. As the world becomes more Facebook-savvy, those connections are much easier to make. How do you distinguish between legal radicalization and terrorist recruitment?"

On October 29, 2008, Shirwa Ahmed, a twenty-seven-year-old

college student who had come to the United States as a teen and graduated from Roosevelt High School in Minneapolis, blew himself up as part of five coordinated suicide bombings in Somalia attributed to the al-Shabaab terror network, one of the many extremist "franchises" that have aligned themselves with al-Qaeda. The bombings killed twenty-nine people and, according to the FBI, earned Ahmed the dubious distinction of being the first U.S. citizen to conduct a suicide bombing. Ahmed was identified by DNA research at the scene of the attack in Somalia, and the FBI helped bring his remains back to Burnsville, Minnesota, for burial (refusing to say at the time whether he was a victim or the attacker). Ahmed's act, made public months later, was a haunting reminder that the "homegrown radicalization" that had proved so troublesome and worrisome in London wasn't a unique British problem.

"A range of socioeconomic conditions, such as violent youth crime and gang subcultures and tensions over cultural integration, may have also played some role in the recruitment process," Phil Mudd, the former CIA counterterrorism officer turned FBI intelligence executive, testified before Congress. "Several of the travelers from Minneapolis came from single-parent households, potentially making them more susceptible to recruitment from charismatic male authority figures." They were helped overseas by others in the community willing to fund jihad—buy the plane tickets (even in some cases posing as the parents of the Minnesotan Somali youth who were under eighteen), pay for the travel, help with passports, and so on. The FBI and the U.S. Attorney's Office in Minnesota empaneled a grand jury to assemble a case against some of the backers. Worshippers at the two mosques suspected of helping in the recruitment subsequently reported being subject to FBI surveillance, and eventually the U.S. Attorney indicted eight men for helping to recruit the Somali youth, one of the largest terrorist networks dismantled since 2001. But while most of the recruitment appears to have occurred in Minneapolis's large Somali population, there are some 200,000 Somalis living throughout the United States—most driven overseas by decades of political turmoil in the Horn of Africa—and FBI agents eventually uncovered evidence of youths who had disappeared from Boston, Portland, Maine, and Columbus, Ohio. (Months after Ahmed's attack in Somalia, it was the same group—al-Shabaab, "the youth"—that U.S. officials feared was targeting Obama's inauguration.)

"The prospect of young men indoctrinated and radicalized within their own communities and induced to travel to Somalia to take up arms, and to kill themselves and perhaps many others, is a perversion of the immigrant story," Mueller said. "It raises the question of whether these young men will one day come home, and if so, what they might undertake here."

In certain ways, the Minneapolis Somali investigation offered precisely the kind of investigative leads leading to actionable intelligence that the Bureau had hoped to build after 9/11: taking a local case, seeing if there were national implications, asking, "Where else is this happening?" and directing national resources to address it. It's precisely the kind of intelligence investigation that didn't happen in the wake of the pre-9/11 Phoenix memo regarding Islamic extremists and flight school training.

The threats continued to multiply. Throughout Obama's first year, at a pace greatly accelerated from previous years, FBI officials took down at least one terrorist plot a month. David Kris, Eric Holder's assistant attorney general for national security, explained in June 2010, "It's been, for us, extremely busy, very hectic, very challenging for a little more than a year now. We are flat out to stop every one of these cold."

In May 2009, a yearlong investigation into a cell of would-be terrorists, aided by a Bureau informant who provided inert weapons and a nonworking Stinger missile rigged by FBI technicians, reached a dramatic conclusion in the Bronx. The four suspects, three of them U.S. citizens, parked what they believed to be deadly car bombs outside two Bronx synagogues and left for Stewart Airport in Newburgh, New York, where they hoped to shoot down an air force plane. As they drove, NYPD vehicles blocked their path and Emergency Services Unit officers converged on their SUV, broke its windows, and hauled them out of the car.

Not long after, Abdulhakim Mujahid Muhammad, a twenty-four-year-old Muslim convert who had changed his name from Carlos

Bledsoe, walked into an army recruiting center in Little Rock, Arkansas, and opened fire. Muhammad, who had converted to Islam shortly after 9/11, had traveled to Yemen, been detained in the country's notorious PSO prison—ground zero for jihadist recruitment—and been interviewed by an FBI agent while incarcerated there. When he returned to the United States, hardened and radicalized, he spent a year living in Little Rock, where his parents ran a tour company, before assembling an arsenal and attacking the recruiting center. In his car, investigators found ammunition and a carefully mapped-out route all the way to Maryland, with additional targets marked along the way.

Muhammad's was just the first of two attacks on military centers that year. In November 2009, U.S. Army Major Nidal Hasan killed thirteen and wounded thirty more at a Fort Hood army facility where troops were preparing to head overseas to Iraq and Afghanistan. Hasan had been in communication with Yemeni radicals, trading e-mails with Anwar al-Awlaki, a fierce Yemeni cleric on the FBI's radar. But his e-mails seemed consistent with work that Hasan was doing for the army on Muslims, and little further attention was paid to him.*

In July, FBI officials swept down on seven men in North Carolina who, the Bureau alleged, had been stockpiling weapons, practicing military tactics, and training overseas with jihadist groups. Having watched group leader Daniel Boyd and his compatriots on and off since 2006, the FBI JTTF decided to move after observing covert training exercises the group conducted on rural land in June and July—a warning sign that harkened back to the Calverton, Long Island, shooting excursions of the Brooklyn cell that eventually targeted the World Trade Center in 1993. The local U.S. attorney, George Holding, said, "These charges hammer home the point that terrorists and their supporters are not confined to the remote regions of some faraway land but can grow and fester right here at home." And yet it was unclear for months what, exactly, Boyd's recruits were planning to do, if anything. Not until September did the U.S. attorney

---

*As one Justice official explains, "If you ever saw the anti-American, extremist vitriol that crosses our desks every day, these didn't even come close."

indict them for a specific plot, alleging that they had intended to target the Quantico Marine Corps Base.

On one of his regular trips through field offices across the country, Mueller swung through the Charlotte division to give the JTTF team an "Attaboy." "The work you did on Boyd was first-rate, start to finish. Some will say they never would have launched an attack, they couldn't have launched an attack, but the fact of the matter is, you never know," Mueller told the Charlotte JTTF team in a private meeting, explaining that he'd been following the case since Boyd had first come on the JTTF's radar in 2006. "You had to take them down."

The Bureau had tried to learn from the intense media reaction to its haste regarding several potential plots and the mixed results of the relevant court cases that followed. The Bureau was accused of acting in haste—the plots were seen as little more than idle chatter, aspirations by groups who had little ability or training to carry out the attacks in actuality. And yet it remains terrifically challenging to balance intent, capability, and probability. One FBI official explains defensively, "If you write them off, they'll surprise you. At some point, these guys will all default to their lowest ability, and even that can be dangerous. You may not be able to shoot down an airliner with a Stinger, but you can still shoot up a shopping mall."

On two consecutive days in September 2009, FBI agents in Dallas and in Springfield, Illinois, arrested men who intended to blow up major buildings, like the cell in Brooklyn earlier in the year. Agents waited until the would-be terrorists had parked the vehicles loaded with explosives (rendered inert already by the FBI) and walked away to escape the detonation. The informant in Dallas, FBI officials explained, had actually tried to talk his supposed collaborator out of the plot, to no avail. ("Look, this is really going to fuck up your life if you go forward with this," the informant told Hosam Maher Husein Smadi before he parked the truck underneath Fountain Place, a sixty-story skyscraper in downtown Dallas.) The FBI had basically been running identical operations in Springfield and Dallas, so the arrests had to be carefully coordinated for the same news cycle, since an arrest in one place might tip the other off. "We had to slow down Smadi while we sped up Springfield," an official explains.

*   *   *

The next case on the FBI's horizon was in an entirely different league from the Brooklyn, Dallas, and Springfield plots, and in fact nearly every other case since 2001. Intelligence and FBI executives concluded that Najibullah Zazi, when they became aware of him in the summer of 2009, was probably only the third core al-Qaeda plotter in the United States since 9/11.*

Standing at the entrance to Zazi's condo complex in Aurora, Colorado, it's hard to imagine that anyone who awoke each morning to such a view could harbor such hatred. The Rocky Mountains, capped with snow, stretch toward the sky off in the distance, and an elementary school sits behind the complex, its playground, filled with frolicking children, abutting the wall of the gated community that perhaps the most dangerous terrorist to enter the United States since 2001 called home.

Zazi had traveled to Pakistan with two high school friends, trained extensively in explosives—agents later recovered page after page of carefully written bomb-making instructions—and met with two of al-Qaeda's senior leaders, Saleh al-Somali, the group's head of external operations, and Rashid Rauf, who recruited Zazi for a martyrdom operation back in the United States. One of Zazi's companions, Zarein Ahmedzay, later explained in court, "We told these two individuals that we wanted to wage jihad in Afghanistan, but they said that we would be more useful to them and to the jihad if we returned to New York and conducted operations there." He added, "They said the most important thing was to hit well-known structures and to maximize the number of casualties."

The intense pressure al-Qaeda was under became clear on November 28, 2008, just days after their meeting in Waziristan, when Rauf,

---

*FBI officials say that of all the terrorist plots disrupted from 2001 to 2009, only two men from Ohio—Iyman Faris, who plotted to destroy the Brooklyn Bridge in 2003, and Nuradin Abdi, who was arrested trying to blow up a shopping mall later that year—had been in contact with the al-Qaeda leadership and prepared to move ahead with their plots without the benefit or knowledge of government informants or U.S. officials.

who had previously been accused of being involved in the 2006 London airplanes plot, became the first British citizen to be killed by the CIA's drone program. Rauf and al-Qaeda's explosives expert, Abu Zubair al-Masri, were killed by three Hellfire missiles fired by a CIA drone into their compound outside the village of Ali Khel, about ten miles from the Afghanistan-Pakistan border.

Returning six weeks later, in January 2009, to New York's JFK Airport from Peshawar, Pakistan, Zazi and his two friends set about planning an attack modeled on the 2005 London subway bombings. Together, they planned to place backpack bombs on the 1, 2, 3, and possibly 6 trains under New York—some of the busiest, most heavily trafficked routes in the subway system. Zazi would have succeeded if not for the trouble he had with the chemical recipes for manufacturing his bomb. The first batch he made in a Colorado hotel kitchenette failed to ignite, forcing him to e-mail one of the al-Qaeda bomb makers for help. The e-mail, flagged by analysts in Washington and forwarded to the Denver JTTF, landed on the desk of FBI supervisor John Scatta on Labor Day, 2009. He saw code words, such as "recipe," that immediately set off alarm bells.

That night, Scatta's surveillance teams arrived outside Zazi's condo. Back at the FBI Field Office, further database and computer checks led the JTTF to decide Zazi wasn't just a "Pizza Hut" lead: He was the real thing. Special Agent in Charge Jim Davis, the former Baghdad legat, ordered all of the Field Office's investigations shut down. They left an agent in Wyoming and two in Colorado to handle crimes on the local Indian reservations; everyone else scrambled toward Denver.

On September 9, a day after renting a car, Zazi got onto I-70, heading east, and quickly hit speeds of over 100 mph, mystifying the FBI surveillance team behind him as to his destination. The Denver JTTF, which was heading the Zazi investigation, now known as Operation Highrise, contacted the Colorado State Patrol, who used Zazi's speed as an excuse to pull him over. During the traffic stop, he informed the Colorado trooper he was driving to New York. "That was the first time that New York came into this investigation," recalls Denver ASAC Steve Olson. "Why is he going to New York? We scramble resources and watch him uninterrupted." For 1,100 miles that day, Zazi sped east. After a few hours of sleep in Ohio, he continued toward New York. FBI agents across the country were on high alert. The SAC in Denver, James Davis (the former Baghdad legat) recalls, "I didn't know whether he was going to New York to be operational or whether he was fleeing to be away from the scene of an attack [in Denver]."

Elaborate surveillance in New York gave way to a comedy of errors amid infighting between the NYPD and the FBI, which ultimately tipped off Zazi that he was being watched. The first clue was a "random" drug checkpoint that the Port Authority Police Department used to stop Zazi's car and search it before he was allowed to cross the George Washington Bridge into New York, on September 11.* As the lawyer for one of Zazi's co-conspirators later wrote, "Even though [Zazi] is not the brightest bulb in the terrorist chandelier, the thinly-transparent ruse of a 'random' checkpoint stop did not fool him." Later, the NYPD towed away Zazi's car, using a parking violation as cover, and Zazi was further tipped off by an imam whom the NYPD approached for information about the terror suspect.†

Zazi aborted the plot in the hours following, throwing away the detonators and other incriminating evidence. "We intend[ed] to obtain and assemble the remaining components to build a bomb over the weekend. The plan was to conduct martyrdom operation on subway lines in Manhattan as soon as the material were ready—Monday, Tuesday or Wednesday," he explained later in court.

Instead, after the twenty-four-year-old would-be martyr became aware of the government surveillance, he flew back to Colorado, by which point leaks from the NYPD had made him the center of a media storm. Camera crews and reporters tracked his movements closely. Back in Colorado, he voluntarily went to the Denver FBI Field Office for three days of lengthy interviews with Special Agent Eric

---

* Subsequent investigation found that the Port Authority Police, who stopped Zazi before he was on the bridge, overlooked nearly two pounds of explosives he had in the car at the time. Whether the police's oversight was intentional or careless is still unknown.

† The NYPD had no regrets as to its actions. As one NYPD executive explains, "You have to understand that from my organization's perspective, if we can just stop the attack from hurting New Yorkers, we consider ourselves successful. The FBI always want to keep operations running longer than we do."

Jergenson; in an adjoining conference room, more agents secretly listened in, and just down the hall, the Operation Highrise command post was running night and day. "One of the great breaks in this case was Zazi's desire to talk his way out of this," Davis recalls. Zazi denied any ties to terrorism or aspirations for an attack during the initial interview, even as other agents simultaneously served a search warrant on his apartment. The media circus followed Zazi and the investigators wherever they went for days. Finally, Davis had had enough: He gave the go-ahead to take Zazi down. Jergenson led Zazi out of his Aurora condo in handcuffs on Saturday, September 19, just five days after he was supposed to have launched his operation, and agents whisked him toward New York. The most serious plot since 9/11 had been averted— but only narrowly, and with a good helping of luck. As Jergenson explains, "My strong belief is that he absolutely would have carried it out. He was trained. He was committed. He was ready to go."

Despite the media circus, the arrest and aftermath were handled markedly differently than many plots of the past: There was no breathless, high-level press conference by Justice Department leaders and Homeland Security officials. Instead, the case was treated more like an old-fashioned FBI case; Obama was confident that the Bureau had things under control and that law enforcement could deal with the matter. As one senior administration official told the *Washington Post,* "[Zazi's case] demonstrated that we were able to successfully neutralize this threat, and to have insight into it, with existing statutory authorities, with the system as it currently operates."

Zazi pleaded guilty in February 2010 to a variety of charges, including conspiring to use a weapon of mass destruction. Several weeks before his plea deal in New York City, Saleh al-Somali, the top al-Qaeda leader Zazi had met with in Pakistan, was killed by another drone strike, becoming the highest-ranking terrorist leader killed in President Obama's first year, a period where the new president had increased the numbers of drones over Pakistan and Afghanistan and killed hundreds of militants.

The Obama administration got a nasty gift on its first Christmas: A would-be Christmas Day bomber, Umar Farouk Abdulmutallab, succeeded in nothing more than burning his own genitals off when his underwear bomb fizzled aboard Northwest Airlines Flight 253, the Amsterdam-to-Detroit plane he'd boarded after a long flight from Africa. Airplane crew members used fire extinguishers to douse the smoke and small fire while other passengers wrestled Abdulmutallab into submission. When worried flight attendant Dionne Ransom-Monroe asked what he was carrying, the Nigerian replied matter-of-factly, "Explosive device."

After being taken into custody when the flight landed safely, he was questioned at the hospital by FBI agents. Over the next several days, he revealed extensive ties to terrorist groups in Yemen.* Agents were dispatched to Nigeria to look into his background; his father had raised concerns with the U.S. embassy there—clearly not taken seriously enough—about his son's ongoing radicalization.

In the wake of the Christmas Day bombing, there was much familiar hand-wringing over the missed signals and the failure of the intelligence community to connect the dots yet again. In a way, the incident underscored the new challenge: the intelligence apparatus was now drowning in information. Although Congress and pundits attacked the failure publicly and trotted out the tired phrase "connect the dots," the key watchword inside government became "signals to noise." How did analysts sort through the mess of data to figure out what was truly important? It was clear, in hindsight, that Umar Farouk Abdulmutallab had been.

For Mueller, the case illustrated the dangers of the voluminous files the Bureau and other agencies have now collected. He knew that somewhere in his Bureau's files the signs of the next attack probably lay; there was simply so much data flowing through the system that it seemed almost inevitable that another Phoenix memo, warnings of an

---

*The FBI and Eric Holder received a great deal of criticism for providing the underwear bomber with a Miranda warning, and yet the Miranda debate, many agents believe, is a false fight, one concocted in Washington for Washington. Even the Bureau's own counterterrorism experts say the Bureau is sometimes too quick to provide Miranda warnings. Take the example of the Christmas Day bomber. "All I lose is his confession. I've got two hundred other witnesses. People just don't understand what they're talking about. I don't need the confession," one counterterrorism agent says.

attack in Yemen harbor, a revealing rumor from a source like Emad Salem, or a set of surveillance photos like those from a shooting range on Calverton, Long Island, existed somewhere. As Art Cummings bemoans, "You're getting three hundred phone calls a day and a thousand e-mails. When someone says, 'You received it?' you don't have any idea."

The Christmas Day incident exposed one quickly remedied hole in the FBI's capabilities. In April 2009, the Bureau had begun the process of creating a specialized High-Value Detainee Interrogation Group, the so-called HIG—a team of trained terrorism interrogators and experts who were uniquely suited for the most important cases. The effort was an attempt to bring the special advantages of the Bureau's interrogation skills to bear in an organized fashion. In hindsight, members of a group like the HIG should have been interrogating the likes of Abu Zubaydah, Mohammed al-Qahtani, and the other al-Qaeda leaders captured after 2001. The new HIG, run by an FBI agent and two deputies—one from the CIA and one from the Pentagon—included three regional teams to ensure quick dispatch to the scene of an unfolding attack. Its guidelines specifically outlined that interrogations must abide by the normal rules and regulations— nothing "extralegal," nothing "enhanced." It's easy to imagine that if it had been formed a decade earlier, the HIG might well have included agents like Jack Cloonan, Ali Soufan, Steve Gaudin, Abby Perkins, and Steve Bongardt.

But the HIG would help only when a terrorist was actually in custody. Solving the data overload, following the right lead among too many, ensuring that the Bureau had the right skill sets—that all still came first. As Mueller has said almost daily since 9/11, "My admonition is, 'No counterterrorism lead goes uncovered.'"

But is that truly possible? And if not, what were Mueller and the Bureau realistically supposed to do?

CHAPTER 16
Hellfires to Handcuffs
A Day in the Life of Terror: May 3, 2010

I know you think what you're doing is right. But it is my job not to let that happen.

— *Jack Bauer, 24, confronting a terrorist*

When anarchist Mario Buda, an Italian immigrant, set out to exact revenge in 1920 for the September 11 arrest and indictment of his friends Nicola Sacco and Bartolomeo Vanzetti, he packed a wagon full of dynamite stolen from a nearby construction site and led his horse to the corner of Wall Street and Broad Street, where J. P. Morgan's firm was headquartered. He left the horse and wagon behind and melted into the crowd, walking past Trinity Church, in whose front yard a young sycamore tree stretched skyward. (The tree would become a key symbol of the church until it was uprooted by falling debris from the World Trade Center towers.) As Buda headed north on foot, the Trinity Church bells tolled for noon. As the final peal of the bell echoed among the caverns of Wall Street, at 12:01 P.M. on September 16, the wagon exploded, killing forty people and wounding two hundred. Nearby, Joseph P. Kennedy, patriarch of the family that would capture America's heart in the sixties, barely escaped injury.

The director of the still nascent Bureau of Investigation, forerunner of the FBI, left Washington on the first available train. William Flynn was known as the nation's premier anarchist-chaser, but modern forensics and investigative techniques were decades away. The Bureau of Investigation, filled with patronage hacks, was still a shadow of what it would become under Flynn's successor, J. Edgar Hoover. The best the detectives and agents working the bombing could do was to go from blacksmith to blacksmith in New York with a horseshoe from the unlucky creature that had drawn the wagon, hoping one smith would recognize his own handiwork. They never caught Buda, who fled the country before investigators could locate him.

Four miles north of Buda's attack, on May 1, 2010, another immigrant, Faisal Shahzad, abandoned his dark blue Nissan Pathfinder in Times Square. Shahzad's explosive device was leaps and bounds beyond what had been available to Buda in 1920, but it was incorrectly assembled and fizzled like a dying firecracker. Soon after street vendors noticed the smoking vehicle and alerted NYPD officers, the bomb squad arrived to take stock. William Flynn would never have been able to anticipate the resources available to his colleagues so many generations later. Yet Shahzad too almost made it out of the country before authorities caught him. He was already on board an Emirates jet at New York's Kennedy Airport, en route to Dubai, when a last-minute computer check alerted authorities to his location. The plane's departure was stopped; customs agents rushed on board and took him in custody at 11:45 P.M. on May 3. "I was expecting you," Shahzad told officers as they approached him on the plane. "Are you NYPD or FBI?"

The day of Shahzad's arrest had already been a busy day in counterterrorism circa 2010, illustrating how much—and how little—had changed since 9/11. That one day illustrated particularly well the strengths and weaknesses, the outright successes and the near misses, that had governed the FBI's daily life under Mueller's tenure. On that Monday, the FBI—and the war on terror, in all its various forms— circled the globe attempting to convict one terrorist, stop the next one, and catch one more.

Standing in court in Mumbai, Mohamed Ajmal Amir Qasab hardly looked like someone who could bring the second largest city in the world to a standstill. He looked very much like the boy he was, just topping five feet, barely out of his teens, dressed in a T-shirt, barefoot, and with shaggy hair. Qasab had appeared very much out of his element during the trial, which had stretched for 271 days and included some 600 witnesses. He had often smiled at his defense attorney and laughed when the courtroom laughed. Yet in the final weeks of the lengthy proceedings, he grew more solemn. Impending doom, it's said, helps to focus the mind.

A number of FBI agents and forensics experts had testified in the trial, although their identities were kept secret from the public in India, and more had been deposed by videoconference from the United States. "FBI investigators have played a vital role in disclosing the truth in this case," special public prosecutor Ujjwal Nikam explained. "The FBI agents and their experts came to the special court and gave evidence, by which we were able to prove that Qasab and his nine associates had come from Pakistan." The testimony and arguments had concluded on March 31; on May 3 he would face the verdict.

India didn't take any chances that his terrorist allies would try to free him or cause trouble during the trial. The trial had been held in a special courtroom built specifically for Qasab's case inside Mumbai's Arthur Road jail, the city's largest and oldest prison. While the Arthur Road facility, just a few miles from the site of Qasab's attacks, is notorious for its overcrowding, the terrorist had been kept isolated, and his trial had been speedy compared to those of most Indian defendants. Housed since the attacks in a custom-made bombproof cell, Qasab didn't even have to venture outside to enter the courtroom; a special tunnel led directly from his cell to the similarly bombproof courtroom.

From their start the year before, the proceedings had always attracted a crowd, but today's gathering was different, even more crowded than usual and bristling with anticipation. Outside, special security forces patrolled the surrounding streets. Barriers of sandbags manned by Indian soldiers protected every approach; rocket teams stood ready to repel any aerial assaults. The whole scene, in its way, was reminiscent of the high-security bunker in which Giovanni Falcone had tried the maxi-trial in the bunker courtroom of Palermo two decades before.

Qasab's two codefendants were brought in first and pronounced not guilty, as the judge had determined that the evidence was insufficient. Then it was Qasab's turn. Dressed in a white kurta, the traditional knee-length shirt of the region, and sporting a light beard, he kept his head bowed and his face expressionless as the judge spoke to him in Hindi. He stood as the judge began reading a summary of his lengthy, 1,500-page finding of guilt. Gasps filled the courtroom as the audience realized Qasab's fate.

Qasab sank into his seat and spent most of the remaining two hours of the hearing slumped at the defense table, covering his eyes with his hand, as if he could block out what was happening around him. The judge, M. L. Tahiliyani, found him guilty on nearly every one of the eighty-six charges he faced. Tahiliyani went on to say that it was clear that the conspiracy to attack Mumbai stretched far beyond the diminutive man standing in his courtroom; dozens, many of them LeT members from Pakistan, had helped plan and execute the attacks. "It was not a simple crime of murder," Tahiliyani told the packed courtroom. "There was a conspiracy to wage war."

Later that week, the same court sentenced Qasab to death—a rare punishment in India.

As the search for the Times Square bomber unfolded back in the United States and just hours hours after Qasab's appearance in the Mumbai courtroom, Bob Mueller flipped through papers and files as his plane settled into its final approach to the one runway of the airport in Sana'a, Yemen. The security detail in the rear of the plane began to check their communications gear and weapons, slipping their radio earpieces in and checking that their sidearms, extra ammunition, and handcuffs were all in the right place. Of course, where they were heading, the handcuffs—more than anything the tool that distinguished their law enforcement mentality from that of the other U.S. forces, who, as an American general had told a previous FBI director, "don't do handcuffs"—would probably be superfluous. If trouble came in the coming hours, it would be fast and loud, and there probably wouldn't be any survivors to take into custody.

Exactly a week before, the British ambassador had narrowly escaped a suicide bombing that targeted his armored convoy as it drove through

Sana'a. Two security guards and a bystander had been wounded; the bomber, who had been standing nonchalantly on the side of the road near a downtown market, carrying a backpack and waiting for the motorcade to pass, died in the blast. Mueller's stop in Yemen would be brief, just a few hours, long enough to lobby the United States' reluctant ally, President Ali Abdullah Saleh, but until the plane departed and was out of surface-to-air missile range, his escorts would remain tense. Hostage Rescue Team operators, who had been sent ahead to plan out the travel routes on the ground, would meet the plane at the airport. The director's protective detail had the routine of these trips down pat. Visiting world trouble spots had been the norm since 9/11. Mueller had lost track of how many visits he'd made to Iraq, Afghanistan, Pakistan, Uzbekistan, Egypt, and other centers in the war on terror. Just ten weeks earlier, the Obama administration had dispatched him to lead talks in Islamabad with U.S., Pakistani, and Afghan officials to encourage greater cooperation on terrorism issues.* According to diplomatic cables, Pakistan believed that the United States always favored India in its relations and had been making life difficult for embassy officials, dragging its feet on renewing visas for U.S. officials, harassing embassy vehicles, shutting down joint training programs, and sabotaging U.S. contractors in the country. Mueller was one of the only U.S. leaders respected enough within Pakistan to try to broker peace.

Yemen, though, was an even more uncertain ally than Pakistan. In the wake of the Christmas Day bombing attempt, many headlines trumpeted that Yemen, Umar Farouk Abdulmutallab's starting point, was "the new front in the war on terror." One U.S. senator had proclaimed after the incident, "Iraq was yesterday's war, Afghanistan is today's war, and if we do not act preemptively now, Yemen will be

---

* According to diplomatic cables leaked in the fall of 2010, Mueller's agenda in the talks with Pakistani interior minister Rehman Malik and Afghan interior minister Hanif Atmar had included "register[ing] U.S. concerns about terrorist threats to U.S. citizens and U.S. interests that emanate from Pakistan, and encourag[ing] continued Pakistani action to counter these threats... [as well as to] acknowledge the sacrifices made by Pakistan's law enforcement agencies and the pressure the terrorist attacks have placed on their resources."

tomorrow's war." Many of the nation's counterterrorism experts just shook their heads. Anyone who'd been following the Obama administration's efforts to shut Guantánamo knew that half the detainees the government still couldn't figure how to handle were from Yemen. The lawless regions of that country were a terrorist factory and had been for years. In fact, President Obama had received a briefing on Christmas Eve on threats emanating from Yemen and the U.S. drone program's counterassaults there. And in January, the United States temporarily closed its embassy in Yemen, given the danger.

Yemen had been a key focus of the war on terror dating back to the millennium, when, as part of the coordinated but failed millennium plot, al-Qaeda members had tried to blow up the USS *The Sullivans,* only to succeed ten months later with the USS *Cole.* Ali Soufan and other members of I-49 had watched the 9/11 attacks unfold from the television of the U.S. embassy in Sana'a. That same fateful day had found Russ Fincher and other agents in Sweden arresting the al-Qaeda leader who had tried to blow up the FBI's *Cole* team in Sana'a, the city Mueller was about to visit. All told, the Bureau's counterterrorism team knew Yemen well; it had had an official presence there since Legat Sana'a opened in 2004, but ever since 2000 agents had had a near constant presence in the country, working one investigation or another.

After his stint interrogating Abu Zubaydah in Thailand, Steve Gaudin had been dispatched to Yemen to help start the U.S. government's "fusion team" with the Defense Department and the CIA. They'd been up and running only a few days when two al-Qaeda members had been killed in downtown Sana'a by the premature explosion of their jury-rigged antitank IED—an IED they'd hoped to use against Gaudin's colleagues. One of the fusion team's main tasks had been to hunt Abd al-Rahim al-Nashiri, a leader of the *Cole* attack. After the CIA's Special Activities Division captured al-Nashiri in the United Arab Emirates, Barbara Bodine's replacement, Ambassador Ed Hull, had conducted a briefing about how Yemen had turned a corner. Steve Gaudin wasn't convinced. "Taking Nashiri off the table is great," he told the ambassador, "but this war is far from over." Gaudin later opened the FBI legat in Sana'a with little more than a folding chair, a card table, a laptop, and an MSAT satellite phone that charged

$6.50 a minute to call Washington. During his years in Sana'a, he investigated cases ranging from terrorism to kidnapped tourists, making a small dent—but only that.

When Mueller traveled around the United States, visiting field offices and speaking at conferences, he often joked about banishing agents who got on his bad side to this desolate outpost not much removed from the twelfth century. "You're gonna love Yemen," he'd say, fixing the agent with a stony stare that was broken only by a twinkle in his eye. Of course, by 2010 the joke didn't work all that well anymore. Yemen was actually now the center of the action, the place where the Bureau's most hard-charging agents wanted to go. It was long past the point when Mueller should have switched his joke to a place like Legat Dakar, in Senegal, or Legat Astana, in Kazakhstan, or perhaps the tiny Fairbanks Resident Agency in Alaska. But Mueller didn't joke much, so changing his small comedy repertoire wasn't in the cards.*

Since he'd taken over as director, Mueller had visited Yemen nearly as much as any other country; he'd developed an almost friendly relationship with President Saleh. After Abdulmutallab's unsuccessful attack, the extremist cleric Anwar al-Awlaki, who was increasingly in the sights of the United States, trumpeted, "Our brother Umar Farouk has succeeded in breaking through the security systems that have cost the U.S. government alone over forty billion dollars since 9/11." Al-Awlaki lived in Yemen's lawless regions, and Mueller was heading to Sana'a to press the government's case for more aggressive actions against the groups spawning people like Abdulmutallab.

The anticolonial fervor of the mid-twentieth century had cast

---

*After Mueller returned to the United States days later, he stood before the graduates of Duke University's Law School, explaining as part of his commencement address that the FBI had several proud Duke graduates in its ranks, such as Steve Chabinsky, the deputy assistant director of the Cyber Division. "[Steve] suggested that I open by saying, 'Good evening. Great to be here in Chapel Hill,'" Mueller told the newly minted JDs. "I quickly realized that it would be like sending Derek Jeter to Fenway to joke about the curse of the Bambino. He would never make it out alive. I could not help but wonder why Steve would try to sabotage my speech. I am sure he will consider the wisdom of his words as he sits at his new desk in Yemen."

Yemen off from its centuries of outside rulers, leaving its native population roughly divided between Shiite tribes to the north and Sunni
tribes to the south. Now, some fifty years after the creation of the
Yemen Arab Republic, the country is referred to in U.S. government
reports as a "perpetually failing state." About twice the size of Wyoming, it has little (legal) economy to speak of, sky-high illiteracy rates,
and a population that seemingly has a national addiction to khat, an
easy-to-grow plant whose leaves contain substances that provide an
amphetamine-like high and whose cultivation uses much of the country's arable land. Most families, according to the government's figures,
spend more annually on khat than on food, and by 4:00 P.M., most of
the nation seems to be high on the large wads of khat stuffed into their
cheeks.

The instability has made Yemen a center of power for one of
al-Qaeda's most powerful and dangerous franchises, al-Qaeda in the
Arabian Peninsula (AQAP). As one FBI executive says, "Yemen is as
much of a nest of vipers as there is in the world right now." Another
intelligence official describes Yemen as "the Harvard School of Radicalization. It doesn't get any better." In fact, Yemen was the site of one
of the earliest known plots linked to al-Qaeda. In December 1992, an
offshoot known as the Aden-Abyan Islamic Army tried to kill Marines
on their way to Somalia for Operation Restore Hope. Even before the
2009 Christmas Day bombing attempt, the U.S. government had been
concerned enough about the rising strength of AQAP to send top
counterterrorism officials to help the Yemeni government attack
AQAP camps and facilities. In response to a December 17 air strike
that reportedly killed thirty-four suspected terrorists, AQAP leaders
had released a video calling for revenge: "We are carrying a bomb to
hit the enemies of God."

Conditions in Yemen continued to deteriorate as conflict in the
northern part of the country reached new heights, and by 2006, a
group called al-Qaeda in the Southern Arabian Peninsula made its
first official appearance. It later merged with the Saudi offshoot to
form AQAP in January 2009. Two of the three leaders of the group
were former Guantánamo detainees who had been repatriated to
Yemen and then promptly released by the government there.

Such releases were not altogether shocking. Yemen, like many of the United States' new "allies" in the war on terror, was hard to judge. One of the chief suspects in the bombing of the USS *Cole*, Jamal al-Badawi, along with twenty-two other al-Qaeda members, had escaped from the national headquarters of the state security force, supposedly by tunneling into the women's bathroom in a nearby mosque. Al-Badawi had confessed to his role in the *Cole* attack after questioning by Ali Soufan in 2001. "He was the guy who recruited the bombers," Soufan later said. "He was the local mastermind." U.S. officials privately doubted the escape story, and the Yemeni government later admitted that allies inside the state security organization had helped the prisoners escape. For al-Badawi, it was at least the second prison break.*

When al-Badawi was captured a year later, the president of the country tried in a meeting with Mueller to claim the multimillion-dollar U.S. government bounty for him. (When Mueller explained that the government doesn't generally grant rewards to other governments, only to private citizens, Saleh quickly replied that a family member of his, a private citizen, had been the one to find al-Badawi.) After al-Badawi pledged allegiance to Saleh, his death sentence was commuted, and he was freed in 2007. Mueller made an unpublicized stop in Yemen during a swing through the region to express his and the government's displeasure with Saleh again, and he left the meeting furious.†

What originally had been a group of some hundred to four hun-

---

* Shortly afterward, Mueller visited the Middle Eastern nation, in part to express the extreme displeasure of the U.S. government at the prison break. After his meeting with President Saleh came the traditional exchange of gifts. Mueller, looking the Yemeni leader in the eye, handed him a pair of handcuffs. The gift, pointed and not particularly diplomatic, could have elicited a response that went either way, yet the president seemed to appreciate Mueller's directness.

† The United States was equally upset when Jaber Elbaneh, another *Cole* suspect who was on the FBI's list of most wanted terrorists, surprised Yemeni court officials by actually showing up at a February 2008 court hearing where charges against him were being adjudicated in absentia. A New Yorker, Elbaneh had trained in Afghanistan with the Lackawanna Six, but instead of returning to the Buffalo area, he traveled directly to Yemen, where he had remained since. After his surprise public appearance in Sana'a, he gave a speech to the judge and walked out of the courtroom unchallenged.

dred AQAP fighters grew quickly amid the khat-fueled lawlessness of Yemen. Besides the Pakistan-Afghanistan border, Yemen had become the top breeding ground for the next generation of Islamic jihadists.

The meetings in Yemen were quick and the motorcades through the streets fast, with the SWAT agents hanging hard on the door handles of their SUVs and fingering their M4 carbines. By nightfall, Mueller's convoy wound safely back to the airport and the plane prepared for takeoff. Mueller folded his long frame into his normal seat, just behind the cockpit, and the engines whined as the jet accelerated away from Sana'a. As the Gulfstream gained altitude, passing out of SAM range, he took a quick glance out the window. Somewhere out there in the seemingly endless desert was Anwar al-Awlaki, the terrorist who at that moment most worried American officials. For all his headlines, bin Laden might still be spiritually important to the jihadist movement, but with his circle of aides continually contracting, he was hardly in the position he'd been a decade before. Al-Awlaki represented a new, more threatening kind of leader, one who was spearheading the Islamic jihad movement via the same technology that was transforming office life and American culture. "The internet has become the new Afghanistan," an intelligence official explains.

Born in New Mexico but raised mostly in Yemen, al-Awlaki had been on the FBI's radar since 1999, when he fell under scrutiny for some of his still unexplained ties to militants, including one al-Qaeda operative who had purchased a battery for Osama bin Laden's satellite phone. Al-Awlaki had ties to Khalid al-Mihdhar and Nawaf al-Hazmi, the 9/11 hijackers, who worshipped at the cleric's mosque in San Diego, and he had been interviewed repeatedly by the FBI after the attacks.*

Al-Awlaki claimed at the time, "We came here to build, not to destroy." But then, as the Bureau closed in, he disappeared back into Yemen in early 2002. He returned to the United States by the end of

---

*One agent later said that "if anyone had knowledge of the plot, it would have been" al-Awlaki, adding, "Someone had to be in the U.S. and keep the hijackers spiritually focused." That said, the case agent who investigated al-Awlaki, Wade Ammerman, believes that the cleric did not know about the attacks.

the year and settled in the Washington, D.C., area, and any sign of compromise or warmth in his feelings toward his homeland quickly dissipated. "This is not now a war on terrorism—we need to all be clear about this. This is a war on Muslims!" the cleric roared in one sermon. Al-Awlaki was under regular surveillance as part of the vast blanket thrown out by the FBI after 9/11, and when agents spotted him crossing state lines with prostitutes, they explored charging him under the Mann Act, a Prohibition-era law—one of the first that the FBI prosecuted in its early days—that prohibits transporting women across state boundaries for "immoral purposes."

Before agents could detain him, the cleric again left the United States, this time for good. After a stint preaching extremism in Britain, he returned to Yemen, where he was arrested in 2006 for participating in an al-Qaeda kidnapping plot. He served eighteen months there in solitary confinement, during which time the FBI again interviewed him. By the end of 2007, he was free again and, in the words of one associate, "harder." After that, al-Awlaki busily became a one-man jihad center, building a network of followers via the internet that included Major Hasan, the Christmas Day bomber, and the Times Square bomber. An intelligence official explains the cleric's appeal to would-be U.S. jihadists: "I don't need to have his sermons translated. This is a guy that sounds like me, looks like me. That's very effective." His DVDs and CDs became bestsellers in extremist circles, and his essay "44 Ways to Support Jihad" was considered one of the movement's key texts. A secret British briefing paper concluded that al-Awlaki had "cemented his position as one of the leading English-speaking jihadi ideologues."

Just weeks before Mueller's visit to Sana'a, al-Awlaki had become the first American citizen to be placed on the CIA's target list for assassination. Barack Obama personally approved the target—perhaps the first time since he had been a teenager that a "presidential finding," as such orders are called, had okayed the assassination of an American citizen. Now, if the CIA's Predator drones could find al-Awlaki, they could kill him. Such attacks were not uncommon in Yemen; in fact, the first drone strike outside Afghanistan had occurred on the barren landscape now below Mueller. In November 2002, Abu Ali al-Harithi, the suspected mastermind of the USS *Cole* plot, had been killed when a Hellfire missile crashed into his convoy. Also killed in the attack was Ahmed Hijazi, aka Kamal Derwish, the spiritual leader who helped recruit the Lackawanna Six. Although Hijazi wasn't the prime target, he had the dubious distinction of being the first American citizen killed by a drone. The government hoped al-Awlaki would be the next.

The CIA's drone program, technically classified and officially denied but too active to be kept secret, had become the Obama administration's favorite antiterror tool, a decade after George Tenet had argued that it would be a "terrible mistake" for the CIA (as opposed to the U.S. military) to operate such weapons in a democratic society. In his first year, Obama had approved more drone strikes than Bush had during his entire eight years in office—partly a reflection of advancing technology, and partly of the sheer number of drones now circling over world trouble spots, more mature intelligence systems that feed the drone's targets, and a sense that ground operations can do only so much. The CIA drones primarily targeted the rural reaches of Pakistan, but attacks in Yemen or in the Horn of Africa were no longer as rare as they once had been. An average of once a week, Obama, through CIA director Leon Panetta, gave the go-ahead for an employee of the Agency operating in one of the drone command posts (sometimes just miles from the White House) to strike with either a Predator drone or the newer, deadlier Reaper model. Estimates for the first-year death toll during the Obama administration ranged as high as five hundred, though no one really knew for sure. But the program was undoubtedly achieving success and was one of the most cost-effective antiterror tools in the U.S. arsenal. Each attack, which cost roughly a quarter million dollars, was a drop in the bucket for the nation's counterterrorism spending and had a comparatively high return. In August 2009, the U.S. killed the head of the Taliban in Pakistan, Baitullah Mehsud, and over the course of Obama's first year it knocked out roughly half of America's twenty most wanted terrorists. The highest cost, perhaps, came in the court of public opinion: The drone attacks resulted in numerous civilian casualties, which made their use increasingly controversial and severely affected support for the United States among the civilian population of Pakistan.

Left to his own devices, Mueller would probably have preferred to hunt al-Awlaki himself in the desert and drag him back to a U.S. courtroom to face American justice, but he was nevertheless a strong proponent of the drone attacks. "Without removing the leadership from the field, we would have had a lot more attacks," Mueller states. "You don't have any alternative. They're in a sanctuary where we don't have control. It's an appropriate form of self-defense."

As Mueller's plane departed from Sana'a, the Mumbai attacker faced justice in India, and the hunt for the Times Square bomber unfolded in the United States, the American drones had already drawn fresh blood. Earlier that morning in North Waziristan, a flight of Predators fired three missiles into a moving vehicle outside the village of Marsi Khel. Four suspected militants died, though U.S. authorities didn't believe they were senior Taliban or al-Qaeda leaders; they were probably just the cannon fodder of global jihad. Therein lay one of the truths of today's threat environment. It was unlikely that Mueller would ever know the names of the four people in that vehicle in North Waziristan; it's possible that Leon Panetta didn't even know for sure when he ordered the Hellfire attack. Any of those four might have become the next Nazibullah Zazi or—more on Mueller's mind today— the next Times Square bomber, both of whom turned out to have trained just miles from Marsi Khel in Pakistan.

The drone strategy was also a recognition of America's maturing government intelligence network, which now purported to know enough about the country's foes that it wasn't worth collecting each and every terrorist out there for interrogation. But it also raised many unanswered questions about what burden of proof preemptive disruption activities should meet; how one charges, prosecutes, and detains foreign suspects in the war on terror; and so on. As one (non-FBI) intelligence official bluntly explains, "It's much less trouble to kill them." But at what cost over the long term?

Normally the seventh floor of the Hoover Building is quiet when Mueller is away. Senior staff members unearth their colored shirts and khaki pants. Yet as Mueller's plane took off from Sana'a, back in Washington, seven time zones earlier, the executive corridor of FBI Headquarters was humming with activity and had been all weekend.

The investigation that had begun moments after Faisal Shahzad had walked away from his Nissan Pathfinder unfolded quickly. Shahzad was no Ramzi Yousef. His Pathfinder, loaded with propane tanks, fireworks, and nonexplosive fertilizer, did little more than smoke when the lit fuse was supposed to trigger the bomb. He watched nearby, waiting for the explosion that never came, then shuffled off to Grand Central Terminal to catch a train back home to Connecticut. He had stupidly left the key to the getaway vehicle he'd parked nearby in the Pathfinder, along with the key to his apartment.

By the next morning, as Mueller was preparing to leave Washington for Yemen, the FBI had traced the car to a dealer in Bridgeport, Connecticut. The investigation was going well enough, and the Yemen visit was deemed sufficiently important, that Mueller proceeded, leaving Deputy Director John Pistole and others in charge. FBI and government teams were chasing leads in Pakistan, Yemen, and Afghanistan, and more experts had been pulled in to track the digital evidence. The registered owner of the Nissan Pathfinder reported that his daughter had recently sold the car on Craigslist; the telephone number of the buyer, who had paid cash and seemed to know the Connecticut area well, popped up in a government database: Faisal Shahzad. The bomber had provided the number when he had been stopped and interrogated by Customs and Border Protection officers as he returned from Pakistan earlier. The customs records turned up a photo, which confirmed that the FBI JTTF was on the right track.

As the pieces came together, what had seemed in the first hours to be the action of a lone wolf, possibly even a domestic militia group, quickly began to lead to Islamic extremists, although a group that hadn't previously been a threat domestically. The Tehrik-e-Taleban (the Pakistani Taliban) was just one of many splinter organizations of the Islamic extremist diaspora that were becoming key to the future of the movement. Within days, the first FBI investigators on Shahzad's trail would be on their way to Pakistan.

In 2009, during a visit to his parents in that country, Shahzad ventured to Waziristan, where affiliates of the T-e-T gave him five days of explosives training before dispatching him back to the United States. Officials have since speculated that the Pakistani militants didn't fully trust Shahzad, which is why he received such an abbreviated course.

594 • G ARRETT M. G RAFF

Yet at the same time they recognized the possible value of an American citizen who could move with ease through his native country. It was an unoriginal strategy. "A lot of these guys head over there because they want to wage jihad and then get turned around to come back here," a former FBI official explains.

Cell phone intercepts helped locate Shahzad, and by Monday his name had been placed on the no-fly list. FBI surveillance teams in Connecticut circled his house as the Justice Department, the Southern District U.S. Attorney's Office, and the FBI in New York and Washington debated whether to take him down. "All we knew was that we had a person of interest—not necessarily that he was the guy," Mueller's chief of staff, John Carlin, explains. "We knew he was involved in that transaction but we didn't yet know he was at the scene." As the hours passed, media leaks made the situation more urgent. The press was beginning to zero in on Shahzad, potentially tipping off the suspect. The decision was made: Snatch him at the first possible opportunity. Yet unbeknown to the surveillance teams, Shahzad, astonishingly, sneaked out of his house and made his way back to New York, where he purchased a ticket at 7:45 P.M. at JFK Airport for that flight to Dubai. Only a "last look" passenger manifest from Emirates Airlines Flight 202 tipped off authorities that he was on the plane, so that agents could thwart his escape and take him into custody, thus avoiding a public relations disaster like the successful international escapes of Mario Buda and Ramzi Yousef.★

And so ended a particularly long day in the age of global terror. Each development, beginning with the drone attack in North Waziristan, continuing through a Mumbai courtroom, a palace in Sana'a, Yemen,

---

★After his arrest, Shahzad was interrogated by the FBI's specialized new High-Value Detainee Interrogation Group, or HIG, which had finally gotten off the ground since the Christmas Day bombing attempt. When the agents began questioning him, he first had a question for them: "Why didn't my bomb work?" A later FBI recreation of Shahzad's bomb, which was exploded in secret in Pennsylvania in June to aid prosecutors, demonstrated that if the bomb had been successful, it would probably have been far deadlier than the Oklahoma City bombing of 1995.

and an aborted bombing plot in Times Square, illustrated the challenges facing counterterrorism officials and Barack Obama's presidency: plots stretching from the mountains of Pakistan, one of the most rural places in the world, aimed at the heart of the third and fifth most populous cities on earth; plots aided by the internet; plots conducted by homegrown radicals and "franchises" of al-Qaeda, which have been increasingly prevalent in recent years. As one intelligence official explains, "None of these cases is alike, but none are dissimilar either. You've got the year of the Somalis and Mumbai, followed by the year of the internet radicals, followed by the year of the Yemenis and Anwar al-Awlaki. Every month, there's another one, pulsing out."

The various plots also illustrated the two main tools of justice available to the U.S. government: handcuffs and Hellfires. If the FBI could get its hands on a seemingly valuable terrorist, it was happy to put handcuffs on him; if it couldn't, the CIA was happy to assassinate him.

When, a few weeks after his arrest, Shahzad arrived in U.S. District Court in Manhattan to plead guilty, he was clear about his motives. "I consider myself a mujahid, a Muslim soldier," he told Judge Miriam Cedarbaum in the same building that had seen terror trials dating back to the 1980s. "I want to plead guilty and I'm going to plead guilty a hundred times over, because until the hour the U.S. pulls its forces from Iraq and Afghanistan and stops the drone strikes in Somalia and Yemen and in Pakistan and stops the occupation of Muslim lands and stops killing the Muslims and stops reporting the Muslims to its government, we will be attacking the U.S., and I plead guilty to that."

One day done. So many more to come.

EPILOGUE
The Next Threat

Our job, if we're going to do it, comes with uncertainty. We've got to play in the gray.
— *FBI agent, discussing the global challenges in 2010*

The tenth anniversary of the 9/11 attacks began like so many other mornings for Robert Mueller—with another sketchy threat looming. President Obama had convened regular meetings of his national security team in the days and hours leading up to the anniversary. Just as they did before Obama's inauguration, they had a "credible but unconfirmed" threat—a tip that emanated from a source tied to the Federally Administered Tribal Areas of Pakistan who had previously provided useful information. He warned of a car-bomb plot involving three individuals, believed to be U.S. citizens, targeting New York or Washington. Security was ramped up. The NYPD searched vehicles trying to enter Manhattan.

Each hour of the anniversary seemed an eternity, but in the end the day passed like every other day since 9/11—peacefully—and sealed an impressive record that owed much to the work of Robert Mueller's FBI: In the ten years after 9/11, not a single American civilian has been killed by a terrorist attack in the United States.

Mueller kept a low profile through the whole anniversary. He had never planned to attend any of the memorial services that day, instead doing what he often did on Sundays: working at the Hoover Building. He'd also skipped the high-profile forums, conferences, and panel discussions about the state of homeland security in the weeks leading up to the anniversary. He had never been a talker.

Bob Mueller was supposed to be playing golf by then—his ten-year term set to conclude a week before—but in the spring of 2011, President Obama had done the once unthinkable: He'd asked Congress to extend Mueller's term. An administration team led by Vice President Biden and advised by Louis Freeh had been interviewing and vetting candidates to replace Mueller for months beforehand. One by one, they eliminated the possible candidates. More than anything, the Obama administration was looking for someone who would be able to consolidate and build upon the reforms of Mueller's tenure, continuing the direction he set since 9/11.

Ten days after U.S. Navy SEALs dropped into a hidden compound in Abbottabad, Pakistan, and killed Osama bin Laden, President Obama stepped into the Rose Garden and surprised nearly everyone with his announcement. Instead of picking a new director, he wanted Congress to pass special legislation to extend Mueller's term for an additional two years. "In his ten years at the FBI," said Obama, "Bob Mueller has set the gold standard for leading the Bureau. Given the ongoing threats facing the United States, as well as the leadership transitions at other agencies like the Defense Department and Central Intelligence Agency, I believe continuity and stability at the FBI is critical at this time."

While enthusiasm on the Hill was slightly muted by what senators such as Chuck Grassley saw as a dangerous precedent—the term limit had been specifically put in place to prevent directors from gathering the political power (and blackmail material) Hoover had once collected—lawmakers quickly rallied around Mueller. In a summer marked overall by bitter partisan battles on Capitol Hill, Mueller's term extension passed the Senate by a vote of 100 to 0. Some agents grumbled at the irony of Mueller, who had enforced upon them the unpopular "five-up or out" policy, extending his tenure, but many agreed that the extension would help solidify some of the changes Mueller's term had produced.

By the end of the month, the U.S. would score a second major victory in the war on terror: Military and CIA drones in Yemen killed Anwar al-Awlaki, as well as another key leader of al-Qaeda in the Arabian Peninsula, the American propagandist Samir Khan. It was a landmark escalation of the U.S.'s preferred tools — Hellfires and handcuffs — killing two American citizens beyond the reach of traditional law enforcement. Mueller still forcefully advocated arrests and trials for terrorism suspects, but he'd years before made personal peace with al-Qaeda militants beyond his agents' grasp dying fiery deaths from drone or SEAL team strikes. That didn't mean, though, he needed to celebrate them. He hadn't been in the Situation Room the night of the bin Laden raid; the FBI still didn't condone assassinations.

Just a few hours after al-Awlaki's death, on Friday, September 30, Mueller crossed Pennsylvania Avenue to attend the installation ceremony for his former chief of staff, Lisa Monaco, as the Justice Department's new assistant attorney general for national security. He sat in the front row, beaming, as Monaco became the fourth such assistant attorney general since the division's creation under the 2005 PATRIOT Act Reauthorization. Toward the rear of the room was Mueller's new chief of staff, Aaron Zebley, the I-49 agent who had helped capture KENBOM planner Khalfan Khamis Mohamed in the South African immigration and refugee center in 2000. More than half a dozen men and women had filled Zebley's office just down the hall from Mueller's seventh-floor suite in the preceding decade.

Across town that same day, Admiral Mike Mullen, the outgoing chairman of the Joint Chiefs, was handing over the military's highest-ranking post to General Martin Dempsey, the fifth Joint Chiefs chair since the 9/11 attacks. Earlier that month, when Leon Panetta became secretary of defense, General David Petraeus took over as the CIA director, the sixth person to hold that post since Mueller began work.

All around Mueller, in fact, the musical chairs of the national security team continued. Mueller and Robert Gates had been the only two national security leaders who had carried over from the Bush administration to the Obama administration. But now Gates himself was gone, retired again and appointed that month as the new chancellor of William & Mary.

Mueller's own deputy director, Tim Murphy, a close ally in headquarters, would be retiring in just a few weeks. Sean Joyce, the executive assistant director for national security, would become Mueller's fifth deputy director.

Bob Mueller had outlasted them all. He was now the longest-serving FBI director since Hoover himself. The Bureau in many ways was now more his than Hoover's: The agent corps solidly consisted of men and women who joined during his tenure, and every executive was someone groomed and promoted under Mueller's guidance.

The General Accounting Office announced in the fall of 2011 that the FBI Headquarters was "functionally obsolete," a conclusion that no one who had worked in the Hoover Building's Brutalist environs would argue against. Listed among the pages and pages of structural complaints about the building—the lack of daylight, the leaking ceilings, the crumbling facade—was a telling statistic about just how much Mueller had reshaped the FBI: In 2001, the FBI Headquarters staff consisted of 9,700 people spread across seven buildings. By the fall of 2011, the FBI Headquarters' ranks included 17,300 employees and contractors working at forty separate sites. Effectively, the FBI's entire growth under Mueller—roughly 8,000 new personnel since 2001—had gone into expanding headquarters and its various national security components, task forces, clearinghouses, and command centers.

Mueller had been energized by the two-year extension—he had felt there was unfinished business to complete. Much of the big strategic stuff was largely under control. The computer upgrades, while still enduring setbacks, were making slow headway. The analyst corps and the Bureau's foreign-language capabilities, while nowhere close to as good as they should have been, were improving. The FBI's intelligence capability, having learned how the NSA and the CIA do intelligence work, was trying to figure out how to do its differently. The Bureau's human resources programs were under way, training new generations of leaders and instilling an education culture in an organization known to dislike such things.

Yet what Mueller called "change fatigue" was spreading across the Bureau—the constant retraining, the new strategies, computer systems, specialties, and the boxes on the organization chart. The skills that helped agents and analysts through the first ninety years of the FBI were not the same as those that will push them through the coming years. "Morale across the Bureau in regards to Headquarters is enormously bad," one agent explains. "There's a feeling: Okay, we get it—now give us a chance to do our job," says one assistant director. During a visit to the Las Vegas Field Office in the summer of 2009, Mueller thanked the assembled agents for recently undergoing the sixteen-hour training on the FBI's new attorney general's guidelines for domestic intelligence investigations, which laid out and updated the process for noncriminal proceedings.

One agent interrupted: "It was sixteen-point-five hours, Director."

"I got it," Mueller said.

Despite the fatigue, the Bureau that Dale Watson had described as being like a slow-turning aircraft carrier a decade earlier was undeniably changing course. As Richard Thornburgh, the former attorney general who has served for years now on Mueller's director's advisory board, explains, "Under the best-case scenarios, this is a thirty-year task. Mueller won't finish it. Mueller's successor won't finish it. If we're lucky, Mueller's successor's successor will finish it. This is a generational change."

The toll of his ten years as director is visible on Mueller's face. As his onetime deputy director Bruce Gebhardt explains, "Bob has consumed himself into the FBI to make it better than it was yesterday." The stress of a thousand Oval Office meetings, some three thousand Threat Matrices, tens of thousands of briefings, scores of congressional hearings, and funerals for six agents killed in the line of duty is now etched around Mueller's eyes. As he says, "When I look ahead, threats are going to have one foot in the U.S. and one foot overseas. When I started out as a prosecutor, maybe one case in ten would intersect with someone in another state. Now in many areas it's not just other states, it's other countries. This is all about putting the Bureau in a posture of predicting the next threat."

In October 2011, Eric Holder awarded Mueller the Levi Award, one of the Justice Department's highest awards, given for "outstanding professionalism and exemplary integrity." The award was named for Edward Levi, who had stepped in after Watergate as President Ford's attorney general and is considered by most scholars and Justice Department observers as the greatest attorney general of the post-war period. For someone who had effectively spent his entire career in the Department of Justice, there could be no greater honor.

In Mueller's typical habit of eschewing public attention, he didn't attend the awards ceremony.

The death of al-Awlaki, just months after bin Laden's killing, seemed in many ways to be a final chapter in the war on al-Qaeda. The terrorist network's operational capability had been degraded by years of drone attacks, arrests, and pressure on the financial networks. Its commanders and leaders were being killed on an almost weekly basis, and al-Awlaki's and bin Laden's deaths removed the most charismatic figureheads of the movement.

Threats from terrorism will no doubt continue as they have for decades since the Munich Olympics and the hijacking of Southern Airways Flight 49. Indeed, reminders of the threat appear regularly. Even as it celebrated al-Awlaki's death, the FBI announced it had broken up an Iranian plot to assassinate the Saudi ambassador and a Massachusetts man's planned attack on the Capitol with remote-controlled airplanes. The following week, in Michigan, Umar Farouk Abdulmutallab pleaded guilty to the 2009 Christmas day bombing of Northwest Airlines Flight 253. The week after, in Somalia, Abdisalan Hussein Ali, one of the score of Somali youths from Minnesota who had left home to join the al-Shabaab terrorist group, blew himself up in an attack on African Union troops in Mogadishu, earning the dubious distinction of becoming only the third American to conduct a suicide bombing.

But after al-Awlaki, the threats seemed different: The days of chaos, of "Pizza Hut" leads, of the constant grinding threat matrices that so bedeviled men like Jim Comey and Pat D'Amuro, seemed relics of the past. The U.S. had figured out how to manage the terrorism threat matrix.

And in that maturation lay Robert Mueller's legacy.

There have been huge cases in other areas during Mueller's tenure—Enron, Global Crossing, Bernard Madoff, Russian spy rings, drug- and gang-related cases of mind-boggling complexity, more than 60,000 bank robberies, and 2,000 civil rights cases. Operation Guard-shack in the fall of 2010 saw 1,000 Bureau personnel descend on Puerto Rico to arrest 133 suspects, most of whom were police officers, on corruption and drug-smuggling charges. The Gambino crime family in New York was virtually dismantled through a series of prosecutions, and fourteen members of the "Chicago Outfit" organized crime group were indicted. In June 2011, Armenian organized crime leader Armen Kazarian became the first known "vor" — the so-called Russian thief-in-law — to be convicted of racketeering in the United States, admitting that he'd helped lead a $100 million Medicare fraud. At the same time, the Bureau's international expansion and operations continued to grow: Just weeks before the SEALs' raid on bin Laden, the FBI conducted its first raid on the ground in Somalia. Agents captured pirate leader Mohammad Shibin, who had led the ransom negotiations for four kidnapped Americans later killed by the band of pirates, and brought him back to stand trial in Norfolk, Virginia.

Some of these other cases have been notable high points for Mueller as director. "The most gratifying days are ones where a child is kidnapped and we're able to help return that child to its family," he reflects. "The days where agents, with their tremendous resources, put their lives on the line to save others."

Russian gangsters, Wall Street con men, bank robbers, crooked government officials, pirates, and drug lords — all of these and more went up against Mueller's FBI, and a fair number of them were taken down by the Bureau. Perhaps they'll read this book in a prison library. Yet history books — this one included — won't likely ever focus on those cases. Counterterrorism and reform within the Bureau will be Robert Mueller's lasting impact, for better or worse.

There will be a moment when the director will exit the Hoover Building for the last time, when he no longer spends his mornings at the White House, when he can stand in the sun and work on his golf game. Robert Mueller will someday go, but the Threat Matrix will remain — evolving, changing, and shifting.

SOURCES, METHODS,
AND ACKNOWLEDGMENTS

This book is the result of more than two years of research on the modern FBI and its international counterterrorism program. I've interviewed hundreds of people who lived through the stories told in these pages, including current and former FBI agents, analysts, staff members, and executives and nearly every living FBI director. While this is obviously an FBI-centric tale, I've also interviewed people throughout the intelligence community, including officers, analysts, and executives of the CIA and the NSA, members of the military and the Department of Defense, officers, detectives, agents, and executives from Homeland Security, Customs and Border Protection, the DEA, the Secret Service, the NYPD, and the Department of Justice ("Main Justice"), including the U.S. Attorney's Offices for the District of Columbia, Eastern District of Virginia, and both the Southern and Eastern Districts of New York, as well cabinet officials and staff at the State Department, the Treasury Department, the National Security Council, the National Counterterrorism Center, Congress, the White House, and a host of other government bodies. All but three of the interviews were conducted in person, generally over the course of many hours. I interviewed many key sources multiple times, and they also helped me check facts during the writing process.

I also relied upon some 100,000 pages of books, reports, articles, and primary sources, as well as court records and FBI and government files, some of which have never been released to the public before. In five instances, I decided, after discussion, to withhold information that could compromise what the intelligence community refers to as "sources and methods." In no cases, though, have I changed any names or created composites of agents. One note on spelling: I have standardized the spelling of Osama bin Laden. The FBI traditionally spells his name Usama bin Laden and abbreviates his name as UBL. I have changed these references to the more traditional spellings, Osama and OBL, even where such spellings appear in written communications or FBI primary sources.

My reporting and writing have been very much aided by those who covered this ground before me. Newspaper and magazine reports, books, and television programs on many of the events covered in these pages greatly helped me to picture and to describe events that I never witnessed. One of the only major players in this story I didn't interview personally was John O'Neill. Luckily, his story has been well told before by Murray Weiss, in *The Man Who Warned America,* and by Lawrence Wright, in *The New Yorker.* I am indebted to the research done by both. The ACLU and Human Rights Watch have also done some impressive work obtaining (under the Freedom of Information Act) and gathering the documents related to the "enhanced interrogation" debate within the government, which has greatly increased the public understanding of the circumstances. I greatly appreciate their persistence in fighting the FOIA battle. The red tape around the Freedom of Information Act can be immensely frustrating, not to mention so slow as to be only minimally useful. For this project, I ended up having to sue the FBI and the Department of Justice to gain access to thousands of pages of files that should have been released publicly. The lawsuit is still ongoing as of 2011, but I hope that in the end it will help encourage the Bureau to change the way it processes FOIA requests relating to foreign nationals.

Throughout the book, I've done my best to recreate conversations that I did not personally hear. Anytime a source speaks in the present tense (*says, recalls, explains,* etc.), that comment represents an after-the-fact recollection made to me in an interview. Past-tense wording (*said, explained, snapped*) represents a comment spoken at the time or a written recollection later. Direct quotations from past conversations have been checked and cross-checked with as many of the sources present as possible; sometimes this has led to irreconcilable differences. For instance, in the dramatic scene at John Ashcroft's bedside in March 2004, sources present in the room recall Bob Mueller saying, "There comes a time in every man's life when God tests him, and tonight you passed your test." Mueller himself refused to speak about the circumstances, except to say that he does not believe it likely that he used the word *God,* since that's not a formulation he normally uses. After discussing the conversation with multiple sources close to the director and the situation in the room, I felt that indeed it doesn't seem in character for Mueller to use the specific *God* phrasing. Thus, in this account, I have him simply say, as one source reported to me, "There comes a time in every man's life when he is tested, and tonight you passed your test."

I have tried, whenever possible, to correct the historical record. There's an almost mythic story now, repeated in Weiss's book and Lawrence Wright's otherwise masterful *The Looming Tower,* that John O'Neill insisted that the U.S. Air Force repaint a transport jet in order to smuggle Ramzi Yousef out of Pakistan and that the air force billed O'Neill $12 million for the mission. Neither part of the story is true, as far as I could determine. As I write in these pages, Yousef was actually flown out of Pakistan on board a private corporate jet lent to the FBI; the air force did not transport Yousef, let alone send O'Neill a multimillion-dollar bill afterward.

Beyond that specific example, heat-of-the-moment reporting is often hindered by incomplete information. Thus, even as I relied on contemporaneous accounts, I tried to re-report as much as was possible years or even decades after the fact. The writers of many contemporaneous accounts did not have access to all subsequently available information; reports, interviews, and transcripts that became available later helped to inform events further. Many times I found inconsistencies or inaccuracies in real-time reporting, as subsequent histories with access to more information will no doubt find in this book. The Kansas City Massacre, for instance, is a great example of how later work has reshaped the view of what actually happened.

For instance, while many contemporaneous articles about Pan Am 103 noted an anecdote that Buck Revell had a son who was supposed to have been on board the plane but had changed flights at the last minute, I was able to confirm that the anecdote was entirely false.

Chris Revell was never scheduled to be on board Pan Am 103 and had in fact returned to the United States from Germany weeks before. Initial reports about the capture of the hijackers of the *Achille Lauro* have U.S. Navy SEALs effecting the capture, yet subsequent time has clarified that it was in fact Delta Force commandos in Sicily who captured the terrorists. At the time of the capture, the U.S. government did not officially acknowledge the existence of Delta Force.

I have done my best to double-check as many of the facts contained here as possible. Nevertheless, there are sure to be errors and mistaken memories in this book. Those are my fault alone. If, as a reader, you notice any, please e-mail me at threatmatrix@garrettgraff .com so that they can be corrected in future editions.

This book would never have happened without Mike Kortan, the Bureau's longtime public affairs agent, who despite being promoted to assistant director in the midst of this project still returned all of my calls and all but one of my e-mails promptly for over two years. I know he did a great deal of advocating for this project behind the scenes while performing all of his other day jobs; I hope he doesn't regret taking my first call in the spring of 2008 and agreeing to help. I am also appreciative of the logistical help I received for over two years from staffers in the Bureau's Office of Public Affairs, including but not limited to Ann Todd, Jeff McCrehan, Ken Hoffman, Shauna Dunlop, Debra Wieerman, Kate Schweit, Lindsay Godwin, Denise Ballew, Anne Beagan, and Ernest Porter, among many others. Before John Miller left for the DNI's office, he was also a big help. The Bureau's historian, John Fox, was helpful in answering some particularly random inquiries.

I also owe very special thanks to Robert Mueller, who, despite his own lack of interest in this project, acceded to it. I know he enjoyed very little of this process—he genuinely prefers never to speak to a member of the press—yet he spoke (mostly) freely with me over a period of two years over dozens of hours we spent together. I did come to know well, though, the way that he'd fix me in the eye after I asked a question and say with steel in his voice, "I'm not going to discuss that with you." Nearly all of his current and former staff at the

FBI, as well as most of the senior executives, contributed at one point or another as well, sharing recollections, opinions, and context with me. Even his protective detail chipped in good-naturedly to help me clean up after a motorcade mishap in Jacksonville, Florida.

Beyond the seventh floor of the Hoover Building, scores of FBI staffers, analysts, agents, and executives, current and retired, gave freely of their time for this project, including days, nights, weekends, early mornings, and late-night phone calls. Some let me invade their homes for hours on end; others wrote me lengthy e-mails to fill in context, digging through old reports, files, and evidence to answer questions and jog memories; others drove me around, taking me to the key sites of old cases. Still others provided personal videos, photos, and journals to aid me in my study. None of them had to, and some were downright reluctant, yet they all answered as many of my questions and pesky follow-ups as they legally could. Fred Stremmel, who understood the history of the Bureau's counterterrorism program better than perhaps anyone else and was incredibly generous with his time, was a tremendous resource. Many of the Bureau sources I interviewed are named in this book; some are not, by coincidence or by design. They are all to be thanked. Among those to whom I can offer more specific public thanks, Leo Taddeo, Alfredo Principe, and the Italian National Police were gracious hosts in Palermo, Sicily, and Neil Mathison, Mike Bobbitt, Amy Stewart, and Attila Szaniszlo showed me around Budapest and granted me access to their world. Former hostage negotiator and New York JTTF agent Christopher Voss was hugely helpful. At Quantico, I'm grateful to James Yacone, the head of the Hostage Rescue Team, for repeatedly granting me access to HRT operators despite his own inclinations. Several former Bureau officials were particularly helpful in reviewing early drafts and bouncing around ideas; I'm in debt to their insights.

Beyond the Bureau, I'm grateful to all of the sources and advisers I leaned on in the U.S. government, the diplomatic and intelligence communities, and nearly a dozen governments around the world. By request, most of them are not named in this book, yet many will see their contributions here. Ben Wittes at the Brookings Institution and Michael Jacobson, then at the Washington Institute, were both extremely helpful in developing my thinking on various parts of this project. My dear friend and colleague Shane Harris, who is one of the country's leading observers of the intelligence community, has been a huge help. My lawyer, Mark Zaid, muckraker that he is, was helpful in navigating the frustrating bureaucracy that is FOIA and working through the lawsuit that we ended up filing to gain access to some of the Bureau's historical records. The information that grew out of the lawsuit provided rich context and important background that never would have surfaced otherwise.

I greatly appreciate the support of *The Washingtonian*'s publisher, Cathy Merrill Williams, who gave me great freedom to pursue this project and never once questioned my random reporting absences and trips away from the office. The Merrill family has been a faithful steward of the magazine for more than three decades and is one of the last media owners in the country to see a publication like ours as first and foremost a public trust. This book owes much to their view that journalism is a public service. Jack Limpert, in whose enormous footprints I now follow at the magazine, filled in for me while I was gone, supported me, and has taught me just about everything I know about my day job; Ken Decell kept everything moving flawlessly without complaint. Thanks as well to the rest of my fantastic colleagues at the magazine, who tolerated my being distracted by this project, especially Sherri Dalphonse, Bill O'Sullivan, Denise Wills, and Mike Leister. Fact-checker extraordinaire Michael J. Gaynor helped me avoid some embarrassing mistakes (those errors that remain, though, are of course my fault alone).

There's also a long list of people who have been critical to my being who and where I am today. Among them: Charlotte Stocek, Mary Creeden, Mike Baginski, Rome Aja, Kerrin McCadden, and Charlie Phillips; John Rosenberg, Richard Mederos, Brian Delay, Peter J. Gomes, Stephen Shoemaker, and Jennifer Axsom; Kit Seeyle, Pat Leahy, Rusty Grieff, Paul Elie, Tom Friedman, and, not least of all, Cousin Connie, to whom I owe a debt that I strive to repay each day. My parents, Chris and Nancy Price Graff, have encouraged me to write since I was a child, instilling in me a love of history and research and an intellectual curiosity that benefits me daily. My mother is the most thorough line editor I've ever been blessed to have.

Thanks also to Adrian, Heather, Gigi, Jenna, Vanessa, and the rest of the crew at Tryst, who served me coffee and croissants each morning as I wrote. This is the second book that I've written sitting at the coffeehouse's beat-up wooden tables.

My very deepest thanks go to Erin Delmore, the spunky Georgetown grad I recruited to help me with my research and reporting and who was my partner during many of the long interviews and road trips. She compiled, sorted, and processed the enormous stacks of research files, reports, records, photos, and interview notes; tallied expenses; filed FOIA requests; gathered photos; tracked down sources; and helped me stay generally organized. At twenty-four, Erin has already gathered one of the best Rolodexes of counterterrorism experts and Pakistani law enforcement sources ever assembled. Erin, you made this book possible; I can't wait to see your own works down the road.

My agents, Tim Seldes and Jesseca Salky, were encouraging and helpful as usual. At Little, Brown, my editor, Geoff Shandler, who helped conceive of this idea and whose enthusiasm for it was infectious even as it spun far beyond its original form, provided an awe-inspiring edit that brought order and flow to the narrative, making the book indubitably better and more pleasurable to read. Geoff's assistant, Liese Mayer, cheerfully helped and edited as well.

Finally, thanks to Katherine, who without complaint allowed me to give this project every free moment I had for two years and cheered me on through it all, although she did say at one point, "How about after this one you take some time off before the next book?"

Katherine, I apologize in advance: I've already started the next one.

NOTES

INTRODUCTION: Public Enemy #1

- The "FBI Pledge for Law Enforcement Officers," instituted by J. Edgar Hoover, was created in 1937 by Hugh H. Clegg, then the assistant director of the FBI's Training Division. First printed in the December 1937 issue of the *FBI Law Enforcement Bulletin*, it was, Hoover explained, "for the voluntary consideration, acceptance, execution, and adherence by all law enforcement officers." All FBI agents were required to sign the pledge until its use was discontinued in September 1980. The violation of this pledge was held up in the government's prosecution of Robert Hanssen as one of the stipulations he violated. History of the pledge is from John Kleinig and Yurong Zhang, *Professional Law Enforcement Codes: A Documentary Collection*, Westport (Conn.): Greenwood Publishing, 1983; Hanssen history is from "Affidavit in Support of Criminal Complaint, Arrest Warrant, and Search Warrants," *U.S. v. Robert Hanssen*, 01-188-A, July 3, 2001.

- Details of the drone strike on Usama al-Kini and Sheik Ahmed Salim Swedan are drawn from Bill Roggio and Alexander Mayer, "Senior al Qaeda and Taliban leaders killed in US airstrikes in Pakistan, 2004–2010," http://www.longwarjournal.org/pakistan-strikes-hvts.php (accessed August 23, 2010). The FBI's Most Wanted Terrorist list is available at http://www.fbi.gov/wanted/terrorists/fugitives.htm.

- Al-Shabaab, see "Designation of al-Shabaab as a Foreign Terrorist Organization," U.S. State Department, February 26, 2008, in *Federal Register*: Vol. 73, Number 53, Department of State, Public Notice 6136; also Stephanie Hanson, "Backgrounder: Al Shabaab," Council on Foreign Relations, February 27, 2009.

- Details of the inaugural day threat and the government's response are pulled from reporting and Martha Joynt Kumar, "The 2008–2009 Presidential Transition Through the Voices of Its Participants," *Presidential Studies Quarterly*, Vol. 39, Issue 4, December 2009, pp. 823–858. Obama's reaction to the threat is pulled from Alter, *The Promise*, pp. 101–102.

- Powers quote from Richard Gid Powers, *Secrecy and Power: The Life of J. Edgar Hoover*, p. 135.

- For the history of the Union Station Massacre, see Robert Unger's impressive piece of investigative reporting, *The Union Station Massacre: The Original Sin of J. Edgar Hoover's*

FBI. The best sources for the early founding of the Bureau—the myths and the realities as Hoover saw them—are Don Whitehead's 1956 *The FBI Story* and Fred Cook's 1964 *The FBI Nobody Knows.* Whitehead's book had the official blessing of Hoover. The most thorough history of the FBI under Hoover is Sanford Ungar's 1976 effort, *FBI: An Uncensored Look Behind the Walls.* The FBI's own historian, John Fox, has also traced the early debate over the creation of the Bureau in "The Birth of the Federal Bureau of Investigation," July 2003, available at http://www.fbi.gov/libref/historic/history/artspies/artspies.htm (accessed August 23, 2010).

- Details of the FBI's case in Antarctica are available at http://www.fbi.gov/page2/july03/071803backsp.htm (accessed August 23, 2010).

- Freeh's instruction to Griglione is from Freeh, *My FBI,* p. 174.

- Ashcroft's relations with the FBI, confirmed through multiple author interviews, is also told in Shenon, *The Commission,* pp. 240–249.

- For more details on the Jeddah suicide bombing see "Prince Muhammad bin Nayef slightly injured in terrorist attack," August 28, 2009, available at http://www.saudiembassy.net/latest_news/news08280901.aspx (accessed August 23, 2010); for more details of the Yemen attack see Sudarsan Raghavan, "British ambassador to Yemen escapes assassination attempt by suicide bomber," *Washington Post,* April 27, 2010.

- Further details and color of the overnight threat-tracking process in the U.S. government is available in Laura Blumenfeld, "Up All Night," *Washington Post,* July 4, 2010.

- The FBI's "Hottest Employers" designation comes from Francesca Di Meglio, "Dream Jobs: College Students Get Real," *BusinessWeek,* April 30, 2010. Mueller's joke is from his commencement address to the Duke University College of Law, Durham, North Carolina, May 15, 2010, available at http://www.fbi.gov/pressrel/speeches/mueller051510.htm (accessed August 23, 2010).

- Senator Jeff Sessions's story from Robert Mueller's 2001 Senate confirmation hearing is from Senate Judiciary Committee, *Confirmation Hearing on the Nomination of Robert S. Mueller, III, to be Director of the Federal Bureau of Investigation,* Senate Hearing 107-514, July 30–31, 2001.

- Palmer bombing from Whitehead, *The FBI Story,* p. 39.

- Information on Daniel Andreas San Diego is from Terry Frieden, "Animal rights activist on FBI's 'Most Wanted Terrorists' list," CNN, April 21, 2009, available at http://edition.cnn.com/2009/CRIME/04/21/fbi.domestic.terror.suspect/ (accessed August 23, 2010).

Chapter 1: *1972*

- *Wonder Years* quote is from *The Wonder Years,* "New Years," episode 104, Season 6, original airdate January 6, 1993.

- The "leap second" history is from the International Earth Rotation and Reference Systems Service (IERS.org).

- Hoover, one of the most fascinating characters of American history, has been the subject of many biographies. The two best are Richard Gid Powers, *Secrecy and Power: The Life of J. Edgar Hoover,* and Athan G. Theoharis and John Stuart Cox, *The Boss: J. Edgar Hoover and the Great American Inquisition.*

- Details of Hoover's final trip to New York were reconstructed from his phone logs with the help of FBI historian John Fox; details of the World Trade Center's opening are from "WTC Timeline," available at http://www.wtc.com/about/wtchistory-wtc-timeline (accessed August 23, 2010).

- The quote from *New York Times* architectural critic Ada Louise Huxtable is pulled from "Jacob K. Javits Federal Office Building," http://www.nyc-architecture.com/SCC/SCC032.htm (accessed August 23, 2010).

- Details of Hoover's funeral are pulled from the memorial tribute volume assembled by the U.S. Congress, as well as "The Long Reign of J. Edgar Hoover," *Time,* May 15, 1972; Richard Nixon, "Eulogy Delivered at Funeral Services for J. Edgar Hoover," May 4, 1972, available at http://www.presidency.ucsb.edu/ws/index.php?pid=3397 (accessed August 23, 2010).

- Reactions to his death and remembrances of J. Edgar Hoover were taken from "Memorial Tributes to J. Edgar Hoover," U.S. Senate 93-68.

- Hoover quote is from Jack Anderson, "The Director," *The New Yorker,* September 25, October 2, and October 9, 1937.

- Story of replacing Hoover is from James Phelan, "Hoover's FBI," *Saturday Evening Post,* September 25, 1965.

- Lyndon Johnson quote from "Remarks Honoring J. Edgar Hoover on His 40th Anniversary as Director, Federal Bureau of Investigation," Washington, D.C., May 8, 1964, available at http://www.presidency.ucsb.edu/ws/index.php?pid=26236 (accessed August 23, 2010).

- Roman emperor joke from Felt, *The FBI Pyramid,* p. 200.

- The story of Gray's brief (troubled) tenure as acting FBI director is told in his memoir, *In Nixon's Web,* as well as Ungar, *FBI,* and Felt, *The FBI Pyramid.*

- The tragedy of the Munich Olympics is best reported in Simon Reeve's book *One Day in September;* as well as E. J. Kahn, "Letter from Munich," *The New Yorker,* September 16, 1972; and Alexander Wolff, "Munich 1972: When the Terror Began," *Time,* August 25, 2002.

- The CIA's first terrorism report is from Naftali, *Blind Spot,* p. 55.

- The hijacking of Southern Airways is primarily recreated from Captain William R. Haas's memoir of the experience, with Ed Blair, *Odyssey of Terror,* as well as Joseph Blank, "We're Taking Over This Plane! And Let's Not Have Any Heroes," in *Reader's Digest's People in Peril;* further details are from Haas's testimony at Congressional Hearing, "Anti-Hijacking Act of 1973," Feb.–March 1973, Serial No. 93-9; as well as 152 pages of FBI documents released under the Freedom of Information Act, and author interviews.

- FAA quote is from Naftali, *Blind Spot,* p. 22.

- Kennedy terrorism use from Naftali, *Blind Spot,* p. 18.

- FAA passenger screening history from Naftali, *Blind Spot,* p. 66

- Felt quote is from *The FBI Pyramid,* p. 12.

- Hoover Law Day quote from "Message from the Director to All Law Enforcement Officials," May 1, 1972, as printed in "Memorial Tribute," U.S. Senate, p. 145.

- TRIBOM investigation is from author interviews and Associated Press, "US agency helped uncover 1973 NYC plot to kill Golda Meir," February 3, 2009.

Chapter 2: *COINTELPRO*

- For more on the FBI's tumultuous 1970s in the years after Hoover's death, there are three main sources: L. Patrick Gray III's memoir, *In Nixon's Web,* written with his son more than thirty years later, which outlines his view of the Nixon years and includes some historically useful Nixon tape transcripts and other primary sources as context; Clarence Kelley's *The Story of an FBI Director* is probably the most honest and conversational memoir of any FBI director. W. Mark Felt chronicled his career in 1979 with the memoir *The FBI Pyramid;* after he was outed as the Watergate source of Bob Woodward and Carl Bernstein, by *Vanity Fair* in a July 2005 article entitled "I'm the Guy They Called Deep Throat," he published *A G-Man's Life: The FBI, Being "Deep Throat," and the Struggle for Honor in Washington* with John O'Connor. All Felt quotations are taken from *The FBI Pyramid* unless otherwise noted. Lastly, Sanford Ungar, just a few years after Hoover's death, wrote a massive history of the Bureau entitled *FBI: An Uncensored Look Behind the Walls.* I'm indebted to his work and research from a previous generation. From a more junior level, at the time at least, Oliver "Buck" Revell records his encounters with Hoover and other Bureau leaders in *A G-Man's Journal.*

- Hoover memorial tribute from "Memorial Tributes," U.S. Senate.

- For more on the evolution of the FBI director confirmation process, see Henry B. Hogue, "Nomination and Confirmation of the FBI Director: Process and Recent History," *Congressional Research Service,* RS20963, March 17, 2005.

- Gray, "right questions," is from *In Nixon's Web,* p. 64.

- After serving as director, Kelley returned to Kansas City and opened a private investigation firm that focused on white-collar matters. David Stout, "Clarence M. Kelley, Director of F.B.I. in the '70s, Dies at 85," *New York Times,* August 6, 1997.

- Richard Gid Powers goes into great detail on COINTELPRO and other post-Hoover challenges in *Broken: The Troubled Past and Uncertain Future of the FBI.*

- Marquise is from author interviews.

- Oliver "Buck" Revell is from Revell's memoir, *A G-Man's Journal,* as well as author interviews.

- Felt is from CBS News, *Face the Nation*, August 30, 1976. Felt and Miller eventually became the highest-ranking FBI officials ever to be convicted of a crime. Both were pardoned by President Reagan in the midst of their appeals.

- Allan Kornblum biography is from Patricia Sullivan, "Allan Kornblum dies; wrote key parts of surveillance act," *Washington Post*, February 15, 2010; Rick Bragg, "Ex-FBI Agent Testifies of Bloody Time in Mississippi," *New York Times*, February 20, 2003.

- For history and more information on the Foreign Intelligence Surveillance Act of 1978, the Federation of American Scientists has compiled a hugely helpful primary source repository at http://www.fas.org/irp/agency/doj/fisa/ (accessed August 23, 2010).

- Giuliani quote is from Naftali, *Blind Spot*, pp. 92–93.

- Reagan inaugural address, January 20, 1981, from http://www.presidency.ucsb.edu/ws/index.php?pid=43130 (accessed August 23, 2010); Reagan's stance on terrorism also covered in "Message to the Congress Transmitting Proposed Legislation to Combat International Terrorism," April 26, 1984, available at www.gwu.edu/~nsarchiv/NSAEBB/NSAEBB55/nsdd138congress.pdf (accessed August 23, 2010).

- The story of the Hanafi Muslim siege of Washington in 1977 is recreated from "The 38 Hours: Trial of Terror," *Time*, March 21, 1977, as well as author interviews and FOIA documents.

- Details of the founding of the Hostage Rescue Team are taken from author interviews as well as Danny Coulson, *No Heroes: Inside the FBI's Secret Counterterror Force*, and Christopher Whitcomb, *Cold Zero: Inside the FBI Hostage Rescue Team*.

- Beirut bombing is from Naftali, *Blind Spot*, p. 129, and Mike Davis, *Buda's Wagon*, p. 78.

CHAPTER 3: *The Pizza Connection*

- Gray poem is from *Thomas Gray, Elegy Written in a Country Churchyard and Other Poems*, New York: Robert Carter and Brothers, 1853, p. 21.

- For those so inclined, Sicily's fascinating history is well worth further examination. I recommend Giuseppe Di Lampedusa, *The Leopard: A Novel* (trans. Archibald Colquhoun), New York: Pantheon, 2007; as well as Peter Robb, *Midnight in Sicily: On Art, Food, History, Travel and la Cosa Nostra*, New York: Picador, 2007. The struggles of Americans there during World War II—including General Patton's own exile—are traced thoroughly in Rick Atkinson, *Day of Battle: War in Sicily and Italy, 1943–1944* (Volume Two of The Liberation Trilogy), New York: Henry Holt and Co., 2007.

- The tragic and inspiring story of Giovanni Falcone is told masterfully in Alexander Stille's *Excellent Cadavers: The Mafia and the Death of the First Italian Republic*, one of the only books I encountered in this project that could rightly be called literature. Stille captures in rich detail the daily struggle that was the fight of Falcone and his brave compatriots. I cannot recommend his book strongly enough. For understanding of Falcone, I'm also grateful to the agents and officers from the Italian National Police for showing me around in Sicily, as well as the FBI's Alfredo Principe.

- The vast majority of the FBI side of the Pizza investigation comes from author interviews with key participants in the FBI, the Justice Department, and the U.S. Attorney's offices. I supplemented these interviews with Ralph Blumenthal's *Last Days of the Sicilians: At War with the Mafia;* James Jacobs, Christopher Panarella, and Jay Worthington, *Busting the Mob: United States v. Cosa Nostra;* and Claire Sterling, *Octopus: The Long Reach of the International Sicilian Mafia.* Sterling did an excellent job piecing together the Mafia story at a time when very few were paying any attention. As background, the FBI issued its own report on "The Sicilian Mafia and Its Impact on the United States" in 1986.

- Details of the trial are taken from Shana Alexander's saga of the trial, *The Pizza Connection: Lawyers, Money, Drugs, Mafia,* as well as author interviews and court records.

- Freeh comments at Quantico Falcone memorial dedication are from http://www.fbi .gov/page2/may06/falcone051706.htm (accessed August 23, 2010).

- The nefarious influence of the Camorra in the region around Naples is told in Roberto Saviano, *Gomorrah,* New York: Farrar Straus and Giroux, 2007. Saviano, a crusading Italian journalist, was placed under police guard after the book was published originally in Italy. It was also made into a documentary movie, directed by Matteo Garrone and released in 2008, which won a Golden Globe for best foreign film.

- The Bureau's tangled history with organized crime under Hoover, beginning with the Apalachin raid, is told in Ungar, *The FBI,* as well as Powers, *Secrecy and Power.*

- Pistone's time as an undercover agent is recounted in his now famous 1987 memoir, *Donnie Brasco: My Undercover Life in the Mafia* (New York, NAL), which a decade later was made into a movie starring Al Pacino and Johnny Depp.

- Commission trial details and quotations from Chertoff, "Prosecution Rebuttal Summation," *Busting the Mob,* p. 125.

- Giuliani quote from Arnold Lubasch, "U.S. Convicts Eight as Members of Mob Commission," *New York Times,* November 20, 1986.

CHAPTER 4: *Operation Goldenrod*

- Reagan and Libya from Ronald Reagan, "Address to the Nation on the United States Air Strike Against Libya," Washington, D.C., April 14, 1986; Qaddafi quote and general history on Libya–U.S. tensions is from Brian Lee Davis, *Qaddafi, Terrorism, and the Origins of the U.S. Attack on Libya,* New York: Greenwood, 1990, p. 186.

- Takeover of *Achille Lauro* is from William E. Smith, John Borrell, and Dean Fischer, "Terrorism: The Voyage of the *Achille Lauro*," and "Terrorism: The U.S. Sends a Message," both *Time,* October 21, 1985, as well as John Tagliabue, "Ship Carrying 400 Seized; Hijackers Demand Release of 50 Palestinians in Israel," *New York Times,* October 9, 1985; Robert Cullen, Rod Nordland, and Theodore Stanger, "Cruising on a Murderous

Cruise," John Walcott et al., "You Can Run But You Can't Hide," and "Getting Even," all *Newsweek,* October 21, 1985. Additional information on *Achille Lauro* is available from Ralph Blumenthal, "Hijacking at Sea: The Achille Lauro, Over Half-a-Century, A Series of Crises and Mishaps," *New York Times,* October 9, 1985.

• Revell's role in the *Achille Lauro* is from *A G-Man's Journal* and author interviews.

• The reaction of the Italian government to the *Achille Lauro* hijacking is explained well in "Italy's Government Is Hijacked," *The Economist,* October 19, 1985. Noesner's role is covered in Noesner, *Stalling for Time,* p. 58.

• Early counterintelligence history and Percy Foxworth from Naftali, *Blind Spot,* pp. 5–8.

• The story of Fawaz Younis's capture is pieced together from a half dozen author interviews, as well as Steven Emerson, "Operation GOLDENROD: The inside story behind the capture of the first terrorist overseas to be brought back to America to stand trial," *Penthouse,* May 1989, p. 38. Revell's *A G-Man's Journal* relates the story, as does Duane "Dewey" Clarridge's memoir, *A Spy for All Seasons,* which chronicles the incident from the CIA's perspective.

• Mughniyeh death from "U.S. Hails Hezbollah Leader's Death," *BBC News,* February 13, 2008, available at http://news.bbc.co.uk/2/hi/7244072.stm (accessed August 23, 2010).

• Meese quote from Kenneth Noble, "Lebanese Suspect in '85 Hijacking Arrested by the F.B.I. While at Sea," *New York Times,* September 18, 1987.

• Younis court proceedings from Lee Hockstader, "Hijacking Confession Is Admissable," *Washington Post,* October 15, 1988.

• Operation Just Cause, the U.S. invasion of Panama, and the trial of Manuel Noriega is a fascinating lost chapter of recent U.S. history. Many of the questions that surfaced after 9/11—the detention of foreign defendants, the use of military power to pursue criminals, and the mixing of the political state and criminal enterprise first emerged in the complicated relationship between Noriega, the DEA, the CIA, and the U.S. government. His case also showed just how hard it could be to figure out what to do with such criminals once their sentences were served—a lesson Barack Obama learned in his first year as president while dealing with Guantánamo Bay. Noriega's U.S. prison sentence wrapped up in September 2007 and yet for nearly three years, the onetime dictator continued to languish in a U.S. prison until the country figured out what to do with him. He was finally extradited to France in April 2010 to face charges of murder and money laundering.

• Quotations from Mueller, Human Rights Watch, and Noriega are from letters released under FOIA by the Department of Justice.

• CISPES accounts from "The FBI and CISPES," a report of the Select Committee on Intelligence, as well as author interviews.

• The best general interest histories I could find on the legal conundrums of wartime were Geoffrey Stone's *War and Liberty: An American Dilemma; 1790 to the Present* and Benjamin Wittes, *Law and the Long War.*

• Cohen exchange from Senate Judiciary hearing, "Oversight of the FBI," February 23, 1988.

- Bush-Revell exchange from *A G-Man's Journal*, p. 247.

- Revell-Specter exchange from Senate hearing, "Oversight of the FBI," February 23, 1988.

- The Kahane assassination is covered in John Miller et al., *The Cell*.

CHAPTER 5: *SCOTBOM*

- For more Pan Am history, there's an excellent and comprehensive website maintained at http://www.panamair.org (accessed August 23, 2010).

- For the SCOTBOM section, I am indebted to Steven Emerson and Brian Duffy's contemporaneous account of the bombing and the initial investigation, *The Fall of Pan Am 103*, which came out just about a year after the attack. The book, though, also highlights why reporting is often called the "first, rough draft of history": It ends believing that the PFLP were involved in the attack. For the Scottish perspective on the attack, London journalist David Leppard's *On the Trail of Terror*, which came out in 1991, was also very useful.

- Some information on the victims of the bombing also comes from Allan Gerson and Jerry Adler's *The Price of Terror*, which traces the victims' families' attempt to gain justice through the legal system against the Libyan government, and a soft-bound memorial book compiled about the victims, *On Eagles' Wings*.

- For a more step-by-step view of the SCOTBOM investigation, see the recent memoir of the lead FBI case agent, Richard Marquise, *SCOTBOM: Evidence and the Lockerbie Investigation*, to whom I'm indebted for his time and guidance in this chapter.

- Technical details and details from the Malta investigation also come from FBI reports on Pan Am 103, released under FOIA.

CHAPTER 6: *JTTF New York*

- The ins and outs of the 1993 World Trade Center bombing have been told very well in several previous works. Contemporaneously, three journalists—Jim Dwyer, Deirdre Murphy, and Peg Tyre—wrote *Two Seconds Under the World*, published in 1994, which puts much of the story together and is particularly vivid about the lives of people inside the towers. Later, after 9/11, three other journalists—John Miller, Michael Stone, and Chris Mitchell—wrote a longer, broader picture of the New York terror operations, *The Cell*. Peter Lance's *1000 Years for Revenge* is a slightly different interpretation; his book, thorough and well researched, goes much further than many agents and investigators involved are willing to go, hinting that Ramzi Yousef may have played a role in the bombing of the Oklahoma City Federal Building and perhaps even the crash of TWA Flight 800—both theories strongly rejected by most investigators.

- The NYPD's own post-9/11 reaction to terrorism was documented in Christopher Dickey, *Securing the City*.

- Details of the La Guardia bombing are from John Springer, "LaGuardia Christmas bombing remains unsolved 27 years later," CNN.com, December 24, 2002, available at http://archives.cnn.com/2002/LAW/12/24/ctv.laguardia/ (accessed August 23, 2010).

- John O'Neill's story has been told well twice before: Murray Weiss, *The Man Who Warned America,* and Lawrence Wright, "The Counter-Terrorist," *The New Yorker,* January 14, 2002.

- The New Afrikan Freedom Fighters bust description and the Laster quote are from Brent L. Smith, *Terrorism in America: Pipe Bombs and Pipe Dreams,* Albany: State University of New York Press, 1994, p. 108.

- Emad Salem's saga is told in Peter Lance, *1000 Years for Revenge,* as well as in Miller et al., *The Cell,* which has Neil Herman as a main figure. The version told here also incorporates author interviews.

- The initial response to the World Trade Center is from author interviews and Dwyer et al., *Two Seconds Under the World.*

- Priscilla Painton, William Mader, and Thomas Sancton, "Who Could Have Done It," *Time,* March 8, 1993.

- The White quote, "I don't give a damn," is from Lance, *1000 Years for Revenge,* p. 136.

- "Did the Serbs do it?" anecdote is from Richard A. Clarke, *Against All Enemies,* p. 74.

- Ramzi Yousef's biographical details are from Simon Reeve, *The New Jackals.*

- "Witches' Brew" raid statements are from Robert McFadden, "Specter of Terror; 8 Seized as Suspects in Plot to Bomb New York Targets and Kill Political Figures," *New York Times,* June 25, 1993.

- William Sessions's trials and tribulations as director of the FBI are told best in Ronald Kessler's work *The Bureau,* which broke many of the allegations against Sessions. See also Chuck Conconi and Harry Jaffe, "Bill and Alice in Wonderland," *The Washingtonian,* March 1993.

- Barr's reaction to Sessions is from "Excerpts from Barr's Memorandum to Sessions," *New York Times,* January 20, 1993.

- Much has been written about Waco and Ruby Ridge, the two domestic debacles that came to define the 1990s for the FBI, and some accounts are more reliable than others. Richard Gid Powers, *Broken,* is a good source, as is Kessler, *The Bureau;* for the Bureau's own perspective, through the eyes of HRT, see Christopher Whitcomb, *Cold Zero,* or Danny O. Coulson and Elaine Shannon, *No Heroes.*

- Clinton's search for Louis Freeh is covered in James Carney, Sharon Epperson, and Elaine Shannon, "The Squeaky Clean G-Man," *Time,* August 2, 1993.

- Freeh's memoir, *My FBI,* is the best source on his career and life. Although the book became a bestseller among Bureau personnel and there were huge lines for Freeh's signings around the country, the title rankled many agents who served with Freeh: "Your FBI? What about the rest of us?"

- Freeh's "intelligence bases" quote is from David A. Vise, *The Bureau and the Mole,* p. 143.

- No one has told the story of the rise of bin Laden and al-Qaeda better than Lawrence Wright, who won the 2007 Pulitzer Prize for Nonfiction for *The Looming Tower*.

- In a then secret 1995 FBI analysis, FBI agents labeled "Ramzi Yousef: A New Generation of Sunni Islamic Terrorists." The analysis continued, "Those involved in the WTC bombing and a second group of extremists who plotted to bomb other landmarks in New York City, including the United Nations building, did not belong to a single, cohesive organization, but rather were part of a loose group of politically committed Muslims living in the area. They were of varying nationalities including Egyptian, Sudanese, Pakistani, Palestinian, and Iraqi."

- Richard Clarke relates his view of the capture of Ramzi Yousef in *Against All Enemies;* the role of the Diplomatic Security Service in Yousef's capture is told in Samuel M. Katz, *Relentless Pursuit*.

- Khalid Sheikh is quoted in Christopher John Farley et al., "The Man Who Wasn't There," *Time,* February 20, 1995.

- The Freeh quote from Oklahoma City is from Vise, *The Bureau and the Mole,* p. 168.

- Freeh's "bomb goes off" quote is from "Terrorism in the United States," April 27, 1995, Hearing, Senate Judiciary Committee, Subcommittee on Judiciary, Terrorism, Technology, and Government Information.

- The incredible story of Donald Hutchings and the other kidnap victims was reported by Sean Langan, "Nightmare in Paradise," *Daily Mail* (London), October 1, 1998, as well as by Ann Hagedorn, *Ransom: The Untold Story of International Kidnapping*, New York: Henry Holt, 1998.

- The Aum Shinrikyo story is from Clarke, *Against All Enemies,* p. 168.

Chapter 7: *Pax Americana*

- The epigraph is from Oliver Wendell Holmes Jr., "The Soldier's Faith," the Memorial Day address at Harvard University, in Richard Posner, ed., *The Essential Holmes: Selections from the Letters, Speeches, Judicial Opinions, and Other Writings of Oliver Wendell Holmes, Jr.,* Chicago: University of Chicago Press, 1992.

- Michael Scheuer relates his own version of his career in the CIA, including his time as leader of Alec Station, in two works written anonymously: 2003's *Through Our Enemies' Eyes: Osama Bin Laden, Radical Islam & the Future of America* and 2004's *Imperial Hubris,* both published by Potomac Books. Scheuer is also a main character in Lawrence Wright, *The Looming Tower.*

- Jamal "Junior" al-Fadl's existence and key role in America's knowledge of al-Qaeda was first reported five years after 9/11 by Jane Mayer in "Junior: The Clandestine Life of America's Top Al Qaeda Source," *The New Yorker,* September 11, 2006.

- O'Neill's early life is taken from Murray Weiss, *The Man Who Warned America.*

- The battle for Somalia is told masterfully in Mark Bowden, *Black Hawk Down*.

- The exact outline of the conversation between O'Neill and Freeh on the flight back from Saudi Arabia is disputed. Wright relates the version here in *The Looming Tower*, which I found reliable according to author interviews as well. Weiss argues that O'Neill would never have spoken to the FBI director like that.

- The Freeh quote about being "victimized" is from "FBI: Troubled House," *PBS Newshour*, April 16, 1997.

- The Bryant quote about Clinton is from Elsa Walsh, "Louis Freeh's Last Case," *The New Yorker*, May 14, 2001.

- Clinton's opinion that "Louis Freeh is a goddamn fucking asshole" is quoted in Bob Woodward, *Shadow*, p. 450.

- In an extraordinary feat of history, historian Taylor Branch privately met with President Clinton throughout his presidency to record contemporaneous observations. Branch's work, published in 2009 as *The Clinton Tapes*, provides a remarkable insight into the evolution of the Clinton presidency and what was on the president's mind. His choice words about Freeh and the FBI are on p. 443.

- Freeh's quote about "vital business" is from *My FBI*, p. 255.

- Freeh's management challenges are noted in Bruce Porter, "Running the FBI," *New York Times Magazine*, November 2, 1997; Nancy Gibbs, et al. "Under the Microscope," *Time*, April 28, 1997; Daniel Franklin, "Freeh's Reign," *American Prospect*, January 1, 2002.

- John Miller's interview of Osama bin Laden is from "Who Is Osama bin Laden?" *Frontline*, PBS, available at http://www.pbs.org/wgbh/pages/frontline/shows/binladen/who/interview.html (accessed August 23, 2010).

- Details about FBI work in Kosovo come from author interviews and Hugh Dellios, "Funeral Ends FBI's Grisly Kosovo Duty," *Chicago Tribune*, July 2, 1999; David Vise, "FBI's Expertise Gets Emotional Test in Kosovo," *Washington Post*, September 20, 1999; Michael Sniffen, "FBI Goes to Work in Kosovo Province," Associated Press, August 1, 1999; David Johnston, "Crisis in the Balkans: Atrocities; F.B.I. Investigators at Sites of 2 Mass Killings," *New York Times*, June 24, 1999; Richard Sisk, "FBI on Hunt for Killers," *New York Daily News*, June 25, 1999; Mike Boettcher, "War crime clues beneath Kosovo rubble; Atrocities 'stagger' FBI investigators," CNN, June 25, 1999, available at http://www.cnn.com/WORLD/europe/9906/25/kosovo.war.crimes/ (accessed August 25, 2010).

- The Livingston quotes are from David A. Vise, *The Bureau and the Mole*, p. 147, and David A. Vise, "New Global Role Puts FBI in Unsavory Company," *Washington Post*, October 29, 2000. The Holbrooke and Haig quotes are from Daniel Klaidman, "Special Report: The FBI's Gambit in Eastern Europe," *Newsweek*, July 11, 1994, and July 18, 1994; Michael Sniffen, "Freeh Trips Signal New Emphasis for U.S. Foreign Policymakers," Associated Press, July 5, 1994.

- The CIA in the 1990s and its struggle for relevance, staffing, leadership, and focus is covered in Timothy Weiner, *Legacy of Ashes*.

- The "Agency is adrift" quote is from John Gentry, "A Framework for Reform of the U.S. Intelligence Community," Aspin Commission on Intelligence Roles and Missions, June 6, 1995, available at http://www.fas.org/irp/gentry/index.html (accessed August 23, 2010).

- Tenet's speech is from "Tenet regrets 'slam-dunk' remark about WMDs," Associated Press, April 28, 2005.

- Taylor Branch from *The Clinton Tapes,* p. 165.

- Clinton's speech is from John Judis, "War on global terrorism was destined to fail," *Australian,* September 9, 2005.

- The Chertoff quote is from "3 Rwandan Rebels Are Arrested in 1999 Killing of 2 Americans," *New York Times,* March 5, 2003.

- Some of the search for Mughniyeh is covered in Adam Garfinkle, "Weak Realpolitik," *National Interest,* Spring 2002, p. 144.

- The Zawahiri quote is from CNN, "Egyptian doctor emerges as terror mastermind," *People in the News,* 2005, available at http://www.cnn.com/CNN/Programs/people/shows/zawahiri/profile.html (accessed August 23, 2010).

- President Bill Clinton, "Statement from the White House Following Grand Jury Testimony," August 17, 1998, is available at http://www.law.umkc.edu/faculty/projects/ftrials/clinton/clintonstatements.html (accessed August 23, 2010).

- Tenet's East Africa "slam-dunk" comment is from Clarke, *Against All Enemies,* p. 184.

- Details of Operation Delenda are from Clarke, *Against All Enemies,* p. 181.

- The Clinton quote on missile strikes is from "U.S. missiles pound targets in Afghanistan, Sudan," CNN, August 21, 1998, available at http://www.cnn.com/US/9808/20/us.strikes.02/ (accessed August 23, 2010).

- O'Neill's and Kallstrom's reactions to the missile strike are from Murray Weiss, *The Man Who Warned America,* p. 221.

- Attempts to deal with bin Laden by the CIA prior to 9/11 are told in George Tenet and Bill Harlow, *At the Center of the Storm,* in chapter 7, "Gathering Storm."

- Steve Coll's *Ghost Wars* is a must-read for anyone interested in this topic, particularly in regards to the complicated calculus of U.S.-Pakistan relations.

- The MacGaffin quote is from MacGaffin, "Spies, Counterspies, and Covert Action," in Jennifer E. Sims and Burton Gerber (eds.), *Transforming U.S. Intelligence,* 2005, p. 84.

- The story of watching bin Laden from an observation drone is from Clarke, *Against All Enemies,* p. 220. When, during a presentation by the CIA about the plan to grab him, Danny Coleman asked what chance of success the plan held, the CIA briefer was blunt: "Slim to none."

- Bin Laden's reward for U.S. assassinations is from Paul Thompson, *The Terror Timeline,* New York: HarperCollins, 2004, p. 77.

• The story of the capture and investigation of Ahmed Ressam was well reported in a seventeen-part series by Hal Bernton, Mike Carter, David Heath, and James Neff, "The Terrorist Within," *Seattle Post-Intelligencer,* June 23–July 7, 2002. Meskini's odd role in the millennium plot was covered in Lorraine Adams, "The Other Man," *Washington Post Magazine,* May 20, 2001.

• Details of the NYPD's Operation Archangel are from John Marzulli, "Secret Plan to Safeguard City Would Mobilize, Seal Site of an Attack," *New York Daily News,* December 30, 1999.

• The story of O'Neill's millennium New Year's Eve is told in Weiss, *The Man Who Warned America.*

• The Qatar details are from Clarke, *Against All Enemies,* p. 152.

• Tenet's "We are at war" memo is taken from Tenet and Harlow, *At the Center of the Storm,* p. 118; the Agency's unpreparedness is covered in David Stout and Mark Mazzetti, "Tenet's CIA Unprepared for Qaeda Threat, Report Says," *New York Times,* August 21, 2007.

• The story of O'Neill's briefcase is from Weiss, *The Man Who Warned America;* Wright, "The Counterterrorist"; and David Johnston and James Risen, "F.B.I. Is Investigating a Senior Counterterrorism Agent," *New York Times,* August 19, 2001.

CHAPTER 8: *The Wall*

• The Sun Tzu quote is from *The Art of War,* Samuel B. Griffith (trans.), New York: Oxford University Press, 1963, p. 145.

• The attack on the USS *Cole* is a terribly poorly reported story; there has been little comprehensive attention given to it by the media, as it was lost in the run-up to 9/11, but it is key to the investigation of the September 11 attack, as well as to the failed opportunities that might have led to the disruption of the plots. The best source of how it fits into the large al-Qaeda narrative was written by the 9/11 Commission in chapter 6 of its report, "From Threat to Threat." The fight to rescue the *Cole* is told in a sixty-minute documentary done by the Military Channel, "Attack on the USS *Cole.*"

• According to Wright, *Looming Tower,* it was Ali Soufan who handed out bottles of water to the Yemeni forces. My reporting leads me to believe it was in fact Special Agent Tim Clemente.

• Details of the Bodine challenges come from author interviews and from Wright, *Looming Tower,* and "FBI Agents Are Leaving Cole Probe in Yemen," *Washington Post,* November 18, 2000.

• Dina Temple-Raston's Yemen joke is from *Jihad Next Door,* p. 47.

• Galligan's recollection of the Bodine-Galligan "three grenades" exchange is from Weiss, *The Man Who Warned America,* p. 348.

- The Clinton quote about trouble with the FBI comes from Taylor Branch, *The Clinton Tapes,* p. 627.
- Sheehan's "Martians" quote is from Richard Clarke, *Against All Enemies,* p. 224.
- See "Countering the Changing Threat of International Terrorism," Report of the National Commission on Terrorism, June 7, 2000, available at http://www.gpoaccess.gov/nct/index.html (accessed August 23, 2010).
- The October 5, 2000, vice presidential debate is available at http://www.debates.org/index.php?page=october-5-2000-debate-transcript (accessed August 23, 2010). The Cheney *Cole* quote from the vice presidential debate is from "Cheney: Swift Retaliation Needed," Associated Press, October 13, 2000.
- The Clarke-Emerson exchange is from Clarke, *Against All Enemies,* p. 214.
- The Washington, D.C., murder rate comes from "District of Columbia Crime Rates, 1960–2008," at http://www.disastercenter.com/crime/dccrime.htm (accessed August 23, 2010).
- The Georgetown Starbucks murders are described in "Starbucks Affidavit," *Washington Post,* March 17, 1999, available at http://www.washingtonpost.com/wp-srv/local/daily/march99/affidavit18.htm (accessed August 23, 2010). The story of the Georgian drunk driver comes from "Ex-Diplomat Gets 7 Years for Death of Teen in Crash," Associated Press, December 20, 1997, available at http://articles.latimes.com/1997/dec/20/news/mn-531 (accessed August 23, 2010).
- The Pickard and Ashcroft stories, confirmed by author interviews, are reported in Philip Shenon, *The Commission,* p. 242.
- The Ashcroft fishing gear story is from "Ashcroft Flying High: Cabinet Members Normally Fly Commercial Airlines," *CBS News,* July 26, 2001, available at http://www.cbsnews.com/stories/2001/07/26/national/main303601.shtml (accessed August 23, 2010).
- The Robert Hanssen saga, which went on to be made into the feature film *Breach* (2007), is traced in great detail by David Vise, *The Bureau and the Mole.*
- The Durbin quote is from Gwen Ifill, "Troubled Legacy," *PBS Newshour,* July 18, 2001.
- The Ashcroft quote about Freeh is from Memorandum for the Record, 9/11 Commission, December 17, 2003, available at http://www.archives.gov/legislative/research/9-11/commission-memoranda.html (accessed August 23, 2010).
- Freeh's Khobar indictment quote is from an untitled FBI press release, June 21, 2001, available at http://www.fbi.gov/pressrel/pressrel01/khobar.htm (accessed August 23, 2010).
- Freeh's Javert-like obsession with the Khobar Towers case was reported in Elsa Walsh, "Louis Freeh's Last Case," *The New Yorker,* May 14, 2001, as well as in Vise, *The Bureau and the Mole,* and Freeh's own *My FBI.*
- The Wilma Lewis quote is from Viveca Novak and Elaine Shannon, "Washington Attorney's Office Upset as FBI Takes Away Bombing Case," *Time,* March 23, 2001.

- Ashcroft's Khobar statement is from "Khobar Towers Indictments Returned," CNN, June 22, 2001, available at http://archives.cnn.com/2001/LAW/06/21/khobar.indict ments/ (accessed August 23, 2010).

- The statistics on Louis Freeh's tenure, as well as his good-bye comments, are taken from FBI, "FBI Director Louis J. Freeh Announced Today that He Is Retiring from Federal Service after Twenty-Seven Years, Effective in June," May 1, 2001, available at http:// www.fbi.gov/pressrel/pressrel01/freeh050101.htm (accessed August 23, 2010).

- President Bush's remark to Woodward is from Bob Woodward, *Bush at War,* p. 39.

- Details of Allan Kornblum's life are from William Grimes, "Allan Kornblum, Counsel to F.B.I., Is Dead at 71," *New York Times,* February 20, 2010.

- A very helpful and thorough history of the wall is in Stewart A. Baker, *Skating on Stilts.* I have relied on author interviews as well as Baker's account to depict some of the tension between Lamberth and the Justice Department.

- The NSA classification change comes from James Bamford, *Shadow Factory,* p. 67.

- A version of the search for Mueller is told in Ronald Kessler's *The Bureau,* his post-9/11 update to his 1994 book, *The FBI.*

- The *Time* quote is from Elaine Shannon et al., "The FBI's Top Gun," *Time,* July 16, 2001.

- The Bush quote comes from "Remarks by the President in Nominating Robert S. Mueller as Director of the FBI," White House, July 5, 2001. Mueller's nomination and early days in the Bureau were covered in Peter Slevin and Dan Eggen, "FBI Nominee Lauded for Tenacity; Mueller Has Wide Support," *Washington Post,* July 30, 2001; Rebecca Carr, "Mueller Pays a Heavy Price for FBI Failures," *Atlanta Journal-Constitution,* June 23, 2002; Stacy Finz, "In the Running for FBI Director," *San Francisco Chronicle,* July 3, 2001; Dante Chinni, "A Turnaround Specialist for a Battered FBI," *Christian Science Monitor,* August 3, 2001; and Eric Lichtblau, "Mueller Brings Platoon Leader Instincts to Job," *Los Angeles Times,* July 6, 2001.

- Although Mueller is hardly mentioned in the book, his class at St. Paul's is the subject of a memoir and book by Geoffrey Douglas, *The Classmates.*

- The St. Paul's prayer book quote is from "Prayer for Courage," *The Book of Common Prayer.* At the time of Mueller's schooling, the Episcopal Church was relying on the 1928 version; the version in use today was introduced in 1979. The "Prayer for Courage" comes from *The Armed Forces Prayer Book,* developed during the Korean War as a supplement.

- Thomas E. Ricks's *Making the Corps* is perhaps the most thoughtful book on the Marine Corps culture. Also useful is Victor Krulak, *First to Fight.*

- The Thucydides quote is from *Thucydides,* translated by Benjamin Jowett, 2nd ed., Oxford, Clarendon Press, 1900, 1.84.

- Material about Kerry's Purple Heart comes from "Service Mettal," available at http:// www.snopes.com/politics/kerry/service.asp (accessed August 23, 2010). Background on Mueller's Marine service is also found in Tom Nugent, "Leatherneck Profile: Robert Swan Mueller III," *Leatherneck,* Volume 85, Number 4, April 2002, p. 20.

- The summer of 2001 is covered in the *9/11 Commission Report*.

- The Kenneth Williams memo is available at "2001 Memo Warned of Bin Laden Aviation Cadre," Smoking Gun, http://www.thesmokinggun.com/documents/crime/2001-me mo-warned-bin-laden-aviation-cadre (accessed August 23, 2010). Circumstances and background on his memo come from the *9/11 Commission Report*, p. 272.

- O'Neill's "KMA day" is described by Weiss, *The Man Who Warned America*, p. 340; his final e-mail to the *Cole* victim's family is described on p. 350.

- The missed opportunities of Khalid al-Mihdhar and Nawaf al-Hazmi are well documented in the *9/11 Commission Report*, p. 266.

CHAPTER 9: *PENTTBOM*

- The Auden quote is from Meryl Gordon, "Comfort Food," *New York Magazine*, June 3, 2002.

- O'Neill's activities on 9/11 are taken from Murray Weiss, *The Man Who Warned America*, and Lawrence Wright, "The Counter-Terrorist," *The New Yorker*, January 14, 2002.

- Clarke's e-mail to Rice is contained in the *9/11 Commission Report*, p. 212.

- A good starting point on Mount Weather's classified and unclassified role in American government is the Federation of American Scientists' resource page, available at http://www.fas.org/nuke/guide/usa/c3i/mt_weather.htm (accessed August 23, 2010).

- Richard A. Clarke relates Watson's telephone call in *Against All Enemies*, p. 13.

- The story of the September 12 meeting exchange comes from Ashcroft's memoir, *Never Again*, p. 133.

- The Ashcroft-Mueller press conference is from "Transcript from Attorney General and FBI Director News Conference," FBI Headquarters, September 14, 2001, available at http://www.justice.gov/archive/ag/speeches/2001/0914pressconference.htm (accessed August 23, 2010).

- The Camp David recounting comes from George Tenet and Bill Harlow, *At the Center of the Storm*, p. 179.

- The Zacarias Moussaoui case is discussed in depth in the *9/11 Commission Report*, p. 273.

- The anthrax letters are a fascinating and still only partially understood case. For more, see Joby Warrick, "Trail of Odd Anthrax Cells Led FBI to Army Scientist," *Washington Post*, October 27, 2008; David Freed, "The Wrong Man," *Atlantic Monthly*, May 2010; and the FBI's own comprehensive report, available at http://www.fbi.gov/anthrax/amerithrax links.htm (accessed August 23, 2010). As this book was going to press, the National Academies of Science were finishing a report on the FBI's handling of the case as well.

- O'Neill's funeral details are from author interviews and Weiss, *The Man Who Warned America*.

- The Wilkerson quote is from Jane Mayer, *Dark Side,* p. 412.

- For more on the "war council" see Yoo's memoir, *War by Other Means,* as well as Charlie Savage, *Takeover;* Jack Goldsmith, *The Terror Presidency;* Barton Gellman, *Angler;* and Mayer, *Dark Side.*

- The Wittes quote is from Benjamin Wittes, *Law and the Long War,* p. 45; Savage from *Takeover.*

- Black's "flies walking across their eyeballs" remark is from Bob Woodward, *Bush at War,* p. 52. The "gloves came off" quote is from John Barry, Michael Hirsh, and Michael Isikoff, "The Roots of Torture," *Newsweek,* May 24, 2004.

- Yoo's "foreign entity" quote is from Alex Gibney, *Taxi to the Dark Side,* 2007. The Goldsmith quote comes from Mayer, *Dark Side,* p. 70.

- Ashcroft's "inclusion" remark is in 9/11 Commission, Memorandum for Record, December 17, 2003, available at http://www.archives.gov/legislative/research/9-11/commission-memoranda.html (accessed August 23, 2010).

- More on James Comey's interesting biography was contained in a *New York* Magazine profile that ran as he prepared to move back to Washington; Chris Smith, "Mr. Comey Goes to Washington," October 20, 2003, available at http://nymag.com/nymetro/news/politics/n_9353/ (accessed August 23, 2010).

Chapter 10: *The Dogs of War*

- The Shakespeare quote is from *Julius Caesar,* Act 3, Scene 1, lines 270–275.

- The CIA's "ghost plane" network after September 11, 2001, has by now been well documented. Five key sources are Stephen Grey, *Ghost Plane;* Trevor Paglen and A. C. Thompson, *Torture Taxi;* Dana Priest, "CIA Holds Terror Suspects in Secret Prisons," *Washington Post,* November 2, 2005; Dick Marty, "Alleged Secret Detentions and Unlawful Interstate Transfers Involving Council of Europe Member States," European Commission Committee on Legal Affairs and Human Rights, June 2006, available at http://assembly.coe.int/Documents/WorkingDocs/doc06/edoc10957.htm (accessed August 26, 2010); and Dana Priest, "Jet Is an Open Secret in Terror War," *Washington Post,* December 27, 2004. Also key has been the work of Jane Mayer, best told in her book *The Dark Side.*

- Louis Freeh's "core values" are available at http://www.fbiacademy.edu/corevalues.htm (accessed August 23, 2010).

- The Baker quote is from Jack Goldsmith, *The Terror Presidency,* p. 72.

- The Tenet quote is from George Tenet and Bill Harlow, *In the Center of the Storm,* p. 232.

- The story of Vice President Cheney's "one percent doctrine" was first reported in Ron Suskind's book on the war of terror, *The One Percent Doctrine.*

- Cheney's first mention of "the dark side" was on *Meet the Press* with Tim Russert, NBC, September 16, 2001.

- Knowles's mission to Afghanistan was covered in Steven Lee Myers, "Seeking Intelligence Trove, FBI Is to Question Captured Fighters," *New York Times,* December 19, 2001; Carol Morello, "FBI Team to Question Detainees," *Washington Post,* December 19, 2001; and Carol Morello, "FBI Starts Processing Detainees in Search for Leads on Attacks," *Washington Post,* December 20, 2001.

- For the context of Mad Dog Mattis's remarks, see John Guardiano, "Breaking the Warrior Code," *American Spectator,* February 11, 2005, available at http://spectator.org/arch ives/2005/02/11/breaking-the-warrior-code/ (accessed August 23, 2010).

- Bush's claim that "Iraq has trained al Qaeda members" is from "President Bush Outlines Iraqi Threat—Remarks by the President on Iraq," Cincinnati Museum Center, Cincinnati, Ohio, October 7, 2002, available at http://georgewbush-whitehouse.archives.gov/ news/releases/2002/10/20021007-8.html (accessed August 23, 2010). Tenet's "He clearly lied" quote is from Tenet and Harlow, *At the Center of the Storm,* p. 353. The story of the Zubaydah cell phone is from John Kiraikou and Michael Ruby, *The Reluctant Spy,* p. 115.

- Zubaydah's medical treatment is covered in Tenet and Harlow, *At the Center of the Storm,* p. 241. Zubaydah's questioning and John Mitchell's role are covered in Katherine Eban, "Rorschach and Awe," *Vanity Fair,* July 2007; Michael Isikoff, "We Could Have Done This the Right Way," *Newsweek,* May 4, 2009; David Rose, "Tortured Reasoning," Vani tyFair.com, December 16, 2008, available at http://www.vanityfair.com/maga zine/2008/12/torture200812 (accessed August 23, 2010); Jason Vest, "Pray and Tell," *American Prospect,* June 19, 2005; and Jane Mayer, "Outsourcing Torture," *The New Yorker,* February 14, 2005.

- The Giglio standard comes from *Giglio v. U.S.,* 405 U.S. 150, 153-54 (1972).

- Padilla's path to terrorism was told in great detail in Deborah Sontag, "Terror Suspect's Path from Streets to Brig," *New York Times,* April 25, 2004. Also useful is Donna Newman, "The Jose Padilla Story," *New York Law School Review,* Volume 48, numbers 1 and 2, 2003 and 2004, p. 39.

- Michael Mukasey's comments on the Padilla case come from "Jose Padilla Makes Bad Law," *Wall Street Journal,* August 22, 2007.

- John Ashcroft's Padilla press conference is from "U.S. Authorities Capture 'Dirty Bomb' Suspect," CNN, June 10, 2002, available at http://archives.cnn.com/2002/US/06/10/ dirty.bomb.suspect/ (accessed August 23, 2010). His full statement is available at http:// archives.cnn.com/2002/US/06/10/ashcroft.announcement/ (accessed August 23, 2010).

- The evolution of the American legal approach to Guantánamo Bay and terrorism is told in Jonathan Mahler, *The Challenge,* as well as in Phillippe Sands, *Torture Team;* the original setup on the island and the surprising efforts the initial crew made to set up the island prison according to international law are detailed in Karen Greenberg, *The Least Worst Place.* Details of agents' living conditions at Gitmo come from Inspector General interviews, as does General Dunlavey's quote.

- Seton Hall University's Mark Denbeaux has done truly impressive work documenting and studying the detainees at Guantánamo Bay. His reports are compiled at http://law

.shu.edu/ProgramsCenters/PublicIntGovServ/policyresearch/Guantanamo-Reports
.cfm (accessed August 23, 2010).

- Wittes's "cannon fodder of international jihad" remark comes from Benjamin Wittes, *Law and the Long War,* p. 86, probably the most thoughtful book yet written on the challenges of terrorism and the American legal system.

- Most of the stories of the military interrogators have been written by those who disagree with the administration's policies and approach. A trio of memoirs by military interrogators emphasizes their proper treatment of detainees: Erik Saar and Viveca Novak, *Inside the Wire;* Chris Mackey and Greg Miller, *The Interrogators;* and Matthew Alexander and John R. Bruning, *How to Break a Terrorist.* For a sympathetic view of America's torture policy, see Marc Theissan, *Courting Disaster,* which was widely rejected by others in the field when it was published.

- The debate over Mohammed al-Qahtani's detention is covered in Jane Mayer, *The Dark Side.*

- The politics of *24* were detailed in Jane Mayer, "Whatever It Takes," *The New Yorker,* February 19, 2007.

- The FBI's specific role in the detainee interrogations is discussed at length in the 400-plus-page report produced by the Office of the Inspector General, *A Review of the FBI's Involvement in and Observations of Detainee Interrogations in Guantanamo Bay, Afghanistan, and Iraq, Special Report,* May 2008, available at www.justice.gov/oig/special/s0805/final.pdf (accessed August 23, 2010).

- Miller and Beaver in Iraq are described by Sands, *Torture Team.*

- Zelikow's "dog that didn't bark" quote is from Mayer, *Dark Side,* p. 280.

- The Ralph DiMaio quote comes from *Amnesty International et al. v. CIA et al.,* Case No. 07 Civ. 5435, U.S. District Court for the Southern District of New York, "Declaration of Ralph S. DiMaio." The Lowell Jacoby quote is from Sands, *Torture Team,* p. 135.

- President Bush is quoted by Jane Black, "Bush's Double Vision on Privacy," Business-Week.com, April 30, 2004, available at http://www.businessweek.com/technology/con tent/apr2004/tc20040430_9115_tc073.htm (accessed August 23, 2010).

Chapter 11: *Threat Matrix*

- The Asa Hutchinson story is from Eric Lichtblau, *Bush's Law,* p. 83. The exact outlines of this story differ in various accounts. Lichtblau's version has Major General Bruce Lawlor handing Hutchinson the note; other accounts have President Bush himself passing the note.

- Ashcroft's "phantoms of lost liberty" quote comes from "Ashcroft: Critics of New Terror Measures Undermine Effort," CNN, December 7, 2001, available at http://archives.cnn .com/2001/US/12/06/inv.ashcroft.hearing/ (accessed August 23, 2010).

- The Jim Rice quote comes from Toni Locy, "As FBI's Mission Has Changed Since 9/11, So Have Its Methods," *USA Today,* October 7, 2003.

- The *Palermo Senator* report comes from author interviews and Robert Mottley, Chris Gillis, and Mark McHugh, "Palermo Senator: Feat of Clay," *American Shipper,* October 2002.

- The FBI bulletin is quoted in U.S. House of Representatives, Permanent Select Committee on Intelligence, "Al Qaeda: The Many Faces of an Islamist Extremist Threat," June 2006.

- The "Ukrainian urinal incident" was first reported in Evan Thomas, "The New Age of Terror," *Newsweek,* August 21, 2006.

- George Tenet's quote about "inclination was to overbrief" comes from George Tenet and Bill Harlow, *At the Center of the Storm,* p. 236.

- The existence of Gebhardt's "I'm amazed and astounded and at a loss to understand" memo was first reported by the *New York Times*'s Eric Lichtblau and was covered in his book *Bush's Law,* p. 89.

- Mueller's exchange with Cheney is from Ron Suskind, *The One Percent Doctrine,* p. 254.

- For the Rumsfeld evidence quote, see, for instance, "Secretary Rumsfeld Press Conference at NATO Headquarters, Brussels, Belgium," June 6, 2002, available at http://www.defense.gov/transcripts/transcript.aspx?transcriptid=3490 (accessed August 23, 2010).

- The Lackawanna Six case is the subject of a very thorough book by NPR's Dina Temple-Raston, *The Jihad Next Door.* Also helpful were Matthew Purdy and Lowell Bergman, "Unclear Danger: Inside the Lackawanna Terror Case," *New York Times,* October 12, 2003; Mark Mazzetti and David Johnston, "Bush Weighed Using Military in Arrests," *New York Times,* July 24, 2009; and Lou Michel, "Lackawanna Officials Say Troops in City Was Bad Idea," *Buffalo News,* July 26, 2009.

- Mueller's testimony comes from Richard A. Clarke, "Finding the Sleeper Cells," *New York Times,* August 14, 2005.

- The story of Brad Doucette's decline was first chronicled by Greg Krikorian, "After 9/11, a Fatal 24/7," *Los Angeles Times,* May 3, 2005.

- Coleen Rowley's story was the subject of a *Time* Magazine feature by Eomesh Ratnesar et al., "How the FBI Blew the Case," June 3, 2002.

- The 9/11 Commission hearing quotations come from Philip Shenon and Eric Lichtblau, "Threats and Responses: The Inquiry; FBI Is Assailed for Its Handling of Terror Risks," *New York Times,* April 14, 2004; as well as Steven Strasser et al., *The 9/11 Investigations: Staff Reports of the 9/11 Commission; Excerpts from the House-Senate Joint Inquiry Report on 9/11; Testimony from Fourteen Key Witnesses, Including Richard Clarke, George Tenet, and Condoleezza Rice,* New York: PublicAffairs, 2004.

- "The Mueller Show" is described in Philip Shenon, *The Commission.*

- The Fitzgerald quote is from 9/11 Commission, Memorandum for Record, March 11, 2004, available at http://www.archives.gov/legislative/research/9-11/commission-memoranda.html (accessed August 23, 2010).

- Harold Ross's time as the editor of *The New Yorker,* including his proclivity for a "new Jesus," is well told in Thomas Kunkel, *Genius in Disguise: Harold Ross of the New Yorker,* Random House, 1995.

- For certain details of Maureen Baginski's tenure at the FBI, I've relied on Elsa Walsh, "Learning to Spy," *The New Yorker,* November 8, 2004, and Chitra Ragavan, "The FBI's 'Vision Lady,'" *U.S News & World Report,* September 27, 2004.

CHAPTER 12: *In the War Zone*

- The Clausewitz quote can be found in Carl von Clausewitz, *On War,* Oxford University Press, 2007, p. 46.

- More on the Wolfowitz-D'Amuro meeting is in Romesh Ratnesar, "Iraq and al-Qaeda: Is There a Link?" *Time,* August 26, 2002.

- Much of what is publicly known about the strange case of the FBI's surveillance of the Thomas Merton Center comes from an ACLU Freedom of Information Act request. The source documents from the request are available at http://www.aclu.org/national -security/aclu-releases-first-concrete-evidence-fbi-spying-based-solely -groups%E2%80%99-anti-war-vie (accessed August 23, 2010). The incident was also a key part of the Inspector General's report, "A Review of the FBI's Investigations of Certain Domestic Advocacy Groups," September 2010, available at http://www.justice.gov/ oig/special/s1009r.pdf (accessed December 23, 2010).

- The letter from Congressman Eliot Engel to Attorney General John Ashcroft, November 24, 2003, is available at http://engel.house.gov/index.cfm?sectionid=66&parentid=64& sectiontree=&itemid=555 (accessed August 23, 2010).

- The Pistole quote is taken from Dan Collins, "FBI vs. the Gray Lady," *CBS News,* November 26, 2003, available at: http://www.cbsnews.com/stories/2003/11/26/national/ main585696.shtml (accessed August 23, 2010).

- Rumsfeld's "inactionable intelligence" anecdote comes from Thomas E. Ricks, *Fiasco,* p. 32. Ricks's book is probably the best history of the Iraq invasion yet written; his 2009 sequel, *The Gamble,* chronicles the "surge" under General David Petraeus.

- The complete "Deck of Cards" is available on the Pentagon's website at http://www .defendamerica.mil/iraq/iraqi55/ (accessed August 23, 2010).

- More on the significance of the May 12, 2003, Riyadh bombing is available from Owen Bowcott and David Pallister, "'The Message Is: You're Not Safe Here,'" *The Guardian* (London), May 14, 2003.

- Sérgio Vieira de Mello's life and death are the subject of Samantha Power's biography *Chasing the Flame,* Penguin, 2008.

- The death of Special Agent Gregory Rahoi was covered by Dan Benson, "FBI Agent Killed in Training Devoted Life to Public Safety," *Milwaukee Journal-Sentinel,* December 16, 2006.

- Details of the life of Raed Al-Banna come from H. G. Reza, "Unlikely Candidate for Car Bomber," *Los Angeles Times,* April 15, 2006.

- Details of the Iraq-U.S. car theft ties come from Bryan Bender, "US Car Theft Rings Probed for Ties to Iraq Bombings," *Boston Globe,* October 2, 2005.

- Details of FBI overtime in war zones come from Office of the Inspector General, "An Investigation of Overtime Payments to FBI and Other Department of Justice Employees Deployed to Iraq and Afghanistan," December 2008, available at http://www.justice .gov/oig/special/s0812/final.pdf (accessed August 23, 2010).

- Piro's interrogation of Saddam Hussein has been covered by Scott Pelley, "Interrogator Shares Saddam's Confessions," *60 Minutes,* January 27, 2008, and by Ronald Kessler, *The Terrorist Watch.* Piro's notes from his interviews have been subsequently released and are available at http://www.gwu.edu/~nsarchiv/NSAEBB/NSAEBB279/index.htm (accessed August 23, 2010).

- Details of Nick Berg's kidnapping are from Ariana Eunjung Cha, "Tape Shows U.S. Hostage Being Beheaded in Iraq," *Washington Post,* May 11, 2004; his father's later comments to the press are from "Father of Beheaded Iraq Hostage Blames Bush Administration for Son's Death," Democracy Now, August 24, 2010, available at http://www.democracy now.org/2004/8/24/father_of_beheaded_iraq_hostage_blames (accessed August 23, 2010).

- Jill Carroll told her story in a multipart series in the *Christian Science Monitor,* available at http://www.csmonitor.com/Specials/Hostage-The-Jill-Carroll-Story (accessed August 23, 2010).

- Rick Atkinson explored the wider battle against IEDs in the *Washington Post*'s series, "Left of Boom," available at http://www.washingtonpost.com/wp-srv/world/specials/leftof boom/index.html (accessed August 23, 2010).

CHAPTER 13: *Showdown*

- The Dies quote is from 9/11 Commission Memorandum for Record, February 4, 2004, available at http://www.archives.gov/legislative/research/9-11/commission-memoranda .html (accessed August 23, 2010).

- The FBI's computer woes are well documented in a series of inspector general reports and congressional hearings. Additionally useful are John Wilke, "How Outdated Filing Hampers FBI Effort to Fight Terrorism," *Wall Street Journal,* July 9, 2002; Eric Lichtblau and Charles Piller, "War on Terrorism Highlights FBI's Computer Woes," *Los Angeles Times,* July 28, 2002; Eric Knorr, "Anatomy of an IT disaster: How the FBI blew it," *InfoWorld,* March 21, 2005, available at http://www.infoworld.com/d/developer-world/anatomy-it -disaster-how-fbi-blew-it-243 (accessed August 23, 2010); Wilson P. Dizard III, "Senators fume as FBI admits Trilogy foul-ups," *Government Computer News,* February 4, 2005; Noah Shachtman, "The Federal Bureau of Luddites," *Slate,* April 6, 2006, available at http://www.slate.com/id/2139274 (accessed August 23, 2010).

- While much has been written about the Comey-Cheney showdown over the so-called Terrorist Surveillance Program, the definitive account of the matter, thus far, is in Barton Gellman's portrait of Vice President Cheney, *Angler.* The only accounts from a participant can be found in Jack Goldsmith, *The Terror Presidency* and Comey's testimony before the Senate Judiciary Committee, "A Hearing on the U.S. Attorney Firings," May 15, 2007.

- Addington's "one bomb away" quote is from Goldsmith, *The Terror Presidency,* p. 181.

- Goldsmith's *The Terror Presidency* is, as one might expect, very instructive about how the new head of OLC approached the issue.

- Comey's remark about "no good lawyer" was first reported in Scott Shane, David Johnston, and James Risen, "Secret U.S. Endorsement of Severe Interrogations," *New York Times,* October 4, 2007.

- The Mueller quote comes from "The New FBI: Protecting Americans Against Terrorism," address to the American Civil Liberties Union 2003 Inaugural Membership Conference, Washington, D.C., June 13, 2003, available at http://www.fbi.gov/pressrel/spee ches/speech06132003.htm (accessed August 23, 2010).

- Mueller's statement to Goldsmith about being an expert on the law is from Goldsmith, *The Terror Presidency,* p. 79.

- Comey's speech can be found in James Comey, "Intelligence Under the Law: Remarks for Law Day at the National Security Agency," May 20, 2005, reprinted in *The Green Bag,* Volume 10, Number 4, Summer 2007, p. 439.

- The Silverman-Robb Commission quotes come from Commission on the Intelligence Capabilities of the United States Regarding Weapons of Mass Destruction, March 31, 2005, Chapter 10, "Intelligence at Home: The FBI, Justice, and Homeland Security." Note: The 2005 so-called WMD Commission is different from the 2008 Graham-Talent Commission, which authored *World at Risk: The Report of the Commission on the Prevention of WMD Proliferation and Terrorism,* New York: Vintage, 2008.

- The Brandon Mayfield case is described well in Eric Lichtblau, *Bush's Law,* pp. 65–74.

Chapter 14: *Culture Clash*

- O'Neill's Londonistan quote is from Evan Thomas, "The New Age of Terror," *Newsweek,* August 20, 2008. Details of the London planes plot are from "Terror in the Skies," *Times* (London), August 13, 2006; Alan Coweel and Dexter Filkins, "British Authorities Say Plot to Blow Up Airliners Was Foiled," *New York Times,* August 10, 2006; Brian Bennett and Douglas Waller, "Thwarting the Airline Plot: Inside the Investigation," *Time,* August 10, 2006.

- The banana anecdote comes from William Saletan, "The Liquid World," *Slate,* August 10, 2006, available at http://www.slate.com/id/2147492 (accessed August 23, 2010).

- The FBI's Las Vegas data mining was first publicized by Rod Smith, "Casinos, Airlines Ordered to Give FBI Information," *Casino City Times,* December 31, 2003. Computer database details come from Ellen Nakashima, "FBI Shows Off Counterterrorism Database," *Washington Post,* August 30, 2006; "Spying on the Homefront," *Frontline,* May 15, 2007; Rod Smith, "FBI's eye on LV vexes lobbyists," *Las Vegas Review-Journal,* November 10, 2005. Additional database details are drawn from Ryan Singel, "Newly Declassified Files Detail Massive FBI Data-Mining Project," Wired.com, September 23, 2009, available at http://www.wired.com/threatlevel/2009/09/fbi-nsac/#ixzz0yH9byRWn (accessed August 23, 2010).

- Mike German's personal story and his unlikely journey from FBI agent to ACLU advocate are detailed in Eric Lichtblau, *Bush's Law,* p. 105.

- Epigram from Rick Atkinson, *The Day of Battle: The War in Sicily and Italy, 1943–1944,* Henry Holt, 2007. p. 380.

- William Jefferson information can be found in Carl Hulse, "Bush Orders Documents from F.B.I. Raid Sealed," *New York Times,* May 25, 2006.

- Freeh's encounter with Tenet is described in George Tenet and Bill Harlow, *At The Center of the Storm,* p. 482.

- The Ashcroft "heart attack" quote comes from 9/11 Commission, Memorandum for Record, December 17, 2004, available at http://www.archives.gov/legislative/research/9-11/commission-memoranda.html (accessed August 23, 2010).

- Supervisor transfer numbers come from Richard Schmitt, "FBI Agents Rebel over Mandatory Transfers," *Los Angeles Times,* May 22, 2006; Kevin Johnson, "FBI Faces High Turnover of Senior Agents," *USA Today,* April 30, 2008; Jerry Seper, "'5 Years Up' Costs FBI Top Managers," *Washington Times,* May 23, 2008.

- FBI departures are described in Andrew Zajac, "Private sector drains FBI talent," *Chicago Tribune,* May 3, 2006. The Mueller-Feinstein exchange is in "FBI Oversight: Hearing before the Committee on the Judiciary," U.S. Senate Serial No. J-109-72, Washington, D.C.: Government Printing Office, May 2, 2006.

- Gebhardt's Antarctica quote comes from Bruce Gebhardt, "Address to the Society of Former Special Agents of the FBI," San Francisco, California, September 16, 2004, available at http://www.fbi.gov/pressrel/speeches/gebhardt091604.htm (accessed August 23, 2010).

- The D'Amuro quote comes from "Terror expertise not a priority at FBI," Associated Press, June 19, 2005.

- The decimation of the FBI's Criminal Division was traced best by an award-winning series by Paul Shukovsky, Tracy Johnson, and Daniel Lathrop, "The FBI's terrorism trade-off," *Seattle Post-Intelligencer,* April 11, 2007. Other key reports have been the Department of Justice Inspector General's dual reports on "The Effects of the Federal Bureau of Investigation's Reprioritization Efforts" (September 2005), available at http://www.usdoj.gov/oig/reports/FBI/a0537/index.htm, and its companion report, "Internal Effects of the Federal Bureau of Investigation's Reprioritization" (September 2004), available at http://www.usdoj.gov/oig/reports/FBI/a0439/index.htm. The Government Accountability Office also reported on the "FBI Transformation," available at http://www.gao.gov/new.items/d041036.pdf (all accessed August 23, 2010); Mueller "smaller white collar" quote is from "Hearing of the Senate Judiciary Committee—Oversight of the Federal Bureau of Investigation," March 25, 2009.

• Kenneth Williams quote on the size of the FBI is from 9/11 Commission Memorandum for the Record, 2003–2004, available at http://www.archives.gov/legislative/research/9-11/commission-memoranda.html (accessed August 23, 2010).

• The FBI's Arabic language challenges are detailed in Dan Eggen, "FBI Agents Still Lacking Arabic Skills," *Washington Post,* October 11, 2006. The Leahy quote and statistics are from "FBI Oversight Hearing Before the Committee on the Judiciary," U.S. Senate, December 6, 2006, Serial No. J-109-122, Government Printing Office, 2007.

• The FBI's human capital efforts have been the subject of two reports by the National Academy of Public Administration, "Transforming the FBI: Progress and Challenges," January 2005, and "Transforming the FBI: Roadmap to an Effective Human Capital Program," September 2005. Two Harvard Business School case studies have also examined the FBI under Mueller: Jan Rivkin and Michael Roberto, "Federal Bureau of Investigation (A)," N9-707-500, and "Federal Bureau of Investigation (B)," N9-707-553, both March 27, 2007.

• Phil Mudd's struggles to change the FBI's mind-set were also covered in Scott Shane and Lowell Bergman, "F.B.I. Struggling to Reinvent Itself to Fight Terror," *New York Times,* October 10, 2006.

• The Sheehan quote comes from Michael Sheehan, *Crush the Cell,* p. 14. The Bloomberg quote is from "Mayor Aims to Quiet Fears over JFK Terror Plot," NY1, June 4, 2007, available at http://www.ny1.com/?SecID=1000&ArID=70351 (accessed August 23, 2010).

CHAPTER 15: *The Arc of Justice*

• The Theodore Parker quotation is from Theodore Parker, "Of Justice and Conscience," in *Ten Sermons of Religion,* Boston: Crosby, Nichols, 1853.

• Details of the Blagojevich arrest come from author interviews and Natasha Korecki, "The FBI agent who ran wiretaps on Blagojevich," *Chicago Sun-Times,* July 6, 2010.

• Eric Holder's challenges appear in Jane Mayer, "The Trial," *The New Yorker,* February 15 and 22, 2010. The "politicized" quote comes from Laura Blumenfeld, "Up All Night," *Washington Post,* July 4, 2010.

• Details of Mueller's encounter with Obama are from Peter Baker, "Obama's War Over Terror," *New York Times Magazine,* January 4, 2010.

• The Hadley quote is taken from Martha Joynt Kumar, "The 2008–2009 Presidential Transition Through the Voices of Its Participants," *Presidential Studies Quarterly,* Volume 39, Issue 4, December 2009.

• Details of the Obama campaign hacking come from author interviews and "How He Did It," *Newsweek,* November 5, 2010.

- For anyone interested in the sprawling chaos of Mumbai, Suketu Mehta's *Maximum City: Bombay Lost and Found,* New York: Knopf, 2004, is a great guide. For the attacks themselves, *Hindu*'s online archives of related documents, including the 69-page police dossier, is an invaluable resource: http://hindu.com/nic/dossier.htm (accessed August 23, 2010). Also helpful were Jyoti Thottam, "India: After the Horror," *Time,* December 4, 2008; Somini Sengupta, "Dossier Gives Details of Mumbai Attacks," *New York Times,* January 7, 2009; Jeremy Hammond, "The Mumbai Attacks: More than Meets the Eye," *Foreign Policy Journal,* December 4, 2008; Zahid Hussain, Matthew Rosenberg, and Peter Wonacott, "Pakistan's Probe Finds Local Links to Attacks on Mumbai," *Wall Street Journal,* December 31, 2008; Aryn Baker and Jyoti Thottam, "The Making of a Terrorist," *Time,* March 16, 2009; Rama Lakshmi, "In Mumbai Terrorism Case, An Emotional, Historic Trial," *Washington Post,* June 22, 2009.

- The NYPD's response to Mumbai is drawn from Patrice O'Shaughnessy, "NYPD learns lessons from Mumbai terrorist attack that killed 174," *New York Daily News,* February 15, 2009.

- The Italian end of the Mumbai investigation was reported on by Anna Momigliano, "Is Nothern Italy a New Haven for Terror Fundraising?" *Christian Science Monitor,* November 23, 2009, and Ariel David, "Italian Police Arrest 2 Linked to Mumbai Attacks," Associated Press, November 21, 2009.

- Information about David Headley is from "Chicagoans Tahawwur Rana and David Headley Indicted for Alleged Roles in India and Denmark Terrorism Conspiracies; Ilyas Kashmiri and Retired Pakistani Major Charged in Denmark Plot," Superseding Indictment, United States Attorney's Office, Northern District of Illinois, January 14, 2010, available at http://www.justice.gov/usao/iln/pr/chicago/2010/pr0114_01a.pdf (accessed August 23, 2010). More information on his case and his ties to U.S. government agencies comes from Joseph Tanfani, John Shiffman, and Kathleen Brady Shea, "American suspect in Mumbai attack was DEA informant," *Philadelphia Inquirer,* December 14, 2009; Sebastian Rotella, "FBI Was Warned Years in Advance of Mumbai Attacker's Terror Ties," ProPublica, October 15, 2010, available at http://www.propublica.org/article/mumbai-plot-fbi-was-warned-years-in-advance (accessed December 3, 2010).

- The FBI's role in India has been covered publicly there in "FBI officials to depose in Kasab's trial: Mumbai police," *Expressindia,* February 9, 2009; "Prosecution lauds help of FBI in 26/11 Kasab trial," Indo-Asian News Service, March 31, 2010; C. Unnikrishnan, "FBI officials to be witnesses in Kasab's trial," *Times of India,* February 9, 2009.

- Obama's inaugural address can be found at http://www.whitehouse.gov/blog/inaugural-address/ (accessed August 23, 2010).

- Details of al-Qaeda's evolution and quotes from Ali come in part from Ali Soufan, "Defeating al-Qaeda and Neutralizing Its Support Network," Washington Institute for Near East Policy, PolicyWatch #1536, June 17, 2009, available at http://www.washingtoninstitute.org/templateC05.php?CID=3074 (accessed August 23, 2010). A useful overall guide to terror plots from 2001 to 2010 is Jena Baker McNeill, James Jay Carafano, and Jessica Zuckerman, "30 Terrorist Plots Foiled: How the System Worked," Heritage Foundation, April 29, 2010.

- Obama's terminology for threats is in Marc Ambinder, "The New Term for the War on Terror," TheAtlantic.com, May 20, 2010, available at http://www.theatlantic.com/poli tics/archive/2010/05/the-new-term-for-the-war-on-terror/56969/ (accessed August 23, 2010).

- Obama's "Daily Economic Brief" is explained further in Mark Hosenball, "The Butterfly Brief," *Newsweek,* February 24, 2009, available at http://www.newsweek.com/2009/02/24/ the-butterfly-brief.html.

- More on Obama's Terror Tuesday tutorials is in Anne Kornblut, "Obama gets weekly tutorials in terrorism," *Washington Post,* May 6, 2010.

- The complicated and confusing Dallas Holy Land Foundation case is described in David Feige, "Pyrrhic Acquittal: The Holy Land Foundation defendants aren't off the hook," *Slate,* October 24, 2007, available at http://www.slate.com/id/2176561 (accessed August 23, 2010).

- "Clean teams" and the Musa quote are from Josh Meyer, "FBI works to bolster cases on Al Qaeda," *Los Angeles Times,* October 21, 2007. Also instructive are Peter Finn, "4 Cases Illustrate Guantanamo Quandaries," *Washington Post,* February 16, 2009, and Michael Isikoff, "The Train Wreck That Didn't Have to Be," *Newsweek,* January 19, 2009.

- For the Ghailani verdict, see Anne E. Kornblut and Peter Finn, "White House unde-terred after Ghailani terror case verdict," *Washington Post,* November 18, 2010; "Obama's Handcuffs," ForeignPolicy.com, http://www.foreignpolicy.com/articles/2010/11/18/ obamas_handcuffs (accessed December 3, 2010).

- Information about tribunals and William Barr comes from Jonathan Mahler, *The Challenge,* p. 25. Mahler's book is also a fantastic resource for the story of Hamdan's legal challenges to the detainee policies.

- Al Megrahi release, Obama quote, and U.S. reaction from Karla Adams, "U.S., Britain Criticize Celebrations for Lockerbie Plotter," *Washington Post,* August 22, 2009.

- President Obama speech to the FBI, White House, "Remarks by the President to Federal Bureau of Investigation Employees," April 28, 2010, available at http://www.whitehouse. gov/the-press-office/remarks-president-fbi-employees-42809 or http://www.realclear politics.com/articles/2009/04/28/obama_speech_to_the_fbi_96250.html (accessed August 23, 2010); Mueller's introduction is available at http://www.fbi.gov/pressrel/speeches/ mueller042809.htm (accessed August 23, 2010).

- Mueller's letter to the Scottish government is available at http://www.fbi.gov/news/ pressrel/press-releases/letter-from-fbi-director-robert-s.-mueller-iii-to-scottish -minister-kenny-macaskill (accessed December 3, 2010).

- Details about the debate about the Pan Am 103 memorial cairn at Arlington are from Allan Gerson and Gerry Adler, *The Price of Terror.*

- Naím's remarks are in Moisés Naím, "Five Wars of Globalization," *Foreign Policy,* January 2003.

• Greg Treverton, "Film Piracy, Organized Crime, and Terrorism," RAND Institute, March 2009; CNN, "U.S. authorities bust cigarette-smuggling ring linked to Hezbollah," July 21, 2000, available at http://archives.cnn.com/2000/LAW/07/21/charlotte.raids.02/.

• "Nigerian scheme" e-mails (and, in a previous era, letters) are a fascinating subset of financial fraud. For an in-depth look, see Mitchell Zuckoff, "The Perfect Mark," *The New Yorker,* May 15, 2006.

• For Brennan's speech, see "A New Approach to Safeguarding Americans," address at the Center for Strategic and International Studies, August 6, 2009, available at http://www.whitehouse.gov/the-press-office/remarks-john-brennan-center-strategic-and-international-studies%20 (accessed August 23, 2010).

• Obama's Cairo University speech, "A New Beginning," June 4, 2009, is available at http://www.whitehouse.gov/the_press_office/Remarks-by-the-President-at-Cairo-University-6-04-09/ (accessed August 23, 2010).

• Al-Zawahiri's quote is from James Sturcke, "Al-Qaida leader releases new tape warning Obama against Bush policies," *Guardian* (London), November 19, 2008.

• Details of the Shirwa Ahmed case are from David Johnston, "Militants Drew Recruit in U.S., F.B.I. Says," *New York Times,* February 23, 2009, and Spencer Hsu and Carrie Johnson, "Somali Americans Recruited by Extremists," *Washington Post,* March 11, 2009.

• Phil Mudd's testimony is in "Statement Before the Senate Committee on Homeland Security and Governmental Affairs," March 11, 2009, available at http://www.fbi.gov/congress/congress09/mudd031109.htm (accessed August 23, 2010).

• Mueller's remarks about the "perversion of the immigrant story" can be found in Address to the Council on Foreign Relations, Washington, D.C., February 23, 2009, available at http://www.fbi.gov/pressrel/speeches/mueller022309.htm (accessed August 23, 2010).

• Kris's quote comes from "Law Enforcement as a Counterterrorism Tool," Brookings Institution, June 10, 2010, available at www.brookings.edu/~/media/Files/events/2010/0611_law_enforcement/20100611_law_enforcement_kris.pdf (accessed December 3, 2010).

• The Bronx synagogue plot is described in Michael Daly, Alison Gendar, and Helen Kennedy, "FBI arrest four in alleged plot to bomb Bronx synagogues, shoot down plane," *New York Daily News,* May 21, 2009. Also useful for understanding the Bureau's evolving approach to terrorism is Eric Lipton, "Recent Arrests in Terror Plots Yield Debate on Pre-Emptive Action by Government," *New York Times,* July 9, 2006.

• Details of the Carlos Bledsoe case come from author interviews and from Steve Barnes and James Dao, "Gunman Kills Soldier Outside Recruiting Station," *New York Times,* June 1, 2009.

• The Boyd case and the Holding quote in Carrie Johnson and Spencer S. Hsu, "Seven Face Terrorism Charges in N.C.," *Washington Post,* July 28, 2009.

• The significance of the Zazi case, as seen by the administration, is explained in Anne Kornblut, "Obama Team Says Zazi Case Illustrates Balanced Approach to Terror Threat," *Wash-*

ington Post, October 6, 2009. Details of the case are outlined in David Johnston and William Rashbaum, "Rush for Clues Before Charges in Terror Case," *New York Times,* September 30, 2009, as well as in William Rashbaum and Karen Zraick, "Government Says Al Qaeda Ordered N.Y. Plot," *New York Times,* April 23, 2010. Probably the best piece yet done on the Zazi case was a special by KMGH-TV investigative reporter Tony Kovaleski.

• Death of Saleh Al-Somali in Joby Warrick and Karen DeYoung, "Top al-Qaeda planner apparently killed in Pakistan," *Washington Post,* December 12, 2009.

• Art Cummings, one of the most influential managers of the Mueller era at the Bureau, is also profiled in Ronald Kessler, *The Terrorist Watch.*

• Barack Obama's "arc of justice" quote is from from Senator Barack Obama, "Remarks on the 40th Anniversary of the Assassination of Dr. Martin Luther King," Fort Wayne, Indiana, April 4, 2008, available at http://open.salon.com/blog/arthur_howe/2009/01/18/the_arc _of_the_universe_is_long_but_it_bends_towards_justice (accessed August 23, 2010).

• Details of the Christmas Day incident are from Eric Lipton, Eric Schmitt, and Mark Mazzetti, "Review of Jet Bomb Plot Shows More Missed Clues," *New York Times,* January 18, 2010; Devlin Barrett, "Details of arrest of bombing suspect disclosed," *Washington Post,* January 24, 2010; Ron French, "Inside Story of Terror on Flight 253," *Detroit News,* March 18, 2010; Richard A. Serrano, "Holder: I made decision on prosecuting airline bomb-attack suspect," *Chicago Tribune,* February 3, 2010. Also useful is "Unclassified Executive Summary of the Committee Report on the Attempted Terrorist Attack on Northwest Airlines Flight 253," Senate Select Committee on Intelligence, May 18, 2010.

Chapter 16: *Hellfires to Handcuffs*

• A remarkably thorough and entertaining telling of the history of VBIEDs is Mike Davis, *Buda's Wagon.* The story of the 1920 Wall Street bombing is also told in Beverly Gage, *The Day Wall Street Exploded: A Story of America in Its First Age of Terror,* Oxford: Oxford University Press, 2009.

• Details of Shahzad's capture are from Jamie Schram and Murray Weiss, "Busted Faisal in a 'cuff' landing at JFK Airport," *New York Post,* May 10, 2010, and Michael Shear, "Speed of arrest in Times Square bomb attempt draws parallels to TV's '24,'" *Washington Post,* May 4, 2010, as well as author interviews.

• Details of Qasab's conviction in Mumbai are from Prachi Pinglay, "Surviving Mumbai gunman convicted over attacks," BBCNews.com, May 3, 2010, available at http://news .bbc.co.uk/2/hi/south_asia/8657642.stm (accessed August 23, 2010).

• The Ujjwal Nikam quote is from Agence-France Presse, "FBI played 'vital role,'" *Straits Times,* April 19, 2009, available at http://www.straitstimes.com/Breaking%2BNews/ Asia/Story/STIStory_365307.html (accessed August 23, 2010).

• The Tahiliyani quote is from Anuj Chopra, "Mumbai gunman guilty of 'act of war,'" *National,* May 3, 2010, available at http://www.thenational.ae/apps/pbcs.dll/article?AID=/20100504/ FOREIGN/705039878/1001/SPORT (accessed August 23, 2010).

- The Qasab death sentence is reported in "Mumbai Attacks: Kasab gets the death penalty," *Times of India,* May 6, 2010, available at http://timesofindia.indiatimes.com/india/Mumbai-attacks-Kasab-gets-the-death-penalty/articleshow/5897555.cms (accessed August 23, 2010).

- For more Yemen background, see Robert F. Worth, "Is Yemen the Next Afghanistan?" *New York Times Magazine,* July 6, 2010. Leiberman quote from Fox News, *Fox News Sunday,* December 27, 2009.

- Mueller's remarks at Duke are from "Duke University College of Law Commencement Address," Durham, North Carolina, May 15, 2010, available at http://www.fbi.gov/pressrel/speeches/mueller051510.htm (accessed August 23, 2010).

- Brennan quote from ABCNews *This Week,* January 3, 2010.

- The Anwar Al-Awlaki quote is from Casey Britton, "Transcript: A Call to Jihad— An Address by Anwar Al-awlaki," WorldAnalysis.net, March 20, available at at http://worldanalysis.net/modules/news/article.php?storyid=1311 (accessed August 23, 2010).

- The "perpetually failing state" quote and other Yemen details are from Jeremy M. Sharp, "Yemen: Background and U.S. Relations," Congressional Research Service, 7-5700, January 13, 2010.

- Badawi details come from Michael Isikoff, "A Terrorist Walks Free," *Newsweek,* October 27, 2010, available at http://www.newsweek.com/2007/10/27/a-terrorist-walks-free.html (accessed August 23, 2010). Mueller's role is from author interviews.

- Anwar al-Awlaki's biographical details are from Scott Shane and Souad Makhennet, "Imam's Path from Condemning Terror to Preaching Jihad," *New York Times,* May 8, 2010.

- Placement of al-Awlaki on the assassination list is from Scott Shane, "U.S. Approves Targeted Killing of American Cleric," *New York Times,* April 6, 2010.

- The Abu Ali al-Harithi missile strike is explained by James Bamford, "He's in the Backseat," *Atlantic Monthly,* April 2006; Walter Pincus, "US missiles kill al Qaeda suspects," *Washington Post,* November 6, 2002; Dana Priest, "U.S. Citizen Among Those Killed in Yemen Predator Missile Strike," *Washington Post,* November 8, 2002.

- Obama's first year and the drone strategy were informed by Jane Mayer, "The Predator War," *The New Yorker,* October 26, 2009, and Peter Baker, "Obama's War Over Terror," *New York Times Magazine,* January 4, 2010.

- The May 3 drone attack was reported in Bill Roggio, "US airstrike kills 4 'militants' in North Waziristan," Long War Journal, May 3, 2010, available at http://www.longwarjournal.org/archives/2010/05/us_airstrike_kills_4_1.php (accessed August 23, 2010).

- A useful timeline of the government's response to the Times Square bombing attempt was compiled by Christopher Weber, PoliticsDaily.com, May 4, 2010, available at http://www.politicsdaily.com/2010/05/04/timeline-of-white-house-actions-following-botched-times-square-b/ (accessed August 23, 2010).

- The Shahzad investigation details are from Mark Mazzetti, Sabrina Tavernise, and Jack Healy, "Suspect, Charged, Said to Admit to Role in Plot," *New York Times,* May 5, 2010; William Rashbaum and Al Baker, "Smoking Car to an Arrest in 53 Hours," *New York Times,* May 5, 2010; James Barron and Michael Schmidt, "From Suburban Father to a Terrorism Suspect," *New York Times,* May 5, 2010.

- Details of Shahzad at the airport are from Al Baker, "As Agents Staked Out, Suspect Fled to Airport," *New York Times,* May 6, 2010; Mark Hosenball, "FBI Surveillance of Times Square Suspect 'Broke Down,'" Newsweek.com, May 5, 2010, available at http://www.newsweek.com/blogs/declassified/2010/05/04/fbi-surveillance-of-times-square-suspect-broke-down.html (accessed August 23, 2010).

- HIG questioning by Kimberly Dozier, "WH adviser: Interrogation team questions Shahzad," Associated Press, May 18, 2010.

- Shahzad's courtroom statement is from *United States v. Faishal Shahzad,* 10-CR-541 (MGC), June 21, 2010.

BIBLIOGRAPHY

Alexander, Matthew, and John R. Bruning. *How to Break a Terrorist: The U.S. Interrogators Who Used Brains, Not Brutality, to Take Down the Deadliest Man in Iraq.* New York: Free Press, 2008.

Alexander, Shana. *The Pizza Connection: Lawyers, Money, Drugs, Mafia.* New York: Weidenfeld & Nicolson, 1988.

Alter, Jonathan. *The Promise: President Obama, Year One.* New York: Simon & Schuster, 2010.

Andrew, Christopher. *For the President's Eyes Only: Secret Intelligence and the American Presidency from Washington to Bush.* New York: HarperPerennial, 1996.

Ashcroft, John D. *Never Again: Securing America and Restoring Justice.* Nashville: Center Street, 2006.

Baker, Stewart A. *Skating on Stilts: Why We Aren't Stopping Tomorrow's Terrorism.* Stanford, CA: Hoover Institution Press, 2010.

Bamford, James. *The Shadow Factory: The Ultra-Secret NSA from 9/11 to the Eavesdropping on America.* New York: Doubleday, 2008.

Bergen, Peter L. *The Osama bin Laden I Know: An Oral History of al Qaeda's Leader.* New York: Free Press, 2006.

Blair, Ed, and Captain William R. Haas. *Odyssey of Terror.* Nashville: Broadman, 1977.

Blumenthal, Ralph. *Last Days of the Sicilians: At War with the Mafia: The FBI Assault on the Pizza Connection.* New York: Times Books/Random House, 1988.

Bobbitt, Philip. *Terror and Consent: The Wars for the Twenty-First Century.* New York: Knopf, 2008.

Botting, James. *Bullets, Bombs and Fast Talk: Twenty-Five Years of FBI War Stories.* Washington, D.C.: Potomac, 2008.

Bowden, Mark. *Black Hawk Down: A Story of Modern War.* New York: Grove Press, 2010.

Branch, Taylor. *The Clinton Tapes: Wrestling History with the President.* New York: Simon & Schuster, 2009.

Brzezinski, Matthew. *Fortress America: On the Front Lines of Homeland Security—An Inside Look at the Coming Surveillance State.* New York: Bantam, 2004.

Burrough, Bryan. *Public Enemies: America's Greatest Crime Wave and the Birth of the FBI, 1933–34.* New York: Penguin, 2004.

Burton, Fred. *Ghost: Confessions of a Counterterrorism Agent.* New York: Random House, 2008.

Bush, George W. *Decision Points.* New York: Crown, 2010.

Chandrasekaran, Rajiv. *Imperial Life in the Emerald City: Inside Iraq's Green Zone.* New York: Vintage, 2006.

Chertoff, Michael. *Homeland Security: Assessing the First Five Years.* Philadelphia: University of Pennsylvania Press, 2009.

Chollet, Derek, and James Goldgeier. *America Between the Wars: From 11/9 to 9/11.* New York: PublicAffairs, 2008.

Clarke, Richard A. *Against All Enemies: Inside America's War on Terror.* New York: Free Press, 2004.

———. *Your Government Failed You: Breaking the Cycle of National Security Disasters.* New York: Ecco, 2008.

Clarridge, Duane R., and Digby Diehl. *A Spy for All Seasons: My Life in the CIA.* New York: Scribner, 1997.

Coll, Steve. *Ghost Wars: The Secret History of the CIA, Afghanistan, and Bin Laden, from the Soviet Invasion to September 10, 2001.* New York: Penguin, 2004.

Cook, Fred J. *The FBI Nobody Knows.* New York: Macmillan, 1964.

Coulson, Danny O., and Elaine Shannon. *No Heroes: Inside the FBI's Secret Counter-Terror Force.* New York: Pocket, 1999.

Davis, Mike. *Buda's Wagon: A Brief History of the Car Bomb.* London: Verso, 2007.

Dickey, Christopher. *Securing the City: Inside America's Best Counterterror Force—the NYPD.* New York: Simon & Schuster, 2009.

Douglas, Geoffrey. *The Classmates: Privilege, Chaos, and the End of an Era.* New York: Hyperion, 2008.

Dwyer, Jim, Deidre Murphy, and Peg Tyre. *Two Seconds Under the World: Terror Comes to America—The Conspiracy Behind the World Trade Center Bombing.* New York: Crown, 1994.

Emerson, Steven, and Brian Duffy. *The Fall of Pan Am 103: Inside the Lockerbie Investigation.* New York: Putnam, 1990.

Faddis, Charles S. *Beyond Repair: The Decline and Fall of the CIA.* Guilford, CT: Lyons, 2010.

Farah, Douglas, and Stephen Braun. *Merchant of Death: Money, Guns, Planes, and the Man Who Makes War Possible.* Hoboken, NJ: John Wiley, 2007.

Farmer, John. *The Ground Truth: The Untold Story of America Under Attack on 9/11.* New York: Riverhead, 2009.

Feith, Douglas J. *War and Decision: Inside the Pentagon at the Dawn of the War on Terrorism.* New York: Harper, 2008.

Felt, Mark. *The FBI Pyramid: From the Inside.* New York: Putnam, 1979.

Felt, Mark, and John O'Connor. *A G-Man's Life: The FBI, Being "Deep Throat," and the Struggle for Honor in Washington.* New York: PublicAffairs, 2006.

Filkins, Dexter. *The Forever War.* New York: Vintage, 2009.

Freeh, Louis J. *My FBI: Bringing Down the Mafia, Investigating Bill Clinton, and Fighting the War on Terror.* New York: St. Martin's, 2005.

Friedman, Benjamin H., Jim Harper, and Christopher A. Preble, eds. *Terrorizing Ourselves: Why U.S. Counterterrorism Policy Is Failing and How to Fix It.* Washington, DC: Cato Institute, 2010.

Friedman, Robert I. *Red Mafiya: How the Russian Mob Has Invaded America.* Boston: Little, Brown, 2000.

Gelbspan, Ross. *Break-ins, Death Threats, and the FBI: The Covert War Against the Central America Movement.* Boston: South End, 1991.

Gellman, Barton. *Angler: The Cheney Vice Presidency.* New York: Penguin, 2008.

Gerson, Allan, and Jerry Adler. *The Price of Terror: One bomb. One plane. 270 Lives. The History-Making Struggle for Justice After Pan Am 103.* New York: HarperCollins, 2001.

Glenny, Misha. *McMafia: A Journey Through the Global Criminal Underworld.* New York: Knopf, 2008.

Goldsmith, Jack. *The Terror Presidency: Law and Judgment Inside the Bush Administration.* New York: Norton, 2007.

Gray, L. Patrick, III. *In Nixon's Web: A Year in the Crosshairs of Watergate.* New York: Times Books, 2008.

Greenberg, Karen. *The Least Worst Place: Guantanamo's First 100 Days.* New York: Oxford University Press, 2009.

Grey, Stephen. *Ghost Plane: The True Story of the CIA Torture Program.* New York: St. Martin's, 2006.

Griffin, Joe, and Don DeNevi. *Mob Nemesis: How the FBI Crippled Organized Crime.* Amherst, NY: Prometheus, 2002.

Gup, Ted. *The Book of Honor: The Secret Lives and Deaths of CIA Operatives.* New York: Anchor, 2001.

———. *Nation of Secrets: The Threat to Democracy and the American Way of Life.* New York: Doubleday, 2007.

Harris, Shane. *The Watchers: The Rise of America's Surveillance State.* New York: Penguin, 2010.

Irons, Peter. *War Powers: How the Imperial Presidency Hijacked the Constitution.* New York: Metropolitan, 2005.

Jacobs, James B., Christopher Panarella, and Jay Worthington. *Busting the Mob: United States v. Cosa Nostra.* New York: New York University Press, 1994.

Jefferys-Jones, Rhodri. *The FBI: A History.* New Haven, CT: Yale University Press, 2007.

Katz, Samuel M. *Relentless Pursuit: The DSS and the Manhunt for the Al-Qaeda Terrorists.* New York: Forge, 2002.

Kelley, Clarence M., and James Kirkpatrick Davis. *Kelley: The Story of an FBI Director.* Kansas City: Andrews, McMeel & Parker, 1987.

Kessler, Ronald. *The Bureau: The Secret History of the FBI.* New York: St. Martin's, 2003.

———. *The FBI: Inside the World's Most Powerful Law Enforcement Agency—by the Award-Winning Journalist Whose Investigation Brought Down FBI Director William S. Sessions.* New York: Pocket, 1993.

———. *A Matter of Character: Inside the White House of George W. Bush.* New York: Sentinel, 2004.

———. *The Terrorist Watch: Inside the Desperate Race to Stop the Next Attack.* New York: Crown Forum, 2007.

Kilcullen, David. *The Accidental Guerrilla: Fighting Small Wars in the Midst of a Big One.* Oxford: Oxford University Press, 2009.

Kiriakou, John, and Michael Ruby. *The Reluctant Spy: My Secret Life in the CIA's War on Terror.* New York: Bantam, 2009.

Krulak, Victor H. *First to Fight: An Inside View of the U.S. Marine Corps.* Annapolis, MD: U.S. Naval Institute Press, 1999.

Kupperman, Robert, and Jeff Kamen. *Final Warning: Averting Disaster in the New Age of Terrorism.* New York: Doubleday, 1989.

Lance, Peter. *1000 Years for Revenge.* New York: ReganBooks, 2003.

———. *Triple Cross: How bin Laden's Master Spy Penetrated the CIA, the Green Berets, and the FBI—and Why Patrick Fitzgerald Failed to Stop Him.* New York: Morrow, 2006.

Lehr, Dick, and Gerard O'Neill. *Black Mass: The True Story of an Unholy Alliance Between the FBI and the Irish Mob.* New York: Harper Paperbacks, 2001.

Leppard, David. *On the Trail of Terror: The Inside Story of the Lockerbie Investigation.* London: Jonathan Cape, 1991.

Lichtblau, Eric. *Bush's Law: The Remaking of American Justice.* New York: Pantheon, 2008.

Mackey, Chris, and Greg Miller. *The Interrogators: Task Force 500 and America's Secret War Against Al-Qaeda.* New York: Back Bay, 2004.

Mahler, Jonathan. *The Challenge: Hamdan v. Rumsfeld and the Fight over Presidential Power.* New York: Farrar, Straus and Giroux, 2008.

Marquise, Richard A. *SCOTBOM: Evidence and the Lockerbie Investigation.* New York: Algora, 2006.

Mayer, Jane. *The Dark Side: The Inside Story of How the War on Terror Turned into a War on American Ideals.* New York: Doubleday, 2008.

Miller, John, Michael Stone, and Chris Mitchell. *The Cell: Inside the 9/11 Plot, and Why the FBI and CIA Failed to Stop It.* New York: Hyperion, 2003.

Moghadam, Assaf. *The Globalization of Martyrdom: Al Qaeda, Salafi Jihad, and the Diffusion of Suicide Attacks.* Baltimore, MD: Johns Hopkins University Press, 2008.

Naftali, Timothy. *Blind Spot: The Secret History of American Counterterrorism.* New York: Basic, 2005.

Naím, Moisés. *Illicit: How Smugglers, Traffickers, and Copycats Are Hijacking the Global Economy.* New York: Doubleday, 2005.

National Commission on Terrorist Attacks Upon the United States. *The 9/11 Commission Report: Final Report of the National Commission on Terrorist Attacks Upon the United States.* New York: Norton, 2004.

Noesner, Gary. *Stalling for Time: My Life as an FBI Hostage Negotiator.* New York: Random House, 2010.

Nucci, Georgia, ed. *On Eagles' Wings: In Remembrance of All Victims of the Lockerbie Air Disaster Who Died on December 21, 1988.* Whippany, NJ: Victims of Pan Am 103, 1990.

Office of the Inspector General. Central Intelligence Agency. *OIG Report on CIA Accountability with Respect to the 9/11 Attacks.* 2005. www.fas.org/irp/cia/product/oig-911.pdf (accessed August 23, 2010).

Paglen, Trevor, and A. C. Thompson. *Torture Taxi: On the Trail of the CIA's Rendition Flights.* Hoboken, NJ: Melville House, 2006.

Pedahzur, Ami. *The Israeli Secret Services & the Struggle Against Terrorism.* New York: Columbia University Press, 2009.

Phillips, Melanie. *Londonistan: How Britain Has Created a Terror State Within.* London: Gibson Square, 2008.

Posner, Gerald. *Why America Slept: The Failure to Prevent 9/11.* New York: Random House, 2003.

Posner, Richard A. *Countering Terrorism: Blurred Focus, Halting Steps.* Lanham, MD: Rowman & Littlefield, 2007.

———. *Not a Suicide Pact: The Constitution in a Time of National Emergency*. New York: Oxford University Press, 2006.

Powers, Richard Gid. *Broken: The Troubled Past and Uncertain Future of the FBI*. New York: Free Press, 2004.

———. *Secrecy and Power: The Life of J. Edgar Hoover*. New York: Free Press, 1988.

Reader's Digest, ed. *People in Peril: And How They Survived*. Pleasantville, NY: Reader's Digest Association, 1983.

Reeve, Simon. *The New Jackals: Ramzi Yousef, Osama Bin Laden and the Future of Terrorism*. Boston: Northeastern University Press, 1999.

———. *One Day in September: The Full Story of the 1972 Munich Olympic Massacre and the Israeli Revenge Operation "Wrath of God."* New York: Arcade, 2000.

Revell, Oliver "Buck," and Dwight Williams. *A G-Man's Journal: A Legendary Career Inside the FBI—From the Kennedy Assassination to the Oklahoma City Bombing*. New York: Pocket, 1998.

Richelson, Jeffrey T. *Defusing Armageddon: Inside NEST, America's Secret Nuclear Bomb Squad*. New York: Norton, 2009.

Ricks, Thomas E. *Fiasco: The American Military Adventure in Iraq, 2003 to 2005*. New York: Penguin, 2007.

———. *The Gamble: General David Petraeus and the American Military Adventure in Iraq, 2006–2008*. New York: Penguin, 2009.

———. *Making the Corps*. New York: Scribner, 2007.

Ridge, Tom, and Lary Bloom. *The Test of Our Times: America Under Siege... And How We Can Be Safe Again*. New York: Thomas Dunne, 2009.

Riebling, Mark. *Wedge: From Pearl Harbor to 9/11: How the Secret War Between the FBI and CIA Has Endangered National Security*. New York: Touchstone, 2002.

Risen, James. *State of War: The Secret History of the CIA and the Bush Administration*. New York: Free Press, 2006.

Rubinstein, Julian. *Ballad of the Whiskey Robber: A True Story of Bank Heists, Ice Hockey, Transylvanian Pelt Smuggling, Moonlighting Detectives, and Broken Hearts*. New York: Back Bay, 2005.

Saar, Erik, and Viveca Novak. *Inside the Wire: A Military Intelligence Soldier's Eyewitness Account of Life at Guantanamo*. New York: Penguin, 2005.

Salisbury, Stephan. *Mohamed's Ghosts: An American Story of Love and Fear in the Homeland*. New York: Nation Books / Perseus Books Group, 2010.

Sands, Philippe. *Torture Team: Rumsfeld's Memo and the Betrayal of American Values*. New York: Palgrave Macmillan, 2008.

Savage, Charles. *Takeover: The Return of the Imperial Presidency and the Subversion of American Democracy*. New York: Back Bay, 2007.

Sheehan, Michael. *Crush the Cell: How to Defeat Terrorism Without Terrorizing Ourselves*. New York: Three Rivers, 2008.

Shenon, Philip. *The Commission: The Uncensored History of the 9/11 Investigation*. New York: Twelve, 2008.

Shorrock, Tim. *Spies for Hire: The Secret World of Intelligence Outsourcing*. New York: Simon & Schuster, 2008.

Sims, Jennifer E., and Burton Gerber, eds. *Transforming U.S. Intelligence*. Washington, DC: Georgetown University Press, 2005.

Singer, P. W. *Wired for War: The Robotics Revolution and Conflict in the 21st Century.* New York: Penguin, 2009.

Smith, I. C. *Inside: A Top G-Man Exposes Spies, Lies, and Bureaucratic Bungling Inside the FBI.* Nashville: Thomas Nelson, 2004.

Sterling, Claire. *Octopus: The Long Reach of the International Sicilian Mafia.* New York: Norton, 1990.

Stille, Alexander. *Excellent Cadavers: The Mafia and the Death of the First Italian Republic.* New York: Vintage, 1996.

Stoll, Cliff. *The Cuckoo's Egg: Tracking a Spy Through the Maze of Computer Espionage.* New York: Doubleday, 1989.

Stone, Geoffrey. *War and Liberty: An American Dilemma; 1790 to the Present.* New York: Norton, 2007.

Suskind, Ron. *The One Percent Doctrine: Deep Inside America's Pursuit of Its Enemies Since 9/11.* New York: Simon & Schuster, 2006.

———. *The Way of the World: A Story of Truth and Hope in an Age of Extremism.* New York: Harper, 2008.

Temple-Raston, Dina. *The Jihad Next Door: The Lackawanna Six and Rough Justice in an Age of Terror.* New York: PublicAffairs, 2007.

Tenet, George, and Bill Harlow. *At the Center of the Storm: My Years at the CIA.* New York: HarperCollins, 2007.

Theoharis, Athan. *The Quest for Absolute Security: The Failed Relations Among U.S. Intelligence Agencies.* Chicago: Ivan R. Dee, 2007.

Theoharis, Athan G., and John Stuart Cox. *The Boss: J. Edgar Hoover and the Great American Inquisition.* Philadelphia: Temple University Press, 1988.

Thornburgh, Dick. *Where the Evidence Leads: An Autobiography.* Pittsburgh: University of Pittsburgh Press, 2003.

Tully, Andrew. *Inside the FBI.* New York: McGraw-Hill, 1980.

Turner, Stansfield. *Burn Before Reading: Presidents, CIA Directors, and Secret Intelligence.* New York: Hyperion, 2005.

Ungar, Sanford J. *FBI: An Uncensored Look Behind the Walls.* Boston: Atlantic Monthly, 1976.

Unger, Robert. *The Union Station Massacre: The Original Sin of J. Edgar Hoover's FBI.* Kansas City, MO: Kansas City Star Books, 2005.

U.S. Congress. House of Representatives. *Memorial Tributes to J. Edgar Hoover in the Congress of the United States and Various Articles and Editorials Relating to His Life and Work.* 93d Cong., 2d sess., 1974. H. Doc. 93-68.

U.S. Congress. Senate. Select Committee on Intelligence. *The FBI and CISPES.* 101st Cong., 1st sess., July 1989. S. Rep. 101-46. http://www.gpo.gov (accessed January 1, 2010).

U.S. Department of Justice. Federal Bureau of Investigation. *The FBI: A Centennial History, 1908–2008.* Washington, DC: U.S. Government Printing Office, 2008.

———. *Report to the National Commission on Terrorist Attacks upon the United States: The FBI's Counterterrorism Program: Since September 2001.* 2004. www.fbi.gov/publications/commission/9-11commissionrep.pdf (accessed August 23, 2010).

———. *The Sicilian Mafia and Its Impact on the United States: Organized Crime Section: Criminal Investigative Division.* Document 92-6235-289. Newark, NJ, 1986.

U.S. Department of Justice. Office of the Inspector General, Federal Bureau of Investigation. *The External Effects of the Federal Bureau of Investigation's Reprioritization Efforts*

(Redacted for Public Release), Audit Report 05-37. 2005. http://www.justice.gov/oig/reports/FBI/index.htm (accessed August 23, 2010).

———. *Federal Bureau of Investigation Legal Attaché Program, Audit Report 04-18*. 2004. http://www.justice.gov/oig/reports/FBI/index.htm (accessed July 23, 2010).

———. *The Federal Bureau of Investigation's Compliance with the Attorney General's Investigative Guidelines (Redacted for Public Release), Special Report*. 2005. http://www.justice.gov/oig/reports/FBI/index.htm (accessed August 23, 2010).

———. *The Federal Bureau of Investigation's Efforts to Hire, Train, and Retain Intelligence Analysts, Audit Report 05-20*. 2005. http://www.justice.gov/oig/reports/FBI/index.htm (accessed August 23, 2010).

———. *The Federal Bureau of Investigation's Foreign Language Program — Translation of Counterterrorism and Counterintelligence Foreign Language Material (Executive Summary Redacted for Public Release), Audit Report 04-25*. 2004. http://www.justice.gov/oig/reports/FBI/index.htm (accessed August 23, 2010).

———. *The Federal Bureau of Investigation's Foreign Language Translation Program (Redacted for Public Release), Audit Report 10-02*. 2009. http://www.justice.gov/oig/reports/FBI/index.htm (accessed August 23, 2010).

———. *Federal Bureau of Investigation's Foreign Language Translation Program Follow-Up, Audit Report 05-33*. 2005. http://www.justice.gov/oig/reports/FBI/index.htm (accessed August 23, 2010).

———. *The Federal Bureau of Investigation's Management of the Trilogy Information Technology Modernization Project, Audit Report 05-07*. 2005. http://www.justice.gov/oig/reports/FBI/index.htm (accessed August 23, 2010).

———. *The Federal Bureau of Investigation's Terrorist Threat and Suspicious Incident Tracking System, Audit Report 09-02*. 2008. http://www.justice.gov/oig/reports/FBI/index.htm (accessed August 23, 2010).

———. *The Federal Bureau of Investigation's Terrorist Watchlist Nomination Practices, Audit Report 09-25*. 2009. http://www.justice.gov/oig/reports/FBI/index.htm (accessed August 23, 2010).

———. *Follow-up Audit of the Federal Bureau of Investigation's Efforts to Hire, Train, and Retain Intelligence Analysts, Audit Report 07-30*. 2007. http://www.justice.gov/oig/reports/FBI/index.htm (accessed August 23, 2010).

———. *The Internal Effects of the Federal Bureau of Investigation's Reprioritization (Redacted for Public Release), Audit Report 04-39*. 2004. http://www.justice.gov/oig/reports/FBI/index.htm (accessed August 23, 2010).

———. *An Investigation of the Belated Production of Documents in the Oklahoma City Bombing Case, Special Report*. 2002. http://www.justice.gov/oig/reports/FBI/index.htm (accessed August 23, 2010).

———. *An Investigation of Overtime Payments to FBI and Other Department of Justice Employees Deployed to Iraq and Afghanistan*. 2008. http://www.justice.gov/oig/reports/FBI/index.htm (accessed August 23, 2010).

———. *An Investigation Regarding Removal of a Tiffany Globe from the Fresh Kills Recovery Site, Special Report, December 2003 (Redacted version released March 2004)*. 2003. http://www.justice.gov/oig/reports/FBI/index.htm (accessed August 23, 2010).

———. *A Review of Allegations of a Continuing Double Standard of Discipline at the FBI, Special Report*. 2003. http://www.justice.gov/oig/reports/FBI/index.htm (accessed August 23, 2010).

————. *A Review of the FBI's Actions in Connection with Allegations Raised by Contract Linguist Sibel Edmonds, Special Report.* 2005. http://www.justice.gov/oig/reports/FBI/index.htm (accessed August 23, 2010).

————. *A Review of the FBI's Handling of Intelligence Information Prior to the September 11 Attacks, Special Report (November 2004; released publicly June 2005) (Redacted for Public Release).* 2004. http://www.justice.gov/oig/reports/FBI/index.htm (accessed August 23, 2010).

————. *A Review of the FBI's Handling of Intelligence Information Related to the September 11 Attacks, Special Report (November 2004; released publicly June 2006).* 2004. http://www.justice.gov/oig/reports/FBI/index.htm (accessed August 23, 2010).

————. *A Review of the FBI's Involvement in and Observations of Detainee Interrogations in Guantanamo Bay, Afghanistan, and Iraq, Special Report.* 2008. http://www.justice.gov/oig/reports/FBI/index.htm (accessed August 23, 2010).

————. *A Review of the FBI's Involvement in and Observations of Detainee Interrogations in Guantanamo Bay, Afghanistan, and Iraq (Revised).* 2009. http://www.justice.gov/oig/reports/FBI/index.htm (accessed August 23, 2010).

————. *A Review of the Federal Bureau of Investigation's Use of Exigent Letters and Other Informal Requests for Telephone Records.* 2010. http://www.justice.gov/oig/reports/FBI/index.htm (accessed August 23, 2010).

————. *A Review of the Federal Bureau of Investigation's Use of National Security Letters, Special Report.* 2007. http://www.justice.gov/oig/reports/FBI/index.htm (accessed August 23, 2010).

————. *A Review of the FBI's Use of National Security Letters: Assessment of Corrective Actions and Examination of NSL Usage in 2006.* 2008. http://www.justice.gov/oig/reports/FBI/index.htm (accessed August 23, 2010).

————. *Review of the Terrorist Screening Center (Redacted for Public Release), Audit Report 05-27.* 2005. http://www.justice.gov/oig/reports/FBI/index.htm (accessed August 23, 2010).

————. *Sentinel IV: Status of the Federal Bureau of Investigation's Case Management System (Redacted for Public Release), Audit Report 09-05.* 2008. http://www.justice.gov/oig/reports/FBI/index.htm (accessed August 23, 2010).

————. *The September 11 Detainees: A Review of the Treatment of Aliens Held on Immigration Charges in Connection with the Investigation of the September 11 Attacks, Special Report.* 2003. http://www.justice.gov/oig/reports/FBI/index.htm (accessed August 23, 2010).

————. *Status of the Federal Bureau of Investigation's Implementation of the Sentinel Project, Report 10-22.* 2010. http://www.justice.gov/oig/reports/FBI/index.htm (accessed August 23, 2010).

U.S. Department of Justice. Office of the Inspector General. Oversight and Review Division. *A Review of the FBI's Involvement in and Observations of Detainee Interrogations in Guantanamo Bay, Afghanistan, and Iraq.* 2008. http://www.justice.gov/oig/ (accessed January 1, 2010).

Vise, David A. *The Bureau and the Mole: The Unmasking of Robert Philip Hanssen, the Most Dangerous Double Agent in FBI History.* New York: Atlantic Monthly, 2002.

Weiner, Timothy. *Legacy of Ashes: The History of the CIA.* New York: Doubleday, 2007.

Weiss, Murray. *The Man Who Warned America: The Life and Death of John O'Neill, the FBI's Embattled Counterterror Warrior.* New York: Morrow, 2003.

Whitcomb, Christopher. *Cold Zero: Inside the FBI Hostage Rescue Team.* Boston: Little, Brown, 2001.

Whitehead, Don. *The FBI Story: A Report to the People.* New York: Random House, 1956.

Wittes, Benjamin. *Law and the Long War: The Future of Justice in the Age of Terror.* New York: Penguin, 2008.

Woodward, Bob. *Bush at War.* New York: Simon & Schuster, 2003.

———. *Obama's Wars.* New York: Simon & Schuster, 2010.

———. *Plan of Attack: The Definitive Account of the Decision to Invade Iraq.* New York: Simon & Schuster, 2004.

———. *Shadow: Five Presidents and the Legacy of Watergate.* New York: Simon & Schuster, 2000.

———. *State of Denial: Bush at War, Part III.* New York: Simon & Schuster, 2007.

Wright, Lawrence. *The Looming Tower: Al-Qaeda and the Road to 9/11.* New York: Vintage, 2006.

Yoo, John. *War by Other Means: An Insider's Account of the War on Terror.* New York: Atlantic Monthly, 2006.

Zegart, Amy B. *Spying Blind: The CIA, the FBI, and the Origins of 9/11.* Princeton, NJ: Princeton University Press, 2007.

INDEX

former officers as traitors, 109–10n
founded as Office of Strategic Services (OSS), 115; FBI predates, 24
"ghost planes" of, 341
interrogation policy, 342, 362–65, 382; "enhanced interrogation," 374, 454n, 548, ("justified") 370, 385, overseas reaction to, 514; value questioned, 526, 533, 550–51 (*see also* "black sites," *above*)
in Iraq, 453; and Saddam Hussein, 455, 457, 462
and Iraq War, 432
in JTTF, 159 (*see also* Joint Terrorism Task Force)
kidnapping by, 216, 514; attempt canceled, 212; attempt fails, 118
National Clandestine Service, 385
and 9/11, 320, 339; 9/11 Commission, 419–20, 422
Obama and, 535, 548–49
and Pan Am bombing, 140, 144–45, 148, 150
stature erodes, 514
Webster as director, 174, 210
in Yemen, 585, 590
CISPES (Committee in Solidarity with the People of El Salvador), 126–31, 160, 163–64, 209
legacy of, 269, 319, 346, 418
Citizens Committee to Investigate the Federal Bureau of Investigation, 62
Civil War, U.S., 129
Clancy, Tom, 305
Clarke, Richard, 193, 199, 232, 260, 267, 302n
and counterterrorism policy, 168–69, 183, 271–72, 296, 314; weekly briefings, 249
and 9/11 and aftermath, 315–16, 420
Clarridge, Dewey, 116
Clausewitz, Carl von, 431
Clear and Present Danger (film), 265
Clemente, James, 379–84, 387, 414
Clemente, Tim, 264
Clinton, Bill, 229–30, 235, 273, 280, 331, 380, 533, 555
assassination threat, 180
counterterrorism policy, 228, 231; and bin Laden, 4, 230, 267; lack of information, 252, 422; Presidential Directive, 192
fires FBI head (Sessions), 176–77
and Freeh, 177–78, 210–11; hostility between, 22, 203–4, 248, 278–79
and Tenet, 323, 330
withdraws troops from Somalia, 199
Clinton, Hillary, 8, 545
Cloonan, Jack, 194–95, 207, 238–42, 250, 579
and al-Libi case, 357, 360
and bin Laden, 179, 196, 205–6, 300, 398
quoted on 9/11, 307–8, 428
CNN (Cable News Network), 134, 315, 472, 537
Coast Guard, U.S., 51, 100, 284, 348, 396
Cohen, William, 230
COINTELPRO (counterintelligence program), 61–64, 128, 280, 319
legacy of, 69–70, 73–74, 128, 163, 209, 269, 295, 418; and constitutional restraints, 346
Cold War, 5, 34, 37, 196, 209
ends, 210, 247

Cole, USS (ADENBOM), 204, 232, 262–69, 339, 372, 585
hints of plotted attack on, 237
importance disregarded, 271
investigation of, 233, 305–11, *passim,* 314–15, 324, 329n, 334, 356, 361, 429; CIA-FBI battle over, 302–3, 306; suspects, 342, 588, 590
Coleman, Danny, 179, 196–97, 231, 309, 311, 401, 468
Colombia, kidnappings in, 468, 470
Colombo family, 80
Combs, Sean "Puff Daddy," 259
Comey, Jim, 279, 284n, 332–33
with Justice Department, 278, 391, 398–400, 484–95, 510, 553; prepares to resign, 482–83, 497
quoted on Mueller and FBI, 412, 415, 417
"Commission," the, 105. *See also* Pizza Connection
Committee in Solidarity with the People of El Salvador. *See* CISPES
Communist Party USA, 63
Communists and Communism, 16, 61
Hoover/FBI and, 34, 58, 76; gatherings wiretapped, 25n
computer use. *See* cybercrime
Constitution, U.S.:
adherence to, 319, 346–47, 509; Lincoln vs., 129
protection of, 288, 433, 491, 493, 495
See also First Amendment; Fourth Amendment; Twenty-second Amendment
Coppola, Leonardo, 81
Corriere della Sera (periodical), 107
Corsi, Dina, 304, 305, 313
Cosa Nostra. *See* Mafia, the
Costa, Gaetano, 84
Coulson, Danny O., 72–76, 120
Cowley, Samuel P., 16
Cox, Archibald, 483
Crimson Tide (film), 415
Croatian separatists, 24, 165, 167, 406
Crouch, George, 350, 356, 554n
Cuba, 61, 380
anti-Castro group (Omega 7), 157, 165, 257
hijacked flights to, 44, 47–48, 51
refugees from, 348
Cuban missile crisis, 66
Cuckoo's Egg, The (Stoll), 477
Cullen, Pete, 532
Cummings, Art, 321–22, 551, 557–58, 579
Customs and Border Protection, 551, 593
Customs Service, U.S., 76, 94, 98, 249, 304
cybercrime, 17, 277, 477, 520, 533, 559
FBI Cyber Division, 559–60, 586n
Justice Department computer crimes unit, 293, 477
See also technology
Czech Republic, 565
Czech intelligence report disputed, 432

Dallas attack planned, 573–74
D'Amuro, Pat, 333–35, 349, 354, 396–97, 428, 432
and interrogation techniques, 364–65, 386
in Nairobi, and KENBOM case, 218, 220–22, 229, 236, 241